Colonialism in Sri Lanka

The Political Economy of the
Kandyan Highlands, 1833–1886

Asoka Bandarage

SECOND EDITION

Vimukti Publishing

Copyright © 1983, 2020 Asoka Bandarage/Vimukti Publishing

First edition published by Mouton/De Gruyter (Berlin) in 1983; reprints by Lake House Publishers (Columbo) in 1985 and Stamford Lake Publishers (Columbo), 2005.

All rights reserved.

www.vimuktipublishing.com

ISBN: 978-1-7349414-0-1

Dedicated to my parents:
to Amma and, in loving memory, Thaththa.

Contents

Preface to the 2nd Edition	xi
Acknowledgments (1st Edition)	xiii

I INTRODUCTION — 1
Development and Underdevelopment: Competing
   Theoretical Perspectives — 2
Development or Underdevelopment?: The Ceylonese Case — 5
Objectives and Limits of the Case Study — 12
Outline of the Book — 14

PART 1: HISTORICAL BACKGROUND — 17

II THE SOCIAL AND ECONOMIC ORGANIZATION OF THE KANDYAN KINGDOM: c. 1591 TO c. 1815 — 18
Modes of Production — 19
Surplus Appropriation: Social Class and Village Organization — 31
Surplus Appropriation: 'Caste Feudalism' — 36
Kandyan Trade and the Effects of European Mercantilism — 41

III THE FIRST PHASE OF BRITISH RULE IN CEYLON: THE MERCANTILIST PERIOD, 1796–1833 — 46
The Establishment of British Rule in Ceylon — 46
The Dominance of British Mercantilism: 1796—1833 — 52
From Mercantilism to 'Free Enterprise': The
   Colebrooke-Cameron Reforms — 58

PART 2: THE PLANTATION IMPACT — 65

IV EXPORT AGRICULTURE IN CEYLON, 1833–1886: AN OVERVIEW — 66
The Origin of Coffee Agriculture: 'Peasant Coffee' — 70
Plantation Coffee — 72
Coconut Cultivation — 82
The Transition from Coffee to Tea in the Kandyan Highlands — 84

V	PLANTATIONS AND THE CONFLICT OVER LAND	87
	The Struggle Over High Lands: Royal and Feudal Villages	87
	The Struggle Over High Lands: Temple Villages	109
	Paddy Lands: Crown Villages	122
	The Paddy Tax and Land Sales	135
	Paddy Taxes and Changing Property Relations	146
	Paddy Lands: Feudal Villages 154 Summary	171
VI	PLANTATIONS AND THE CREATION OF A LABOR FORCE	174
	The Attempt to Create a Sinhalese Labor Force	174
	The Migratory Labor Force from South India	195
	Recruitment, Control, and Reproduction of Estate Labor 201 Summary	220
VII	PLANTATIONS AND THE COLONIAL STATE	222
	The Colonial Administration	222
	The Facilitation of the Plantation Enterprise by the Colonial State	236
	Infrastructure Needed for Paddy Agriculture	255
	Sources of Government Revenue	260
	Colonial State Policy and the Subsistence of the Peasantry	266
	Summary	274

PART 3: CONCLUSIONS AND THEORETICAL IMPLICATIONS 275

VIII	THE COLONIAL TRANSFORMATION OF THE KANDYAN HIGHLANDS: SOCIO-ECONOMIC DIFFERENTIATION AND STRATIFICATION	276
	The Incorporation of the Highlands into the World Capitalist Economy	277
	Indigenous Capital and Regional Differentiation	279
	Socio-economic Differentiation in the Kandyan Highlands	286
	The Articulation of Modes of Production	287
	Backwardness in Paddy Agriculture	297
	The Colonial State and the Subordination of Traditional Political Authority	302
	Class, Caste, and Ethnic Configurations in Colonial Kandy	306

IX	**THEORETICAL CONCLUSIONS: THE CHARACTERIZATION OF THE COLONIAL POLITICAL ECONOMY**	322
	Development Perspectives	322
	Underdevelopment Perspectives	329
	Characterization of Colonial Social Formations: The Neo-Marxist Debate	332
	Debate on the Mode of Production	344
	The Specificity of the Colonial State	349
	Towards a Theoretical Synthesis	352
X	**NEOCOLONIALISM IN SRI LANKA, 2020**	358
	Post-Colonial Developments	359
	Neocolonialism and Geopolitical Rivalry	364
	UNHRC Resolution	369
	The Millenium Challenge Cooperation Compact	373
	U.S. Military Exapansion	381
	The Way Forward	386
	APPENDICES	390
	REFERENCES	403

List of Figures

5:1 The Effects of Colonial Land and Tax Policies on Property
 Relations in the Kandyan Village Economy   172
8:1 The Articulation of Modes of Production in Colonial Kandy 289
8:2 The Transition from Feudal to Colonial Economy
 (1820s–1880s)   300
8:3 Economic Sectors, Social Classes, Ethnic Groups
 and Castes in the Kandyan Highlands - circa 1848   308

List of Maps

Ceylon   XIV
The Principal Coffee Estates, circa 1880   98
Roads and Railways Constructed Under the British, 1814–1913 248

List of Tables

2:1	Sinhalese Land Measurements	22
4:1	Quantity of Ceylon Coffee Produced and Prices, 1834–1842	73
4:2	Average Annual Migration of Indian Estate Laborers, 1841–1890	74
4:3	Coffee Production in Ceylon, 1844–1847	75
4:4	The Ceylon Coffee Industry, 1850–1869	77
4:5	The Ceylon Coffee Industry, 1880–1886	78
4:6	Export of Coconut Produce from Ceylon, 1870–1910	82
4:7	Areas Under Tea and Coffee (Acres), 1883–1886	85
5:1	Crown Lands Surveyed and Sold: Central Province, 1844–1860	98
5:2	Ownership of Cultivated Plantation Coffee Lands	98
5:3	Land Sales in Central Province: 1868–1887	107
5:4	Temple Lands: 1876	112
5:5	Commission Under Ordinance No. 10 of 1856	113
5:6	Land Owned by Several Members of the Grain Tax Commission of 1878	136
5:7	Paddy Lands Sold by the State for Nonpayment of the Paddy Tax, 1880–1892	139
5:8	Peasant Coffee, 1880–1886	143
5:9	Grain Tax Collections: Nuwara Eliya District, 1856–1884	144
5:10	Description of Lands Sold for Nonpayment of Paddy Tax: Nuwara Eliya District, 1882	147
5:11	Tribute Paid by Tenants of the Village of Nivitigala to the Overlord — Doloswala Dissawa	158
5:12	Deity Temples (Dēwālēs) in the Sabaragamuwa Province and their Revenues	162
5:13	List of Cases Instituted by the Lay Incumbent (Nileme) of the Deity Temple (Dēwālē) Against its Tenants	167
6:1	Value of Imported Goods in Ceylon 1839–1893	185
6:2	Percentages of Sinhalese and Tamils in the Estate Population, 1871, 1881, 1891	190
6:3	Sinhalese Population Resident on Estates, 1871, 1881, 1891	190
6:4	Sources of Immigration into Ceylon from South India	198
6:5	South Indian Labor Immigration, 1851–1854	200
6:6	Migration of Indian Estate Laborers, 1839–1886	202
6:7	Rice Imports, 1837–1872	212

6:8	Comparative Statement of Costs to Planter of a Coolie (Estate Laborer) in British Guiana, Mauritius, and Ceylon (1871)	218
7:1	Extract of Return of Crown Land Sales, 1840	232
7:2	Receipts from Road Ordinance Collections in Labor and Money, 1882–1884: Central Province	253
7:3	Public Works Expenditure of the State, 1867 and 1877	259
7:4	Government Revenues: 1840–1886	261
7:5	Government Revenues from Grain Taxes, 1823 and 1876	263
7:6	Incidence of Taxation in Terms of a Day's Income on Heads of Families	267
7:7	A Statement of the Several Old Taxes Repealed after the Arrival of Lord Torrington and the Expected Loss of Revenue, 1847 and 1848	269
7:8	A List of Several New Taxes Imposed since the Arrival of Lord Torrington . . . Estimate of the Amount of Revenue Expected from the same, 1847 and 1848	271
7:9	Areas Cultivated by Estates and Peasants, Census Years, 1871–1891	273
8:1	Waste Land Use and Ethnic Group, 1860–1889	282

Preface to the 2nd Editon

The first edition of Colonialism in Sri Lanka was published in 1983 by Mouton Publishers. The Sri Lankan edition of the book was published by Lake House Publishers in 1985. In 2005, Stamford Lake Publishers issued a reprint, along with a Sinhala version, Sri Lankawe Yatathvijithavadaya, translated by the late Mrs. Sita Kulatunga. As all of these editions are now out of print, and as the topic is as relevant now as it was 37 years ago, Colonialism in Sri Lanka is being re-published with an update chapter in this second edition. I hope it continues to contribute to the discourse on the roots of current crises that lie in European colonialism, and to the search for alternative and sustainable models of social and political evolution.

Based on an extensive use of primary sources, the book provides a detailed account of the absorption of Sri Lanka into the emerging global capitalist economy in the nineteenth century. Its well-documented discussions of land expropriation, plantation development, the use of state violence – and the different effects of these forces on local social classes and ethno-religious groups – sheds light on key universal themes of colonial capitalist development. In particular, the theoretical chapters of the book synthesizing debates on colonial political economy continue to be entirely relevant to current discourses.

The book's discussion of the origin, processes and evolution of globalization is more relevant now than ever, in order to understand current political and economic crises, and the necessity to turn towards bio-regional, ecological and equitable ways of living in both Sri Lanka and the world at large. This contemporaneous view is the particular focus of the new chapter, 'Neo-Colonialism in Sri Lanka, 2020,' written especially for this edition, which discusses the current challenges of globalization facing Sri Lanka.

I would like to thank all the individuals who have helped bring this 2020 edition of Colonialism in Sri Lanka to fruition. In particular, I would like to extend my appreciation to Mahinda Gunasekara and Anil Amarasekara, who provided relevant contact information; and to Niroshana Jayasundera, former CEO of Stamford Lake Ltd., who has given his support to keep the book in print over the years. Similarly, I am grateful to Walter De Gruyter publishers in Berlin for returning rights to the book to me, and for their help in accessing files of the first edition. A sincere thank you also to Dr. Dov H Levin of the University of Hong Kong, for clarifying the election interference of the 1950s and 60s briefly discussed in Chapter 10.

Finally, I would like to express my deep gratitude to Paul Mayhew for editing the new chapter, and for preparing this work for re-publication. Without his interest, experience and talents, this edition would not have seen the light of day.

Asoka Bandarage
Lovettsville, Virginia
June 2020

Acknowledgments (1ˢᵗ Editon)

This study would not have been possible without the financial and intellectual support of a number of institutions and individuals. It gives me great pleasure to express my gratitude to them here.

An earlier version of this study was presented as my Ph.D. dissertation at Yale University. From Yale's Concilium for International Area Studies I received a Dissertation Research Fellowship for archival research. Subsequently I received a Summer Faculty Fellowship from the National Endowment for the Humanities to do further research in Sri Lanka. I have also received funds from Brandeis University to help cover costs of typing, photocopying, etc. The Center for European Studies at Harvard University provided me with an office during the summer of 1981 when I was doing revisions for this book. I express my thanks to all these institutions for their generous support. While at Yale I had the good fortune to work with a committee of very helpful and congenial thesis advisors: Professors, Wendell Bell (chairman), John Low-Beer, James Scott, and Keith Hart. My own capacity to complete the first version of this work depended to a large extent on their support and to them I express my deep gratitude. I wish particularly to thank Wendell Bell for helping me develop a more critical attitude towards my own biases and assumptions; to John Low-Beer for his intellectual support throughout the period of my graduate studies at Yale, to Jim Scott for his patience and encouragement which enabled me to get started and develop this project; and to Keith Hart for his great interest and tremendous support without which it would have been impossible for me to continue. I worked closely with Keith in formulating some of the central arguments of this study and to him I owe an enormous intellectual debt.

As it will become apparent to the reader, this book has depended to a great extent on the painstaking historical research of several generations of Sri Lankan scholars. Among them I wish specifically to thank Dr. Michael Roberts, who provided me with a most insightful and extensive commentary on an earlier draft of this work. Many of the criticisms and observations made by him have been considered in many more places than I can begin to mention and I believe that Michael Roberts' comments have helped strengthen the arguments I make in this book. I wish also to thank Dr. Kumari Jayawar- dena for her useful comments on an earlier draft and her encouragement and, to Mr. U. K. Sumanandasa for sharing ideas and

Acknowledgments (1st Editon)

information relevant to this work. My father, Mr. D. S. Bandarage, read an earlier draft and gave me valuable comments which I have accepted with great appreciation.

My appreciation also goes to my colleagues at Brandeis, Peter Conrad, Paula Rayman and Irv Zola, for their helpful advice in bringing this study to fruition and to Chitra, Shanti, and Dilan Abeygoonawardena for their hospitality when I lived in their home while doing research in England. Thanks are also due to Elizabeth Bouche for typing the manuscript and to Paul Solstrom for doing the index for the book with much care and interest.

Finally, I would like to thank my teachers at Visakha Vidyalaya, Bryn Mawr College and Yale University for their encouragement at different stages of my intellectual development.

Asoka Bandarage
Cambridge, Massachusetts
January 1982

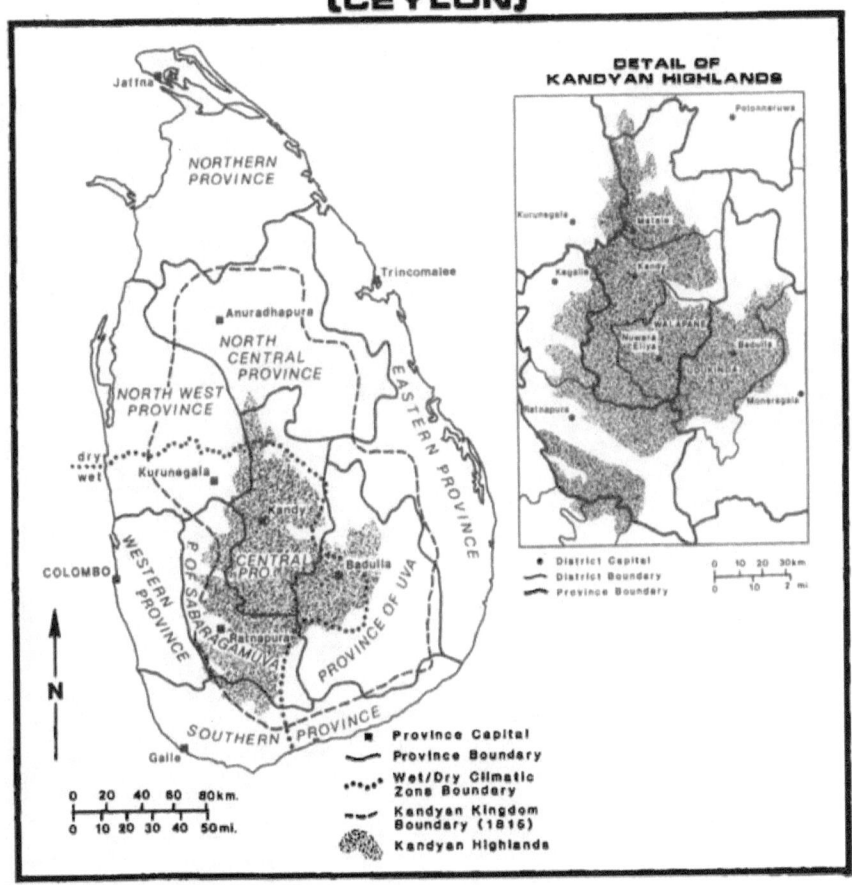

Prepared by Clark University Cartographic Service/USA

I. Introduction

The economic, political, and cultural expansion of the West into Asia, Africa, and Latin America since the late fifteenth century set in motion processes of fundamental socioeconomic transformation in those societies. The earlier period, when the European powers exercised direct political control over the colonies is generally referred to as the period of 'classical colonialism'. The socioeconomic structures set in place during classical colonialism continue to wield determining influences on the lives of people in the contemporary Third World.[1] A wide variety of theoretical perspectives has sought to grasp the nature of that colonial transformation and its long-term implications for the evolution of Third World societies. The result is the lively ongoing theoretical debate in the sociology of development and underdevelopment.

The central issue that concerns this study is the impact of the British plantation economy and colonial political authority on the Kandyan Highlands of Ceylon (Sri Lanka),[2] during the nineteenth century. This subject, in itself, is not new. Although this study has brought together a number of important colonial documents that have not been utilized by previous writers, most of the facts and events covered in this book are relatively familiar to students of Ceylonese history. But earlier studies have attempted neither a synthetic analysis of the various aspects of the British colonial impact on Ceylon nor an interpretation of the general dynamic of the colonial transformation in the context of changes in the international political economy. What is also glaring in its absence is an attempt to relate the transformations which took place in the island to the current debate on development and underdevelopment in the Third World.[3] This study has been undertaken with the objective of filling several such gaps in the existing literature. It seeks to provide a

---

1. The term, Third World, refers very broadly to the colonial and neocolonial nations of Asia, Africa, and Latin America. See Keith Buchanan, "Delineation of the Third World", in Ingolf Vogeler and Anthony R. de Sousa (eds.), *Dialectics of Third World Development* (Montclair: Allanheld Osmun, 1980) and Peter Worsley, "One World or Three? A Critique of the World System of Immanuel Wallerstein", *Socialist Register*, 1981.
2. As this book deals with the British colonial period of the island's history, its colonial name, Ceylon, rather than its Sinhala name, Sri Lanka, will be used throughout. Note also that Kandy is a European derivation from the Sinhala term *kanda uda rata* "The country above the mountains".
3. An example is K. M. de Silva (ed.), *History of Ceylon*, vol. 3 (Colombo: University of Ceylon Press Board, 1973).

theoretically informed interpretation of the British colonial impact on Kandyan Ceylon during the nineteenth century. It also seeks to make a contribution to the wider debate on development and underdevelopment in the Third World on the basis of the Ceylonese case study.

In this introductory chapter we will outline very briefly and broadly the development and underdevelopment perspectives on social change in the Third World. We shall then proceed to discuss some of the previous studies on Ceylon which have a bearing on the subject of this book in relation to those two broad and competing development and underdevelopment perspectives. A more detailed and incisive discussion of these theories will be undertaken in the concluding chapter where an attempt is made to test, refine, and reformulate some of the existing theories on the basis of the Ceylonese case materials. In the final chapter some suggestions are also made towards the formulation of a more synthetic and holistic approach to the study of colonialism and Third World social formations.

Development and Underdevelopment: Competing Theoretical Perspectives

The dominant social science perspective on the nonwestern world, commonly referred to as the 'development' or 'modernization' school, derives its assumptions from the historical experience of capitalist development in the West. It argues that the western nations have laid the foundation for the transformation of the Third World through the diffusion of capital, technology, values, and organizational forms. It assumes that the West, in alliance with native elites, will ensure that these 'backward' nonwestern societies will traverse the same path of socioeconomic development as the western nations themselves did.[4]

A highly influential variant of the modernization/development perspective is the dual economy/dual society theory. It was formulated to explain the apparent contradiction between the backwardness of most nonwestern economies and the 'modernizing' presence of the West in those nations. Theorists working within the framework of 'dualism' posit two completely separate western/modern and nonwestern/traditional sectors and attribute the back-

---

4. Each of the theories sketched in the Introduction will be discussed more fully in Ch. IX of this book. See note 1, Ch. IX, for bibliographic references to the modernization/development perspective and its critiques.

Introduction   3

wardness of the latter to its supposedly primitive values and traditional social structures.[5]

The underdevelopment perspective which has been formulated during the last few decades as a reaction against the dominant development perspective has inverted some of the basic presuppositions of the earlier school. It points out that the fundamental barriers to Third World development lie not in the supposedly traditional social structures and values of the indigenous societies, but in the exploitative relationship imposed upon them by the West. According to André Gunder Frank, the underdevelopment of the colonial or 'satellite' nations is the result of the very development of the western 'metropolitan' nations.[6] Similarly, within the satellite or peripheral nations themselves, the development of the dominant economic sectors, regions, and social classes is achieved at the expense of the subordinated small-scale sectors, backward regions, and lower social classes. For Frank, and many other theorists of his persuasion, underdevelopment in the Third World is the result of western capitalist penetration and is synonymous with dependency on the West.[7]

Although underdevelopment has been presented as the converse of development, these writers have not depicted underdevelopment as a state of economic or social stagnation. Rather, it is presented as a process of change which does bring forth a certain amount of economic growth and prosperity for the dominant sectors and social classes of the peripheral nations. But it is pointed out that this growth is externally oriented or dependent on the West and satisfies neither the long-term needs of the Third World countries as national entities nor the interests of the majority of their people. The dynamic of underdevelopment set in place by the West, these theorists argue, leads to increasing internal inequalities and unevenness between social classes, economic sectors, and regions, as well as growing international disparities between the already rich metropolitan countries and the poor countries of the periphery.[8]

Inequality and unevenness are features intrinsic to capitalist development — whether it be in the metropolitan West or the nonwestern peripheries.[9] But some theorists such as Samir Amin, Hamza Alavi, and Jairus Banaji have argued that there is a fundamental difference in the capitalist develop-

---

5. See notes 4, 5, 6 in Ch. IX of this book for bibliographic references to the dual economy theory and its critiques.
6. André Gunder Frank, *Capitalism and Underdevelopment in Latin America: Historical Studies of Chile and Brazil* (New York: Monthly Review Press, 1967), *passim*.
7. Ibid., *passim*. See notes 15, 16 and 17 in Ch. IX, in this book for more bibliographic references to the underdevelopment perspective.
8. Frank, *Capitalism and Underdevelopment, passim*.
9. See, for example, Sanjaya Lall, "Is 'Dependence' a Useful Concept in Analyzing Underdevelopment?" *World Development*, vol. 3, nos. 11 and 12 (1975).

ment taking place in the Third World from that which took place (and is continuing to take place) in the West.[10] The reasons for these differences they claim must be sought in the external imposition of capitalism into the colonies and the resultant imperialist relationship. As Gunder Frank has also argued, it is this exploitative relationship which has structured and continues to shape the processes of social change in the Third World. In attempting to place the uneven and unequal logic intrinsic to capitalist expansion within the peculiarity of the metropolitan-satellite relationship, Amin, Alavi and other neo-Marxist theorists have begun to characterize the socioeconomic structures which have emerged in the Third World as distinct forms of 'peripheral', 'dependent', or 'colonial' capitalism.[11]

The task of specifying the precise features of colonial capitalist development is a difficult one which is still at a conjectural stage. The specificity of colonial capitalist development cannot be sought at the level of theory alone. Some of the major problems with both development and underdevelopment theories are the abstract and overgeneralized nature of their formulations and the insufficiency of empirical observation. The colonial transformation is a highly differentiated process which has varied across such factors as time, country, region, precolonial socioeconomic structures, and strategies of European economic, political and cultural domination. We need concrete historical and/or anthropological analyses of alternative particular cases of the colonial transformation before the available macrosociological perspectives can be refined and more synthetic and comparative theories of Third World social change can be built upon. This is not to argue for narrow empiricism or the endless postponement of theoretical formulations, but to stress the necessity for a balance between the specificity of historical and anthropological studies, on the one hand, and the broad generalizations of macrosociology, on the other. Such a balance is essential if we are to move beyond simplistic depictions of underdevelopment as a situation which is identical everywhere in the Third World from the sixteenth to the twenty-first century.[12]

---

10. Samir Amin, *Unequal Development: An Essay on the Social Formation of Peripheral Capitalism* (New York: Monthly Review Press, 1976); Hamza Alavi, "India and the Colonial Mode of Production", *Socialist Register* (1975); Jairus Banaji, "For a Theory of Colonial Modes of Production", *Economic and Political Weekly*, vol. VII, no. 52 (December 23, 1972).
11. Amin, *Unequal Development*, especially Ch. 4 and 5; Alavi, "India and the Colonial Mode", *passim;* Hamza Alavi, "India: Transition from Feudalism to Colonial Capitalism", *Journal of Contemporary Asia*, vol. 10, no. 4 (1980).
12. See Ian Roxborough's *Theories of Underdevelopment* (Atlantic Highlands: Humanities Press, 1979) for a discussion of the problem of overgeneralization in underdevelopment theories.

Introduction

Peter Evans' recent work, *Dependent Development: The Alliance of Multinational, State, and Local Capital in Brazil*, has been a stepping stone in the direction towards greater specification of the heterogeneous and multistructured Third World social formations.[13] His analysis of Brazil has helped identify a particular variant of dependent capitalist development which is specific to the contemporary period and the more industrialized Third World nations such as Brazil and Mexico. On the basis of his intensive historical case study, Evans identifies a category of Third World nations which he calls the 'semi-periphery' and he distinguishes it structurally from the more numerous and less industrialized peripheral nations.

The objective of this book however, is to provide a historical case study of the earlier and more numerous variant of peripheral or colonial capitalist development which involved both direct political control by the metropolitan nations and the transformation of the indigenous societies into primary producers through export agriculture. In analyzing the installation of the capitalist mode of production in the Kandyan Highlands and the ensuing 'articulation' between pre-existing and superimposed economic and political structures, this study seeks to contribute to our understanding of 'classical colonialism'. A careful study of the origin and evolution of the earlier colonial processes is essential before we can begin to understand their neocolonial evolution, their political manifestations, or the strategies necessary to overcome them. It is in the spirit of seeking answers to contemporary social problems of Sri Lanka and comparable problems elsewhere in the Third World that this historical study has been undertaken. It is also hoped that the general frame of analysis developed in this study would be of relevance to future students of colonialism and social change in the Third World.

Development or Underdevelopment?: The Ceylonese Case

The subject of this book, namely the impact of the plantation economy and British political rule on precolonial Ceylonese society, is the most controversial issue in the historiography of colonial Ceylon. It has been debated by nineteenth-century planters, state officials and nationalists and continues to be debated by contemporary politicians and social scientists. Although the protagonists of this debate do not identify themselves as such, we can very

---

13. Peter Evans, *Dependent Development: The Alliance of Multinational, State, and Local Capital in Brazil* (Princeton, N.J.: Princeton University Press, 1979).

broadly divide them into two schools of thinking which coincide with the development/modernization and underdevelopment frameworks outlined earlier.

The claim that the western presence in the colonies is mutually beneficial to the colonizer and the colonized is not a new formulation. It was widely used by the Europeans to justify their rule over nonwestern peoples. Hugh Clifford, a governor of colonial Ceylon, summed up this modernization/ development point of view when he said in 1929,

> Though the British capital invested in Ceylon may pay dividends to shareholders in all parts of the world, the investment of that capital in the Island, the trade and business which is thereby created, and the annual expenditure which the working and maintenance of its properties necessitates, all contribute to the internal income of the country, add to the general wealth and directly and indirectly benefit materially its indigenous population.[14]

The notion that colonial rule was beneficial to Ceylon as a nation and the majority of its people has been uncritically upheld by Ceylonese historians of an earlier generation such as H. A. J. Hulugalle and G. C. Mendis.[15] Contemporary writers who share this general modernization point of view defend the plantations and colonial rule against the attacks of their opponents by pointing out that: plantation development in Ceylon did not result in a large-scale expropriation of the Sinhalese peasantry; the lands alienated for plantations were in fact forest and high lands of marginal usefulness to the peasants; land sales by the natives themselves were responsible for much of the alienation; the colonial state did not administer its land legislation to the letter of the law; the state allocated separate land for slash-and-burn agriculture and pasturage; and, the land scarcity which occurred in the Kandyan villages in the twentieth century was the result of economic relationships within the village rather than the result of plantation expansion.[16] In taking the defense of

---

14. Hugh Clifford, "Some Reflections on the Ceylon Land Question", *Tropical Agriculturist* 68 (1927), pp. 301–02. Compare this with the self-legitimating ideology of multinational corporations operating in the Third World today. See, for example, Richard J. Barnet and Ronald E. Muller, *Global Reach: The Power of the Multinational Corporations* (New York: Simon and Schuster, 1974), esp. Part 2.
15. H. A. J. Hulugalle, *British Governors of Ceylon* (Colombo: Associated Newspapers of Ceylon, 1963), p. 2, and G. C. Mendis (ed.), *The Colebrooke-Cameron Papers: Documents on British Colonial Policy in Ceylon, 1796–1833* (Oxford: Oxford University Press, 1956), Introduction, pp. ix and xi. For a nationalist critique of these procolonial views, see Tennakoon Vimalananda, *Buddhism in Ceylon under the Christian Powers and the Educational and Religious Policy of the British Government in Ceylon 1797–1832* (Colombo: M. D. Gunasena, 1963), Preface, p. ii.
16. Clifford, "Some Reflections", p. 301. Donald R. Snodgrass, *Ceylon: An Export Economy in Transition* (Homewood, Ill.: Richard D. Irwin, 1966), p. 55; Lalith Jayawardena, "The Supply of Sinhalese Labour to Ceylon Plantations (1830–1930):

Introduction

plantations and the colonial state to an extreme, Lal Jayawardena has argued that British land policy did not dispossess the Sinhalese peasantry; instead, it created a class of high land peasant proprietors.[17] These arguments of Jayawardena and others will be evaluated against historical evidence presented in the subsequent chapters of this book.

Those who have applied the dual economy model to the Ceylonese case, such as Donald Snodgrass and T. Jogaratnam, argue that the Ceylonese plantation economy was/is a classic example of an 'enclave economy' using foreign capital, foreign labor, and even foreign supplies including the food to feed the estate labor force. They go on to claim that there were neither 'positive spread effects' nor 'negative backwash effects' from the plantation sector to the indigenous village sector.[18] Snodgrass argues that the village sector remained backward in spite of the growth of the plantation sector.

> The co-existence of so poor an economy in general and a peasant sector in particular with a prosperous estate sector raises a serious question. It is clear that the estates did not create the poverty. But even so, why did they not eliminate it?[19]

Snodgrass has not explained *why* the plantations failed to eliminate the poverty and backwardness of the village economy. He has simply alluded to the 'traditional' backwardness of an undifferentiated village or peasant sector.[20] That the plantation presence created a dualistic economy consisting of an advanced, capital-intensive, export sector on the one hand and a stagnant, technologically-backward, labor-intensive, subsistence sector on the other, with relatively few interconnections between them, has been the common characterization of the Ceylonese economy. Even a Marxist writer such as Satchi Ponnambalam has failed to overcome such long held, dualistic assumptions.

> By the time coffee collapsed in the 1880s, there had emerged in the country a dual economy. One was a highly developed, organized, foreign-owned, capitalistic, plantation economy producing for export in the central highlands. The other was a tradition-bound, primitive, self-sufficing, subsistence, peasant economy, producing for domestic consumption in the remainder of the Wet and Dry Zone areas of the

A Study of Imperial Policy in a Peasant Society" (Ph.D. dissertation, Cambridge University, 1963), *passim;* Michael Roberts, "The Impact of the Waste Lands Legislation and the Growth of Plantations on the Techniques of Paddy Cultivation in British Ceylon: A Critique", *Modern Ceylon Studies* 1 (1970), pp. 157–98; Patrick Peebles, "Land Use and Population Growth in Colonial Ceylon", in James Brow (ed.), *Contributions to Asian Studies* 9 (Leiden: E. J. Brill, 1976), pp. 64–80.

17. Jayawardena, "The Supply of Sinhalese Labour", pp. 266–67.
18. Snodgrass, *Ceylon,* p. 59; T. Jogaratnam, "The Role of Agriculture in the Economic Development of Ceylon", *University of Ceylon Review* 20 (April 1962), pp. 132, 135–37.
19. Snodgrass, *Ceylon,* p. 55.
20. *Ibid.,* p. 55.

country. These two co-existed in splendid isolation, establishing no contact whatsoever between them. The former grew under the patronage of the colonial government, while the latter, being orphaned as it were continued to stagnate. This pattern of dualism, which the coffee era left as its legacy, continued to be the central characteristic of Sri Lanka's economy up to the time of independence in 1948. Even the post-Independence governments have continued to work within the framework of this dualism left by the early British colonial period.[21]

One of the primary objectives of this study is to expose the empirical invalidity and theoretical inadequacy of these facile dualistic assumptions that have dominated social science analyses of Ceylon until now. We shall attempt to do this by delineating the multiple linkages that developed between the plantation and the village and by demonstrating that the European plantation economy was established at drastic expense to the Kandyan peasantry and local food production.

However, the claim that the poverty and the backwardness of the peasant sector in Ceylon was caused by the plantations and that the colonial impact, in general, had an underdevelopmental rather than a developmental effect on the native society, is not a wholly new point of view. In fact, by the second decade of the twentieth century, a vociferous group of nationalists (consisting mainly of a small group of western-educated Ceylonese) were propagating this view in Ceylon. The colonial governor, Hugh Clifford, noted in alarm

> ... that a local school of thought has grown up in the Island which teaches with persistent reiteration the doctrine that the tea and rubber estates are a parasitic growth, which is battening upon the colony's lifeblood; that they have worked no appreciable benefit to the indigenous inhabitants of the country; and that they owe their existence to a systematic series of acts of expropriation and spoliation.[22]

Many contemporary social scientists also hold the view that plantation development resulted in a large-scale expropriation of the Sinhalese peasantry.[23] Some have compared it to the Enclosure Movement in England;[24]

---

21. Satchi Ponnambalam, *Dependent Capitalism in Crisis: The Sri Lankan Economy, 1948–1980* (London: Zed Press, 1980), p. 8.
22. Clifford, "Some Reflections", pp. 301–02. For a good discussion of the evolution of a nationalist perspective during the twentieth century, see Vijaya Samaraweera's recent article, "Land, Labor, Capital and Sectional Interests in the National Politics of Sri Lanka", *Modern Asian Studies*, vol. 15, no. 1 (1981).
23. J. B. Kelegama, "The Economy of Rural Ceylon and the Problem of the Peasantry", *Ceylon Economist* (September 1959), pp. 341–70; I. H. Van Den Driesen, "Land Sales Policy and Some Aspects of the Problem of Tenure: 1836–1886, Part 2", *University of Ceylon Review* 15 (1957), pp. 26–52; Ceylon Parliament, *Sessional Papers* (henceforth denoted as SP) 1951, No. 18, "The Report of the Kandyan Peasantry Commission", pp. 69–77; A. B. Perera, "Plantation Economy and Colonial Policy in Ceylon", *Ceylon Historical Journal* 1 (July 1951).
24. Ralph Pieris, "Society and Ideology in Ceylon during a 'Time of Troubles', 1796–1850, III", *University of Ceylon Review* 10 (January 1952).

Introduction

others have pointed out that this expropriation curtailed dry grain cultivation and pasturage, thereby endangering peasant subsistence.[25] Buddhadasa Hewawitharana and S. B. D. de Silva, two economists who do not agree with the large-scale expropriation theory, claim nevertheless that the shortage of pasture land for plough animals and soil erosion caused by the clearing of forests for plantations, in turn, led to a serious retrogression in the technology of peasant paddy production.[26] It has also been argued, most commonly by Sinhalese politicians, that the hiring of South Indian labor by the plantations robbed the Kandyan peasantry of employment opportunities. Some of these underdevelopment and nationalist arguments will be examined in the light of historical evidence in later chapters of this book.

The work of all writers on the British colonial period in Ceylon, however, cannot be adequately understood by placing them within the development or underdevelopment perspectives. The writings of Michael Roberts, a leading historian of nineteenth-century Ceylon, is a case in point. Roberts (as well as Lal Jayawardena) has challenged the simplistic assertion of nationalist writers that plantation development resulted in a large-scale expropriation of the Sinhalese peasantry during the nineteenth century.[27] He has also helped widen the focus of the debate on British colonialism in Ceylon by examining the introduction of private property rights and the emergence of a native capitalist class. Roberts' studies of indigenous capitalist development, a subject neglected by both dual economy and nationalist writers, have made a tremendous contribution to the historical study of British Ceylon.[28] But while recognizing that the results of British rule were both 'sweet and sour' and that

---

25. N. K. Sarkar and S. J. Tambiah, *The Disintegrating Village* (Colombo: Ceylon University Press Board, 1957), pp. xiii-xiv.
26. Buddhadasa Hewavitharana, "Factors in the Planning and Execution of the Economic Development of Ceylon" (Ph. D. dissertation, University of London, 1964), pp. 222-23; S. B. D. de Silva, "Investment and Economic Growth in Ceylon" (Ph.D. dissertation, University of London, 1962), pp. 192-94; see also the article by Angelika Sievers, "Geographical Aspects of Peasant Tradition and Plantation Industry in the Kandyan Hill Country", in *Conference on Ceylon* (Philadelphia: University of Pennsylvania, 1967).
27. Roberts, "The Impact of the Waste Lands Legislation;" Michael Roberts, "Some Comments on Ameer Ali's Paper," *Ceylon Studies Seminar*, no. 3b 1970/72 Series; Jayawardena, "The Supply of Sinhalese Labour," *passim*.
28. See, for example, Michael Roberts, *Facets of Modern Ceylon History through the Letters of Jeronis Pieris* (Colombo: Hansa Publishers, 1975) and his chapter "*Elite Formation and Elites, 1832-1931*", in K. M. de Silva (ed.), *History of Ceylon*, vol. 3, pp. 263-84. Patrick Peebles has also made a significant contribution to our understanding of the phenomenon of indigenous capitalism. See his "Land Use and Population Growth", in *Contributions to Asian Studies*, vol. 9 (Leiden: E. J. Brill, 1976), and "The Transformation of a Colonial Elite: The Mudaliyars of Nineteenth-Century Ceylon" (Ph. D. dissertation, University of Chicago, 1973).

the colonial society in Ceylon contained "both unblended and blended elements of the old and the new,"[29] Roberts, like most other historians writing on Ceylon, has failed to provide an interpretation of the general dynamic and direction of colonial capitalist development in the island.

A number of village case studies undertaken by sociologists and anthropologists on the Kandyan Highlands during the post-Independence period (i. e., since 1948) have a bearing on the subject of this book. These studies of mid- and late-twentieth-century Kandyan villages, in fact, point to the further evolution of many of the social forces and economic and political structures that emerged during the nineteenth century and are identified in this study. For example, the 1957 study by Sarkar and Tambiah and more recent work by Barrie Morrison, Tudor Silva, Newton Gunasinghe, et al.,[30] document the rapid commercialization of the Kandyan village economy, the increasing landlessness of the cultivator class, the concentration of land among noncultivating, often absentee, landowners, and, the expansion of wage labor relations.

Barrie Morrison and Tudor Silva have argued that as the focus of the Kandyan village socioeconomic organization shifts away from paddy cultivation, the village has become increasingly dependent on outside employment and other external sources for its very survival. In other words, the paddy-centred 'traditional' village is in a process of disintegration. As noted earlier, it is the origin and general dynamic of this process of transformation during the nineteenth century that this book seeks to demonstrate. However, in studying social change in the contemporary Kandyan Highlands, Barrie Morrison and Tudor Silva have not provided an adequate theoretical analysis of the dialectics of underdevelopment in those villages. For example, they have not explored the roles played by the propertied and salaried classes and the expanding

---

29. Michael Roberts, "Some Aspects of Economic and Social Policy in Ceylon, 1840–1871" (D. Phil. thesis, Oxford University, 1965), p. 414.
30. N. K. Sarkar and S. J. Tambiah, *The Disintegrating Village*; Barrie M. Morrison, M. P. Moore and M. U. Ishak Lebbe (eds.), *The Disintegrating Village: Social Changes in Rural Sri Lanka* (Colombo: Lake House Investments, 1979), especially case studies by Morrison and Tudor Silva on the Kandyan Highlands: Newton Gunasinghe, "Agrarian Relations in the Kandyan Countryside", *Social Science Review*, no. 1, September 1979; and, Newton Gunasinghe, "Production Relations and Classes in a Kandyan Village", *Modern Ceylon Studies*, vol. 6, no. 2 (July 1975). For discussions of changing political structures and kinship organization in the Kandyan villages during the post-Independence period see the works of Robinson and Yalman respectively. Marguerite S. Robinson, *Political Structure in a Changing Sinhalese Village* (New York: Cambridge University Press, 1975). Nur Yalman, *Under the Bo Tree: Studies in Caste, Kinship and Marriage in the Interior of Ceylon* (Berkeley: University of California Press, 1971).

Introduction

world capitalist economy in the disintegration of the traditional Kandyan village.[31]

Working within a neo-Marxist framework, Newton Gunasinghe has grappled with some of the broad analytical issues in the characterization of the contemporary Kandyan village social structure. The focus of his work is on the changing social relations of production in the village economy. While there is little description or analysis of the sources of the changes themselves, he correctly points to the dynamic of underdevelopment in motion in the Kandyan villages. Gunasinghe argues that although some feudal or 'archaic' social relations of production still persist in the Kandyan countryside, feudalism as a mode of production has been dismantled giving way to a peripheral form of capitalism in the contemporary Kandyan village.[32] To this extent, he confirms our own findings on the nineteenth-century transformations in the Kandyan Highlands. In line with the analyses of Hamza Alavi and other writers on India, Gunasinghe claims that a peripheral capitalist 'mode' has become dominant in the Kandyan region.[33]

We shall return to these theoretical issues in our final chapter where it will be argued that the concept of a colonial or peripheral capitalist *mode* by itself is inadequate for understanding the complexity and heterogeneity of Third World social formations structured by colonialism. In our conclusions we will point out that the concept of peripheral capitalism must be placed firmly within the wider context of the capitalist world economy and the imperialist relationship. We will also argue that the analysis of peripheral capitalism must be complemented by the methodological approach popularly known in Marxist academic circles as the 'articulation of modes of production'.[34] In this study we have combined the 'articulation' approach with a number of theoretical constructs derived from the underdevelopment perspective in providing a dialectical analysis of British colonialism in Ceylon during the nineteenth century.

---

31. Morrison, "Meegama: Seeking Livelihood in a Kandyan Village", and Silva, "Welivita: The Demise of Kandyan Feudalism", in *The Disintegrating Village*, ed. by Morrison, et al. See also my review of this collection of studies, Asoka Bandarage, review of *The Disintegrating Village* in *Pacific Affairs*, vol. 54, no. 3 (Fall 1981).
32. Gunasinghe, "Agrarian Relations", p. 21.
33. Ibid., p. 21. See also Alavi, "India and the Colonial Mode;" Banaji, "For a Theory of Colonial Modes".
34. The articulation approach is discussed in Ch. IX of this book.

Objectives and Limits of the Case Study

Reverting now to the colonial transformation of the Kandyan Highlands to be examined in this book, it should be noted that most of the supporters and opponents of Ceylon's plantation economy mentioned earlier, have arrived at their respective conclusions on the basis of an examination of the policy and practices of Ordinances No. 12 of 1840 and No. 1 of 1897, introduced by the colonial administration in Ceylon. These were undoubtedly the main instruments of land appropriation. However, a consideration of the effects of these ordinances alone is insufficient for an understanding of the overall effects of the colonial impact on Kandyan society. Other measures used by the British to replace users' rights and joint rights to land with absolute private property rights, such as the Partition Ordinance, Kandyan Marriage Ordinances, Land Registration Ordinance, the campaign against slash-and-burn agriculture, registration of feudal properties, etc., need to be taken into account as an ensemble. In addition, the effects of colonial taxation on property relations and surplus appropriation need to be explained in accounting for the changes in land tenure. It is only by looking at the confluence of these various colonial policies and their effects, that the full range of the plantation impact on Kandyan society can be assessed. In doing so, a very broad meaning needs to be given to the definition of the 'estate or plantation revolution', i. e., a meaning which goes beyond narrowly economic influences and which takes into account the changes in the power structures and the class and ethnic configurations in the society as well.

We shall argue throughout this book that underdevelopment cannot be understood at the level of economic structures alone. It has to be understood at the levels of political and ideological structures as well. The role of the colonial state was indispensable for the creation and the development of the British plantation economy. In addition to the tasks of surplus appropriation, political control of the population and legitimation of the colonial social order, the colonial state played a decisive role in mediating between opposing modes of agricultural production and social classes. The incorporation of the native aristocracy, without whose support the colonial administration would have come to a standstill, was also an important achievement of the nineteenth-century colonial state.

A major shortcoming of previous studies (both the dualist and nationalist variants) on British colonialism in Ceylon outlined earlier, is that they have assessed the effects of colonial policy and practice on a supposedly undifferentiated peasant society. However, the recognition of the hierarchical nature of precolonial Sinhalese society and the differential impact of colonial policy on the diverse social classes, yields an infinitely more complicated

Introduction

picture. Dualistic perspectives based on polar opposites, plantation and village or modern and traditional sectors, are inadequate for an understanding of the complexity of the colonial impact. This study attempts to present a synthetic analysis which takes into account the different sectoral, class, as well as ethnic configurations created by the plantation economy and the colonial state in Kandyan Ceylon.

However, it has not been possible to examine all of the important and relevant aspects of British colonialism in Ceylon in this book. For example, the cultural and psychological changes (which were slower in the Kandyan Highlands than in some other regions of the island) that accompanied the expansion of market forces, Christian missionary activity and western education have not been examined here. Furthermore, an analysis of the colonial impact on the sexual division of labor and sexual stratification in Kandyan society has not been possible, largely due to the almost total absence of historical materials on this subject.

To return to the primary focus of this study, namely the installation of the capitalist plantation mode of production, it must be noted that the plantation economy was the raison d'être of British colonialism in Ceylon. The production of cash crops for the world market transformed Ceylon into a classic case of an 'export-propelled' economy closely tied to the world capitalist economy. The superimposition of the profit-maximizing, foreign-owned, land- and labor-intensive coffee plantations upon the largely self-sufficient village economy brought forth a veritable social revolution on the island. Its effects on precolonial land tenure and social stratification were among the most revolutionary. The impact of this 'estate revolution' extended beyond the regions where plantations were physically present and beyond the narrowly economic influences. The effects of plantations, however, were differentially felt in the diverse ecological regions of the island. Furthermore, the specific form that the plantation impact took was necessarily conditioned by the nature of the pre-existing socioeconomic organization in each ecological and/or cultural region. The plantation impact was most direct and dramatic on the Central or Kandyan Highlands of the precolonial Kandyan kingdom, which had been relatively isolated prior to British rule and where plantations were later opened up by the British. It is for these reasons that this study has been focused primarily on the Kandyan Highlands, the heartland of the British plantation economy.

The time period dealt with is essentially the period of initial contact between the British and the Kandyan society in the Central Highlands. During the fifty or so years between 1833 and 1886, British political authority was consolidated and routinized, and the plantation economy firmly established. It was during this period that Ceylon was incorporated into the capitalist world economy as a primary producer. This then was a period of revolutionary social change. It was during this period that the colonial economic and political framework was firmly set in place. In fact, many of the major political and economic problems facing Sri Lanka today, such as the inherent instability of her export economy, land hunger of the peasantry, and the marginal status of the South Indian estate labor force, for example, can be attributed to the persistence of the colonial socioeconomic structures established during the period covered here.

The year 1833 is a commonly accepted landmark in the history of the island. The Colebrooke-Cameron Reforms which provided the juridico-political framework for capitalist agricultural development in Ceylon were introduced that year, making it, therefore, a convenient starting point for this study.

Eighteen eighty-six is generally considered the turning point when the Ceylon plantation economy shifted from coffee to tea agriculture. For the first time in her history, the volume of tea exports from Ceylon surpassed her coffee exports in the year 1886. In a broader sense, this change also signifies the beginning of the transition to the twentieth century. While the principal focus here is on the earlier coffee plantation economy, it will be pointed out that the patterns and structures which emerged during the 'coffee era' of Ceylon's plantation history were continued essentially intact into the later period when tea displaced coffee as the primary export crop.

Outline of the Book

Part 1 presents the essential context into which the plantation economy and the colonial state were later inserted. Chapter II gives a brief account of the precolonial socioeconomic organization of the Kandyan Highlands. Chapter III covers the first phase of British rule, namely the mercantilist period up to about 1833.

Part 2 is the main body of the work. Chapter IV provides a historical overview of the development of plantations between 1833 and 1886. Chapters V, VI, and VII analyze successively the problems of land, labor, and the role of the colonial state in the installation and development of the plantation economy.

Part 3 contains the conclusions of the study and an evaluation of some of the major theories in the sociology of development and underdevelopment. Chapter VIII provides an integrative analysis of different modes of production and political structures as well as the changing class, caste, and ethnic confi-

Introduction

gurations in the Kandyan Highlands. Chapter IX is a critical discussion of development and underdevelopment theories on the basis of the Ceylonese case materials. Finally, some suggestions are presented towards the development of a more comprehensive approach to the study of colonialism and Third World social formations.

Part 1: Historical Background

This section presents the historical background necessary for an understanding of the colonial impact on the Kandyan Highlands. It is an account of the socioeconomic organization of the Kandyan kingdom and the European mercantilist activities which preceded the opening up of plantations in the 1830s.

II. The Social and Economic Organization of the Kandyan Kingdom: c. 1591 to c. 1815

Almost a century after the arrival of the Portuguese in Ceylon and the loss of Sinhala political sovereignty in the coastal lowlands, the Kandyan kingdom emerged in the Central Highlands of Ceylon in defiance of European rule, the spread of Christianity, and European mercantilism. This new state, the very birth of which was in resistance to European domination, took upon itself the task of preserving the Sinhalese Buddhist heritage of the ancient civilization that had flourished in the dry-zone from around the third century B.C. to about the twelfth century A.D.

The Kandyan kingdom, particularly its core region, the Central Highlands, was largely an ethnically homogeneous society of Sinhalese Buddhists. But in spite of its claims to a pristine Sinhalese Buddhist identity, South Indian Hindu influences ranging from popular religious practices to the selection of South Indian princes (from the Nayakkar dynasty) to the Kandyan throne, were well established in the kingdom. The Kandyan kingdom also attracted other non-Kandyan elements into its midst from the coastal lowlands, especially those groups who were persecuted by and discontented with European rule, such as Muslim traders, members of the cinnamon peelers caste (*salagama*), and several other castes inhabiting the coastal lowlands.

The Kandyan period/society was only one particular historical form and not necessarily the most typical social formation (if there was any such) of precolonial Ceylon. It is, however, the specific form upon which the British plantation economy was directly imposed in the mid-nineteenth century and is therefore discussed in detail here.

Nominally, at least, the Kandyan kingdom comprised the major portion of the island's interior (see Map p. XIV), including the regions of the north-central dry zone where the hydraulic civilization had once flourished. But the effective political authority over these outlying regions was in the hands of local feudatory powers such as the *vanniyars*.[1] The focus of our attention will be

---

1. S. Pathmanathan, "Feudal Polity in Medieval Ceylon: An Examination of the Chieftancies of the Vanni", *Ceylon Journal of Historical and Social Studies* (henceforth *CJHSS*) 2 (July-December 1972): 118–30. See also, C. R. de Silva, "Some Comments on the Political and Economic Conditions in the Kingdom of Kotte in the Early Sixteenth Century", *Ceylon Studies Seminar* 1969/70 Series, no. 10, p. 5.

Social and Economic Organization of the Kandyan Kingdom: 19

limited to the heartland of the Kandyan kingdom, i.e., the Central or Kandyan Highlands around the capital of Kandy where a distinct form of social organization evolved. We will discuss the decisive features of the Kandyan socioeconomic organization such as its modes of production, division of labor, forms of surplus appropriation, and class structure.

The Kandyan Highlands consist largely of the contemporary Central and Sabaragamuwa Provinces and a part of the Uva Province. The large portion of the Central Highlands belongs to the southwestern wet zone of the island which receives between 100 to 200 inches of rain annually. The southeastern border of the Highlands which belongs to the island's dry zone receives fifty to seventy-five inches of rainfall per year. The mountains of the interior which range from five thousand to six thousand feet above sea level formed a natural fortress surrounded by forests (See Map p. XIV).

A striking characteristic of the Kandyan kingdom was its sparse population. Frequent wars against the Portuguese and then the Dutch in the coastal lowlands, deadly epidemics and polyandrous marriages, and of course the low levels of economic production and social welfare, were probably causes of the small population size. According to the British Census Report of 1824, the population of the Kandyan kingdom was 256,835. The population of Kandy, the capital city in 1818, was 3,000.[2]

Modes of Production

The ordinary Kandyan village consisted of a tract of paddy land (*kumburu*), a few small gardens surrounding the homes (*vatta*), a tract of periodically cultivated dry grainland (*hēn*) and a tract of forest (*käle*). The methods of production and tenurial relations in the permanently cultivated paddy land differed significantly from that of the periodically cultivated dry grain land as well as the small gardens surrounding peasant homesteads.

Without entering into the neo-Marxist debate on the definition of a mode of production here,[3] for the purpose of this discussion, we shall define a mode of production as a system of production characterized by distinct productive forces (including labor organization and technology), and distinct social relations of production (including property relations and surplus appropriation). On the basis of these broad criteria, we can distinguish two

---

2. S. B. W. Wickramasekara, "The Social and Political Organization of the Kandyan Kingdom" (M. A. thesis, University of London, 1961), p. 2.
3. See ch. IX of this book for a discussion of this debate and a further definition of mode of production.

modes of agricultural production in precolonial Kandy: feudalistic paddy agriculture and communalistic dry grain or high land agriculture.[4] The symbiotic relationship between these two modes of production was extremely important, particularly from the point of view of peasant subsistence. How it was subsequently disrupted by the intrusion of the plantations and market forces during British rule will be examined in later chapters of this book. Let us now turn our attention to the organization of paddy and high land agriculture in the Kandyan Highlands during the precolonial period.

Paddy Agriculture

Unlike the ancient dry zone civilization from which it claimed descent, the Kandyan economy was not based on an extensive hydraulic system. There were, of course, minor village tanks, but nothing akin to the gigantic irrigational complexes that existed in the dry zone were needed in the wet zone Highlands. Changed ecological conditions led to adoption of different methods of production. Following the collapse of the hydraulic works around the twelfth century A.D. and the shift of population centers away from the dry zone, greater reliance came to be placed on the cultivation of dry grains using slash-and-burn techniques to meet minimum subsistence needs.[5] Wet rice continued to be the primary crop, but it was dependent on seasonal rains (rather than on stored water) and was commonly grown on the terraced fields of mountain slopes.[6] In the dry zone regions of the Kandyan Highlands such as the Uva region, however, tanks were still necessary for wet rice cultivation.

As in the earlier historical epochs, land was held in individual or joint family shares (*pangus*); but cultivation was conducted communally by the villagers. In the absence of wage labor, a system of reciprocal labor exchanges known as *attam* had evolved to meet the seasonally fluctuating demand for labor in paddy cultivation. These reciprocal methods of labor mobilization and organization suited the labor-intensive methods of production in irrigated plough agriculture.[7]

---

4. Although closely related to agricultural production, craft production in Kandyan society is not discussed here.
5. S. Arasaratnam, *Ceylon* (Englewood Cliffs, N. J.: Prentice-Hall, 1964), p. 70.
6. For a description of the methods of rice cultivation, see Robert Knox, *An Historical Relation of Ceylon*, reprinted in *The Ceylon Historical Journal* 6 (July 1956–April 1957), Part 1, Ch. 3. Appendix I in this study discusses Knox and his work.
7. Newton Gunasinghe, "Social Change and the Disintegration of a Traditional System of Exchange Labour in Kandyan Sri Lanka", *Sociological Bulletin* 25 (September 1976), p. 168.

Social and Economic Organization of the Kandyan Kingdom:

As noted earlier, being sparsely populated, labor, not land, was the scarce factor of production in the Kandyan kingdom.[8] In addition to the guaranteed access to the use of land (discussed below), the producers owned the tools and implements of production (e.g., the plough) which were few and simple; they also had control over the productive process in general.[9] Methods of production were primitive and yields in paddy agriculture quite low. The specific property relations and forms of surplus appropriation in Kandy, which we shall discuss shortly, inhibited improvements in agricultural technology and generalized commodity production.

Property Relations in Paddy Agriculture

Theoretically, the king was the 'lord of the soil' (*bhupati/puthuvisvami*). But in practice, his claim to the unpaid services of the inhabitants was based on the wide diffusion of rights to cultivate 'his' land.[10] Given the scarcity of money, the king was not able to pay for services rendered to him. Instead, he gave out differential rights to the land to various individuals and groups in the society in return for his own right to extract their services and produce. In other words, land had to be given out in order to rule.[11]

For this reason, individuals were allowed, or even encouraged, to open up new land for cultivation. Due to the difficulties of opening up new land for wet rice cultivation (or 'asweddumizing' the land) those who did so, were given prescriptive rights to the land quite readily by the monarchical state. It was a well-established theory in Kandyan society that a person who brought virgin land under cultivation, *ipso facto* got title to it.[12] As Ralph Pieris notes,

> Royal forests could not be cultivated without the express permission of the king through one of his *adhikāramas* [chief ministers]. The cultivator could improve such land or convert it into paddy fields, but notice was required since *rājakāriya* [duty to the king] would be assigned to the newly cultivated land. According to Davy no duty was paid for the reclaimed land during the life of the original cultivator, presumably in recognition of the difficulty of bringing forest or waste land into cultivation for paddy crops, and to encourage the opening up of such land. The pro-

---

8. Wickramasekara, "The Social and Political Organization", p. 2.
9. Compare Mahmoud Mamdani's observations on pre-colonial Uganda, *Politics and Class Formation in Uganda* (New York: Monthly Review Press, 1976), p. 25.
10. de Silva, "Investment and Economic Growth", p. 27.
11. For discussion of the theme "land to rule", see the articles in Robert Eric Frykenberg, (ed.), *Land Control and Social Structure in Indian History* (Madison: University of Wisconsin Press, 1969), especially the article by Walter C. Neale on "Land is to Rule."
12. L. J. de S. Seneviratne, "Land Tenure in the Kandyan Provinces", *Ceylon Economic Journal* 9 (1937), p. 15.

prietor was free to sell or otherwise alienate this land, but the new proprietor was liable to perform *rājakāriya*.[13]

As C. K. Meek has pointed out, in precapitalist societies, land *per se* has no value; only the expenditure of labor on the land creates value.[14] In the case of regularly cultivated paddy fields, there was a complex tenurial system involving hierarchical, not absolute property rights. A number of individuals from the cultivator to the feudal overlord (including the king) had claims to the shares of the produce of the land on the basis of their respective functions in the society. As S. B. D. de Silva notes,

> Individual ownership *per se*, was less important than the rights and exemptions pertaining to a given tenure in regard to such matters as the payment of taxes or performance of services. The fact that emphasis was placed on functional rather than ownership aspects was reflected in the conventional unit of land measurement *amuna* which was not a uniform measure of land surface, but related to an area of land capable of yielding a given output of grain, which naturally varied according to fertility, location, etc., given technique of production.[15]

The compilations made by Hans-Dieter Evers show that the basic Sinhalese land measurement, the *amuna*, varied by region (district), crop and the techniques of production (paddy or high land agriculture), whereas the acre, the measurement of land introduced during the colonial era, was a uniform measure of land surface.

Table 2:1

Sinhalese Land Measurements
(Approximate Acre-Equivalent of One Amuna)*

District	Paddy Fields	High Lands
Kandy	2 acres	2 acres
Kegalle	–	5 acres
Kurunegala	–	40 acres

Sinhalese land measures are further broken down: 1 ȳala = 12 amuna; 1 amuna = 4 pala; 1 pala = 10 las (kuruni). (Amuna, pala, las, and kuruni are usually abbreviated as a-p-l-k).

*These compilations are based on studies done during the 1950s and 1960s.

Source: Hans-Dieter Evers, "Temple Lands and Rājakāriya: The Kandyan Lankātilaka Raja Maha Vihāraya," *Ceylon Studies Seminar*, 1969/70 Series, no. 6, p. 2.

13. Ralph Pieris, *Sinhalese Social Organization: The Kandyan Period* (Colombo: Ceylon University Press Board, 1956), p. 46.
14. C. K. Meek, *Land Policy and Practice in the Colonies* (London: Oxford University Press, 1946), p. 23.

Social and Economic Organization of the Kandyan Kingdom: 23

To return to our discussion of hierarchical rights to paddy lands, it should be noted that in general the cultivator's usufructary right could not be disturbed by the overlord, who enjoyed tribute exacting rights over the land as long as the cultivator paid the rent. In fact, alienability of land was restricted by a number of customary practices. Lands liable to forced labor service to a feudal lord, for example, could not be disposed by the overlord without the sanction of the king or a superior in the feudal administrative hierarchy.[16] The caste specificity of forced labor services attached to paddy landholdings made land transfers between individuals of different castes impossible. Furthermore, land sold or mortgaged could always be bought back or redeemed by the original landholder or his/her heirs. As a British interpreter of Kandyan law, F. A. Hayley, later claimed,

> It would seem therefore that Sinhalese law proper unaffected by European ideas or judicial decisions, knew nothing of renunciation, but permitted revocation in every case, with the exception perhaps of dedications to religious establishments.[17]

Nevertheless, disputes over land and land transfers were not totally unknown in precolonial Kandy. U. A. Gunasekara notes that such disputes were caused by the lack of regular revision of land registers, absence of primogeniture (hence land being divided among all heirs) and frequent changes in marital ties.[18]

Land disputes also emanated from the broad division of tenurial rights of paddy cultivators into heritable (*praveni*) rights held in perpetuity and temporary (*maruvena*) rights held at the will of the overlord.[19] As Wickramasekara notes, these two 'ideal types' of tenure could have been made the basis for arguments in the event of a conflict between feudal overlord and cultivator.[20] In fact, 'temporary' tenants who desired security struggled to establish 'heritable' rights in perpetuity over the land they cultivated.[21] This was due to the fact that in theory though not always in practice, the temporary tenants

---

15. de Silva, "Investment and Economic Growth", p. 27. The definition of *amuna* as "an area capable of yielding a given output of grain" as given by S. B. D. de Silva is not quite correct. Sowing area seems to be closer to its Sinhala meaning.
16. F. A. Hayley, *A Treatise on the Laws and Customs of the Sinhalese* (Colombo: H. W. Cave, 1923), p. 4.
17. Ibid., p. 305.
18. U. A. Gunasekara, "Land Tenure in the Kandyan Provinces of Ceylon" (B. Litt. thesis, Oxford University, 1959), p. 67.
19. Wickramasekara, "The Social and Political Organization", p. 180.
20. Ibid., p. 180.
21. Pieris, *Sinhalese Social Organization*, p. 69; Gananath Obeysekara, *Land Tenure in Village Ceylon: A Sociological and Historical Study* (Cambridge: Cambridge University Press, 1967), p. 218.

could be removed from the land at the overlord's will. In other words, the temporary tenant was more or less a sharecropping tenant who was required to pay feudal tribute and whose rights to the land were revocable. But it should be stressed that in both types of tenure — temporary and hereditary — the lord-serf relationship involved extra-economic coercion and the exaction of a surplus in the form of labor services, rent in kind and, less often, in money.

Obeysekara's claim that "acquisition of *praveni* title implies ownership of property, unmediated by suzerainty to an overlord, and the compulsory performance of services contractually required by the tenant"[22] is not correct. Tenants with heritable rights could hold their lands in perpetuity only as long as they paid feudal tribute to the overlord. In other words, land disputes in precolonial times pertained to customary hierarchical rights, not private property ownership. Private property rights in land were introduced only during the nineteenth century by the British. As Gunasinghe has argued, "serfdom is the obligation of the producer to perform stipulated services independent of his volition subjected to force; in this sense Kandyan tenants were *de facto* serfs."[23]

Although land disputes and land transfers did take place in precolonial times, they were relatively rare. This was because the very existence of the feudal lord *qua* overlord depended on the land being cultivated by tenants. In the absence of a market for land or wage labor, it was in the interest of the landlord that the tenants remained tied to the soil. As Jairus Banaji has argued, in precapitalist agriculture "the low productivity of labor . . . had to be compensated by expanding the surface under cultivation. This in turn depended on the lords' ability to mobilize and retain labor power on the land."[24]

In practice then, temporary tenants (*nilakārayas*), too, were allowed to cultivate the land for successive generations like the permanent tenants (*pangukārayās*). As written titles to land were rare, the distinction between hereditary and temporary tenure became difficult to make, particularly with the passage of time.[25] The long-standing patronal relationship between the lord and the tenant also made eviction of tenants difficult and contributed to the security of tenure of the cultivators. As Pieris notes,

---

22. Ibid., p. 218. His claim may be applicable to 'free villages'. See p. 36 in this chapter.
23. Gunasinghe, "Agrarian Relations", p. 11.
24. Jairus Banaji, "Modes of Production in a Materialist Conception of History," *Capital and Class* 3 (Autumn 1977), p. 18.
25. Pieris, *Sinhalese Social Organization*, p. 178.

Social and Economic Organization of the Kandyan Kingdom: 25

> But it often happened that these servants [*nilakārayās* or temporary servants], though liable to dismissal, were seldom evicted, having acquired as it were, a birth right by long residence and possession, and being content to perform the customary services to the lord.[26]

In spite of the factors contributing to the security of tenure, desertions by hereditary and temporary tenants were not infrequent. It is true that permanent avenues of escape, such as politically autonomous towns, were absent in the Kandyan Highlands.[27] But as Robert Knox, the foremost authority on precolonial Kandyan society observed, when tribute exaction became especially oppressive, it was customary for cultivators to run away into the jungle in order to avoid taxes and punishment by the feudal lords or the king.

> But if any find the duty to be heavy, or too much for them, they may leaving their house and land, be free from the king's service, as there is a multitude do. And in my judgment they live far more at ease, after they have relinquished the king's land, than when they had it.[28]

Likewise, a Grain Tax Commission appointed by the subsequent British administration noted in retrospect that

> Every man might escape taxation by the simple process of abandoning his tenement and this was not infrequently done. Nor was this by any means a privilege to be despised in a country, where land was more plentiful than tenants to occupy it.[29]

Indeed the maintenance of cultivators on the land was a problem central to feudal societies everywhere, and the conflict over rent between lords and serfs was the chief expression of class struggle in feudal societies. James Scott has observed this in relation to southeast Asian kingdoms, and Mahmoud Mamdani, in relation to precolonial Uganda.[30] In most of these kingdoms, any serious misrule, such as the attempts by the royalty to expand surplus appropriation unjustly was likely to lead to spontaneous revolt under the aegis of a rival claimant to the throne.[31] Stewart Gordon has pointed out that agricultural producers in precolonial Asian kingdoms were in the habit of negotiating taxes with state officials and overlords. Gordon implies that by paying more during good harvests and less during bad ones the cultivator class attempted to maintain a certain equilibrium in their subsistence.[32] How-

---

26. Ibid., p. 63.
27. Gunasinghe, "Agrarian Relations", p. 11.
28. Knox, *An Historical Relation*, p. 69.
29. *SP* 1890, No. 28 "Report of the Grain Tax Committee", p. ii.
30. James C. Scott, *The Moral Economy of the Peasant* (New Haven, Conn.: Yale University Press, 1976), p. 54; Mamdani, *Politics and Class*, p. 29.
31. Mamdani, *Politics and Class*, p. 29.

ever, there is little evidence of peasant revolts over rent or rent negotiations between overlords and tenants in the precolonial Kandyan kingdom.

High Land Agriculture

As suggested earlier, "free access to cultivable land is the supreme safety valve in a feudal economy"[33] characterized by inefficient methods of production. The uncultivated forest land in particular was a source of supplementary subsistence which provided timber, honey, and other forest products for the Kandyan peasant cultivators. Even more crucial as a means of subsidiary subsistence was 'swidden' or slash-and-burn agriculture.[34]

The uncertain weather conditions, the labor intensity of paddy cultivation, the ready availability of land, among other factors, made dry grain cultivation on unirrigated high lands (*goda bim*, as opposed to irrigated *mada bim* where wet rice was cultivated) a popular subsidiary pursuit. Slash-and-burn agriculture (*hēn* in Sinhala and *chena* as anglicized by the British), is a simple system of cultivation, involving the rotation of soil and relatively little exertion of labor. Villagers would communally slash and burn a portion of the village forest, hoe the ground and broadcast the seeds.[35] After the dry grains were harvested, the land was abandoned for a period ranging from five to twenty-five years, until it reverted to forest and was recultivated. Among the dry grains grown on chena land were finger millet or *kurakkan (elucine-coracana)*, maize, hill paddy (*elvi*), legumes, and many varieties of beans. Chena cultivation, then, guaranteed the peasantry a minimum security of subsistence when paddy crops failed and/or when claims of overlords on their rice crops became excessive.[36] During the slack season in wet rice cultivation, hoe agriculture became the primary occupation of the peasantry and their chief means of sustenance. Furthermore, it should be noted that the yields in dry grain cultivation were proportionately much higher than in paddy agriculture. Economic historian Ameer Ali, has noted that,

---

32. Stewart Gordon, "Recovery from Adversity in Eighteenth-Century India: Rethinking 'Villages', 'Peasants' and Politics in Pre-Modern Kingdoms", *Peasant Studies*, vol. 8, no. 4 (Fall 1979), p. 78.
33. de Silva, "Investment and Economic Growth", p. 48.
34. Ibid., p. 48. Where the popular term 'swidden' comes from is not clear.
35. For an account of the methods of slash-and-burn cultivation in Kandy, see Pieris, *Sinhalese Social Organization*, p. 86.
36. See Scott's observations on Southeast Asia, *The Moral Economy*, pp. 62–63.

According to the Blue Books, of about 450,000 acres of cultivated land in 1833 [throughout the island] nearly 100,000 had been under chena farming. And in view of the fact that there was only about 212,000 acres which had been under paddy that year, one can conclude that there was one acre of chena land for every two acres of paddy. Thus it was a "complementary and indispensable" element in Sri Lanka's rural economy.[37]

As noted elsewhere (Appendix 1), the agricultural statistics in the Blue Books were notoriously unreliable. But it is fair to surmise that given the periodic nature of chena cultivation and the difficulty of locating swidden plots hidden away in remote jungle areas, the Blue Books of the colonial administration may have underestimated rather than overestimated the acreage under chena crops. What is quite clear, however, is that chena agriculture was an integral part of the village economy and peasant subsistence. As James Scott has pointed out in relation to southeast Asia, it was one of the important 'fallback' activities of the village economy. He notes that,

> The existence of these options in a traditional peasant society gives it a certain elasticity – a capacity to absorb for a short time at least, crop failures and the claims of outsiders. A critical fact about these options is that, they are, even in normal times, an established part of local activity and their intensification does not greatly disturb the web of village life.[38]

Like in paddy agriculture, in chena too, a system of communal agricultural labor prevailed. The labor for jungle clearing, for example, was shared among fellow chena cultivators. However, the division of the chena plots into temporary individual or household shares during each chena cycle seemed to have been the common practice. Moreover, each cultivator was entitled only to the yield from his temporary plot.[39]

A further category of high land agriculture that contributed to peasant subsistence was garden (*vatta*) cultivation.[40] The vegetables, fruits, and spices that were grown on the small plots surrounding the peasant homes were important supplements of the peasant diet. When villages expanded, high lands which were previously used for shifting agriculture were turned into permanent home gardens. According to customary law, the gardens

---

37. A. C. M. Ameer Ali, "Rice and Irrigation in the Twentieth Century", *The Ceylon Historical Journal*, vol. 25 (October 1978), p. 253.
38. Scott, *The Moral Economy*, pp. 62–63.
39. H. W. Codrington, *Ancient Land Tenure and Revenue in Ceylon* (Colombo: Ceylon Government Press, 1938), p. 4.
40. Kotelawala identifies paddy, chena, and garden as the three main forms of agriculture in the Dutch-controlled south-west coastal belt. D. A. Kotelawala, "Agrarian Policies of the Dutch in South-West Ceylon, 1743–1767", *A. A. G. Bijdragen* 14 (1967), p. 4.

belonged to the households that cultivated them. A surplus was not systematically collected on them, although cultivators often presented their overlords with fruits and vegetables from their gardens.

Property Relations in Chena Cultivation

Except for the sequestered forests of the king (*tahansi käle*), especially the thick forest belt maintained to separate the Kandyan kingdom from the European ruled lowlands, all forests were potentially cultivable by the people.

Occasionally high lands were granted explicitly as 'appurtenances' to a paddy field, usually by the king to a feudal overlord. But even where such high land appurtenances to paddy fields were explicitly recognized, their precise extent, boundaries, or location were not stated in land rolls, deeds, or other legal documents. The vagueness of individual rights to chena land and high land in general is apparent in the wording of title deeds. For example, a deed of 1685 "made over the field Lambabarana with the buildings and plantations belonging thereto, the four hen [chena] thereto appurtenant,"[41] and a decree (*sittu*) of 1774 made over "two *pelas* and three *lahas* [both land measurements] of field [paddy field] together with the garden and the house and the high and low gardens."[42] This vagueness of individual rights to high lands corresponded to the temporary and shifting nature of swidden cultivation. The more precise boundaries and rights to paddy fields, on the other hand, reflected the settled and permanent nature of paddy agriculture.

As several writers have argued, chena land tenure was not identified by any standard criteria, but rather by local practice. For example, L. J. de S. Seneviratne says that where population was scanty and the area for chena practice large, communal ownership of forest land was recognized; but where land was scarce, chena land was held in individual shares. Given the low density of population and lack of competition for land in the Kandyan kingdom, Seneviratne concludes that "it is very likely that in early times, the chena tract was enjoyed in common."[43] Pieris too says that "Hen was forest which people were at liberty to clear for cultivation."[44]

As noted earlier, a chena became to temporary property of the person who cultivated it during the cultivation period. When not in cultivation, it

---

41. Quoted by Hayley, *A Treatise*, p. 4.
42. Ibid., p. 96.
43. Seneviratne, "Land Tenure", p. 38.
44. Pieris, *Sinhalese Social Organization*, p. 48.

Social and Economic Organization of the Kandyan Kingdom: 29

reverted to being village jungle. Seneviratne notes, "the possession of the chena became tangible only once in seven or eight years and in the interval, the land reassumed the character of ownerless jungle."[45]

It appears then that alongside the well-developed hierarchical tenurial rights to paddy fields (*mada idam*), there was a more communal sense of village rights to the category of land known as high land (*goda idam*), which included forests and chenas. That uncultivated forest and periodically cultivated swidden land was generally considered the common property of the village adjoining it, was recognized by a prominent official of the British colonial government in 1871.

> In many villages, especially in Matale North, the whole of the hen land is held in common and there is strong ground for believing that prior to the acquisition of the Kandyan territories by the British Government, individual possession of hen land was unknown; all hen which the villagers were allowed to cultivate being strictly common land belonging to the village. So clearly was this recognized that in some of the early records of this Government the word hen was ordinarily rendered "commons."[46]

The entire system of tribute exaction or surplus appropriation in the Kandyan kingdom was organized around the possession of paddy lands.[47] Even if the overlords wanted to exact tribute from the cultivators on the basis of chena landholdings within their respective feudal villages, they lacked the ability to do so. Ronald Herring's observation in relation to colonial and postcolonial Ceylonese conditions, is also applicable to the precolonial situation (although in precolonial times market relations were relatively undeveloped).

> The expropriation of the surplus of *chena* requires a great deal of effort relative to rewards compared to wet paddy where tenants can be concentrated physically and there are economies of scale in collecting and marketing the crop.[48]

As several writers have noted, in addition to supplementing the peasant diet, chena agriculture afforded the producer class a sense of relative political autonomy. John Harris has claimed that shifting cultivation connotes independence and freedom to the cultivators and was therefore preferable to paddy cultivation.[49] We noted earlier that when taxation on paddy lands became excessive, cultivators ran away to the jungles. Many who did so, resorted to slash-and-burn agriculture to maintain their livelihood.

---

45. Seneviratne, "Land Tenure", p. 38.
46. *AR* 1871, "Report of the Service Tenures Commissioner", J. F. Dickson, p. 370.
47. Knox, *An Historical Relation*, p. 69.
48. Ronald Herring, "Redistributive Agrarian Policy: Land and Credit in South Asia" (Ph. D. dissertation, University of Wisconsin-Madison, 1976), p. 404.
49. John Hariss, "Agriculture in the Economic Development of Sri Lanka", in *Agricul-*

But in spite of the many economic and political advantages of chena cultivation, a class of cultivators dependent entirely on chena did not emerge in the Kandyan Highlands. The traditional attachment of peasants to their ancestral paddy fields, the prestige associated with wet rice cultivation as the ritually highest caste occupation (discussed below), the self-identity of the Sinhalese as a nation of rice cultivators (*goiyas*), the preference for the consumption of rice over other grains, are the more popular explanations for this anomaly. The overdrawn image of the Sinhalese as a nation of rice cultivators and rice eaters constituted an important element in the ideological control exercised by the overlords in keeping peasants tied to the paddy fields. A more tangible reason for the nonemergence of a producer class dependent solely on chena, was the tighter political control exercised by the state and the feudal overlords over the cultivators in the Kandyan Highlands, and the repressive measures taken to ensure labor adhesion to paddy cultivation. To reiterate, the economic and political hegemony of the feudal overlords as a class rested on the cultivators being tied to their paddy fields.

In contrast, in the outlying regions of the Kandyan kingdom, such as parts of the former dry zone civilization, the insufficiency of water and the difficulties faced by the state and the feudal lords in exercising control, contributed to the emergence of relatively autonomous tribal groups (*varigé*), dependent primarily and sometimes exclusively on shifting cultivation for their subsistence.[50] James Brow's observations with regard to chena cultivation in the North Central Province during the twentieth century are applicable to the practice of swidden agriculture in the precolonial Kandyan Highlands as well.

> ... chena cultivation is egalitarian. It is undertaken by the smallest continously cooperating economic unit, the household, on land that is not individually owned and which is equally accessible to all. The capital requirements are minimal, an axe, a mamoty [hoe] and a sickle being the only necessary tools ... it is restricted only by the amount of manpower that the individual household can muster. It is largely geared to subsistence and provides few opportunities either for monetary profit or the elevation of one villager above his fellows. In all these respects ... it differs from paddy cultivation.[51]

---

ture in the Peasant Sector of Sri Lanka, ed. by S. W. R. de A. Samarasinghe (Peradeniya: Ceylon Studies Seminar, 1977), p. 41.

50. James Brow, "The Changing Structure of Appropriations in Vedda Agriculture", *American Ethnologist*, vol. 5, no. 3 (1978), p. 448. See also James Brow, "The Impact of Population Growth on the Agricultural Practices and Settlement Patterns of the Anuradhapura Veddahs", in *Contributions to Asian Studies*, ed. by James Brow, vol. 9 (Leiden: E. J. Bill, 1976), p. 81.

51. Ibid., p. 90.

Social and Economic Organization of the Kandyan Kingdom: 31

What is clear then is that both in terms of the productive forces and the social relations of production, paddy and chena agriculture differed sharply from each other. Paddy was labor intensive and required more elaborate techniques of production and labor organization. Property relations in paddy were hierarchical in that a class of overlords who had superior rights to the land exacted a surplus from the cultivators. In contrast, chena was labor extensive and relied on extremely simple methods of production and forms of labor mobilization. Property relations in chena were communal. Surplus appropriation by the overlords being generally absent, cultivators could enjoy the entire yields from their temporary chena plots.

Paddy and chena then signified two distinct feudal and communal modes of production. The feudalistic paddy agriculture was clearly the dominant mode. It was the locus of the politico-economic (as well as the ritual) organization of Kandyan society. The communalistic chena mode was a subordinate and supplementary mode of production. It is not correct, however, to view chena agriculture as a survival of a prefeudal mode of production that had existed prior to the development of plough-based wet-rice agriculture.[52] Paddy and chena were cultivated side by side by the same class of cultivators in the Kandyan Highlands. Chenas were cultivated during the slack season in paddy and when paddy fields failed to produce a crop. As a safety valve of peasant existence, swidden agriculture complemented paddy. However, as noted earlier, chena also represented a realm of political autonomy for the cultivator class providing the peasants a sphere wherein they could resist harsh surplus appropriation by the feudal overlords. The class struggle over rent between the overlords and the cultivators needs also to be understood in the context of this 'articulation' or fluctuating balance of forces between the dominant feudal and subordinate communal modes of production.[53]

Surplus Appropriation: Social Class and Village Organization

The villages of the Kandyan kingdom were identified by their overlordship: villages belonging to the crown (*gabadāgam*); to the feudal aristocracy

---

52. Boserup's hypothesis that increasing demographic pressure leads to a unilineal progression from hoe to plough agriculture needs historical verification. See Ester Boserup, *Woman's Role in Economic Development* (New York: St. Martin's Press, 1970), Ch. 1.
53. See discussion of the articulation of modes of production in Ch. IX of this study.

(*nindagam*); and the Buddhist temples (*vihāragam*). The king could transfer crown/royal villages to the nobility or revoke villages already granted to them. But the villages granted to the temples were irrevocable.[54]

Although these villages differed from each other in terms of overlordship, they were basically similar in terms of their internal socioeconomic organization. For example, all villages were comprised of both paddy and chena modes of production. Tribute exaction in the form of rent in kind (rarely in money) and forced labor services (on the basis of caste) characterized all villages. The specific labor services owed by the tenants to their overlords, however, tended to vary according to the role and status of the respective overlord within the larger society.

Crown Villages (*gabādagam*)

The king held certain villages for his personal maintenance. The tenants of these villages were liable to cultivate the king's share of the village paddy fields (*gabada muttettu*) and/or perform specialized labor services and supply pingo loads of produce (*kada rajakāriya*) to the king's storehouses.[55]

In addition, cultivators were obliged to perform corvée labor for the state. It is uncertain as to how much labor was exacted as corvée labor. It seems that an individual's share could have varied anywhere from thirty days to three months per year.[56] The labor thus exacted was used for defense and the construction of the irrigational infrastructure as well as items of conspicuous consumption for the royalty such as magnificent lakes and palaces.

Villages of the Aristocracy (*nindagam*)

Due to the shortage of cash, the remuneration of officials with land grants for their services to the state increased during the Kandyan period. In making such land grants, the rights of tribute exaction from the producer class were transferred from the king to the nobility. The villages so obtained were known as *nindagam*.[57]

---

54. H. L. Seneviratne, *Rituals of the Kandyan State* (Cambridge: Cambridge University Press, 1978), p. 8.
55. Wickramasekara, "The Social and Political Organization", p. 171.
56. Ibid., p. 171.
57. Gunasinghe distinguishes between villages held by the nobility *qua* nobles dissociated with any office (*nindagam*) and villages held by the nobles as officials of the state

Social and Economic Organization of the Kandyan Kingdom: 33

The expansion of aristocrats' villages strengthened the authority and the local autonomy of the aristocratic-administrative class vis-à-vis the direct producers as well as the central authority of the king. There was a continuous struggle between monarchical and feudal authority throughout the Kandyan period.[58] The localized power of the feudal lords was a prerequisite for the maintenance of royal authority. But the king attempted to control the power of the nobility by constant reallocation of feudal properties among different families, by revoking grants already made and, by giving preferential treatment to those aristocrats most loyal to himself. While the king wanted to maintain the aristocracy simply as a class of administrators, the aristocracy for their part struggled to consolidate their power independent of the king. It was a faction of these ambitious aristocrats who conspired with the British and finally managed to get rid of the Kandyan king in 1815.

Temple Villages (vihāragam and devālagam)

The key to the transformation of the Buddhist clergy (sangha) from the position of mendicants to that of feudal overlords in Sinhalese society lies in the land grants made to temples by the king and state officials. The granting of lands/villages to Buddhist temples was an innovation created to cope with hardship incurred during famines, when the laity could not support the monks.[59] But by the Kandyan period, the generosity shown to the Buddhist clergy in the form of land grants had become highly extensive.[60] Such gift-giving to the clergy was encouraged by the clergy themselves who stressed that generosity shown to them (dāna) was one of the highest forms of meritorious behavior available to the lay disciples of the Buddha.

In the Kandyan kingdom there were two categories of temple villages corresponding to two catagories of temples: the villages belonging to Buddhist temples (vihāragam) and villages belonging to deities venerated by Buddhists (devālagam). It needs to be pointed out that although Buddhism is atheistic in principle, deity worship came to be incorporated into the practice of Sinhalese Buddhism over the centuries since its introduction to Ceylon in

---

(badavadili), in "Agrarian Relations", p. 9. Following the more common usage in the literature on the Kandyan period, the term *nindagam* will be used to refer to both types of villages in this work. See Pieris, *Sinhalese Social Organization*, p. 60.

58. For Max Weber's discussion of patrimonial versus feudal authority, see Reinhard Bendix, *Max Weber: An Intellectual Portrait* (New York: Doubleday, 1962), p. 360.
59. H. C. Ray (ed.), *History of Ceylon* (Colombo: Ceylon University Press, 1960), vol. 1, p. 244.
60. Hayley, *A Treatise*, pp. 530–32.

the third century B.C. The incorporation of deity worship and cults is partly explainable by the fact that Buddhism being "essentially philosophical and rationalistic provided no consolation or relief for the mundane distresses and crises of life."[61]

However the temples of the Buddha and the deities worshipped by Buddhists were kept apart.[62] While the former were administered largely by the Buddhist clergy themselves, the latter were managed by lay incumbents (*nilemēs*) drawn from the feudal aristocracy. Knox observed the wealth and influence of the temples when he said

> Unto each of these pagodas, there are great revenues of land belonging: which have been allotted to them by former kings, according to the state of the kingdom; but they have much impaired the revenues of the crown, there being rather more towns belonging to the church, than unto the king.[63]

The tenant cultivators of temple lands were exempt from many of the services that other villagers owed to the state. The relatively lighter tax burden, due partly perhaps to the spiritual association, made many cultivators prefer attachment to temple villages rather than to royal or aristocrats' villages. There were cases where cultivators themselves granted their lands to temple villages in order to avoid payment of certain taxes to the state.[64] Due to the irrevocability of temple villages by the king, many aristocrats too preferred to grant their lands to temples headed by blood relatives. This allowed them to continue enjoying the produce and services of the cultivators of those villages.[65]

The alliance between the nobility and the higher clergy was such that certain aristocratic families gained hereditary rights to some of the most influential positions within the clerical organization. Partly as an effort to counteract this powerful alliance, the king stipulated that no lands could be granted to temples without his prior approval. This, however, was not always heeded. The consolidation of 'monastic landlordism', in turn, led to a process of economic differentiation within the clerical (*sangha*) community. An important development that contributed to this process during the Kandyan

---

61. S. J. Tambiah, "Ceylon", in *The Role of Savings and Wealth in Southern Asia and the West* (Paris: UNESCO, 1963), p. 122; see also Kitsiri Malalgoda, "Millennialism in Relation to Buddhism", *Comparative Studies in Society and History*, vol. 12, no. 4 (October 1970), p. 426.
62. Hayley, *A Treatise*, pp. 530–32; Hans-Dieter Evers, "Buddha and the Seven Gods: The Dual Organization of a Temple in Central Ceylon", *Journal of Asian Studies*, vol. 27, no. 3 (May 1968), p. 541.
63. Knox, *An Historical Relation*, p. 116; see also Hayley, *A Treatise*, p. 558.
64. Knox, *An Historical Relation*, p. 118.
65. Seneviratne, *The Ritual*, p. 8.

Social and Economic Organization of the Kandyan Kingdom: 35

period was the appointment of heads of temples (*vihārādhipati/adhikari*) and the selection of their successors according to the tradition of 'pupillary succession' (*sisyānu sisyaparamparāva*).

> This so-called "pupillary succession" (*sisyānu sisyaparamparāva*) was widely used to retain the monasteries, in the hands of certain influential families. ... For a number of monasteries, another rule of succession termed (*jnātisisparamparava*) ... became valid. Under this rule, only a relative of the deceased *vihārādhipati* could succeed him. Thus a layman could be the successor to a deceased monk, provided he was ready to take up the robes.[66]

A basic component of pupillary succession was the matrilineal transfer of temple property from an incumbent clergyman to his sister's son who was ordained under him.[67] Although the clergy continued to be celibate and remained confined to the monastic life of their order, the mechanisms of pupillary succession and matrilineal transfer of property ensured the concentration of temple property in the hands of the aristocratic families. This close alliance between the clergy and the nobility strengthened the power of the feudal overlord class vis-à-vis both the king and the cultivator class. For example if a tenant refused to perform his duty, the clergy (who did not mete out physical punishment) had only to appeal to the feudal chief of the district to have the tenant punished.[68] On other occasions, the nobility could depend on the clergy for support in their intrigues against the king.

In addition to the close relationship to the nobility, the higher echelons of the Buddhist clergy had a special relationship to the state as well. Buddhism was the state religion. The king, as the protector of Buddhism and the monastic order, provided the temples with extensive land grants and also participated actively in temple ritual. The Buddhist clergy in turn provided the dominant ideology justifying the status quo. Structural inequalities in the society based on caste, social class (and also sex) were legitimated by the Buddhist concept of cause and effect (*karma*) and the knowledge implicit therein that "a violation of this order was considered a negation of the harmonious mystical order of things, generating repercussions endangering all."[69]

---

66. Heinz Bechert, "Theravada Buddhist Sangha: Some General Observations on Historical and Political Factors in Its Development", *Journal of Asian Studies* 29 (1969-1970), pp. 767-68.
67. Gunasinghe, "Agrarian Relations", p. 10.
68. W. M. G. Colebrooke and C. H. Cameron, *The Colebrooke-Cameron Papers: Documents on British Colonial Policy in Ceylon, 1796-1833*, 2 vol. ed. by G. C. Mendis (London: Oxford University Press, 1956), vol. 1, p. 131.
69. de Silva, "Investment and Economic Growth", p. 29; see also Malalgoda, "Millennialism", p. 430.

Adding to the differentiation along class lines, a sectarianism based on caste (discussed below) also developed within the Buddhist clergy during the Kandyan period. The powerful *Siam* sect (so called because it first received higher ordination [*upasampadā*] from Siam) refused to ordain any but the high caste, *govi*, men. Two other sects, *Amarapura* and *Ramanya*, were established in the nineteenth century, as a reaction against this caste elitism.

The monastic organization then departed very radically from the Buddhist disciplinary code for the clergy (*vinaya*), which is antiproperty and anticaste to the core and was completely integrated into the class and caste-based feudal social structure of Kandy. The Buddhist clergy had become not only a powerful ideological authority but also an important feudal economic and political force in the society.[70]

'Free' Villages

It seems that in addition to the villages under the overlordship of the king, the nobility and the clergy, there was yet another category of villages known as 'free' villages (*korālagam*). The inhabitants of these were not considered serfs of any particular overlord and they seem to have been eminently proud of their 'free' status.[71] However, the number of such villages, their origin, or their relationship to the state are not clear. There is not sufficient evidence to establish the cultivators of these villages as a class of independent peasant proprietors or yeomanry in Kandyan society.[72]

Surplus Appropriation : 'Caste Feudalism'

The particular form of social relations of production known as 'serfdom' is characteristic of the relationship between the direct producers (tenant serfs) and the surplus-appropriating class (overlords) in 'feudal' societies.[73] The defining feature of 'feudalism' is that the overlords' rights to tribute exaction is

---

70. Tambiah, "Ceylon", p. 121.
71. Pieris, *Sinhalese Social Organization*, p. 25.
72. Gunasinghe, "Agrarian Relations", p. 9. Compare Hamza Alavi's observations on independent peasant proprietors in precolonial India in "India: From Feudalism", p. 370.
73. Karl Marx, *Pre-Capitalist Economic Formations*, pp. 125–39; for Max Weber, however, the defining feature of feudalism was the politico-juridical relationship between

extra-economic, i.e., it is not defined by their roles in the production process, but by other roles they play in the society as administrators, clerics, etc. Feudal overlords generally do not play a role in economic production but leave it entirely in the hands of the cultivators themselves.

In the West European and Japanese feudal societies, tenant cultivators often held land in exchange for military service for their overlords. Although constant warfare was a feature of Kandyan society (particularly against the foreign rulers of the lowlands) the forestial and mountainous nature of the Kandyan Highlands made guerilla warfare the most suitable form of military strategy for the kingdom. This state of military affairs did not therefore lend itself to the emergence of a class of feudal lords whose political power was largely dependent upon the possession of expensive military equipment and armor.[74] It is noteworthy, however, that protracted warfare to keep out the European rulers from the coastal lowlands "converted the people of the kingdom into a potential militia and made the intervention of the state much more intense in the daily existence of the people."[75]

The feudal aristocracy in Kandyan Ceylon held land and tribute-exacting rights on the basis of their administrative positions in the Kandyan state. The Kandyan state was essentially an 'agrarian bureaucracy' organized along the land tenure system of the society. The complex administrative apparatus of the state with the monarch at its apex was divided into three sectors: the royal household/palace (*māligāwa*); the territorial administration (*rata*); and, departments (*bādda*). The royal household was managed by the personal officials of the king. The largest unit in the territorial administration was the province (*disāva*). This in turn was divided into smaller units such as *korales*, *pattus* and villages or *gamas*. Each of these units was headed by a state official drawn from the aristocratic-administrative hierarchy. The various departments of the state such as the elephant catchers (*kuruve*) and transport (*madige*), supplied specialized services required by the state. They were each headed by state officials in charge of exacting the forced labor services of specific caste groups attached to their departments.[76]

In Kandyan Ceylon, tribute was paid largely in personal labor services rather than in cash or kind. This was due to several important reasons, among which the shortage of cash, the smallness of the social surplus, difficulty of storing grain, and the absence of a market economy were the most decisive.

---

the vassal and the sovereign. See Max Weber, *The Theory of Social and Economic Organization*, ed. by Talcott Parsons (New York: Free Press, 1964), pp. 373–81.
74. Wickramasekara, "The Social and Economic Organization", p. 35.
75. Gunasinghe, "Agrarian Relations", p. 12.
76. Pieris, *Sinhalese Social Organization*, Part 1.

Furthermore, the feudal overlords found that exaction of personal labor services helped enhance their retinues and their direct authority over the people.

The most distinctive feature of Sinhalese feudalism was that the exaction of labor services was organized along a caste system. E. R. Leach has termed it 'caste feudalism' and has suggested that the stasis of the precolonial Sinhalese economy was due to the *caste* nature of its feudalism.[77]

Caste can very broadly and briefly be seen as both a system of differentiation of society into hereditary occupational groups and a ritual stratification of those groups along a continuum of purity and pollution.[78] In the Sinhalese caste system, the cultivator caste (*govi*) is the numerically largest and the ritually highest caste. The feudal aristocracy belonged to the elite subcategory within the *govi* caste, commonly referred to as the *radala*. The numerous artisan/service castes such as the blacksmiths (*ācari*) and potters (*badahala*), etc., were placed below the *govi* caste in the caste hierarchy. But there was/is no unanimity regarding the precise status of some of the 'low' or service castes (see Appendix 2). As Pieris notes.

> But it must be noted that "The caste system" was far from being a clearly defined hierarchy in which the various castes were graded in an immutable order of precedence. While there was no doubt as to the superiority of the "good people" [*govis*], there was no unanimity regarding the precise status of some of the low castes.[79]

Caste differences apart, all members of the producer class, i.e., the tenant cultivators obliged to pay tribute to feudal overlords, were first and foremost subsistence rice cultivators. In fact, the cultivator caste and the service castes cultivated their paddy fields according to identical techniques. Neither is there evidence which suggests that the cultivator or *govi* caste had more land than the service castes. In drawing a distinction between the categories of class and caste, Robert Knox pointed out that

> The highest, are their noblemen, called Hondrews. . . . 'Tis out of this sort alone, that the king chooseth his great officers and whom he imploys in his Court, and appoints for Governors over his Countrey. Riches are not here valued, nor make any the more honourable. For many of the lower sorts do far exceed these Hondrews in Estates. But it is the birth and parentage that inobleth.[80]

The economic homogeneity of the 'peasantry' as tillers of the soil was a striking feature of Kandyan social life. It should be noted that the term

---

77. E. R. Leach refers to caste feudalism in both India and Ceylon in his "Hydraulic Society in Ceylon", *Past and Present*, no. 15 (1959), pp. 2–26.
78. For a comprehensive account of the Sinhalese caste system, see Bryce Ryan, *Caste in Modern Ceylon: The Sinhalese System in Transition* (New Brunswick, N. J.: Rutgers University Press, 1953).
79. Pieris, *Sinhalese Social Organization*, p. 176.
80. Knox, *An Historical Relation*, p. 106.

Social and Economic Organization of the Kandyan Kingdom: 39

peasantry will be used in this book in a general sense to refer to all direct producers on the land. As just noted, the producer class or peasantry was economically homogeneous in the precolonial era. But, as we shall discuss later, in addition to the pre-existing caste differences, the peasantry began to be economically differentiated, in terms of their access to land, during the subsequent British colonial period.

The two broad social classes in Kandyan society, then — the lords and the serfs — were distinguishable primarily in terms of their hierarchical rights to land. The numerous caste groups, on the other hand, were differentiated not in terms of property relations, but in terms of the forced labor services they formally owed to their feudal overlords as potters, drummers blacksmiths, etc., and the ritual status associated with those services. It is plausible that these caste differences within an otherwise homogeneous peasantry inhibited the emergence of class consciousness and collective action among the cultivator class.

We must turn to Robert Knox once again to understand how caste was utilized for the satisfaction of the technical division of labor in the feudal economy and how the utilization of caste for this purpose in turn inhibited structural transformations of Kandyan social institutions.

> The country being wholly his, the king farms out his land not for money but for service. And the people enjoy portions of land from the king and instead of rent they have their several appointments, some are to serve the king in his wars, some in their trades, some serve him for labourers and others are as farmers to furnish his House with the fruits of the Ground; and so all things are done without cost and every man paid for his pains: that is, they have lands for it....
>
> Many towns are in the king's hand, the inhabitants whereof are to till and manure a quantity of the land according to their ability, and lay up the corn for the king's use. These towns the king often bestows upon some of his nobles for their encouragement and maintenance, with all the fruits and benefits that before came to the king from them. In each of these towns there is a smith to make and mend the tools of them to whom the king hath granted them, and a potter to fit them with earthen ware, and a washer to wash their cloaths, and other men to supply what there is need of. And each of these hath a piece of land for this their service, whether it be to the king or the lord; but what they do for the other people they are paid for. Thus all that have any place or employment under the King, are paid without any charge to the king.[81]

When the services of a particular caste were no longer required, it was given a new occupation by the state. Similarly, when the need for a new service emerged, either a new subcaste was created or the functions of an already existing caste were adjusted (usually by the king) to meet the new services required. There was, then, as in the Indian caste system, "ample

---

81. Ibid., pp. 68–69.

scope for fission and fusion *within* each major group" (emphasis added).[82] But this *inner* flexibility of the caste system made caste a barrier to *structural* transformation of the economy and society.

It has been argued that the fundamental stasis of feudalism based on caste (as opposed to, say, feudalism of the West European or Japanese types), was one of the factors that inhibited indigenous economic development through the growth of trade and reinvestment.[83] The assignment of each member of the society at birth to a caste-specific vocation and the caste endogamous nature of most villages, made labor mobility and entrepreneurship difficult.

A peculiar feature of the Sinhalese caste system was that all castes were primarily subsistence cultivators, and that economic specialization was restricted to subsidiary pursuits. This, coupled with various other restrictions placed by caste inhibited the extension of the technical division of labor.[84] Although the division of labor was highly specialized (along caste lines) and complex, the technology of production remained backward. The social surplus being small, the society was not able to support a non-agricultural population freed from the function of subsistence production. As S. B. D. de Silva has observed,

> The stagnation of agricultural technique which was associated with the virtual absence of a professional class of whole-time artisans, exempt from the absorbing task of growing their own food and hence free to specialize in devising or improving agricultural implements, was both a cause and an effect of the meagre size of the grain surplus.[85]

Furthermore, ' the caste system hindered individual economic relations by preventing loan transactions between people of different castes and discouraged industry by forbidding the use of luxury articles by lower layers of society."[86] A very significant share of the slender economic surplus was devoted to conspicuous consumption and especially to the construction of large monuments by the royalty and the nobility, rather than to reinvestment in agriculture and the expansion of economic production. This did not escape Knox's keen eye.

> The king often employs his people on vast works and that will require years to finish, that he may inure them to slavery, and prevent them from plotting against him, as haply they might do if they were at better leisure. Therefore he approved not that his

---

82. Pieris, *Sinhalese Social Organization*, p. 171.
83. de Silva, "Investment and Economic Growth", p. 29.
84. Ibid., p. 35.
85. Ibid., p. 30.
86. Ibid., p. 30.

people should be idle; but always finds one thing or other to be done, tho the work be to little or no purpose.[87]

Max Weber's famous hypothesis that Asiatic religions, particularly Buddhism, which represents the most pure type of 'other worldly mysticism', lacks the 'premiums' for the development of a rational ethic conducive to the growth of western-style capitalist entrepreneurship needs mentioning here.[88] Extending Weber's thesis to Sinhalese society it could well be argued, that the premium for 'nonaction' in this world enunciated in the Buddhist doctrine and perhaps overemphasized by the clergy, may have been a contributory factor in the economic stasis of Kandyan society.

However, several important qualifications need to be interjected here. Economic stasis was not characteristic of all periods in the historical evolution of Sinhalese Buddhist society. Many of the dry-zone hydraulic societies which preceded the Kandyan kingdom achieved high levels of technological progress and agricultural development. It should also be pointed out that for Sinhalese Buddhists caste does not represent a doctrinal principle. It is possible to hypothesize, then, that the barrier to economic dynamism rested not so much in the 'other worldly mysticism' of the Buddhist doctrine as in the caste principle of social organization which was a secular — specifically Hindu — concept incorporated into religious practice.

Most western social scientists (and western-trained local scholars) starting with Max Weber have attributed the backwardness of nonwestern economies to internal factors, largely to psychological characteristics. How external forces, especially European colonialism, contributed to economic stasis of nonwestern societies has long been neglected. This is precisely the objective of this book: to delineate the nature of external impact on Kandyan society during British rule. Before we approach that central theme in later chapters, we shall briefly discuss here the effects of trade and Dutch mercantilism on Kandy in the period preceding British conquest and direct colonial rule.

Kandyan Trade and the Effects of European Mercantilism

Trade contact is a vent through which a self-sufficient village economy can be undermined. Paul Sweezy has pointed out that external trade played a

---

87. Knox, *An Historical Relation*, p. 70.
88. Max Weber, *The Religion of India* (Glencoe, Ill.: Free Press, 1958), p. 4.

decisive role in the reorganization of domestic production and the transition from feudalism to capitalism in western Europe.[89] But the impact of trade contact varies with the nature of the external impact itself and the nature of the internal social organization. European mercantilism seems to have had an 'involuting', rather than a transformative effect on Kandyan feudalism. A discussion of its impact on the coastal lowlands which were under the direct political control of the mercantile powers for over three centuries, i.e., the Portuguese (1505–1666), the Dutch (1666–1796), and, the British (1796-c. 1833), is beyond our scope here.[90]

While a certain amount of foreign trade was characteristic of the Sinhalese economy from a very early time on, trade had increased with the shift of populations and kingdoms from the dry zone to the wet zone since about the thirteenth century A.D. When Sinhalese sovereignty was forced to withdraw into the landlocked interior in order to safeguard its independence from the Europeans, external trade became essential to sustain a modicum of economic prosperity and vitality and even political autonomy. Contrary to the popular view that the Kandyan kings deliberately maintained the self-sufficiency of the Kandyan economy and insulated it from outside forces, historian Arasaratnam has argued that the policy of the Kandyan state was directed explicitly at the maintenance of external links via trade.[91] Arasaratnam is one of the few writers who has attempted to *explain* the increasing self-sufficiency and insulation of the Kandyan economy during the seventeenth and eighteenth centuries, rather than attributing it simply to 'traditional backwardness .

S. B. D. de Silva presents a convincing analysis of the relationship between caste and the stasis of precolonial Sinhalese economy. However, his ahistorical approach towards precolonial social formations prevents him from seeing that the stasis of the Kandyan economy was not necessarily characteristic of other periods or forms of precolonial Sinhalese economy. Furthermore, he attributes the stasis simply to internal factors thus failing to see how

---

89. Paul Sweezy, "A Rejoinder", in *The Transition from Feudalism to Capitalism* (with Introduction by Rodney Hilton) (London: New Left Books, 1976), p. 106. Sweezy's hypothesis has been challenged by Maurice Dobb, et al., who argue that the internal struggle over rent between lords and serfs was the primary cause for the transition from feudalism to capitalism in western Europe. See Maurice Dobb, *Studies in the Development of Capitalism* (New York: International Publishers, 1963), p. 42.
90. For an enlightening discussion of the intensification of feudal social relations in the coastal lowlands during European mercantile rule, see E. Reimers, "Feudalism in Ceylon", *Journal of the Royal Asiatic Society (Ceylon)*, vol. 31, no. 81 (1928).
91. S. Arasaratnam, "The Kingdom of Kandy: Aspects of its external Relations and Commerce, 1658–1710", *CJHSS*, vol. 3, no. 3 (July-December 1960).

Social and Economic Organization of the Kandyan Kingdom: 43

external factors such as European mercantilism, may have contributed to the intensification of the feudal basis of the social structure and the economy.[92] It is important to interject here that such a strengthening of existing social structures resulting from the impact of external trade was not peculiar to the Kandyan case. For example, Robert Brenner has pointed out that in the case of Eastern Europe ". . . during the late medieval and early modern period, the powerful impact of the world market for grain gave a major impetus to the tightening of peasant bondage at the same time as it was stimulating the development of capitalism in the West."[93]

From the inception of the Kandyan state (circa 1591), there had been regular trade with the outside world, particularly in commodities used by ordinary people: "Paddy was sometimes brought in and sometimes taken out, especially from the Eastern ports, depending on the relative demand and supply in Ceylon and India."[94] The main article of import was cloth; and of export, arecanut. Each trader and middleman dealt in both articles and much of the negotiations took the form of barter. In addition, Kandyans also imported some basic necessities such as salt and dried fish and exported spices such as pepper and cinnamon.[95] Michael Roberts' remarks on the precolonial trading patterns in the island are particularly applicable to the Kandyan Highlands.

> . . . a segment of the population (particularly the Moors) specialized in trading activities and sections of the population were familiar with market transactions. While some (perhaps most?) of the transactions took a non-monetary form, it is evident that monetary exchanges also occurred. Nevertheless, the impression remains that its use was limited. The first British Governor [of the coastal lowlands] was struck by the fact that there was "so little" trade. . . . The internal overland trade was restricted by limitations of transport. The principal form of transport was pack cattle (*tavalam*) . . .; river transport being available to a few localities only. . . . There were obvious limitations to the volume of any trade which relied on such freighting facilities.[96]

Given these essential features of Kadyan trade, that is, the import of manufactured goods, the export of natural goods, the predominance of

---

92. de Silva, "Investment and Economic Growth", p. 32.
93. Robert Brenner, "Agrarian Class Structure and Economic Development in Pre-Industrial Europe", *Past and Present*, no. 70 (February 1976), p. 43. See also Robert Brenner's "The Origins of Capitalist Development: A Critique of Neo-Smithian Marxism", *New Left Review*, no. 104 (July-August 1977), esp. section 3. Compare Pierre Philip Rey's position on the impact of trade on the precapitalist lineage mode of production as discussed by Aiden Foster-Carter in "Can We Articulate 'Articulation'?" in *The New Economic Anthropology*, ed. by John Clammer (New York: St. Martin's Press, 1978), pp. 217–31.
94. Arasaratnam, "The Kingdom of Kandy", pp. 109–11.
95. Michael Roberts, "Some Comments on Ameer Ali's Paper", *Ceylon Studies Seminar*, no. 3b, 1970/72 Series, p. 4.
96. Ibid., p. 5.

barter over monetary exchanges and limitations in transport it could not affect the relative self-sufficiency of the village economy or the occupational specialization based on caste. Nevertheless, this trade was important to the Kandyan king who lacked a navy of his own and had therefore to rely on contacts to the outside world through the Hindu and Muslim traders from the South Indian coasts who were the main participants in overseas trade.[97]

During their rule over the coastal lowlands of Ceylon, the Portuguese attempted to capture the Kandyan kingdom and exercise control over its trade. The Kandyans, however, succeeded in resisting political and economic control by the Portuguese. But with the subsequent rulers of the coast — the Dutch — the Kandyans were less successful. Here, we shall be concerned only with the impact of Dutch mercantilism (which reigned over the coastal lowlands between 1666 and 1796) on the Kadyan kingdom.

The Dutch, who followed a more systematic commercial policy than the Portuguese in Ceylon, were obsessed with securing a monopoly of trade throughout the island. This called for the subordination of the Kandyan kingdom which provided a considerable amount of the food supply of the lowlands and about two-thirds of the total exports from Ceylon. Furthermore, a number of the seaports that were central to this trade were still under the control of the Kandyan monarch and had to be taken over in order to establish Dutch monopoly over the island's trade.[98]

In spite of the desperate resistance put up by the Kandyan king, the Dutch managed to usurp control over the external trade and seaports of the Kandyan kingdom. All Kandyan products had now to be sold to the Dutch, and all articles the kingdom imported from the outside world had to be obtained from the Dutch as well.

While this policy increased the profits of the Dutch East India Company which ruled the coastal belt of the island, it reduced the Kandyan kingdom to a subordinate position of isolation and autarky, despite its continued political independence. According to Arasaratram,

> The tremendous efforts at survival of the seventeenth century and the subsequent pressure of the Dutch weakened the Kandyan kingdom, leaving it by the end of the eighteenth century an anachronistic remnant of Sinhalese power. Dutch mastery of all lucrative sources of wealth in the country left nothing with which this kingdom could rebuild itself. Its products were all channelled to Dutch ports at prices well below market value. Land was the only source of revenue in the kingdom, and good arable land was not abundant. Communication in the mountainous terrain was very difficult, and villages and districts developed as independent economic entities, with little surplus production and no means of disposing of this surplus....

97. Arasaratnam, "The Kingdom of Kandy", pp. 112–13.
98. Ibid., pp. 114–16.

Social and Economic Organization of the Kandyan Kingdom: 45

... The Kandyans fell into an intellectual and material stagnation, knew nothing of the world around them, and were steeped in ancient tradition. *Their economic organization became more feudal; chiefs, as Dissavas and other officers, wielded ever greater authority over the people.* [emphasis added] [99]

It is clear that the effect of Dutch mercantilism on the Kandyan economy was forced isolation and involution, rather than economic expansion. This meant that with the decline of commerce, the money supply of the state, which had not been great to begin with, was further reduced. It meant also that the state had to pay its officials increasingly with land grants in lieu of money. As noted earlier, land was the basis of political authority in Kandyan society. The increase in land grants to the nobles and the accompanying decentralization of political power tended to strengthen the power of the feudal lords over the tenants.[100] The feudal lords intensified the exaction of personal labor services. The general trend was towards the strengthening of the caste system (along which forced labor exaction was organized) and greater oppression of the cultivator class.

99. Arasaratnam, *Ceylon* (Englewood Cliffs, N. J.: Prentice-Hall, 1964), p. 147.
100. Ibid., p. 147.

III. The First Phase of British Rule in Ceylon: The Mercantilist Period, 1796-1833

This chapter recounts the capture and consolidation of political authority in the coastal lowlands and the Kandyan kingdom by the British, the main trends in economic and social development between 1796 and 1833, and the reforms introduced by the Colebrooke-Cameron Commission of Inquiry in 1833. This will provide the essential historical background for understanding the effects of plantation agriculture which commenced in the 1830s. A comprehensive examination of the controversial issues pertaining to the early period of British rule in Ceylon, 1796–1833, however, is not the objective of this chapter.

The Establishment of British Rule in Ceylon

Capture of the Maritime Provinces by the British: 1796

The initial attraction of Ceylon for the British was in her strategic location on the east-west trade route and as a naval base for the British Indian Empire. The rivalry between the British East India Company and the French in India, and the importance of the natural harbor of Trincomalee, on Ceylon's eastern coast for the command of the Malabar and Coromandel coasts of India, led to the capture of Trincomalee by the British in 1782.[1] But it was the political developments in Europe during the wars of revolution that resulted in the eventual annexation of the coastal lowlands of Ceylon by the British after the expulsion of the Dutch in 1796.

Being only a temporary possession captured to protect British interests in India against the French, Ceylon was at first administered by the East India Company as part of the Presidency of Madras. But in order to provide a more efficient government and to increase the chances of holding it permanently, the British imperial government made Ceylon a crown colony in 1802 in spite

---

1. K. M. de Silva, "The Coming of the British to Ceylon, 1762–1802", in *History of Ceylon*, ed. by K. M. de Silva vol. 3, pp. 3–6.

The first phase of British Rule in Ceylon 47

of the objections of the East India Company, which had governed the coastal lowlands until then. The Peace of Amiens, signed between England and France during the same year, confirmed British possession of maritime Ceylon.

Cession of the Kandyan Kingdom

In the early years of their rule in the coastal lowlands, the British relaxed control that had been imposed by the Dutch over the external trade of the Kandyan kingdom by allowing the Kandyan king to use some of the island's sea ports.[2] This move was motivated by desire to convince the Kandyan king that British presence in Ceylon would be beneficial to him. However, once their political authority was entrenched in the coastal lowlands, the British sought to subjugate the Kandyan kingdom. Among the reasons for this were the needs to: reduce insecurity and expenditures involved in guarding the frontiers; gain direct access between the western and eastern coasts of Ceylon; and control the products of the Kandyan kingdom. But the Kandyan monarch remained unmoved by diplomatic pressures and resisted subordination to the British. As elsewhere in the nonwestern world, resistance by the native ruler (in this case, the Kandyan king) brought forth formal political annexation by the militarily and technically advanced nation (Britain).[3]

The British had attempted to annex the Kandyan kingdom several times between 1803 and 1815 but failed in the face of guerilla resistance by the Kandyans. But when a faction of the Kandyan aristocracy opposed to the king solicited the British to intervene, the British came in and, exploiting this opportunity, they deposed the Kandyan king. Moreover, the British 'liberators' usurped the Kandyan throne for themselves; an outcome unanticipated by the Kandyan aristocratic conspirators! The justification given by the British for their intervention was the desire to rescue the Kandyan people from the tyranny of their king, Sri Vickrama Rajasinghe, and to project and promote Buddhism, the religion of the people, which the tyrannical king had neglected.[4] But as J. S. Furnivall, the early theorist of colonialism. has

---

2. K. M. de Silva, "The Kandyan Kingdom and the British – The Last Phase, 1796 to 1818", in *History of Ceylon*, ed. by K. M. de Silva, vol. 3, p. 15.
3. For a discussion of the decisive factors for formal empire building, see D. K. Fieldhouse, *Economics and Empire: 1830–1914* (London: Weidenfeld and Nicolson, 1973), p. 154.
4. K. M. de Silva, "The Kandyan Kingdom", pp. 24–25. See also Malalgoda, "Millennialism", p. 433.

pointed out, colonizing powers tend to "justify their activities on moral grounds and colour them with the warm glow of humanitarianism" even though their primary motive was "the search for material advantage."[5]

We lack sufficient evidence of the magnitude of the tyranny inflicted by Sri Vickrama Rajasinghe on the Kandyan people or the level of popular resentment against him. But the consensus among Ceylonese historians is that the deposal of the king was due to aristocratic opposition rather than popular rebellion. For example, K. M. de Silva says

> Sri Vickrama Rajasinghe's rule for all the drama and the political turmoil associated with it, was singularly and significantly free of any such demonstrations of the people's dissatisfaction. The people gave little or no support to the advancing British army in 1815, and demonstrated no enthusiasm at the cession of the Kandyan kingdom to the British. Thus the political turmoil in the Kandyan Kingdom in 1814-15 can by no stretch of the imagination be called a rebellion of the people.[6]

When the people were deeply dissatisfied with their ruler over a political, economic religious, or other issue. they resorted to riots or rebellions. These popular rebellions were not inspired by any particular ideology or a desire to restructure the existing social order, but by the immediate collective need to show disapproval.[7] But according to K. M. de Silva and other writers, no such mass revolt took place in 1815. It was rather the intensification of the power struggle between monarchical and feudal interests in Kandy, and the emergence of Britain as the dominant force in the South Asian region, that led to the alliance between the aristocracy and the British, and the subsequent cession of the Kandyan kingdom.[8]

It appears that the aristocratic disaffection with the king grew out of those policies of the absolutist monarch which threatened the interests of the feudal chiefs as a social class. The king had on occasion "conferred superior office on men of a lower status than that from which it was customary to fill such positions,"[9] which was obviously a cause for much grievance among the nobility. In addition, the king sometimes took measures to restrain the chiefs from exercising their powers over the people arbitrarily.

Apparently, the aristocratic opposition to the king gained greater momentum with the disenchantment of prominent Buddhist clergymen (*bhikkus*)

---

5. J. S. Furnivall, *Colonial Policy and Practice: A Comparative Study of Burma and Netherlands India* (Cambridge: Cambridge University Press, 1948), p. 6.
6. K. M. de Silva, "The Kandyan Kingdom", p. 25. See also, Colvin R. de Silva, *Ceylon Under the British Occupation*, 2 vols. (Colombo: Colombo Apothecaries, 1953), vol. 1, p. 158.
7. K. M. de Silva, "The Kandyan Kingdom", p. 26.
8. Ibid., pp. 12-16.
9. P. E. Pieris, quoted in ibid., p. 22.

The first phase of British Rule in Ceylon

with Sri Vikrama Rajasinghe. However, as K. M. de Silva has pointed out, there is insufficient evidence to determine whether the alienation and opposition of the clergy were caused by the king's religious policies, or the clergy's kinship ties to the aristocracy.[10] It was probably due to a combination of both these as well as other factors.

As noted above, on deposing the Sinhala monarch, the British annexed the Kandyan Kingdom instead of securing the throne for the puppet king chosen by the aristocracy. As Colvin R. de Silva has remarked,

> The Kandyans [i.e., the aristocracy] had turned with too facile readiness to the idea of bringing in the foreigner to settle their political differences. That pitcher went once too often to the well. The convenient arbitrator became the permanent master. The Kandyans accomplished their own political doom.[11]

It has been pointed out that the Portuguese and the Dutch who ruled maritime Ceylon prior to the British, were unable to conquer the Kandyan kingdom because of the inadequacy of their own military resources rather than any inherent military strength of the Kandyan kingdom. In contrast, by 1815, the British were not only the most formidable imperial force in the world, but also the dominant force in the South Asian region.[12] It is important to note, however, that the Kandyan kingdom was ceded, not conquered by the British. It was political acumen rather than military strength that led to the British success in taking Kandy.

The Kandyan Convention of 1815

By the Kandyan Convention of March 2, 1815 (Appendix III), signed by the British and members of the Kandyan feudal-administrative class, the kingdom was turned into a British colony. However, the Brtish recognized the political necessity of providing guarantees to those groups and individuals who had assisted them in pacifying the kingdom which hitherto no European power had been able to conquer. It was for these reasons that the British tactfully agreed to govern according to the customary laws and institutions of the kingdom and particularly to maintain the "rights, privileges and powers" of the chiefs, the Buddhist religion and the Sangha.[13]

---

10. Ibid., pp. 22–23.
11. Colvin R. de Silva, *Ceylon Under British Occupation*, vol. 1, p. 158.
12. K. M. de Silva, "The Kandyan Kingdom", p. 13.
13. The Proclamation of 2nd March, 1815 or the Kandyan Convention in *A Revised Edition of the Legislative Enactments of Ceylon*, vol. 1 (Colombo: Government Printer, 1923), pp. 59–60.

The Kandyan Convention was aimed at conferring legitimacy on British rule in the Kandyan kingdom. It enabled the British colonial state to present itself as the rightful successor to the Sinhalese monarch. In fact, as noted earlier, the very reason given by the British for their intervention was the liberation of the people from their oppressive king who violated the customs and conventions of Kandyan society. The justification then was that the British would be more Kandyan than the Kandyan king himself!

However, during the course of the nineteenth century, Kandyan interests which the British promised to uphold and the European capitalist interests that the colonial state in fact chose to foster began to clash with each other. In later chapters we will consider how the colonial state adapted Kandyan customs and institutions to further the British political and economic interests and the contradictions and dilemmas that arose during that process.

The Great Rebellion of 1817–1818

The British established a separate administrative structure for the Kandyan Provinces by superimposing a British Board of Commissioners on the native feudal administration. They also maintained intact the basic institutions of Kandyan society. However, dissatisfaction with British rule soon spread among the feudal nobility, the Buddhist clergy and the peasantry. As Colvin R. de Silva has pointed out, the primary reason for the feudal dissatisfaction was loss of their status in society.[14] The superimposition of a European administrative class above the entire feudal administrative hierarchy meant that all feudal chiefs were now compelled to pay homage and obeisance even to a common British soldier, whereas in pre-British times the nobles were subordinate only to the Kandyan monarch. Furthermore, the British sought to curtail some of the emoluments and powers of the chiefs.

The Buddhist clergy (*sangha*), too, became dissatisfied with the alien Christian government and the severance of the historical link between the state and Buddhism. The Sinhalese monarchs personally took part in religious ceremonies; they paid homage to the clergy particularly by bestowing large land grants to the temples for the maintenance of the clergy. The clergy soon came to realize that the British officials who were Christians could not replace the Kandyan king. Nor were the British prepared to give the clergy the veneration they were accustomed to receive from the Kandyan kings.[16]

---

14. Colvin R. de Silva, *Ceylon Under British Occupation*, vol. 1, p. 160.
15. Ibid., p. 160.
16. G. C. Mendis, *Ceylon Under the British* (Colombo: Colombo Apothecaries, 1944), p. 16.

The first phase of British Rule in Ceylon

It seems that the masses of the people were not favorably disposed towards the British either. The substitution of an alien race in place of the monarch that they had deified, the dimuniution of the dignity of their chiefs who were their patriarchal lords, probably contributed to the peasants' own loss of national pride and growing antipathy towards the British.[17] Moreover, it is likely, that even at this early stage of British rule, the manner in which the British began to abuse traditional institutions such as corvée labor (*rājakāriya*) caused great hardship to the producer classes and contributed to their desire for the restoration of Kandyan monarchy.

The revolt that ensued quickly spread throughout the Kandyan Provinces. This revolt, considered the "most formidable insurrection during the whole period of British occupation in Ceylon,"[18] is generally known as the Great Rebellion of 1817–1818. All segments of the Kandyan population — many factions of the aristocracy, the clergy and the peasantry — seem to have participated in this effort to drive out the British.

The rebellion sparked off when a Muslim population in the outlying provinces of Bintanna and Vellassa persuaded the British to appoint a Muslim headman in order to escape payment of levies to their Sinhalese governor (*dissava*). The Sinhalese governor naturally objected to the reduction of his income and authority. So, when a pretender to the Kandyan throne named Vilbave appeared, the governor and his people supported him. Though there was no pre-arranged plan, once the revolt began, many other Kandyan chiefs who were dissatisfied with the British joined the rebels. Before long, only a few chiefs remained loyal to the British.[19] It was only with the utmost severity and repression that the British put down the rebellion.

Historians agree that the Great Rebellion of 1818 was a postpacification revolt in which all segments of the Kandyan population came together to drive out the common enemy and restore the precolonial social order.[20] The rebellion was not simply a feudal reaction but also a popular nationalist revolt. Some of the reasons for the alliance between the overlord and cultivator classes in this instance, will be discussed in Chapter VIII.

Consolidation of British Political Authority in Kandy: 1818

Following the standards of English constitutional law, the British treated the 1815 Kandyan Convention as any other ordinary treaty capable of amen-

---

17. Colvin R. de Silva, *Ceylon Under British Occupation*, vol. 1, p. 162.
18. K. M. de Silva, "The Kandyan Kingdom", p. 32.
19. Mendis, *Ceylon Under the British*, p. 16.
20. Michael Roberts, "Variations on the Theme of Resistance Movements: The Kandyan

dment by subsequent legislation.²¹ This the British did by passing the Proclamation of 1818. The object of introducing the new Bill was to bring the rebellious Kandyan Provinces more firmly under British control and to curtail the powers and the privileges of the Kandyan chiefs. For example, British officials known as Government Agents, rather than the feudal chiefs, were now made the central figures of the provincial administration. Furthermore, the protection afforded to Buddhism was reduced, in effect, by being extended to other religions as well.

In addition, the British experimented with several alternative strategies to offset the power of the feudal chiefs. One such was the attempt to institute a free peasantry. This they tried to do by releasing the tenant cultivators of the former crown villages (*gabādagam*) from forced labor duties and having them pay a grain tax instead. In subsequent chapters we shall consider the relative successes and failures of such methods used by the British to counteract the authority of the native chiefs.

The changes introduced by the Proclamation of 1818, along with the network of roads built to link the interior and the coast, opened the Kandyan Highlands to increasing influences from the outside world. However, it was with the introduction of a plantation economy around the third decade of the nineteenth century, that the isolation of the Kandyan kingdom was completely broken down. This process included the incorporation of Kandy into the world economy and the adaptation of precolonial social institutions to satisfy the needs of the colonial plantation economy and industrializing Britain.

The Dominance of British Mercantilism: 1796-1833

Merchant capital flourished independently in many parts of the world before they were colonized by Europeans. But its modern history starts in the sixteenth century when European merchant capital created the framework for the capitalist world market.²²

Rebellion of 1817–18 and Latter Day Nationalism in Ceylon", *Ceylon Studies Seminar*, no. 9 (1970/1972 Series), p. 21. See also, S. Arasaratnam, *Ceylon*, p. 152 and K. M. de Silva, "Nineteenth-Century Origins of Nationalism in Ceylon", in *History of Ceylon*, vol. 3, ed. by K. M. de Silva, pp. 249–61.

21. K. M. de Silva, "The Kandyan Kingdom", p. 27. See also the Proclamation of 21st November, 1818, in *A Revised edition of the Legislative Enactments* vol. 1, pp. 60–64.

22. Geoffrey Kay, *Development and Underdevelopment: A Marxist Analysis* (London:

The first phase of British Rule in Ceylon

From the beginning of historic times Ceylon had been an entrepôt in east-west trade. This trade had always been in the hands of non-Sinhalese traders such as South Indians and Arabs. Arabs had frequented Ceylon for many centuries as middlemen in east-west trade. By the fourteenth century, with the shift of Sinhalese capitals to the southwest and the local monarchs' search for new sources of revenue and political support, these Muslim traders had begun to arrive in larger numbers and to play an important role in the local economy and the royal court.[23]

The Arab traders who began coming to Ceylon starting around the tenth century A.D. were probably descendants of Arab settlers in the Malabar coast of India, rather than direct arrivals from the Middle East. They formed trading communities along the southwestern coast of the island and by integrating their interests with those of the local sovereign, gained a virtual monopoly of the island's import-export trade. While their imports included textiles and luxury goods, their exports consisted largely of ivory, precious stones, cinnamon, and pepper.

One of the features that distinguished these Muslim traders from the Europeans who displaced them in the sixteenth century was that the Muslims were not military powers. Being politically and militarily subordinate to the local rulers, they had to ingratiate themselves by paying tribute to the local monarchs and by performing diplomatic services for them: "The main concern of these Arab merchants was none other than to see that the local sovereign did not allow himself to be cajoled by their rivals."[24]

These Arab merchants formed themselves into separate but permanent settlements along the island's coast. Having thus become a local population, they did not export the profits of their trade abroad as did the European mercantilists who subsequently usurped the Arabs' trade monopoly in Ceylon and the Indian Ocean region.

During the early years of their rule in Ceylon, the British (first the East India Company and then the colonial state), continued the mercantilist policies inherited from their Portuguese and Dutch forebears. The British continued the cinnamon trade intact, maintaining the state monopoly and the use of compulsory labor services of the *Chaliya* or *Salagama* caste of cinnamon

---

Macmillan, 1975), p. 94. Immanuel Wallerstein, however, is emphatic that sixteenth-century Portuguese mercantilism in Asia did not develop the preconditions for Asia's incorporation into the European world market. *The Modern World System: Capitalist Agriculture and the Origins of the European World Economy in the Sixteenth Century* (New York: Academic Press, 1974), pp. 343–44.

23. H. C. Ray (ed.), *History of Ceylon* (Colombo: Ceylon University Press, 1960), vol. 1, part 2, pp. 711–12.
24. Ibid., pp. 711–12; see also C. R. de Silva, "Some Comments on the Political and Economic Conditions".

peelers. The state monopolies in salt and tobacco were also continued. Some of the other state monopolies in arrack and toddy (both alcoholic beverages derived from coconut), pearl fishery and gem digging were rented out, i.e., the right of collecting the 'government's share' or, in other words, the task of surplus appropriation, was auctioned to the highest bidder.[25]

British mercantilist policies, like the Portuguese and Dutch policies before them, encouraged trade, but discouraged investment and the development of agricultural enterprise. For example, when a greater volume of exports was needed, the surplus extracted from the producers (in labor and in kind) was increased instead of improving the social and/or technical bases of production. In other words, systematic methods of production were not developed. The meagre attempts made by some Dutch and British state officials to cultivate cash crops in plantations before the 1830s were not very successful. As a subsequent British Commission of Inquiry in Ceylon remarked in 1833:

> . . . Besides the system of monopoly maintained and in some cases extended by the government, the power exercised by the Governor of regulating duties and imposing taxes has been injurious to commerce and to the influx and accumulation of capital. . . .[26]

The position of the British mercantilist state on traditional institutions, such as compulsory labor, was, to say the least, ambiguous. The liberal-humanitarian and laissez-faire interests encouraged the abolition of forced labor and its replacement with a grain tax. But the shortages in both labor and state revenue led to the continued use of forced labor for such things as the construction of roads and collection of cinnamon. It is important to remember that while the Kandyan Convention of 1815 confirmed the right of the British to continue precolonial institutions, it did not grant them the right to adapt those institutions to suit the requirements of European trade. As we will observe later, it was precisely by such adaptations of traditional institutions that the British managed to survive politically and expand economically.

The continuation of forced labor helped maintain the authority of the native aristocratic class or headmen over the cultivators. The headmen were employed by the British to supervise forced labor exaction on behalf of the colonial state. This practice tended to validate the indigenous caste hierarchy upon which forced labor exaction was organized. As we shall examine later, it was the British who made corvée labor a truly compulsory and universal

---

25. Vijaya Samaraweera, "Economics and Social Developments Under the British, 1796–1832", in *History of Ceylon*, vol. 3, ed. by K. M. de Silva, p. 49.
26. G. C. Mendis (ed.), *The Colebrooke-Cameron Papers*, vol. 1, p. 190.

The first phase of British Rule in Ceylon

system of labor exaction in Ceylon.[27] According to one British official stationed in the Four Korales of the Kandyan Provinces,

> ... that the road service is felt by the people as oppressive, that it interferes with their occupations, retards every little project of improvement and limits their industry to cultivating only what is requisite to satisfy their actual wants, that it deters people from settling in the province and that to so many of the Headmen the road service is a source of considerable emolument in conniving at the absence of those who can pay for the indulgence and which form the difficulty of getting evidence to prove it, the Government Agent finds it out of his power to check.[28]

The mercantilist policies of the state, and their reinforcement of feudal institutions, inhibited the emergence of an entrepreneurial class, European or native. The strict prohibition against Europeans buying land outside the limits of Colombo (the capital) was in essence a ban against European capital investments in Ceylon.[29] Renting was one of the only fields effectively open to local capital and was dominated by the aristocratic-administrative class of the maritime provinces known as the *Mudaliyars*, Muslim and low-country Sinhalese traders, and the South Indian money lending caste of *Chettiyars*.[30] However, as we will discuss in later chapters, the mercantilist policies of the British in the 1820s and early 1830s, encouraged a certain amount of smallholder cash crop cultivation, especially coffee, by peasants in the gardens surrounding their village homesteads.

The primary interest of the mercantilist state was revenue. The extension of already existing taxes and the imposition of new ones such as the tax on coconut trees were aimed at augmenting the revenue. The state depended on a host of middlemen tax collectors — renters, British officials and native headmen — for revenue collection. Lack of state control over these collecting agents resulted in indiscriminate expropriation from the peasant cultivators who bore the brunt of the tax burden.

As elsewhere in the colonies, the harshness of surplus appropriation under mercantilism (also known as 'booty capitalism') provoked a number of peasant revolts. The most widespread of these revolts took place in the maritime provinces in 1797 against the British East India Company. Company rule was so unpopular that finally it had to be replaced by direct imperial rule in 1802. The abuse of compulsory labor and other violations of customary practice, led

---

27. Ibid., p. 58; Colvin R. de Silva, *Ceylon Under British Occupation*, vol. 2, Ch. 6 passim.
28. The evidence of Lieut. Taylor, Government Agent (henceforth G. A.) for the Four Korales, quoted in Colvin R. de Silva, *Ceylon Under British Occupation*, vol. 2, p. 159.
29. Samaraweera, "Economic and Social Developments", p. 49.
30. Ibid., pp. 55–56.

to open resistence against the British in the newly acquired Kandyan Provinces as well.[31]

European Merchant Capitalism

The coastal lowlands of Ceylon were under European mercantile rule for over three hundred years from 1505 to about 1833, whereas the Kandyan kingdom was under its sway for less than twenty years (from 1815 until the plantation economy was set in place in the 1830s). In classifying this early period of colonial domination as mercantilist, we need to specify the structural components of merchant capitalism or mercantilism.

Merchant capitalism is not a distinct mode of production in that it does not create specific productive forces or social relations of production.[32] It usually imposes itself upon pre-existing modes of production at the level of exchange or relations of distribution. However, through its activities in the sphere of exchange, mercantilism can foster changes in existing socioeconomic structures. This according to Marx would be the 'nonrevolutionary path' to capitalist development. The 'revolutionary path' to capitalism, on the other hand, would involve more direct transformations of the social relations of production.[33]

European mercantilism in the colonies consisted of straightforward pillage and plunder or unequal trade (buying cheap and selling dear). European mercantile dominance over the southwestern coastal region of Ceylon resulted in increasing 'cash consciousness' and land transfers among the natives, particularly the local headmen class.[34] But, by and large, in Ceylon as in most other colonies, mercantilist expropriation did not lead to structural transformations of the indigenous society.

Geoffrey Kay's claim that "in the underdeveloped world . . . the existing economic structures had been broken down by merchant capital in its era of supremacy before 1800,"[35] is certainly overdrawn, at least in relation to Ceylon. As a matter of fact, the harshness of surplus extraction under Euro-

---

31. Mendis, *The Colebrooke-Cameron Papers*, p. 190.
32. For a distinction between capital and capitalism as a mode of production see Ernesto Laclau, "Feudalism and Capitalism in Latin America", *New Left Review*, vol. 67 (May-June 1971), p. 28.
33. Karl Marx, *Capital*, ed. by Frederick Engels (New York: International Publishers, 1967), vol. 3, p. 334. My thanks to Jon Saxton for helping me locate this reference.
34. Kotelawala, "Agrarian Policies of the Dutch", *passim*.
35. Kay, *Development and Underdevelopment*, p. 9.

The first phase of British Rule in Ceylon

pean mercantile rule led to the reinforcement of precapitalist institutions such as corvée labor and caste services rather than their demise.[36] Mercantile rule inhibited agricultural development and injured peasant subsistence.

The distinctiveness of mercantilism must also be sought at the level of the state, particularly in its expanded role in the economy and the manner in which the appropriated surplus was utilized. In Ceylon, the European mercantilist state relied very heavily on state monopolies and trade restrictions for the augmentation of its revenue. It took no responsibilities whatsoever towards local food production (unlike the precolonial Sinhalese state) and took little interest in the expansion of export agriculture (as did the subsequent colonial capitalist state).

A surplus had historically been expropriated from the peasantry by the native overlords and the precolonial state. In contrast, European mercantilism set in motion a process whereby an increasing portion of the surplus appropriated was no longer available locally, but exported to the imperial countries. It is true that the surplus expropriated during the precolonial era was largely used towards the conspicuous consumption of the overlord class rather than reinvestment in the economy. The 'economic drain' from the colonies during the mercantile period, on the other hand, contributed to the accumulation of capital in the West and the industrialization of the imperial nations.[37] This process of surplus export created the framework for a world market within which structural changes in the imperialist and colonial societies were later to take place.

The Conflict Between Mercantilism and 'Free Enterprise'

While mercantilist ideas held sway during the early period of British rule in Ceylon, by the mid 1830s they came to be challenged by laissez-faire ideas. A conflict of interests developed within the British community in Ceylon between the mercantilist-statist side and the liberal-free enterprise side. This debate within the colony reflected the larger conflict taking place in contemporary Britain between mercantilist interests and the rising industrial bourgeoisie.

With the cession of Kandy and the consolidation of political authority, the British began slowly to develop a permanent interest in the island. Following

---

36. Compare the impact of trade on the second serfdom in Eastern Europe. See Robert Brenner, "Agrarian Class Structure", p. 43 and "The Origins of Capitalist Development", Section 3.
37. For discussion of the economic drain from India see Alavi, "India: From Feudalism", pp. 386–87.

the protests made by a number of governors in the island, in 1812, the Colonial Office permitted Europeans and their descendants to purchase or receive land grants from the state up to 4,000 acres.[38] (The Proclamation announcing this decision — the Government advertisement of July 21, 1812 — applied only to the Maritime Provinces as the British had not yet captured Kandy.) British governors, notably North (1798–1805), Barnes (1824–1831), and Horton (1831–1837) encouraged private enterprise in export agriculture. As early as 1801, North had declared that "the establishment of private property is the object of all my institutions."[39] During his term of office, Governor Barnes provided many incentives for export agriculturists by exempting their land, exports, imports, and labor from taxation.[40] He set an example to other Europeans by opening up a coffee plantation himself in the Kandyan Highlands. His greatest contribution to commercial development however, was in the construction of roads connecting the interior and the coast which opened up the Kandyan Highlands to European capitalists.

What emerges from the above discussion is that while in the early years of British rule mercantilism reigned, in the second and third decades of the nineteenth century, new and conflictual economic interests and ideologies were emerging in colonial Ceylon.

> From the beginning of its establishment, the Crown government displayed a duality of thought in the formulation of its economic policies. On the one hand, like Madras, i.e., East India Company it embraced the inheritance of a monopoly structure and developed and intensified it to a degree not even achieved by the more mercantilist Dutch. On the other, it was bent upon fostering private enterprise in the colony. These policies were not mutually compatible and they often conflicted. The monopoly proclivities were usually triumphant, but at times the interests of private enterprise received precedence, as in the oft cited instance of coffee.[41]

The conflict between mercantilist and free enterprise was largely resolved when the 'free enterprise' side triumphed with the Colebrooke-Cameron Reforms of 1832–1833.

From Mercantilism to 'Free Enterprise': The Colebrooke-Cameron Reforms

As historians often note, stages of history do not come in neat packages. The seeds of the new historical periods are formed in the earlier ones, while

---

38. Samaraweera, "Economic and Social Developments", pp. 55–56.
39. Quoted in Colvin R. de Silva, *Ceylon Under British Occupation*, vol. 2, p. 364.
40. Mendis, *The Colebrooke-Cameron Papers*, vol. 2, pp. 279–80.
41. Samaraweera, "Economic and Social Developments", p. 55.

The first phase of British Rule in Ceylon

many aspects of the older periods linger on and shape the new.[42] Still, specific events can and do signify turning points in historical development. In Ceylon, it was the Colebrooke-Cameron Reforms of 1833 that provided the politico-juridical framework for the 'modernization', specifically the capitalist development of Ceylon, and provided a definite watershed in the history of the island. However, it must be noted that these Reforms were not without ambiguities and, when put into effect, did not always yield the anticipated results.

As pointed out earlier, by the third decade of the nineteenth century, British authority was firmly established in the Indian Ocean.[43] Ceylon's location was by itself no longer the compelling reason for the British presence in the island. With the conquest of Kandy and the suppression of the Great Rebellion of 1818, problems of internal security were largely eliminated and economic interests came to the fore.

In spite of increased taxation of the producer classes, the deficit in the colonial state budget continued. The Colonial Office in London wanted to make Ceylon a self-financing colony; moreover, a profitable one. These interests prompted the appointment of a Royal Commission of Inquiry to make recommendations for the improvement of the revenue, the administration and the judiciary in Ceylon. Of the two members of the Committee, William Colebrooke, the investigator of revenue and administrative matters, was an unmistakable proponent of laissez-faire; and Charles Cameron, the legal advisor, was a noted Benthamite.[44] Colebrooke was the principal member of the Commission; Cameron's concerns and activities were restricted to his area of professional training — the judiciary.

Before examining the specific recommendations of this Commission, (which the Colonial Office named the Commission of Eastern Enquiry), it is important to place them in the light of developments in the imperial center — Britain — at the time, specifically the emerging dominance of industrial over mercantile enterprise. The restrictive trade practices and monopolistic-privileges that sustained the commercial explosion of the sixteenth and seventeenth centuries were built around the slave trade and monopolistic trading companies (e.g., British East India Company). However, these could not provide the most effective environment for a nation on its way to becoming 'the workshop of the world.' Pressures put by industrial interests on the British government succeeded in having the trade monopoly of the East India Com-

---

42. Harry Magdoff, "Colonialism (c. 1450 — c. 1970)", in *The New Encyclopaedia Britannica*, 15th edition., s.v , pp. 879–906.
43. Fieldhouse, *Economics and Empire*, p. 100.
44. Eric Stokes, *English Utilitarians and India* (Oxford: Clarendon Press, 1959), p. 321.

pany, the foremost commercial corporation, abolished in 1813 and its commercial operations terminated in 1833.[45] As Harry Magdoff has noted, the transformation of the old colonial and mercantilist commercial system was completed when in addition to the abolition of slavery and the slave trade, the protectionist Corn Laws and the Navigation Acts were repealed in England in the late 1840s.[46]

The triumph of industrial capitalism over merchant capitalism heralded a new colonialism and a world economy based on an international division of labor and the extension of capitalist relations of production. The European nations which had hitherto remained buyers of colonial products now became producers of industrial goods. The colonies were turned into suppliers of raw materials for European industry and food for the growing European urban populations.[47] The colonies also became markets for European goods. This process had far-reaching effects on the economies and social structures of the colonial areas which had been left essentially intact during the preceding centuries of European mercantilist expropriation.[48]

The victory of industrial capitalism was echoed in the new economic thought — classical economics. 'Laissez-faire et laissez-aller' became the slogan of this economic school. As Magdoff points out, Adam Smith's theory expounded in *The Wealth of Nations* in 1776, that monopolies and trade restrictions did not increase, but decreased national wealth, was adopted as official ideology of the British government in 1846, fifty-six years after Smith's death.[49]

It is important to understand that these new ideas did not develop in isolation from empire building. In fact, Eric Stokes points out that to a large extent laissez-faire doctrine, political liberalism, and evangelism, emerged in response to Britain's "Indian connection."

> Indeed, considering the general public indifference to Indian affairs, it is remarkable how many of the movements in English life tested their strength and fought their early battles upon the Indian question. To Adam Smith the hated "mercantile system" found its embodiment in the East India Company, which he attacked in an unusual furore of denunciation. The cause of Free Trade was to a large extent fought out in the struggle for the abolition of the Company's commercial functions. It was the same with other contemporary movements of ideas. Evangelicalism, the rock upon which the character of the nineteenth-century Englishman was founded, owed much of its impetus to the Indian connextion.[50]

45. Alavi, "India: From Feudalism", p. 384.
46. Magdoff, "Colonialism", p. 890.
47. Ibid., p. 890. For a different explanation of the same phenomena, see W. Arthur Lewis, *The Evolution of the International Economic Order* (Princeton, N. J.: Princeton University Press, 1973), pp. 8–11.
48. Magdoff, "Colonialism", p. 890.
49. Ibid., p. 888.
50. Stokes, *English Utilitarianism*, p. xii.

The first phase of British Rule in Ceylon

As mentioned earlier, surplus exported from the colonies during the mercantilist phase was crucial for capital accumulation and the rise of industrialism in Britain. This fact, along with Eric Stokes' observations, noted above, raises an important theoretical question. The question, whether Britain's "Indian connection" (and by extension the Ceylon connection) was simply a consequence of capitalist expansion in Britain or a causal factor in the very emergence of capitalism in Britain, however, cannot be dealt with here.[51]

Be that as it may, let us return to the main trend of thought in this chapter. As Stokes has pointed out, it was the liberal strand of nineteenth-century utilitarianism as represented by Jeremy Bentham, rather than its more authoritarian strand represented by John Stuart Mill, that the Colebrooke-Cameron Commission introduced to Ceylon in 1833.[52]

The Colebrooke-Cameron Reforms

Very broadly, the provisions of the Colebrooke-Cameron Reforms can be summarized as follows:[53] *Administrative Unification*: The island was divided into five provinces — East, West, North, South, and Central — and each province was placed under the authority of a British Government Agent. The entire native administrative hierarchy was subordinated to the British Government Agent or the "G.A." This move further broke down the isolation of the former Kandyan kingdom and restricted the authority of the native headman class. *Judicial Unification*: A uniform system of modern/western courts of law were superimposed on the ancient village councils (*gamsabhas*). These new courts were made the defenders of new legal concepts such as private property rights. *Representative Government*: Executive and Legislative Councils were introduced to advise the Governor and thereby to reduce his autocratic powers. The 'unofficial' membership of the Legislative Council came to be filled by members of the European planter community in the island. In later years westernized native elites were gradually included. *English Education*: A system of English schools was introduced for the purpose of creating a loyal, westernized, native elite who could be employed cheaply

---

51. Alavi questions what he calls Wallerstein's Eurocentered theory of the modern world system on similar grounds. See Alavi, "India: From Feudalism", p. 381.
52. Stokes, *English Utilitarianism*, p. 321.
53. For a valuable discussion of these Reforms, see Colvin R. de Silva, *Ceylon Under British Occupation*, vol. 2, Ch. 18 *passim*. See also V. K. Samaraweera, "The Commission of Eastern Enquiry in Ceylon, 1822–1837: A Study of a Royal Commission of Colonial Inquiry" (D. Phil. dissertation, Oxford University, 1969).

in the lower echelons of the colonial bureaucracy.[54] The statement enunciated by Macaulay in introducing his famous educational reforms to British India in 1835, could easily have been attributed to Colebrooke, whose reforms were similar to Macaulay's in both spirit and substance.

> ... to form a class Indian in blood and colour, but English in tastes, in opinions, in morals and in intellect; a class who could serve as interpreters between the government and the masses, and who, by refining the vernaculars, would supply the means of a widespread dissemination of western learnings.[55]

Colebrooke's reforms were highly significant for the politico-juridical as well as the cultural 'modernization' of Ceylon. Colebrooke recognized that forcible control over the native population could not be maintained in the long-run without convincing them of the supposed superiority of the British race and the civilizing influence that the British could impart to the natives. Thus, with the introduction of Colebrooke's educational reforms, the dissemination of an English education and western values and lifestyles among privileged natives, became a cornerstone of British colonial policy in the island.

Most important from the point of view of the island's economy and social structure, however, were the economic reforms introduced by Colebrooke. He curtailed the direct participation of the state in the economy by abolishing state monopolies in cinnamon and other exports, by reforming customs duties so as to encourage private exports of commercial crops, and by getting the state to sell off its cinnamon, coffee, and pepper plantations to private interests.[56]

Colebrooke thus envisioned a new economic role for the colonial state. Instead of its former role as direct participant in the economy, he expected it to become a facilitator for private enterprise. Its function was to create an environment conducive for capitalist development through appropriate changes in the native tax structure, land tenure, labor mobilization, and the curtailment of native opposition to British policy and authority.[57] As we shall discuss later, the Ceylon plantation economy did not simply grow out of free market forces. From its very inception, the plantation economy was built upon the restrictive policies of the colonial state such as its legal monopoly over forest and high lands and the extra-economic coercion at its disposal. As

---

54. Mendis, *The Colebrooke-Cameron Papers*, vol. 1. See also L. A. Wickremeratne, "Education and Social Change, 1832 to c 1900," in *History of Ceylon*, ed. by K. M. de Silva, vol. 3.
55. Quoted in Eric Ashby's *Universities: British, Indian, African: A Study in the Ecology of Higher Education* (Cambridge: Harvard University Press, 1966), pp. 51–52.
56. Mendis, *The Colebrooke-Cameron Papers*, vol. 1, "Introduction", pp. xxxvii-xli.
57. Ibid., p. xli.

we shall examine later, although in theory Colebrooke advocated free enterprise, in practice he ensured that the colonial state could step in whenever capitalist interests were threatened.

In setting the foundation for capital investment in Ceylon, Colebrooke lifted the precolonial and mercantilist restriction on land alienation and encouraged the sale or grant of 'crown' land (discussed later) to private buyers. He thus set the basis for private property rights in land. Colebrooke also recommended the establishment of a Bank of Deposits to facilitate finance for economic development.[58] To his credit, Colebrooke did not distinguish between native and European capital in introducing these reforms.

However, it is important to note that Colebrooke was not totally averse to the continuation of free land grants to capitalists by the state. K. M. de Silva has argued that it was the influence of Edward Wakefield rather than the Colebrooke reforms that introduced the principle of crown land sales to Ceylon.[59] The Wakefieldian theory which claimed that land in the colonies should be sold rather than granted freely was becoming acceptable in the Colonial Office at this time.

It needs to be pointed out that while Colebrooke sought to disassociate the state from direct participation in the economy, he allowed European government officials to engage in commercial agriculture in order to make up for the reductions he made in their salaries. What happened in the long-run was precisely what Colebrooke sought to avoid, that is, the involvement of state officials in plantation development at the expense of their official duties. This issue will be discussed in detail in Chapter VII.

Colebrooke opposed the precolonial system of compulsory labor services to the state (*rājakāriya*) on economic, political, and moral grounds.[60] He felt that by preventing labor mobility and the emergence of voluntary or free wage labor, it discouraged economic development; that arbitrary exploitation of the peasantry incited them to rebellion against the British government; that it was inhumane and unjust for a modern, 'civilized' state to exact forced labor.[61] The underlying motive in attempting to free forced labor was the

---

58. Vijaya Samaraweera, "The Colebrooke-Cameron Reforms", in *History of Ceylon*, vol. 3, ed. by K. M. de Silva, p. 86.
59. K. M. de Silva, "The Third Earl Grey and the Maintenance of an Imperial Policy on the Sale of Crown Lands in Ceylon, c. 1832–1852", *Journal of Asian Studies*, vol. 27, no. 1 (November 1967), p. 10. See Marx's discussion of Wakefield's views in Marx, *Capital*, ed. by Frederick Engels, 3 vols. (New York: International Publishers, 1967), vol. 1, chapter on "The Modern Theory of Colonisation", pp. 766–67.
60. G. C. Mendis (ed.), vol. 1, "Report of Lieut. Colonel Colebrooke upon the Compulsory Services to which the Natives of Ceylon are Subject", *passim* and "Introduction", p. xxxvii.
61. Ibid., *passim*.

creation of the wage labor force needed for capitalist economic development in the island.[62]

Wage labor, which emerged in Western Europe in a gradual process of evolution, Colebrooke attempted to create externally by administrative fiat. But as we shall observe later, because the social and economic prerequisites for the emergence of wage labor were absent in Ceylon, Colebrooke's attempt by and large failed. Furthermore, it must be recognized that the abolition of forced labor introduced by Colebrooke was only partial. It was not extended to the villages of native headmen (*nindagam*) and the Buddhist temples (*vihāragam* and *devālagam*), and the colonial governor was allowed to reserve the right to recall compulsory labor services during emergencies.[63]

The intention of the liberal reformers seemed to have been to carry out a 'dual mandate', that is, to develop both British capitalist interests and the welfare of the masses. Some of them, particularly Colebrooke, saw no contradiction in the two interests and genuinely believed that the two goals were mutually compatible. Colebrooke's expectation that the abolition of forced labor would simultaneously create a wage labor force and free the peasants from feudal bondage, is a case in point. But as the words of James Stuart, the Master-Attendant of the colonial state (1825–1855), reveal, the British were not entirely ignorant of the inherent contradictions between capitalist profits and the welfare of the people.

> We profess to govern for the exclusive good of the natives of the country and devote our attention almost exclusively to make the culture of the soil profitable to European adventurers.[64]

In the rest of this book we shall demonstrate how, at each turn, the humanitarian impulse was subordinated to capitalist interests and the need for political stability. What followed during the nineteenth century was not harmony, but conflict, between capitalist and peasant interests.

---

62. Ibid., *passim*.
63. "Service by Tenure" was abolished with qualifications by the Order in Council of 12th April, 1832. See *A Revised Edition of the Legislative Enactments of Ceylon*, vol. 1, pp. 68–72. Governor North first attempted to abolish forced labor in the maritime provinces by introducing the Charter of Justice in 1801, but was unsuccessful. See Mendis, *The Colebrooke-Cameron Papers*, vol. 2, p. 170.
64. Quoted in Mendis, *The Colebrooke-Cameron Papers*, vol. 1, p. 57.

Part 2: The Plantation Impact

Part 2 contains the discussion of the substantive issues of this book. It presents analytically organized historical descriptions of the process of plantation development and colonial rule. Chapter IV provides a synopsis of the main events and trends in Ceylonese export agriculture between 1833 and 1886. Chapters V, VI, and VII discuss the nature of land, labor, and juridico-political requirements of the coffee plantation economy, how they were met, and their effects on the Kandyan village economy and social structure.

IV. Export Agriculture in Ceylon, 1833-1886: An Overview

This chapter provides a brief historical synopsis of export agricultural development in Ceylon during the nineteenth century. The emphasis is on the plantation, the dominant export agricultural strategy adopted in the island. The chronological overview of periodic trends and significant events in the nineteenth-century plantation history presented here, it is hoped, would help the reader follow the more conceptually organized discussions on land, labor, and infrastructure pertaining to coffee plantations that follow in Chapters V, VI, and VII. This chapter is based on secondary sources, specifically the writings of Ceylonese historians.

A plantation or estate can be described as a large parcel of land on which hundreds of laborers are regularly imployed in the systematic cultivation of a single cash crop for sale in the market. The labor used in plantations can be slave, indentured or wage labor. The average size of a planation in Ceylon has tended to vary with the availability of land and the nature of the crop. According to some writers, the nineteenth-century coffee plantations in Ceylon ranged from a small unit covering a little more than twenty to thirty acres, to large properties of cver 1,000 acres each.[1] In the Ceylonese context, a smallholding was usually a plot less than ten acres in size producing cash crops. They were usually cultivated by the owners and their families, although some native capitalists also maintained smallholdings.

With the spread of the industrial revolution in Western Europe in the late eighteenth century, a shift occurred in the trade between imperialist nations and their colonies. As we noted earlier, during the mercantile period of European colonialism, the European nations were buyers of colonial produce such as spices, sugar, as well as slaves (from India they got manufactured goods, mainly cotton textiles). The advance of industrialization, however, turned the imperial nations into sellers of machine-produced goods. Concomitantly, a change took place in the demand for colonial produce. The demand for spices was replaced by the search for raw materials such as cotton, wool, vegetable oils and fats, jute and dyestuffs needed for European industry; and food such

---

1. Michael Roberts and L. A. Wickremeratne "Export Agriculture in the Nineteenth Century," in *History of Ceylon*, ed. by K. M. de Silva, vol. 3, pp. 92-93.

Export Agriculture in Ceylon

as wheat, coffee, tea, cocoa, meat, and butter needed for the growing urban populations of industrial Europe.[2] It is in the context of this new international division of labor and the extension of capitalist relations of production and distribution that the origin and development of the Ceylonese plantation economy must be understood.

As noted earlier, Ceylon participated in international trade since very early times. When population centers moved to the southwest, this trade expanded. Under Portuguese, Dutch, and British mercantilism, some efforts were made to increase production of spices, particularly cinnamon and pepper, for export.

The first plantation in Ceylon was established by the Dutch in 1769 for securing assured supplies of cinnamon. At the time the British arrived in 1796, there were several other small-scale plantations as well as smallholdings in Ceylon's coastal lowlands.

> Thus it was the trade in cinnamon that occasioned the emergence for the first time in Ceylon of the two types of producing units — plantations and smallholdings — which today characterize the organization of agricultural production in the country.[3]

However, these state-owned plantations remained a mere handful in number and they relied on forced labor of specific castes such as the *salagama* cinnamon peelers. Throughout Dutch and British mercantile rule, the extraction of spices as feudal tribute continued to be the basis of profits. But from the point of view of the 'modernization' of Ceylon, the most significant development that took place was the establishment of private coffee plantations dependent on wage labor by the Europeans around the third decade of the nineteenth century. In fact, according to Sinhalese folklore,

> The rise and progress of coffee planting in Ceylon is undoubtedly the most remarkable phenomenon that the island has ever seen since the days when ... the yakhos [aborigines] were compelled to make way for the human race [Aryans].[4]

The demise of cinnamon and the rise of coffee exports from Ceylon during the third decade of the nineteenth century can best be understood by looking at the changing pattern of exports from the colonies to the metropoles referred to above, i.e., the shift from spices to food. On the recommendation of the Colebrooke Commission, the colonial state's monopoly in cinnamon was abolished, and in its place a high tax or duty on cinnamon exports was introduced around 1833. This led to an increase in the price of Ceylon cinnamon in the world market. It was no longer able to compete with the inferior and

2. Magdoff, "Colonialism," p. 490.
3. Gamani Corea, *The Instability of an Export Economy* (Colombo: Marga Institute, 1975), p. 51.
4. From *The Ceylon Miscellany* of 1866 quoted in D. M. Forrest's *A Hundred Years of Ceylon Tea* (London: Chatto and Windus, 1967), p. 26.

less expensive cinnamon varieties from other colonies. It was the restructuring of Ceylon's cinnamon trade along laissez-faire principles that sealed its decline and paved the way for the rise of private coffee production.[5]

While there are differences of opinion as to the origin of coffee cultivation in Ceylon, there is a consensus that it was the Dutch colonial state which attempted its systematic cultivation.[6] But being confined to the coastal lowlands and to precapitalist social relations of production, coffee planting did not succeed under the Dutch.

Coffee did not establish a clear ascendancy until the 1840s. European plantation enterprise in the period 1823–1840 was characterized by experimentation in a variety of cash crops such as indigo, cotton, and sugar in different localities.[7] With the conquest of Kandy, a soil and climate ideally suited for coffee cultivation became available in the sparsely populated Central Highlands. These factors contributed to the dramatic rise in coffee production in Ceylon in the late 1830s.

In the period before 1833, the British colonial state cultivated its own coffee plantations in the Kandyan Highlands, especially in the region known as the Sath (Seven) Korale, under the management of its provincial officials. The government apparently made use of the corvée labor (*rājakāriya*) services of the Sinhalese peasantry who inhabited the neighboring villages. No permanent staff, costs of feeding or housing of laborers were therefore involved. In fact, the Lieutenant Governor of the colony, Campbell, remarked in 1824 that coffee was being cultivated by the government "without the cost of a pice [coin]."[8]

However, Colebrooke and other liberals perceived that due to both technical and political reasons, forced labor could not be used for large scale plantation agriculture. The constant care and attention needed for the efficient cultivation of coffee was not compatible with forced labor. Indeed, slave and indentured labor were used by European planters in many parts of the world. But due to a variety of reasons which we shall discuss in subsequent chapters, the Kandyan peasantry could not be forced into laboring on the European plantations.

---

5. Roberts, "Export Agriculture," p. 93.
6. John Ferguson, *Ceylon in the Jubilee Year 1887* (Colombo: 1887), pp. 59–61.
7. Roberts, "Export Agriculture," p. 93.
8. I. H. Van Den Driesen, "Coffee Cultivation in Ceylon (1)," *The Ceylon Historical Journal*, vol. 3, no. 1 (July 1953), p. 36. Van Den Driesen is the foremost historian of coffee agriculture in Ceylon. I am indebted to his work for much of the information on the coffee plantation economy used in this chapter. I wish also to thank Donald Snodgrass for very kindly lending me his notes of Van Den Driesen's unpublished book manuscript on the history of coffee agriculture in Ceylon. I have, however, relied on Van Den Driesen's published work and unpublished Ph.D. dissertation rather than his unpublished book manuscript.

Export Agriculture in Ceylon

The exaction of compulsory labor from the cultivator class had historically been under the authority of the native headmen. The use of compulsory labor on European plantations then would have necessitated close cooperation between the native chiefs and the European planters and administrators. But given the tenuousness of the relationship between the native headmen and the British following the 1818 rebellion, such a transfer of compulsory labor onto the plantations was not possible. Instead, Colebrooke sought to release a free wage labor force for the plantations by abolishing compulsory labor to the state. But as we shall discuss later, a free labor force could not be created simply by legislation.

Before its abolition in 1833 by the Colebrooke Commission, the British followed a policy of making land grants in freehold (*sinnakara*) to European and native entrepreneurs. Over 50,000 acres of land were granted to Sinhalese alone, most of which went to the *Mudaliyar* or aristocratic class in the maritime provinces.[9] The granting of these lands was probably politically motivated as well. However, we do not know how much of this land was converted to commercial agriculture by the *Mudaliyars*.

The first large-scale coffee plantation was established by George Bird, a retired British government official around 1824. In addition to 400 acres of land near Kandy, Bird received a loan of 4,0000 rix dollars from the government.[10] Most of the early planters were government officials. The most notable among them was Governor Barnes who pioneered plantation agriculture in Ceylon with his road construction and legislative reform programs. In addition to the contributions made by individual governors and other state officials, the colonial state as an institution, played a key role in the fostering of plantation agriculture in Ceylon.

> The examples of discriminatory taxation, remission of customs duties state experiments and the like, show clearly, that the notion that a plantation coffee industry (large scale) could be successfully developed, did not spontaneously "grow up" in Ceylon. For while it is true that private enterprise played an important part in setting up the coffee industry, the numerous measures adopted by the government show us that the latter was the agent which deliberately fostered the movement, supplied much of the driving force and opened the way to individual initiative.[11]

More will be said of the role of the state in the establishment and development of the Ceylonese plantation economy in later chapters, especially Chapter VII.

---

9. Peebles, "Land Use and Population," pp. 70–71.
10. Van Den Driesen, "Coffee Cultivation," p. 34. The rix dollar was a currency used by the Dutch and also the British during the early years of their rule.
11. Ibid., p. 38.

The Origin of Coffee Agriculture: 'Peasant Coffee'

Some writers, particularly those who stress the beneficial effects of European plantation development on the natives, hold the opinion that smallholding coffee or 'peasant coffee' agriculture in Ceylon was a by-product of plantation development.[12] But there is reliable evidence which suggests that smallholder coffee production in fact preceded plantation coffee production. In the early decades of the nineteenth century, the Europeans had neither the capital nor the knowledge to cultivate coffee very differently from the native peasant cultivators. It can be hypothesized that the Europeans in fact learned to grow coffee from the successes and failures of peasant producers.[13] Until the middle of the 1830s, the volume of peasant coffee exports exceeded the volume of plantation exports. Van Den Driesen has observed that peasant producers responded very quickly to government inducements and favorable prices. Between 1820 and 1824, peasant coffee exports increased by over 100 percent from 539,662 pounds to 1,213,603 pounds.[14] Van Den Driesen has also estimated that during the prosperous 1850s and 1860s, the area under peasant coffee accounted for between 1/5 to 1/4 of the annual output and it brought an annual income of between £250,000 and £300,000 for the peasant growers.[15] Both Van Den Driesen and Ameer Ali have pointed out that peasant coffee played an important role in the commercialization and monetization of the village economy, particularly in the Kandyan Highlands where coffee thrived best.[16] We shall now consider briefly why plantations became the dominant mode of coffee production in spite of the earlier successes of peasant smallholder production.

Peasant coffee was often grown in the gardens surrounding the village homes and along the roadside. Being only a *subsidiary* to rice cultivation, peasants did not cultivate coffee systematically. They often neglected the coffee bush during its growth, collected the berries prematurely, and damaged them by wetting.[17] Peasant coffee therefore was not able to command as

---

12. Snodgrass, *Ceylon*, p. 38. See also Hugh Clifford, "Some Reflections," pp. 9–10.
13. Colin Leys found this to be the case in colonial Kenya, *Underdevelopment in Kenya: The Political Economy of Neo-Colonialism*, (Berkeley: University of California Press, 1975), p. 29.
14. Van Den Driesen, "Coffee Cultivation," pp. 38–39.
15. I. H. Van Den Driesen, "Some Trends in the Economic History of Ceylon in the 'Modern' Period," *CJHSS*, vol. 3 (1960), p. 16.
16. Van Den Driesen, "Coffee Cultivation," p. 36 and A. C. L. Ameer Ali, "Peasant Coffee in Ceylon during the Nineteenth Century," *CJHSS*, Vol. 2, No. 1 (January-June 1972), pp. 57–58.
17. Van Den Driesen, "Coffee Cultivation," p. 33.

Export Agriculture in Ceylon

good a price in the London market as did the plantation varieties. In fact, the market price for peasant coffee was consistently lower than that for plantation coffee. Another reason perhaps was that being a relatively powerless group in the society, the peasant coffee growers were not in a position to command a good price from the middlemen traders who bought their products. Furthermore, as peasant coffee production was supplementary to wet-rice production, peasants were unable and unwilling to produce at the large scale required to be competitive in the world market. The distributors of peasant coffee found their supplies to be unreliable compared to plantation supplies. Plantations, of course, produced exclusively coffee, and exclusively for export.

The complexity of the precolonial division of labor which required that peasant labor services be attached to wet-rice fields also added to the difficulty of transferring a larger share of peasant labor from wet-rice cultivation to cash crop production for export. Moreover, peasant cultivators were accustomed to a relatively unmonetized self-sufficient economy and lifestyle. Their cash needs being few, they could not have been induced to take up large-scale systematic cash crop cultivation at this time.

During the preceding mercantilist period, Europeans found that it was politically expedient and economically sound to have peasants cultivate cash crops and for them (the Europeans) to extract these crops for sale in the world market. In other words, it involved making profits at the level of distribution rather than production as the Dutch did in Java under the oppressive 'Culture System' during most of the nineteenth century.

But getting Sinhalese peasants to produce a larger and more reliable supply of coffee was difficult. Excessive use of state force in surplus exaction had already culminated in several peasant revolts.[18] These difficulties were compounded by the fact that if the British wanted greater control over peasant coffee supplies, they would have had to break the monopoly which Muslim traders enjoyed as middlemen collectors and sellers of peasant coffee.[19] It was after the Europeans usurped their foreign trade, that the Muslims moved heavily into local trade. They brought in supplies from the outside world which were often bartered for peasant coffee. In addition, they became moneylenders to the Sinhalese villagers. With the expansion of the cash economy and the growth of a market for land in the nineteenth century, these Muslim

---

18. This was particularly the case under the rule of the British East India Company in the coastal lowlands between 1796 and 1802. See G. C. Mendis, *The Colebrooke-Cameron Papers*, p. 190.
19. Ameer Ali, "Peasant Coffee," p. 50.

traders were able to make greater inroads into the village economy by buying up village land.

In contrast to the difficulties in expanding and controlling peasant coffee production, a number of factors such as the availability of extensive supplies of land in the Kandyan Highlands and cheap supplies of labor from South India, as well as the consolidation of British political authority in the island made plantation coffee production a viable enterprise for the Europeans in the 1830s. Plantations seemed to them both a more efficient and more reliable source of cash crops than smallholder export production which was a subsidiary pursuit of the rice cultivating Sinhalese peasantry that was controlled by local middlemen. As we shall see, the choice of the plantation over the smallholding as the *dominant* agricultural strategy had far-reaching implications for the social class formation and political processes in the colony.

Plantation Coffee

The dramatic rise of plantation coffee in the late 1830s was due to the confluence of a number of favorable external factors. Following protests from Ceylon, the British government finally abolished the discriminatory customs duties on Ceylon coffee. The duties on Ceylon and West Indian coffee were thus equalized at 6d. per pound. Ceylon's competitive position in the world coffee market was thereby greatly improved.[20]

The decrease in the consumption of wine coincided with an increase in the demand for coffee in Great Britain and over a great part of western Europe around this time. In 1801, the individual consumption of coffee in Britain was one ounce per annum per person; in 1841, it had risen to eleven pounds and five and one half ounces, giving a big boost to coffee production in the colonies.[21]

According to Van Den Driesen, the refusal of West Indian slaves to work on coffee plantations following emancipation and the subsequent decline of West Indian coffee production increased the world market demand for Ceylon coffee.[22] We do not have sufficient evidence on this particular relationship between the emancipation of slaves elsewhere and Ceylon coffee, but do know that following the demise of West Indian coffee, some coffee planters did come to Ceylon from Jamaica and helped extend coffee cultivation in the

---

20. Van Den Driesen, "Coffee Cultivation," p. 41.
21. Ibid., p. 41.
22. Ibid., p. 41.

Export Agriculture in Ceylon

island. For example, R. B. Tytler, a tropical agriculturist who studied Jamaican coffee cultivation methods, introduced them to Ceylon around 1837.[23]

These exogenous factors, combined with the favorable politico-juridical framework set by the colonial state lifted the serious barriers that had existed towards large-scale coffee cultivation until then. The supportive measures provided by the colonial state such as the abolition of restrictions on land sales, construction of roads and provisions for the immigration of a plantation labor force from South India will be discussed in subsequent chapters. Since the mid-1830s, both coffee production and prices increased dramatically. By the 1840s, what is commonly known as the era of 'coffee mania' or 'king coffee' had dawned in Ceylon.

Table 4:1

Quantity of Ceylon Coffee Produced and Prices

Year	Bushels	Price per Bushel
1834	138,800	15s.3d.
1835	161,976	152.3d.
1836	190,162	22s.6d.
1837	223,697	22s.3d.
1838	220,735	30s.
1839	365,062	25s.
1840	858,000	32s.2d.
1841	956,850	36s.
1842	1,254,263	45s.

Source: I. H. Van Den Driesen, "Coffee Cultivation in Ceylon (1)," *The Ceylon Historical Journal*, vol. 3, no. 1 (July 1953), p. 42.

We lack statistical evidence on the distribution of coffee production between plantations and peasant smallholdings. But based on the study of official despatches (correspondences) between Ceylon and England, Van Den Driesen concludes that although smallholder production continued to increase, the expansion in overall production at this time, was largely due to the rise of plantations.[24]

The frantic rush to open up coffee plantations in the Kandyan Highlands created a land market, a phenomenon new to Sinhalese society. Most lands

---

23. Ibid., p. 41.
24. Ibid., p. 43.

that were sold were 'crown' lands, i.e., land supposedly belonging to the state. Van Den Driesen estimates that between 1833 and 1843, approximately 258,072 acres of crown land were sold.[25] Not all land sales statistics are broken down by region or type of buyers — European/native; planter/smallholder. But again on the basis of official despatches, Van Den Driesen concludes that crown land sales were largely in the planting districts, notably the Central Province and were made to European planters.[26]

As coffee plantation production prospered, more British capital came to be invested in Ceylon at this time. According to Van Den Driesen's estimates, the annual investment of British capital between 1838 and 1843 was approximately £100,000 per year. Around 1844, the minimum cost of setting up a plantation was about £3,000.[27] During the same period, roughly 130 coffee estates were opened up in the Central Province alone.[28]

The abolition of corvée labor in 1833 did not create the anticipated free labor force. In the face of the Kandyan peasantry's resistance to wage labor, the planters had to resort to the import of cheap labor from South India. The immigration and subsequent settlement of South Indian laborers in the Kandyan Highlands is a phenomenon inextricably linked with the development of plantation agriculture in Ceylon. The issue of labor supply for the plantations will be taken up in detail in Chapter VI.

Table 4:2

Average Annual Migration of Indian Estate Laborers, 1841—1890
(thousands)

Period	Immigration	Emigration	Balance of Migration
1841–1850	39	17	12
1851–1860	57	31	26
1861–1870	68	53	15
1871–1880	102	83	19
1881–1890	54	55	−1

Source: A. C. L. Ameer Ali, "Changing Conditions and Persisting Problems in the Peasant Sector under British Rule in the Period 1833–1893," *Ceylon Studies Seminar*, 1970/72 Series, no. 3a, p. 3.

25. Ibid., p. 43.
26. Ibid., p. 43. See also Tables 5:1, 5:2, 8:1, in this book for available breakdowns by size, region, and ethnicity of buyers.
27. Snodgrass, *Ceylon*, p. 26.
28. Van Den Driesen, "Coffee Cultivation," p. 43.

Export Agriculture in Ceylon

The period of 'coffee mania' also saw the rapid extension of a network of roads linking the planting districts of the interior to the ports of the coastal lowlands (Map. p. 248). The government bore the costs of road construction which, as will be discussed later, were passed on to the peasantry via taxes. The proportion of government revenue derived from plantation-related sources such as crown land sales, export and import duties, road and bridge tolls, and port dues, greatly increased from the 1840s on.[29]

But this era of prosperity did not last very long. Between 1845 and 1849, the Ceylon coffee industry faced severe economic depression, the first wave of which came between 1844 and 1846 caused a sharp decline of coffee prices in Great Britain. As the differential duty on British grown coffee was lifted in 1844 Javanese and Brazilian coffee began to enter Britain in larger quantities, thereby leading to a general reduction of coffee prices.[30] The market value of coffee exports from all countries having been equalized, the only advantage Ceylon possessed now was her low cost of production — essentially the low wage rates.[31] But in spite of this decrease in profits, the margin was still large enough for those planters who had already purchased land to continue production, as exemplified by the following statistics.

Table 4:3

Coffee Production in Ceylon, 1844—1847

Year	Total Acreage Under Coffee (acres)	Coffee Exports cwts.	Value £
1844	25,198	133,957	267,663
1845	36,051	178,603	363,259
1846	46,150	173,892	328,791
1847	56,832	293,221	456,625

Source: I. H. Van Den Driesen, "Coffee Cultivation in Ceylon (1)," *The Ceylon Historical Journal*, vol. 3, no. 1, July 1953, p. 51.

The second fall in prices which came between 1847 and 1849 was caused primarily by the depression in England. As incomes in England declined, the

---

29. I. H. Van Den Driesen, "Some Aspects of the History of the Coffee Industry in Ceylon with Special Reference to the Period, 1823–1885," unpublished Ph.D. dissertation, University of London, 1954, p. 535.
30. Van Den Driesen, "Coffee Cultivation," pp. 49–50.
31. Speculum, pseud. [G. Wall], *Ceylon*, p. 116.

English either cut down on their coffee drinking or resorted to the use of cheaper admixtures of coffee and chicory. As prices declined, Ceylon planters were not able to control their supplies as recently opened plantations now began to bear fruit.[32] Given that the coffee bush takes three years to bear fruit, once planted, the planters had little control over its yield.

The fall in prices and the depression in England adversely affected the Ceylon plantations. From 1846 onwards, capital began to flow into Ceylon in diminished quantities and credit from the London financial houses too became increasingly scarce.[33] The increasing inability of the planters to pay their laborers on time discouraged the immigration of South Indian laborers to Ceylon plantations. Total arrivals declined from 73,401 in 1845 to 29,430 in 1849.[34]

Government revenue which was heavily dependent on the coffee industry was seriously depleted by the depression. Less was spent on construction projects by the state and the increased rates of internal carriage contributed further to the planters' woes. Under these circumstances, a number of estates were forced to close down. Between 1847 and 1849, as much as ten percent of the plantations and twenty-five percent of the total area under coffee went out of production. In addition, a substantial number of estates that had become unprofitable were sold off at nominal prices.[35] The effects of the depression were most severely felt by the plantation sector — the planters, the financial agencies which had advanced credit in anticipation of commissions on crops, sections of the mercantile community engaged in plantation-related activities such as transport, and the colonial state.[36]

But the impact of this depression on peasant producers was different. As Van Den Driesen notes, the depression in England served to reduce peasant coffee growers' income by curtailing one of their *supplementary* sources of income; however, it did not, as in the monocultural plantation sector, curtail an only source of income.[37] But the effects of the depression were passed on to the peasantry indirectly by the colonial state via a series of new taxes. With the imposition of these taxes by Governor Torrington, the strong antigovernment feelings of the peasants which had been building up for decades flared into open rebellion in 1848. These issues will be taken up in subsequent chapters.

32. Van Den Driesen, "Coffee Cultivation," p. 51.
33. Ibid., p. 53.
34. Ibid., p. 53.
35. Ibid., p. 56.
36. Ibid., p. 57.
37. Ibid., pp. 56–57.

Export Agriculture in Ceylon

By 1850, the signs of recovery of coffee agriculture began to appear. Between 1850 and 1870, Ceylon coffee enjoyed a period of boom and prosperity. One of the reasons behind this was the increasing efficiency of plantation coffee production. During the depression, new techniques had been experimented with and a greater knowledge of soil and climate necessary for coffee was acquired; wasteful expenditure was curtailed. According to a contemporary observer, in 1857, an acre of forest land could be brought under crop for one tenth of its cost in 1844.[38] Undoubtedly, technological improvements contributed to increasing productivity of labor and the profitability of plantation production.

During the 1850s and 1860s, coffee consumption in Britain increased again. A great deal of capital came into Ceylon and credit became readily available. As the immigration of labor, land sales, government revenue and road building all increased, coffee production and its profits also soared.

Table 4:4

The Ceylon Coffee Industry, 1850–1869
(Annual Figures and Annual Averages)

Year	Export Volume (000 cwts.)	Export Unit Value (shillings/cwt.)	Area Planted (000 acres)
1850–1854	344	48	59
1855–1859	537	51	138
1860–1864	615	52	199
1865–1869	939	66	243

Source: Donald Snodgrass, *Ceylon: An Export Economy in Transition* (Homewood, Ill.: Richard D. Irwin, Inc., 1966), p. 20.

Peasant coffee producers also took advantage of the favorable market conditions and advances made in production techniques. It seems that at least some coffee smallholders adopted scientific methods of production developed in the European plantations.[39] The increase in the quantity of peasant coffee exported, from 114,962 cwts. in 1856, to 195,291 cwts. in 1866, has been attributed partly to the adoption of more systematic methods of production by peasant growers.[40]

38. Tennent quoted by I. H. Van Den Driesen, in "Coffee Cultivation in Ceylon (2), "*The Ceylon Historical Journal*, vol. 3, no. 2 (October 1953), p. 156.
39. Ibid., p. 160.

The sudden collapse of Ceylon coffee from the height of its success in the 1860s and 1870s was caused by *Hemileia Vastatrix*, the coffee leaf disease commonly referred to as the 'coffee blight'. It was first detected in 1869 and spread rapidly all over the coffee districts. Although the yield per acre began to decline due to the disease, prices remained sufficiently high and planters kept expanding into high virgin forest land for some years. While previously the belief was that heights between 4,000 and 4,500 feet were best for coffee, it was now found that it thrived remarkably well in elevations up to 5,000 or even 5,500 feet. In spite of the leaf disease, the competition for forest land and land prices increased.[41]

But as acreage increased, the crop still began to fluctuate due to the spread of the leaf disease. Planters tried various measures to arrest its spread, including increase in the use of manure, experimentation with new coffee varieties including Liberian. These measures in turn raised the costs of production.[42]

As if the leaf disease were not enough, prices began to decline as a result of the increase in the supply of coffee from Brazil to the world market and the 'Great Depression' in Britain between 1879 and 1884. These factors in combination brought forth the ultimate downfall of the Ceylon coffee industry. The collapse of the Oriental Bank in Ceylon which had wide planting connections in 1883 symbolized the demise of coffee.

Table 4:5

The Ceylon Coffee Industry, 1880–1886

Year	Acreage	Exports (cwts.)	Value (£)
1880	252,431	656,595	3,333,739
1881	252,431	437,233	2,137,326
1882	220,000	466,173	1,803,151
1883	174,000	307,244	1,358,536
1884	150,000	302,808	1,188,285
1885	127,000	320,975	1,244,996
1886	98,000	184,044	831,563

Source: I. H. Van Den Driesen, "Coffee Cultivation in Ceylon (2)," *The Ceylon Historical Journal*, vol. 3, no. 2, October 1953, p. 167.

40. Ibid., p. 160.
41. Ibid., pp. 163–64.
42. Ibid., p. 165.

Export Agriculture in Ceylon

As plantation after plantation went out of production, capital was removed from the island and estate laborers were sent back to South India in droves. Government revenue declined and many branches of local enterprise associated with planting were adversely affected. As Van Den Driesen has observed, "The economic development of the country in consequence was sharply arrested for almost a decade,"[43] thus making the dangers of an export strategy based on monoculture self-evident.

The peasant growers were completely wiped out by the leaf disease. As noted, the planters were able to delay the collapse of their coffee by extending estates into higher elevations. The peasant growers, however, were not able to compete with planters to buy new land. According to Van Den Driesen, the early collapse of peasant coffee was due solely to the leaf disease. The Depression in England in the 1880s had no part in the downfall of peasant coffee as peasant growers were independent of bank loans and other forms of financial assistance from abroad.[44] But the economic downfall made itself felt on the peasantry with great severity because of the harsher enforcement of taxes by the colonial state at this time. This issue will be discussed in Chapter V.

Capital and Ownership of Coffee Plantations

Before we conclude our overview of the history of coffee agriculture in Ceylon, it is necessary to provide some information on the ownership and capital investment in Ceylon's coffee plantations.

The ownership of coffee plantations was almost entirely British. Among the reasons why native capitalists were confined to plantation-related service activities (such as transport) and coconut cultivation in the nineteenth century was the extreme reluctance on the part of British banks and the 'agency' houses managing plantations to extend credit to Ceylonese.[45]

As Jonathan Levin has observed, "the most significant characteristic as far as development of the export economy is concerned, however, was their remittance of income."[46] One of the prominent features of Ceylon's plantation economy — and of colonial economies in general — was that profits were exported and were not necessarily reinvested in the colonies. As we have seen, capital was quickly removed during times of crises or depression. The adverse

---

43. Ibid., p. 167.
44. Ibid., pp. 168–69.
45. Snodgrass, *Ceylon*, p. 26.
46. Jonathan Levin, *The Export Economies*, p. 6.

effects of this pattern of capital investment led a contemporary observer, Ferguson, himself a pioneer British planter in nineteenth-century Ceylon, to lament,

> The accumulated profits made during the time of prosperity, which elsewhere, e.g., England, form a reserve fund of local wealth, to enable the sufferer from present adversity to benefit by past earnings, were so far as the planters were concerned, wanting in Ceylon. There was no reserve fund of past profits to fall back upon, no class of wealthy Europeans enriched by former times of prosperity ... circulating the liquidated profits of former industry, when the period of adversity and depression arrived..... Ceylon, in fact, in the best days used to be a sort of incubator, to which capitalists sent their eggs to be hatched and whence a good many of them received from time to time an abundant brood, leaving sometimes but the shells for our local portion.[47]

No statistical details are available on rates of return on capital during the coffee period. A rough and conservative estimate puts profits at twenty five percent of sales.[48] As noted above, these profits were not reinvested in Ceylon to generate industries or local agriculture. Rather, the profits were remitted to the imperial country and eventually contributed to the dynamic of capitalist development there. Here lies the fundamental difference between capitalist development in the imperial nations and the colonies.

Yet another significant feature about capital in Ceylon's plantations was that it was largely "self generating, once the coffee industry had been established on a prosperous footing."[49] After the initial decades very little or no capital was brought in; instead profits were exported to Britain. As Edwin Craig notes,

> ... very little foreign capital was involved in the development of the coffee plantation system. British investors were capital-shy throughout the coffee era. Although very little capital was required for the establishment of a coffee plantation – labour was hired cheaply to clear the land; the plant required little care during the gestation period; only seasonal labour was necessary for harvesting – *that which was needed was supplied out of the savings of workers in the government service [European officials]. The costs (greatly reduced by the use of compulsory labor) of road construction and maintenance were paid out of tolls and taxes or the gains from exports.* [Emphasis added][50]

The colonial state played a crucial role in capital accumulation in the colony, particularly during the early years when the plantation economy was being set up. As we shall examine later, the surplus extracted from the natives

---

47. Ferguson quoted in Snodgrass, *Ceylon*, pp. 27–28.
48. Snodgrass, *Ceylon*, p. 27. See also N. Ramachandran, *Foreign Plantation Investment in Ceylon, 1889–1958* (Colombo: Central Bank of Ceylon, 1963), p. 41.
49. Snodgrass, *Ceylon*, p. 26.
50. Edwin Craig, Jr., "Ceylon," in *Tropical Development, 1880–1913*, ed. by Arthur Lewis (London: George Allen and Unwin Ltd., 1970), p. 225.

Export Agriculture in Ceylon

by the colonial state in the form of forced labor, taxes, etc. were largely transferred to the plantation sector in the form of infrastructure, police protection and the bureaucracy necessary to maintain the plantation economy.

As noted earlier, most of the early coffee planters in Ceylon were in fact government officials. The majority of these early British planters were small proprietors who had to obtain a good part of their capital in the form of advances on future crops from British owned banks and agency houses. But as the participation of government officials in plantation agriculture was discouraged after the mid-1840s, a new breed of resident proprietors became dominant.

Since the third quarter of the nineteenth century, joint stock corporations began to swallow up many of the former partnerships and individual proprietorships.[51] Some of the former owners became paid employees of the companies and remained on the estates as managers. During the twentieth century, a few agency houses which supervised the operation and management of estates had come to own many of Ceylon's plantations.[52] However, individual proprietorship rather than corporate ownership and management of estates was the norm during the coffee era.

Although Ceylon coffee plantation agriculture was relatively short-lived (less than seventy years in all), it set the pattern of development for the subsequent major plantation crop — tea. The features which have remained basic to the dominant plantation 'system' in Ceylon were fashioned by coffee during the nineteenth century. Donald Snodgrass has neatly summarized these characteristics of the dominant plantation sector.

> British ownership and management of most estates, including almost all the largest ones; provision of finance by British banks and "agency houses"; large-scale factory-style operation of the estates using massive forces of industrial labour specially imported for the purpose; control of the import-export trade by the British; virtually complete reliance on imported supplies of capital equipment, estate supplies and even food for the labour force; virtually complete reliance on foreign, especially British markets for the product.[53]

It is true that the coffee plantation economy established itself as a foreign enclave upon the Sinhalese village economy. It used foreign capital, foreign labor, imported food supplies, and equipment. The only direct incursion was on native land. But in spite of this superficial duality and separation between the plantation and the village, the two sectors were in fact interlinked in many fundamental ways. The objective of this study is precisely to delineate

---

51. Snodgrass, *Ceylon*, p. 27.
52. Ibid., pp. 27, 38.
53. Ibid., p. 21. Most plantations are now owned by the state or local capitalists.

those underlying linkages and cleavages between the foreign enclave economy and the pre-existing village economy and social structure. In doing so we shall question the highly overdrawn dualistic picture of the foreign plantation and the native village painted by Snodgrass and other writers. We shall argue that Sinhalese labor did play a select role in crucial spheres (jungle clearing, transport, carpentry, etc.) of the coffee plantation economy, particularly during the early critical years. The role of peasant coffee in Ceylon's export agriculture during the nineteenth century has already been discussed in this chapter. Furthermore, local people, especially the emerging native capitalist class developed a substantial stake in coconut and later, during the twentieth century, in rubber cultivation. Although coconut agriculture was not strictly a plantation enterprise, a discussion of its features and evolution is necessary to complete our overview of nineteenth-century export agriculture in Ceylon.

Coconut Cultivation

Since 1870, the export of coconut products from Ceylon steadily increased in relation to total exports. Acreage under coconut increased from approximately 200,000 acres in 1860 to 600,000 by 1900.[54] As Table 4:6 shows, by 1910, coconut exports came to constitute roughly a quarter of total exports from Ceylon and coconut had become the second largest export commodity from the island.

Table 4:6

Export of Coconut Produce from Ceylon, 1870–1910

Year	% of Total Exports
1870	4
1880	9
1890	15
1900	17
1910	24.5

Source: S. Rajaratnam, "The Growth of Plantation Agriculture in Ceylon, 1886–1931," *Ceylon Journal of Historical and Social Studies*, vol. 4, no. 1, January-June 1961, p. 9.

54. S. Rajaratnam, "The Growth of Plantation Agriculture in Ceylon, 1886–1931," *CJHSS*, vol. 4 (1961), p. 9.

Export Agriculture in Ceylon

But hardly any of the features of the dominant coffee (and later tea) economy described by Snodgrass applied to coconut. Coconut trees flourish in sandy soil near the seashore. Hence the greater part of the coconut cultivation was/is to be found along the western and southwestern coastal belt, the Jaffna Peninsula and the Eastern coastline rather than the Kandyan Highlands where coffee and tea flourished successively.[55]

Unlike coffee and tea, coconuts were grown largely on smallholdings and peasant gardens with very little systematic cultivation. Rajaratnam notes that only about ten percent of the coconut acreage was in units large enough to be called plantations.[56] These were largely in the hands of local capitalists. But this should not blur the fact that many local capitalists themselves owned smallholdings rather than plantations. Unlike in coffee and tea, the smallholding was the characteristic unit in coconut cultivation.

The labor on both coconut smallholdings and plantations was almost exclusively local peasant labor. Coconut cultivation did not require a year-round residential labor force and the labor of Sinhalese villagers was utilized to meet the periodic needs of coconut cultivation.

A crucial feature that distinguished coconut agriculture from the dominant export agriculture — coffee — was that it was largely a local enterprise both in terms of labor and ownership. As Rajaratnam argues, it was in the sphere of distribution of coconut products that foreigners played an important role: "European enterprise in coconut was limited to marketing; several firms already established in the coconut trade of South India processed and marketed some of the exports from Ceylon."[57]

Coconut cultivation played a major role in native capitalist development and social class formation in the coastal lowlands of Ceylon during the British colonial period.[58] What is extremely significant, however, is that although coconut became a significant aspect of the export agriculture of nineteenth-century Ceylon, being a native enterprise, it did not wield a commensurate influence on the determination of policies or the activities of the colonial state. It was the dominant European agriculture based first in coffee, then tea, that wielded a determining influence on the colonial state and the evolution of the colonial political economy.

In the spectrum of export agriculture in colonial Ceylon ranging from coffee dominated by the European plantation mode to coconut dominated

---

55. Ibid., p. 9.
56. Ibid., p. 9.
57. Ibid., p. 9.
58. See Douglas de Silva, "The Growth of the Coconut Industry," in *Liberation and Coconut*, Part 1, *Logos*, vol. 18, no. 1 (March 1979).

by the native smallholder unit, *rubber* agriculture came to occupy a middle position. Although the rubber plant was introduced into the island in 1886 when coffee collapsed, its systematic cultivation did not begin until the turn of the century. In other words, rubber in Ceylon is a twentieth century export crop. The area under rubber expanded from a mere 1,750 acres in 1900 to 220,000 acres in 1913. In Ceylon, rubber was generally cultivated in areas ranging in elevation from about fifty to two thousand feet above sea level. In other words, rubber required a lesser altitude than coffee or tea and a higher altitude than coconut.[59] Rubber thrived best (and continues to do so) in the southwestern foothill areas such as the Kegalle, Ratnapura and Kurunegala districts which lie between the elevations of the Kandyan Highlands and the lowlands of the southwestern coast. A substantial proportion of the rubber acreage came to be held by natives both in the form of plantations and smallholdings.[60] European ownership of rubber, however, was confined to large plantations. While the labor used on native rubber holdings was largely peasant labor of Sinhalese villagers, European rubber planters employed South Indian labor in addition to native labor.

The Transition from Coffee to Tea in the Kandyan Highlands

As noted above, the locus of coconut and rubber cultivation was not the Kandyan Highlands but the lesser altitudes in the coastal lowlands and the southwestern foothills respectively. Let us now return to our original focus on the Kandyan Highlands and the collapse of coffee agriculture in the 1880s. In their search for a profitable substitute during the declining years of coffee, the planters experimented with a variety of cash crops such as cinchona, cocoa, and tea. They cultivated these usually on abandoned coffee estates or interspersed with coffee. It was tea which eventually became the successor to coffee as Ceylon's foremost plantation crop. The first tea plantation was opened in 1867. However the period 1867–1870, was the heyday of Ceylon

---

59. G. H. Pieris, "Economic Geography of Rubber Production in Ceylon," unpublished Ph.D. dissertation, Cambridge University, 1965, p. 77.
60. Rajaratnam, "The Growth of Plantation Agriculture," p. 13. See also Rajaratnam's thesis on the "History of Plantation Agriculture of Ceylon, 1886–1931: With Special Reference to Tea and Rubber," unpublished M.Sc. thesis, London School of Economics, 1961.

Export Agriculture in Ceylon

coffee, and planters paid little attention to tea. In 1870, there were only 250 acres of tea.[61] It was in the late 1880s, with the decline of coffee, that planters turned seriously to tea cultivation. As Table 4:7 clearly demonstrates, the rise of tea paralleled the decline of coffee cultivation in Ceylon.

Table 4:7

Areas Under Tea and Coffee (Acres), 1883–1886

Year	Tea	Coffee*
1883	19,797	250,740
1884	57,626	202,869
1885	120,728	167,677
1886	164,728	89,813

Source: S. Rajaratnam, "The Growth of Plantation Agriculture in Ceylon, 1886–1931," *Ceylon Journal of Historical and Social Studies*, vol. 4 (1961), p. 6.
*While the figures in this table pertain only to plantation coffee acreage, the statistics in Table 4:5 include smallholder or peasant coffee acreage as well.
**Note the disparity between the acreage under plantation coffee for 1883, 1884, 1885 as given in Table 4:7 and the total coffee acreage (which should be greater) as given in Table 4:5.

In the early stages of tea cultivation in the 1880s, a number of difficulties confronted the tea planters. Failure of coffee had ruined many a planter and credit was difficult to obtain. Tea took three to six years to mature; it required greater capital outlay for factory and machinery than faster yielding crops such as cinchona; and being a perennial (unlike coffee), it required a permanent labor force. There were not many experienced tea planters and even the Tamil laborers from South India preferred their familiar work on coffee estates. Furthermore, it was difficult to obtain large quantities of tea seeds from Assam.[62]

By about 1883, a number of forces converged to make tea cultivation profitable. One was the increasing demand for black tea over green tea in the British market.[63] Another reason was the reduction of the price of sugar at this time, which also encouraged tea consumption in Britain.[64]

Tea was found to flourish in a wider range of altitudes than coffee. In fact, the soil and climate of Ceylon, particularly in the Kandyan Highlands, was found to be more suited for tea than coffee. The yields in Ceylon tea plan-

61. Rajaratnam, "The Growth of Plantation Agriculture," p. 5.
62. Ibid., p. 6.
63. S. Rajaratnam, "The Ceylon Tea Industry, 1886–1931," *CJHSS*, vol. 4 (1961), pp. 170–71.
64. Ibid., p. 171.

tations were greater than that of the older tea estates of Assam, and they often exceeded 500 lbs. of made tea per acre.[65] Tea planters shared few of the difficulties which had faced the coffee pioneers once the wholehearted conversion to tea began. There was land in plenty, not only that which required conversion from coffee, but also virgin forest land that had been bought for coffee, but had been left uncultivated. The rapid expansion of tea acreage continued until about 1897, on average, 20,000 acres brought under cultivation each year.[66]

However, the tea boom brought to the fore once again the conflicts over land and labor between plantation and peasant interests which had been dormant during the collapse of coffee. In many respects, the new dominant export crop, tea, continued the political and economic structures set in place by coffee, well into the twentieth century.[67]

---

65. Rajaratnam, "The Growth of Plantation Agriculture," p. 6.
66. Ibid., p. 7.
67. See, for example, the pamphlet on *The Tea Trade* (London: World Development Movement, 1980), esp. section on Sri Lanka.

V. Plantations and the Conflict Over Land

In this chapter we shall consider the impact of the colonial land and tax policies and their implementation on the land tenure arrangements of the Kandyan village economy. Our specific focus will be on the relationship between colonial politico-economic developments (specifically plantation expansion) and the changes in the property relations and surplus appropriation in the Kandyan Highlands during the nineteenth century.

In Chapter II, we distinguished two dynamically integrated modes of production in the Kandyan village economy — paddy and high land agriculture.[1] We also distinguished two broad categories of villages — royal (*gabadāgam*) and feudal villages. Feudal villages, we noted, comprised of those held by the nobility (*nindagam*), the Buddhist temples (*vihāragam*) and the temples of deities worshipped by Buddhists (*dēvalagam*).

We shall discuss the impact of colonial land and tax policies on each category of these lands. First we shall consider state policies and practices towards the high lands (*goda bim*) belonging to both royal and feudal villages. We shall pay special attention to the actions taken by the state towards the properties of the temple villages. Colonial land and tax policies towards the paddy lands (*mada bim*) in the royal villages differed significantly from the state's position towards the paddy lands in the feudal villages. We shall therefore discuss the changes introduced into the paddy lands of the royal and feudal villages separately.

The Struggle Over High Lands: Royal and Feudal Villages

Land Requirements of Plantations

When opening up coffee plantations, British planters had to take into account not only the ecological needs of the crop, but also the availability of

---

1. The cultivation of home gardens was also a subsidiary form of peasant subsistence. While our concern here is on the colonial impact on paddy and high lands, we shall refer to its effects on peasant gardens where relevant.

vast tracts of uncultivated land and the labor required for clearing and preparing it. The Kandyan Highlands of the island were selected for soil and climate, and abundant uncultivated forest as well as the periodically cultivated high lands (*goda idam*) land ideally suited for coffee. The irrigated low lands (*mada idam*) used for wet rice cultivation, being unsuited for coffee cultivation, were of no direct interest to the planters.

During the initial phase of plantation development, planters preferred land in the lower elevations of the mountainous regions. This preference was due to the fact that the lower elevations consisted of much land that had already been cleared for shifting cultivation by the Kandyan peasants and did not therefore demand a heavy outlay of labor for conversion into coffee estates.[2]

By the middle of the nineteenth century, however, world demand for coffee, as well as planters' scientific knowledge of its cultivation increased. Forest lands in the higher elevations were found to be as good, if not better suited for coffee cultivation than the swidden lands on lower elevations. Another fact which undoubtedly contributed to the expansion of plantations into the 'wilderness of the peak' and away from the villages was the persistent conflict between planters and peasants over boundaries and cattle trespassing. K. M. de Silva says that had the planters continued to buy up abandoned swidden plots, and had the myth about the 1,700 feet contour being the desirable maximum height for coffee cultivation not been exploded in the 1840s, disputes over land sales between planters and peasants would have become more formidable than they actually did.[3] According to D'A Vincent's 1882 Report on Forest Administration, coffee plantations were principally at high elevations between 3,000 and 5,000 feet.[4] On the other hand, historian S. B. W. Wickramasekara notes that precolonial Kandyan villages were situated mostly at elevations less than 3,000 feet.[5]

A great portion of the high lands turned into coffee estates, particularly during the later phases of plantation expansion, were virgin forests at high

---

2. Great Britain, Parliament, *Parliamentary Papers* (henceforth *BPP*) *1850*, vol. 12. Evidence of Geroge Ackland before the British Parliamentary Committee of Inquiry on the Rebellion of 1848, p. 20.
3. K. M. de Silva, "The 'Rebellion' of 1848 in Ceylon," *CJHSS*, Vol. 7, No. 2 (July-December 1964), p. 152. See also *BPP 1850*, Vol. 12, p. 23 and A. C. L. Ameer Ali, "Peasant Coffee," p. 55.
4. Ceylon, Legislative Council, *Sessional Papers* (henceforth SP), *1882*, No. 68, pp. 22, 24.
5. Wickramasekara, "The Social and Political Organization," p. 79; see also Michael Roberts, "A Selection of Documentary Evidence as Aids for the Lecture on 'The Administration of the Waste Lands Ordinance No. 12 of 1840 and its Impact on the Coffee Period, 1840–1880s'," *The Archives Lecture Series* (20 June 1969), pp. 15–16.

Plantations and the Conflict over Land

elevations rather than forests which had been subjected to swidden or chena cultivation. However, except for the sequestered royal forests of the Kandyan monarch (*tahansi käle*), cultivators had users' rights to all forest lands surrounding their villages. Furthermore, all forests were potentially cultivable as chenas. We shall discuss how the spread of plantations, private property rights, peasant cashcropping (and population increase) curtailed chena cultivation and ultimately wiped out the cultivators' usufructary rights to forests and other high lands.

How Land Was Obtained for Plantations

The early British coffee planters received large land grants from the colonial state free of payment in freehold (*sinnakara*). We do not have figures on the total extent of these grants, but do know, for instance, that Major George Bird and Governor Barnes received large tracts of land near Kandy for coffee cultivation.[6]

Soon after the Kandyan rebellion of 1818 valuable forest lands were conferred on native chiefs who had been loyal to the British. Later these came to be known as 'British Grants.'[7] But according to George Turnour, the Revenue Commissioner for the Kandyan Provinces, no specific land grants were made to natives in the interior for purposes of commercial agriculture *per se*.[8] Land grants to natives were not supposed to exceed thirty-six acres although a few headmen in the coastal lowlands did receive much larger grants. In fact, Peebles documents that land grants to prominent families in the lowlands 'created a category of landed proprietors with landholdings of unprecedented extent.'[9]

A number of factors including the injunctions of the Colebrooke Commission, increasing demand for land, land surveying costs incurred by the state, and native opposition to land alienation, led to the abolition of free land grants by the colonial state. In its place, a minimum upset price of five shillings an acre was imposed on land disposed to the planters by the colonial state. The influence of the theories of Edward Gibbon Wakefield probably

---

6. Van Den Driesen, "Coffee Cultivation in Ceylon (1)," p. 34.
7. Ceylon, *Administrative Report* (henceforth *AR*), *1876*, Report on the Sabaragamuwa District.
8. Great Britain, Colonial Office 416 Series, No. 21 (henceforth denoted as *CO* 416/21, etc.), p. 117.
9. Patrick Peebles, "Land Use and Population Growth," p. 71, Table 1. See also Michael Roberts, "Some Comments," p. 7. The British also created a class of loyal native proprietors in India through large land grants.

also played a significant role in this change of policy. A cardinal doctrine of the Wakefieldian theory of colonization was that land in the colonies should be sold and not freely granted to agriculturists. Wakefield's impact on Ceylon's land policy seemed to have been made through his disciple, Earl Grey, who was Under Secretary at the Colonial Office between 1831 and 1834 and Secretary of State for the Colonies between 1846 and 1852.[10]

First, as free grants and then at the give-away price of five shillings an acre, the early British planters, almost all of them government officials, were able to accumulate vast tracts of land in the Kandayn Highlands. Many planters bought up land not merely for immediate cultivation, but for its real estate value as well. A large proportion of land bought from the Crown was later resold to other parties at huge profit margins.[11] Since much land had already been sold at twenty shillings or more in the private land market, the colonial state raised its minimum upset price to twenty shillings in 1844.[12]

During the initial years of plantation development, the planters had almost a free hand in the choice of location and extent of their plantations, or 'estates', as they were popularly known in Ceylon. A planter would choose a plot of land and have it surveyed at his own expense. The government would then carry an advertisement in the local newspaper for three months and the land would be put up for auction on the appointed day. It was an established custom that others would not outbid the land away from the planter who had originally selected it and had it surveyed. The land was sold at the prevailing minimum upset price. What delayed land disposal, barring disputes with natives, of course, was usually the inadequacy of the Survey Department which was very much understaffed.[13]

The 'Crown Land' Question

The most vexatious and controversial issue facing the British plantation interests in Ceylon was the question of native rights to land, particularly the forest, swidden, and pasture land that were suited for plantation development.

Let us recapitulate our earlier discussion of precolonial Kandyan land

---

10. K. M. de Silva, "The Third Earl Grey," p. 5. See also Karl Marx's discussion in *Capital*, vol. 1, Chapter 33. See also ch. 3, p. 63 in this work.
11. *BPP 1847–1848*, Vol. 42, Sir Emerson Tennent's Report on Finance and Commerce, p. 96.
12. *BPP 1850*, vol. 12, Evidence of Jonathan Forbes before the British Parliamentary Committee of Inquiry on the Ceylon Rebellion, p. 274.
13. Van Den Driesen, "Coffee Cultivation in Ceylon (1)."

Plantations and the Conflict over Land

tenure. All uncultivated/ unoccupied land in precolonial Kandy was theoretically 'crown' land belonging to the king. But as land was plentiful and not a commodity, the king did not prohibit cultivation of his lands except the sequestered royal forests (*tahansi käle*).[14] According to the customary law of Kandyan society, peasant cultivators had users' rights to the high lands surrounding their villages regardless of the overlordship of the village — royal or feudal.[15] Due to the difficulties of collection, taxes were generally not levied on swidden lands and village gardens. As discussed earlier, this helped guarantee a minimum subsistence for the peasantry.

In contrast, plantation development along capitalist lines presupposed absolute proprietary rights, fixity of tenure, and land as a commodity. It was when the colonial administration applied these modern legal terms to the former Kandyan kingdom that the old and the new systems of land tenure began to clash. In the words of Lord Stanmore, Governor of Ceylon (1883–1890),

> ... But with the growth of ideas of exclusively individual and alienable property, a different state of things has grown up. On the one hand, the villager who has occasionally cultivated a patch of land in the adjacent forest claims it (often impudently) as his own individual property, whilst on the other hand, the Crown claims that absolute possession of all parts of the forest not shown to be already alienated, and claims with the possession, the full right of disposing of it and of regarding neighboring paddy owners using it, as trespassers.[16]

It is well to remember that recognition of users' rights to land was not a feature peculiar to Kandyan society. It was characteristic of precapitalist societies in general,[17] and the clash between users' and owners' rights is an inevitable outcome in the transition from precapitalist to capitalist forms of land tenure.[18]

In making a literal interpretation of the feudal maxim that 'all uncultivated land belongs to the king', the colonial state, as the successor to the Kandyan king, proceeded to sell vast tracts of forest and swidden lands in the Central Highlands to planters and speculators in freehold. The Kandyan peasants, however, due to ignorance of colonial legal interpretations and/or in defiance of colonial authority, continued to practice shifting cultivation, collect forest produce, and graze their animals on the high lands in the

---

14. *CO* 54/345, No. 46 of 29 August 1859, Evidence of Turnour, p. 128.
15. F. A. Hayley, *A Treatise*, pp. 126–28.
16. *CO* 54/643, June 11, 1897, Stanmore's Memorandum, p. 3.
17. Meek, *Land Law and Custom*, pp. 12, 26–30. See also Furnivall, *Colonial Policy*, p. 3.
18. Ibid., p. 12. See also Mamdani, *Politics and Class Formation*, p. 42.
19. *SP 1873*, No. 29, Correspondence on the Subject of the Conservation of Crown Forests, p. 9.

customary manner. There is ample evidence on the resulting conflicts between planters and peasants over the ownership and use of high lands as well as the difficulties experienced by the colonial state in resolving these conflicts. In an official correspondence to the Secretary of State for the Colonies, Governor Gregory expressed his sympathy for the plight caused the peasantry by such crown land alienation.

> In these patches the natives obtain their fence sticks, wood for fuel and for building and shelter for their cattle, and it is almost tantamount to expulsion to clear them. On the other hand, their fertility makes them to be sought after by the planters.[19]

What is clear from the remarks of Gregory and others is that while colonial officials were aware of the ill effects of high land expropriation on the peasantry, they were not prepared to subordinate planter interests to that of the peasants. The conflict over lands between planters and peasants sometimes took violent form as George Ackland, an experienced coffee planter who managed thirty-five estates, stated before the British Parliamentary Commission inquiring into the peasant rebellion of 1848 (this rebellion will be discussed in Chapter 8),

> Upon one occasion when I first settled in the Valley of Doombera where the natives are very superstitious, and generally speaking troublesome to deal with, they threatened to murder my people; they burnt down a new house that was built; the headman (native chief) himself told me that he would never allow us to settle there. This was the first plantation that was made in the interior upon any extensive scale. They also complained that their grazing lands were claimed by the government, and that they attributed to the coffee planters making their applications to purchase land; therefore upon these grounds they were dissatisfied.[20]

Likewise, P. E. Wodehouse, one-time Assistant Colonial Secretary and also a prominent planter, stated before the same Parliamentary Commission,

> I said that when European settlers come into a country, in which up to this day, the natives have lived exactly, as they like among themselves, it stands to reason that all the views of a European settler should be at variance with theirs. For example his estate may be surrounded with land which they have for generations looked on as common property; he gets into disputes with them immediately respecting the trespass of their cattle and it is almost impossible to define any fair line between the rights of the natives in respect of that ground and the rights of the Europeans whose cultivation is injured.[21]

During the land rush when the forests and swidden lands in the Kandyan Highlands were being sold off to European planters by the colonial state, the natives too began to press their claims to the lands being sold or already

---

19. *SP 1873*, No. 29, "Correspondence on the Subject of the Conservation of Forests," p. 9.
20. *BPP 1850*, Vol. 12, p. 19.
21. Ibid., p. 140.

Plantations and the Conflict over Land

disposed to planters and speculators by the state. George Turnour, a prominent government official, has mentioned an incident where certain lands at Pussellewa which formed the 'magnificent coffee estates' of Messrs. Worms, Barron, Delmar and Major Bird were claimed by natives.[22] As Turnour went on to point out, the inability of the planters to produce clear titles to land to counteract such native claims, discouraged land buying among capitalists.[23] The selling of land to which they had no title deeds in the European juridical sense by natives of all classes (nobility, clergy, peasantry) complicated the land issue even further.[24] As Governor Ward (1855–1860) subsequently wrote to the Secretary of State for the Colonies,

> The Government had so peacefully slumbered over its rights that twenty years after the occupation of the Kandyan provinces when European enterprise first sought in coffee cultivation a new field for the investment of capital, the local authorities were startled to find that they, literally, had not the power to give a good title, even to the most unscrupulously preserved Royal Forests – grants had been made to European capitalists at an early period but every inch of land was contested by native claimants and the grantees were compelled to obtain by process of law the title which the government was powerless to give them, or to compromise with their opponents, a proceeding which only doubled the number of frivolous claims.[25]

It must be emphasized that the necessity to assert Crown rights to land arose only with the development of plantations and resultant competition for land in the 1830s. The situation was not a creation of government neglect as the above statement suggests, but a result of new capitalist economic forces active in the colony.

The Crown Lands Ordinance

The colonial state attempted to resolve the conflict over high lands once and for all through legislation. The instrument used was Ordinance 12 of 1840, commonly known as the Crown Lands Encroachment Ordinance, (Appendix IV.). Its chief architect was George Turnour, the well-known authority on Kandyan land tenure. The objective of the Ordinance was to define a

---

22. *CO* 54/345, No. 46 of 29 August 1859, from Turnour's letter of 15 October 1836 quoted in Enclosure No. 4, p. 173.
23. Ibid., p. 175.
24. Michael Roberts, "Land Problems and Policies, c. 1832 to c. 1900," in *History of Ceylon*, ed. by K. M. de Silva, vol. 3, p. 121.
25. *CO* 54/345, No. 46 of 29 August 1859, Letter from Governor Ward on "Chena Lands."

set of criteria for determining Crown and private rights to 'waste lands' and to create the machinery for ejection and/or punishment of encroachers.[26] The ultimate objective, of course, was to enable the state to provide secure and fixed titles to purchasers of land and thereby to lay the framework for private property rights and capitalist agricultural development in Ceylon.[27]

The notorious Clause 6 of the Crown Lands Ordinance presumed that all uncultivated and unoccupied lands belonged to the Crown:

> And it is further enacted that all Forest, Waste, Unoccupied and Uncultivated Lands shall be presumed to be the property of the Crown; until the contrary thereof be proved; and all chenas and other lands which can be only cultivated after intervals of several years shall, if the same be situated within the Districts formerly comprised in the Kandyan Provinces (wherein no Thombo have been heretofore established) be deemed to belong to the Crown and not to be the property of any private person claiming the same against the Crown.[28]

Thus the Ordinance proceeded to place the burden of proving 'private' rights to these lands by criteria set forth by itself:

> ... except upon proof only by such person or sannas or Grant for the same, together with satisfactory evidence, as to the limits and boundaries thereof, or of such customary Taxes, Dues or Services having been rendered within twenty years for the same, as have been rendered within such period for similar lands being the property of private proprietors in the same District.[29]

Those who could not furnish proofs of ownership, i.e., title deeds (*sannas*) and tax receipts, were to be ejected from the land and crops and buildings on them were to be confiscated. The penalty for disobedience to an order of ejection was a fine of £5 and a maximum of fourteen days imprisonment.[30] The recognition of prescriptive rights to land held in uninterrupted possession was deliberately not extended to the Kandyan Provinces.[31] As Van Den Driesen has pointed out, the recognition of prescriptive rights would have drastically reduced supplies of land available to planters in the Kandyan Highlands.[32]

---

26. Ibid., p. 24. See also Roberts, "Land Problems," p. 121.
27. *CO* 54/345, No. 46 of 29 August 1859, p. 24.
28. The Crown Lands Ordinance No. 12 of 1840, reprinted in *A Revised Edition of the Legislative Enactments*, vol. 1, pp. 120–23.
29. Ibid., pp. 122–23.
30. Ibid., p. 123.
31. Ordinance No. 9 of 1841 in *A Revised Edition of the Legislative Enactments*, vol. 1, p. 124.
32. I. H. Van Den Driesen, "Land Sales Policy and Some Aspects of the Problem of Tenure – 1836–1886; Part II," *University of Ceylon Review*, vol. 15 (June-December 1956), p. 40.

Plantations and the Conflict over Land

Difficulty of Proving 'Ownership' Under the Crown Lands Ordinance

As many colonial government officials themselves subsequently pointed out, the colonial administration was demanding proof of ownership to a category of land which had customarily been considered communal village land. Obviously, Ordinance 12 of 1840 was designed to abolish users' rights to high lands. As the Assistant Government Agent of the Badulla District reiterated,

> ... strictly speaking, any private right which existed under the Kandyan Government with respect to chenas, not founded on a sannas or grant was rather the right to cultivate, than a title to the soil cultivated.[33]

When the precolonial Kandyan king made land grants to members of the aristocracy or the clergy, only the location, extent and boundaries of the paddy fields (*mada idam*) being granted were generally specified on the accompanying title deeds. Only vague references were made to the appurtenances of those paddy fields, i.e., the portions of village high lands used for supplementary agriculture and pasture, by peasants.[34] Furthermore, not all land grants were accompanied by written deeds. But now, the Crown Lands Ordinance demanded written deeds as proof of ownership. Most peasants who had only users' rights could not furnish title deeds to prove ownership to 'their' lands. Where written deeds were available, they were generally in the hands of overlords who had received grants from the Kandyan king. The terms of the Crown Lands Ordinance, then, were clearly biased in favor of the overlords, particularly the administrative or headman class. As a colonial official, J. Bailey himself pointed out, "Sannases are only found in families of some consideration. The boundaries are so vaguely described in them that it is impossible as a general rule to define the land indicated within fifty acres or so."[35]

In addition, historian Van Den Driesen has noted that the deeds given to the clergy and the nobility were engraved on copper, while those granted to common people were on fragile ola leaves and did not survive long.[36] More important is the fact that while deeds in precolonial times conferred hierarchical (often tribute-exacting rights) and not private ownership rights, the British recognized these deeds as proof of private property rights. The overlords who had greater access to title deeds now were in a stronger position to

---

33. *CO* 54/345, Memorandum by J. Bailey, p. 122.
34. See, for example, title deeds quoted by F. A. Hayley in *A Treatise*, pp. 96, 108.
35. *CO* 54/345, Memorandum by J. Bailey, p. 122.
36. Van Den Driesen, "Land Sales Policy," p. 41.

claim absolute ownership rights to the same land that cultivators had held customary users' rights.

The second category of proof accepted by the state towards the recognition of private rights to high lands was receipts for taxes, dues, or services rendered within the twenty years prior to the introduction of the Crown Lands Ordinance in 1840. But in Kandy there was no equivalent of the registers of ploughed fields (*hī-lēkam-miti*) for nonploughed or swidden lands. As we have noted, the precolonial Kandyan state (and the colonial state) did not generally exact taxes from chena lands. The British collected taxes only on hill paddy (*elvi*) grown on swidden fields. But hill paddy constituted only a small portion of the total chena cultivation.[37] Furthermore, no labor services were exacted on the basis of high land holdings *per se*.[38] The second category of proof of ownership to high lands demanded by the colonial state then (i.e., tax receipts), seems to have been largely nonexistent.

Clause 7 of the Crown Lands Ordinance stated that a person possessing land was entitled to a certificate (which later came to be known as a 'Certificate of Quiet Possession' or C.Q.P.) upon making an application to the Crown.[39] But the conditions for acceptance of these applications were generally stringent, requiring a declaration of the extent of the native right, the manner in which the land was acquired, and a survey of the land. It is plausible that only natives working for the colonial administration and knowledgeable of colonial law, such as the headmen, were therefore in a position to apply for these certificates.

Theoretically, the Crown Lands Ordinance and colonial land policy in general, allowed any person, European or native, to buy land. In practice, however, many factors mitigated against the peasants buying crown land. Even when some peasants did find the cash to buy high land, the cumbersome and bureaucratic method of land sales prevented many of them from making the purchases.[40] But, in general, most peasants did not have the required cash to buy land from the colonial state. Moreover, for peasants to agree to buy land from the European state would have signified in essence defeat and renunciation of their age old users' rights — renunciation of a traditional way of life — in short, moral defeat, on top of economic setback.

37. *CO* 54/345, p. 330. Bailey is uncertain if taxes were levied on elvi crops before 1840. Ibid., p. 41.
38. *CO* 54/345, Memorandum by J. Bailey, p. 330.
39. Clause 7 in Ordinance No. 12 of 1840 in *A Revised Edition of the Legislative Enactments*, pp. 120–23.
40. A. C. L. Ameer Ali, "Changing Conditions and Persisting Problems in the Peasant Sector under British Rule in the Period 1833–1893," *Ceylon Studies Seminar*, 1970/72 Series, no. 3a, p. 7.

Plantations and the Conflict over Land

Ludovici, a contemporary Burgher (Burghers are a Eurasian community descendent from the Dutch) critic of the colonial state, pointed out that the colonial state exercised its power to debar peasants from buying land.

> Great mass of people debarred from competing at government sales and not only the high upset price, but the discretion, which the Government exercises to accept or refuse an offer accounts in a most unwholesome manner the freedom of the market.[41]

While such direct interference by the colonial state in the land market does not seem to have been a common practice, it does suggest that the operation of the land market was not always free.

Land Sales Under the Crown Lands Ordinance

On the basis of the legal justification acquired through the Crown Lands Ordinance, the government continued to alienate vast amounts of forest land to planters. We do not have a breakdown on the proportion of crown lands sold that were actually converted into estates. However, the proliferation of land sales in the planting districts suggests that a large proportion of crown lands sold were converted into coffee plantations. According to D'A Vincent's estimates, between 1833 and 1880 (i.e., roughly the span of the coffee period), a yearly average of 25,000 acres of crown land was sold, mostly to European capitalists. The total amount of revenue realized by these sales was Rs. 18,716,890, at an average of 31 shillings an acre.[42] According to historian Patrick Peebles' estimates, crown land sales between 1833 and 1889 comprised roughly ten percent of the surface area of the island.[43]

It is obvious from Table 5:1 that the total extent of land and the average size per lot bought by the Europeans far exceeded that purchased by the numerically preponderant native buyers. According to compilations made by Michael Roberts, during the period from 1868 to 1906 Europeans bought seventy percent of the crown land acreage sold in Central Province, the primary coffee (and later tea) planting region in the country.[44] A great portion of the lands bought by the Europeans were turned into coffee plantations.[45]

---

41. Ludovici, *Rice Cultivation*, p. 122.
42. *SP 1882*, No. 68, p. 10.
43. Peebles, "Land Use and Population," p. 71. Compare Peebles' estimates with D'A Vincent's in *SP 1882*, No. 68, p. 10.
44. Roberts, "Some Comments," p. 11, (n. 2).
45. Roberts, "A Selection of the Documentary Evidence," p. 14; Jayawardena, "The Supply of Sinhalese Labour," pp. 266–67; Roberts, "Some Comments," pp. 9–14; Peebles, "Land Use and Population," p. 75.

Part 2: *The Plantation Impact*

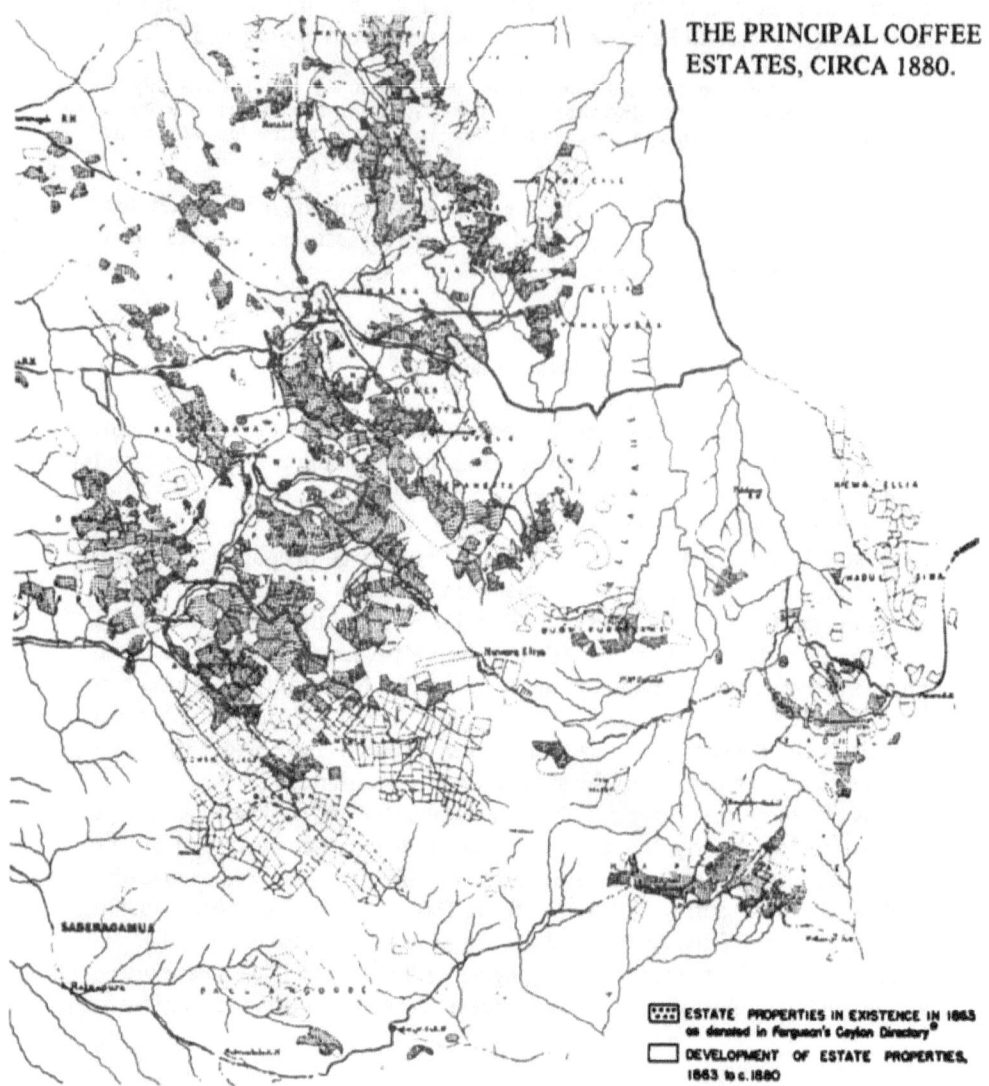

Map originally published for A. M. Ferguson —
Ceylon Observer Office — London by J. Hoddon & Co., London.

Special thanks to Michael Roberts who made available his copy of this map for purposes of reproduction.

Plantations and the Conflict over Land

Table 5:1

Crown Lands Surveyed and Sold: Central Province, 1844–1860

	Number of Lots	Extent (Acres)	Sold £	Fees £
Europeans	750	79,172	116,293	13,648
Natives	1,514	10,471	25,796	3,702

Source: *Ceylon Legislative Council, Sessional Paper*, No. 3 of 1860, Report of the Survey Department.

Table 5:2

Ownership of Cultivated Plantation Coffee Lands

	1871–1872		1880–1881	
	Acres	Percent	Acres	Percent
1. Total	195,627	100	256,500	100
2. Non-European	12,642	6.4	20,352	7.9
3. European	182,985	93.6	236,148	92.1

Source: Michael Roberts, "Export Agriculture in the Nineteenth Century," *History of Ceylon*, vol. 3 ed. by K. M. de Silva, (Peradeniya: University of Ceylon, 1973, p. 97.

As Table 5:2 suggests, very few non-Europeans converted their land into coffee *plantations*. However, many did cultivate coffee smallholdings. Europeans bought the greater share of crown lands in the plantation regions of the hill country, while in the nonplantation regions of the island, natives purchased the greater share of the crown land.[46] An examination of the ethnic background of these non-European land buyers and the uses they made of the lands thus purchased will be included in our discussion of native capitalist activities in Chapter VIII.

Reverting our attention to the issue of crown land sales to European planters in the Kandyan Highlands, it must be emphasized that the Crown Lands Ordinance was not able to resolve the high lands problem in a definitive manner. The statistics showing large-scale land sales to Europeans tell only one side of the story. The battle over high lands between contending interest groups raged throughout the colonial period. Peasants continued to cultivate dry grain and/or coffee on crown land; both the direct producers of the soil –

---

46. Ibid., p. 75; Roberts, "Some Comments," p. 12.

the peasantry — and the native overlords, the clergy, and the nobility, contested titles to land expropriated by the state and themselves made land sales to planters and speculators.

The conflict over land between plantation owners and natives took many forms. A common conflict has been described by P. D. Millie, an early coffee planter in Ceylon. He says that when a surveyor went in to prepare village land for sale, the peasants surrounded the surveyor without violence: bewailing and lamenting they finally threw themselves on the ground exclaiming "Pass over our bodies, our dead bodies, before you measure and sell the hunting ground of our forefathers."[47]

Another common conflict occurred over the construction of roads to European estates through native land. In fact, the colonial state passed special legislation giving planters the right to build private roads to their estates through neighboring village lands (this is discussed in Chapter VII). Colonel Watson, who faced native opposition in attempting to trace such a road to an estate in 1844, has stated his experience quite vividly:

> I entered into conversation with the spokesman who was an *aratchi* [village headman] and told him the advantages the road would be to himself and the surrounding villagers. He became very excited and in a very insolent manner said "who sent you white people here, we did very well without you; look there" (pointing to a coffee estate) "that forest was mine"; then to a sugar plantation "that was mine"; then to open ground upon which some estate cattle were grazing "that was mine"; you have levelled our forests; seized our *chenas* and now you are turning our paddy fields into roads. But we have a man up there (pointing to the Knuckles range of the mountains about 12 miles distant) who will soon get rid of you; he will cut the ... (drawing his hand across his throat with a vicious smile) of everyone of you.... This statement of the aratchis betrayed the voice and feelings of the Kandyans in general.[48]

The words of the native headmen quoted above and Colonel Watson's commentary on the incident bespeak of the hostility between the ruler and the ruled. This incident also indicates the discomfort and fear experienced by the colonizers due to the lack of legitimacy to their rule.

In discussing a particularly important aspect of the conflict over high lands, we shall next go on to look at the colonial state's campaign against swidden or chena cultivation and the compromises made by the state in the face of peasant resistance.

---

47. P. D. Millie, *Thirty Years Ago* (Colombo: 1878), Ch. 20 (no pagination).
48. Quoted in Ralph Pieris, "Society and Ideology," p. 89.

Plantations and the Conflict over Land

The Campaign Against Chena Cultivation

The continued 'encroachment' by peasants on forest and swidden lands which the state considered 'crown land' (on the basis of the Crown Lands Ordinance) threatened plantation expansion. D'A Vincent stated in 1882,

> In the most thickly populated parts of the Island, and especially in the Kandyan districts, the people ... have annually encroached on the Crown forest until not only do they now chena beyond the boundary of the village common-land but they also cut such timber as they require at great distances from their villages. It must before long become a question how far those rights of these people extend and whether the division amongst shareholders of what was village common-land, is to go on to an unlimited extent.[49]

Along with its efforts to appropriate high lands then, the state carried on a general policy of preventing swidden cultivation, particularly in the planting regions. Swidden agriculture was condemned as a 'primitive' form of cultivation destructive of the soil; its produce was declared to be of no nutritional value; and the land-extensive nature of shifting cultivation was claimed to make cultivators indolent. The following remarks by C. R. Buller, Government Agent of the Central Province, shed much light on the ignorance and antipathy of the colonial administration towards swidden cultivation.

> The cultivation of chena, is I consider, more injurious than otherwise to the country; it is destructive of the soil and renders it unfit for any purpose for seven, eight or ten years; and the crop of inferior grain usually raised on it, cannot, in any degree, compensate for the injury done to the land; it provides the native with a coarse kind of food, which he would soon abandon were he to apply himself to the cultivation of more valuable production (such as coffee, coconut, potatoes, etc.), from the proceeds of which he could purchase rice and other more nutritious substitutes; and the time and labour he now devotes to the cultivation of such unwholesome food as korakan [finger millet], would be spent much more profitably to himself, and with far greater general benefit, were they expended on the roads and public works, or in aiding the well-directed efforts of landed proprietors towards the public welfare.[50]

While chena cultivation was highly irrational from the point of view of the planters and the colonial state, it was quite rational from the peasants' point of view. As noted earlier, swidden was the safety valve to peasant subsistence. Where irrigation and paddy harvests failed, and/or taxes on paddy fields were extremely onerous, the peasants had necessarily to turn to shifting cultivation to stay alive.[51] Moreover, swidden plots could potentially be converted into home gardens as villages expanded. We have also noted that swidden crops

---

49. *SP 1882*, No. 68, p. 52.
50. *BPP 1847-1848*, vol. 42, Enclosure in Emerson Tennent's "Report on Finance and Commerce," p. 120.
51. Ludovici, *Rice Cultivation*, p. 26; *AR 1884*, Report of Baumgartner, p. 67A.

were easier to cultivate than wet-rice and they yielded proportionately greater harvests. Furthermore, the validity of the colonial administration's attacks against slash-and-burn agriculture, such as the low nutritional value of dry grain crops is open to serious doubt.[52]

Colonial administrators also argued that an increase in the number of people dependent on shifting cultivation would contribute to an increase in the numbers leading unsettled lives and thereby to lawlessness in the country.[53] But swidden, though important, was only a supplementary form of agriculture for the peasants of the Central Highlands. These people were not nomads; they led settled lives as wet-rice cultivators in their ancestral villages.[54] The argument that chena should be curbed in order to prevent lawlessness in the country was again a fictitious one, fabricated to justify the alienation of high lands by the state for sale to planters and speculators.

Some provincial officials did, however, acknowledge the importance of swidden for the subsistence of the peasantry. They pointed out that peasants turned to shifting agriculture not out of indolence, but out of despair particularly over the neglect of irrigational and other facilities necessary for wet-rice cultivation. A few provincial officers condemned the colonial state pointing out that it was unjust and inhumane to curtail chena cultivation indiscriminately when the peasants had no alternatives.

> In some parts of Kandyan Districts, where the muddy lands are of small extent and the means of irrigation scanty, people have been compelled to cultivate chenas largely in order to obtain the means of subsistence.[55]

Constraints on Peasant Coffee

The conflict between planters and the peasantry over land must not simply be interpreted as a struggle between subsistence and cash crop production. The struggle over high lands represented, at least to a small extent, a conflict between two modes of cash crop production, namely smallholder cash cropping and plantation production.

The Kandyan peasantry was quick to respond to the forces of commercialization and monetization that came with colonial rule. As a matter of fact,

---

52. Ronald Herring, "Redistributive Agrarian Policy," p. 406.
53. *SP 1871*, No. 3, "Report on Timber Reserve," p. 6.
54. Michael Roberts, "Grain Taxes in British Ceylon, 1832–1878: Problems in the Field," *Journal of Asian Studies*, vol. 27 (1968), p. 810.
55. *CO 54/345*, No. 46 of 29 August 1859, pp. 233–34; also *SP 1873*, No. 15, "Papers Relating to the Cultivation and Survey of Chena Lands," p. 5.

Plantations and the Conflict over Land

it was the Kandyan peasantry who were the pioneer coffee growers in Ceylon. They were growing coffee for export decades before the plantations came on the scene. Between 1800 and 1804, the average peasant coffee exports were 1,116 cwts., while between 1822 and 1825, exports had increased to 10,246 cwts.[56] As Roberts notes, "The scale of production went up greatly from the 1830s ... and had reached a peak of 148,000 to 218,000 cwts. in the period 1865–69."[57] In fact it was the earlier success of peasant coffee that encouraged Europeans to undertake large-scale cultivation on estates.

When plantations started expanding into the higher elevations of the Kandyan Highlands, the smallholders who lacked the cash and the influence necessary to compete with the planters in purchasing crown land, failed to follow suit. Furthermore, the clearing of the hilltops for plantations disturbed the ecology and agriculture on the peasant lands in the villages below.[58] Colonial legislation such as the Bill against coffee stealing (see Chapter VII) also favored plantation coffee over peasant coffee.

Native Land Claims

In addition to cultivating chenas (and sometimes 'peasant coffee') on high lands that the Crown claimed as its own, natives also laid claims to lands sold by the state to planters and speculators. Litigation became rampant and the security of title to plantation property was threatened. Sir Emerson Tennent, the Colonial Secretary, voiced the colonial administration's alarm over rampant native 'encroachments' and land claims in the following manner: "These fraudulent and vexatious proceedings not only discourage minor capitalists from settling in the colony, but they greatly embarrass and disconcert the local arrangements of the Government."[59]

The object of the natives — both overlords and peasants — was to make quick money before the state expropriated their land. It is important to note that encroachers on crown high lands were not always Kandyan peasants, but also enterprising men from the coastal lowlands.[60] The influx of new groups further exacerbated the confusion over high lands. Bailey, the Government

---

56. Ameer Ali, "Peasant Coffee," p. 50.
57. Roberts, "Some Comments," p. 24.
58. Ameer Ali, "Peasant Coffee," p. 55; see also Angelika Sievers, "Geographical Aspects of Peasant Tradition," *passim*.
59. *BPP 1847–1848*, vol. 4, Tennent's Report. See also *CO* 54/345 of 29 August 1859, p. 334.
60. Ariya Abeysinghe, *Ancient Land Tenure to Modern Land Reform in Sri Lanka* (Colombo: Centre for Society and Religion, 1978), vol. 1, p. 91.

Agent of the Badulla District, commented in 1859 on the thriving private land market, the changes in land ownership and the negative effects of these changes on the British plantation enterprise in the following manner.

> Land is daily increasing value and its value is daily being more appreciated. Chenas are fast changing hands, eagerly purchased by Moormen and Chetties and converted into plantations [smallholdings]. The Kandyans too are fast losing that wholesome respect for Government which would induce them to acquiesce in its orders and if we delay, we shall have to contest every foot of the ground.[61]

What is evident from the foregoing discussion is that the Crown Lands Ordinance was only partially successful in achieving its aims. While it allowed the state to expropriate vast tracts of land for the plantations, it also unleashed social forces and conflicts that threatened the hegemony of the British in the island. Some of these conflicts over land surveys and the construction of roads to estates through villages, have already been referred to earlier.

According to Van Den Driesen, the resentment of expropriated native landholders at first took the form of isolated outbreaks of violence such as the tearing down of boundary fences and cutting down of coffee trees.[62] Van Den Driesen suggests, that these rebellious acts must soon have assumed considerable proportions, because the colonial state was constrained to pass an Ordinance specifically to prevent injuries to and thefts of plantation property. According to Clause 14 of this Ordinance — Ordinance 6 of 1846 — any person who "unlawfully or maliciously cut, broke, barked, uprooted, or otherwise destroyed trees on a plantation could be imprisoned with or without hard labor for any period not exceeding one year, and if a male, to corporal punishment not exceeding fifty lashes."[63] Some planters whose properties were trespassed and damaged probably exerted pressure on the colonial state to pass this legislation. Legislation such as this (and others discussed in Chapter VII) which relied on the coercive power of the state were commonplace measures in the establishment of a politico-juridical basis for capitalism in Ceylon and elsewhere.

Repressive legislation, however, could not quell the rising tide of resentment against colonial rule and plantation expansion. Many contemporary observers and subsequent writers have commented on the direct relationship between the crown land policies and the popular rebellion of 1848.[64] The evidence that H. L. Layard, a high government official and a prominent coffee planter, gave before the British Parliamentary Committee inquiring

---

61. *CO* 54/345 of 29 August 1859, p. 31.
62. Van Den Driesen, "Land Sales Policy," p. 42.
63. Ibid., p. 42.
64. Ibid., pp. 42–43.

Plantations and the Conflict over Land

into the Ceylon rebellion of 1848, illuminates this relationship remarkably well. Layard here talks of "encroachment" of Europeans and the colonial state on native lands, rather than of native encroachments on plantations and crown lands, as was customary among colonial administrators and planters.

Q. 6210: Will you state your opinion generally as to the causes of those disturbances?
A: I should be disposed to divide those causes according to the sections of population amongst whom the disaffection existed. With reference to the Kandyan Province, I should state that the causes were in the first instance the *encroachment by the Europeans as well as by the Government upon the lands and ultimate sale to the Europeans.*

Q: 6211: When did those encroachments on the part of the Europeans and Government begin?

A: They commenced prior to my arrival in the island in 1841; in about 1840 and 1841 were the first encroachments ...

Q.6212: How did the Europeans encroach upon the lands?

A: *By purchasing from the Government those lands, which were, as it is stated, available for native cultivation and pasturage.*

Q.6213: You used the expression "the encroachment of Government upon lands." Did the natives consider the lands belonging to them and that the Government interfered with them and sold them to Europeans?

A: Hitherto the natives had free access to the lands; but the Government, the moment they found the lands could be disposed of to advantage, ascertained how far the natives had a claim to the lands and where the natives could not establish a legal claim, the Government sold the lands, upon the application of the European settlers.

Q.6214: Were those sales conducted to a great extent?

A: To a very large extent.

Q.6215: In what provinces were they?

A: Principally in the Central Provinces.

Q.6216: Were those lands belonging to the temples or belonging to natives especially?

A: In some instances there were portions of land which had been appropriated or claimed by the temples, and in others, and in most cases there were lands which had been appropriated or claimed by native villagers.

Q.6217: You think that was one of the causes of the discontent?

A: I think it was a very probable cause. [emphasis added][65]

The neglect of the needs and repression of the rights of the natives, particularly the cultivators, did not come about due to mere ignorance on the part of the British officials. It resulted primarily from the incompatibility of the interests of British private capital and that of the peasantry. In referring to the injury caused the peasantry, Emerson Tennent, the Colonial Secretary, sighed at what he accepted to be the inevitable costs of capitalist agricultural

---

65. *BPP 1850*, Vol. 12, Evidence of H. L. Layard before the British Parliamentary Committee inquiring into the 1848 rebellion in Ceylon, p. 226.

development: "It must be obvious that these are grievances to which we can apply no remedy, because they arise out of legitimate causes which it would be injudicious in us to control, I mean to check coffee-planting."[66]

Compromises in the Implementation of Crown Lands Legislation

In challenging the populist view that colonial land policy led to the large-scale expropriation of the Kandyan peasantry, several contemporary writers have pointed out that the Crown Lands Ordinance of 1840 (and the subsequent Waste Lands Ordinance – No. 1 of 1897) were not implemented to the letter of the law. The colonial state's extreme dependence on the native aristocratic-administrative class for the implementation of its policies (discussed later in this chapter), and the defiant and widespread squatter movement, these writers argue, made it impossible to fully exercise the provisions of the various repressive land ordinances.[67]

In attempting to reduce the encroachment problem to manageable proportions, the colonial state did in fact introduce several concessionary measures. These included sale of swidden lands to people who had already brought them under cultivation; grant of right for shifting cultivation on payment of taxes or purchase of government licenses, and the issue of "certificates of quiet possession" (under Clause 7 in Ordinance 12 of 1840) to applicants with "legitimate" claims to high lands.[68] Although some of these concessions conflicted with the most stringent stipulations of the Crown Lands Ordinance (for example that proper titles be obtained *before* undertaking shifting cultivation), the colonial state found it politically expedient to introduce them.

It is obvious that these compromise measures amounted to land *sales* rather than free land grants to the natives or a recognition of their users' rights. Only natives with money were therefore able to take advantage of these opportunities to establish private ownership to high lands. The Government Agent of the Central Province, Braybooke, noted in his Administration Report for 1867 that the licensing rate for swidden cultivation at one shilling an acre was too high given the poverty of the people, and the uncertain nature of shifting cultivation.[69]

---

66. Emerson Tennent, quoted in Van Den Driesen, "Land Sales Policy," p. 45.
67. Roberts, "A Selection of the Documentary Evidence," pp. 5 and 9; Jayawardena, "The Supply of Sinhalese Labour," Ch. 5, *passim*.
68. Roberts, "A Selection of the Documentary Evidence," p. 14.
69. *SP 1873*, No. 15, p. 25.

Michael Roberts has compiled statistics on the extent of 'encroached' land that was later sold to private individuals in freehold by the colonial state.[70]

Table 5:3

Land Sales in Central Province, 1868–1887

	Lots	Acres
Encroachments sold or given at a valuation	1221	4,390
Granted at half the value	1109	4,823
Certificates of Quiet Possession	2936	9,671
Total	5266	18,884

Source: Michael Roberts, "A Selection of the Documentary Evidence as Aids for the Lecture on The Administration of the Waste Lands Ordinance No. 12 of 1840 and its Impact on the Coffee Period, 1840–80s," *The Archives Lecture Series*, Ceylon (June 20, 1969), p. 14.

Michael Roberts and Lal Jayawardena claim that a great portion of land thus obtained by the natives was later converted into cash crop production, probably 'peasant coffee'.[71] As noted earlier, compared to the size and extent of crown land purchased by European planters, the sales made to natives were much smaller in size per unit and total extent (see Tables 5:1 and 5:2, for example).[72]

In challenging the view popular among Ceylonese writers that colonial land legislation resulted in the large-scale expropriation of the Kandyan peasantry [73] Lal Jayawardena has argued instead that colonial land policies created a class of high land peasant proprietors which did not previously exist.[74] Jayawardena goes even further in claiming that the colonial state carried on a deliberate policy towards 'conserving' the peasantry who were threatened by market forces beyond their control and their own irrational proclivities towards selling their lands to outsiders. Jayawardena assigns to the colonial state a paternalistic role (vis-à-vis the peasantry), neglecting to note that it was colonial legislation that unleashed those threatening market forces by turning land into a commodity.[75] Further more, Jayawardena fails to recognize that while a very large amount of the high lands to which peasants

---

70. Roberts, "Some Comments," p. 17.
71. Roberts, "A Selection of Documentary Evidence," p. 14; Jayawardena, "The Supply of Sinhalese Labour," pp. 266–67.
72. See also Roberts, "Export Agriculture," p. 97.
73. Please see Ch. I, notes 23, 24, 25 of this book for references to this popular view.
74. Jayawardena, "The Supply of Sinhalese Labour," Ch. 5, *passim*.
75. Ibid., p. 254 and Ch. 5, *passim*.

had customary users' rights were expropriated by the state only a very small portion of these was resold to the peasantry in freehold.

Michael Roberts, on the other hand, has argued that "individuals from a middling-lower strata in the rural sector had successfully acquired crown land."[76] In the absence of sufficient data on the class background of native land buyers, this assertion must remain at best a hypothesis. What needs to be emphasized is that the smallness of the high land plots purchased by natives from the Crown does not necessarily indicate a 'middling-lower' social class status of the buyers as Roberts seems to suggest.[77] As he himself notes, many well-to-do non-Europeans (including Chettiyar moneylenders) bought small high land plots which they converted into coffee smallholdings.[78] It is, however, likely that where individuals from the lower strata acquired crown land, they did so largely through illegal encroachments (as discussed earlier) rather than through purchases from the Crown.

As suggested earlier, illegal encroachment on high lands was about the most vexatious problem facing the planters and the colonial officials in the Kandyan Highlands during the expansion of coffee plantations. In a further attempt to bring the encroachment problem under control, the colonial state devised a scheme of demarcating village high land reserves during the 1850s. The inherently conflictive task of sorting out the distribution of these reserves was left to the villagers themselves.[79] This probably intensified land disputes within the village as well. The attempt to control defiant native populations by restricting them to 'native reserves' was a fairly common colonial practice not peculiar to Ceylon. The 'native reserves' policy in Ceylon was quite mild in comparison to the much harsher policies carried out (even today) by Europeans in many parts of Africa, the Americas and Australasia.[80] The planter community in Ceylon, however, was not pleased with this arrangement to demarcate village high land reserves as it was potentially threatening to plantation expansion.[81]

The confluence of a number of forces such as the policy of chena reserves just referred to, the laxity of provincial administrators in implementing the Crown Lands Ordinance, the availability of paddy fields, home gardens, and,

---

76. Roberts, "Some Comments," p. 12.
77. Ibid., p. 12.
78. Ibid., pp. 12 and 24–25 (n. 3).
79. Roberts, "The Impact of the Waste Lands Legislation," p. 171.
80. For example, the present and past policies in South Africa, Brazil, the U. S. See also Meek, *Land Law and Custom*, p. xxv, and Leys, *Underdevelopment in Kenya*, p. 31.
81. Millie, *Thirty Years Ago*, Ch. 20; Roberts, "A Selection of the Documentary Evidence," p. 12.

Plantations and the Conflict over Land

of course, encroachments on high lands, prevented the absolute dispossession of the Kandyan cultivators and delayed the emergence of a wage-earning class. Thus a large-scale expropriation of the peasantry akin to the Enclosure Movement in England did not take place in nineteenth century Ceylon. The issue of the non-emergence of a regular wage-earning class among the Kandyan peasantry during the nineteenth century will be discussed in the next chapter.

The policy of selling high land in freehold, however, completely eliminated the customary communal village rights to high lands by the end of the century. A British provincial administrator observed in 1871 that there were very few villages in the Kandyan coffee districts where the common right to village high lands had not been totally extinguished.[82]

In addition, from about the 1870s on, very few permits were given out for swidden cultivation. Although a certain amount of illicit shifting cultivation still continued, the role of swidden cultivation had been greatly reduced in the wet zone of Ceylon by the end of the century.[83] A major reason for the demise of chena cultivation was of course the expansion of coffee plantations. Yet another reason was the increasing importance of peasant cash cropping and the substitution of cash crops (especially peasant coffee) for swidden crops on the still available high lands by the peasant cultivators. Although plantations did not directly impinge on the village gardens, the restrictions placed on the free access to uncultivated land by the state, constrained the expansion of peasants' garden cultivation as well.

The Struggle Over High Lands: Temple Villages

Extensive monastic properties was one of the striking features of precolonial Kandy. Prior to the operation of the Temple Lands Commission (to be discussed in this chapter) from 1856 to 1868, sixty percent of the land in the Sabaragamuwa District alone belonged to the Buddhist temples.[84] It must be brought to mind that there were essentially two categories of temple properties — those belonging to Buddhist temples (*vihāragam*) and others belonging to the temples of deities worshipped by Buddhists (*dēvalagam*).

---

82. *AR 1871*, Report on Nuwarakalawiya quoted in Roberts, "Waste Lands Legislation," pp. 180–81.
83. Michael Roberts, "Aspects of Ceylon's Agrarian Economy in the Nineteenth Century," in *History of Ceylon*, ed. by K. M. de Silva, vol. 3, p. 159.
84. Michael Roberts, "Grain Taxes in British Ceylon, 1832–1878: Problems," p. 812.

When a land rush emerged in the wake of plantation development, the planters and the colonial state began to covet the vast tracts of forest and swidden land well suited for coffee and held by these temples. Emerson Tennent, the Colonial Secretary, was outraged that the clergy were laying claim to high lands indiscriminately and selling them, when in fact, as he (and the colonial administration) claimed, these high lands belonged to the Crown.

> The most perceptible evil which flows from the privileges thus accorded to the temples, is the facility which it affords for fraud on the Government, the temples laying claim indiscriminately to lands of every description, and to any extent; lands which are in reality, the property of the Crown but which are daringly seized and openly sold by the temples; the Government owing to the want of surveys and to the ease with which sannas (or native deeds) can be forged, being really powerless against this system of dishonesty.[85]

As Tennent noted, Kandyan chiefs and clergy were laying claim to vast tracts of high lands based on titles which appeared vague and questionable in the eyes of the British. Furthermore, they were selling high lands to which they did not have alienable rights under Kandyan law. The Temple Land Commissioners subsequently appointed by the colonial state to investigate this confused state of affairs noted that "The priests are some of them very wealthy indeed, amassing wealth appears to be their sole object and aim; they are large money lenders and with two exceptions are all of them of the Siam Samagam."[86]

The claim of the British investigative team that the amassing of wealth was the 'sole object' of the Buddhist clergy was an exaggeration. But there is no doubt that the clergy were violating the Buddhist disciplinary code by engaging in mundane pursuits such as the selling and renting of land. Note also that as the Commissioners have stated, most of the monks engaging in rentier and mercantile activities belonged to the sect known as *Siam Samagam/Nikaya*, which recruited members exclusively from the *govi* or cultivator caste considered the highest caste among the Sinhalese.

The Temple Lands Commission

Several attempts had been made by the British since 1819 to define and register temple properties.[87] However, it was with the passing of Ordinance

---

85. *BPP 1847–1848*, Vol. 42, p. 97.
86. *SP 1863*, No. 11, "Report of the Temple Land Commissioners," pp. 370–71.
87. *SP 1876*, No. 18, "Buddhist Temporalities Commission Report," Appendix A; see also Roberts, "Land Problems and policies," p. 133.

Plantations and the Conflict over Land

No. 10 of 1856, aimed at the registration and settlement of temple properties, that definite steps were taken by the colonial administration to bring the temple land situation under control.[88] The activities of the Temple Lands Commission was restricted to the Kandyan Provinces where both temple lands and the demand for them by planters were the most extensive. The tasks of the itinerant Temple Lands Commission included the examination of the temples' claims to land, expropriation of high lands, and the extension of the paddy tax to wet-rice lands in cases where the temples did not have 'proper' titles. The costs of surveying the land were to be shared between the state and the particular temples involved.[89]

Ordinance No. 10 of 1856 was similar to Ordinance No. 12 of 1840 in that the burden of proving title again fell on the native landholders. Kandyan kings often made only verbal land grants to temples; where written titles had been given, their wording with respect to the high lands was extremely vague. Furthermore, as the temple villages were exempt from payment of grain taxes to the state, it is conceivable that they were not listed in the government tax records of ploughed fields (*hī lekam miti*) either.[90]

Due to these difficulties faced by the temple overlords in providing evidence acceptable to the Commissioners, a large proportion of the temple land claims came to be rejected. It is likely that in trying to gain as much land as possible, the temple lords exaggerated their customary claims. On the other hand, it also appears that the high survey fees discouraged many monks and lay incumbents of deity temples (*nilemēs*) from pursuing their land claims. Both the verbal and statistical evidence on temple lands alienated indicate that most of the temple land claims rejected were in fact high lands which were ideal for coffee plantations. This suggests, that one, if not the primary motive in registering temple lands by the colonial state was to release high lands for coffee plantations. As the Temple Lands Commissioners reported,

> In the case however of the Sapperegama Maha Dewale which is the largest claim in the District and comprise a great quantity of villages, the Basnayake Nileme has, after communication withdrawn the claim of the Dewale in the village of Panecla to a very large extent of forest land, admirably adapted for coffee cultivation and already, I believe applied for....
>
> The Basnayeke Nileme of Ammaduva Kattregam Dewale has under similar circumstances withdrawn his claim to a very large tract of forest on the borders of the Southern Province. I have also rejected a small tract of valuable forest in the village of Ammaduva. There will be a considerable amount of forest rejected at Bottumbe well fitted for coffee cultivation.[91]

88. *A Revised Edition of the Legislative Enactments*, vol. 2, p. 646.
89. Roberts, "Land Problems and Policies," pp. 132–33.
90. *SP 1861*, No. 2, "Report of the Temple Lands Commissioner."
91. *SP 1863*, "Report of the Temple Lands Commissioner for 1862," p. 14.

Similarly, the *Colombo Observer*, the organ for the planter community which kept a close watch over the activities of the Temple Lands Commission noted with satisfaction.

> Now that Mr. Tottenham's staff has jointed him, we fancy next year will present a largely increased acreage under the head Temple Lands. A large proportion of the lands thus released will we doubt not, be useful for coffee cultivation.[92]

In addition to rejecting the claims of Buddhist monks and lay incumbents to high lands, the Commissioners also rejected a considerable amount of their claims to wet-rice lands (*mada idam*) in the temple villages. The tithes to be collected by the colonial state from these paddy fields, as the Temple Commissioners noted, were "no unimportant addition" to the state revenue.[93]

Table 5:4 gives approximate figures of the lands held by temples in those provinces (including non-Kandyan Provinces) where the Temple Lands Commission carried out its activities. These figures represent in effect the amount of land to which the colonial state granted ownership rights to the temples.

Table 5:4

Temple Lands: 1876

Province	Acres
Central	239,232
Western	75,303
North Western	58,360
North	1,583
Southern	1,559
Total	376,037

Source: Report of the Buddhist Temporalities Commission, Ceylon Legislative Council, Sessional Paper, No. 18 of 1876, p. 41.

However, the above figures do not tell us how much land the temples had prior to the expropriations made by the Temple Lands Commission. As Table 5:5 demonstrates, between 1856 and 1864, the Temple Lands Commission rejected approximately fifty-five percent of total temple land claims, the majority of which were claims to high lands. Approximately sixty percent of high lands claimed were expropriated by the state.

---

92. *The Colombo Observer*, January 29, 1866.
93. *SP 1863*, "Report of the Temple Lands Commissioner for 1862," p. 14.

Table 5:5

Temple Lands Registered/Rejected by the Temple Lands Commission Under Ordinance No. 10 of 1856

	(2)			(3)			(4)			(5)	
	Registered	Paddy Fields		Rejected			Registered	Highlands (includes gardens, chenas, forests)		Rejected	
District	Amunams	Pelas	Kurunis	Amunams	Pelas	Kurunis	Amunams	Pelas	Kurunis	Amunams	Pelas	Kurunis
Kandy	1,313	2	0	906	3	1	2,382	0	1¹/₃	4,297	1	4
Matale	604	3	6	683	3	7	1,054	1	6	5,657	3	7
Nuwara Eliya	222	0	1	157	1	0	320	0	0	999	3	2
Ratnapura	2,090	1	5	1,388	0	6	6,234	3	3	12,672	0	1¹/₄
Kegalle	1,246	2	9	553	0	6¹/₄	3,985	1	6	1,293	2	5
Badulla (Uva Province)	2,183	2	6	898	0	7	5,749	1	0¹/₃	5,388	0	4¹/₂
Anuradapura	251	0	7	3	0	0	1	0	0	1,001	1	0
Polonnaruwa	11	0	0	130	2	0	0	0	0	302	0	4
Kurunegala	4,831	3	6	3,716	0	9	8,067	2	4	8,481	1	2
Puttalam	10	0	0	112	0	1	60	2	0	80		
Southern Province (Hinidum Pattu)	13	1	7	3	3	6	123	3	7	142	2	2
Totals	12,778	2	7	8,553	0	3¹/₄	27,978	3	7²/₃	40,316	1	2

Source: Compiled from Tables appended to the Temple Lands Commissioners' Reports from 1857–1864 and published in the "Report of the Commission on Tenure of Lands of Viharagam, Dewalagam and Nindagam," Ceylon Parliament Sessional Paper 1 of 1956, Appendix A.

Results of Temple Lands Registration

As Table 5:5 indicates, in the short run, the temples lost a little over half of the land to which they had customary rights due to the implementation of the Temple Lands Registration Ordinance.[94] As noted above, much of the land thus expropriated by the state was uncultivated forest or periodically cultivated chena lands suited for coffee. The alienation of these lands prevented the clergy and the lay incumbents of the deity temples from leasing or selling those lands to planters and speculators or from converting them to cashcropping on their own.

Although the rejection of temple land claims by the Commission reduced the total amount of temple lands held by the overlords by half, in the long run the activities of the Commission benefitted the temple lords in an important respect. In the process of making its inquiries into temple land tenure, the Comissioners dug up evidence against tenants who had been defaulting on their feudal obligations to the overlords.[95] This evidence now gave the overlords a renewed legitimacy to demand that the tenants pay their customary tribute in labor, kind, or cash.

The reactivation of feudal tribute through the registration of temple lands must be seen in historical context. As noted in Chapter II, conflict between lords and serfs over rent was the primary form of class struggle in precolonial Kandyan society. With the arrival of the British, the authority of the aristocracy and the clergy in the society began to decline.[96] The tenant cultivators in turn became lax about paying tribute to their overlords. In fact, by the middle of the nineteenth century, some of the specialized services performed by tenants for their lords had become obsolete and were not being enforced. Moreover, the Revenue Commissioner of the Kandyan region, George Turnour, noted that the abolition of forced labor in the royal villages (*gabadāgam*) and its substitution with a grain tax in 1818 (discussed later) had the indirect effect of loosening the feudal nexus in the villages of the aristocrats and the temples (*nindagam* and *vihāragam*) as well.[97]

But now in the 1860s, the land registration scheme of the colonial state helped strengthen feudal social relations which had been weakening in the wake of monetization and commercialization of the economy and the di-

---

94. Roberts, "Aspects of Ceylon's Agrarian Economy," p. 161.
95. *SP 1863*, No. 11, p. 6; see also Gunasinghe, "Agrarian Relations," pp. 19–20.
96. Kitsiri Malalgoda, *Buddhism in Sinhalese Society 1750–1900: A Study of Religious Revival and Change* (Berekeley: University of California Press, 1976), p. 181.
97. Turnour's Report quoted by Colvin R. de Silva in *Ceylon under the British*, vol. 2 pp. 388–99.

munition of the authority of the feudal lords. This reactivation of feudal authority in the temple villages was not entirely an unintended consequence of the colonial state's efforts to obtain high lands for the European plantations. As will be seen in later chapters, the strengthening of feudal relations was in line with the new and more favorable policy the colonial state adopted towards the feudal aristocracy following the rebellion of 1848.

Alienation of high lands by the colonial state reduced the amount of swidden and pasture land that had hitherto been available to the peasant cultivators of the temple villages. While expropriation of temple lands by the state reduced the sources of income of temple overlords, it cut right into peasant subsistence.[98] Furthermore, it wiped out the peasantry's usufructary rights to the alienated lands thereby diminishing their sense of political autonomy traditionally associated with swidden agriculture. The reduced access to the village common lands then tied the peasantry more firmly to their paddy fields and thereby to the direct control and supervision of the feudal lords. No doubt many peasants continued to ,encroach, that is, cultivate chenas and graze their animals on the lands taken over by the Temple Lands Commission. But, as Hans-Dieter Evers notes,

> The registration of temple lands had a very stabilizing effect on the system .... Once a certificate had been issued and the services connected with temple lands put down in writing, the mighty judiciary machine of the colonial government could be used to maintain the status quo. The extent of vihāragam and dēvalagam is therefore today, 1964–66, more or less the same as in 1857.[99]

However, the activities of the Temples Lands Commission did not simply reinstitute feudal social relations, but changed the 'status quo' within which these relations operated. As the subsequently appointed Buddhist Temporalities Commission noted in 1876, Ordinance No. 10 of 1856 put into effect by the Temple Lands Commission gave temple overlords absolute ownership and the right of land alienation which they did not have under Kandyan customary law. The Buddhist Temporalities Commission lamented that "with European ignorance we applied our own notions of the law of property to those of Orientals,"[100] and went on to point out that under the cover of British law, the temple overlords were now freely selling land and timber with complete disregard for the customary users' rights of the cultivators.[101]

---

98. Van Den Driesen, "Land Sales Policy," p. 52.
99. Hans-Dieter Evers, "Temple Lands and Rājakariya: The Kandyan Lankātilaka Raja Maha Vihāraya," *Ceylon Studies Seminar*, 1970/71 Series, no. 6, p. 5.
100. *SP 1876*, No. 18, "Buddhist Temporalities Commission Report," Appendix, p. 38.
101. Ibid., p. 38.

Historian Kitsiri Malalgoda too suggests that it was the tenant cultivator class that stood to lose from these new political and economic developments which threatened their guaranteed access to land.

> In fact along with registration, the government gave up all interest in temple lands. The result was that temple authorities who hitherto had been entitled merely to the usufruct of the lands dedicated to them, were now vested with absolute rights. Many monks in the Kandyan provinces found it irresistible to use these rights to their personal advantage. And there was no effective authority to stop them; the ecclesiastical authorities were much weaker than they had been before, and the secular authorities (i.e., the government) remained inactive in this regard for a long time to come.[102]

This state of affairs undoubtedly intensified the conflicts over land rights between the temple overlords and their tenants. The overlords, who now enjoyed private property rights to high lands conceded by the Temple Lands Commission, began to look upon the cultivators using the swidden, forest and pasture lands of the temple villages, as 'encroachers', in the same manner as the planters and the colonial state did towards the cultivators asserting their customary users' rights. In contrast, during precolonial times, when land was plentiful and was not a commodity, temple overlords had paid little heed to their village high lands and had allowed the peasants to do as they pleased with them, as long as the cultivators paid tribute on the wet-rice fields.

Differential Effects of Colonial Land Legislation on the Native Social Classes

In the long run, then, colonial state policies towards temple lands were advantageous to the temple overlords and detrimental to the peasant cultivators. Although some feudal families and clergy lost their customary hierarchical rights to a vast extent of high lands, in general, many of them were able to strengthen their hold over the remaining lands, often at the expense of the cultivators' usufructary rights.

On the basis of island-wide land sales data, Patrick Peebles concludes that crown land sales tended to increase the class disparities within the native population.

> Crown land sales . . . were unequally distributed among the Ceylonese population. A few prominent Ceylonese families accumulated enormous estates. Further analysis identified two sets of intermarried families, one *karāva* caste, and one *goyigama* caste, who puchased a disproportionate share of Crown land purchased by Sinhalese elites . . . . Even at the village level, The crown land must have contributed to inequality, since only a minority of cultivators could have purchased any land at all.[103]

---

102. Malalgoda, *Buddhism in Sinhalese Society*, p. 178.
103. Peebles, "Land Use and Population," p. 75.

Plantations and the Conflict over Land 117

As Peebles notes, not all natives who acquired crown land were from the traditional Sinhalese aristocracy. Several other Sinhalese and non-European groups who had accumulated money through plantation-related mercantile and other activities bought high lands (as well as paddy lands) in the Kandyan Highlands. They bought lands not only from the colonial state but also from native land sellers — feudal lords and cultivators. As noted earlier, by comparison with the purchases made by European planters, the total extent and size per plot bought by these non-Europeans were much smaller. As we shall argue later, these groups constituted a subordinate capitalist class.

The *karava* artisan caste from the coastal lowlands was one of the foremost Sinhalese groups to invest in land in the interior.[104] Several mercantile groups from India including Indian Tamils, Chettiyars, Borahs and Parsis also purchased land from the colonial state and native land sellers in the Kandyan Highlands during the nineteenth century.[105] A substantial amount of land thus bought was converted into coffee smallholdings. Roughly a third or more of the acreage under so-called 'native coffee' was in fact under the control of Chettiyars and other mercantile groups from India.[106] The long-term implications of the arrival of these entrepreneurial groups to the Highlands will be considered in Chapter VIII.

Among the natives who stood to gain most from the implementation of colonial land legislation was the native administrative stratum (headmen), often drawn from the aristocratic sub-caste known as the *radala*. (Not all headmen, however, had the honor of being considered a *radala*.)

As noted earlier in our discussion of the Crown Lands Encroachment Ordinance, both the written title deeds which were required as proof of ownership to land and the familiarity with the colonial legal system necessary for applying for a C.Q.P. (Certificate of Quiet Possession) were much more readily avilable to the headmen than the cultivators. As we will discuss in Chapter VII, many feudal aristocrats were employed by the colonial state in the administration of the colony. These headmen who were familiar with colonial law and administrative practices had a distinct advantage over the peasants, the clergy, and those aristocrats disassociated from the colonial administration, in competing to establish their rights over land.

As contemporary observers and secondary writers have noted, the colonial state was very heavily dependent on the native headmen, particularly for the

---

104. For an interesting account of the entrepreneurial activities of perhaps the wealthiest *karava* businessman in the nineteenth century, see Michael Roberts, *Facets of Modern Ceylon History*.
105. Abeysinghe, *Ancient Land Tenure*, p. 97.
106. Roberts, "Some Comments," pp. 24–25 (n. 3).

implementation of the Crown Lands Ordinance. P. D. Millie, the coffee planter, observed that the consent of the *Ratemahatmaya* (superior officer in the Kandyan administrative hierarchy) was necessary for most land sales. He further observed that in the inlying villages there was a common saying pertaining to the power of the native headmen which went "might is right or rather shall be."[107]

The chiefs or headmen were the key link between the colonial administration and the mass of cultivators. Given the dependence of the British administrators on the native headmen, it is not surprising that the British were compelled to adopt a more liberal stand vis-à-vis their claims to land over those of the cultivator class. In fact, the evidence available suggests that the duty of implementing the Ordinance contributed to the augmentation of the headmen's authority over the producer class and to increasing the headmen's access to private property. Michael Roberts has described the indispensable role played by the native headmen in crown land appropriation.

> Not only was the sale of land dependent on the report of the *ratemahatmayas* and other headmen (no land was auctioned without a report on the allotment from the chief headmen of the district), but the application of the Ordinance and its avowed aim of preventing encroachments depended largely on the headmen. There is reason to think that, in the coffee period, the headmen tended to favour the local interests against those of the Crown — with presumably, their kith and kin, as the main beneficiaries. G.A.'s and A.G.A.'s were driven to despair at their helplessness.[108]

In a letter to the Colonial Secretary the Government Agent of the Central Province pointed out that while the Crown Land Ordinance presses very hard upon the "numerous and poor section of the population," the wealthier natives would sometimes defeat the claims of the government by providing fraudulent receipts, surveys and well-drilled witnesses.[109] From the scattered evidence available in the colonial documents, it appears that it was the native overlord class rather than the cultivators who made the most extensive claims to 'crown land' based on customary rights. A.C. Lawrie, a senior Puisne Judge of colonial Ceylon, has cited the case of one Angammana Ratemahatmaya who sold crown land to a Moorman (Muslim) on the basis of a forged title deed (*sannas*).[110] It was not unusual for the state to postpone land sales to planters due to challenges put up by large feudal village (*nindagam*) proprietors on the basis of loosely worded grants.[111] In the Sabaragamuwa District 'valuable

---

107. Millie, *Thirty Years Ago*, Ch. 20.
108. Roberts, "A Selection of the Documentary Evidence," p. 12; see also Roberts, "Some Comments," p. 18.
109. *CO* 54/345, No. 46, pp. 318–19; see also, Abeysinghe, *Ancient Land Tenure*, p. 93.
110. A. C. Lawrie, *A Gazeteer of the Central Province of Ceylon* (excluding Walapane), 2 vols. (Colombo: Government Printer, Ceylon, 1896, 1898), vol. 1, pp. 56–57.
111. *AR 1882*, "Report on Sabaragamuwa," p. 47A.

Plantations and the Conflict over Land   119

forest land' (by which the British meant land suited for plantation coffee) was being claimed by chiefs and headmen, for example the Mahawaletenne family, on the basis of 'British grants' conferred on them for their loyalty to the British during the Kandyan rebellion of 1818.[112] The introduction of the Land Registration Ordinance (discussed later) and the appointment of the Temple Lands Commission (discussed earlier), represent some of the attempts made by the colonial state to control what it considered to be illegal land transactions on the part of feudal overlords.

In the midst of this confusion created by colonial land policies aimed primarily at providing private property rights to European planters, the native feudal lords attempted to gain absolute ownership rights to land for which they only had hereditary tribute exacting rights under precolonial law. There were numerous incidents where clergy and nobility sold or rented land to which the cultivators also had hereditary users' rights. As pointed out before, when land became a valuable commodity, conflict and instability in the lord-serf relationship sharply increased. It seems that the native overlords were anxious to rent or sell their lands to outsiders (such as *karavas* and Chettiyars) not simply to escape expropriation by the Crown, but also to escape 'encroachments' by the peasant cultivators attempting to assert their own rights. Thus the native overlords became the largest private land sellers and renters in the Kandyan Highlands. This state of affairs is well illustrated by the land transactions of one Kandyan chief, Parantala Ratemahatmaya, noted in the Buddhist Temporalities Commission Report of 1876.

> Threw off the robes and ceased to be a priest in 1849; has held several incumbencies, first Degaldoru Vihare, then Selawa Vihare. . . . Explains his connexion with the lease of the coffee land Duniwilkana belonging to the Degaldoru Vihare. He and his fellow priests after he had thrown off the robes, *in order to protect the interests of the vihare, the waste land belonging to which was being encroached upon and the timber felled by natives leased the land to an European planter to be planted with coffee*, first for a small rent, and afterwards, under a fresh agreement for £300 a year. [emphasis added]¹¹³

The threat posed by the peasant encroachers to land buyers (especially European planters and speculators and also some non-European rentier groups) and native land sellers (especially the largest native land sellers — the nobility and the clergy) brought the interests of the European planters and the native overlords together on several occasions. This is made clear in a Memorial of 1859 which was the product of a coalition of "chiefs, priests,

---

112. *AR 1876*, "Report on Sabaragamuwa," p. 40; see also *AR 1882*, "Report on Sabaragamuwa," p. 50A.
113. *SP 1876*, No. 18, "The Report of the Commissioners Appointed to Inquire into the Administration of the Buddhist Temporalities," p. xxix.

European residents and other inhabitants of the Central Province."[114] It was sent to the Secretary of State for the Colonies in Britain for reconsideration of the tenuous position in which the memorialists had been placed either as proprietors of forest and swidden lands (i.e., overlords) or as purchasers (i.e., planters) who had converted the land into coffee cultivation, due to illegal claims and peasant encroachments. The Memorialists pointed out that the Crown Lands Ordinance No. 12 of 1840, the very instrument which had been designed to establish private property rights and secure titles to land was contributing to the proliferation of illegal claims and insecurity of property. The Memorialists went on to plead that the Crown Lands Ordinance, therefore, be repealed.[115]

Arguing against the repeal of the Crown Lands Ordinance, Henry Ward, the Governor of Ceylon at the time, pointed out that ". . . the native element involved in the introduction of the Memorial represented the vendors, clergy and nobility whose interests were in this instance identical with those of the Europeans who were the buyers."[116]

Instead of repealing the Crown Land Ordinance as requested by the Memorialists, the colonial state introduced several new legislative enactments aimed at a more efficient application of the principles of private property and fixity of tenure as laid down in the Crown Lands Ordinance. These included the Land Partition, Land Registration, and several other ordinances. They are discussed in detail in Chapter VII.

The Land Registration Bill in particular was aimed at providing security of title to land transacted and to prevent 'illegal' claims by natives.[117] Where illegally claimed land had already been sold by the natives, the purchasers (who in the majority of cases were European planters), were granted outright ownership rights and the original pruchase price was collected from the illegal sellers. Such direct intervention by the state helped ease the fears that both the planters and the native overlords had about 'encroachments' by peasant cultivators. Van Den Driesen claims that since the passage of the Land Registration Bill in 1863, "no more protests emanated from the planting fraternity or their representatives in the Legislative Council" and concludes that the Land Registration Ordinance was successful in achieving its avowed aim of providing fixity of tenure for private property owners.[118] But notwithstanding the Land Registration Bill and Van Den Driesen's conclusions about its

---

114. *The Examiner*, February 16, 1859.
115. Ibid. See also Van Den Driesen, "Land Sales Policy," p. 49.
116. *CO 54/345* of 29 Aug. 1859, p. 30.
117. *SP 1863*, No. 4, "Land Registration," p. 3.
118. Van Den Driesen, "Land Sales Policy," p. 51.

Plantations and the Conflict over Land

success, the battle over high lands continued throughout the coffee era and into the subsequent tea period of Ceylon's plantation history.

Collapse of Coffee and the Transition to Tea

As coffee agriculture collapsed in the late 1870s, plantations were ruined and most planters went bankrupt. The majority of coffee plantations were sold off cheaply and from the late 1870s to the second half of the 1880s, there was a sharp drop in land sales. During this period there was a corresponding relaxation of government control over 'crown land' and the persecution of peasant 'encroachers'. But when, in the 1880s, tea was found to be a successful substitute for coffee, a renewed interest in land buying and selling emerged. The conflict over land between contending interest groups which had been dormant during the collapse of coffee came to the fore once again.[119]

It is important to point out that although the individuals involved were not the same, the interest groups involved in the land conflict during the tea era were essentially the same as they had been during the coffee era — being the planters, the colonial state, the native overlords, local capitalists, and the peasant agriculturists.

A new legislative instrument, Ordinance No. 1 of 1897, "Relating to claims to Forest, Chena, Waste and Unoccupied Lands" was passed, this time to safeguard the interest of tea planters and to prevent native encroachment and illegal sale of crown lands. In essence, this new ordinance, commonly referred to as the "Waste Lands Ordinance" was a reenactment of Clause 6 of Ordinance No. 12 of 1840. It stated that, "All forest, waste and unoccupied or uncultivated lands which can be only cultivated after intervals of several years, shall be presumed to be the property of the Crown, until the contrary there of be proved."[120]

Lord Stanmore (who had earlier been a Governor of Ceylon), among others, opposed this Bill during its drafting stages. Stanmore pointed out that a village could not exist by paddy cultivation alone, and that if village swidden lands were taken away, the peasant cultivators would in effect be deprived of their means of subsistence.[121] But in spite of these arguments and the experiences of the coffee era, Ordinance No. 1 of 1897 was put into effect. In this particular instance, as in many others during the colonial period

---

119. *CO* 54/643, June 11, 1897, "Enclosure No. 1: Petition of Landowners."
120. Clause 23a of Ordinance No. 1 of 1897 in *A Revised Edition of the Legislative Enactments*, p. 392.
121. *CO* 54/643, June 11, 1897, p. 4.

of Ceylonese history popularly known as the 'Planter Raj', the interests of planters determined policy formation. But the very necessity for the passage of this Ordinance suggests that the conflict over high lands was far from resolved and that it continued well into the twentieth century.

Paddy Lands: Crown Villages

In precolonial Ceylon, the cultivators were liable to pay ground rent to the king and/or his political and spiritual representatives — the nobility and the clergy — who received land grants from him. With the shift of population centers from the dry zone to the wet zone, the collapse of the hydraulic works and the retrogression of paddy cultivation between the thirteenth and sixteenth centuries, the predominant form of tribute exaction also began to change from one of tithes in kind to one of personal labor services to the overlords.

At the time the Kandyan kingdom was ceded to the British in 1815, tribute exaction there took primarily the form of caste-defined labor services. Furthermore, tribute was being exacted only on wet-rice lands (*mada idam*). Swidden, forest, pasture, and garden plots collectively known as high lands (*goda idam*) and considered the appurtenances of paddy fields were not liable to separate taxation.

Through the Proclamation of November 21, 1818, promulgated following the unsuccessful Kandyan rebellion, the colonial state abolished forced labor (*rājakariya*) attached to paddy landholdings in crown villages (*gabadāgam*). A grain tax of one-tenth of the produce to be annually supplied to royal storehouses was substituted in place of personal labor services. The districts which were loyal to the British during the 1818 rebellion were made liable only for one-fourteenth of the annual produce, whereas the lands of the leaders of the rebellion, if and when restored to them, were required to pay one-fifth of their annual produce to the colonial state.[122]

Sufficient explanation is not available in the colonial documents for this change made in the form of surplus appropriation in the royal villages, from

---

122. Proclamation of November 21, 1818, in *Colebrooke-Cameron Papers*, ed. by G. C. Mendis, vol. 2, pp. 235–36; see also Turnour's Evidence before the Colebrooke Commission, *CO* 416/20, p. 88.

Plantations and the Conflict over Land

forced labor services to payment in kind. The colonial state's desire to reduce its dependence on the native chiefs through whom compulsory labor services had to be exacted, the state's interest in augmenting its revenue, extension of the cash economy, abolition of caste-specific labor services that were of no use to the British — are all plausible reasons for this change in the predominant form of tribute exaction.

The Proclamation of 1818 specifically exempted the temple villages (*vihāragam*) and villages of headmen in office (*nindagam*) from payment of the grain tax to the state.[123] In addition, Regulation No. 4 of September 21, 1829 introduced by Governor Barnes to promote export agriculture, exempted from taxation all land growing coffee, cotton, sugar, indigo, opium, and silk. This Regulation also exempted the products of these lands from export duties.[124]

In the Kandyan Province, no taxes were collected on dry grain or swidden crops, except hill paddy (*elvi*). Where taxes were collected on hill paddy, its collection was not systematic as in the case of wet paddy.[125] Hill paddy alone accounted for an insignificant portion of swidden agriculture and peasant subsistence. *Kurakkan* (Sinhalese term for elucine coracana or finger millet) and other grains such as maize were the principal swidden crops. In the discussion that follows, our concern will be limited to the tax on paddy or wet rice.

Under British colonial rule, only a certain category of land, namely wet-rice land (*mada idam*), formerly belonging to crown villages (*gabadāgam*) and cultivated by a particular class of cultivators, i.e., owner-cultivators, was made liable to pay the land tax to the state.[126] It is to this category of land that we turn our attention now.

When compulsory labor was again abolished in the crown villages in 1833 by Colebrooke, the lords' fields (*mutettus*) or those paddy fields cultivated by tenants entirely for the benefit of the precolonial king, were sold off to private individuals by the colonial state. It is not clear at all who these private buyers were. As European planters had no use for wet-rice fields, we can surmise that the buyers of Crown paddy fields were natives with cash — either cash cropping peasantry, feudal lords, traders or money lenders.

The tenants (*pangukārayās*) of the crown villages who were thus relieved of their customary labor services and made liable for the paddy tax, gained

---

123. G. C. Mendis (ed.), *Colebrooke-Cameron Papers*, vol. 2, pp. 236–37.
124. Ibid., pp. 279–80.
125. *SP 1880*, No. 22, "Report of the Dry Grain Commission," pp. 1–6.
126. Roberts, "Some Comments," p. 21.

freehold rights to their hereditary land shares (*praveni pangus*). The British thus turned the hereditary tenants of the crown villages into a class of small-scale owner-cultivators.

> When in 1832 *Rajakariya* was abolished, the mutettu fields were all sold and the pangukarayas being thus relieved of their duty (for the mutettu land was sold simply without any appurtenant rights) became virtually the owners of their pangus.[127]

Whether the tenants at will cultivating temporary plots (*maruvena pangus*) were also turned into owner-cultivators is not made clear in the available colonial documents.

Forms of Surplus Appropriation

Redemption

In the mid-1830s, following the recommendation of Colebrooke, permission was given to paddy landholders in the Central Province to redeem their paddy tax in perpetuity by paying the equivalent of ten years' value of the tax on their respective fields.[128] This proved to be both a speedy and a convenient method of revenue collection for the colonial administration which was short of both revenue and personnel at the time.

Roughly £18,329 were collected as redemption fees by the state during the short period that the redemption scheme was in operation between 1835 and 1842. Unconfirmed sources place the total area redeemed at 21,000 paddy acres. It has been pointed out that only the richer landholders were able to make use of the opportunity for redemption. However, there is insufficient information on who these rich landholders actually were.[129] But there is evidence that with the expansion of the cash economy, particularly the production of coffee by peasants, more and more people were able to make use of the redemption option.

---

127. Extract from the Memorandum by Sharpe, Assistant Government Agent (henceforth AGA), Badulla, in *SP 1870*, No. 18, "Papers on Service Tenures, 1869–1870;" see also Roberts, "Impact of Waste Lands Ordinance," p. 166.
128. Mendis (ed.), *Colebrooke-Cameron Papers*, vol. 1, "Report of Colebrooke upon the Revenues," p. 84; see also *SP 1890*, No. 17, "The Grain Tax Ordinance," p.v; *BPP 1850*, Vol. 12, Evidence of Jonathan Forbes, p. 275; Michael Roberts, "Grain Taxes in British Ceylon, 1832–1878: Theories, Prejudices and Controversies," *Modern Ceylon Studies* (1970), pp. 119–20.
129. The estimates on redemption were taken from Roberts, "Grain Taxes in British Ceylon, 1832–1878: Theories," p. 121; see also Roberts, "Aspects of Ceylon's Agrarian Economy," p. 148.

Plantations and the Conflict over Land

The permission to redeem was availed of to some extent in 1836, 1837 and 1838. In 1839 few proprietors had recourse to this privilege. The number has since been on the increase and it is probable that in future the advantage will be duly appreciated and more generally secured.[130]

But concerned over the loss of state revenue, the colonial administration did away with the redemption option once and for all in 1842.[131]

Besides the redemption option which was quickly discontinued, there were essentially three other methods of grain tax collection in nineteenth-century Ceylon — renting, *aumani*, and commutation systems.[132] All these three methods involved the estimation of the value of the land or its potential crop by government nominees known as 'assessors.' In some districts, the local headmen themselves were the assessors.[133] As in the case of implementing the Crown Lands Ordinance, the British administration depended very heavily on the native headmen class for implementation of its taxation policies.

> ... British revenue administration depended on a host of minor officials, particularly the headmen. Distrusted, yet influential and essential, they were a collaborating class without which the British administration would have ceased to move....[134]

This indispensability gave the native headmen much room to manipulate British tax policy to their own advantage, often at the expense of the peasant owner-cultivators. How they did this, we shall discuss in later sections of this chapter.

Renting

Under the renting system, the right to collect the paddy tax was sold to the highest bidder at an auction.[135] The renting system was the most convenient method of revenue collection for the state. The state received its share of one-tenth of the produce in money from the renter or revenue farmer. It was the renter who was responsible for collecting the paddy from the cultiva-

---

130. *Ceylon Blue Book 1841*, Introductory note on land revenue quoted in Roberts, "Grain Taxes in British Ceylon, 1832–1878: Theories," p. 121; see also *BPP 1850*, Vol. 12, Evidence of Jonathan Forbes, p. 275.
131. Roberts, "Grain Taxes in British Ceylon, 1832–1878: Theories," pp. 121–22.
132. Roberts, "Grain Taxes in British Ceylon, 1832–1878: Problems," p. 814.
133. Ibid., p. 814.
134. Ibid., p. 815; see also Emerson Tennent's views on the subject in *BPP 1847–1848*, Vol. 42 and Ludovici's views in *Rice Cultivation*, pp. 133–34.
135. For a description of the operation of the renting system, see Emerson Tennent's Report in *BPP 1847–1848*, vol. 42, p. 67; Ludovici, *Rice Cultivation*, p. 134; Gananath Obeyesekere, *Land Tenure in Village Ceylon*, pp. 109–10; *BPP 1850*, Vol. 12, Evidence of Wodehouse, p. 139.

tors on the threshing floor and for selling it to recover monies he had already paid the state. The functions of the renter as a middleman considerably eased the administrative burden of the colonial state.[136]

Although convenient from the point of view of the state, the renting system was inherently corrupt and injurious to peasant interests. As the renters were required to purchase the right to collect the paddy tax by auction before paddy was harvested, only those possessing substantial sums of money were able to bid for renting rights. Quite often renters were wealthy outsiders — usually traders. Renters often being the merchant capitalists of the village, the peasant cultivators had to turn to them for advances of seed paddy and cash, as well.[137] As one critic of the renting system pointed out, the multiple functions of the renter in the village economy and his wealth and influence enabled him to "bind the cultivators under a system of social serfdom."[138]

Collusion among assessors, renters, and headmen and resultant extortion and oppression of the cultivators became characteristics of the renting system.[139] Furthermore, government legislation further helped augment the power of the renters over the cultivators. For example, Ordinance No. 14 of 1840 gave renters the right to sue cultivators in the District Court for omissions and irregularities in their payments.[140] Sir Emerson Tennent, the Colonial Secretary, himself attacked the renting system in no uncertain terms. His observations are worth quoting at some length.

> It would be difficult to devise a system more pregnant with oppression, extortion and demoralization than the one here detailed. The cultivator is handed over to two successive sets of inquisitorial officers, the assessors and the renters; whose acts are so uncontrolled, that abuses are inevitable, and the intercourse of the two parties is characterized by rigour and extortion on the one side, and cunning and subterfuges of every description on the other.
> Every artifice and disingenuous device is put in practice to deceive the headmen and assessors as to the extent and fertility of the land and the actual value of the crops and they, in return, resort to the most inquisitorial and vexatious interference, either to protect the interest of the Government, or privately to further their own. Between these demoralizing influences, the character and industry of the rural population are deteriorated and destroyed. The extension of cultivation by reclaiming a portion of waste land only exposes the harassed proprietor to fresh visits from the headmen and a new valuation by the Government Assessor, and where annoyance is not the leading object, recourse is had to corruption in order to keep down the valuation.

136. Roberts, "Grain Taxes in British Ceylon, 1832–1878: Problems," p. 816.
137. Ibid., p. 819; *SP 1867*, No. 4, p. 22. The colloquial Sinhala term for such village trader cum moneylender today is *mudalali*.
138. Ludovici, *Rice Cultivation*, p. 136.
139. Ibid., p. 134.
140. Obeyesekere, *Land Tenure*, pp. 110–11.

But no sooner has the cultivator got rid of the assessor than he falls into the hands of the renter, who under the authority with which the law invests him, finds himself possessed of unusual powers of vexation and annoyance. He may be designedly out of the way when the cultivator sends notice of his intention to cut; and if the latter, to save his harvest from perishing on the stalk, ventures to reap it in his absence, the penalties of the law are instantly enforced against him. Under the pressure of this formidable control, the agricultural proprietor, rather than lose his time or his crop in dancing attendance on the renter or submitting to the multiform annoyance of his subordinates, is driven to purchase forebearance by additional payments.[141]

The system of revenue collection through renters was in use in the coastal regions since Dutch times. It has been claimed that while renting was introduced to the Kandyan Provinces after 1815, it was applied with greater severity there than in other regions of the colony. The harsher oppression of the Kandyan peasants under the renting system has been attributed to their alleged ignorance, 'purely agricultural' and long-suffering nature, and to the opportunistic character of the men from the coastal lowlands who often became the renters in the Kandyan districts.[142] But given the independent character of the Kandyan peasantry and their keen sense of justice, the absence of comparative data on the operation of the renting system in the Maritime and Kandyan Provinces, and the frequent disparagements of the Kandyan character in colonial documents, we need to be cautious of such assertions. However, the point that renters were often outsiders is a significant one. The absence of kinship ties, a sense of community or reciprocal obligations towards the Kandyan cultivators gave these outsiders the 'freedom' to exploit the peasants unscrupulously.

Aumani System

Unlike renting, the *aumani* or *amani* (information on the origin or the English translation of this term is not available) system of paddy tax collection was restricted to certain areas of the Kandyan Provinces. Where this method of tax collection was in operation, government personnel rather than renters collected the state's share of the paddy crop directly from the cultivators. As under the renting system, theoretically the tax was not collected when the fields did not produce a crop.[143] Apparently government officials believed that the *aumani* system was as oppressive to the cultivator as the renting system and perhaps more important from the administration's point

141. *BPP 1847–1848*, Vol. 42, pp. 67–68; see also Speculum, *Ceylon*, p. 45.
142. Roberts, "Grain Taxes in British Ceylon, 1832–1878: Problems," p. 814.
143. Ibid., p. 814; *SP 1890*, No. 17, pp. iv-v.

of view, it yielded much less revenue than the renting system. The reasons for these beliefs, however, are not clearly expressed in official documents.[144] The *aumani* system was in operation only for a short period of time during the early years of British rule in Kandy, roughly between 1815 and the early 1830s. It was done away with around 1832 when the operation of the commutation system of paddy tax collection was widened in the area.

Commutation of the Paddy Tax

Commutation of tribute or the transfer of the method of payment from kind to its cash equivalent, signifies a change in the direction of monetization of the economy. As other writers have also noted, money rent is usually a transitional form of surplus extraction which attaches itself to agrarian relations when feudal social relations are disintegrating and when land is being converted into a commodity.[145] Such deliberate changes are generally introduced when the activities of the state become more elaborate as they did in colonial Ceylon with the development of the plantation enterprise. Under the commutation system, the government share of one-tenth of the paddy crop was collected by state officials. But unlike in the renting and *aumani* arrangements, the paddy fields were subjected to a fixed annual payment, regardless of whether the field was cultivated or not. The commutation option had to be taken up by a whole district for a specified number of years. It is not clear how the cultivators of a given district arrived at such a collective decision and what role the headmen played in such deliberations.[146]

Commutation settlement was first introduced in some districts of the Central Province in the late 1820s, by George Turnour who was the Revenue Commissioner of the Kandyan Provinces at the time.[147] Among the reasons given for the introduction of this system were the humanitarian interest of saving the cultivator from the oppression of the renter. It was also believed that a fixed annual tax (as opposed to a variable tithe such as involved in the renting and *aumani* systems) would stimulate peasant cultivators to abandon their supposedly indolent habits and to increase production.[148] But as we

---

144. Roberts, "Grain Taxes in British Ceylon, 1832–1878: Problems," p. 814.
145. See, for example, Newton Gunasinghe, "Production Relations and Classes in a Kandyan Village," *Modern Ceylon Studies*, vol. 6, no. 2 (1975), pp. 120–21.
146. *SP 1876*, No. 30, "Paddy Commutation," p. 35.
147. *Ceylon Blue Book 1867*, p. 20; see also Roberts, "Grain Taxes in British Ceylon, 1832–1878: Problems," p. 822.
148. Ibid., p. 822; *AR 1882*, "Report of Sabaragamuwa District," p. 48A.

Plantations and the Conflict over Land

shall discuss later, a fixed annual tax went against the very subsistence requirements of peasant existence.

In the early years, the state allowed the payment of commuted paddy tax to be made either in money or kind.[149] The tithes paid in kind were delivered to government store houses. We lack details on the manner in which the colonial state disposed of the tax collected in grain except for a few references to the inconveniences of collection in kind.

> Hitherto, the grain collected has been stored by the government, and either sold or used for the subsistence of the troops, a practice both inconvenient and injurious; inconvenient from the necessity of establishing grain stores throughout the country, and of providing for the transport of grain; and injurious as depriving the landholders of the principal market of the interior, in the supply of the troops.[150]

In later years, the paddy tax collected in kind was probably sold either to local traders or directly to European planters (who used it to feed their immigrant estate labor) or used by the state to feed its own immigrant wage laborers in the Public Works Department.

In the early years of the operation of commutation, the state made a twenty-five percent deduction in the sum to be paid if it was paid within the year in which the tax was due.[151] In addition, cultivators were given the option of paying their paddy taxes in coffee, cinnamon, or pepper.[152] These measures demonstrate the colonial government's distinct interests in extending the use of money and the cultivation of cash crops.[153] Although the colonial administration did not explicitly state so, as Ameer Ali points out, "the grain tax was a typical measure designed to persuade and even to force the traditional sector to enter the cash nexus."[154]

The commutation of the paddy tax was optional until 1878. But it was widely accepted in the Central Province. In the Kandy District, out of 19,628 acres paying the tax, 18,150 acres were under voluntary commutation.[155] A number of reasons may account for the greater readiness of the peasants in the Kandyan Highlands to accept commutation. The alleged harsher enforce-

---

149. *Ceylon Blue Book 1867*, p. 29.
150. Mendis (ed.), *Colebrooke-Cameron Papers*, "Report of Colebrooke upon the Revenues," p. 82.
151. *SP 1876*, No. 30, p. 24.
152. Ibid., p. 24; see also *Ceylon Blue Book 1867*, p. 24.
153. Roberts, "Grain Taxes in British Ceylon, 1832-1878: Problems," p. 832.
154. Quoted in Roberts, "Some Comments," p. 18. Roberts, however, questions this assumption. The attempt to force natives to enter the cash nexus through taxation was a common colonial practice. See, for example, R. M. A. Van Zwanenberg, *Colonial Capitalism and Labor in Kenya: 1919-1939* (Nairobi: East African Publications Bureau, 1975), Ch. 3.
155. *SP 1889*, No. 34, p. 7; see also *SP 1878*, No. 29, "Papers Relating to Grain."

ment of the renting system in the Kandyan Provinces, and the peasants' desire to be rid of the renters may be one. Furthermore, registration of paddy lands in the commutation registers was regarded as a valuable index to land ownership and therefore a goal worthy in itself.[156] With the rise of a land market and new concepts of private property, securing proofs of ownership to ancestral property acceptable to the British, such as the registration in the commutation registers, became a central concern of the peasantry. But perhaps the most important reason why the commutation system was quickly and widely accepted by the Kandyan peasantry was their ability to pay the tax on their paddy fields with cash or cash crops.

Cash crops, especially smallholder coffee, which was the great monetizer of the Kandyan village economy, were grown on the gardens and swidden plots of the peasants.[157] Between 1820 and 1824, 'peasant coffee' exports increased by over one hundred percent from 539,662 lbs. to 1,213,603 lbs.[158] Van Den Driesen estimates that during the prosperous 1850s and 1860s, the area under peasant coffee accounted for between one-fifth to one-fourth of the annual output and that it brought an annual income between £250,000 and £300,000 for the peasants.[159] It is quite clear that commutation of the paddy tax encouraged peasant coffee cultivation and participation in the market economy. Colonial administrators were aware of this relationship between the commuted paddy tax and peasant cashcropping. "Many villagers in the wet and dry zone highlands paid their paddy tax during the nineteenth century from proceeds of their coffee, coconut and vegetable gardens."[160]

In referring to the 'luxuriance of native coffee' in the mid-nineteenth century, the Assistant Government Agent of the Badulla District elaborated that "It put in circulation among the villagers annually in this District as much as Rs.600,000. It was this that ensued the cheerful payment of taxes, crowded the court room with suitors and filled the pockets of arrack renters."[161]

The rate of commuted paddy tax varied from district to district ranging from 33/4d. to 9d. per *parrah* (a parrah is approximately three-quarters of a bushel) of paddy.[162] The colonial government almost always raised the rate of commutation each time a new settlement was made. For example, the rate

156. *SP 1876*, No. 30, p. 19.
157. Ameer Ali, "Peasant Coffee," p. 50.
158. Van Den Driesen, "Coffee Cultivation in Ceylon (1)," pp. 38–39.
159. I. H. Van den Driesen, "Some Trends in the Economic History of Ceylon in the 'Modern' Period," *Ceylon Journal of Historical and Social Studies* 3 (1960), pp. 1–17.
160. *SP 1877*, "Grain Tax Commutation," Appendix, No. 68, p. xcvii.
161. *AR 1885*, "Report of Badulla District," p. 19a.
162. Roberts, "Grain Taxes in British Ceylon, 1832–1878: Problems," p. 824.

Plantations and the Conflict over Land

of commutation throughout the Central Province was doubled in 1864. The justification given for this increase was that since the previous rate had been fixed, the market price of paddy had doubled in the Central Highlands.[163] But on closer examination, one finds that 1864 was a year of financial difficulties for the Ceylon plantation enterprise and that the doubling of the paddy tax at this point may have been triggered off by the increased revenue needs of the state.[164]

By the 1840s, the state no longer permitted the payment of the commuted tax in kind, and commuted dues had to be paid entirely in cash. In the 1860s, the remissions which had been given in earlier years for the prompt payment of commuted taxes were also abolished. Thus the commutation system was made more strict and efficient.[165]

The doubling of the tax and the abolition of the system of remissions and payments in kind led to frequent defaults in paddy tax payments and accumulation of arrears on the part of the peasant cultivators. In a further attempt to streamline its revenue collection, the colonial state passed Ordinance No. 5 of 1866 which enabled the state to evict defaulting tenants from their lands and to sell those lands to recover taxes due.[166] As we shall discuss later in this chapter, the execution of the clauses of this ordinance had disastrous consequences for the owner-cultivators of paddy fields.

The Debate Over a General Land Tax

The inherent injustice of taxing only one category of land, and the one belonging to the most impoverished segment of the population at that, was recognized by some members of the colonial administration. Colebrooke who undertook a careful inquiry of the sources of state revenue had this to say about the paddy tax as early as 1833:

> This tax which is collected only on the grain crops throughout the island and not upon other articles of colonial produce, is objectionable from its undue pressure on one branch of agriculture, and that of the first importance to encourage, also from the extensive establishments required for its collection, and from the vexatious interference of the revenue farmers and native headmen.[167]

---

163. Ibid., p. 825.
164. Speculum, Pseud. [George Wall], *Ceylon: Her Present Condition: Revenues, Taxes and Expenditore* (Colombo: Colombo Observer Press), 1868, pp. 129, 11.
165. Roberts, "Grain Taxes in British Ceylon, 1832–1878: Problems," pp. 826–27.
166. Ibid., p. 826.
167. Mendis (ed.), *Colebrooke-Cameron Papers*, "Report of Colebrooke upon the Revenues," p. 82.

Emerson Tennent went further and suggested in his 1848 Report on the Finance and Commerce of the Island that a general land tax should be substituted in place of both the tax on home-grown paddy and the customs duty on imported rice.[168] The duty on imported rice fell heavily on the planters who imported rice to feed their estate labor force. We shall not be concerned with the customs duty on imported rice here, but will take it up in Chapter VII.

In spite of the suggestions of Tennent, any alteration of the tax structure, particularly the introduction of a general land tax to cover all cultivated lands was unanimously and most vociferously opposed by the powerful European planting community.[169] A land tax, they feared, would encompass not only their cultivated coffee acreage, but also their vast stretches of uncultivated lands.[170] Unlike the customs duty on rice (the chief mode of taxing the plantation enterprise — to be discussed) which varied with the amount of rice imported, a land tax, they argued, would remain fixed regardless of the vagaries of the world market and the Ceylon coffee enterprise. Other objections the planters had against the land tax were the difficulty and expense that would be involved in making a cadastral survey; the possible evasion of all taxation by those classes not possessing land; and the generally adverse effects of a land tax on the European plantation system which they considered to be the life blood of the Ceylonese economy.[171]

In making their case, planting interests obviously exaggerated the importance of the plantation economy for the colony; whereas, in fact, its benefits were largely restricted to a few groups — the planters, the colonial state, and those native social classes closely associated with colonial economic and political interests. The planters also played up the need for an extensive cadastral survey as a prerequisite for the introduction of a land tax, when in fact a simple and inexpensive survey could have been devised. In claiming that a general land tax would leave the landless population untaxed, these interest groups failed to take into account the sundry taxes such as the road tax, salt tax and stamp duties (discussed in later chapters), which fell on all classes regardless of their relationship to land.

Many of the native headmen who were large landed proprietors paid no land taxes on their feudal villages (*nindagam*); nor did the Buddhist clergy

---

168. *BPP 1847–1848*, Vol. 42, p. 67; *SP 1876*, No. 30, p. 26.
169. Roberts, "Grain Taxes in British Ceylon, 1832–1878: Theories," pp. 132–33.
170. Ibid., p. 125.
171. Ibid., pp. 130–31; *SP 1890*, No. 17, "The Grain Tax Ordinance of 1878," p. viii; Obeysekere, *Land Tenure*, p. 112.

Plantations and the Conflict over Land

pay dues on their temple villages (*vihāragam*). As stated earlier, the headmen had a direct role to play in the exaction of taxes due from the paddy fields of the peasant cultivators. In outlining their role in paddy tax collection, Governor Havelock said,

> It is upon information supplied by chiefs and headmen holding office that the assessment of the paddy tax is mainly based. And these chiefs and headmen not only in the Kandyan Province but also in the Maritime Provinces are the collectors of the paddy tax and receive a commission on their collections amounting in the aggregate to about Rs.500,000 or 5 percent of the proceeds of the tax.[172]

It is easy to understand then, why the headmen had a vested interest in retaining the grain tax and in opposing a general land tax.[173] We saw earlier how the European planter lobby in the colony and the large native landholders in the Central Province came together in 1859 to send a Memorial to the Secretary of State for the Colonies asking that the Crown Lands Ordinance be repealed. In this instance when a general land tax was being talked about as a possible method of increasing government revenue, once again the European planting interests and a new and influential segment of the local landowning classes joined forces in their opposition to the substitution of the paddy tax with a general land tax. The victory of this united opposition is reflected in the recommendations of the Grain Tax Commission appointed by the Legislative Council in 1878 to inquire into the collection of the grain tax and to make suggestions for a new tax structure for the colony.[174]

Most of the members of the Grain Tax Commission, appointed to consider a general land tax, were large landholders.[175] Table 5:6 gives the approximate extent of land owned by four of the Ceylonese members of the Grain Tax Commission of 1878.

Like most other members of the emerging native capitalist class, these landowners were not coffee planters, but were predominantly coconut planters, in the Maritime Provinces. Of those listed in Tabel 5:6, all but Coomaraswamy, who is a Ceylon Tamil, are low-country Sinhalese. Given the extent of land held by Alwis (2,500 acres), it is not surprising that he championed the opposition to the land tax in the Legislative Council. He put forward two principle arguments. First, the paddy tax was traditional and hence acceptable to the people. Second, an extension of the tax to previously untaxed

---

172. *SP 1892*, No. 3, pp. 3–4; see also Roberts, "Grain Taxes in British Ceylon, 1832–1878: Theories," p. 131.
173. Obeyesekere, *Land Tenure*, p. 115.
174. *SP 1878*, No. 29, "Papers Relating to Grain Taxes."
175. One observes parallel situations in contemporary advanced capitalist societies. Note, for example, the appointment of corporate representatives themselves to government agencies responsible for the regulation of corporations.

chenas and gardens, would, in essence, tax the curry as well as the rice of the peasantry (curry products allegedly being grown on chenas and gardens).[176] In other words, the native landed class, as did the British on most occasions, justified their actions on grounds of humanitarianism towards the poor.

Table 5:6

Land Owned by Several Members of the Grain Tax Commission of 1878

Members	No. of Properties	Extent (acres)	Extent (uncult.)	Coffee	Coconut	Cinnamon
Alwis	19	2,500	?	–	2,250	250
Coomaraswamy	1	200	?	–	200	–
Dias	8	1,711	852	–	697	162
Perera	3	142	?	–	142	–
Totals	31	4,553	852	–	3,289	412

Source: Michael W. Roberts, "Grain Taxes in British Ceylon, 1832–1878: Theories, Prejudices and Controversies," *Modern Ceylon Studies*, vol. 1, 1970, p. 130.

The conclusions reached by the Grain Tax Commission were based on replies to a questionnaire given to twenty-five European officials, three Ceylonese officials (above the headmen rank), two Europeans, seven Ceylonese (who were not public servants) and forty chiefs and headmen.[177] Not only were these European officials and native headmen called upon to represent 'public opinion' on the paddy tax often ignorant of conditions at the grassroots level, but, as noted above, there was a definite conflict of interests between the peasantry and the large landed classes (both European and native) on the issue of taxation.

As to be expected, then, a general land tax was not recommended by the Grain Tax Commissioners in 1878. Instead, upon their recommendation, the "utterly indefensible" renting system was abolished and a system of *compulsory* commutation or forced payment in cash was introduced via a new legislative enactment — Ordinance No. 11 of 1878.[178] The purported aims of Ordinance No. 11 of 1878 were to relieve the peasant cultivator through the elimination of the renter, and to offer him greater choice of methods in

---

176. Roberts, "Grain Taxes in British Ceylon, 1832–1878: Theories," pp. 130–31.
177. Ibid., p. 131.
178. Ibid., p. 131; see also, "The Grain Tax Ordinance of 1878," reprinted in Obeyesekere, *Land Tenure*, Appendix, pp. 297–304.

Plantations and the Conflict over Land

paying the commuted paddy tax. Its effects on the peasantry, however, were disastrous.

The new compulsory commutation offered a choice between an annual fixed commutation (like the earlier voluntary commutation) and a crop commutation. In the case of the crop commutation, the paddy tax was to be collected only in years when the fields produced a yield. In both cases — fixed and crop commutation — the tax was to be collected under the supervision of district officers, known as Grain Commissioners, and the tax was in all cases to be paid in cash. The government reserved the right to seize the land, crops, and movable property of defaulters as set forth in Ordinances No. 5 of 1866 and No. 6 of 1873. These ordinances prescribed "the order in which the property of public defaulters may in certain cases be seized and sold."[179]

Ordinance No. 11 of 1878, or the compulsory commutation ordinance, was not introduced to all provinces of the island immediately upon passage. The planting regions, particularly the Uva Province (which was carved out of parts of Central, Southern, and Eastern Provinces in 1886) and the Central Province were brought under compulsory commutation in 1887 and 1888 respectively.[180] During the decade 1878–1888, the older voluntary commutation system with its fixed annual charges still prevailed in these two provinces.

The Paddy Tax and Land Sales

The last quarter of the nineteenth century was a period of famines and widespread poverty for the peasant cultivators of the planting regions.[181] The ultimate reason for this was the collapse of the Ceylon coffee enterprise and the depression in England. The leaf disease which destroyed Ceylon coffee was first detected around 1869 and spread rapidly all over the coffee planting districts. It is believed that planters were able to withstand the spread of the disease longer than the peasant coffee growers by extending their estates on to higher elevations. Peasants, however, were not able to compete with plan-

---

179. See "Ordinance No. 6 of 1873," in *A Revised Edition of the Legislative Enactments*, vol. 1, pp. 623–24.
180. *SP 1889*, No. 15; see also Roberts, "Grain Taxes in British Ceylon, 1832–1878: Problems," p. 834.
181. L. A. Wickremaratne, "Grain Consumption and Famine Conditions in Late Nineteenth-Century Ceylon," *CJHSS*, vol. 3, no. 2 (July-December 1973), p. 29.

ters for new land. By the mid 1870s, peasant coffee was on its way out and, by the late 1880s, it was completely wiped out.[182]

In addition to the coffee-leaf disease, prices for Ceylon coffee began to decline as a result of the increase in the Brazilian coffee supply to the world market and the Great Depression in Britain between 1879 and 1884.[183] When the Ceylon coffee industry suffered its first serious depression in 1846–1848, Governor Torrington imposed a series of new taxes on the peasants. The peasant protest that ensued culminated in the rebellion of 1848.[184]

When the demise of coffee led to a reduction of government revenue in the late 1870s, the state once again turned to taxing the peasants more heavily. But this time, instead of imposing new taxes, the government sought to maximize revenue from already existing sources.[185] It is against this background that the imposition of compulsory commutation and the harsher and more efficient enforcement of grain tax collection in general, need to be understood.

During times of prosperity, district officers were lax in the collection of revenue and let arrears accumulate on taxes due from the peasants. Thus a large percent of the tax collections of each year constituted arrears from previous years. In the Central Province, forty-five percent of the land revenue collected between 1871 and 1872 consisted of arrears.[186] In addition, the injunctions of Ordinances No. 5 of 1866 and No. 6 of 1873, which empowered the state to recover taxes from defaulting tenants by selling their lands, were not strictly enforced.[187]

But in the late 1870s and 1880s, when faced with a financial crisis, the government began to enforce tax collection and the strictures of the above ordinances to the letter. John F. Dickson, who became the Government Agent of the Central Province in 1882, championed the campaign against the accumulation of paddy tax arrears. In his words,

> If every one knows that the tax must be paid, that it must be paid punctually, that if it is not so paid, compulsory powers will be put in force without delay; that this involves costs and sale of property at a great sacrifice and possibly eviction from the land ... then the rule will be that one will pay promptly and without attempt at procrastination.[188]

---

182. Van Den Driesen, "Coffee Cultivation in Ceylon," pp. 168–69.
183. Ibid., p. 167.
184. Ibid., p. 167.
185. D. Wesumperuma, "The Evictions under the Paddy Tax and Their Impact on the Peasantry of Walapane, 1882–1885," *CJHSS*, vol. 10 (1970), p. 131.
186. *AR 1883*, "Report of the Central Province," by G. A., John F. Dickson, Part I, p. 6A.
187. Wesumperuma, "The Evictions," p. 132.
188. *SP 1890*, No. 27, p. 9.

Plantations and the Conflict over Land

During J. F. Dickson's administration in the Central Province, grain taxes were strictly and harshly enforced; arrears were collected and government revenues were thus increased. During the first two years of his administration, arrears on commuted paddy taxes were reduced from Rs. 182, 822 in 1881 to Rs. 97, 220 in 1883; and arrears on road taxes (discussed in Chapter VII) from Rs. 21, 599 in 1881 to Rs. 12, 187 in 1883.[189]

However, having lost their sources of cash, i.e., 'peasant coffee' and supplementary wage-labor opportunities on the estates due to the collapse of coffee, many peasants were unable to pay the taxes due to the state at this time. As the Assistant Government Agent of the Badulla District remarked in his Administration Report of 1883,

> It was particularly unfortunate for the people that just at the time the general depression in the agriculture and trade in general of the district began, their liabilities were increased by the new commutation. Though relief in many instances was given, it was not until two or three years had elapsed and there still remain many cases of over-taxation, while the rates generally being based upon the value of padi estimated in a year of prosperity are now considered and felt to be too high.[190]

The colonial state in the meantime sought to enforce Ordinance No. 5 of 1866 to the letter by evicting defaulting cultivators from their lands and selling the lands to recover taxes. What resulted was expropriation, destitution, and, in some cases, death due to starvation.

It must be recognized that expropriation and sale of peasant land for nonpayment of taxes was a wholly new practice that was introduced by the British. In precolonial times, as land had no value of its own, defaulting cultivators were not evicted but probably subjected to physical punishment. Many peasants ran away to remote areas or jungles in order to avoid taxes and corporal punishment. In some instances they may have attempted to renegotiate the tax burden with officers of the state, although there is no evidence of such attempts in precolonial Kandy.

Paddy Land Expropriation by the State

As Table 5:7 shows, the sale of paddy lands belonging to defaulting cultivators by the colonial state was not a phenomenon restricted to the plantation regions.[191] The widespread land sales in Batticaloa, a nonplantation

---

189. *AR 1883*, "Report of the Central Province," Part I, p. 6A.
190. *AR 1883*, "Report of the Badulla District," by Aelian King, p. 26A.
191. See also compilation of evidence from reports of G. A.'s and A. G. A.'s throughout the country, in C. S. Salmon, *The Grain Tax in Ceylon: Reports for the Years 1885, 1886, 1887, 1888 and 1889* (London: Cassell, 1890); for figures on land

region in the Eastern Province may have been related to the emergence of capitalist relations of production in paddy agriculture and the concentration of paddy lands in a few hands in that region. Some of the reasons for the widespread paddy land sales in two other districts where coffee was not a major crop, the Galle and Matara Districts of the Southern Province, have been provided by Obeysekere in his study of changing land tenure patterns in Madagama, a village in the Southern Province.[192]

The collapse of peasant coffee was the precipitating factor in peasants' inability to pay the commuted paddy tax in the coffee growing regions. Paddy land expropriations, however, were unevenly spread in those regions. As Table 5:7 points out, paddy land sales seem to have been extensive in the Ratnapura, Nuwara Eliya, and Badulla Districts. It is significant to note that land sales were greatest in the dry zone areas of the Highlands. The neglect of irrigation crucial for paddy cultivation in those regions along with the failure of coffee, contributed to peasant inability to pay taxes. The comparatively lower land sales figures for Kandy and Matale Districts in the Central Province, two other coffee producing areas, could be explained by the fact that a high proportion of paddy fields there were untaxed as they belonged either to temples or headmen in office or were wholly redeemed from tax payments by the cultivators when the redemption scheme was in operation between 1835 and 1842.[193] However, on averaging paddy land sales between 1881 and 1885 in the Central Province, the primary plantation region, Obeysekere concludes,

> ... so, that in a period of five years in the Central Province alone there were 13,863 sales of parcels of land. According to the Census of 1881 and 1891 there were in this province 54,387 and 56,009 adult cultivators respectively. Assuming that each cultivator represented a family, one in about four families lost a parcel of land. This again is a conservative estimate since we have no data on private sales which may have accounted for a much larger number. Once again, if each sale represented a share in a common estate, the consequence of these sales no doubt seriously altered the structure of traditional land tenure system.[194]

As Wesumperuma notes, within the coffee planting region, the peasant cultivators in the Udukinda Division of the Uva Province and the Walapane Division of the Nuwara Eliya District (in the Central Province) seemed to have been the most hard hit by paddy land sales by the state.[195] In the following pages, we shall point out the approximate extent of lands sold

    sold for nonpayment of the grain tax, see also *SP 1889*, No. 48, "Grain Tax Commutation," pp. 83–85.
192. Obeyesekere, *Land Tenure*, esp. Chapter 5.
193. Roberts, "Some Comments," p. 21. See also AR 1886, Report on Nuwara Eliya District, p. 37A.
194. Obeyesekere, *Land Tenure*, p. 121.
195. Wesumperuma, "The Evictions," p. 132.

Table 5:7

Paddy Lands Sold by the State for Nonpayment of the Paddy Tax, 1880–1892

District	(1) Total No. of Lots Under Paddy Cultivation	(2) No. of Lots Sold for Nonpayment of Paddy Tax	(3) % of Col. 2 to Col. 1	(4) Total Extent Under Paddy in Acres	(5) Total Extent of Land Sold in Acres	(6) % of Col. 5 to Col. 4
Colombo	45,072	513	1.1	57,484	633	1.1
Kalutara	28,902	2,476	8.5	45,273	3,355	7.4
Negombo	17,505	109	0.6	14,932	89	0.5
Kegalle	44,201	491	1.1	21,408	110	0.5
Ratnapura	25,476	6,359	24.9	26,539	2,443	9.2
Galle	31,384	4,832	15.3	45,887	4,036*	8.7
Matara	28,622	1,949	6.8	45,997	1,974	4.2
Hambantota	9,715	337	3.4	20,118	352	1.7
Kandy	35,852	739	2.0	19,130	344**	1.7
Matale	17,723	317	1.7	9,912	135	1.3
Nuwara Eliya	18,848	2,372	12.5	?	747	–
Badulla	29,307	9,433	32.1	17,787	5,408	30.4
Jaffna	?	168	–	?	108	–
Batticaloa	4,797	1,198	24.9	65,773	18,002	27.3
Trincomalee	1,391	1	0.0	7,814	16	0.2
	338,795	31,294	9.2	398,054	37,751	9.4

This table was compiled on the basis of information in the *Sessional Papers* and *Administration Reports* of the period 1880–92. The number of lots and the extent of fields under paddy cultivation varied from year to year. However, once a commutation settlement was effected to last for seven years the variations in [the figures on record] were few. Columns 1 and 4 are from the statistics for the year 1889 – the year of the Select Committee on Grain Tax.
*Without the acreage of 151 lots sold in 1891 and 1892 because no information is available.
**Without the acreage of 26 lots sold in 1891 and 1892.

Source: Michael Roberts, "Some Comments on Ameer Ali's Paper," *Ceylon Studies Seminar*, No. 3b, 1970/72 Series, p. 20.
N. B.: Roberts' compilations are based on Wesumperuma's tabulations. See D. Wesumperuma, "Land Sales Under the Paddy Tax in Ceylon," *Vidyodaya*, vol. 2, no. 1, January 1969.

due to default on the paddy tax in these regions. We shall then discuss the relationship between the grain tax, changing property relations and peasant subsistence there.

According to one estimate, of the total land area of the Udukinda District of the Uva Province (Uva was made into a separate province only in 1886) 22½ percent was sold by the Crown between 1882 and 1885 for default of the paddy tax.[196]

Of the 3,244 paddy fields sold, 985 were bought by villagers (obviously those who had the cash to do so), while the rest (approximately 70 percent) passed into the hands of outsiders. Of the latter, 694 fields were bought by low-country people, 446 by Moors and Tamils, 670 by headmen, and 145 infertile fields bought by the Crown were returned to their original owners in the Jubilee year (1887). These fields in total were sold for just 22 percent more than the taxes due on them, which suggests that the fields were infertile — in which case they should not have been taxed — or that they were sold off very cheaply by the state to recover its dues.[197] If in fact the fields were sold very cheaply, as the available evidence suggests was the case, the non-European buyers of these small peasant plots were the ones to derive the greatest advantage from the miserable plight of the cultivator class.

Apparently these sales deprived 2,930 heads of household representing 14,650 persons (approximately 49 percent of the population of Udukinda) of their means of livelihood. Of these persons, 599 or 20 percent were compelled to leave the area while 2,000 became tenants on the lands of others (presumably the new owners) and 127 were absolutely destitute.[198]

C. J. R. Le Mesurier, the Assistant Government Agent in the Nuwara Eliya District, who was known for his sympathy for the peasants (and perhaps the only British official in whose honor the peasants named a village — Mesuriegama), first brought the plight peasants in the Nuwara Eliya district, particularly Walapane, into light when he reported in his Administration Report for 1886,

---

196. *SP 1891*, No. 4, pp. 5–12; see also Wesumperuma, "The Evictions," p. 132 and Obeyesekere, *Land Tenure*, p. 119.
197. Obeyesekere, *Land Tenure*, p. 119.
198. Ibid., p. 119.

Plantations and the Conflict over Land   141

I am able to give some startling figures as the result of the policy of selling up the unfortunate villagers for their arrears of commutation tax during the four years preceding 1886. I find that out of a total of 18,848 fields in the district, 2,889 have been sold for default that is to say, over 15 percent of the fields have forcibly changed hands in four years. Of the fields sold, 1,900 are now cultivated, and 989 — that is about 8 percent of the number in constant cultivation at the last commutation (12,148) — have been abandoned. In the case of the fields sold, 1,048 of the late owners are dead, and 382 with their families have left the district. In 1881, the population of the villages in which the sales have been held was 34,216; it is now as near as can be ascertained, 30,693 — a decrease of over 10 percent of the fields sold, 1,001 have been purchased by resident Kandyans, 1,260 have been purchased by low countrymen and Moors, and 628 by the Crown.[199]

Long before the much publicized Walapane evictions took place in the 1880s, Leopold Ludovici, the prominent critic of the colonial government, pointed out in 1867 that while other branches of 'native industry' were progressing, paddy agriculture had been retrogressing. He saw the paddy tax as a principal reason for this retrogression.[200] Yet another critic of the government, George Wall, writing under the pen name, Speculum, pointed out that contrary to the official view that the natives were by nature indolent, it was the paddy tax that created indolence among the peasantry by making them abandon cultivation for fear of increased taxation on higher yields.[201]

Following the publication of Le Mesurier's Report, grain taxes in Ceylon became a public issue. The Ceylon government was severely criticized, especially by the abolitionists of the Cobden Club of England who found food taxes, particularly when falling on those least able to pay, morally reprehensible. Of the several tracts written calling for the repeal of the paddy tax, C. S. Salmon's, *The Ceylon Starvation Question*, and George Wall's, *The Grain Tax or Native Distress in Ceylon: Its Cause and Remedy*, written under the pseudonym, Jus, are the most noteworthy.[202]

---

199. Although Le Mesurier does not give names, these figures seem to cover several areas within the Nuwara Eliya district such as Walapane, Gangapālāta and Uda Hēwahēta. See, *AR 1886*, "Report on the Nuwara Eliya District," by C. J. R. Le Mesurier, p. 37A.
200. Ludovici, *Rice Cultivation*, p. 101.
201. Speculum, *Ceylon*, p. 81.
202. C. S. Salmon, *The Ceylon Starvation Question* (London: Cobden Club, 1891); Jus, *The Grain Tax or Native Distress in Ceylon: Its Cause and Remedy* (Colombo: Ceylon Independent, 1889). George Wall was the editor of the newspaper *Ceylon Independent*.

The Evictions in Walapane

Following the exposé by Le Mesurier and subsequent agitation by opponents of the paddy tax, the Ceylon government appointed R. W. D. Moir, the Government Agent of the Central Province in 1889, to investigate the whole episode. Moir, who held pro-grain tax views, disagreed with Le Mesurier on the extent of the destitution (and the deaths) caused by the operation of grain tax commutation in Walapane.[203]

However, Moir, Le Mesurier, Baumgartner (who was the Assistant Government Agent of Nuwara Eliya during the years when the land sales took place), as well as contemporary headmen and other witnesses who gave evidence before Moir, agreed on the causes of paddy land sales and the eviction of the cultivators. They were unanimous over the principal cause being the collapse of native coffee. Moir stated

> ... distress among the people began to manifest itself when the coffee crops failed on which they chiefly depended. I believe that it was the destruction of the coffee plant both in native gardens and on estates which was the origin of the poverty stricken condition in which so many of the people in Walapane and Uda Hewaheta now are, and that but for the failure of coffee crops there need have been no arrears and no forced sales.[204]

Similarly, one witness who appeared before Moir, Boragolle Ganetirala, Registrar of Marriages of Udapalata in Walapane, said, "Gradually coffee failed and the people fell into poverty, the produce of fields being insufficient to pay the tax and support the people."[205]

The sharp drop in the market price of peasant coffee around this time further reduced the cash incomes of the peasantry and their ability to pay the paddy taxes to the colonial state.

As noted above, at the very time that the peasantry lost their cash resources, the colonial government started to collect the arrears due on their taxes. As Le Mesurier wrote,

> The failure of the coffee crops was undoubtedly the cause of the non-payment of the tax in the first instance, but it was the subsequent harrying of the people for their arrears of tax that was the cause of their ultimate widespread misery and distress.[206]

In addition to the more systematic application of the law, that is, more rigorous tax collection, the state also increased both the rate of commutation

---

203. *SP 1889*, No. 29.
204. *SP 1889*, No. 29, Report of R. W. D. Moir, G. A. for the Central Province, p. 3.
205. Ibid., p. 21; see also Wesumperuma, "The Evictions," p. 135.
206. *SP 1889*, No. 29, p. 19.

Plantations and the Conflict over Land

of the paddy tax, i.e., the market value assigned to paddy, and the rate of assessment of the paddy fields, i.e., the estimated output of the fields.[207] The moderate commutation rates of the 1830s and 1840s had been raised in 1856 to 66½ cents per bushel in the Nuwara Eliya District. In 1864, they were again raised to Rs. 1.00 per bushel in Walapane.[208] As noted earlier, the sharp increase in the rate of commutation in 1864 was most likely related to the financial crisis of the plantation sector and the increased revenue needs of the colonial administration at that time.

Table 5:8

Peasant Coffee, 1880—1886

Year	Exports (cwts.)	Price (per cwt.) (shillings)
1880	44,753	70
1881	29,769	70
1882	35,499	47
1883	14,823	47
1884	11,886	47
1885	20,611	49
1886	10,046	63

Source: I. H. Van Den Driesen, "Coffee Cultivation in Ceylon (2)," *Ceylon Historical Journal*, vol. 3 (1953), p. 167.

In the late 1850s and 1860s, the peasants were able to pay the high commutation rates because of the prosperity of native coffee then.[209] The very fact that the peasants had to rely on their coffee crops to pay their paddy taxes shows that the paddy tax was pitched too high.[210] Le Mesurier pointed out in 1887 that the price of paddy at harvest time on the threshing floor ranged from 50 cents to 87½ cents per bushel in the Nuwara Eliya District. However, the Grain Tax Commissioner had fixed Rs. 1.20 as the rate of assessment under the Grain Tax Ordinance.[211] In addition, Moir himself concurred with Le Mesurier that the assessments of the fields were too high.

> It is not by means of money rate alone, however, that an increase in the grain tax was brought about in 1864. On the re-assessment of the fields Government share in kind

---

207. Roberts, "Grain Taxes in British Ceylon, 1832–1878: Problems," p. 828.
208. Wesumperuma, "The Evictions," pp. 135–36.
209. Ibid., p. 136.
210. Roberts, "Grain Taxes in British Ceylon, 1832–1878: Problems," p. 833.
211. *AR 1887*, "Report on the Nuwara Eliya District," by Le Mesurier.

was also in many cases materially increased, the general effect being to raise the tax from 1,335,13sh. (Rs. 13,356.50 cents) under the settlement in operation from 1857 to 1863, to £3,039.17sh.10d. (Rs. 30,398.02 cents) — an increase of 128 percent. I concur with my Assistant therefore in the opinion that one reason why the land owners allowed the grain tax to fall into arrears was that the tax was excessive.[212]

The following statistics on the total revenue collected from the grain tax in the Nuwara Eliya District (of which Walapane was a Division) shows roughly a little over a doubling of the rate of commutation at each assessment.

Table 5:9

Grain Tax Collections: Nuwara Eliya District, 1856—1884

1856 (under the old assessment of 1838)	Rs. 5,840.24
1857 (under the new assessment of 1856)	Rs.10,119.44
1867 (under the new assessment of 1864)	Rs.21,524.04
1884*	Rs.46,591.90

*Year of assessment not given

Source: D. Wesumperuma, "The Evictions under the Paddy Tax and Their Impact on the Peasantry of Walapane, 1882—1885," *Ceylon Journal of Historical and Social Studies*, vol. 10, 1970, p. 136.

There is enough evidence to support the thesis that the increase in the total revenue from the paddy tax was not due to the expansion of acreage under paddy, but due to the increase in the commutation rates and assessments of fields. As Le Mesurier's previously quoted reports indicate, the productivity and extent of paddy fields in fact declined over the years. One reason for this was the decrease of the regular flow of water needed for wet-rice cultivation due to forest clearings for plantations (and swidden agriculture). Baumgartner, who was the predecessor of Le Mesurier in the position of Assistant Government Agent in Nuwara Eliya, stated

> There can be no doubt, I think, that the clearing of almost all the high slopes at the head of this valley as coffee estates, Greymont being one of the newest, has seriously affected the water-supply of the fields below and disregard or at least ignorance of this probable result was shown when so much forest was sold to be opened as estates.[213]

Le Mesurier succinctly summarized the causes of peasant distress in Walapane when he said that,

---

212. *SP 1889*, No. 29, p. 3.
213. *AR 1884*, "Report on the Nuwara Eliya District," by AGA Baumgartner, p. 66A.

Plantations and the Conflict over Land

The causes of the large arrears outstanding at the beginning of 1881 are now clear. They were first, the over-assessment of the fields; second the injury to the water supply by the clearing of forests for estate and chena cultivation; third, sickly nature of the population; and fourth and principally, the failure of the coffee crops.[214]

When their primary means of subsistence — paddy — and their cash resources — coffee — were cut off, the peasants naturally turned to that safety valve of peasant subsistence — swidden or chena cultivation. But as Baumgartner reminds us, chena acreage was greatly reduced in the coffee planting regions due to the alienation of high lands by the Crown and the prohibition of shifting cultivation.[215] Baumgartner and other officials stationed in the planting regions noticed that having lost their paddy fields and their chenas too, the peasants had to turn to yet a more primitive form of subsistence, essentially the gathering of jungle roots and leaves.

> In Walapane the people dependent on chena crops suffered through the partial failure of the kurakkan, which in many villages did not develop its seed properly but withered up .... Except in Oyapalata the food supplies of the people of Walapane were certainly scarce and inadequate, and I had personal opportunities of observing that people were gathering jungle leaves for their subsistence.[216]

As Le Mesurier noted, some families in the Badulla District became simply destitute when evicted from their paddy fields. A conversation that the sympathetic Le Mesurier had with such a destitute family — a man, woman, and child — wandering along the Lower Badulla road, is a poignant expression of peasant suffering caused by the paddy tax.

> Q. Who are you?
> A. We are the people of Walapane.
> Q. Why have you left your village?
> A. Because we have lost all our property.
> Q. How did that happen?
> A. We are allowed to run into arrears with our paddy tax for two or three years. It was then called up all of a sudden. No mercy was shown us, and all our property was sold.
> Q. What are you doing now?
> A. We are in search of employment and means of livelihood.
> Q. Where are you going to?
> A. Nowhere in particular.
> Q. Why do you not go and work on a tea or on a coffee estate?
> A. We have tried this, but we never got anything for our work, all our earnings were taken by our *kangani* [labor supervisor on plantations] for debts he said. It is "debt" always "debt" with us.[217]

---

214. *SP 1889*, No. 29, Appendix 3, p. 3.
215. Ibid., p. 3.
216. *AR 1884*, "Report of the Nuwara Eliya District," by Baumgartner, p. 67A; see also *AR 1888*, "Report of the Uva Province," by G. A., F. C. Fisher, p. 223A.
217. *AR 1887*, Report of the Assistant Government Agent for Nuwara Eliya, quoted by Ameer Ali in "Changing Conditions," p. 13.

Thus, a once prosperous peasantry producing coffee for the world market, was reduced to starvation and destitution by the combined effects of the collapse of their cash crop production and harsh enforcement of commuted taxes by the state. Unlike plantation agriculture, which was strictly monocultural being confined to coffee, peasant production was diversified — consisting of paddy, cash crops (especially coffee), and chena crops. But the protection from market forces that should have accrued to the peasant despite the collapse of coffee was not realized because of the intervention of the colonial state at that time with harsher taxation. While the collapse of peasant coffee reduced the peasants' cash incomes, it was the harsh enforcement of colonial taxation that deprived them of their subsistence. As James Scott has pointed out in relation to southeast Asia, colonial taxes were usually enforced without consideration of the highly variable economic conditions of the peasant cultivators. Scott says,

> There is little doubt that the *average* burden of the colonial government on a peasant's income was greater than that of the indigenous governments that had preceded it. The growing average fiscal levy of the colonial state, though symptomatic, misses the most oppressive features of taxation in terms of peasant subsistence needs. The distinctiveness of colonial taxes lay not so much in the fact that they were higher, but in the nature of those taxes and the blind rigor with which they were imposed. [emphasis in original][218]

Paddy Taxes and Changing Property Relations

The Queen's Advocate of Ceylon argued in 1878 that whereas it was wrong to impose a grain tax in England where property was unevenly distributed, in Ceylon where property was evenly distributed and conditions of life equal and simple, the imposition of a grain tax was justifiable.[219] However, it was British policy introduced to promote plantation agriculture and the grain tax in particular, that contributed, to the generalization of private property rights and increasing inequality in the distribution of property and wealth in the village economy. As Le Mesurier pointed out, the eviction of peasants from their lands for nonpayment of paddy taxes resulted in the stagnation of paddy agriculture, changes in ownership of land, emigration, destitution and in some cases, even death resulting from starvation.[220] In the following pages,

---

218. Scott, *Moral Economy*, p. 92.
219. *SP 1878*, No. 37, p. iv.
220. *AR 1888*, "Report of the Nuwara Eliya District," by Le Mesurier, p. 76A.

Table 5:10

Description of Lands Sold for Nonpayment of the Paddy Tax: Nuwaru Ellya District, 1882

(1)	(2)	(3)	(4)	(5)	(6)		(7)		(8)	(9)	(10)	(11)	(12)
Village	Name of Land	Sowing Extent	The Unpaid Amount of Tax for which the Land was Sold	For what Period	Land Sold for		Market Value of Land		Date of Sale	Name of Owner	Name of Purchaser	Purchaser's Connection with Government. If any	Remarks
					Rs.	c.	Rs.	c.					
Kohoka	Kombal Arawa	2 pelas			2	60	200	0	Aug. 1882		Puncha	—	More than 500 fields were sold in the Nuwara Ellya district, but headmen do not give information and people are also afraid to give information. Full lists should be got from Government.
Yatipalata	Migha Arawa	3–1/2 pelas	Less than 18c.		12	0	400	0	July 1882		Mr. Soysa	For Head Clerk of Nuwara Ellya Kacheheri Korala	
Udagampahaha	Field No. 2,050	1 amunam	Less than 50c.	Arrears from 1879 to 1881, three years.	26	50	600	0	do.		Babappuhami	Head Clerk	
Yatipalata	Narande Arawa	2 pelas			8	0	250	0	do.		Mr. Gunawardena	Ratemahatmaya	
Ukutula	No. 1,047	3 pelas			12	0	300	0	do.		Mr. Eriyagama	Korala	
Udugampaha	No. 1,595	1 pela			6	50	150	0	do.		Babappuhami	For Head Clerk	
Yatipalata	Ulpotekumbura	2 pelas	Less than Rs. 20		8	12	300	0	do.		Mr. Soysa	—	
Kohoka	Dimbul Arawa	2–1/2 pelas			3	50	400	0	do.		Bastian Appu		
Oyapalata	Damunagaha-ela	2–1/2 pelas			12	0	350	0	do.		Mr. Soysa	For Head Clerk	
Pallegampaha	Field No. 170	6 kuranies			3	0	100	0	do.		Mr. Banda	Clerk	
Kohoka	Field No. 866	1 pela			6	0	100	0	Aug. 1882		Babappuhami	Korala	
		Total	Rs. 20.68		100	22	3,150	0					

Source: SP 1890 No. 27, "Further Papers Relating to the Alleged Deaths from Starvation in the Nuwara Ellya District," Enclosure of Letter no. 957/160, p. 7.

we shall only be concerned with changes in ownership and property relations in paddy agriculture.

As noted earlier, the aims of the commuted paddy tax were the augmentation of government revenue, the reduction of the burden of tax collection and the expansion of the cash nexus. As Le Mesurier suggests, the introduction of new property relations in paddy agriculture was not a great concern or deliberate aim of the British although they were not averse to the final outcome.

> Considering the enormous number of fields that have changed hands during the last few years in those Districts into which the commutation system has been introduced, I hardly think it will be denied that the Grain Tax Ordinance has effected a revolution in the ownership of land that was not contemplated by its framers.[221]

Much of the paddy fields expropriated by the Crown for nonpayment of taxes, were sold to private individuals. Table 5:10 shows that the fields thus expropriated were very small in extent (Column 3) and that value of the unpaid taxes on them were also extremely small (Column 4). It is also obvious that the lands were sold well below the market price (compare Columns 6 and 7), and in most cases the purchasers were various headmen who worked for the colonial government (Column 11).

> All the fields of which the tax was too heavy had been already sold by the Crown ... or had become the property of wealthy owners who bought them for a mere song at the default sales. ... The fields are generally sold for a little more than the tax due and the Crown only buys it when there are no bidders.[222]

We have noted that the headmen played an indispensable role in assessing the value of fields, supplying information to British officials and in collecting taxes. They were thus placed in an ideal position to maneuver land sales to their advantage. There is plenty of evidence which shows that they did so, and that a great proportion of the lands of defaulting peasant cultivators were bought by headmen and their relatives at very low prices. A petition signed by over one hundred villagers of Walapane stated that,

> The Ratemahatmaya, Corales and Aratchys [officials of the native administrative hierarchy] of the said (Walapane) District without taking due tax from their fields yearly as usual, although they offered and upon false plea the said headmen obliged to sell their fields for trifling sums and purchasing from them ... by which means they become rich and the petitioners are principally living by kurukkan [dry grain] cultivation and he who not bribed the Ratemahatmaya such persons are, not allowed to cultivate highlands. ... That the petitioners are ready and willing to prove all these things at the enquiry.[223]

221. *AR 1887*, "Report of the Nuwara Eliya District," by Le Mesurier.
222. *AR 1888*, "Report of the Nuwara Eliya District"; see also S. B. D. de Silva, "Investment and Economic Growth," p. 197.
223. Ceylon National Archives 47/210 series quoted in Wesumperuma, "The Evictions," p. 140.

Plantations and the Conflict over Land

We mentioned previously that the colonial government's attempt to pass an additional portion of the revenue burden on to the peasantry in 1848 resulted in a peasant rebellion that year. For reasons that we cannot discuss at length here, the harsher enforcement of taxes in the late 1870s and 1880s did not lead to a similar rebellion. However, there were isolated acts of protests, petitions (as the one referred to above), thefts, and instances when peasants joined together to evade payment of the taxes.[224]

In addition to the purchases made by local headmen, a large percentage of lands sold for tax defaults were bought by outside speculators, generally low-country Sinhalese and Muslim traders. F. C. Fisher, the Government Agent of the Uva Province, wrote in 1888,

> Continued the sale of lands seized for the nonpayment of tax. Twenty-three lands in the Udapalata division were sold at about Rs. 4 the acre and twenty-eight allotments of land in the Dambawinipalata at an everage of Rs. 3.58 the acre. Twenty-two lands remain unsold, and will have to be taken over by the Crown. Nearly all the purchases were made as usual by Moors and low-country Sinhalese.[225]

The processes of land expropriation and concentration that were set in motion led to increasing social differentiation within the village. An important feature of the new social relations which has shown up again and again in our discussions is the increasing importance of non-Kandyan ethnic groups such as low-country Sinhalese, Chettiyars and Muslims in the Kandyan village economy.

Crown land sales contributed to social differentiation within the village in yet another respect. This happened when the colonial state, or more accurately its local representatives, the village headmen, sold the paddy fields which were jointly held by several co-owners without consideration of the complexities of co-ownership. During the precolonial era, when private property ownership was absent, land, particularly paddy fields, were jointly held in undivided shares by several co-owners, usually family members. But now, when one shareowner failed to pay the paddy tax, the entire field was sold thereby expropriating the shares of the others as well. The practice of alienating jointly-held land in undivided shares in a context when one and all were clamoring to establish private property rights to land, left room for much fraud, disputes and litigation among villagers. As Obeysekere notes, these conflicts resulting from the operation of the paddy tax had drastic consequences for the traditional system of land tenure based on joint

---

224. Ibid., p. 138; see also *AR 1882*, "Report of the Sabaragamuwa District," p. 48A.
225. *AR 1888*, "Report of the Province of Uva," p. 230A.

ownership and contributed to the eventual changes in village social relations, including the loosening of kinship ties.[226]

Private Land Sales

The colonial state was not the only party that expropriated peasant paddy fields in order to recover taxes due. Private parties, notably renters and creditors, also expropriated peasant land to recover debts from defaulting peasants. Private land sales (rarely recorded in government statistics) had increased dramatically since the introduction of the renting system of tax collection and the spread of monetary transactions. Obeysekere's comments on the effects of private land sales on Madagama, a village in the Southern Province bordering the plantation regions, are applicable to the Central and Uva Provinces as well.

> There is therefore warrant for inferring that this type of sale — to kinsmen or shareowners, or outsiders, constituted a very important category of land sales, probably even more important than government sales. If so, the changes in land ownership during this period must have been of the most radical character, altering considerably the traditional land tenure arrangements and the power structure of the society.[227]

As renters were often moneylenders and traders as well, they were able to expropriate peasant lands for nonpayment of both paddy taxes and loans. Besides, peasants often mortgaged their lands to these speculators in order to get sufficient cash to pay government taxes and meet other expenses.[228] When peasants failed to pay back mortgages, land fell into the hands of the lenders. Usury hastened the emergence of new forms of stratification and the transformation of old economic relations in the village economy.[229] S. J. Tambiah's observation with regard to the twentieth century is relevant here because the commercialization of the landlord-tenant relationship that he describes, as we can see, had its origins in the nineteenth-century colonial period.

> The point to be noted is that within the peasant agricultural field it is commercial and credit operations that provide the most effective basis for accumulations by non-cultivators and correspondingly the chief channel for draining the peasants'

---

226. Obeyesekere, *Land Tenure*, pp. 125–26; see also *AR 1888*, "Report of the Nuwara Eliya District," p. 76A and *AR 1886*, "Report of the Southern Province," p. 52A.
227. Obeyesekere, *Land Tenure*, p. 125.
228. Jus, *The Grain Tax*, p. 6.
229. S. B. D. de Silva, "Investment and Economic Growth," p. 197.

Plantations and the Conflict over Land   151

wealth through marginal profits. These profits are finally invested in land, again which results in a transference of land from the actual cultivator to a *rentier* group.²³⁰

Many contemporary observers and subsequent writers have also noted the backwardness of paddy agriculture in colonial Ceylon and the fact that paddy was the least profitable investment for capital. In fact, Ludovici observed that the 'capitalist class' in paddy agriculture was only a nominal capitalist class and that they did not apply their wealth to agricultural improvements. He went on to say that they did not directly participate in decisions of agricultural production, but merely collected their share of the produce from the cultivators. Raising of the crop and payment of state taxes, were left to the cultivators themselves.²³¹ What Ludovici observed in 1867 are the peculiar features of 'rentier capitalism'. What is significant to note with respect to rentier capitalism in paddy agriculture was that while property relations changed significantly, methods of agricultural production remained stagnant and in some cases even retrogressed.²³² Ludovici also said,

> ... the eagerness with which native capitalists buy up good paddy land in the rural districts is therefore not from the expectation of any large profits, but partly because the investment is safe and partly because they have no other channel into which to turn their capital.²³³

Native capitalists did have a few other channels to invest their capital. These were the production of export crops (usually smallholder coffee or coconut) and plantation related commercial activities such as transport and arrack renting. But the question still remains, if paddy was so unprofitable, as all concerned seemed to agree it was, why did the village headmen and particularly outsider merchant capitalists continue to buy up the small scattered paddy plots of defaulting peasant cultivators? One obvious reason that we have already noted was the extremely low price at which these fields could be obtained. But a more complex reason for this situation was the tradition of 'land to rule'.

As we noted in our discussions of precolonial land tenure, the overlords' power in the feudal society was determined by the ability to control the tenants on their paddy lands. This relationship between land and rule did not disappear overnight with the conversion of land into a commodity and the expansion of market forces and the cash nexus. In fact, as we noted earlier,

---

230. Tambiah, "Ceylon," p. 85. See also p. 110.
231. Ludovici, *Rice Cultivation*, p. 139.
232. de Silva, "Investment and Economic Growth," pp. 280–81.
233. Ludovici, *Rice Cultivation*, p. 131; see also de Silva, "Investment and economic Growth," p. 158.

some of the land policies of the colonial state, such as the temple land registration scheme, had the indirect effect of reactivating fedual labor services and thereby the control of the temple lords over their tenants.

The colonial state, we observed, sold off the paddy fields of the defaulting cultivators (in the former royal villages) because neither the state nor the European planters had any use for these wet-rice lands. In contrast, the village headmen and outsider rentier capitalists were quick to buy up these paddy plots from the state or directly from the cultivators themselves. For the headmen, the acquisition of more and more paddy lands became a strategy for maintaining their traditional authority over the people, an authority they feared was disappearing in the wake of monetization and commercialization of the rural economy. For the petty capitalists from elsewhere, the low-country artisan castes such as the *karava*, and non-Sinhalese groups such as the Chettiyars and the Muslims, the acquisition of paddy fields promised an avenue for prestige and status which they sorely lacked in the Kandyan context. Paddy land transfers then, did not lead to a simple replacement of traditional lord-tenant relations by capitalist contractual relations. Instead the old relations were reconstituted on a new basis within the expanding market economy under the aegis of the colonial state. As Obeysekere notes,

> The crucial issue is why should wealthy landlords in the first place be interested in buying these small scattered shares in outside villages or invest their money in mortgage contracts when they are aware of the economic worthlessness of the transactions? The answer, obviously, is that motives more powerful than economic ones are at work, motives pertaining to power and prestige. The control over tenants, while economically of little importance, enhances the status of individuals and families in the power structure of the region. It is to the ideology of power, derived from traditional feudal norms still possessing great vitality and contemporary relevance, that we must now turn.[234]

An endemic feature of the traditional lord-tenant relationship was that in addition to the economic obligation of cultivating the lord's fields and paying him rent, the tenant was liable to perform all sorts of personal services which were often defined by caste. Tambiah points out,

> In fact, the power of feudal overlordship rested precisely in this command over services, which was an intrinsic aspect of the wealth and resources at the command of the superior. Landlordship today in many parts of Ceylon carries with it the same command over the tenant. In the twentieth-century context of overpopulation and landlessness this command can be exploited all the more and the *traditional obligations of a landlord more easily forgotten.* [emphasis added][235]

We can imagine that when paddy fields passed into the hands of non-Kan-

---

234. Obeyesekere, *Land Tenure*, p. 215; see also Michael Roberts, "Aspects of Ceylon's Agrarian Economy," p. 158 and "Elite Formation and Elites, 1832–1931," in *History of Ceylon*, ed. by K. M. de Silva, vol. 3, *passim*.
235. Tambiah, "Ceylon," pp. 65–66.

dyans such as the low caste *karavas* or Muslim traders, the extremely status-conscious Kandyan peasants became reluctant to perform personal services to their new landlords. Reversals occurring in the traditional status hierarchy and the loss of patronage due to the entry of outsiders resulted in conflicts between the tenants and their new landlords.

We noted a littler earlier the important observation made by Obeysekere that wealthy Ceylonese (and Indians) bought up paddy fields for reasons pertaining to power and prestige. But this observation is not consistent with the projection that Obeysekere makes when he says that "More research on the Grain Tax would show, we think, that its effects, when combined with the loss of the structural prerequisite would have been analogous to that of the Enclosure Movement in England."[236] As a matter of fact, only in a few cases did the expropriation of paddy fields lead to a physical removal of the cultivators from their ancestral paddy fields. Whereas a segment of the Kandyan peasantry became a casual and shifting labor force working for a supplementary income on the coffee (and later tea) estates or emigrated to towns, the large majority of the expropriated cultivators remained on the land as tenant sharecroppers of the new landlords.[237] Admittedly, the peasants' security on the land was now quantitatively and qualitatively reduced, but they nevertheless remained a paddy cultivating peasantry by and large. Baumgartner's observations regarding the Southern Province were equally applicable to the plantation regions in the Kandyan Highlands. "Those whose lands have been sold generally continue as cultivators under other proprietors, as sometimes under the new proprietor of their own land, more especially when the purchaser is as too often the case, a Moorman."[238]

This situation partly explainable by the fact that when many peasants were being expropriated in the 1880s, the coffee plantations were also collapsing due to the leaf disease. Even if some of the expropriated paddy cultivators were willing to become an estate labor force at that point, the plantations were in no position to absorb them. In fact, unable to cope with the leaf disease, the planters were sending their imported labor force back to India at this time.

Perhaps more important from the point of view of the nonemergence of a 'surplus polulation' in the village economy and consequences similar to that of the Enclosure Movement in England, is the fact that 'passive rentiership' prevented the development of capitalist methods of production in paddy agriculture.[239] For a number of complex reasons, among which the tradition of 'land to rule' is one, the landlords — both the headmen and the merchant

236. Obeyesekere, *Land Tenure*, p. 127.
237. Wesumperuma, "The Evictions," p. 142.
238. *AR 1886*, "Report of the Southern Province – Matara District," p. 91A.
239. Tambiah, "Ceylon," p. 111.

capitalists — were content to leave the production process in the hands of the cultivators. It remained labor intensive, archaic and the result was an extremely low level of labor productivity.

Abolition of the Paddy Tax

In spite of the recommendation of a Legislative Committee in 1890 that the Paddy tax be continued, the newly arrived Governor Havelock abolished the paddy tax in 1892. The fact that the tea industry was booming at the time and state revenues were increasing were probably significant for Havelock's decision. It was also noted that at this time the collections from the paddy tax were declining and that the administrative costs involved in making the collections were increasing.[240] The annual loss of Rs. 500,000 incurred by the state due to the abolition of the paddy tax was made up by quietly introducing a series of new taxes including a stamp tax, as well as salt and import duties, which again fell most heavily on the peasantry.[241] However, in abolishing the paddy tax, Governor Havelock admitted what its critics had been saying throughout the century: "Paddy tax is an obnoxious tax. It is a tax that presses on one particular class of cultivators and one particular industry."[242]

Paddy Lands: Feudal Villages

Paddy Tax to the State

Following the patterns of precolonial land tenure, Proclamation 1818 specifically exempted the temple villages (*vihāragam*) and villages of headmen in office (*nindagam*) from payment of the paddy tax to the state. When a village was not exempt from taxation, the overlord rather than the tenant bore the ultimate responsibility of paying the tax due to the state.[243] In those cases where the overlord paid the tax, he usually recovered it from the cultivators. It was often the case that aristocrats not holding office registered their lands under the names of relatives, either headmen in office or clergy-

---

240. *SP 1892*, No. 3, p. 146.
241. Ibid., p. 146.
242. Ibid., p. 5.
243. Roberts, "Grain Taxes in British Ceylon, 1832–1878: Problems," p. 813.

Plantations and the Conflict over Land

men, in order to avoid payment of the paddy tithe.[244] This was one of the reasons why so much of the paddy lands in the Kandyan Provinces was exempt from taxation. According to Emerson Tennant's estimates, nearly one third of the paddy lands in the former Kandyan kingdom belonged to temples, which meant that they were tax exempt.[245] But, we noted earlier, that between 1856 and 1864 the Temple Lands Commission expropriated over 8,500 amunams of paddy fields claimed by the temples, thereby reducing the total amount of wet-rice fields exempted from that tax (Table 5:5, Column 3).

The Debate Over Forced Labor in the Feudal Villages

Although exempt from state taxation, the cultivators of feudal lands were liable to pay feudal tribute to their respective overlords in caste-defined labor services, as well as in kind and occasionally in cash.

Since forced labor to the state (*rājakariya*) was abolished in 1833, various British interest groups began to debate the pros and cons of maintaining compulsory labor in the feudal villages. Planters and some colonial officials pointed out that land held under feudal tenure was unproductive and inimical to agricultural development. The planters, as Colebrooke did in abolishing forced labor to the state, anticipated a release of a wage labor force upon the abolition of compulsory labor in the feudal villages.[246] Others, including Christian missionaries, pointed out that serfdom was antithetical to the principles of moral justice and should therefore be abolished.[247] Emerson Tennant, who was apprehensive about the authority that native headmen wielded over the people, claimed that forced labor augmented the arbitrary authority of the feudal lords and compulsory labor in the feudal villages should therefore be replaced by a commuted tax. Tennant argued that

> The important point, however, in this question, and the one which most urgently requires legislative adjustment is the social condition of the tenants of these lands, who are now the serfs of the temples, and subjected to compulsory labour and a variety of feudal services and contributions as the tenure of their fields. As no such

---

244. *BPP 1847–1848*, Vol. 42, Emerson Tennent's Report, p. 96; Roberts, "Land Problems and Policies," p. 813.
245. *BPP 1847–1848*, Vol. 42, p. 97; see also Roberts, "Aspects of Ceylon's Agrarian Economy," p. 157.
246. Memorandum on "Service Tenures," by the Queen's Advocate in *SP 1869*, No. 18, p. 12; *AR 1871*, "Report of the Service Tenures Commissioners," by J. F. Dickson, p. 384; *SP 1876*, No. 18, Analysis of Evidence in the "Report of the Buddhist Temporalities Commission," p. 2.
247. *SP 1876*, No. 18.

tenure is no longer tolerated elsewhere in the island, and as the courts of law have in some instances refused to recognize the claim to enforce it, I am of the opinion that the priesthood would not offer any serious opposition to its abolition, and the substitution of a money-rent; thus converting their tenants into leaseholders, on a footing with all other cultivators throughout the island and elevating their position above their present state of dependence and servitude.[248]

Several other British officials, including the Service Tenures Commissioner, J. F. Dickson, and C. P. Layard, the Government Agent of the Western Province, suggested that the entire system of serfdom should be completely abolished in the feudal villages. They argued that these villages should be taken over by the government as far as possible and, as Tennant did earlier, suggested that they should be placed on the same footing as the former crown villages (gabadāgam) making the cultivators pay one-tenth of the share of the paddy crops to the government.[249]

In spite of these sound arguments and suggestions, other high officials of the colonial administration were reluctant to interfere with the feudal authority of the chiefs and the clergy over the people. They feared that a change in the balance of political forces in the country resulting from the abolition of feudal labor, might not necessarily be in their own favor. Meek's observations regarding the relationship between landholding and political power in other colonies are quite applicable to the situation faced by the colonial administration in Ceylon.

> ... land legislation is not easily designed simply to further agricultural production but it is also influenced by the desire to maintain or re-adjust political forces, resulting from the manner in which property is held. A re-adjustment in the manner in which property is held often leads to a change in the balance of political forces.[250]

Since the Rebellion of 1818, the British did experiment with indirect and imperceptible means to reduce the powers of the native chiefs (discussed in Chapter VII). But they did not dare make deliberate alterations in the feudal relationship between lord and serf, particularly in the early period of British rule, i.e., prior to the introduction of British capital, when the feudal bond was still intact and strong. As the astute George Turnour, Revenue Commissioner of the Kandyan Provinces, noted in 1829, forced labor had not lost its legitimacy among many tenants.

> The natives in general are still very decidedly attached to their religious institutions, so much so, that the local Government has hitherto considered it politic to give them every support and countenance, with the object of conciliating the people and of preserving the tranquility of the country. Any interference with a view to change

---

248. *BPP 1847-1848*, Vol. 42, pp. 97-98.
249. *SP 1876*, No. 18, pp. 40 and 52.
250. Meek, *Land Law and Custom*, p. xix.

Plantations and the Conflict over Land 157

would certainly be regarded by the chiefs and people as well as by the priests, as subversive of those institutions.[251]

In addition, as we have seen in relation to the implementation of British land and tax policies, the colonial state found the native chiefs indispensable for governing the colony. The abolition of feudal labor due to the chiefs then would have called for a revamping of the precolonial social order and a substitution of a new one. As Governor Horton explains, the British had neither the finances nor the political will to do this.

> ... the whole native machinery in the internal Government had been created by the exaction of personal services, the abrogation of which would necessarily leave the country without a police, and without the means of carrying on all those details of judicial and executive duty which are provided for in other countries by municipal and local regulations, for the protection of property and the preservation of the public peace. Secondly compulsory service was so interwoven with the other institutions of the country, the interests of the chiefs, and the maintenance of their religious establishments that its abrupt abolition would occasion disruption — it appears certain that so soon as the Government relinquishes its feudal claims on the gratuitous services of the inhabitants....[252]

Necessity for Reform

By the late 1860s, the effects of economic changes in the larger society began to make themselves felt on the lord-serf relationship in the feudal villages as well. As land became a commodity, feudal overlords began to sell high lands to outsiders without regard to the users' rights of the direct producers. We have seen how the activities of the Temple Lands Commission, particularly the grant of ownership rights to overlords of temple villages, tended to sharpen conflicts over land between temple lords and tenants. Similarly, Mitford, the Government Agent of the North Western Province, pointed out in 1868 that since the introduction of capital into the island, feudal overlords had begun to sell land to outsiders — Europeans, Muslim traders, low-country Sinhalese — and that these sales caused great hardship to the cultivators in the feudal villages. For example, Mitford showed that tenant cultivators were now forced to travel great distances to perform menial services for their new absentee landlords who had purchased their paddy fields from their feudal overlords.[253] Mitford also pointed out that when several buyers jointly bought feudal land, they each asserted their claims to the labor services of the tenant cultivators, thereby greatly increasing their service burden.[254]

251. Evidence of George Turnour, *CO* 416/20, pp. 105–06.
252. Quoted in Colvin R. de Silva, *Ceylon under the British*, vol. 2., p. 410.
253. *SP 1869*, No. 18, "Papers on Service Tenures," pp. 12 and 14.
254. Ibid., pp. 12–14.

Part 2: The Plantation Impact

Table 5:11

Tribute Paid by the Tenants of the Village of Nivitigala to Their Overlord — Doloswala Dissawa

(1) Situation or Names	(2) Extent A. P. K.	(3) Ridies.	(4) Pice.	(5) Rice. M.	(6) Salt. M.	(7) Curry stuff. M.	(8) Oil. M.	(9) Ghee. M.	(10)
Lekam	9 3 9	33	11	..	..	..	..	..	Furnishes Adookku Pehidoon to the village and followers for 10 days during Peranera, and also in cases of any other ceremony in his Walauwe, devil dance, & c.
Disawe Lekam	3 3 2	33	11	..	..	..	..	..	
Panapure Nile	20 2 4	42	..	90	10	10	2	2	
Kahangoda Nile	17 1 4	42	..	90	10	10	2	2	Do. do. do.
Tepalegoda Nile	15 1 3	42	..	90	10	10	2	2	Do. do. do.
Muruddewela Nile	15 2 3	42	..	90	10	10	2	2	Do. do. do.
Reygaleperesse Nile	6 3 2	25	15	85	10	10	2	2	Do. do. do.
Yaligaleperese Nile	8 2 6	25	15	85	..	10	2	2	Do. do. do.
Hamanharipanse Nile	8 0 8	25	15	85	10	10	2	2	Do. do. do.
Kandawarasse Nile	5 0 4	25	15	85	10	10	2	2	Do. do. do.
Hendarapitigey Gewatte	3 3 0	3	14	5	..	..	16	16	For the foregoing 8 miles receives 160 cocoanuts.
Godegey Gewatte	2 2 8	3	..	5	1/2	1/2	..	..	And two cocoanuts.
Halkandeliegy Gewatta	3 0 8	3	..	5	1/2	1/2	..	..	Watches at the Walauwe for 2 terms of thirty days each, and carries loads or performs other medial services.
Ulian Pangua of Garadewatte Gamea	3 1 8	3	14	..	81½	81½	..	..	
Leanegey Gewatta	2 2 2	3	..	5	1/2	1/2	..	..	Do. do.
Pallendigey Ganwasame	2 1 0	3	14	..	..	..	..	..	Do. do.
Potwattegey Ulianwasan	3 2 8	3	14	..	..	..	..	..	Do. do.
Delgaha Ulian Pangua	2 2 0	6	6	..	..	..	..	..	Do. do.
Polgahalenna Ulianpangoo	3 3 2	3	14	..	..	..	..	..	Do. do.
Appallagey Ulianpangoo	3 3 0	3	14	..	..	..	..	..	Do. do.
Bopellegoda Ulianpangoo	3 3 4	3	14	..	..	..	..	..	Do. do.
Murulenkande Ulianpangoo	3 2 8	3	14	..	..	..	..	..	Do. do.
Kirulliegy Ulianpangoo	2 1 4	3	14	..	..	..	..	..	Do. do.
Polwalle Ulianpangoo	2 1 4	3	14	..	..	..	..	..	Do. do.
Kammalpitie Ulianpangoo	3 1 0	3	14	..	..	..	..	..	Do. do.
Gelanie Ulianpangoo	2 3 0	6	14	..	..	..	..	..	Do. do.

Plantations and the Conflict over Land

Name						Services
Homapangua a dunukadu	1	0	0	2	8	Conveys the orders for the services of all the people of the village.
Niggahapangua Wasame	1	0	0	2	3	Do. do. do.
Talegahapangua	1	2	2	2	8	Do. do. do.
Mehelme duhukanpangua	1	0	0	...	...	Do. do. do.
Loggepangua a dunukan	2	0	0	3	6	Do. do. do.
Mahawelepangua	1	0	0	...	...	
3 Blacksmiths	6	1	8			Construct platform for the Ganladda when he attends Perahera at Rittagey. Present an areca knife each, and make any iron works when required, on being furnished with iron and charcoal.
3 Silversmiths	6	1	2			Present a chunam box each, and make any work when required, on being furnished with the metal, gold, silver, brass or copper.
4 Potters	5	1	0			Furnishes a pingo load of chatties as a present at New Year, and also supply the people of the village with chatties to bring cakes or oil to the Walauwe, and give as many chatties as required to the Walauwe, as well as tiles, which they must put on the roof.
Pahamune Selankaree	2	3	2			Builds sleds, furnishes firewood and water during Perahera, and attends at any journey.
The two Washers	1	3	8			Puts up white cloth at the lodgins and furnishes fresh cloths.
The two Twaduwas	11	0	7			Supplies 4 flag staves; the personal services rendered by the people of this village, including the Pelkareas, cannot be particularized, they being obliged to cultivate the fields and chenas, and after doing all the works, store the produce, improve the gardens, cut ditches, and do any other service which may be required from them.
Kandekotepangua	2	1	7			Watches at the Walauwe for two terms of thirty days each, and carries loads or performs other menial services. Furnishes 1,500 jagery ball, smaller sizes.
Udakorewite Unduhakuru	0	1	2	...		Conveys the order for the services of all the people of the village.
Eluwanegey Gewatta	6	1	3	20		
Edanhellegeypangu	2	3	5	5		
	216	0	1			

Source: SP 1869–70 No. 18 "Papers on Service Tenures," Memo. No. 2 by Mitford, 11 Jan. 1869.

Table 5:11, taken from Mitford's report on feudal service tenure, provides a good picture of the socioeconomic organization of one particular feudal village (Nivitigala) before the introduction of tenure reforms in 1870. Column 1 gives the name and/or caste-specific economic function of the tenants; Column 2, the extent of feudal land held by each; Columns 3 and 4, the tribute paid to the overlord (Doloswala Disawe) in cash; Columns 5–9, tribute paid in kind; Column 10, the caste-specific forced labor services owed to the lord.

The Services Tenures Ordinance: 1870

In 1870, the colonial state finally appointed a Commission – the Service Tenures Commission – to inquire into the alleged 'fraud and deception' of feudal overlords as reported by Mitford and other officials and to suggest remedies for these evils. The Commissioners registered the caste-specific feudal labor services and tithes in kind or cash due to the overlord from each paddy landholding in the feudal villages and allocated a monetary sum that could be paid by the tenants in lieu of compulsory labor and tithes in kind.

Thus, without abolishing feudal tribute altogether or in principle, the colonial state attempted to 'modernize' it by providing the tenants the option of commutation. This option was made available by enacting Ordinance No. 4 of 1876.[255] The colonial state hoped that this arrangement would help extend the cash economy while yet maintaining feudal tribute which was also the means of remunerating the headmen for their services to the colonial state. It is important to note that following the popular rebellion of 1848, the colonial state took great pains to make the native chiefs a collaborating class in the administration of the country and did not necessarily want to loosen their authority over the people.

Without a doubt the newly introduced commutation scheme helped augment the cash incomes of some headmen and Buddhist clergy. Table 5:12 shows that commutation dues paid by tenants became the most important source of cash income of the deity temples (*dewalēs/devalēs*) of Sabaragamuwa following the introduction of the commutation Ordinance No. 4 of 1870 (see Column 3). This Table also shows that renting 'boutiques' or small retail shops was a chief source of income for these deity temples.

---

255. "An Ordinance to Define the Services Due by the Praveni Tenants of Wiharagama, Dewalagama, and Nindagama Lands, and to Provide for the Commutation of those Services," in *A Revised Edition of the Legislative Enactments*, vol. 1, pp. 770–78.

Plantations and the Conflict over Land

But on the whole, relatively few tenants seemed to have taken up the opportunity to commute their feudal labor services into cash payments. This was because the tenant cultivators soon realized that commutation offered them few benefits. Ameer Ali has argued that this was partly because the Ordinance was introduced at a time when the main cash crop of the peasantry — coffee — was already suffering from disease and decline and the peasants had no alternative cash resources.[256] There is little evidence which suggests that even prior to the spread of the coffee leaf disease the tenants of the feudal villages had been growing coffee as widely as the cultivators of the former royal villages.

The Proclamation of 1818 turned many of the cultivators of the former royal villages into a class of owner-producers. However, this newly gained independence was a highly tenuous one. Quite often it resulted in the expropriation of the owner-cultivators' lands due to their failure to pay the paddy tax to the state or loans to their creditors. In comparison, the tenant cultivators in the feudal villages who continued to be serfs, nevertheless enjoyed a certain modicum of security and stability. In other words, transformation of property relations were much slower in the feudal villages than in the former crown villages. Ameer Ali attributes the persistence of patron-client relations as a factor in the reluctance of many tenants in the feudal villages to take up the commutation option.

> To the peasants getting free from the service to Nindagama-lords meant not only losing their favors in times of difficulties, but sometimes also earning their enmity. In cases of those lords who were still functioning as responsible government officers or village headmen, the peasants did not dare to take a risk.[257]

In spite of the reluctance of many tenants to take up the commutation option provided by the Service Tenures Ordinance, it did have a significant impact — albeit a negative one — on the tenants' relationship to the land and thereby to the overlords. As the colonial administration itself later admitted, the 1870 Ordinance was not successful in easing the tension between the overlords and the tenants as it was purported to do; rather, it exacerbated the tensions which had already been increasing due to the intrusion of economic forces underway in the larger society. As the Buddhist Temporalities Commission appointed in 1876 to inquire into the state of affairs in the temple villages noted, "The priests and lay incumbents of the dewala are now absolutely irresponsible; no one can touch them."[258] The Commissioners blamed

---

256. Ameer Ali, "Changing Conditions," p. 25.
257. Ibid., p. 25.
258. *SP 1876*, No. 18, Appendix, p. 38.

Table 5:12

Deity Temples (Dēwālē) in the Province of Sabaragamuwa and their Revenues

(1) No.	Name of Déwalé	(2) Number of Pangus*	(3) Annual Income from Commutation Services	(4) Annual Income from Fields and Gardens Exclusively its Own	(5) Annual Income from Rents of Boutiques at the Perahera	(6) Annual Income from Offerings	(7) Total
			Rs.	Rs.	Rs.	Rs.	Rs.
1	Maha Saman Dēwālē	659	13,379	2,500	1,000	250	17,129
2	Alutnuwara Katragam Dēwālē	156	4,900	450	200	100	5,650
3	Boltumbe Saman Dēwālē	52	943	200	50	50	1,243
4	Anmaduwe Katragam Dēwālē	28	388	120	400	100	1,008
		895	19,610	3,270	1,650	500	25,030

Remarks. The Maha Saman Déwalé was additionally entitled to receive one-half of the income of the Saman Kovila on the top of the top of the Peak, the annual offerings of which amount on an average to 2,500 rupees.
*Pangus are paddy land shares.

Source: SP 1876, No. 18, 'Report of the Buddhist Temporalities Commission' — Appendix.

Plantations and the Conflict over Land

the 1870 Ordinance for the corruption and irresponsibility of the temple lords. The Commissioners pointed out, for example, that commutation which was to have been voluntary was on occasion forced upon the tenants by the overlords eager to increase their cash incomes. For example, the Commissioners noted that

> In the Province of Seven Korales the late incumbent of Madawala Vihare, a temple endowed with upwards of 400 acres of rice land, induced the tenants to commute their service for a money payment and appropriated the revenues to the maintenance of his mistress..... And the incumbent of Godigomuwa temple bought for himself out of the revenues, a large garden and built a handsome house, in which he keeps two mistresses.[259]

The disparagement of the clergy and the Buddhist religion was perhaps a motive of the British Commissioners in making statements such as the above. It is true, however, that during the colonial period with the loss of state patronage and the weakening of ecclesiastical authority, many Buddhist clergymen had declined into a state of moral degeneration. The Service Tenures Ordinance only helped make matters worse by allowing the clergy to engage in economic pursuits prohibited by the Buddhist disciplinary code (*vinaya*) for the monks. The commutation option provided by the colonial state then provided the Buddhist clergy or the *sangha* the sanction and a readymade mode of adaptation to the new market economy. In addition to the commutation fees exacted from the tenants, the sale of high lands (to planters and speculators) and the lease of buffaloes and shops, enabled the clergy to participate in economic activities, a participation which undoubtedly affected their spiritual pursuits.[260]

We noted in our discussion of precolonial Kandy that the caste-specificity of the feudal division of labor and the fact that the land was not valued in itself prevented the emergence of a land market there. But now, under the terms of the commutation ordinance, feudal lords could alienate the lands of defaulting tenants. They could either establish private property rights to those lands or sell them to outsiders to recover taxes due. Buying and selling of feudal lands then became a profitable enterprise. Furthermore, under the new policies introduced by the British, land shares (*pangus*) could also be exchanged between people of different castes as cash could be paid in lieu of caste services.

In practice, many injustices crept into the operation of the new monetized system. For example, when land shares with low caste duties traditionally attached to them were bought by high caste people, the latter managed to

---

259. Ibid., Resumé of the Evidence of the Temple Lands Commission, p. 173.
260. Ibid., pp. xxix; see also Roberts, "Waste Lands Ordinance," p. 167.

pay a commutation fee far below that assigned by the Service Tenures Commissioners to those plots. The Buddhist Temporalities Commission which inquired into the operation of the Service Tenures Ordinance noted in 1876 that,

> ... the more influential tenants have converted their services into nominal payments; while the services of the low-caste tenants remain the same as in former times. This has produced great inequality and has reduced the value of temple property.[261]

We can hypothesize, then, that commutation and the monetary transactions and land transfers that it engendered had differential effects on the various castes in the feudal villages; the artisan castes rated as low being more badly affected than the higher *govi* caste. Part of the reason for this was also the desire on the part of overlords while adopting commutation to yet retain the specialized services of these 'low' castes such as drummers and palanquin bearers, as these services could only be performed by them.

Tenant resistance to these changes was not uncommon. When outsiders, especially from low castes and non-Kandyan groups, bought feudal lands, the hereditary cultivators accustomed to paying deference only to their caste superiors, often refused to perform duties or pay dues to the new landlords. A. C. Lawrie, a prominent British judge in colonial Ceylon, has documented several such cases of peasant resistance. For instance, when a feudal family by the name of Kapuwatte sold their land to a low-country Sinhalese by the name of Don Domingo Wijesinghe, the hereditary tenants on the land refused to acknowledge Wijesinghe as their lord or to cultivate his fields. Wijesinghe was finally compelled to sell the land that had cost him much money and trouble. The tenants refused to do service for the next purchaser either and continued to cultivate the lands practically free from service obligations.[262]

What is clear then is that commutation very sharply increased the elements of conflict and tension in the feudal lord-serf relationship. Even the Service Tenures Commissioner, J. F. Dickson, who generally defended government policy and practice, noted the contradictions created.

> The Ordinance [Service Tenures Ordinance of 1870] *will I think be beneficial in upholding the chiefs' families* but I am not able to agree with those who charged the landlords with tyranny and cruelty to their tenants. No such case has occurred here. *I think it is questionable whether the Ordinance has done the tenants any good at all.* [emphasis added][263]

Tenants on feudal lands often complained that the commutation fees assigned by the Service Tenures Commission to their land shares were too high.

---

261. Ibid., p. 40.
262. Lawrie, *A Gazeteer*, vol. 1, p. 62.
263. "Report of the Service Tenures Commissioner," quoted in *AR 1871*, "Report of the Galle District," by Lee, AGA, p. 384.

Plantations and the Conflict over Land 165

They also pointed out that the Commissioners assigned commutation fees per land share without regard to the fact that each land share was jointly held by several individuals. Thus, when it came to ascertaining the fees due from each share, violent disputes erupted among co-owners. The fact that the introduction of commutation into the feudal villages created more confusion than it resolved and, that it caused hardship to the very tenants that it purported to free from serfdom, is evident from a Memorial sent to the governor by the tenants of the Demon Temple of Sabaragamuwa.[264] While it is clear that the Memorial was instigated by some influential people personally opposed to the lay incumbent of this particular temple, Iddamalgoda Nileme, the Government Agent of the Western Province, C. P. Layard, himself acknowledged the legitimacy of the tenants' grievances.

> It is also certain that since the passing of the Ordinance No. 4 of 1870, *the revived claim to services, which were becoming obsolete*, the generally high rate at which their services have been valued for the purposes of commutation, and the necessity imposed upon tenants to commute by pangus, which is almost prohibitive of the relief intended to be afforded have rendered temple tenants generally very impatient of their condition. [emphasis added][265]

The list of court cases instituted by the Iddamalgoda Basnayaka Nilemē against the tenants of his Demon Temple of Sabaragamuwa illustrates the exacerbation of the lord-tenant conflict alluded to by Layard. Column 1 in Table 5:13 lists the court cases instituted by overlord Iddamalgoda for nonperformance of duties or nonpayment of commuted value of those duties by his tenants; Column 2 shows the defense made by the tenants and gives an idea of the general confusion caused by the application of fixed annual commutation fees to land shares held in rotation by several tenants; Colomns 3 and 4 show the results of the cases and whether the lands of the tenants were seized for default and whether they were to be sold to recover the payments due.

In our discussion of temple land registration by the colonial state in the period 1856–1864 we noted that during the early part of the century tenants in feudal villages had begun to ignore some of the services they were obliged to perform for their overlords. As Layard also noted, some feudal services had become obsolete. But the temple land registration scheme and the Service Tenures Ordinance helped reactivate those decaying service obligations and thereby strengthened the hold of the overlords over their tenants. Table 5:13 (Column 1) shows that tenants of the Maha Saman Deity Temple had been neglecting some of their service obligations and that many even questioned the legitimacy of their overlord (Column 2). But now, under the protection derived

264. *SP 1876*, No. 18, Appendix C.
265. Ibid., p. 52.

from the new Ordinance, the incumbent overlord was demanding that the tenants either perform their feudal services or pay up the commuted value assigned to those services by the Service Tenures Commissioners in 1870. It seems that even where the tenants paid up the commuted fee, they could not always avoid the performance of the labor services, as they continued to live and cultivate the lord's fields in the traditional manner. In some cases, the tenants now became subjected to a 'double burden', personal labor services and cash taxes to the overlord. It seems that some feudal lords even began to demand taxes on chena plots which were traditionally tax-exempt — a demand that many tenants continued to resist (Table 5:13, Column 2).

We noted in Chapter II, two distinct types of tenants in precolonial Kandy: hereditary tenants (*pangukārayo*) and temporary or tenants at will (*nilakārayo*). According to precolonial customary law, the lords could alienate only the lands of the temporary tenants as the hereditary tenants held their plots in perpetuity. But we noted that in practice, given the absence of a land market and the lords' desire in keeping tenants tied to their paddy fields, even the temporary tenants remained relatively secure on the land. But now, the Services Tenures Commission of 1870, made the security of both groups of tenants much more tenuous. This was because the overlords were now given the right to expropriate the lands of any tenant — hereditary or temporary — for nonperformance of services or the nonpayment of commuted fees. Thus the Service Tenure Ordinance provided the basis for the overlord to dispossess the cultivator of his means of production and to establish himself on a new economic or contractual basis as a rentier capitalist. This also gave the overlord the right to sell the land to outsiders.

Indeed as overlords gained the right to alienate land, many peasants who failed to pay their commuted fees lost their rights to hereditary lands. The customary users' rights of the cultivators were not guaranteed by the Service Tenures Ordinance introduced by the British. Furthermore, the commutation introduced into the feudal villages was a fixed annual commutation which did not take into account the inevitable changes in the tenant cultivators' ability to find cash from season to season. On the other hand, the Ordinance provided the basis for the conversion of the overlords' hierarchical tribute exacting rights into absolute private property rights.

It is important to take note of the fact that although peasant resistance to exploitation by the overlords increased at this time, most peasants did not question the legitimacy of feudal tribute exaction. What they objected to was not the principle of feudal tribute but its subversion by their feudal lords and new absentee landlords. Perhaps, for most tenants in the feudal villages, feudal justice — by which was meant the adherence to customary law and recip-

Table 5:13

Court Cases Instituted by the Lay Incumbent (Nilemē) of the Maha Saman Deity Temple (Dēwālē) Against its Tenants

(1) Cause of Action, Date of Institution, and Number of Case.	(2) Defence	(3) Result	(4) Whether writ issued, and if so, have lands been sold in satisfaction of writ.
February 27th, 1874. No. 9,066. — For non-performance of services as tenants of Amnwala Balingaya Ulian Panguwa for the year 1873.— Claims commuted value of the Panguwa, 11 rupees and 50 cents.	Nil	Judgment for plaintiff by consent.	Writ not issued.
April 18th, 1874. No. 9,203. — For nonperformance of services as tenants of Kalingavage Panguwa (Uliyan) for the year 1873.— Claims commuted value 17 rupees and 20 cents.	The 4th defendant denies his liability to pay the amount claimed, on the ground that he is the owner of only 1/4 of Kanattewattahena belonging to the Panguwa mentioned in the plaint, and that it being a Hena he is not subject to pay anything as regards services, and further urges that the plaintiff is not the lawful Basnayaka Nilame of the Maha Sanan Dewale.	Judgment entered against 1st defendant by consent, plaintiff waives other defendants, save the 4th, who is absolved with costs.	Writ not issued.

April 28th, 1874. No. 9,206. — For nonperformance of services as tenants of Bopetta Gamwasam Panguwa for the year 1873.— Claim, commuted value 63 rupees and 35 cents.	The defendant pleads performance of services and says that the plaintiff refused to accept the Penum. & c., which the defendant rendered.	Judgment for plaintiff as claimed with costs.	Writ issued and amount partly recovered by sale of crops, and writ is now reissued to recover the balance.
April 29th, 1874. No. 9,210. — For nonperformance of services as tenants of Hangomawe Minum Panguwa for the year 1873.— Claim, commuted value 34 rupees and 80 cents.	Nil	1st defendant admits claim — 2nd and 3rd in default. Judgment for plaintiff as claimed with costs.	Writ issued and lands of defendants seized, but not sold yet.
No. 9,211. — For nonperformance of services as tenants of Hangomnwe Wahumpura Panguwa for the year 1873.—	Nil	The 1st, 2nd, 3rd, 5th, 6th, 7th, 8th, and 9th defendants present, 3rd and 5th defendants admit claim. 4th defendant reported a resident at Kandy, and 10th defendant dead. Judgment for plaintiff against 1st, 2nd, 3rd, 5th, 6th, 7th, 8th, and 9th defendants, as claimed, with costs.	Writ issued and lands of the defendants sequestered, but not sold yet.
No. 9,255. — For nonperformance of services as tenants of Weerahim Gamwasam Panguwa for the year 1873. — Claim, commuted value rupees 38 and 75 cents.	The 1st defendant pleads performance of service for the year 1873, it being his Tattumaru turn of possession — 2nd, 3rd, 5th, 6th and 7th defendants deny their liability to pay the amount claimed, and 14th defendant pleads that he holds no property subject to the services of the Maha Saman Dewale.	The plea of the 5th defendant that chena lands are not liable, is not maintainable at law. Payment not being proved, judgment for plaintiff as claimed with costs.	Writ issued and lands sequestered, but not sold

Plantations and the Conflict over Land

No. 9,256. – For non-performance of services as tenants of Hangomuwe Manawatage Ulian Panguwa. – Claim, commuted value 24 rupees and 35 cents.	The 5th defendant further says he is the owner of an individed 1/6th of Dunkarukalehena of this pangu, and it being a hena he is not liable to any payment as regards services, and that the plaintiff is not the lawful Basnayaka Nilame of the Maha Saman Dewale.	Judgment entered against the 5th defendant by consent against 1st, 2nd, 3rd, 6th, 7th and 8th defendants by default, and 9th absolved from the instance with costs.	Writ issued, returnable 14th October, 1876.
	1st, 2nd 5th, 6th, and 9th defendants say, they are not liable to pay the claim – 5th defendant further says, that he performed the services for the year in question – the 9th defendant syas he is possessed of no lands within the Dewalegama, and that the plaintiff is not the Basnayaka Nilame as alleged.		

Source: SP 1876 No. 18 "Buddhist Temporalities Commission Report," p. 68.

rocal obligations by lord and serf — was more important than the elusive 'freedom' promised by the commutation option introduced by the British. Certainly tenant resistance was a form of class struggle in colonial (and precolonial) Ceylon; however, it was not revolutionary, rather, it was restorative in that it looked to the past, not the future.

Although many peasant cultivators lost their hereditary rights to land following the introduction of commutation into the feudal villages, a physical expropriation of the cultivators from the paddy fields (perhaps anticipated by the planters) did not necessarily take place. This was largely because in order to continue their traditional authority over the people, the feudal overlords wanted to retain the tenants on the land. An alternative source of labor to work these lands would certainly have been difficult to obtain. Even the outsiders who bought up paddy plots in the feudal villages preferred to retain the hereditary tenants as sharecroppers rather than drive them out. The results of the introduction of commutation into the feudal villages then were in many respects similar to the outcome in the former royal villages. As in the latter, the principle of 'land to rule' and the extraeconomic sanctions associated with it were not entirely wiped out by the introduction of cash and market relations. In fact, colonial policies resulted in the grafting of new contractual and monetary relations upon the pre-existing hierarchical rights without completely abolishing them.

The adaptation of the Kandyan feudal lords to the modern world of cash and markets was largely as rentier rather than entrepreneurial capitalists. As we shall explore later, colonial state policies towards local agriculture wielded a determining influence on the particular forms of adaptation made by the feudal lords (and the emerging native entrepreneurial groups) within the colonial political economy. While their role as rentier capitalists did not contribute to the expansion of agricultural production and technology, it nevertheless allowed them to simultaneously enjoy both 'feudal' authority and the advantages of new market relations and the cash nexus.

What is clear from the foregoing discussion is that through the activities of the Temple Lands Commission, the Service Tenures Commission and the introduction of commutation, the colonial state was able to 'tear away' precapitalist social relations from its feudal context and subordinate it to the control of the colonial state and the interests of the dominant market economy and the plantation sector.[266] As described earlier, in the process of this subordination a fundamental transformation of the feudal social relationship was set in motion. In other words, the feudal basis of the lord-serf relation-

---

266. See also Gunasinghe, "Agrarian Relations," pp. 15–21. On the cultural adaptations made by some feudal lords, see Wickremeratne, "Education and Social Change," p. 179.

ship was undermined. Hans-Dieter Evers' claim then that "monastic landlordism ... has survived the onslaught of British colonialism more or less by default..."[267] is not entirely accurate. What emerged in the feudal villages, to use Charles Bettleheim's phrase, was a contradictory process of 'conservation-dissolution.'[268] The theoretical implications of this dialectic, we shall turn to, in our conclusions in Chapter IX.

Summary

Irrigated paddy lands (*mada bim*) used exclusively for wet rice cultivation signified a feudal mode of production in precolonial Kandy. Dry lands or high lands (*goda bim*) on the other hand constituted chena land, virgin forest land and pasturage. High lands, and chena in particular, signified a communal mode of production. This chapter has discussed the effects of colonial land and tax policies on property relations in paddy and high lands. These effects are broadly summarized in Figure 5:1.

The colonial state expropriated vast tracts of forest as well as periodically cultivated chena lands belonging to both the royal and the feudal villages. The peasant cultivators thereby lost their users' rights to those lands. Feudal lords (especially the temple overlords) lost a large portion of the high lands to which they had rights of overlordship. For the rest, they received private property rights. Most of the high lands alienated by the state were sold to planters who turned them into coffee estates. A smaller portion of high lands were sold to feudal lords and local enterpreneurs in freehold.

The introduction of private property rights and the concept of land as a commodity, wiped out the communal village rights to high lands. Furthermore, due to the confluence of crown land expropriation, plantation and smallholder cash crop production, the extent and significance of swidden agriculture was drastically reduced. Thus the safety valve of peasant subsistence — chena — and the political autonomy traditionally associated with chena cultivation were gradually lost.

Turning to paddy lands, we observed that the colonial state did away with forced labor in the royal villages and substituted a paddy tax in its place. The cultivators were in effect given freehold rights to their ancestral paddy fields.

---

267. Hans-Dieter Evers, "'Monastic Landlordism' in Ceylon: A Traditional System in a Modern Setting," *Journal of Asian Studies*, vol. 28, no. 4 (August 1969), p. 685.
268. Charles Bettleheim, "Theoretical Comments," in Arrighi Emmanuel, *Unequal Exchange: A Study of the Imperialism of Trade* (New York: Monthly Review Press, 1972), pp. 297–98.

But most of these cultivators could not retain their ownership rights to these lands for very long. Default on their commuted paddy tax led to the expropriation of many peasant lands by the state. The state in turn sold these lands to headmen and outsider merchant capitalists. Many peasants also lost their lands through private sales to creditors, merchants, and headmen. The intrusion of these cash and market relations, however, did not completely wipe out extraeconomic features of the landlord-tenant relationship; nor did the alienation of land necessarily lead to a physical removal of the peasantry from their land.

Figure 5:1

The Effects of Colonial Land and Tax Policies on Property Relations in the Kandyan Village Economy

	High Land (*goda bim*)	Paddy Land (*mada bim*)
Royal Villages (*gabadāgam*)	Crown expropriation of land to which cultivators had users' rights; some cultivators gain freehold rights. Long-term effects: Plantation expansion; curtailment of swidden (and garden) cultivation; restriction of peasant cash cropping.	Imposition of commuted tax. Long-term effects: Expropriation of cultivators for nonpayment of tax to the state or indebtedness to merchants. Emergence of rentier-tenant relations.
Feudal Villages (*nindagam vihāragam* and *dēvalagam*)	Crown expropriation of land to which feudal overlords have tribute exacting rights and cultivators have users' rights; overlords gain freehold rights to some lands. Long-term effects: Plantation expansion and curtailment of swidden cultivation; land sales by feudal overlords to planters and speculators.	Voluntary commutation of paddy taxes and labor services. Long-term effects: Expropriation of cultivators for non-payment of commuted dues. Emergence of rentier-tenant relations.

Voluntary commutation of forced labor services and rent in kind were introduced by the colonial state to feudal villages — *nindagam, vihāragam* and *dēvalagam*. Here too, default on commuted taxes led to the loss of the customary rights of the tenant cultivators. Again, the gradual dispossession of the peasantry did not necessarily lead to their physical removal from the land. In fact, 'feudal' authority was strengthened, albeit within a new politico-economic framework and a new contractual economic basis.

What becomes clear is that private property rights and contractual cash relations were introduced into all categories of land, although at different times and with varying rigor. Thus property and class relations in all categories of land — high lands, paddy lands, royal, and feudal lands — began slowly to converge in the same direction. Customary rights to village high lands were quickly wiped out because of the direct threat they posed to plantation expansion. On the other hand, the traditional extraeconomic features of the lord-tenant relationship, such as the exaction of personal labor services, were maintained in many villages. But the subordination of the lord-tenant relationship to the cash nexus, market forces, private property rights, and the exigencies of the colonial state and the plantation economy laid the basis for a structural transformation of property relations, surplus appropriation, and the class relations in the Kandyan Highlands.

VI. Plantations and the Creation of a Labor Force

In this chapter, we turn to the manner in which the European coffee planters in the Kandyan Highlands procured, controlled and reproduced their labor supply. One particular interest here is to see if any linkages were forged and what cleavages occurred between the plantations and the Kandyan village economy in the process of procuring labor for the coffee estates.

Plantation agriculture has long been heavily dependent upon the extent and character of the available labor supply.[1] Plantation coffee in particular requires a large, regular, and well-disciplined labor force. During coffee harvests, labor requirements increase tenfold. When this increased demand for labor could not be met, the ripened coffee berries had to be left to rot on the bushes, causing heavy losses to the planters.[2]

In this chapter we consider why the planters found it necessary to *create* an estate labor force; the efforts taken by the colonial state to convert the Sinhalese peasantry into a labor force for the plantations; the relative failure of those efforts; the procurement of an immigrant labor force from South India by the planters; and, the advantages that accrued to the planters from the employment of immigrant laborers.

The Attempt to Create a Sinhalese Labor Force

At the time plantations were opened up in the Kandyan Highlands of Ceylon, the precolonial economy there was not characterized by unlimited supplies of labor.[3] Labor, not land, was the scarce factor of production in the precolonial economy. Unlike in neighboring South India, there were no landless agricultural labor castes in Kandy. The Kandyan artisan castes themselves were primarily wet-rice cultivators who possessed their own means of produc-

---

1. V. D. Wickizer, *Coffee, Tea and Cocoa* (Stanford: Stanford University Press, 1951), p. 449.
2. *Colombo Observer*, April 5, 1866.
3. Note that the situation in Kandy contradicted the assumptions of the dual economy model of labor supply applied to many nonwestern societies by Arthur Lewis, et al. W. Arthur Lewis, "Economic Development with Unlimited Supplies of Labour", *The Manchester School* (May 1954).

Plantations and the Creation of a Labor Force   175

tion and could not, therefore, be induced to become plantation labor. The elaborateness and complexity of the precolonial division of labor, especially its caste-specificity as well as the absence of agricultural labor castes in Kandy, made it extremely difficult to create the wage labor force needed by the plantations.

In contrasting feudal Ceylon with rapidly industrializing England in the midnineteenth century, an English writer wrote,

> In England the study of statesmen is to find employment for the poor; while in Ceylon the difficulty is to find poor to employ. England has not sufficient land to produce food for its manufacturing people; while Ceylon has not sufficient labouring population to cultivate the soil for English capitalists and has none to spare for manufacturing purposes.[4]

Similarly, in 1847, the Colonial Secretary, Emerson Tennent, in a Desptach home to the Secretary of State for the colonies, noted in alarm,

> In looking to the prospects and future advancement of the colony; we cannot close our eyes to the fact that the extensive operations now in progress, the large investment of capital, the resort of settlers and the application of European energy to convert the forests of the interior into productive plantations are all dependent on a steady supply of labour; they have been undertaken on that expectation, and their success or defeat must be contingent on its realization. Yet at this moment the planters have not the slightest assurance for the uniform continuance of that supply; but on the contrary, they have already been made aware of the risques they run from its capricious fluctuations as well as the possibility of its total interruption.[5]

Most planters and colonial officials rationalized the labor scarcity by disparaging the Sinhalese peasantry as indolent and as lacking economic incentives.[6] References to the laziness of the Sinhalese, particularly the Kandyans, abound in colonial documents. One example is the statement made by Governor Robinson at the opening session of the Legislative Council in 1866,

> The wants of the native population of the Island are few and easily supplied by an occasional day's work in their own gardens or paddy fields. Their philosophy, their love of ease and indolence or their limited ideas, whichever may be the real cause, render them perfectly content with what they already possess;...[7]

---

4. J. Steuart, *Notes on Ceylon and its Affairs During a Period of Thirty Eight Years Ending in 1855*, quoted in Ralph Pieris, "Society and Ideology," p. 81.
5. *Co* 54/235, April 21, 1847, pp. 17–18 and 47.
6. Ibid., p. 15; see also statement by Governor Maitland, quoted in Ralph Pieris, "Society and Ideology," p. 79.
7. Address by Robinson quoted in Ludovici, *Rice Cultivation* p. 1. See also Michael Roberts, "Indian Estate Labour in Ceylon during the Coffee Period, 1830–1880," (part 1), *The Indian Economic and Social History Review*, vol. 3, no. 1 (March 1966), p. 2.

Use of Compulsory Labor During the Mercantilist Period

Given the reluctance of Kandyan peasants to work on European plantations, one option the British could have taken was to force them to do so. Indeed, various forms of forced labor, ranging from slavery to debt bondage, were used to tie labor to plantations throughout the world. As we noted in Chapter III, in the early years of their rule in Ceylon, the British (as the Dutch had done earlier) used precolonial corvée labor for purposes of road construction, cinnamon collection, etc.

Under the precolonial kings, corvée labor was exacted primarily for the construction of irrigation works and items of conspicuous consumption such as lakes and religious edifices. As noted, under the British, forced labor came to be used primarily for mercantile and related activities. In justifying the use of compulsory labor for mercantile ends, an officer of the East India Company (which ruled the coastal lowlands until 1802), wrote, "from the habitual indolence of the Natives and the cheapness of the necessities of life upon Ceylon, there is no other effectual way of calling forth their labour."[8]

Observing the use of involuntary labor since the abolition of slavery in many parts of the world W. Kloosterboer has noted that employers or the state generally resort to the use of compulsory labor where there is both a labor shortage and an open resource situation, with respect to peasant land.[9] Both these conditions were present at the time the British annexed the Kandyan Highlands. These factors (and the lack of government funds to remunerate wage labor), rather than the alleged laziness of the natives, necessitated the use of compulsory labor by the colonial state during the mercantilist period.

Construction of roads was indispensable for commercial development and the consolidation of British political authority in the island. Corvée labor, therefore, came to be used primarily for road building and maintenance. In 1832, there were in the Kandyan Provinces 3,000 laborers compulsorily employed in the construction of public works, of which 1,000 were at work on the Kandy-Trincomalee road alone.[10]

There is evidence that the exaction of corvée labor by the British was unusually severe and that they often violated customary principles in doing so. The subversion of customary practices in exacting corvée labor provoked defiant resistance on the part of the Kandyan peasantry. A case in point was the refusal of the peasants of the Walapane district to come to Kandy for

8. Lord Hobart, Governor of Madras, quoted by Vijaya Samaraweera in "Economic and Social Developments," p. 61.
9. W. Kloosterboer, *Involuntary Labour Since the Abolition of Slavery* (Leiden: E. J. Brill, 1960), p. 205.
10. Colvin R. de Silva, *Ceylon Under the British*, vol. 2, p. 441.

'public work' (which under the British meant almost exclusively road construction), as it was contrary to precolonial norms to travel long distances for corvée duty.[11]

Compulsory road service was so abhorrent to the peasants that cases are reported where many people employed substitutes to perform their own quota of service at higher rates than those paid by the government (ordinarily, however, the government did not pay for forced labor).[12] Colonial tribute exaction was so severe in its effects on the peasants that some Kandyan chiefs were compelled to report to the Colebrooke Commission in 1832, "That the rents they pay in a year are as large as the contributions to the late pre-colonial Government in 10 years, besides the services they perform which are also heavier than those formerly enacted."[13]

However, Colebrooke saw that most chiefs who were responsible for the exaction of corvée labor from the peasants themselves abused their authority. For this reason, and perhaps more significantly because he perceived corvée labor to be economically wasteful or inefficient, Colebrooke decided to abolish it. He hoped that its abolition would release the voluntary or free wage labor force that would be more suited for capitalist agricultural development in the island.

The use of forced labor on the plantations was difficult due to both technical and political reasons. Coffee production requires constant care and attention, not always compatible with forced labor. Furthermore, the exaction of compulsory labor was, as noted, under the authority of the native aristocratic-administrative class. Any attempt to make plantation work compulsory on the peasantry would have called for a complete revamping of the precolonial land tenure and authority arrangements. Given the antipathy of the Kandyans towards road service, their general antagonism towards the British as expressed by the rebellion of 1818 and other minor rebellions around the same period, and the dependence of the British on the native chiefs for labor exaction, a transfer of customary forced labor onto the plantations was well-nigh impossible.

Conservation or Dissolution of the Peasantry?

Given that conditions contributing to the emergence of a voluntary wage labor force for the European plantations were absent in the village economy,

---

11. G. C. Mendis (ed.), *Colebrooke-Cameron Papers*, vol. 2, p. 190.
12. C. R. de Silva, *Ceylon Under the British*, vol. 2, p. 404.
13. Quoted in Mendis (ed.), *Colebrooke-Cameron Papers*, vol. 1, p. 106.

such conditions had to be created by administrative fiat. Van Zwanenberg has enumerated some of the factors that necessitated peasants' participation as wage laborers on the European plantations of colonial Kenya: 1) cash needs determined by the level of taxation and demand for imported goods; 2) comparative returns to effort from sale of cash crops, other commodities, and wage labor; 3) wages offered by the plantations.[14] To these must be added the availability of land for peasant cultivation as a determinant factor in their decision to work as laborers on the estates.

Although for purposes of discussion we need to separate colonial state policies towards the procurement of land from the procurement of labor for the plantations, in practice, they were inextricably linked. In addition to making land available for planters, the alienation of high lands (used by peasants for swidden cultivation and pasturage), was also motivated by the state's desire to reduce peasant economic independence and thereby induce them to work on the estates. In opposing the Waste Lands Ordinance No. 1 of 1897, Lord Stanmore, who had served earlier as a Governor of Ceylon (1883–1890), pointed out that

> There are two schools of thought ... one which holds that the maintenance of the village communities and smallholders is of vital importance to the wellbeing and independence of the native community, and another which desires to see all such lands in the hands of the Crown, to be sold by it for profit, and the villages converted into tenants at will working for wages. I strongly hold the first view. Most planters and many officials hold the latter and this ordinance will enable them to realize what seems to be desirable.[15]

In contrast to Stanmore, George Turnour, the first Revenue Commissioner of Kandy, held the dominant planter-official view (described above by Stanmore). Turnour also recommended the partition and sale of the minute and scattered paddy fields held by peasant cultivators as it could help release a labor supply for the plantations.

> To a limited extent voluntary laborers might be obtained at the rates at which private individuals engage them, but if landed property were rescued from the minutely subdivided condition into which it has fallen, the supply of voluntary labour would be greater.[16]

Provincial officers of the state were delighted to see signs of an emergent 'surplus' population in the planting regions. One such officer, an Assistant Government Agent of the Kegalle District, did not hide his preference for peasants working on the estates rather than cultivating cash crops in their own gardens.

14. Van Zwanenberg, *Colonial Capitalism*, p. 287.
15. *CO* 54/635, quoted in Jayawardena, "The Supply of Sinhalese Labour," pp. 16–17; see also *CO* 54/643, June 11, 1897.
16. Turnour's evidence before the Colebrooke Commission, *CO* 416/20, p. 90.

Plantations and the Creation of a Labor Force 179

> I hope that indirect good may be the result (of the diversion of traffic from the Kandy road to the railway which deprived the villagers of a market for the produce of their gardens) if men are induced to seek labour on the coffee plantations. The early age at which marriages are contracted tends to keep the people poor and to prevent the men leaving their homes, but want of food is the best cure for this evil and though a secure [sic] remedy it is the only one.[17]

While colonial taxation had as its aims the increase of state revenue and the extension of the cash nexus, it was also motivated by the desire to create a wage labor force out of the Sinhalese peasantry. The attempt to create a wage labor force for European agriculture through taxation was a common colonial practice.[18] The compulsory road tax introduced in 1848 is a good example. All males between the ages of 18 and 55 were made liable to pay this tax either by road service for six days per year or by commuting it to a cash payment of Rs. 1.50.[19] A week's labor on a coffee estate, it was anticipated, could yield this sum of money for the average peasant.[20] The colonial state sought to realize several of its major interests, that of construction of roads, absorption of the peasantry into the cash economy and creation of labor for estates through this tax. (The road tax is discussed in detail in Chapter VII.)

We have seen that the commutation of the paddy tax compelled the subsistence producing paddy cultivator, either to grow his own cash crops or work on plantations to obtain the money necessary to pay cash taxes to the state.[21] We have also noted that the collapse of 'peasant coffee' led to the expropriation of paddy fields of defaulting peasants. In hailing the 'beneficial' effects of such expropriation for creating an estate labor force, the Assistant Government Agent of the Badulla District, Aelian A. King, wrote in his Administration Report of 1883,

> It is probable that few sales will result in much change for the worse as regards the owners, while the good of the greater number will, there is [reason] to anticipate be advanced. A section of the community composed of pauper proprietors who are unable to cultivate their lands for want of energy and want of means and who instead of benefitting their neighbours are a positive burden to them, will be got rid of. If they behave like sensible people, they will thus become of much more use to them-

---

17. From the Administration Report of the AGA of the Kegalle District for 1870, quoted by Eric Meyer in "Between Village and Plantation: Sinhalese Estate Labour in British Ceylon" (uncorrected advance copy); *Colloques Internationaux du Centre National de la Recherche Scientifique* — Paris, No. 582 (1978), pp. 5–6. I am grateful to Eric Meyer for sending me a copy of this paper.
18. Van Zwanenberg, *Colonial Capitalism*, pp. 76–103.
19. *A Revised Edition of the Legislation Enactments of Ceylon*, vol. 1, p. 391; ibid., p. 411 for legislation on the commutation of the road tax.
20. Meyer, "Between Village and Plantation," p. 6.
21. Ameer Ali, "Peasant Coffee," pp. 57–58.

selves and to the community in their changed circumstance. There is plenty of work for them, if they choose to seek it.²²

King asserts that paddy cultivators remain poor because they are lazy ('for want of energy') and because they lack land ('want of means'). We noted earlier that the widespread paddy land sales in the Badulla District where King was stationed were a primary factor in the poverty and destitution of the peasants. We also noted that even if these expropriated cultivators wanted to work on the estates there was no work available for them given that coffee was rapidly collapsing at the time.

Echoing the view of many of their contemporaries in Ceylon, A. M. and J. Ferguson, the foremost journalists and record keepers of the Ceylonese plantation enterprise in the nineteenth century, stated that the only way to raise revenue in an 'oriental land' is to tax the one or two articles which are indispensable to the masses. They further justified their views with the claims that "the pinching of the stomach is morally good because it will induce the peasants to work on plantations."²³ These several examples show that British officials and planters were willing to let the peasants starve as long as they could find a regular and cheap labor force for the plantations.

The general policy of the colonial administration to create an estate labor force out of the Sinhalese peasantry during the early decades of plantation development far outweighed the interest shown by individual officials such as Stanmore (quoted on page 178) in later years to conserve the peasants on the land. It should be noted that even Stanmore expressed his opposition to the government's land policies, only upon retirement from the position of Governor of Ceylon.

Lal Jayawardena a student of British colonial rule in Ceylon, has argued, however, that the conservation of the peasantry was the motive force of colonial land policy and practice.²⁴ While it is true, as we observed in Chapter V, that sympathetic provincial officials such as Le Mesurier and Baumgartner expressed a desire to conserve the peasantry on the land, theirs was not the dominant official view. Jayawardena, for example, has given far greater weight to official *pronouncements* of good will towards the peasantry than to the actual implementation of colonial land and tax policies which (in conjunction with the new market and monetary relations intruding into the

---

22. *AR 1883*, Report on the Badulla District by Aelian King, AGA, p. 26A.
23. A. M. and J. Ferguson, *Taxation in Ceylon with Special Reference to the Grain Taxes: The Important Duty on Rice Balanced by a Local Excise Levy and the Proposal to Substitute a General Land Tax*, quoted in Obeysekere, *Land Tenure*, p. 113.
24. Jayawardena, "The Supply of Sinhalese Labour," Ch. 5, *passim*.

Plantations and the Creation of a Labor Force

village), in the long run contributed to the expropriation of peasant high lands and paddy fields.[25] However, in this study we have not denied that other classes of natives, headmen, and merchant capitalists, derived considerable advantage from colonial land and tax policies and their implementation.

The interest among some officials in conserving the peasantry, emerged largely following the 1848 rebellion when the colonial state became worried about peasant agitation. Since that rebellion, and particularly as state revenues began to increase during the coffee boom of the 1850s and 1860s some colonial governors such as Henry Ward (1855–1860) and William Gregory (1872–1877) became concerned with improving paddy agriculture and the welfare of the peasants.[26] Furthermore, by the middle of the nineteenth century, the employment of immigrant labor on European estates had become an established practice (see Tables 6:5 and 6:6). From then on, the concern of the planters and the officials began gradually to shift away from the earlier focus on creating a Sinhalese estate labor force to making the supply of labor from South India more reliable.

It is interesting to note that even those colonial administrators most committed to conserving the peasantry, were in fact even more concerned about the procurement of South Indian labor for the plantations. In supporting the planters' demand that the colonial state build a railway for the transportation of South Indian labor (a massive project and the first ever railway to be built in Ceylon), Governor Ward wrote in 1858, "We [planters and officials] must sink or swim together, and have no doubt that we shall *swim* with proper co-operation which shall not be wanting on my part" [emphasis in original].[27]

On the face of it, the efforts made by the British to create a Sinhalese labor force for the plantations and their avowed interest in conserving the peasantry – at least on the part of some officials – may seem antithetical. But on closer examination, one finds that these two interests were not necessarily so contradictory.

This apparent paradox, that is, to simultaneously create an estate labor force and conserve the peasantry, can best be understood in relation to the constant efforts made by planters everywhere to keep the costs of production

---

25. Ibid.
26. See S. V. Balasingham, *The Administration of Sri Henry Ward, Governor of Ceylon 1855–60* (Dehiwala: Tissara Prakasakayo, 1968), p. xiv and B. Bastiampillai, *The Administration of Sri William Gregory, Governor of Ceylon, 1872–77* (Dehiwala: Tissara Prakasakayo, 1968), p. viii.
27. CO 54/340, Private letter from Ward to [Lord Stanley?], 14 April 1858, quoted in Roberts, "Indian Estate Labour in Ceylon," p. 18. See also Ch. XI on Henry Ward in Hulugalle's *British Governors of Ceylon*, which reveals that the plantation enterprise was Ward's primary concern.

down to a minimum. In making attempts to lower their costs of production, planters and colonial administrators shifted the costs of reproducing the labor force of the European sectors (plantations and mines) to the native village economies. But such a shift was possible only if the village economies and the peasantries were conserved to some extent. In other words, the European colonizers wanted to maintain the estate labor force as a semipeasantry that could bear a part or most of the costs of its own reproduction through subsistence activities on village land. The interest of European capital then was not in wiping out the peasantry or the village economies in their entirety, but, rather, in changing and moulding the village economies to suit their own expansionary needs.

Thus the sugar planters and the colonial state in Guyana encouraged the emergence (since there was no pre-existing peasantry there) of a peasant sector that could bear a part of the costs of reproducing the plantation labor force.[28] Similarly in Kenya, attempts were made to develop peasant squatter settlements that would complement the needs of the European plantations.[29] In Southern Africa, migrant mine workers were allowed to retain ties to their home villages which bore a part of the costs of reproducing the migrant labor force and the totality of the subsistence needs of their wives and children. As Arrighi and others have argued, it was precisely because of the conservation of the peasant subsistence economy that the European sector could establish the tradition of paying a single wage over a family wage per worker.[30] The attempt to maintain wage workers of European plantations (and mines) as a semipeasantry on the land then, was/is a common colonial strategy. Claude Meillassoux points this out quite clearly when he says that,

> The agricultural self-sustaining communities because of their comprehensiveness and their raison d'être are able to fulfill functions that capitalism prefers not to assume in the underdeveloped countries: the functions of social security. The cheap cost of labour in these countries comes from the super-exploitation, not only of the labour from the wage-earner himself but also of the labour of his kin-group.[31]

Obviously, the shifting of the responsibilities of social security and labor reproduction to the subsistence sector has enormous implications for changes

---

28. Jay R. Mandle, *The Plantation Economy: Population and Economic Change in Guyana, 1838–1960* (Philadelphia: Temple University Press, 1973), pp. 34–36.
29. Van Zwanenberg, *Colonial Capitalism*, p. 215.
30. G. Arrighi, "Labour Supplies in Historical Perspective: A Study of the Proletarianization of the African Peasantry in Rhodesia," *The Journal of Development Studies*, vol. 6, no. 3, 1970, p. 200. See also Harold Wolpe, "Capitalism and Cheap Labour-Power in South Africa: From Segregation to Apartheid," in *The Articulation of Modes of Production*, ed. by Harold Wolpe (London: Routledge and Kegan Paul, 1980).
31. Claude Meillassoux, "A Marxist Approach to Economic Anthropology," in *The Articulation of Modes of Production*, ed. by Wolpe, pp. 197–98.

Plantations and the Creation of a Labor Force

in the precolonial sexual division of labor and the position of women — a subject we cannot investigate here. However, it is important to stress that the impetus for the evolution of a semiproletarian/semipeasant class in the colonies cannot simply be attributed to the profit maximizing behavior of the European capitalists alone. The emergence of a new shifting or migrant class was in part a peasant response to the demands made by the new colonial political economy. Many peasants were forced to work for wages in order to pay taxes to the colonial state or satisfy some of their newly-acquired consumer tastes. They did not, however, want to give up the emotional ties to family and community and the attachment to their ancestral land. The decision to straddle two sectors of the newly-evolving colonial economy was not simply a European imposition on nonwestern cultivators; it was partly the peasantry's own rational response to changing socioeconomic realities.

Returning now to the situation in nineteenth-century Ceylon, it seems that at least a few officials of the colonial administration envisioned the creation of a semiproletarian/ semipeasant class among the Sinhalese cultivators. Lal Jayawardena shows that this possibility was entertained by some members of the colonial administration, particularly the provincial officials.

> This . . . illustrates the basic dichotomy of British policy towards the native population. On the one hand, as exemplified by the attitude of the Government Agents, they wanted the native to remain a peasant. This meant seeing that he had enough land to maintain himself in the manner in which he was accustomed — as Davidson put it — "equal strangers to opulence and poverty." On the other hand, they wanted him to improve his lot to shake himself out of his lethargy; this meant placing the European in his vicinity. He could work voluntarily on the Estate if he chose or learn habits of thrift and enterprise by imitation and wean himself away from wasteful chena cultivation on to a more profitable crop. On this view, paternal interference with the free purchase and sale of private land would only hamper enterprise. The compromise solution for which they were groping was one where the European was near enough to the native to influence him, but not so near as to dispossess him.[32]

It is crucial to note that although planters and officials constantly complained about the difficulty of obtaining Kandyan labor for the estates, they did not express a wish to create a residential labor force out of the Sinhalese peasantry. As noted earlier, labor needs on the coffee estates were seasonal, the greatest demand being during harvest time. A Kandyan semiproletariat who would meet the fluctuating labor needs of the coffee estates, but who nevertheless did not require dwellings, medical care and food from the planters, would have ideally suited the planter's profit maximizing needs.

---

32. Jayawardena, "The Supply of Sinhalese Labour," p. 145.

The colonial state took many steps to satisfy the labor needs of the planters. Taxation of the peasantry, as noted earlier, was one such move. Given the seasonal increase in the labor requirements of coffee cultivation, the colonial state in places such as Kenya synchronized colonial tax collection with the harvest season in coffee thereby compelling natives to work on the estates during the harvest time to earn enough money to pay their taxes.[33] We do not have information on the scheduling of cash tax collection in colonial Ceylon to be able to say if a similar collusion occurred between the planters and the administration in colonial Ceylon. But we do have evidence which shows that the confluence of state policies (including taxation) and the extension of the market economy managed to create new cash needs in the Sinhalese peasantry.

Cash Needs of the Sinhalese Peasantry

Peasants needed cash to pay their taxes to the colonial state such as the paddy and road taxes, and to purchase a few imported items such as English textiles, kerosene oil, and match boxes which came to be widely used in the villages during the nineteenth century.

Prior to the colonial period, Kandyan villagers obtained cloth from the weaver caste within the village or from itinerant peddlars (often Muslims) in exchange for agricultural produce. But as Ameer Ali notes, "With the increasing import of cheap cotton textiles from Manchester, the native weaving and spinning industries had almost entirely ceased to exist."[34] This can be seen in the decline of handlooms in the island from 3,972 in 1850 to 1,222 in 1890.[35] Governor Gordon (1883–1890) wrote in one of his private Despatches to the Colonial Office in London,

> Whatever we have succeeded or failed in doing in the East we have at least accomplished one thing thoroughly — the extinction of native taste and native art and to a great — a very great — extent, native manufacture. It is cheaper to import hideous woolen shawls of black and red checked "MacGregor tartan," than to manufacture native clothes and muslins. Consequently, the common people, now wrap themselves up in these ... "plaid" shawls instead of the national "comboy."[36]

33. Van Zwanenberg, "Colonial Capitalism," p. 88. Many other strategies were adopted in Kenya to induce peasants to work on European plantations. One such was the payment of peasants' taxes to the state directly by the planters themselves. Ibid., p. 91.
34. Ameer Ali, "Changing Conditions," pp. 14–15.
35. Ibid., p. 15.
36. Governor Gordon, quoted ibid., p. 15.

Plantations and the Creation of a Labor Force

Along with imported textiles, the use of imported kerosene oil also spread rapidly among village households during the nineteenth century. "Between 1883 and 1887 kerosene oil was imported to an annual average value of nearly Rs.274,00 which increased to nearly Rs.566,000 between 1888 and 1892."[37] Kerosene became a popular substitute for coconut oil which had traditionally been the chief source of fuel. Along with kerosene, came the use of imported matches.

Table 6:1

Value of Imported Cotton Goods in Ceylon, 1839–1893
(Mostly from England)

Period	Annual Averages
1839–1843	£ 161,064
1844–1848	195,582
1849–1853	202,411
1854–1858	337,138
1859–1863	606,978
1864–1868	787,440
1869–1873	850,247
1874–1878	757,042
1879–1883	544,636
1884–1888	472,805
1889–1893	532,570

Source: A. C. L. Ameer Ali, "Changing Conditions and Persisting Problems in the Peasant Sector under British Rule in the Period 1833–1893," *Ceylon Studies Seminar*, 1970/72 Series, no. 3a, p. 15.

How Peasants Met Their Cash Needs

'Peasant coffee' was the primary source of monetizing the Kandyan village economy. It helped peasants pay their cash taxes to the state and buy the few imported articles of consumption noted above.[38] Governor Ward observed the importance of their coffee gardens when he said,

---

37. Ibid., p. 16: see also Roberts, "Aspects of Ceylon's Agrarian Economy," p. 148.
38. Ameer Ali, "Peasant Coffee," pp. 57–58; see also D. Wesumperuma, "The Migration and Conditions of Immigrant Labour in Ceylon, 1880–1910," unpublished Ph.D. dissertation, University of London, 1974.

Many peasants have small coffee gardens which they cultivate with their wives and children and the amount received for what is termed "native coffee" varies from £250,000 to £300,000. It is with this money as I believe that the improvements in native houses, dress and habits of living originated.[39]

What is interesting to note is that the newly acquired cash needs encouraged the Kandyan peasants primarily to take up smallholder cash cropping rather than hiring themselves out as wage labor on the European coffee estates or producing paddy for the market. To the extent that smallholder cash crop production — especially coffee — took away peasant labor from the plantations, it posed a competitive threat to the dominant plantation mode of production. Furthermore, the cultivation of their own cash crops (which was something that was not allowed the peasants in some other European colonies) gave the Kandyan peasantry a sense of economic as well as cultural autonomy. To quote Governor Ward once again,

With regard to the native population, although the improvement in their means and habits is marked and has had no small influence upon the increase of the Revenue, *it is impossible to rely upon them for any supply of organized labour* out of their usual routine. They will work by contract in clearing jungle; the whole of the paddy and coconut cultivation of the Island is in their hands; they convey the entire coffee crop from the Estate to the port of shipment; *but they will not work for hire upon the Estates themselves* Many have small coffee gardens . . . .
And though Oriental felling and customs still remain in their sway, there is a curious dash of European feeling, a consciousness of legal rights . . . . [emphasis added][40]

It should be remembered, however, that the 'autonomy' derived from peasant cash cropping was a rather precarious one. We saw, for example, that when peasant coffee collapsed and the cultivators were no longer able to pay their cash taxes and personal debts, the colonial state and moneylenders, expropriated their paddy fields. It should also be noted that not all of the lands designated as native coffee smallholdings belonged to the peasantry. Although the small coffee gardens surrounding their homes belonged to the peasants, a substantial amount, roughly over a third of the larger smallholdings (ten acres or over) were owned by non-European entrepreneurial groups such as Chettiyars and "Kanganies" (Indian labor supervisors on the European coffee plantations).[41] It is not clear on what basis these groups cultivated their coffee smallholdings — wage labor, sharecropping, or leasing. Given the difficulty of obtaining wage labor from the Kandyan peasants, it can be hypothesized that they resorted to renting and other non-wage forms of labor exaction.

39. Ward's Despatch quoted in *The Colombo Observer*, November 26, 1866.
40. Ward's Despatch to the Secretary of State for the Colonies cited in *The Colombo Observer*, November 26, 1866; see also *BPP*, Vol. 42, 1847–1848, p. 49.
41. Roberts, "Some Comments," pp. 24–15, (n. 3).

Plantations and the Creation of a Labor Force

To turn once again to Governor Ward's remarks quoted above, we observe that in addition to peasant coffee cultivation, the local peasantry did perform some of the more specialized and skilled tasks associated with plantation development such as jungle clearing and the transportation of supplies to and from the estates. In addition, they were employed in the construction of buildings as masons and carpenters.[42] As Governor Ward observed, it was regular and routine labor on the coffee estates that the Sinhalese peasants refused to perform.[43]

Sinhalese Labor on the Coffee Estates

Both Michael Roberts and Eric Meyer have pointed out that those writers who have applied the 'dual economy' thesis to Ceylon (that the Ceylon economy consists of two entirely separate plantation and village sectors) tend to underestimate the role of Sinhalese labor in Ceylon's plantation economy.[44] While this stems partly from the assumptions of the dual economy theorists, it is also confounded by the difficulties of numerically estimating the Sinhalese labor force on the coffee estates, which was largely shifting or nonresidential. The observations made by the Census enumerators in 1891 point out that although the Sinhalese peasantry did not become a permanent or residential labor force (a development that planters did not necessarily require for reasons discussed earlier) a significant number of them became a shifting proletariat.

> It must however be noted that the number of Sinhalese enumerated is not a safe guide to the number of Sinhalese labourers employed on an estate. Sinhalese do not readily go into "lines" and the Sinhalese labour for the most part comes from the neighbouring villages. At the Census time too, large numbers of the Sinhalese returned to their homes to be set down on the village schedules.[45]

It is interesting to note that a large percentage of the resident Sinhalese laborers on the coffee plantations came from the low-country coastal areas rather than the neighboring Kandyan villages. Obviously, the low-country Sinhalese could not commute between village and estate as the Kandyans probably did in larger numbers. Some of the low-country Sinhalese who came

---

42. Van Den Driesen, "Some Aspects of the History," p. 117. Michael Roberts, "Elite Formation and Elites," pp. 280–82.
43. Ward's Despatch in *The Colombo Observer*, November 26, 1866.
44. Roberts, "Aspects of Ceylon's Agrarian Economy," p. 163 and Meyer, "Between Village and Plantation," p. 1; for discussion of dual economy theory and its application to Ceylon see Chapters 9 and 1 in this book.
45. Ceylon Government, *Census of Ceylon,* 1891, p. 42.

to work on the plantations were absconders trying to avoid payment of the road tax (from which the plantation laborers were exempt) and other escapees from the law.[46]

It is generally believed that the majority of the Sinhalese who sought estate work were members of the low-country artisan castes.[47] Given the specialized and skilled nature of the work performed by most Sinhalese for the plantations, this hypothesis seems highly plausible. We know, for instance, that an artisan caste from the southwestern coastal town of Moratuva (*Moratuva karawas*) held a monopoly of the carpentry jobs associated with estate development. Michael Roberts has pointed out that the special skills of the *karavas* helped them amass wealth to join the newly emergent local capitalist class in unusually large numbers.

> The extraordinary degree to which *karavas* from Moratuva figure among the national elite provides other clues to the success of the *karavas*. Since a large number of the Moratuva *karavas* were carpenters and cartwrights at the beginning of the nineteenth century, it can be argued that their artisan background had given them the motivations and abilities needed to seize the economic opportunities of subsequent decades ... their advance could also be explained in terms of the vantage points they secured for themselves by being the first low country Sinhalese to take up the entrepreneurial opportunities in the central highlands associated with the coffee trade, coffee culture, and the servicing of plantations.[48]

In addition to the *karavas*, two other low-country Sinhalese castes that were among the first to seize the new economic opportunities which opened up with plantation development were the *durāvas* and the *salagamas*.[49] All three of these castes, i.e., the *karavas*, *durāvas*, and the *salagamas* migrated from South India to the southwestern coastal areas of Ceylon at various times between the thirteenth and eighteenth centuries. As Roberts has argued, their comparatively late inclusion within the Sinhalese social structure perhaps made them "less bound to paddy cultivation and more familiar with market devices, less hidebound by tradition, more mobile, and more flexible in their attitudes."[50] Their functional position within the precolonial economy as artisans, and the status accorded to them as newly-arrived low castes then, helped them adapt more readily to the new economic opportunities that opened up with plantation development. Having made their money through

---

46. Meyer, "Between Village and Plantation," p. 4; see also *AR 1888*, Report for the Nuwara Eliya District, p. 78A.
47. Ludovici, *Rice Cultivation*, p. 124; Van Den Driesen, "Some Aspects of the History," p. 177.
48. Roberts, "Elite Formation and Elites," pp. 281–82.
49. Ibid., p. 280. Duravas are the caste of 'toddy tappers'. See Appendix II.
50. Ibid., pp. 280–81.

Plantations and the Creation of a Labor Force

such occupations as carpentry, transport, and arrack (liquor) renting, they went on to invest this wealth in coconut estates and western education. In this manner they became a dominant group within the native capitalist class.[51]

Transition to Tea and the Increase of Sinhalese Estate Labor

In the period of tea plantation expansion since the mid-1880s, there was an increase of resident Sinhalese labor on the plantations. The year round and greater care needed by tea as compared to coffee and the larger economies of scale in tea production, restricted the peasantry's ability to cultivate tea. Furthermore, with population increase, dwindling swidden and forest lands, changing property relations and greater cash needs, the dependence of the Sinhalese peasantry on estate labor for their livelihood began also to increase. It seems that estate labor began to replace both shifting cultivation and peasant coffee as the most important supplementary occupation of the paddy cultivators during the tea period. The Government Agent of the Uva Province wrote in 1887,

> The tea enterprise is now giving wages to a large number of Sinhalese who are yearly manifesting a much greater readiness than formerly to work for hire. This is a hopeful sign, partly the result of lessons of adversity and partly the effect of the operation of the new Road Ordinance which is familiarising them with manual labour other than paddy field work and depriving it in their eyes of its degrading character.[52]

It is clear from the Table 6:2 that Sinhalese wage labor on the estates increased significantly between 1881 and 1891, i.e., with the shift to tea. This is also substantiated by the figures compiled by Eric Meyer. While the residential Sinhalese labor force on the estates indicated by Meyer's figures (in Table 6:3) rose only slowly, the nonresidential Sinhalese labor force increased dramatically during the twentieth century. Even today, the Sinhalese working on the estates are largely a semiproletarian group. Meyer notes, "From 1931 to 1946 the Tamil population on estates decreased by 3.9 %, whereas the low-country Sinhalese increased by 53 % and the Kandyans by 109.7 %."[53]

---

51. For the biography of one such *karava* entrepreneur, Jeronis Pieris, see Roberts, *Facets of Modern Ceylon History*.
52. *AR 1887*, Report of the GA for the Uva Province; see also Meyer, "Between Village and Plantation," p. 9.
53. Ibid., p. 1.

Table 6:2

Percentages of Sinhalese and Tamils in the Estate Population*

	1871		1881		1891	
	Male	Female	Male	Female	Male	Female
Sinhalese (low country and Kandyan)	4.87	1	4.07	1.54	8.46	5.76
Tamil (Ceylon and Indian)	91.5	96	92.98	96.12	88.36	91.51

*Percentages of other ethnic groups in the estate population such as the Europeans, are not available.

Source: Ceylon Government, *Census of Ceylon*, 1891, p. 41.

Table 6:3

Sinhalese Population Resident on Estates*
(% of Total Estate Population)

1871	3.3%
1881	3.0%
1891	7.2%

*Includes all estates

Source: Eric Meyer, "Between Village and Plantation: Sinhalese Estate Labour in British Ceylon," Colloques Internationaux du Centre National de la Recherche Scientifique, Paris, no. 582, 1978, p. 1.

Statistically speaking, the assertion made by Lal Jayawardena and Donald Snodgrass that the "Sinhalese never became a plantation proletariat" is true.[54] But as Eric Meyer says, such a statement needs to be qualified.

> Finally if one means by "proletariat" a class of workers which has no access to the land and is left with its sole labour force, it can be said that the Sinhalese estate proletariat never became a large category during British times. But if we take into account the non-resident labour force, which kept some ties with village lands though inadequate for its subsistence, we may assuredly say that there was a large unstable class always shifting between village and plantation, whose function in the economy of the village and in that of the plantation must have been important if not essential.[55]

54. Jayawardena, "The Supply of Sinhalese Labour," quoted in Meyer, "Between Village and Plantation," p. 1; Snodgrass, *Ceylon,* p. 59.
55. Meyer, "Between Village and Plantation," p. 5.

Inadequacies of Sinhalese Labor Supply

It is clear that a significant number of Sinhalese, particularly low-country Sinhalese, became a semiproletariat on the estates providing largely the more skilled and specialized services needed for plantation development. However, the large numbers needed for regular and routine labor, particularly during coffee harvests, were not forthcoming. The essentially shifting and supplementary character of Sinhalese labor made both planters and officials anxious about the viability of the plantation enterprise. Emerson Tennent said of Kandyan peasants in 1848 that "the cultivation of their own rice land renders their services uncertain and always irregular and unsatisfactory;"[56] and P. E. Wodehouse (a planter and one-time Assistant Colonial Secretary) stated that "you cannot very often depend upon the native labor; they will at certain seasons go to work upon their rice fields, whatever you may offer them."[57]

The availability of Sinhalese peasant labor for the estates depended on the timing of labor needs between plantation and peasant agriculture. The coffee berries on the estates ripended at the same time as those on the peasant home gardens. Peasants got busy with the picking and selling of their own coffee. Besides, they had to tend to their rice fields and chena plots. How could they have been on the plantations at the same time?

At the beginning of the twentieth century, the unreliability of Sinhalese labor had not changed although Sinhalese were then working in larger numbers on tea estates. Their participation increased because tea was not as conducive to smallholder production as coffee. But as colonial officials noted, ". . . the only unsatisfactory point about them is that they are somewhat unreliable. If a shower of rain comes down, they will clear off in half an hour. And they require a good deal of humoring."[58]

The unreliability of Sinhalese peasant labor, however, was not a labor problem peculiar to the British planters of colonial Ceylon. Kloosterboer points out that in Indonesia, the Dutch were not up against a shortage of laborers as much as against the difficulties of irregular labor. The Indonesians worked for the Dutch only when it was absolutely necessary to do so to meet their immediate cash requirements.[59] Similarly, Van Zwanenberg shows that in colonial Kenya, peasants preferred to work on European estates for short periods rather than on a permanent basis.[60]

56. *CO 54/235*, April 21, 1847, pp. 16–17.
57. *BPP 1850*, Vol. 12, p. 138.
58. *Reports of the Proceedings of the Labour Commission (1908)*, quoted by Meyer, "Between Village and Plantation," p. 8.
59. Kloosterboer, *Involuntary Labour*, p. 44.
60. Van Zwanenberg, *Colonial Capitalism*, p. 73.

In explaining the causes for the unreliability of Sinhalese labor, Emerson Tennent said that want of good faith on the part of the planters as employers, their breach of labor contracts, nonpayment of wages on time, and unkindness in their general treatment of laborers contributed to the reluctance of the Sinhalese to work regularly on the estates.[61] But the planters characteristically attributed the reluctance of Sinhalese to work on European estates solely to their traditional values.

> The (Kandyan) has such a reverence for his patrimonial lands, that were his gain to be quadrupled, he would not abandon their culture.... Besides working for hire is repulsive to their national feelings, and is looked upon as almost slavery. The being obliged to obey orders, and to do just what they are commanded is galling to them.[62]

But as Michael Roberts has pointed out, the harsh treatment meted out to laborers by the planters and the low wages offered served to further local aversion to routine labor on the estates.[63] In addition to its unreliability, the planters found Kandyan labor to be costly. Given the availability of alternative sources of cash, the Kandyans would work only for the going market price for labor. Furthermore, the Sinhalese who worked on the estates had to be paid higher wages than the imported South Indian laborers. For example, in 1908 the plantation wage rate for Sinhalese ranged between 33 and 75 cents per day, whereas the Tamil wage rate (for men) ranged only between 33 and 37 cents.[64] We can surmise that during the earlier coffee period when Sinhalese labor was even more scarce, there was a similar if not a greater disparity between Sinhalese and Tamil wage rates. But it is not clear whether the few Sinhalese who performed the same field work as the imported laborers were also paid higher wages than their foreign counterparts.

Given the specificity of Sinhalese labor, there emerged a functional division of estate labor between the Sinhalese and the imported South Indian Tamils. The Sinhalese, especially the low-country artisan castes, monopolized the higher-paid skilled jobs, such as jungle clearing, masonry, carpentry, and transport services, while the South Indians were relegated to the menial, low-paid routine work as field hands. Emerson Tennent pointed out in 1848 that £5 was the average monthly wage of carpenters, masons, and mechanics, while the average monthly wage for laborers was only £1 per month.[65] It is important to recognize that the objection of the Sinhalese was not towards

---

61. *CO 54/235*, April 21, 1847, p. 6.
62. C. R. Rigg, "Coffee Planting in Ceylon," quoted by K. M. de Silva, *Social Policy and Missionary Organizations in Ceylon, 1840–1855* (London: Longmans, 1965), p. 236.
63. Roberts, "Indian Estate Labour on the Estates," (part 1), p. 1.
64. Meyer, "Between Village and Plantation," p. 8; see also K. Thiagaraja, "Indian Coolies in Ceylon Estates," *The Indian Review*, March 1917, p. 182.
65. *BPP 1847–1848*, Vol. 42, Tennent's Report.

Plantations and the Creation of a Labor Force   193

manual labor *per se*, as the planters claimed it was, but towards hiring themselves out regularly as field hands and towards living on the estates.[66] The status differences between the Sinhalese peasantry and the Indian Tamils were associated with the ethnically defined tasks they each performed within the hierarchically structured colonial economy. More will be said of this in Chapter VIII.

Although most planters and state officials dismissed Kandyan peasants as indolent and backward, the more astute among the British noted the consciousness of customary and legal rights and underlying antipathy on the part of the Kandyans towards colonial authority. The British were generally suspicious of the Kandyans. Jonathan Forbes, a British official and a long-term resident in Kandy, said of the Kandyan peasantry, "... though they are credulous, and are generally very intelligent and particularly well acquainted with any duties which they may be called on to perform or any privileges that they were entitled to..."[67]

An early British planter, exasperated by the independence enjoyed by the Kandyan peasants, complained in a letter home in 1848,

> You would really be surprised to know the extraordinary state of independence in which these people live. I can assure you it is my conviction that almost two thirds of the population snap their fingers at the English (so little dependent are they upon them).[68]

The Relative Failure to Create a Sinhalese Labor Supply

The formal abolition of compulsory labor in royal villages in 1833 and the subsequent land and taxation policies of the colonial state did not release the anticipated wage labor force for the coffee plantations. The efforts of the colonial state, such as its tax policies, in conjunction with the general dynamic of the market economy did turn a significant number of Sinhalese peasants into a shifting and casual labor force for the European coffee estates. But this semiproletariat was insufficient in number, too expensive and highly unreliable from the planters' point of view. The primary commitment of these shifting Sinhalese laborers was to their paddy fields and coffee gardens. Moreover, they preferred to do the skilled and specialized services needed on the estates rather than the routine work which increased tenfold during harvest time.

The reason for the relative failure of the British to create a regular estate labor force out of the Sinhalese peasantry cannot be attributed to the alleged

---

66. Colvin R. de Silva, *Ceylon Under the British*, vol. 2, p. 405.
67. *BPP 1850*, Vol. 12, p. 273.
68. *Extracts of Letters from Ceylon (1848)*, quoted in Ralph Pieris, "Society and Ideology," p. 81.

peasant-oriented policies of the colonial state.[69] As we demonstrated in Chapter V, the colonial state in fact alienated more land that the peasantry had held on customary tenure than it resold to them in freehold. Although some peasants lost complete access to land during the coffee period, most experienced the process of dispossession only gradually. Many peasants were able to retain access to some land, especially through encroachments on high lands. Village headmen and outsider merchant capitalists who gained private property rights to peasant paddy plots retained the hereditary tenants on the land as sharecropping tenants rather than driving them out. As discussed earlier, although the cultivators' tenurial relationship to the land was significantly altered within the new politico-juridical framework introduced by the British, a physical separation of cultivators akin to the results of the Enclosure Movement in England did not take place. Some of the traditional land sharing arrangements, such as the system of rotation of paddy fields among co-owners, also helped retain a potentially surplus population in the village.[70]

The argument put forward by S. B. D. de Silva to explain the nonemergence of a surplus population in the Sinhalese village economy needs also to be mentioned here. De Silva claims that the peculiar nature of labor use in paddy agriculture, particularly the resilience of its backward methods of production in absorbing increasing numbers of people (albeit at decreasing levels of labor productivity) precluded the release of a surplus population that could be employed on the plantations.[71] This argument, however, is not wholly consistent with the fact that during the twentieth century when the land to man ratio declined with rapid population increase, Sinhalese peasants became a semiproletariat on the tea and rubber estates in much larger numbers than they did during the coffee era.[72] In many ways, de Silva's explanation is similiar to the 'agricultural involution' thesis advanced by Clifford Geertz in relation to Java. Geertz has argued that the Javanese village economy was able to maintain a rising population on a dwindling land supply by stretching out or 'involuting' the traditional methods of production at decreased standards of living.[73]

The confluence of these several factors prevented the emergence of a large-scale estate proletariat among the Sinhalese peasantry by the end of the nineteenth century. Given the efforts of the colonial state to create a regular

69. Jayawardena, "The Supply of Sinhalese Labour," Ch. 5, *passim*.
70. For a good discussion of two systems of land sharing known as *tattumaru* and *karamaru*, see Obeysekere, *Land Tenure in Village Ceylon*, pp. 18–36.
71. S. B. D. de Silva, "Investment and Economic Growth," Ch. 21, *passim*.
72. In a recent study, a number of writers have argued that many Sri Lankan villages are no longer paddy-centric. Most of the population make their livelihood through other agricultural and nonagricultural pursuits. Morrison, et al., *The Disintegrating Village*.
73. Clifford Geertz, *Agricultural Involution: The Process of Ecological Change in Indonesia* (Berkeley: University of California Press, 1963), p. 80.

estate labor force out of the peasantry, this then was a defeat for both the colonial state and the planters. But the major reason why the state did not exert greater coercion towards this end (as colonial states did in many other parts of the world) was that a comparatively larger, cheaper, more reliable, and docile migrant labor force was available from South India.

The Migratory Labor Force from South India

The unreliability, costliness and alleged rebelliousness of Sinhalese labor were constantly contrasted with the merits of South Indian labor by the British planters of Ceylon. On the relative merits of the two groups as estate labor, one planter had the following words to say;

> As to the comparative merits of the two races as labourers, the low-country Sinhalese certainly (*pace* the Colonial Secretary) make useful and energetic carpenters, sawyers, felling contractors and handymen; but for carrying on the regular routine of a coffee estate and for giving the least possible trouble (except in "re" coast advances) I do not believe a race could be *invented*, more suited to our wants than the docile and intelligent Tamils. [emphasis in the original] [74]

The 'docility' of immigrant labor was not an inherent trait of Tamil character as the Ceylon planters easily concluded. Rather it was/is a structural feature of migratory labor and a global phenomenon in capitalist development. Gunnar Myrdal's generalization on the advantages of a foreign labor force for plantations is highly applicable to the Ceylonese case. "Foreign laborers isolated in unfamiliar surroundings were more docile, more easily organized for effective work and were permanently attached."[75] The advantages of cheap, nonunionized foreign labor were not limited to the European plantations and mines in the nineteenth century. One observes them in the farms and factories of contemporary advanced capitalist societies as well.

Writing on the 'labour problem' in the tropical colonies in 1899, W. Alleyane Ireland theorized that commercial development of these colonies was possible only if there was either an extraordinary density of population or a pool of imported contract labor.[76] It was the latter that made plantation development possible in nineteenth-century Ceylon.

---

74. "Correspondence," in *The Colombo Observer*, November 16, 1866.
75. Gunnar Myrdal, *Asian Drama*, quoted in J. E. Goldthorpe, *The Sociology of the Third World: Disparity and Involvement* (New York: Cambridge University Press, 1975), p. 74.
76. W. Alleyane Ireland, "The Labour Problem in the Tropics," (New York: 1899), p. 3.

There existed in the southern districts of India at the time coffee plantations were being opened up and developed in Ceylon, a class of agricultural laborers, by and large propertyless and easily exploitable. These unskilled laborers existed in sizable proportions even before the British occupation of that country. Work opportunities available to them were mostly in agriculture and menial services, but scarce and utterly ill-rewarding. Labor of this category belonged to castes such as *Palli, Pallan, Paraiyan* and *Cheruman*, rated as low in the Indian caste system. They consisted of about ten to fifteen percent of the South Indian population at the beginning of the nineteenth century.[77] During the nineteenth century, this class of agricultural laborers increased in absolute numbers, and in proportion to the total agricultural population. This was due to a number of factors including natural population growth; disintegration of village handicrafts (particularly weaving, because of cheap British imports); new property relations that came in the wake of monetization and commercialization; retrogression of peasant agriculture; and, lack of alternative opportunities for work.[78]

In terms of relative access to land these South Indian agricultural laborers were much worse off than their kandyan contemporaries in Ceylon. In fact, landless agricultural labor was absent in the precolonial Kandyan kingdom. As noted earlier, labor not land was the scarce factor of production in precolonial Kandy. In contrast, the agricultural labor castes of South India were compelled to work regularly for hire to make ends meet. During the course of the nineteenth century, they began to leave their villages in search of work wherever work was available, especially in the European-owned plantations of the West Indies, Mauritius, Malaya, and neighboring Ceylon.

Following the emancipation of slaves in the West Indies, South Indians (and also Bengalis), and Chinese were recruited as indentured labor for plantations all over the colonies.[79] Arthur Lewis has pointed out that about fifty million people left India and China mainly to work as indentured laborers in tropical plantations mines, communications, and construction projects during the second half of the nineteenth century. According to Lewis, the very low wages paid – roughly a shilling a day – barely sufficient to maintain

---

77. D. Wesumperuma, "The Migration," *passim*.
78. Ibid., pp. 28–31. See also Dharma Kumar, *Land and Caste in South India: Agricultural Labor in the Madras Presidency during the Nineteenth Century* (Cambridge: Cambridge University Press, 1965), pp. 63, 139.
79. Barbara Bradby points out that the nineteenth-century sugar and cotton plantations in Peru drew imported labor from China because of the "relatively advanced state of destruction of natural economy in China compared with Peru at that time," Barbara Bradby, "The Destruction of Natural Economy," in *The Articulation of Modes of Production*, ed. by Wolpe, p. 117.
80. Lewis, *The Evolution*, pp. 14–15.

Plantations and the Creation of a Labor Force 197

these workers, set the price of tropical commodities very low in the world market.[80] In addition, Gail Omvedt notes,

> In contrast to the Europeans, Indian low caste laborers not only suffered long hours on ship journeys, toiled in disease-ridden conditions to provide sugar, coffee, tea and raw materials for the industries of Europe, and built up the major export industries of several countries — they also ended up having only a precarious basis as a low-status and distrusted minority in the societies they entered, and sometimes with no citizenship at all.[81]

In her important article on labor migration in colonial India, Gail Omvedt questions the popularly held view that the South Indian laborers who migrated to plantations abroad constituted a class of 'free' laborers or a true proletariat. She points out that these laborers were not 'free' in the Marxist sense, in that they still had some claims to land and the obligations to landlords that went with those claims. They were not always free to sell their labor to any employer they chose, either.[82] In other words, as Omvedt argues, they were only semiproletarianized, being still tied to feudal social relations.

> Far from being an indication of labour mobility, of "proletarianized" peasants "dispossessed" from the land, they reveal the opposite, the relative immobility of peasant society, in which labour migrants retain their ties and claims to the land keeping their families on the land and returning to it, and in which their lowest strata — the adivasis and Adi Dravidas — were clearly tied to the landlords as well through debt-bondage......
>
> Many of those classed as agricultural laborers had claims to small plots of land too small to support them; still others were unrecognized tenants working for moneylender landlords on land that had once been theirs and to which they still had a customary claim....[83]

While it is unlikely that the South Indian laborers who migrated to plantations as far away as the West Indies were able to retain ties to their land and landlords in the South Indian villages, those who migrated to neighboring Ceylon (and perhaps Mauritius and Malaya) certainly did so, at least during the nineteenth century.

South Indian Labor Migration to Ceylon

Almost the whole bulk of the Indian emigrant labor force in Ceylon was drawn from a few Tamil districts of Southern India, such as Ramnad, Madras, Malabar, and Tanjore.[84] The following figures, which give the sources of labor

81. Gail Omvedt, "Migration in Colonial India: The Articulation of Feudalism and Capitalism by the Colonial State," *The Journal of Peasant Studies*, vol. 6, no. 2 (1980), p. 189.
82. Ibid., p. 202.
83. Ibid., pp. 200 and 202.
84. Ibid., p. 199; see also Kumar, *Land and Caste*, p. 138.

emigration for the period 1921–1935, are not without direct relevance to the character and style of emigrant labor procurement in the nineteenth century since, even then, the sources of labor for the coffee estates of Ceylon were the same. The chief characteristics of these South Indian districts, as pointed out in Table 6:4, were their poor agricultural conditions, absence of alternative occupations, and surplus agricultural population.

Table 6:4

Sources of Immigration into Ceylon from South India

Districts	General Character of Rural Economy	Plantation Laborers	Free Laborers
		Average Annual No. of Immigrants (1921–1935)	
Tinnevelly	Poor agricultural conditions and no subsidiary occupation	2,267	42,898
Ramnad	Same as Tinnevelly	6,092	15,618
Trichinopoly and districts around it	Landlordism, defective land tenure, rice cultivation, no subsidiary occupation	73,052	17,375
Arcot, Madras, Chingleput, etc.	Better land tenure, development of small-scale industries	11,331	5,035
Travancore, Cochin, Malabar		545	15,984

Source: N. V. Sovani, *Economic Relations of India with South-East Asia and the Far East* (Bombay: Oxford University Press, 1949), p. 139.

The definition of 'free labor' used in the above table is not quite clear. It is plausible that the 'free laborers' listed in this table refer to those South Indians who came to Ceylon on their own rather than through formal recruitment as plantation labor. These unrecruited migrants came either to trade or to take up sundry wage labor jobs available in government construction projects, such as the Colombo harbor.

Whatever the traditional patterns of labor mobility from India to Ceylon were, the systematic recruitment of wage laborers from South India began only with the development of plantation agriculture. However, as Kuruppu points out, it was not the British Government or the European planter who first drew upon South Indian labor for working a staple industry in Ceylon. There is evidence that a caste of weavers known as the *Chaliyas*, who came from Malabar, were later made to specialize in cinnamon peeling by the

Plantations and the Creation of a Labor Force

Sinhalese king, Rajasinghe, during the precolonial era.[85]

The early experiments of the British in recruiting Indian labor to Ceylon ended in failure. In 1828, the founders of the Ceylonese plantation economy, Governor Barnes and Major Bird, recruited 180 laborers from South India. Due to the harsh treatment meted out by the employers, within a year almost all the laborers deserted.[86] In theory, South Indian labor migration to Ceylon plantations was free or voluntary. But in practice, it did not remain a spontaneous movement of people. During the early stages of recruitment, a great amount of inducement had to be made by professional recruiters to motivate South Indians to emigrate despite the poverty-stricken conditions in which they existed. Various coercive, nonmarket elements had to be employed for the maintenance and control of South Indian laborers on the coffee estates. As Kuruppu remarks,

> It was that labour as a class makes its appearance in modern Ceylon highly regimented and for all practical purposes in semi-slavery with few or no individual rights and liberties and all this with its overwhelmingly foreign extraction.[87]

The fluctuations of the labor supply to the Ceylon plantations apparent in Table 6:5 were attributable to a number of factors. Among them the prosperity or distress of agriculture in South India, and conditions in the Ceylon coffee industry and the world market, were significant. The dramatic decline in immigration in 1853 was caused by the good agricultural harvests in South India, whereas, the increase in arrivals starting in 1854, resulted from the generally poor harvests there.[88] As a contemporary newspaper report stated, one reason for the fluctuation of South Indian labor emigration to Ceylon was the changing cash needs of the laborers, i. e., cash to pay taxes to their landlords and the colonial state back in India. "The labour supply was larger in 1854 than in previous years because with the failure of the rice crop, the peasants needed to find money to pay their land tax."[89]

A number of significant facts are revealed by the figures in Table 6:6. One is the very dramatic increase in the arrivals and net inflow of South Indians over the course of the nineteenth century as plantations expanded — except during down turns in the plantation economy as during the collapse of coffee during the period 1880–1886. The transient laborers of the early decades

---

85. N. S. G. Kuruppu, "A History of the Working Class Movement in Ceylon," *The Ceylon Historical Journal*, vol. 1, no. 2, (October, 1951), p. 130.
86. Ibid., p. 133.
87. Ibid., p. 139.
88. For a discussion of this particular relationship, see Speculum, *Ceylon*, p. 14.
89. *The Ceylon Times*, September 26, 1854, quoted in K. M. de Silva, *Social Policy*, p. 264.

rarely brought wives or children. But later, as an Indian community began slowly to evolve on the estates, more families came. This is particularly evident with the shift from coffee to tea (beginning in the mid-1870s) which requires a year-round labor force. Many who arrived as immigrants with the hope of saving money and returning to India, were not able to do so; many never saw India again.[90] As we shall discuss later in this chapter, the Indian laborers were tied to a system of debt bondage on the estates from which neither they nor their descendants were generally able to escape.

Table 6:5

South Indian Labor Immigration, 1851–1854

Year	Men	Women	Children	Total
1851	28,224	1,003	273	29,500
1852	50,843	2,226	770	53,839
1853	36,582	2,042	653	39,227
1854	54,014	9,006	4,301	67,321

Source: I. H. Van Den Driesen, "Some Aspects of the History of the Coffee Industry in Ceylon with Special Reference for the Period 1823–1885," unpublished Ph.D. dissertation, University of London, 1954, p. 244.

The functional division of labor in the colonial economy and cultural differences (including language and religion) kept the South Indian estate laborers apart from the Sinhalese peasantry in the neighboring villages. But it did not prevent small segments of the Indian estate labor force from moving into the peasant sector by leasing or purchasing land for smallholder production of coffee as well as garden vegetables.[91] It seems that South Indian labor supervisors or *kanganis* who had accumulated cash were more prone to making such incursions into the Sinhalese village economy than the ordinary estate laborers or 'coolies'. There were also movements in the reverse direction. A few cases of Sinhalese peasants working on the estates and doing so-called Tamil 'coolie' or field work are on record.[92] Such exchanges of economic roles were gradually complemented by cultural identities associated with those newly-acquired roles. As Meyer has observed in relation to the Sinhalese who became resident laborers on the European estates, "It seems that on the plantations where the Tamils were an overwhelming majority the

---

90. Snodgrass, *Ceylon*, p. 25.
91. Roberts, "Aspects of Ceylon's Agrarian Economy," p. 164; see also Roberts, "Some Comments," pp. 24–25, (n. 3).
92. Meyer, "Between Village and Plantation," pp. 4 and 9.

resident Sinhalese had to conform to the dominant model; so much so in some cases they lost their social identity."[93] Meyer substantiates his point with a quote from a European planter who noted "I had thirty Sinhalese on Somerset working as Tamils, calling themselves Tamils and working under Tamil names. All talked Tamil, but not among themselves."[94]

Recruitment, Control and Reproduction of Estate Labor

Labor Recruitment

The indenture system which was widely used around the world for recruiting laborers to plantations following emancipation, contractually bound the immigrant laborer to serve a particular employer for a specific period, usually between three to five years.

Although Ceylon government legislation provided for indenture contracts for periods over three years, planters preferred contracts with their laborers that lasted only a month at a time.[95] This was due to a number of factors including the seasonal labor needs of coffee; the planters' interest in creating competition among labor for employment; and the relative success of labor recruitment through intermediary labor contractors (discussed shortly). Thus, the Indian immigrant laborers in Ceylon (and in Burma and Malaya) were considered 'free' and had the legal right to quit their employer's service at a month's notice. They were also free to move between their homeland in South India and their work place in Ceylon, unrestricted by regulations of the governments of India and Ceylon.[96]

Emigration to Ceylon was exempted from the strictures of the Indian Emigration Ordinance on several grounds, especially the kinship ties between recruiters and laborers (discussed below); the belief among colonial administrators that welfare protection available for immigrant laborers was quite adequate; and the consideration of migration to Ceylon as an age-old internal or pan-Indian phenomenon.[97] "Ceylon has been taken as it were into the

---

93. Ibid., p. 9.
94. Ibid., p. 9.
95. Wesumperuma, "The Migration," pp. 52–55.
96. Ibid., p. 37.
97. Ibid., pp. 40–49.

Table 6:6

Migration of Indian Estate Labourers, 1839–86
(Annual Averages, Rounded to Nearest Hundred)

Period	Arrivals			Departures			Net Inflow		
	Men	Women and Children	Total	Men	Women and Children	Total	Men	Women and Children	Total
1839–42	4,800	400	5,300	6,400	500	6,900	−1,500	−100	−1,600
1843–49	46,600	1,500	48,100	23,500	800	24,300	23,100	800	23,800
1850–59	48,600	7,500	56,100	36,300	2,700	39,000	12,200	4,900	17,100
1860–72	52,400	17,300	69,700	54,700	12,400	67,100	−2,300	4,800	2,600
1873–79	82,603	32,813	115,416	85,066	19,026	104,092	−2,463	13,787	11,324
1880–86	36,659	9,423	46,152	43,233	12,310	55,543	−6,574	−2,817	−9,391

Sources: Donald Snodgrass, *Ceylon: An Export Economy in Transition*, p. 26 and I. H. Van Den Driesen, "Some Aspects of the Coffee Industry in Ceylon with Special Reference for the Period 1823–85," pp. 244, 272 and *CO* 54/235, pp. 4–6.

Plantations and the Creation of a Labor Force

Tamil heart; Ceylon is no more foreign to the Trichinopoly labourer than Madura or Ramnad and very much less so than Malabar or Mysore."[98]

As Gail Omvedt has pointed out, labor recruitment for Ceylon plantations which first took the form of indenture — formal contracts which bound labor to an employer for a stipulated period of time — was soon replaced by a more informal system of recruitment which bound the laborers through debt to intermediary labor contractors known as *kanganis*. In fact, this method of labor recruitment and control, the 'kangani system', was first developed in Ceylon and later adopted in several other British colonies.[99] Omvedt also notes that this switch from indenture to labor contracting coincided with the shift of plantation ownership from individual proprietors to monopoly and corporate forms of ownership. In other words, Omvedt suggests that the expansion of metropolitan capital abroad relied on 'semi-feudal' methods of labor recruitment and control such as the kangani system.[100]

The Kangani System

The kanganis, or labor headmen (like their counterparts the *mistris, sardars*, and *jobbers* in colonial India) were usually drawn from among the estate laborers themselves and preferably from the same districts and villages in South India.[101] As the Clifford Commission inquiring into immigrant labor in Ceylon noted in 1908, the kangani system

> ... provided the soundest basis for the recruitment of labour and was of purely patriarchal character in its origin and principles. The *Kangany* or labour headman was in the beginning, and still is in a large number of the older and more solidly established estates, the senior member of a family group composed of his personal relatives to whom may be added other families drawn from villages in South India, from the vicinity of which he and his relatives came.[102]

Planters gave out cash advances to the kanganis to recruit and transport laborers from their villages in South India to the plantations of the Kandyan Highlands. Much of these cash advances given to the laborers at the time of recruitment went for debt clearance rather than towards the improvement of living conditions of the labor recruits or their families. In many cases

---

98. N. V. Sovani, *Economic Relation of India with South-East Asia and the Far East* (Bombay: Oxford University Press, 1949), p. 139.
99. Omvedt, "The Migration," pp. 192–93.
100. Ibid., p. 194.
101. Sovani, *Economic Relations*, p. 39.
102. The Clifford Commission on Immigrant Labour (1908), quoted in Kuruppu, "A History," p. 135.

the kangani had not only to clear the debts to his landlord, moneylender, and the colonial state back in South India, but also to "get the prospective migrant certified by the headmen before he or she could leave for Malaya, Ceylon etc."[103]

The cash advances given out by the planters to attract laborers were entered in the estate debt account as charges against the kangani and he was in turn to recover those advances from 'his' laborers.[104] Thus on arrival, the laborer was already indebted to the kangani and tied to the plantation in order to pay back the debts.[105] In other words, the laborer had moved from debt bondage in his South Indian village to debt bondage on the Ceylon plantation. This cycle of indebtedness worked to the great advantage of the coffee planters since it guaranteed labor return each season and it placed no constraints on them to pay higher wages or improve working conditions.

Labor Transport and Maintenance

On arrival at the estates, the labor gangs were forced to live huddled together four or five persons to an eight by ten feet room. Rows of such rooms, commonly referred to as the 'lines', constituted the residences of the laborers on the plantations. Thiagaraja, who observed the working and living conditions of laborers on the tea estates, noted that laborers worked ten continuous hours a day on the fields without a break and earned wages which were scarcely sufficient to live on.[105] It can be assumed that the conditions on the earlier coffee estates were as bad, if not worse.

Government legislation purported to benefit laborers, could not do so, particularly in the face of powerful opposition from the planters. For example, Ordinance No. 5 of 1841, which was introduced to make both the employer and employee equal before the law, in fact made the employer liable to civil proceedings and the employee to criminal proceedings in cases of violations of obligations towards each other.[106] Similarly, Ordinance No. 11 of 1865 benefitted the planters by granting them a firmer hold over their laborers.[107] As in colonies elsewhere, here too the illiterate workers who

---

103. Omvedt, "The Migration," p. 198.
104. K. M. de Silva, *Social Policy*, p. 239; Van Den Driesen, "Some Aspects of the Coffee Industry," p. 18.
105. Thiagaraja, "Indian Coolies," p. 182.
106. Michael Roberts, "The Master Servant Laws of 1841 and the 1860s and Immigrant Labour in Ceylon," *CJHSS*, vol. 8 (1973), p. 25.
107. Ibid., p. 37.

had no bebefactors to represent their interests did not have the sophistication to use the law even when it could offer them some protection.[108] As Michael Roberts remarks,

> Lords of their domains, the planters were faced by timid immigrants bred under authoritarianism and with no conception of trade union organisation. Where legislation fell short of the radical it was rather such factors as the heavy demand for labour, the scope for desertion and the enlightened self-interest and humanitarianism of planters, than any legislation that would have tended to soften the treatment of the immigrants.[109]

'Enlightened self-interest' and 'humanitarianism' were quite rare in the treatment of labor. As far as the planters were concerned, Indian laborers represented 'human nature in an uncultivated state' and they disparagingly referred to them as 'coolies'. P. D. Millie, an early planter, has said that when coolies complained to them that their pay was short, the planters usually ordered them off 'with a cuff and a kick.'[110]

The colonial state and the planters blamed each other for the deplorable conditions of travel, living, ill health, and the high mortality rate of the Indian immigrants ". . . of about 1,447,000 emigrants to Ceylon in the early years of 1843–1867, 350,000 were unaccounted for and presumed dead."[111] Emerson Tennent compared the condition of the estate laborers to that of West Indian slaves.

> The condition of the coolies on the estates and their treatment by their employers was not in every instance or in every particular such as humanity or even policy would have required in order to encourage and secure a continuation of their resort to Ceylon.[112]

The influx of weak and emaciated Tamil laborers from the famine-stricken districts of India introduced cholera and small pox into the country.[113] Due

---

108. Van Zwanenberg, "Colonial Capitalism," p. 89.
109. Roberts, "The Master Servant Laws," p. 37; see also Roberts, "Indian Estate Labour," *passim*.
110. P. D. Millie, *Thirty Years Ago*, Chapter 3.
111. Omvedt, "The Migration," p. 189.
112. CO 54/235, Tennent's Despatch to the Secretary of State for the Colonies; see also Thiagaraja, "Indian Coolies," p. 181. For the debate on the issue of state vs. planter responsibility and neglect of estate labourers, see K. M. de Silva, "Indian Immigration to Ceylon, The First Phase, c. 1840–1855," *CJHSS*, vol. 4, no. 2 (July-December 1961); I. H. Ven Den Driesen, "Indian Immigration to Ceylon – The First Phase, c. 1840–1855 – A Comment," *CJHSS*, vol. 7, no. 2 (July-December 1964); and K. M. de Silva, "Tennent and Indian Immigration to Ceylon, 1846–1847 – A Rejoinder," *CJHSS*, vol. 9, no. 1 (January-June 1966).
113. *AR 1877*, Report of the AGA for the Nuwara Eliya District; see also Michael Roberts, "Observations on Computations of the Mortality Rates among Immigrant Indian Labourers in Ceylon in the Coffee Period," *CJHSS*, vol. 9, no. 1 (January-June 1966); and D. M. Forrest, *A Hundred Years of Ceylon Tea*.

to the hazards to public health and the threat to the labor supply itself caused by the diseases carried by the immigrant laborers, the colonial state began to take some responsibility for the transportation of estate laborers since the 1850s.[114] The state's efforts to impose quarantine restrictions, however, affected the free flow of labor into the island and resulted in recurring clashes between the state and the planters.[115] Of the two main immigration routes, i.e., the Mannar-Matale (or the north route) and the Tuticorin-Colombo route, the former was closed by the state due to health hazards in 1899. In addition, the state organized a 'Coolie Medical Fund' and transferred a part of the export duties collected on coffee, tea, etc., towards medical facilities for the laborers.[116]

Labor Control

The labor headman or kangani was the indispensable middleman in both the recruitment and the control of plantation labor. To the planter, he was the labor recruiter and the labor supervisor; to the laborer, he was the immediate employer and the patriarchal head of his labor gang.[117]

There were generally two types of labor headmen or kanganis: a 'sub-kangany' with a relatively small labor gang consisting of family members and close relatives and a 'head-kangany' with several sub-kangany gangs under his control and supervision.[118] Sub-kanganis worked on the fields with their labor gangs and drew daily wages like all other laborers. The head-kangany, however, did not do field work, but supervised and organized labor gangs for which he received a monthly wage from the estate.[119] In addition, kanganis often collected from each laborer a trifling portion of their pay for supposedly representing the interests of labor.[120]

While the relationship of the kanganis to the planters was largely contractual, their relationship to the laborers was solidified by ethnic and kinship ties. As Goldthorpe observed, this only helped widen the gulf between the planters and the laborers. "The gulf between the European upper caste and

---

114. Snodgrass, *Ceylon*, p. 25.
115. Wesumperuma, "The Migration," pp. 58-64.
116. *SP 1880*, No. 9; *SP 1881*, No. 30; *SP 1881*, No. 35.
117. Wesumperuma, "The Migration," p. 79.
118. Ibid., p. 180.
119. Ibid., p. 82.
120. Van Den Driesen, "Some Aspects of the Coffee Industry," p. 181.

Plantations and the Creation of a Labor Force 207

the masses of unskilled workers was widened by the use of middlemen who were often 'Oriental aliens'."[121]

The immigrant laborers were drawn from a background of peasant agriculture where the process of production was not directly controlled by the landlords. Understandably then, they found the adjustment to the highly regimented working conditions of the plantations, under the direct supervision of labor headmen, very difficult.[122] In spite of the familiar references to the docility of the Tamil laborers, one hears also of individual acts of rebellion such as absenteeism, desertion, coffee stealing, and neglect of tools.[123] Coffee stealing in particular may have been a rational means of augmenting one's meagre income in a situation in which there was a ready market for coffee. The miserable working and living conditions and the continuous cycle of indebtedness (discussed below), perhaps induced these acts of resistance and survival on the part of laborers.

Among the main labor problems faced by the planters was the poor turnout for work and heavy turnover of the labor force.[124] One of the measures adopted by the planters to ensure labor turnout was the offer of 'commissions' to kanganis. A commission, also called 'head' or 'pence' money, varying between two and four cents, was given to the kangany for each laborer of his gang that turned up for work every day.[125]

> In addition to the recruiting fees, the recruiters – kanganies – are given "pence money." On every cooly (male or female) working, the recruiters – kanganies – get 6 cents (about one anna) a day . . . .
>
> For instance, if 100 coolies work a day, the kangani gets Rs.6 that day . . . .
>
> Again in addition to recruiting fees and "pence money" the kanganies are also decently paid. There are sub-kanganies under the kanganies, who have their own standard arrangements, and they are also well off.[126]

Thus the kanganies were placed in a powerful position vis-à-vis both the laborer and the planter. The kanganis were notorious for keeping much of the cash advances given by the planters and for extracting more money than was due from the laborers in debt repayment.[127] The economic incentives offered

---

121. Goldthorpe, *The Sociology*, p. 49.
122. Wesumperuma, "The Migration," p. 212.
123. *SP 1864*, No. 1, p. viii; see also Millie, *Thirty Years Ago*, Chapter 4; Kuruppu, "The History," p. 136. On coffee stealing by estate laborers, see *SP 1873*, No. 11, p. 9.
124. Wesumperuma, "The Migration," p. 341.
125. Ibid., p. 182.
126. Thiagaraja, "The Indian Coolies," p. 184.
127. Wesumperuma, "The Migration," p. 82.

by the planters, such as 'head money', drove the kanganis to use force in compelling laborers to turn up for work.

While the kanganis played an indispensable role in supplying and controlling the labor force, this very role gave them the power to create instability in the supply of labor. For example, they used their power and influence in shifting labor gangs between estates to suit their own interests.[128] K. M. de Silva says there was a category of labor headmen who earned their living entirely by 'crimping' laborers from one estate to another, and that they were most active during periods of labor scarcity.[129] Another writer, Wesumperuma, comments on the inequities in the system of labor recruitment and control in the following manner.

> The working of the system therefore not only explains the debt servitude and the absence of economic progress among the working class in a period of striking prosperity in the industry in which they worked; but it also helps to explain the rise of the Chetties and the kanganies as economic elites in the plantation region. The labourers acceded to the set-up because they were drawn from the poverty stricken and illiterate sections of the population in South India who, were quite used to a life of indebtedness which was repaid by them with their manual labour.[130]

Debt Bondage

One of the chief characteristics of the Ceylonese plantation economy was that the fluctuations in the demand and supply for labor did not affect the wages of laborers. The wage rate remained generally fixed. For example, Wesumperuma notes that between 1880 and 1910, the daily wage rates remained unchanged, although there were sharp fluctuations in the demand and supply of labor.[131]

The labor market was dominated by cash advances rather than wages. Planters preferred to compete for labor with offers of larger cash advances instead of outright payment of higher wages. Unlike wages, cash advances tied the laborer to the plantation and ensured the planter his labor supply.[132] Cash advances included coast advances or the sums given out by the kangani on recruitment back in the South Indian village, as well as sums given out by the planters (via the kanganis) to laborers upon arrival at the estates.

For the laborers, the cash advances were the primary means of bridging the gap between low wages and their accumulated debts. But these advances only tied them into a cycle of debt bondage. It was in months of peak work on the

---

128. Ibid., p. 342.
129. K. M. de Silva, *Social Policy*, p. 240.
130. Wesumperuma, "The Migration," p. 344.
131. Ibid., p. 167; Van Den Driesen, "Some Aspects of the History," p. 203.
132. Wesumperuma, "The Migration," p. 344.

Plantations and the Creation of a Labor Force

estates that cash advances were most readily available from the planters. At other times, the laborers had to turn to credit from the labor headmen or Chettiyar moneylends from South India.[133] The cash advances obtained from the kanganis and the Chettiyars carried high interest rates. The outcome was the extraction of a large portion of the laborers' wages by their creditors, mainly other South Indian immigrants who also came to Ceylon to participate in the new economic activities unleashed by the opening up of plantations.

Planters did not pay wages directly to the laborers. Instead, wages were given to the labor headmen who in turn were to pay the laborers at their own discretion. This again left ample room for corruption and extortion. The laborers earning low wages, roughly eighteen shillings a month in the 1850s and carrying huge debts, were therefore hardly in a position to remit money to their villages in South India. Thiagaraja's observations with regard to the tea estates were equally applicable to the situation in the earlier coffee estates.

> There is absolutely not a single cooly on any one estate without debts. The only question is about the difference of amount. The debt of each cooly varies from Rs.50 to Rs.200 and more. Seldom does a cooly owe less than Rs.50.
>
> The average debt of a cooly is roughly Rs.100. These debts are said to be accumulated in different ways. First, the amount advanced by the kangany before recruiting and the travelling expenses. Secondly value of things brought from the kangany from time to time. Thirdly, cash lent by kangany during illness and on other occasions.[134]

The entrenchment of debt bondage is most clearly reflected in what came to be known as the 'tundu system'. 'Tundus' were chits of paper on which the debt each laborer owed to the estate was written down by the planter or the kangany. A laborer was not able to quit an estate (which he/she often sought to do) unless he/she paid back the debt marked on the 'tundu' to the planter or his intermediary. So much for the freedom and mobility of wage labor in Ceylon's coffee plantation economy!

> ... the iniquitous *tundu* system (abolished only in 1921) which tied down the labourer to an estate and deprived him of mobility. By this system the miserably paid and exploited labourer who invariably incurred a large debt to the *kangany* and to his employer was unable to seek new employment unless he discharged his debt to his former employer.[135]

133. Thiagaraja, "The Indian Coolies," p. 183. For a discussion of debt-bondage (*enganche*) on a Peruvian sugar plantation, see C. D. Scott, "Peasants, Proletarianization and the Articulation of Modes of Production: The Case of Sugar Cane Cutters in Northern Peru, 1940–1969," *The Journal of Peasant Studies*, vol. 3, no. 3 (April 1976).
134. Thiagaraja, "The Indian Coolies," p. 183. See also Kumar, *Land and Caste*, p. 142, and Omvedt, "The Migration," p. 208.
135. Kuruppu, "The History," p. 136.

It is important to interject here that even the pitiful remittances sent back by the laborers went for repayment of debts to creditors back at home. Omvedt has observed that after decades of migration, those South Indian regions such as Tanjore which were the primary districts of labor supply to plantations in Ceylon (and elsewhere) still remained poor and backward.[136] However, it must be noted that the substantial savings that kanganis and Chettiyars sent back to India helped increase their wealth and power in their home villages.[137] Furthermore, as we noted earlier, many kanganis and Chettiyars who accumulated wealth through the exploitation of Indian estate laborers and Kandyan peasantry (through renting and usury) invested some of their wealth in coffee smallholdings, vegetable gardens and less often in paddy fields in Kandyan villages.

'Rice Money'

One of the means that the planters used to ensure labor turnout for work was the partial payment of wages in rice, which was the staple food of the laborers. When the laborers failed to work the required number of days, their rice rations were curtailed. When the laborers fell ill and could not turn up for work they were not given their rice supplies either.[138] The Labour Commission of 1908 admitted that the average laborer working five to seven days a week would not have worked as much had the rice supply, i.e., his/her very subsistence, not depended on the number of days worked.[139] In the early years of the twentieth century, the quota of rice given per week was "men, 1/4 bushel each, women 1/4 and 1/8 each on alternate weeks and young working boys and girls, 1/8 of a bushel each."[140] The ratio of wages for men, women and children during the tea period was generally 5:4:3. During the earlier coffee period, covered in this study, however, the use of female and child labor was not very great. Jean Grossholtz notes that women and children who worked on the coffee plantations did not receive wages of their own as their labor was counted in calculating the man's wage.[141] This of course was not a practice peculiar to plantations in the colonies but a commonly used stra-

---

136. Omvedt, "The Migration," p. 208.
137. Ibid., p. 197.
138. Thiagaraja, "The Indian Coolies," p. 181.
139. Wesumperuma, "The Migration," p. 213.
140. Thiagaraja, "The Indian Coolies," p. 181.
141. Jean Grossholtz, "Forging Capitalist Patriarchy: The Effect of British Colonial Rule in Sri Lanka," unpublished manuscript, pp. 255–59. I would like to thank Jean Grossholtz for lending me a copy of this manuscript.

tegy of profit making and patriarchal control in the early factories of industrializing England.[142] The sexual and age-based division of labor and the specificity of the exploitation of women and children were crucial to the profitability of the plantation economy. An examination of these issues, however, is beyond the scope of this book.

The receipt of part of their wages in rice and the accumulated debts that had to be paid to various creditors, left the laborers with hardly any cash to meet their other expenses such as clothing, curry ingredients, ceremonial expenses, etc. They therefore bartered a part of their rice ration for sundry items with traders.[143] The planters supplied rice to the laborers at a fixed rate generally below the retail market price. Price of rice fluctuated often, but the planters bore these changes without passing them on to the laborers. Emerson Tennent's observations on this subject are worth quoting in some detail.

> In Ceylon, it is a very general custom upon the estates in the Hill country of the interior (...) for the proprietor, in hiring his coolies and labourers, to engage not only to pay them a certain amount of wages, but to provide them at his own risk with a certain amount of rice sufficient for their consumption, to be delivered to them on the plantation at one fixed and invariable price. This price varies from 5s. a bushel to 6s. or even higher, according to the remoteness of the locality and the increased expense of carriage, and at this rate it is continued to be issued to the cooly during the whole term of his engagement. But all the fluctuations of the market in the meantime affect the risk of the employer alone, both during periods of scarcity when price is high and during the rainy season when the carriage becomes extravagantly dear. I have myself known the price of rice to amount up to 12s., 15s., and even 20s. a bushel within 30 miles of Kandy, yet still the planter must issue to his labourers at the stipulated cost. From the best information I can collect, I have reason to believe that on estates 20 miles distant from Kandy, the habitual loss to proprietors is, on average 1s.6d. to 2s. a bushel, but taking it at the smaller sum, and supposing each proprietor to have 300 coolies in his employment, his annual loss on this one item would amount to 270£ per annum; one third of which at least would be saved to every estate by the abolition of the import duty of 7d. per bushel.[144]

Notwithstanding planters' protests to the contrary, Michael Roberts has noted that "through the years the planters made a 'considerable profit' from the system of partial payment of wages in rice."[145] The planters found that

---

142. Western feminist scholars are now doing important research on the role played by patriarchal authority in the rise of capitalism, particularly in the early factories of England. See, for example, Maria Teresa de Sousa Fernandes, "Women and the Wage Labor System — A Theoretical Approach to the Sexual Division of Labor," esp. part 4, unpublished Ph. D. dissertation, Brandeis University, 1981.
143. *The Colombo Observer*, November 12, 1866.
144. *BPP 1847–1848*, Vol. 42, Emerson Tennent's Report on Finance and Commerce, pp. 62–63.
145. Roberts, "Indian Estate Labour," part 2, p. 118.

in the long run it was advantageous to keep wage rates fixed and to bear the fluctuations of the market price of rice themselves. They realized that once the wages of laborers were raised to meet rising costs of rice, it would be difficult to bring them down once the price of rice fell.[146] Furthermore, the partial payment in rice guaranteed the minimum subsistence of the laborers and also their turn-out for work.

The system of labor control and remuneration in Ceylon's plantations was essentially a patriarchal system based on debt-bondage. Labor supply and retention on the coffee plantations were in fact guaranteed by nonmarket, coercive methods. It is not entirely correct to say that the debt bondage developed on the plantations was a precapitalist relationship. It probably never existed before and was a peculiar innovation feasible only within the framework of colonial capitalism. It is interesting to note in this regard that social relations of production that evolved in the expansion of capitalism were not purely capitalist in that they did not always require the creation of a proletariat in the strictly Marxist sense i.e., free from the means of production and free to sell labor to any employer. Like the Ceylon plantations, the textile factories of colonial India were heavily dependent on *jobbers*, a different type of patriarchal headmen. Similarly, Peruvian plantations devised *enganche*, a form of debt bondage for recruiting and controlling labor. In the early factories of England, the patriarchal authority of male heads of households were adapted for the control and supervision of the labor of women and children.[147] 'Precapitalist' social relations of production ranging from slavery to sharecropping were also widely employed in capitalist agriculture in the United States.

Table 6:7

Rice Imports to Ceylon, 1837–1872

Period	Amount (cwts.)	Value (£ '000)
1837–1839	798	167
1840–1849	1,689	296
1850–1859	2,728	323
1860–1869	4,197	1,186
1870–1872	4,794	1,558

Source: Donald Snodgrass, *Ceylon: An Export Economy in Transition* (Homewood, Ill.: Richard D. Irwin, Inc., 1966), p. 31.

146. Wesumperuma, "The Migration," p. 210.
147. See Omvedt, "The Migration"; Scott, "Peasants, Proletarianization and the Arti-

Plantations and the Creation of a Labor Force

It is fair to say that the system of debt bondage based on the patriarchal authority of the kanganis and the partial payment of wages in rice were the very bases of the plantations' profit planning and control systems. This system was so successful from the planter (and kangani) point of view, that it was carried on to the subsequent tea period of Ceylon's plantation history without fundamental changes. It was much later during the tea period that the kangani system and the payment of wages in rice began slowly to change.

Imported Rice

As Table 6:7 shows, rice imports continued to climb up during the nineteenth century. Of the rice imported, the major portion went to feeding the estate laborers in the coffee estates. A significant portion also went into feeding the urban population engaged in plantation-related service activities.[148] The small urban population in Ceylon in the nineteenth century included South Indian immigrants, as well as Sinhalese and native Tamil peasants drawn from the villages. Most of them worked in transportation, construction, and trade. These people depended almost entirely on imported rice for their subsistence.

> Three million out of five million bushels of rice imported went to Tamil immigrants. The rest went to feed traders, contractors, carpenters, and others who found it more profitable to buy imported grain rather than engage in their own cultivation.[149]

But what is more ironic is that during the course of the nineteenth century, the rice growing Sinhalese peasantry themselves came to depend more and more on imported rice. Emerson Tennent pointed out in 1848 that the native peasantry's dependence on imported rice was not restricted to periods of harvest failures, but was a habitual one.

> ... a large proportion of the agricultural population both in the interior and on the coast are compelled not merely on occasions of the failure of their own crops from drought or inundation, but habitually to subsist on the imported rice with all its charges for duty, freight and carriage.[150]

While the self identity of the Sinhalese peasants, and the Sinhalese as a community of people, was tied up with paddy cultivation and the glories of the ancient wet-rice producing hydraulic civilization, in reality a lot of the Sinhalese peasants depended on other grains, especially swidden crops such as kurukkan and at times even on jungle produce for their subsistence.[151] Fur-

culation of Modes of Production"; de Sousa Fernandes, "Women and the Wage Labor System."
148. *SP 1878*, No. 29, p. 13.
149. GA of the Western Province quoted in the Supplement to *The Colombo Observer*, November 19, 1866.
150. *BPP 1847–1848*, Vol. 42, p. 61.
151. *AR 1883*, Report for the Badulla District, p. 27A.

thermore, the rice producing Kandyan peasants often had less rice to eat than the Tamil estate laborers. The rice supply of the estate laborers was guaranteed as part of their wage. But the native peasants had no such guarantees of their minimum rice requirements.[152] In contrast, their paddy plots were expropriated for nonpayment of taxes and the irrigation necessary for rice cultivation was neglected by the colonial state.

Much of the rice imported to Ceylon came from India and Burma (until 1937, Burma was administratively a part of India).[152] The only regions within Ceylon that produced a surplus of rice to be exported to the planting districts, were the Batticoloa District in the Eastern Province and the Hambantota District in the Southern Province.[154] A discussion of the distinct social and technical organization of rice production in these regions is beyond the limits of this study. Suffice it to mention that the rice supplied from these regions was insufficient to meet the rice requirements in the rest of the island, particularly on the coffee estates.

In discussing the procurement of rice for plantation labor, it would seem pertinent to offer a note of explanation on the South Indian business community/caste of Chettiyars, commonly referred to as the Chetties.[155] They came to Ceylon during the development of plantations to perform distinctive functions as financiers and traders in the colonial economy. As credit bankers to the planters, estate laborers, Sinhalese peasantry and native capitalists, the Chettiyars' economic activities straddled both plantation and village sectors. The planters, for instance, obtained rice supplies for their labor force on credit from the Chettiyars and paid them back after their export earnings came in.[156] The Chettiyars were an integral element of the Ceylon plantation enterprise.

The financial and trading activities of the Chettiyars were not confined to India and Ceylon, but extended to Burma, Malaya and other South East Asian countries as well.[157] Hans-Dieter Evers has pointed out that in adapting themselves to the colonial economies, this precapitalist moneylending caste

---

152. *AR 1883*, report for the Central Province, p. 10A.
153. Sovani, *Economic Relations*, pp. 4–5.
154. Roberts, "Aspects of Ceylon's Agrarian Economy," pp. 155–56; see also Herring, "Redistributive Agrarian Policy," Ch. 9, *passim*.
155. Morris D. Morris has questioned the relevance of the concept of caste to describe the Chettiyars. He suggests that community is perhaps a more appropriate epithet. "Values as an Obstacle to Economic Growth in South Asia: An Historical Survey," *The Journal of Economic History*, vol. 27 (December 1967), p. 604.
156. Wesumperuma, "The Migration," p. 210; see also *SP 1934*, No. 8, "The Report of the Banking Commission."
157. Hans-Dieter Evers, "From Subsistence to Generalized Commodity Production: A Study of the South Indian Money Lenders and the Expansion of the Colonial Mode

Plantations and the Creation of a Labor Force 215

played an important intermediary role. They helped advance the colonial economic interests and also extended the cash nexus into the village economy.[158] In Ceylon, their activities included 'renting' of the paddy tax (discussed in Chapter V), smallholder cash crop production (especially coffee), moneylending, and trading (especially imported rice).[159] As speculators, they also dealt in gold, and still do.

We have also noted in the previous chapter that when peasants failed to pay their paddy taxes or loans, the Chettiyars were able to expropriate their paddy lands as renters or creditors. The Chettiyars also bought paddy fields that the Crown sold in order to recover the commuted taxes from defaulting Sinhalese paddy cultivators.

Reasons for the Importation of Rice

As mentioned earlier, the supply of rice to the plantations was the monopoly of the Chettiyars. Being South Indians themselves, they had established sources and networks for the procurement, transportation, and distribution of rice from India. Given the dependence of the planters on the Chettiyars for obtaining rice on credit, and the reliability of their supplies, neither the planters nor the colonial state made any substantial efforts to develop regular local supplies or to break the monopoly of the Chetties. As Emerson Tennent observed, "... owing to the present unequal distribution of capital, the entire trade in rice, its importation and sale, are exclusively in the hands of those who have a free command of money."[160]

Another important reason why rice was imported in large quantities was that the colonial state maintained the cost of imported rice at the same level as home grown rice. This was done essentially by imposing a low customs duty on imported rice. We noted earlier the Colonial Secretary, Emerson Tennent's complaints in 1847 that the customs duty on imported rice at 7d. per bushel was too high. However, it must be noted that this levy remained fixed at 7d. per bushel throughout the nineteenth century, while the tax on home grown paddy was increased at regular intervals.[161]

of Production," unpublished paper read at the seminar on "Underdevelopment and Subsistence Reproduction in Southeast Asia," University of Bielefeld, West Germany (April 21–23, 1978).
158. Ibid., p. 4.
159. Samaraweera, "Economic and Social Developments," p. 49; Roberts, "Aspects of Ceylon's Agrarian Economy," p. 149; Michael Roberts and L. A. Wickremaratne, "Export Agriculture in the Nineteenth Century," in *History of Ceylon*, ed. by K. M. de Silva, vol. 3, p. 98.
160. *BPP 1847–1848*, Vol. 42, p. 61.
161. Ludovici, *Rice Cultivation*, p. 126.

One of the arguments made by the laissez-faire proponents within the colonial administration for keeping the customs duty on imported rice at a minimum was that if it were raised it would give local paddy cultivators special protection and an unfair advantage over imported rice![162] This was of course a fabrication devised to protect planter interests. By exerting their considerable influence on the colonial administration, the planters managed to keep down the duty on imported rice and thereby the price of imported rice at a minimum. For example, as a colonial official pointed out, Indian rice was selling at approximately Rs.3.50 per bushel in Kandy in 1883 — a remarkably low price for that year.[163]

Yet another reason for the continued importation of rice to feed the estate laborers perhaps was their preference for familiar varieties of rice from India such as *cocanada mill, kallunda, sulai, pakkudi*, etc.[164] But the fact of the matter was that the immigrant labor had never had reason to develop a taste for local rice as their supplies had always been obtained by the planters from India.

Ameer Ali has clearly described the complicated relationship between the partial payment of estate wages in rice, the importation of rice, and the effects of rice imports on irrigation and the neglect of local rice production.

> The Indian workers were already a physically weakened lot. Therefore they had to be fed properly if the employers were to enjoy the maximum productivity of their labor. Cash wages would not solve the problem because the Indians were in the habit of collecting every cent with the hope of returning someday to their motherland. Therefore it was wiser to remunerate them more in kind and less in cash. But this system made a very important difference in the nature of the demand for rice.
>
> ... since the employer supplied this article to his entire labor force, the demand of the employer was qualitatively greater and was beyond the normal supply capacity of a local supplier. Therefore, instead of depending on any one risky local source or undergoing the inconvenience of drawing on several local sources, the employer made his demand on the merchants in Colombo, who in turn made theirs on the Indian market. ... This explains why the planters had no interest and opposed every attempt of the Government to engage in irrigation works.[165]

The most simple reason why the planters did not obtain locally-produced rice was that there was hardly a local surplus available. As mentioned before, the rice cultivators themselves had often to turn to imported rice for subsistence. Although the primary occupation of the vast majority of the Sinhalese peasantry continued to be paddy cultivation, paddy was often a below-subsis-

---

162. *BPP 1847–1848*, Vol. 42, p. 61.
163. *AR 1883*, Report for the Badulla District, p. 27A.
164. Ameer Ali, "Rice and Irrigation," p. 261.
165. Ibid., pp. 261–62.

Plantations and the Creation of a Labor Force 217

tence production (discussed in Chapter VIII). This was not simply because foreign capital neglected domestic food production, but also because the planters positively discouraged paddy production in Ceylon. The generalization made by Arthur Lewis is quite applicable to the Ceylonese case. "There was no revolution in domestic food production, so LDCs became importers of food. Finance and trade in primary products were dominated by foreigners, who looked outward rather than inward."[166]

Given the international devision of labor and factor endowments within the British empire, it made sense for British capital to ignore local food production. The interest in local food production emerged only when supplies from India and Burma were threatened or when other crises developed. When labor and food supplies from India became precarious, planters as well as government officials came up with schemes for settling the South Indian laborers on 'crown land' neighboring the plantations. This was a strategy successfully adopted by planters and the states in other colonies such as British Guyana.[167]

The objectives behind this suggestion to settle Tamil labor in Ceylon were to secure a ready supply of labor and to make the laborers grow their food themselves. The final aim, of course, was to bring down the planters' costs of production. Subsequent to the rebellion of 1848, Emerson Tennent went so far as to suggest that the rebellious Kandyans be expelled from the disturbed districts (which were the richest planting areas) and that the immigrant laborers be settled on their lands instead.[168] Similarly, the Report of the Committee appointed to inquire into irrigation and rice cultivation in 1867 recommended settling Indian laborers in the interior planting regions.

> ... surrounded by coffee estates and situated on the high-way used by Tamil immigrants. The Committee believes that good localities may be found in this part of the Central Province for the settlement of Malabar coolies as cultivators of the soil. Not only might estate labourers be induced to locate themselves as rice cultivators but measures might be adopted for the introduction of small Tamil communities from the opposite coast of India.[169]

The subsistence agricultural interests and efforts of the immigrant estate laborers, however, never extended beyond the raising of vegetables in garden plots around the 'lines' they lived in. Any real attempts to settle the South Indians on Kandyan lands would have been fatal to the British since it would

---

166. Lewis, *The Evolution*, p. 70. (LDC$_s$ = Less Developed Countries).
167. Mandle, *The Plantation Economy*, pp. 34–36.
168. *BP* pp. *1850*, "The Third Report on Ceylon," p. 253; K. M. de Silva, *Social Policy*, p. 130.
169. *SP 1867*, No. 4, pp. 13 and 50.

have intensified the conflict between the native peasantry and the British, a conflict which had already culminated in the peasant revolt of 1848. Just as the colonial state's efforts to make the Sinhalese peasantry into a *reliable* semiproletariat working for the European coffee estates failed by and large, the interest of a few government officials such as Tennent to turn the Indian estate laborers into a semipeasantry in the Kandyan Highlands (or elsewhere in Ceylon) never materialized.

But all in all, the costs of labor in the Ceylon coffee plantations were comparatively lower than the labor costs of planters in other British colonies such as Guyana and Mauritius during the same period.

Table 6:8

Comparative Statement of Costs to Planter of a Coolie (Estate Laborer) in British Guiana, Mauritius and Ceylon (1871)*

	Wages per Year	Total Cost Per Year Per Coolie
British Guiana	£ 18–5–0	£ 23–10–0
Mauritius	£ 6–0–0	£ 18–14–6
Ceylon	£ 10–4–0	£ 12–4–0

*Approximate figures.

Source: *CO* 54/463, Robinson to Kimberley, No. 60, 28 February 1871, Memo by Fairfield, 28 February 1871, in Michael Roberts, "Indian Estate Labour in Ceylon During the Coffee Period (1830–1880)," *The Indian Economic and Social History Review*, vol. 3, no. 1 (March 1966), p. 31.

As noted earlier, the laborers on the coffee estates were predominantly male immigrants who had left their families back in South India. The planters paid these workers only a single wage; not a family wage. Since the labor force was a semipeasantry, the bulk of the costs of reproducing the labor force was borne by their village economies. What the British failed to do with the Kandyan peasantry – turn them into a reliable semiproletariat – they managed to do with the immigrant Sough Indians. Omvedt's observations are useful here in understanding the nature of the 'articulation' that resulted between the plantation economy of Ceylon and the village economies of South India which supplied the plantation labor force.

> This generally implies also a sexual division of labour between the sectors in which women and families remain in the villages while males (and to a certain extent adult working women) migrate to become workers; it also implies the lack of a *family wage* which is the main mechanism through which cheap labour and thus cheap raw

materials and consumer goods for developing European capitalism can be maintained. It is continuing ties to the land, including ties of feudal dependence, that makes this possible, and thus imperialism in its colonial phase maintains a situation of dependent and blocked production not only through the direct thwarting of native industry but also through the maintenance of agrarian feudalism.[170]

Whether this articulation resulted in the 'maintenance of agrarian feudalism' in the labor exporting South Indian villages, as Omvedt argues it did, or if it contributed to a transformation of feudal social relations, is not a question that can be answered here. It calls for a specific analysis of the relationship between labor migration and changes in the internal socioeconomic organization in labor-exporting districts such as Tanjore, Malabar, Ramnad, etc.

Turning now to Ceylon, it should be noted that following the transition from coffee to tea cultivation, the migrant Indian workers on the Ceylon plantations became a wholly residential labor force. This was largely due to the year-round labor requirements of tea production. As women and children were employed in much larger numbers on tea estates, immigrants now came in families. It was estimated that by 1938, sixty percent of the 'Indian' labor force on the estates had become a part of the permanent population of the island.[171] Although they came to be counted with the permanent population, they remained and continue to remain a separate community of people confined to the estate enclaves. Their contacts with the Kandyan peasantry in the neighboring Sinhalese villages and their ethnic counterparts, the Ceylon Tamils, in the Northern and Eastern Provinces of the island were minimal.

It was only in 1939, following the intervention of the Indian government and due to the growing nationalist cries of Sinhalese politicians to repatriate the Indian laborers, that the South Indian labor immigration to Ceylon came to be stopped. This ban on further immigration marks the turning point when the estate labor force began to develop the characteristics of a true proletariat. Until that time they were bound by economic and kinship ties to their ancestral villages in South India and their hopes of returning to the motherland sooner or later. Furthermore, the prospects of permanent settlement in Ceylon tended to dissipate and break down the patriarchal control of the kanganis as recruiters. Likewise, the system of payment in rice was progressively eliminated.[172]

---

170. Omvedt, "The Migration," p. 186.
171. Sovani, *Economic Relations*, p. 39.
172. Visakha Kumari Jayawardena, *The Rise of the Labor Movement in Ceylon* (Durham, N. C.: Duke University Press, 1972), p. 334.

Reverting to the period under review in this book, that is the coffee period, the estate laborers then could at best be rated only as semiwage labor. The only 'true' proletariat, if any, at the time was the small urban labor force centered around Colombo. It was not until the last decade of the century, after the advent of tea, that the emergent proletariat began to manifest a sense of organizing and organized action.

Summary

The Kandyan peasantry did not become a permanent wage labor force on the coffee estates. This is attributable to a number of economic, political, and cultural reasons, most significantly the availability of alternative and traditional means of livelihood. Some of them became shifting and seasonal estate laborers. Low-country Sinhalese, particularly the artisan castes, were however more readily attracted to the plantation system's skilled occupations and provided the specialized services required for estate development.

As for the poineer gangs and regular 'coolies' they needed, the British colonizers found in the poverty-stricken South Indian agricultural labor castes, the cheapest possible resident labor force procurable at the time. Unlike the Kandyan peasantry that the planters rated as unreliable and rebellious, these Indian laborers were not only amenable to discipline, but being foreign were perhaps more prone to pay the white masters the homage and obeisance generally denied to them by the Kandyan peasantry.

The proximity to home, short-term contracts and comparatively higher wages (in relation to South India) being offered were the inducements that drew South Indian labor to the Ceylon plantations. Besides, these laborers had few other opportunities to make money to pay their debts (to landlords, moneylenders, and the colonial state) and generally to make ends meet.

The relationship between planter and laborer was not strictly a contractual relationship between capital and wage labor. The use of labor headmen or kanganis as labor recruiters and supervisors, the coercion, debt-bondage, and the partial payment of wages in rice used to maintain labor on the estates, added nonmarket, patriarchal elements into the social relations of production within the plantations.

Almost all of the rice needed to feed estate labor was imported from India and Burma. The estate laborers were not turned into a semipeasantry in Ceylon producing their own food. But as a migrant labor force they continued their ties to their villages in South India. This enabled the planters to shift a substantial portion of the costs of reproducing their labor to the South Indian village economies and thereby reduce the costs of production on the plantations.

With respect to most of their labor and food requirements, the European coffee plantations remained largely independent of the Sinhalese peasantry. The availability of a regular and cheap supply of rice from India and the low customs duty on imported rice tended to inhibit local rice production. In the long run, a substantial segment of the native population, including many Sinhalese paddy cultivators themselves came to rely more and more on imported rice for their very subsistence.

VII. Plantations and the Colonial State

The purpose of this chapter is to examine the role of the colonial state in the creation and development of Ceylon's plantation economy and how that role in turn shaped the policies of the state towards the village economy during the nineteenth century. Some of the politico-juridical and economic activities of the state in providing land and labor for the plantations have already been described in Chapters V and VI. This chapter will present a more comprehensive analysis of the structure of the colonial state and its role in plantation development in nineteenth-century Ceylon.

The Colonial Administration

The Native Headmen

The British came to Kandy in 1815 allegedly to liberate the Kandyans from their tyrannical king. Upon the cession of the Kandyan kingdom, the British signed the Convention of 1815 with the native aristocracy, (Appendix III). This Convention, which conferred legitimacy upon British rule, made the British Crown the successor to the Kandyan monarch. As stated in the Convention, the British agreed to govern according to the feudal institutions and customs of the Kandyan kingdom.

> The Dominion of the Kandyan Province is vested in the Sovereign of the British Empire, and to be exercised through the Governor or Lieut. Governors of Ceylon for the time being and their accredited Agents, saving to the Adigars, Dessaves, Mohottals, Coralas, Vidhanas and all other chief and subordinate Native Headmen, lawfully appointed by the authority of the British Government, the Rights, Privileges and Powers of their persons and property, with their Civil Rights and immunities, according to the laws, and customs established and in force amongst them.[1]

The succession of the colonial state to the role of the precolonial monarch proved inherently more difficult than anticipated by either the British or the

---

1. Clause 4 of the Kandyan Convention, reprinted in C. G. Mendis (ed.), *Colebrooke-Cameron Papers*, vol. 2, p. 228.

Kandyan aristocracy. Even before British political authority had been established in the Kandyan Highlands, discontent began to spread among all classes of the Kandyan population. Some of the reasons for this dissatisfaction have been pointed out in Chapter III. Violation of Kandyan customs and severe damage to national pride resulted in the 1818 Kandyan rebellion, aimed at expelling the British.

Following the suppression of the rebellion, the British sought to further reduce the powers and privileges of the native chiefs. The British were highly suspicious of the chiefs and considered them to be their staunchest political opponents.[2] The Proclamation of 1818 promulgated after the suppression of the rebellion, aimed specifically at the reduction of the authority of the Kandyan aristocracy.[3] P. D. Kannangara has pointed out that following the suppression of the rebellion, a separate government distinct from that of the Maritime Provinces was established in the former Kandyan kingdom; and that the British Governor of Ceylon assumed full powers over the Kandyan Provinces without the interposition of a Legislative Council. Kannangara goes on to say that "These arrangements led to the superimposition of a loose form of European authority over a good part of the feudal organization that had belonged to the former monarchs."[4]

In addition to reducing the traditional powers of the aristocracy as administrators or representatives of the state, the British also sought to reduce their authority as landlords over the peasant cultivators.[5] The abolition of forced labor (*rājakāriya*) in the crown villages (*gabādagam*) and the creation of a class of peasant proprietors in 1818 was motivated at least partly by the desire of the British to create a class of loyal natives who could potentially be a countervailing force to the aristocracy. Turnour, the Revenue Commissioner of the Kandyan region, subsequently pointed out that, whether intended or not, the introduction of a grain tax in lieu of forced labor in the crown villages in 1818 led indirectly to the loosening of the feudal bond between lords and serfs.

2. K. M. de Silva, "The Development of the Administrative System, 1833 to c. 1910," in *History of Ceylon*, ed. by K. M. de Silva, vol. 3, p. 221.
3. Proclamation of 1818, reprinted in Mendis (ed.), *Colebrooke-Cameron Papers*, vol. 2, pp. 231–43; see also M. L. Marasinghe, "Kandyan Law and British Colonial Law: A Conflict of Tradition and Modernity – An Early State of Colonial Development in Sri Lanka," unpublished paper presented at the Fifth Congress of the International Sociological Association, Uppsala, Sweden, 1978, pp. 13–14; Colvin R. de Silva, *Ceylon Under the British*, vol. 1, p. 197.
4. P. D. Kannangara, *The History of the Ceylon Civil Service, 1802–1833* (Dehiwala-Ceylon: Tissara Publishers, 1966), p. 99.
5. Colvin R. de Silva, *Ceylon under the British*, pp. 398–400.
6. Turnour's Report quoted ibid., pp. 398–99; see also Colebrooke's Report on Administration in Mendis (ed.), *Colebrooke-Cameron Papers*, vol. 1, p. 49.

No derangement could I presume have been intended in the relations which subsisted between the proprietor of the village and his dependents as individuals or as regarded their private rights. Yet such was the construction put upon the enactment by the dependents who from the moment they paid their tythes to Government, ceased to render either dues or labour to the proprietor. The tone of the Proclamation and the universal cessation of contributions from *Palakarayas* (tenants) (at least in this province Sabaragamuwa) made the proprietor consider the sacrifice on their part resolved on by Government and they have submitted without remonstrance.[6]

The tenurial changes introduced in 1818 were not applied to the villages of the temples (*vihāragam* and *dēvalagam*) or of the nobility (*nindagam*). But as Colvin R. de Silva has pointed out, some of the tenant cultivators of temple villages also took the opportunity to shake off some of their service obligations to the feudal overlords (clergy and aristocratic lay incumbents) in the wake of changes taking place in the royal villages.[7]

Commissioner Colebrooke, appointed by the imperial government to devise new administrative arrangements for Ceylon in 1829, like many of the colonial officials in Ceylon, showed a hostility towards the hereditary privileges of the high caste native headmen. He wanted the subordinate positions in the European civil service to be opened to natives without regard to caste, which within the native administration was the determinant of status. He argued, instead, that a competent knowledge of the English language and an education in English be made the necessary criteria for recruitment to the civil service.[8] Colebrooke's intention clearly was to nurture a Europeanized elite that would be loyal to the British. In fact, Colebrooke's 1833 reforms in the sphere of education were a first step towards the emergenc of a westernized native elite. The *Ceylon Journal*, the short-lived liberal newspaper, printed and published by the colonial government (until 1833) saw little doubt of the fitness of the Kandyans for the "boons of civilization."[9]

> A body of men respectable from superior education and poverty is absolutely necessary as a means of good government; and aware of the advantages that have occurred from such a class in our own country, I cannot for a moment think that there is anything in the Kandyan character to prevent similar advantages following their formation in this Island.[10]

---

7. Colvin R. de Silva, *Ceylon under the British*, p. 400. See also discussion in Ch. V, of this book.
8. Report of Colebrooke on Administration, Mendis (ed.), *Colebrooke-Cameron Papers*, vol. 1, pp. 69–70; see also K. M. de Silva, "The Development," p. 221.
9. P. R. Pieris, "The Sociological Consequences of Imperialism with Special Reference to Ceylon," unpublished Ph. D. dissertation, University of London, 1950, p. 333. Ralph Pieris's study is focused on the cultural aspects of imperialism – the "contact between dominant and subordinate cultures," pp. 15–16.
10. *Ceylon Journal*, January 11, 1832, quoted ibid., p. 333.

However, the low-country Sinhalese and the Northern Tamils (from the Jaffna Province) were the first to avail themselves of these avenues of mobility. English education and civil service opportunities were not readily resorted to by the more conservative Kandyans, especially the aristocracy who wanted to hold on to their feudal bases of authority. During the nineteenth century, no significant westernized elite emerged in Kandy. The Kandyan aristocracy was by and large confined within the bounds of local society, although many of them took advantage of the land and tax policies of the colonial state.

Like Colebrooke, Emerson Tennent, the Colonial Secretary during the late 1840s sought to reduce the authority of the native headmen class. He criticized their powers on grounds of moral justice, administrative efficiency and political expediency. Tennent's views reflect the dominant attitude among the British towards the native aristocracy during the period between the rebellions of 1818 and 1848.

> I would likewise recommend, as far as possible the discontinuance of the present monopoly by the native chiefs of all local employment, not for the sake of income, but for the assertion of power and the pride of authority. Their number is unnecessarily great, their example prejudicial and their multiplications of inferior officers whilst it secures a sinecure for the chiefs, tends to neutralize responsibility and to diminish the efficiency with which Government ought to be served. . . .
>
> Generally speaking, there is but little real sympathy between the headmen as a body and the people. They look upon the latter as separated from them by an hereditary inferiority, and they assert their own pre-eminence by every possible means. The same alienation from the body of the people, seems to have characterized them at all periods. The Modliars were the ready abettors of Portuguese fanaticism and Dutch rapacity, and both rewarded them by confirming their exclusive privileges. The policy of successive British Governors has been directed to the obliteration of these unjust and artificial distinctions and the power of the headmen has been reduced by the commutation of feudal tenures, and the suspension of ancient titles of rank but still more by the abolition of the Raja Karia, or compulsory labor on public works, which as the people worked under the direction of the Modliars gave the latter a direct and unlimited authority.[11]

Change of Policy Towards the Native Headmen

Following the rebellion of 1848, a British Parliamentary Committee was appointed by the imperial government to inquire into the causes of that revolt. Witness after witness testifying before the Committee claimed that the disintegration of the authority of the native aristocracy was the fundamental factor in the uprising of 1848. Had their authority over the people not been

---

11. *BPP 1847–1848*, Vol. 12, pp. 96–97.

reduced by the colonial state, the argument went, the chiefs would not have incited the people to rebel. Major Skinner, the head of the Public Works Department at the time, explained that

> The headmen generally are placed in an anomalous position. The Government expects them to keep their several districts in good order by the exercise of their influence; they have no positive legally recognized authority, but by their influence they are expected to keep their districts in good order; but literally they have not the means of doing it, for our policy has completely undermined their authority.[12]

K. M. de Silva, an historian who has done extensive research on the 1848 rebellion, does not accept the above explanation. He agrees that British policy since the 1818 rebellion succeeded in reducing the powers of the aristocracy. But according to him, "The loss of their former powers and privileges had not resulted in any appreciable decline in the influence of the chiefs over the people."[13] We shall also point out later that the headmen had little to do with the rebellion.

Whatever the causes of the rebellion of 1848, the fact that it occurred made the British realize that they had essentially failed in their attempts to build a collaborating class in the Kandyan Highlands that could be an effective countervailing force against the aristocracy.[14] The British also learned from bitter experience that given the relative self-sufficiency of the indigenous economy and the elaborateness and complexity of its social structure, the local headmen were indispensable as a collaborating class to maintain British authority and expand British capital. Following the rebellion, British administrators finally conceded their dependence on the native headmen. "We have no alternative but to use the native as a means for carrying out our government and the higher he stands in his own esteem and in the respect of others, the more effective instrument shall we find him."[15] Major Skinner, the head of the Public Works Department, who had experienced difficulties in exacting peasant labor for road construction, saw a clear need for the headmen in carrying out the functions of his department.

> With a population as that of Ceylon, which is diffused generally over the country in small villages averaging fifteen or twenty houses each, and with a country almost inaccessible to us, as a matter of course it is impossible to govern the colony without the instrument of the native chiefs and headmen.[16]

---

12. Evidence of Major Skinner before the British Parliamentary Inquiry on the Ceylon Rebellion of 1848, *BPP* 1850, Vol. 12, p. 280.
13. K. M. de Silva, "The Development," p. 221.
14. Ibid., p. 220.
15. *BPP* 1850, Vol. 12, "Appendix to Minutes of Evidence," p. 350.
16. Evidence of Skinner in *BPP 1850*, Vol. 12, p. 285.

Plantations and the Colonial State

A few British officials continued to argue that the system of hereditary chieftanship as an instrument of administration was irreconciliable with British ideas of parliamentary government and the practices of modern bureaucracy. But given the political realities facing them in the 1850s, official opinion turned overwhelmingly towards the restoration of the powers and privileges of the native headmen.[17]

By midnineteenth century, the Kandyan aristocracy had resigned themselves to the permanency of British rule. They also began to covet the political and financial benefits to be accrued from collaborating with the British. For example, K. M. de Silva has pointed out that the Irrigation Ordinance of 1856, introduced by the colonial state to provide for the revival and extension of village tribunals (*gamsabhas*) helped augment the power of the chiefs over the cultivators.[18] This was because the Ordinance enabled the headmen to preside over the tribunals. We also observed earlier that in the long run, the activities of the Temple Lands and Service Tenures Commissions and the implementation of the Crown Lands Ordinance helped strengthen the political and economic authority of the feudal lords over their tenants.

Governor Gordon (1883–1890), firmly believed that it was safe to admit the aristocracy as junior partners into the administration of the country. He attempted to cultivate the aristocracy as a countervailing force to the emergent western educated elite. Gordon saw the westernized elites, who were beginning to demand the 'Ceylonisation' of the exclusively British higher echelons of the Ceylon civil service in the 1880s, as a potentially more dangerous threat to British hegemony than the feudal aristocracy.[19]

> Gordon was purposeful in his policy of an aristocratic revival. He disregarded the claims of better educated men of other social groups and the emerging castes to equality of opportunity. By the end of the century not only were all posts of President of village Tribunals in the hands of the Kandyan chiefs or the *Mudaliyars* in the low country, but all six Sinhalese Police magistrates in 1901 were members of the same aristocratic groups.[20]

The use of the native administrative class as intermediaries proved profitable to the colonial state both politically and financially. The native headmen were unpaid officials of the state. Their emoluments consisted of feudal tribute exacted from the tenant cultivators in the form of forced labor, payment in kind and/or cash. Through the continuation of this feudal practice (although altered by the commutation option), the colonial state was able to pass on a considerable part of the costs of administration directly to

---

17. K. M. de Silva, "The Development," p. 221.
18. Ibid., pp. 220–21.
19. Ibid., p. 221.
20. Ibid., p. 221.

the peasantry. Turnour, the Revenue Commissioner, justified this practice before the Colebrooke Commission in 1829 by claiming that the chiefs themselves preferred feudal tribute from tenants to pecuniary compensation from the state, because it ensured that the tenants would remain under their direct authority. Turnour went on to explain that the chiefs realized that should their serfs be relieved from feudal duties, they would be obliged to pay high wages to obtain alternative sources of labor to work their lands.[21]

The Incorporation of Native Headmen into the Administration

The British superimposed their own civil service on the native administrative hierarchy without fundamental changes in the latter's structure and personnel. Although not a part of the civil service, the subordinated native administrative hierarchy became an integral part of the colonial administration at the provincial level.

At the top of the native administrative hierarchy in the Kandyan region were the chief headmen (*Dissāwas*) in charge of the largest territorial units known as the *Dissāwas*; below them were the superior headmen known as *Ratēmahatmayās* and *Koralēs* in charge of units known as *Ratas* and *Kōralēs* respectively; still below them were the village headmen (*Aračchi/Vidhānas*) who were in charge of the smallest units of administration, the villages (*gamas*).[22]

As we have noted earlier, the native headmen performed a wide variety of functions on behalf of the colonial government. The British provincial officials (Government Agents and Assistant Government Agents) who were often ignorant of the native languages and customs, were entirely dependent on the chiefs, particularly the village headmen who were most familiar with grassroots activities. As George Turnour enumerated before the Colebrooke Commission, the headmen were

> ... employed in regulating the attendance and superintending the labour of the people employed on the roads and other public works. They collect the Grain Tax and are charged with the police of the country. The subordinate headmen are under the direction of the superior headmen and all under the orders of the Agents of Districts. They attend also as assessors to the Courts of Justice.[23]

In addition, it should be remembered that the services of the headmen were indispensable for locating and obtaining the 'crown' high lands which were to be converted into coffee plantations.

21. *CO* 416/20, Evidence of Turnour (1829), p. 103.
22. K. M. de Silva, "The Development," p. 219.
23. *CO* 416/20, Evidence of Turnour (1829), p. 119; see also *AR 1867*, Report of the Badulla District by W. E. Sharpe, p. 29.

Plantations and the Colonial State

Newton Gunasinghe has noted that the Kandyan chiefs who were incorporated into the colonial administration following the 1848 rebellion were drawn not from the first or highest echelon of the Kandyan aristocracy but the second, and "sometimes from the ranks of petty chieftancies."[24] Many of the highest aristocratic families had lost favor with the British since the 1818 rebellion. Many of these families were extinguished because of banishment or land confiscation by the British or due to lack of progeny. The Commissioner of Public Works, Major Skinner, noted that the first Adigar (highest officer of the Kandyan court), Molligoda and his son both died victims of alcoholism "and the name of a once high and powerful family is now extinct."[25] Moreover, as Ralph Pieris has observed, many of the symbols of the highest echelons of the nobility, their dress and appellations for example, came to be arrogated by petty headmen during the British period.[26]

As Gunasinghe points out, the power of the 'new aristocracy' like that of their predecessors rested on the control of land and bureaucratic positions.[27] But it must be emphasized that the distinguishing feature of the new aristocracy was that its authority was determined by and dependent upon its relationship to the colonial state. In other words, heredity was no longer sufficient to exercise *radala* or aristocratic status; it had to be legitimated by the British. We shall return to the issue of the subordination of native political authority in Chapter VIII.

The European Officials

The European wing of the colonial administration, the civil service, was numerically not very large. It consisted of a few highly influential officials such as the governor, the colonial secretary, the auditor-general, heads of administrative departments, the judiciary, the heads of the military stationed in Colombo, and the provincial officials stationed outside the capital.

The governor enjoyed an authoritarian position in the colony. In theory he was subject to the control of the Secretary of State for the Colonies (at the

---

24. Gunasinghe, "Agrarian Relations," p. 20.
25. Quoted in Pieris, "Society and Ideology in Ceylon," p. 96.
26. Ibid., p. 98.
27. Gunasinghe, "Agrarian Relations," p. 20.

Colonial Office in London) in all matters concerning the administration of the island.[28] As one historian puts it,

> In practice the governor of Ceylon enjoyed almost absolute power; the checks were in the beginning negligible. Although the Governor was expected to consult his Executive Council in the task of administration, he could reject its advice provided he explained his action satisfactorily to the Secretary of State for Colonies. Laws were made in the form of Ordinances with the Legislative Council's advice and consent, but with an unofficial majority the Governor could usually carry through his views.[29]

Given the enormous powers at his disposal, the governor could exercise much discretion in making government policies. But the overall thrust of the colonial state's activities, namely the facilitation of British capitalist expansion, was determined outside the island. Individual governors had to act within the limits demarcated by the needs of British capital. The governor had to subordinate all other interests to the primacy of commerce and the maintenance of law and order. This the local governors understood very well. At a banquet given in his honor by the Ceylon Association of London, which was largely an organization of Londoners connected with Ceylon's tea plantations, the newly appointed governor, West Ridgeway, said before he left for Ceylon in 1895,

> To put it shortly, one of the primary duties of the Governors is the promotion of commerce. Commerce is the bond of union between all parts of the empire — commerce is the *raison d'etre* — but I suppose I am speaking to the converted.[30]

The provincial officials of the colonial state were the Government Agents in charge of the nine provinces and the Assistant Government Agents in charge of the twenty one subdivisions of those Provinces. As the representatives of the state, these officers were entrusted with the tasks of maintaining law and order, revenue collection, and implementing land and tax laws.[31] Barely knowing the native language and customs, these European officials would have found it impossible to carry on their functions without the native headmen.

In the early years of British colonial rule, government officials were indistinguishable from the planters, but following the reforms of 1845 (to be discussed shortly), there was some distancing between the civil service men and the planters. However, even then Government Agents could exercise their own discretion in local administration only within the boundaries set by British capital, the Colonial Office and the Governor of Ceylon.

28. S. V. Balasingham, *The Administration of Sir Henry Ward*, p. xiv.
29. B. Bastiampillai, *The Administration of Sir William Gregory*, p. viii.
30. Quoted by Hulugalle, in *British Governors of Ceylon*, p. 3.
31. K. M. de Silva, "The Development," pp. 217–18.

Plantations and the Colonial State

As noted above, during the early phase of plantation development, that is, until about the middle of the century, almost all European officials of the state were also coffee planters. The pioneer planters Governor Barnes and Major Bird are examples. These officials used the authority of their official positions to introduce legislation conducive to plantation development. Such measures taken by Governor Barnes as the exemption of all land devoted to cash crops from custom duties and the utilization of forced labor for road construction are cases in point. Much of the initial capital for plantations also came from the salaries of these British officials in Ceylon.[32]

The Reforms of Colebrooke in 1832 also helped extend official participation in commercial agriculture. While Colebrooke cut back on the salaries and pensions of civil servants, he allowed them to make up for that loss through investments in commercial agriculture.[33]

Table 7:1 shows the amount of land sold by the colonial state to various government officials in the course of a single day, in a single district in the Central Province following the passage of the Crown Lands Ordinance in 1840. During the early days of the 'land rush' in the Kandyan Highlands, such large-scale appropriations were prevalent. We see here the familiar names of Turnour, architect of the Crown Lands Ordinance; C. R. Buller, the Government Agent of the Central Province who carried on a vehement attack against chena cultivation; Captain Skinner, the Commissioner of Roads; Stewart Mackenzie, the Governor of Ceylon (1837–1841). Much of the land thus bought at the giveaway price (set by the state) of five shillings an acre, was resold to other parties by these government officials at £2 an acre.

The evidence given by Ackland, a prominent coffee planter, testifying before the British Parliamentary Committee inquiring into the rebellion of 1848 helps further validate the thesis that the early British in Ceylon consisted of a single 'planter-official' class.[34] Not only does Ackland's evidence reveal the complete identification of the state with economic enterprise, it also shows that there was no independent judiciary in colonial Ceylon. (Note that several judges are listed as buyers of crown land in Table 7:1.)

Q.3191 (Hume)	You have stated that cattle were sometimes shot and disputes took place; who were the parties to redress any grievance or complaint in that case?
A. (Ackland)	The Government servants and officials; the Government agents in some districts or the district judges, if it be a place where they have separate authority.
Q. 3192 (Hume)	Were the district judges themselves coffee planters?
A. (Ackland)	Everybody was a coffee planter in Ceylon, from the Governor

---

32. Van Den Driesen, "Coffee Cultivation in Ceylon (1)," p. 38. See also ch. 4, p. 80 in this study.
33. K. M. de Silva, "The Development," p. 213.
34. The term planter-official is attributed to Van Den Driesen.

Table 7:1

Extract of Return of Crown Land Sales, 1840

		Acres
District of Upper Bulatgammu, or Ambagammoon, all sold at 5 s. per acre	The Hon. W. O. Carr (Judge) and Captain Skinner (Commissioner of Roads)	862
	The Right Hon. the Governor, Mr. Stewart Mackenzie	1,120
	F. B. Norris, Esq. (Surveyor-general) and others	762
	Hon. G. Turnour (Government Agent, Kandy, Acting Colonial Secretary)	2,217
	H. Wright, Esq. (District Judge, Kandy), and G. Bird	1,751
	Sir R. Arbuthnot (Commander of the Forces) and Captain Winslow (A. D. C.)	855
	T. Oswin, Esq. (a District Judge)	545
	C. R. Buller, Esq. (a Government Agent, now of Kandy)	764
	Capt. Layard (on the Staff) and friends	2,264
	P. E. Wodehouse, Esq. (Government Agent, and Assistant Colonial Secretary)	2,135
	Acres	13,275
	At 5 s.	£3,320

All sold in one day, and the Ambegammoon Road surveyed and began forthwith. Much of the above land was resold to other parties at 2£ per acre, for it was well known that Government would carry on this line of road.

Source: British Parliamentary Papers, Vol. 12, 1850, p. 303.

Plantations and the Colonial State 233

	on downwards, except Lord Torrington and Sir Colin Campbell [successive Governors].
Q. 3193 (Hume)	Was Sir Emerson Tennent? Colonial Secretary.
A. (Ackland)	I do not think he was.
Q. 3194 (Major Blackall)	Then in the case of any complaint between themselves and the Europeans, they had to go to another coffee planter to seek redress?
A. (Ackland)	Yes.
Q. 3195 (Major Blackall)	Were all coffee planters appointed magistrates for that purpose?
A. (Ackland)	No, but public servants became coffee planters.
Q. 3196 (Major Blackall)	Then that would affect their character in the eyes of the natives?
A. (Ackland)	I should think very injuriously.[35]

The practice of appointing Britishers already resident in the island to official positions was common in the early years of colonial rule. In this way effective control of many of the most coveted jobs in the higher bureaucracy practically fell in the hands of two British families resident in Ceylon, the Layards and the Templars who came to be known as the "family compact."[36] A Captain Layard and friends are listed in Table 7:1 as landbuyers.

We see then that at least in the early years of British rule in Ceylon, the colonial administration was far from the impersonal bureaucratic type of authority identified by the renowned sociologist, Max Weber. But it is well to remember that Weber himself acknowledged that the British Empire was basically an administration of 'notables'. He pointed out that the Empire provided a vast system of public assistance to the British governing classes, usually the younger sons of the gentry who did not inherit the ancestral estates (due to the operation of the law of primogeniture) and were therefore sent off to the colonies.[37]

The early colonial administration in Ceylon represented a personal form of rule by a few notables. We have seen the names of Turnour, Layard, Skinner, Barnes, Buller, Wodehouse, pop up again and again with regard to political, economic, juridical, and other matters in the colony. George Ackland quoted above, was himself a merchant, a planter, a member of the Legislative Council and proprietor of *The Colombo Observer* which was the organ of the planter community and the semi-official newspaper of the government.[38]

In the mid-1840s, the Colonial Office in London began to acknowledge that the neglect of official duties by the civil servants in Ceylon stemmed

35. *BPP 1850*, Vol. 12, p. 20.
36. K. M. de Silva, "The Development," p. 214.
37. Hans H. Gerth and C. Wright Mills (eds.), *From Max Weber: Essays in Sociology* (New York: Oxford University Press, 1958), p. 210; Ralph Pieris, "Some Neglected Aspects of the British Colonial Administration in the Early Nineteenth Century," *Ceylon Historical Journal*, vol. 2, nos. 1–2 July and October 1952), p. 73.
38. *BPP 1850*, Vol. 12, p. 2.

largely from their involvement in plantation agriculture. In 1844–1845, Lord Stanley, the British Secretary of State for the Colonies, ordered the civil servants in Ceylon to dispose of their properties and issued a strict prohibition against their participation in commercial activities.[39] The Governor of Ceylon at the time, Colin Campbell (1841–1847), modified this ruling by allowing civil servants to keep their estates provided they did not manage them. He thereby introduced the principle of separation of ownership and management. Campbell attempted to discourage further commercial investments on the part of officials by declaring that official promotions for those with planting interests would be delayed.[40] In attempting to separate civil servants from the plantation enterprise, Governor Campbell also offered increases in salaries and pensions.[41] As noted earlier, the native wing of the colonial administration was remunerated by tribute exacted from the peasantry, rather than salaries paid from the colonial treasury (a few of the highest chiefs did receive fixed salaries). The cheapness of the native administration no doubt helped the colonial state increase its outlays on salaries for the European officials.

In a public statement made in 1929, Governor Hugh Clifford stressed that no colonial officials held land in the island at that time.[42] Back in 1849, George Ackland observed that the process of extricating public servants from coffee planting was extremely difficult and despite Campbell's orders, the formal separation between the bureaucracy and commercial enterprise was not yet effected.[43] In a recent study, political scientist Jean Grossholtz notes that notwithstanding this formal separation, civil servants in Ceylon continued to retain ties to capitalist enterprise and the ability to benefit from them.[44] As the earlier quoted statement of Governor Ridgeway indicates, whether officials had private interests in capitalist agriculture or not, in their official status they were expected to uphold commerce as the *raison d'être* of colonial government.[45]

Michael Roberts has observed a gradual distancing between the planters and the civil servants following the reforms and the new recruitment patterns introduced into the civil service in the mid-1840s.[46] In fact these civil service men who were generally better educated developed a sense of superiority

---

39. K. M. de Silva, "The Development," p. 214.
40. Grossholtz, "Forging Capitalist Patriarchy," p. 116.
41. K. M. de Silva, "The Development," pp. 214–15.
42. Hugh Clifford, "Some Reflections," p. 287.
43. *BPP 1850*, Vol. 12, p. 20.
44. Grossholtz, "Forging Capitalist Patriarchy," p. 117.
45. See page 234 and footnote 30 in this chapter.
46. Michael Roberts, communications to author.

Plantations and the Colonial State 235

towards the planters. Nevertheless, the linkages within the small European community far outweighed the cleavages within it along educational and occupational lines. Attempts to maintain their distance from the native population and to cultivate a sense of racial superiority necessitated that the different factions of the white community band together. This they did through the social links maintained at the European-only tennis and other social clubs such as the Colombo Club, Prince's Club, and the Kandy Club.[47] Intermarriages that took place between the planters' and civil servants' families also helped reinforce the sense of community among the white colonizers.

Notwithstanding the firm commitment of the colonial state to the plantation enterprise differences and even clashes did emerge from time to time between the officials and the planters. Most of these differences occurred over the allocation of state revenue. The planter lobby tried its best to pass on the costs of roads, and medical care for labor, on to the state. While the profitability of the plantations was the only concern of the planters, the colonial state had to take care of other matters too. For instance, the state had to ensure that the native headmen class remained sympathetic to British rule and that the peasantry were kept under control. This meant that the state could not give in to each and every demand made by the planters.

The most serious clash between the state and the planters occurred during the term of Governor MacCarthy (1860-1863). MacCarthy, who was noted for his parsimony and laissez-faire views, was charged with neglecting roads needed by the plantation sector.[48] This charge culminated in the resignation of all six unofficial members of the Legislative Council and in what Michael Roberts has called 'the first constitutional reform movement in the island.'[49]

In spite of the formal separation between the state and the plantation economy and the occasional clashes between individuals in these two spheres, the European planter community continued to enjoy an extremely influential position in the colony. It was the most powerful pressure group in Ceylon and was represented by the Chamber of Commerce established in 1837 and the Planters Association established in 1854. The latter organization was called 'a power in the state' by one of its contemporary critics, George Wall.[50] Members of the planting community found ample representation in the Legislative Council and it also became a custom for the governor to consult the planters on all matters of importance in the colony.[51] Planter pressure, for example, was decisive in the government's decision not to intro-

47. Ibid.
48. Hulugalle, *British Governors of Ceylon*, p. 98.
49. Michael Roberts, communications to author.
50. Speculum, *Ceylon*, p. 122.
51. K. M. de Silva, "The Development," p. 236.

duce a general land tax and not to raise the import duty on rice. While bearing in mind the qualifications of the 'planter-official' hypothesis noted earlier, we can still agree with Van Den Driesen that

> "The problems of the planter came to be regarded as synonymous with those of the country.... Thus did Ceylon dance to the coffee growers' tune for the greater part of the nineteenth century.'[52]

In fulfilling its commitment to the plantation sector, the state was often compelled to take actions that were detrimental to the village sector, particularly the peasant cultivators. The dualistic policy and practice of the colonial state vis-à-vis these two sectors can be demonstrated by examining its politico-juridical and economic functions during the nineteenth century. It should be remembered, however, that although colonial state activities were motivated primarily by the desire to expand European capital, the white planters were not the only ones to benefit from them. The more privileged segments of the native population also benefitted.

It is extremely difficult to separate the various functions of the state from each other. But for purposes of this discussion, we shall examine in turn the state's actions in meeting the land, labor and infrastructural requirements of the plantation sector.

The Facilitation of the Plantation Enterprise by the Colonial State

The Provision of Land for Plantations

The colonial state's claims to both land and paddy taxes were based on the legitimacy it derived as the successor to the precolonial Sinhalese monarch. In accepting the feudal maxim that the king/state was the 'lord of the soil' literally, the colonial state assumed the position of 'grand seigneiur'. The legitimacy of the Crown Lands Ordinance of 1840 was based entirely on this assumption. As Michael Roberts has observed,

> The British believed commonly that state over-proprietorship had characterised medieval European policy and tended to equate Asian societies with European feudalism. Thus James Stuart Mill claimed that in India 'the property of the soil resided in the sovereign.' Similar concepts were applied to Ceylon as well. Significantly, as Oriental scholar-official George Turnour was among the earliest proponents (in 1835)

---

52. Van den Driesen, "Some Trends," p. 2.

of the theory that the king of Ceylon had been "the absolute owner of every acre of land in the country." Practices derived from Kandyan and Dutch times were used to bolster this proposition. In the policy discussions on the subject of 'Waste Lands' and encroachments, a Governor noted that the Crown had "a catholic right to all the lands not proved to have been granted at an earlier period" and this concept was incorporated in the Crown Lands Encroachment Ordinance of 1840.[53]

The unqualified assumption that 'all land belonged to the king' was clearly erroneous. However, it was tremendously useful to the colonial state as a justification for its policy measures.[54] Feudal claims such as these were used by the colonial state towards the establishment of private property rights and capitalist agriculture. But far from completely eradicating the feudal norms and institutions. the colonial state built itself and the plantation economy upon selected aspects of the precolonial social structure. Those aspects of the precolonial society that conflicted with the interests of the colonial state and commercial agriculture, such as the users' rights to forest, pasture and swidden lands were either ignored or curtailed, while the assumption that the king was the owner of all uncultivated land was accepted literally. But in subordinating and adapting precolonial institutions to suit the purposes of capitalist development, these institutions and customs (such as the theory that all land belonged to the king) were fundamentally transformed.

It is necessary to interject here that the colonial state justified its right to the paddy tax also on the basis of its assumed role as the successor to the precolonial monarch. The colonial state claimed that under British rule, the paddy tax was greatly reduced and was more beneficial to the native cultivators than it had ever been under the Sinhalese rulers. In the absence of comparative quantitative data, these assertions cannot be tested. But on the basis of the discussion in Chapter V, we can conclude that the paddy tax was certainly not beneficial to the paddy cultivators. Even after the exposé of the large-scale evictions and starvation resulting from the paddy tax in many regions in the late 1870s and 1880s, the colonial state continued to justify the paddy tax on the basis of customary usage.

53. Roberts, "Land Problems and Policies," p. 124; see also K. M. de Silva, "Studies in British Land Policy in Ceylon, I: The Evolution of Ordinances 12 of 1840 and 9 of 1841," *CJHSS*, vol. 7 (1964), p. 124.
54. Roberts, "Land Problems and Policies," p. 124. In India too, the colonial state legitimized its claim to a large share of the surplus from Indian agriculture by propagating the myth that in Mughal India the land was the property of the Emperor. See Hamza Alavi, "India," p. 186. Similarly, Alex Gordon has pointed out that in Indonesia, the Dutch colonial state made all waste land crown property by passing the State Land Law of 1870, "Stages in the Destruction of Java's Self-Supporting Rural Economic System," unpublished paper read at the Seminar on "Underdevelopment and Subsistence Reproduction in Southeast Asia," University of Bielefeld, West Germany, 21–23 April 1978. Similar examples can be found for other colonial areas, including Africa.

> That a levy by the Crown of a portion of the grain grown on paddy lands has been made from time immemorial, that in its origin it was a rent and not a tax, that it was heaviest under the rule of the native sovereigns, that it has been continuously reduced during the occupation of the Island by the English, that as last settled by the Ordinance No. 11 of 1878 it is lighter than at any previous time and that at present it is the survival in a modified and more beneficient form of the rent exacted by the ancient kings as lords paramount of the soil.[55]

In responding to the demand of critics that the land tax should be extended to the plantations, the Grain Tax Commissioners of 1878 claimed that while plantation owners had purchased their lands in private property rights, the paddy cultivators were merely the former tenants of the Crown and had no legal right to be exempted from the age old ground rent due to the sovereign.[56] Another argument set forth by Governor Gregory was that as the peasants held their high lands free of taxation, it was entirely justifiable to tax their paddy fields. This argument was again based on the precolonial practice of taxing only the wet rice fields (*mada idam*) and not the appurtenant high lands (*goda idam*).

> The fact that other land is exempted from this rent or tythe is no reason that all land should be so exempted. It is not the case that the paddy grower is unjustly treated, for he receives his share of benefit by the uplands which he holds free of tax.[57]

The fact that the Crown Lands Ordinance of 1840 demanded titles and receipts of taxes paid on high lands; that it denied or restricted peasants' access to high lands; that it created a situation — a land market — that never existed in precolonial times, was conveniently forgotten in justifying the paddy tax on the basis of customary practice.

The Provision of the Politico-Juridical Framework for Private Property

As we noted in Chapter V, the creation of private property rights in land and a land market through the instrument of the Crown Lands Ordinance did not prove easy for the colonial state. The peasantry in particular challenged the claims of the colonial state on the basis of their precolonial users' rights. The state found it necessary therefore to pass an assortment of other auxiliary legislation such as the Private Roads Bill, Coffee Stealing Bill, Land Registration Ordinance, Partition Ordinance, Kandyan Marriage Ordinances, etc., in order to protect the newly established private property rights.

---

55. *SP 1890*, No. 17, "The Grain Tax Ordinance, – 1878," p. 38.
56. *SP 1878*, No. 29, "Papers Relating to Grain," p. 18.
57. Ibid., p. 9.

Plantations and the Colonial State

The Private Roads Bill and the Coffee Stealing Bill very clearly point to the conflict between plantation and peasant interests and the partiality of the colonial state towards the former. The Land Registration, Partition, and Kandyan Marriage Ordinances were clearly part of the routinization of private property rights. As such they were more useful to those who had access to the colonial bureaucracy. This meant also that these registration ordinances had differential effects on the various social classes in the native society.

The Private Roads Bill

When three planters could not obtain access to a tract of land purchased from the Crown because natives owning the adjoining swidden land refused a road to be built through their land or sell their land to the planters, access was secured through the intervention of the state which passed a legislative enactment, Ordinance No. 17 of 1861. This bill allowed construction of private roads to estates through native landholdings. The Colonial Secretary, Newcastle, showed a keen awareness of the class bias of this legislation when he said,

> I must observe that legislation of this kind, the effect of which is to take away one man's property, not for public purpose, but for the benefit of another man, requires to be very carefully watched and not least so when it is for the benefit of a member of the ruling class.[58]

Bill Against Coffee Stealing

Similarly, Ordinance No. 8 of 1878, passed in order to prevent coffee stealing, helped planters at the expense of native cultivators. This Ordinance made the possession of more than a bushel of coffee without a sale note, a penal offense. Stealing of coffee from European owned estates had become an organized and systematic enterprise in which plantation laborers, petty traders, and neighboring villagers took part.[59] This Ordinance, aimed at preventing such stealing, required that even the peasant coffee cultivator prove that his coffee was his own. In principle, then, this Ordinance was similar to the Crown Lands Ordinance in that the burden of proving that the coffee was their own or was 'honestly received'/bought was placed on the producer/-possessor. The Ordinance also prohibited the loading of coffee between six in

---

58. *SP 1862*, No. 2, "Native Rights," p. 5.
59. *SP 1873*, No. 11, "Correspondence on the Subject of Coffee Stealing," p. 5.

the evening and five in the morning. People convicted of coffee stealing were committed to imprisonment with hard labor.⁶⁰ We lack statistical evidence on the extent of convictions made under this Ordinance, it is plausible, however, that it discouraged smallholder coffee production. Also important is the class bias of this legislation – in favor of the planters. The Chief Justice at the time himself noted that,

> There is a natural prejudice in the public mind against special criminal legislation on behalf of a particular kind of property especially when the owners of that kind of property belong mainly to a single class of the community. But if you show that you are doing no more for it than has been already done for another kind of property belonging to a different class of the community, that prejudice must in reasonable minds, be very much diminished and need no longer be an obstacle to measures for securing the administration of sustained justice.⁶¹

The Land Registration Ordinance

In Chapter V, we mentioned that in 1859 a coalition of landed proprietors consisting of European planters and native overlords presented a memorial to the Secretary of State for the Colonies pleading that the Crown Lands Ordinance be repealed. Instead of repealing the Ordinance, the colonial state introduced several new legislative enactments aimed at a more efficient application of the principles of private property and fixity of tenure as laid down in the Crown Lands Ordinance. Among them was Ordinance No. 8 of 1863 which provided 'for the registration of titles to land and of all deeds affecting land in the colony.'⁶² The objectives of the Bill were to secure certainty of title to landed property and provide for the registration and ultimately to 'prevent the heavy losses sustained by capitalists for want of reliable information.' Under this Ordinance, arrangements were also made to survey each district; investigate all land claims in them, and register allotments of ascertained owners and issue certificates of ownership to them.⁶³

According to Van Den Driesen, the Land Registration Bill enabled the state to lay claim to properties that were 'illegally' claimed or encroached upon by natives. Where the illegally claimed land had already been sold, the buyers (who were often planters) were given outright ownership rights and the original sale price was collected from the illegal sellers.⁶⁴

60. *SP 1873*, No. 10, "Coffee Stealing," pp. 3–9.
61. *SP 1873*, No. 11, p. 6.
62. *SP 1863*, No. 4, "Land Registration," p. 3; see also Van Den Driesen, "Land Sales Policy, (2)," p. 50.
63. Ibid., p. 50.
64. Ibid., p. 51.

Plantations and the Colonial State

There is little evidence in colonial documents which validate Van Den Driesen's conclusions that the Land Registration Ordinance succeeded in returning lands encroached by natives to planters. However, it is clear, that the Ordinance was introduced to strengthen private property rights which were being assailed by rampant encroachments and illegal land sales.

The Partition Ordinance

The Kandyan institution of undivided or joint ownership of land (usually among family members), came into conflict with the capitalist concept of individual private property ownership introduced by the British. Under the precolonial arrangements, paddy cultivation was carried on jointly without a physical subdivision of the family plot. On the other hand, the Kandyan system of bilateral inheritance tended to increase the subdivision of the ancestral property into smaller and smaller units. The Kandyan system of inheritance often came into conflict with the systems of private property and primogeniture, familiar to the British.[65]

The British administration felt that the system of joint ownership of land and the minute fragmentation of ownership units were impediments to the extension of private property rights, agricultural development and the emergence of wage labor.[66] Ordinance No. 10 of 1863, or the 'Partition Ordinance,' was passed in order to give "every inducement to landowners to seek a division, or if the extent (was) small and the number of proprietors great, a sale of the lands so held."[67] Any one of the two or more owners was given the right to compel partition or sale of land jointly held, and owners refusing to allow partition had to appear in court to explain why a partition or sale of the jointly held property should not be carried on, as asked for by another co-owner.

The Partition Ordinance became a "notorious instrument of land grabbing" for indigenous capitalists. This was not necessarily the intention of the British in passing the Ordinance; it was one of its unintended consequences. Upon purchase of property, the new owners who had acquired the land through partition were able to eject tenants whose families had held the land for centuries. Foreclosures of mortgages and debts also became means through

---

65. Roberts, "Land Problems and Policies," pp. 123, 90–97; see also *CO* 416/20, Evidence of George Turnour.
66. *CO* 416/20, p. 96.
67. Quoted in Roberts, "Land Problems and Policies," p. 124.
68. Roberts, "Aspects of Ceylon's Agrarian Economy," p. 50.

which cultivators lost their shares in land to financiers.[68] The Partition Ordinance, along with the commuted paddy tax, contributed to the emergence of new property and class relations in the village economy. These new legislative instruments introduced by the British, contributed to incessant disputes over land. As Governor Ward himself observed, the proverbial love of litigation of the Sinhalese was not an inherent cultural trait, but one induced by the new laws and the alien and cumbersome judicial procedure.

> Sinhalese are using machinery of oppression that we have placed within their reach, that nearly the whole population are habitually in the Courts and that our criminal statistics should show no less than 17,000 accused persons in a single year.[69]

Registration of Births and Marriages

Ordinance No. 13 of 1862, pertaining to the registration of births and deaths and the series of ordinances introduced in order to register Kandyan marriages, also complemented the administration's policy of creating a juridical framework in support of private property rights.[70]

The abundance of land and its ready availability for use in precolonial Kandyan society made conflicts over land relatively rare occurrences. Labor, on the other hand. was scarce and a number of labor sharing schemes had been devised by the cultivator classes. These included reciprocal labor sharing arrangements in paddy cultivation known as *attam*, joint ownership of property, and polyandrous marriage.

In precolonial Kandy, there was no registration of marriages in the western legal sense; cohabitation between a man and a woman of the same caste and rank was accepted by the community as 'proof of marriage'. Similarly, divorces were obtained easily through mutual consent.[71]

The practice of polyandry, or the taking of one wife by several 'associated husbands', usually brothers, was a fairly common practice among the cultivator classes in the Kandyan Provinces. One of the basic reasons for this was economic. As tribute exaction was made on landshares held by cultivators rather than on individuals in the form of head taxes, the practice of joint cultivation enabled several men to share the corvée labor duties (*rājakāriya*) attached to a given plot of land. Furthermore, it ensured that while one man

---

69. *CO* 54/474, No. 38 of 4, February 1872, Governor Henry Ward to Earl of Kimberley.
70. Roberts, "Land Problems and Policies," p. 123.
71. *Papers on the Custom of Polyandry as Practiced in Ceylon* (Colombo: Government Record Office, 1898), pp. 5–13.

Plantations and the Colonial State

was away on duty to the state, there was another or several men to take care of the family cultivation.[72]

However, the reasons for polyandry were not entirely economic. The practice of female infanticide (which the British outlawed), and the sexual division of labor in Kandyan society also contributed to the emergence of polyandrous arrangements.[73] These are issues that need greater investigation. Here, we are concerned only with the impediments that polyandrous marriage placed on the extension of private property rights in land and the attempts made by the colonial state to combat them.

The ready availability of land and the custom of holding land jointly by family members precluded the need for clearly defined means of establishing paternity and inheritance rights during precolonial times. The children of polyandrous unions referred to each of their mother's husbands as 'father'. Such arrangements made it difficult to trace paternity and inheritance. This in turn made the application of the Land Registration, Partition, and other Ordinances difficult. In addition, the absence of certificates of births, deaths, and marriages made disputes over land inheritances and land claims extremely cumbersome to deal with.

As an effort to resolve some of these difficulties, the colonial state passed Ordinance No. 13 of 1859, or the 'Kandyan Marriage Ordinance', and several subsequent amending ordinances making polyandry and polygyny illegal and unregistered marriages invalid.[74] As the District Judge of Kandy noted, British intentions on this matter were largely economic. "That whatever the Legislature does in the matter, it should proceed with the sole object of settling Civil Rights of property, rather than such disreputable dogmas of morality."[75] Here again, the interests of the British and the Kandyan cultivator class came into conflict. The efforts to get people to register marriages were largely unsuccessful in spite of the harshness of the law which stated that,

> Any person, resident in the Kandyan provinces being married who shall marry any other person during the life of the former husband or wife, whether the second marriage shall have taken place in such Kandyan provinces or elsehwere and every person counselling, aiding and abetting such offender, shall be guilty of an offense

---

72. Ibid., pp. 5–13. See also *SP 1959*, No. 16, "Report of the Commission on Marriage and Divorce," Appendix A, p. 175.
73. For other possible reasons for polyandry, see Pieris, "Society and Ideology," p. 81.
74. Ordinances No. 13 of 1859 and No. 3 of 1870, in *A Revised Edition of the Legislative Enactments*, vol. 1, p. 751.
75. *SP 1869–1870*, "Papers Relating to the Operation of the Kandyan Marriage Ordinance," p. 19: see also Supplement to *The Colombo Observer*, November 19, 1866.

and being convicted thereof shall be liable to be imprisoned, with or without hard labour for a period not exceeding three years. . . . [76]

The relative failure of the British in enforcing the Marriage Ordinances during the nineteenth century was due to the extreme difficulty of obtaining a divorce under its terms and the payment of fees involved in obtaining marriage licenses.[77] On the other hand, the fact that the British transformed corvée labor (*rājakāriya*) into a capitation tax divorced from land tenure (to be discussed later in this chapter) reduced the economic advantages of polyandry. The introduction of private property rights, a land market and western values contributed to the gradual demise of polyandry. These larger socioeconomic forces operating in the society were more successful in wiping out polyandry than the Marriage Ordinance which attempted to change things overnight. Once again, the British found that existing social structures could not be changed simply by administrative fiat.

What is perhaps most interesting about the Kandyan Marriage Ordinance is that it was initiated by some members of the Kandyan aristocracy. This Ordinance had its roots in a Memorial sent by a group of aristocrats entreating the British to do away with the customs of polyandry and polygyny.[78] The British were happy to comply given their interest in wiping out the barriers to private property and the 'uncivilized' customs of the natives. It was then that the Kandyan Marriage Ordinance of 1859 was enacted.

It seems that like the British, the aristocracy, too, was desirous of strengthening their newly acquired private property rights to land. The behavior of the aristocrats in this instance has also to be understood in the context of the ideological control exercised by the colonial power. A specific motive in asking for the abolition of polyandry was the desire of this particular group of aristocrats to ingratiate themselves with the colonial ruler.[79] Let us also bring to mind that this was not the only occasion when the interests of the British — specifically the planters — and the native chiefs converged. These two groups came together in 1859 in sending a Memorial demanding that the Crown Lands Ordinance be repealed.

Once the Ordinance was passed, members of the aristocratic-administrative class were the first to register their marriages.[80] This is understandable given

76. Ordinance No. 3 of 1870 — "An Ordinance to Amend the Laws and Marriages in the Kandyan Provinces," in *A Revised Edition of the Legislative Enactments*, vol. 1, p. 751.
77. *SP* 1869, No. 21, p. 23 and *SP* 1869, No. 27, p. 5.
78. *SP* 1959, "Report of the Commission on Marriage and Divorce," Appendix A.
79. Ibid., p. 176.
80. *AR* for the Kegalle District by Sharpe, quoted in *SP* 1869, No. 3, "Papers Relating to the Operation of the Kandyan Marriage Ordinance."

Plantations and the Colonial State

that polyandry was largely restricted to the cultivator classes to begin with and that the native headmen class was much more familiar with the various laws being passed by the colonial administration. In encouraging the native headmen to register their marriages, some Government Agents in the Kandyan Provinces began to appoint only 'married' (i. e., properly registered) candidates to administrative positions. The intention of these British provincial officials was to cultivate a class of natives who were attached to the government's point of view and whose behavior in turn would set an example to the masses of the cultivators.[81]

The Attempted Provision of Labor for the Plantations

In Chapter VI, it was pointed out that the colonial state attempted to create a labor supply for the plantations out of the Kandyan peasantry by alienating their high lands (*goda bim*) and by imposing a series of cash taxes on them. But for reasons discussed earlier, a steady and regular supply of labor could not be obtained from the peasant cultivators.

Unlike the colonial governments of plantation colonies in the West Indies and Mauritius, the Ceylonese state stopped short of state sponsorship of the recruitment and supply of labor to the plantations. Throughout the nineteenth century, the planter lobby in Ceylon agitated for state sponsorship of labor immigration.[82] But proximity of the sources to labor supply in South India and the relative ease of labor recruitment, prevented the direct participation of the colonial state in this matter. Laissez-faire ideology was often invoked by government officials in justifying the noninvolvement of the state.[83] The fact that labor migration into Ceylon was considered inter-Indian migration by the British government in India and that it did not come under the strictures of the Indian Emigration Ordinances also helped Ceylon planters obtain their labor easily and without resort to state sponsorship. However, the state did recruit the Indian laborers known as the 'road coolies' that it used for construction work in its own Public Works Department.

The colonial state did provide the planters the institutional means and supports needed for controlling and retaining the laborers on the plantations. These were quite important given the tendency on the part of laborers to abscond without repaying debts. With the enactment of Ordinances No. 5 of

---

81. *AR 1863*, Report of O'Grady, G. A. for the North Western Province, quoted in *SP 1869*, No. 3, p. 16.
82. K. M. de Silva, *Social Policy*, Chap 8, p. 243.
83. Wesumperuma, "The Migration," p. 52.

1841 and No. 11 of 1865 — the Master-Servant Laws — the state granted the planter a firm bold over his laborers. The partiality of these laws to the planter becomes obvious when one considers the fact that the planter was made liable only to civil proceedings, but the laborer to criminal proceedings, for breach of a labor contract.[84]

With the introduction of the 'tin ticket system' of labor transportation in 1901, the colonial state came to take on a more central role in the conveyance of South Indian labor to the Ceylonese plantations. The tin ticket referred to the metal token given to each laborer as the pass or ticket for their use of government-owned transportation (specifically the railways), and as the indicator of the estate to which he/she was being taken. It was a system of cash on delivery in which the state bore the initial expenses of transporting the package being delivered, i. e., the laborer. The costs of transportation were later recovered by the state from the planters who in turn debited the costs to the laborers themselves![85]

The Provision of Infrastructure Needed by the Plantations

One of the greatest contributions of the colonial state to the establishment and consolidation of the Ceylonese plantation economy was the provision of the necessary infrastructure — roads, railways, ports, hospitals for estate laborers etc.

In their efforts to keep out the Europeans, the precolonial Kandyan kings had the Highlands deliberately isolated from the European ruled coastal lowlands of the island. A thick forest belt prohibited to cultivators (*tahansi kālē*) was maintained between the mountainous core of the Kandyan kingdom and the Maritime Provinces. No roads were allowed to be built that could link the two areas.[86]

In contrast, the construction of communication networks, particularly roads, was a *sine qua non* for the consolidation of British political authority and commercial development in the Kandyan Highlands. The 1818 rebellion in Kandy impressed upon the British the importance of a network of roads for breaking down the isolation of the Highlands and for controlling possible guerrilla warfare in that region.

Once plantation development got under way in the 1830s, the need for roads linking the coffee estates to the sea ports in the coastal lowlands be-

---

84. Roberts, "The Master Servant Laws," p. 25.
85. Wesumperuma, "The Migration," p. 86.
86. Pieris, *Sinhalese Social Organization*, p. 46.

came urgent. Given the dependence of the estates on imported supplies, labor, and foreign markets for sale of coffee, the very profitability of the coffee enterprise came to rest on the availability of an efficient communications system. In outlining the aims of the 'Road Ordinance' introduced in 1848, Earl Grey, the Secretary of the State for the Colonies, made quite clear the administration's commitment to providing roads needed for plantation development.

> The construction and maintenance of roads was one of the heaviest charges upon the Colonial Treasury; yet so far from being advisable to curtail (this) work ... it was of the highest importance to the progress and prosperity of Ceylon that the roads should be improved and many new ones made. The imperfection of the existing means of transit and the consequently heavy expense of bringing down their produce and of sending supplies to the higher country, which is the best adapted for the growth of coffee, was one of the greatest difficulties with which the planters had to contend.[87]

The response of the colonial state to the infrastructural needs of the plantation sector was overwhelming. Governor Barnes, the pioneer road builder of Ceylon, had the Colombo-Kandy road constructed by 1820.[88] By the midnineteenth century, an entire network of roads was completed between the planting regions and the coast. By 1867, the first railway line was completed between Kandy and Colombo.[89] The impressive communication network developed by the colonial state in the nineteenth century was largely concentrated in the planting region. (See Map, p. 248).

Undoubtedly, the natives, particularly the cashcropping peasantry and those groups engaged in commerce and transportation, also benefitted from the roads and railways built by the state. In fact, as mentioned earlier, members of certain low-country Sinhalese castes, such as the *karava*, found in the plantation-related transportation activities a basis for their entry into the emergent local capitalist class.[90] But as some Europeans themselves acknowledged, roads and railways were constructed with the British plantation enterprise in mind and, the plantations were the chief beneficiaries of the new communications system.[91] For example, while pointing out that the newly constructed railway reduced planters' costs of production, Governor Robin-

---

87. Quoted in K. M. de Silva (ed.), *Letters on Ceylon*, p. 8.
88. L. A. Wickremaratne, "The Development of Transportation in Ceylon, c. 1800–1947," in *History of Ceylon*, (ed.) K. M. de Silva, vol. 3, p. 303.
89. Indrani Munasinghe, "The Colombo-Kandy Railway," *The Ceylon Historical Journal*, vol. 25, Nos. 1–4, October 1978.
90. Michael Roberts, "The Rise of the Karavas," *Ceylon Studies Seminar*, 1968/69 Series, Paper No. 5, *passim*.
91. *BPP 1850*, Vol. 12, Evidence of Ackland, p. 44.

Part 2: The Plantation Impact

ROADS AND RAILWAYS CONSTRUCTED UNDER THE BRITISH, 1814–1913

Source: G. C. Mendis, *Ceylon Under the British*.
Colombo: The Colombo Apothecaries Co., Ltd., 1944, p. 93.

Plantations and the Colonial State

son (1865–1872) also noted in 1869 that the natives could "never derive any direct advantage unlike the European commercial class from the railway."[92]

Sources of Revenue and Labor for Road Construction

The question that we need to investigate now is how and where the state obtained the labor and the money necessary for these large-scale construction projects.

In the period prior to the Colebrooke Reforms, all roads were built with the forced labor (*rājakāriya*) of the peasants. In 1832, Colebrooke formerly abolished forced labor to the state with the anticipation that it would release a wage labor force among the Sinhalese peasantry. But for reasons discussed earlier, such a labor force did not emerge. When a depression in the coffee industry reduced government revenue, Governor Torrington reinstated compulsory labor in the form of a road tax via Ordinance No. 8 of 1848 or the Road Ordinance. This Ordinance required that all males between the ages of eighteen and fifty five (except those specifically exempted such as laborers residing in plantations and Buddhist monks) labor on road construction six days per year or pay an annual commuted fee of Rs.1.50.

> Every male inhabitant between the ages of 18 and 55 years shall be liable to perform six consecutive days' labour in each year upon the thoroughfares in this colony, or on works necessary for the formation, repair, or improvement thereof, or in the collection and preparation of materials required for any such purpose, or any work sanctioned by the Legislative Council under the authority of this Ordinance.[93]

Although the road tax was greatly resented by the peasantry and was a decisive factor in the eruption of the 1848 rebellion, the colonial state maintained this tax well into the twentieth century. Indeed, this tax conferred great advantages on the state and the plantation sector. George Ackland, the British planter, stated quite bluntly before the British Parliamentary hearings on the 1848 rebellion that the practical effect of the Road Ordinance was to transfer the expense of making roads from the colonial treasury to the people at large.[94] In a situation of labor scarcity, the road tax provided the state with a ready-made source of labor for road maintenance and construction. Governor Barnes had earlier asked "who ... was there so fit to undertake the task as the people themselves?"[95] Forced labor was exacted under the Road

---

92. Quoted in Wickremaratne, "The Development of Transportation," p. 309.
93. As stated in Ordinance No. 10 of 1861 — The Amending Ordinance No. 8 of 1848, *A Revised Edition of the Legislative Enactments*, vol. 1, p. 391.
94. *BPP 1850*, Vol. 12, p. 44.
95. Quoted in Samaraweera, "Economic and Social Development," p. 60.

Ordinance by the native headmen. As the continuation of this practice helped maintain their own precolonial authority over the people, the headmen acquiesced to the orders of the British without protest.

On the other hand, the road tax was so abhorrent to the peasantry that some of them worked on the coffee estates principally to avoid it (the road tax it must be reiterated was not levied from the estate laborers).[96] Most Kandyan peasants preferred to pay the commuted tax rather than labor on the roads. Between 1876 and 1880, out of an average of 517,000 people bound to work on the roads, 85 percent opted to commute.[97] It seems that some peasants insisted on commuting the labor dues even when they did not have the cash to pay, as during the collapse of peasant coffee in the early 1880s.[98] The result of defaulting on the road tax (and the paddy tax) was the sale of their paddy fields by the state in order to recover monies due.

Out of total public work expenditures in 1867, approximately 15 percent was derived from funds collected under the Road Tax Ordinance.[99] In addition to supplying labor, the road tax also helped augment government revenue and extend the cash nexus into the village economy. Part of the cash collected in the form of the road tax (largely from the native peasantry) was used to pay the Indian laborers that the state imported to work on its construction projects. These laborers worked in separate labor gangs and probably had no contact with the Sinhalese peasantry who also worked on the roads under the supervision of their own Sinhalese headmen.

The planters, who were constantly in search of avenues to pass on more of their financial responsibilities to the peasantry, kept demanding that the commutation rate of the Road Tax (revenue from this tax being used for plantation related infrastructure) be increased.[100] Meanwhile, large numbers of peasants who had defaulted on their road tax payments were being imprisoned by the state.[101]

The colonial state exacted labor for road construction on the basis of the feudal right of the state to corvée labor. Here again the colonial state used feudal legitimacy to further its own end of extending the market economy and private enterprise. In so doing, it deliberately changed the fundamental character of precolonial labor exaction. Samaraweera's observations with regard to the use of forced labor by the British during the earlier mercantilist

---

96. *AR 1888*, p. 78A.
97. *SP 1882*, No. 4, "Road Ordinance Commission Report," p. 5.
98. *AR 1883*, "Report for the Badulla District," p. 28 A.
99. *The Ceylon Blue Book*, 1867.
100. *SP 1864*, No. 6, p. 10.
101. *SP 1882*, No. 4, p. 5.

Plantations and the Colonial State

phase (1796–1833) can also be extended to the operation of the Road Ordinance since 1848.

> Although some officials strongly felt that *rajakariya* was incompatible with the concepts of order and justice they had known – "so opposed to our national prejudices" was a recurring phrase in early correspondence – it was not a rejection or an abolition of the institution that was considered by the British, but a more efficient and remunerative employment of it to further their policies. This entailed a considerable modification, and in some respects even an extension of the institution, which strikingly changed its character and transformed it to the true compulsory services system it became under the British.[102]

In precolonial times the legitimacy to exact corvée services (*rājakāriya*) was derived from the fact that at least a part of the labor thus exacted was used towards the benefit of the peasantry themselves, e. g., the construction and maintenance of irrigational works necessary for peasant paddy cultivation and subsistence. In discussing the nature of capital accumulation in the colony, a contemporary critic of the colonial state pointed out the different uses to which corvée labor was put by the colonial and precolonial states.

> But if they (the native rulers) taxed the people severely and worked them slavishly, they repaired the tanks, and protected vigilantly the sources of their own wealth and power. They may have oppressed the people perhaps and have devoted too large a share of their earnings to the luxury of their own courts; *but they did not export the profits of industry either to alienate them permanently to foreign uses or to invest them temporarily in foreign securities*, whilst their own national enterprise was starving for want of capital. [emphasis added][103]

This is an extremely important observation. The critic, George Wall, did not deny that precolonial overlords exacted tribute from the cultivators. What he objected to was the export of accumulated surplus by the British for economic development outside Ceylon. The colonial state refused to extend forced labor exacted under Ordinance No. 8 of 1848 for the construction of infrastructure needed for paddy agriculture, specifically irrigation works. As an afterthought, Emerson Tennent, the Acting Governor, proposed that tank construction too be included under Ordinance No. 8 of 1848. But the Secretary of State for the Colonies, Grey, rejected the proposal to associate roads and irrigation works by saying that the labor required for tanks differed materially from that needed for road construction.[104] While it is correct that the labor required for tank construction differed from that for roads, the truth of the matter is that the peasant cultivators loathed road construction but were accustomed to and willing to engage in irrigation projects which

---

102. Samaraweera, "Economic and Social Developments," p. 60.
103. Speculum, *Ceylon*, p. 75.
104. *The Colombo Observer*, April 5, 1866; see also *SP 1867*, No. 4, p. 240.

were of direct benefit to themselves.[105] Secretary Grey later indicated that the use of native labor for irrigation works be made the subject of separate legislation.[106] This, Governor Ward subsequently attempted to do, but without much success.

In precolonial times, corvée labor was a form of service tenure. Each landholding was required to supply a specified number of individuals for a given number of days per year to labor on behalf of the state. The evidence of a British military official in Ceylon, Jonathan Forbes, before the British Parliamentary Committee on the 1848 rebellion help clarify the nature of precolonial corvée labor exaction.

Q.6939: What was the nature and extent of the rajakariya before? In the Kandyan kings' time it was limited by the authority which they had over the nation, so that they could never trespass very far; under our Government it was exceedingly severe sometimes.

Q.6940: What was the amount and extent of the labour required from the people generally when the rajakariya was in force? It was according to the portion of land they had; every piece of land was divided into portions, each portion had to furnish one man probably, for road service; it might by three or four months that they were called out.

Q.6941: Am I to understand you to say that they might sometimes be called away from their homes to work at forced labour for a period of four months? Not one individual; according to the size of the land which he held he was liable to be called on.[107]

The Road Ordinance of the British subverted precolonial labor exaction by divorcing corvée labor from landholding. While in pre-British times it had been a form of service tenure, the British made it into a universal capitation or head tax for males.[108]

During periods of famine and depression, the peasants were allowed no relief from the road tax. J. F. Dickson, the Government Agent of the Central Province who spearheaded the campaign for the efficient collection of grain taxes in the 1880s, extended his efforts to the prompt collection of the road tax as well. The following figures show that the total revenue from the road tax steadily increased and that between 1882 and 1884 there was a large increase in the number of persons who labored instead of paying the com-

---

105. *BPP 1850*, Vol. 12, Evidence of Jonathan Forbes, p. 26; On the Sinhalese peasantry's willingness to engage in irrigation construction, see *The Colombo Observer*, November 8, 1866 – The Editor's Reply.
106. Michael Roberts, communications to author.
107. *BPP 1850*, Vol. 12, p. 276. Forbes also authored two books, *Eleven Years in Ceylon* (London, 1840) and *Recent Disturbances and Military Executions in Ceylon* (London, 1850).
108. Ibid., p. 275.

Plantations and the Colonial State

muted road tax. This is significant because it illustrates the relationship between the collapse of peasant coffee, the loss of peasant cash incomes, and the necessity to pay the road tax in labor at this time.[109]

Table 7:2

Receipts from Road Ordinance Collections in Labor and Money,
1882–1884: Central Province (in Rupees)

	1882	1883	1884
Collected in Money	–	85,948	79,257
Arrears in Money	–	11,023	7,509
Value of Labor Furnished	–	19,658	30,987
Total	100,008	116,630	117,753

Source: Ceylon Government, Administration Report of the Government Agent for the Central Province, J. F. Dickson (1884), p. 34A.

Private Roads, Medical Care and Railways

Not all of the infrastructure essential to plantation development was provided directly by the labor or the cash taxes of the peasantry. As expenditures in infrastructure increased, the state attempted to introduce a system of partial self-finance whereby planters themselves were required to bear a portion of the expenses towards private roads to estates, hospitals for estate labor, and railways.

The introduction of the principle of partial self-finance, however, was not easy. While the state was committed to a strict policy against deficit financing, the planters too were committed to keeping down costs of production to a minimum. It was after much debate that the state managed to get the planters to pay part of the costs of private roads to estates, hospital care for laborers, etc. Having finally got the plantes to accept the fact that branch roads diverted from public roads were "constructed for the benefit of the planters and the advantages which the villagers derive from them will be remote,"[110] the state worked out a grants-in-aid system whereby the state and the planters each bore a part of the costs of construction of private roads to estates.[111]

109. *AR 1884*, Report of the G. A. for the Central Province – J. F. Dickson, p. 34A.
110. *SP 1886*, No. 7, "Branch Roads," p. 3.
111. Ibid., p. 3.

Similarly, with the passing of Ordinance No. 14 of 1872, 'the Estate Medical Wants Ordinance,' the state passed on a portion of the medical costs of the estate laborers to the planters.[112] In explaining the action of the government, Governor Gordon pointed out that the large majority of the native population was unaffected by the coffee industry and it was therefore unjust to shift the burden of medical care of the 'coolies' on to the peasantry.[113]

We have seen, however, that the majority of the peasantry, at least in the Kandyan Highlands, were affected by the many changes, such as the new market economy and private property rights that came with coffee plantation expansion. We have also seen that the peasantry did bear a significant amount of the infrastructural costs of the plantations through forced labor, loss of land, and cash taxes. An obvious example of this shift of burden is the rural police tax. A special rural police force was maintained by the state for the exclusive protection of plantation interests from the thefts and attacks of neighboring villagers. However, the peasant villagers themselves were required to pay this tax. The Government Agent for the Sabaragamuwa District wrote in 1874 that the rural police tax was a most unpopular tax, that the villagers saw it as an unjust imposition and it was therefore very difficult to collect.[114]

Similarly, there was no secret about the fact that the railway was introduced to benefit the planter community.[115] It was the agitation by the planter community that led to its very construction. The expenses for railway construction were met through several means. The export duty on coffee which Governor Torrington had abolished during the 1848 crisis was reintroduced in 1858 and a special fund was created out of the coffee duties to be used specifically to meet the obligations of railway construction.[116] The government also made substantial amounts of money available out of its general revenue towards the railway.[117] In addition, the newly founded Ceylon Railway Company raised capital almost entirely in London by sale of debentures.[118] These measures also signify the further expansion of British finance capital at this time.

---

112. *SP 1872*, No. 1, "Correspondence Relating to the Medical Treatment of Coolies."
113. *SP 1881*, No. 30, p. 2.
114. *AR 1874*, "Report for the Sabaragamuwa District," p. 71.
115. *AR 1884*, Report of the G. A. for the Central Province – J. F. Dickson, p. 41A.
116. Wickremaratne, "The Development of Transportation," p. 308.
117. Ibid., p. 309.
118. Ibid., pp. 308–09.

Infrastructure Needed for Paddy Agriculture

The colonial state's policies towards the infrastructure needed by the plantation sector were systematic and impressive. Pressure by the planter community was no doubt instrumental in sustaining continued state support. On the other hand, there was neither a comparable peasant lobby nor a sustained commitment on the part of the colonial state to provide the infrastructure, particularly irrigation, needed by paddy producers. In fact, the planters who depended on imported supplies of rice to feed the estate laborers "opposed every attempt of the Government to engage in irrigation works."[119] The planter lobby saw the solution to the local rice shortage not in improved irrigation, but in improved transportation.[120] The planters' concern was with the availability of a regular and cheap source of rice for their laborers. As far as they were concerned, importation of rice was far more reliable than dependence on local supplies. The legacy of importing rice begun by the planters has continued to plague the island during the postcolonial era.

Available evidence suggests that the wholehearted commitment of the state to providing infrastructure for the plantation sector resulted in the relative neglect of the paddy sector. We have seen, for example, that the compulsory labor exacted under the Road Ordinance was not extended to irrigation works. In the period before 1850 when roads were being constructed on a massive scale, almost no irrigation projects were undertaken.[121] It is widely believed today that the abolition of compulsory labor (rājakāriya) by Colebrooke in 1832 hastened the decline of the irrigational infrastructure necessary for paddy cultivation.[122]

The amount spent on irrigation varied with the whims of individual governors and the general state of the revenue. As Government Agent, Bailey, remarked in 1858,

> I have dwelt on the ruinous condition of such works of irrigation as are still in use. We have ourselves to blame for this, for not only has the Government never devoted a fair portion of revenue towards the rest of these works but by inattention to the agricultural system of the people tacitly permitted the national customs which, under the native government were the means of keeping all works for irrigation in repair, to fall into disuse.[123]

Many of the critics of the colonial government such as Leopold Ludovici also pointed out, "... surplus balances have year after year been quoted as

---

119. Ameer Ali, "Rice and Irrigation," p. 262.
120. Ibid., p. 260.
121. *SP 1890*, No. 3, p. 56.
122. Roberts, "Land Problems and Policies," p. 140.
123. Quoted in *SP 1890*, No. 3, "Reports of the Central and Provincial Irrigation Boards for 1888," p. 3.

the index of our prosperity. But how little of the annual expenditure represents items voted for the advancement of the native agriculture."[124]

Irrigation works for paddy agriculture for the large part, are needed only in the dry zone of the country. Most Sinhalese peasants lived in the wet zone during much of the nineteenth century when most parts of the dry zone remained sparsely populated and malaria-ridden. In precolonial times, vast networks of irrigation were available when populations were concentrated in the dry zone of the island. With the collapse of irrigational works and the shift of population centers to the wet zone beginning in the thirteenth century, paddy cultivation became dependent on seasonal rains rather than on water stored in tanks. A greater part of the Kandyan Highlands, the region under study in this book, belongs to the wet zone. A smaller part of the Highlands, the drier leeward side, including parts of Uva, Walapane and Uda Hewaheta belonging to the dry zone (see Map, p. XIV.) is dependent on irrigation for paddy agriculture. We discussed earlier that it was in these regions that paddy land expropriation caused the greatest misery to the cultivators. The brief discussion on the irrigation policies of the colonial state which follows next is not restricted to the Kandyan Highlands, but applies to the island in general.

A host of factors prompted the state to undertake improvements in irrigation during the 1850s. The rebellion of 1848 brought to light peasant grievances and the necessity to do something about them. Governor Ward and Governor Gordon, noted for their sympathy towards the peasants, looked upon the restoration of irrigation works as a 'moral obligation' on the part of the state.[125]

The entire scheme of restoring tanks in the dry zone was undertaken with the hope that once irrigation was provided, people from the more populated wet zone areas would migrate to the dry zone.[126] Emerson Tennent entertained the more fanciful idea that once the tanks were restored, the South Indian estate laborers could be settled in the dry zone thereby providing the planters with a more readily accessible supply of labor.[127] It was also believed that the restoration of irrigation works would put an end to chena cultivation, much despised by the British.[128] Another important reason for the colonial administration's concern with improving paddy cultivation at this time was the scarcity of imported rice from India due to the famine condi-

---

124. Ludovici, *Rice Cultivation*, p. 15.
125. Michael Roberts, "Irrigation Policy in British Ceylon During the Nineteenth Century," *South Asia*, No. 2 (August 1971), p. 51.
126. Ameer Ali, "Rice and Irrigation," p. 266.
127. Roberts, "Irrigation Policy in British Ceylon," pp. 48–49.
128. Roberts, "Land Problems and Policies," p. 140.

tions there and the resultant 'rice riots' in the urban areas of Ceylon. Ameer Ali notes,

> In June 1866 the usual monthly import of rice fell from 300,000 to 30,000 bushels. Stocks were exhausted. The price of a bushel of rice therefore went up to 15s. and in some places even to 17s.6d. As a result, the population of Colombo, Kandy and Galle attempted to break open the shops, and thereby forced the Governor to call in the military.[129]

During the second half of the nineteenth century, governors such as Ward and Robinson attempted to restore irrigation works by greater financial allocations and revival of ancient institutions associated with water management such as the village councils (*gamsabhas*).[130]

Where efforts were made to restore ancient irrigation works, the colonial state followed a strict policy of self-finance. The costs of irrigation works were to be recovered from the cultivators in the form of a water rate.[131] It should be noted that such a stringent policy of self-finance was not applied towards the construction of roads, railways, and ports needed primarily by the planters. In addition to the water rate, each adult male inhabitant of the villages served by the restored works was bound to contribute not more than ten days of labor for construction purposes.[132] This was imposed over and above the compulsory road service, (or its commuted equivalent) that all males were already required to perform. According to Roberts, "the water rate had yielded only 11.9 percent of the expenditure on the larger irrigation works in the period 1871–1904; while the land sales [paddy land sales by the state?] had yielded a further 13.4 percent."[133]

Although the state was not able to recoup all of its expenses through the water rate, Ludovici found it to be a death blow to paddy agriculture.[134] But he is not explicit why this was so. We can only speculate that the water rate was pitched too high, that it was exacted with severity and cash taxes in general made peasant security on the land precarious.

By passing Ordinance No. 2 of 1887, the colonial state attempted to allocate one fourth of the proceeds of the paddy tax towards the restoration of irrigation works.[135] This particular scheme was devised largely as a justification for the continued exaction of the controversial paddy tax at a time when the opposition to it was mounting. As mentioned earlier, the colonial

129. Ameer Ali, "Rice and Irrigation," p. 259.
130. Michael Roberts, "The Paddy Lands Irrigation Ordinances and the Revival of Traditional Irrigation Customs, 1856–1871," *CJHSS*, vol. 10 (1967), pp. 114–30, *passim*.
131. *SP 1872*, No. 2, p. 6.
132. Report of the Census of Ceylon – 1931, p. 22.
133. Roberts, "Land Problems and Policies," p. 141.
134. Ludovici, *Rice Cultivation*, p. 181.
135. *SP 1890*, No. 17, p. vii.

state exacted the paddy tax on the basis of customary usage. But custom called for the utilisation of the paddy tax towards the maintenance of paddy agriculture and peasant welfare. There is no indication in Ordinance No. 2 of 1887 how the other three-fourths of paddy tax revenues were to be spent; for example, what percent was to be ploughed back into paddy cultivation and what percent was to be used to maintain the plantation sector and the colonial state.

We cannot enter into a detailed discussion of the results of the irrigational projects undertaken by the colonial state here. Suffice it to point out that a large number of contemporaries agreed that during the nineteenth century, many of the ancient irrigation works remained in disrepair and the beneficial effects of the state's irrigation projects (except perhaps in the Eastern Province and the Hambantota District in the Southern Province where a wholly different set of conditions prevailed) were minimal. The Irrigation Ordinance of 1856, introduced by Governor Ward, was only partially brought into operation; nearly all Government Agents and Assistant Government Agents agreed that the Irrigation Ordinance of 1861, too, was defective and that it brought forth only limited results.[136]

The average yield per acre of paddy did increase after the passing of the Irrigation Ordinance of 1856. But Ameer Ali concludes that in the context of forty years of irrigation expenditure the actual gain made at the end of the century was not a significant achievement. He goes on to say that the acreage expanded was not very significant either.[137] In other words, the wide fluctuations in the seasonal production of paddy and the continuous increases in rice imports continued to be the main characteristics of the Ceylonese economy in the nineteenth century. Ameer Ali attributes the failure of the state's irrigational efforts largely to the fact that "A spurt of enthusiasm and a sympathetic feeling towards the 'natives' rather than any economic consideration ... seems to have been the driving force behind the entire scheme."[138]

This was in sharp contrast to the policies of the colonial administration towards the provision of land, labor, and infrastructure for the plantation enterprise. In those efforts, 'economic consideration', or the profitability of the plantations reigned above all else and sustained support from the state was always forthcoming. The local peasantry was not oblivious to the dualistic policies of the state vis-à-vis the plantation and paddy sectors. The Assistant Government Agent of the Sabaragamuwa District, F. R. Saunders, reported in 1869 that the state had lost its credibility among the paddy cultivators; that they no longer believed in the excuses given by the state such

---

136. *SP 1890*, No. 3, p. 7.
137. Ameer Ali, "Rice and Irrigation," p. 274.
138. Ibid., p. 272.

Plantations and the Colonial State

as lack of funds and land surveyors for failure to implement the proposed irrigation schemes. Saunders reported, "Had the scheme (they say) been for the immediate benefit of Government, instead of to assist us, such as the Temple Lands Scheme, how quickly would surveyors be found."[139]

Irrigation is only one of the inputs needed to raise paddy yields. Others include fertilizers, high yielding seed varieties, advanced techniques, as well as land tenure arrangements conducive to expanded production. But as Ameer Ali notes again, "The Colonial Government rarely legislated or interfered in these aspects. Therefore, its attempts to improve the rice economy of the country through irrigation schemes were a piece-meal affair and not the outcome of a comprehensive plan."[140]

Table 7:3

Public Works Expenditures of the State (for the entire Island)

		1867	1877
1)	Percent of total public work expenditure derived from Road Ordinance Funds and Private contributions	15.2%	10.2%
2)	Of the funds derived from Road Ordinance Funds (and private contributions) percent spent on roads, streets, bridges and canals	99.2%	96.6%
3)	Percent of total public work expenditure spent on roads, streets, bridges and canals	73.8%	82.5%
4)	Percent of total public works expenditure spent on irrigation	.2%	6.3%

Source: *The Ceylon Blue Book*, 1867, 1877.

In contrast, the colonial administration provided direct support to the development of agricultural inputs and techniques for plantation agriculture through such important measures as the establishment of the Royal Botanical Gardens for scientific experimentation of cash crops at Peradeniya (near Kandy).[141] The colonial administration was greatly concerned with finding a substitute cash crop for coffee when it was being wiped out by the leaf disease in the late 1870s. A favorable report on tea was issued as a Government Sessional Paper in 1867 to encourage the cultivation of tea on the

---

139. *AR 1869*, "Report for the Sabaragamuwa District," p. 20.
140. Ameer Ali, "Rice and Irrigation," p. 274.
141. Rajaratnam, "The Growth of Plantation Agricultures," p. 1.
142. Ibid., p. 5.

plantations of the Kandyan Highlands.[142] Most government officials, like Governor Gregory (1872–1877) who were in office during the time coffee was collapsing, took a personal interest in finding a suitable substitute(s) for coffee.[143] It is also instructive to note here that coconut, which was predominantly a local cash crop, though contributing significantly to export earnings, did not receive commensurate support from the colonial state. European plantation crops, first coffee, then tea (and also rubber) wielded an almost exclusive and determinant effect on the colonial state and the shape of the colonial political economy.

If we take roads and irrigation to represent the central infrastructural needs of plantation and paddy production respectively, the colonial state's relative expenditures on these two items help shed some light on its role vis-à-vis these two sectors of agricultural production. As our figures in Table 7:3 pertain only to fiscal years 1867 and 1877, we are unable to make long-term assessments.

Given the parsimony of the planters and other monied classes in the colony, it can be safely assumed that their private contributions to state revenue were insignificant (Row 1). 15.2 percent and 10.2 percent of the total expenditures on public works in 1867 and 1877 respectively, came directly from the Road Ordinance Funds. It is unclear if the value of the uncommuted tax, i.e., the forced labor services of the peasantry was included in these calculations (Row 1). Almost all of the funds collected under the Road Ordinance went towards the construction and maintenance of roads, streets, and bridges, which were of primary importance to the planters (Row 2). The vast portion of all public works funds were spent towards roads (Row 3), while only a very small amount was allocated towards irrigation projects which were of primary importance to the paddy cultivating peasants. There was, however, a significant increase in sums spent on irrigation between 1867 and 1877.

Sources of Government Revenue

Having considered some of the items of state expenditure towards plantation and paddy agriculture, we now need to examine the sources from which the state derived the revenue necessary for these expenditures. Two of the main sources of revenue exacted from the peasantry, the paddy and the road taxes, have already been discussed.

---

143. Ibid., p. 1.

It is important to note that all of the state's revenues were derived from local sources. The colonial administration received no financial support whatsoever from the imperial government even in times of severe economic setbacks. Rather, in addition to the profits exported by the plantation enterprise, the colonial government was required to make an annual financial contribution of approximately £177,000 to the home government as payment for the British garrison stationed in Ceylon.[144] Speculum (George Wall) pointed out that during times of depression, the annual military contribution, among other factors, cut directly into the state's outlays on irrigation.

> In the present exhausted condition of the country, the Government could not undertake any immediate large outlay on Irrigation works, without some special provision. The exactions of the Home Government for Military contribution; the drain on local resources for Railway payments; the increased cost of the establishments; and the creation of new offices of patronage have brought the relation between the revenue and expenditure into an alarming position.[145]

Van Den Driesen has listed crown land sales, export and import duties, railway receipts (since 1867) as the chief avenues through which the coffee industry contributed to the state revenue in the nineteenth century.[146]

Table 7:4

Government Revenues: 1840–1886 (Averages in Rupees)

Year	Land Sales	Coffee Duty*	Import Duty on Rice
1840–1849	13,387	5,724	60,552
1850–1859	49,174	5,672	92,218
1860–1869	980,514	40,341	136,527
1870–1879	881,542	–	166,450
1880–1886	39,126	9,423	185,204

*For a few years between 1848 and 1859, and between 1870 and 1882, no export duty was levied on coffee.

Source: I. H. Van Den Driesen, "Some Aspects of the History of the Coffee Industry in Ceylon with Special Reference to the Period 1823–1885," unpublished Ph.D. dissertation, University of London, 1954, pp. 541–42.

---

144. *SP 1878*, No. 29, p. 12.
145. Speculum, *Ceylon*, p. 106.
146. Van Den Driesen, "Some Aspects of the History," p. 535.

In the following pages, we shall discuss crown land sales and export and import duties as these particular sources of state revenue help highlight the differential policies of the colonial administration towards surplus exaction from plantation and paddy agriculture.

Land Sales

A large percentage of the state revenue derived from land sales came from the purchase price paid by European planters and speculators for crown land. We have seen that the natives too bought (and sold) such land. Thus crown land sales were not exclusively sources of income from the plantation sector or the Europeans. Jonathan Forbes, admitted before the British Parliamentary Committee of 1849 that the object of the colonial state in Ceylon was not so much the revenue to be gained from land sales, as the encouragement of the plantation enterprise.[147] Furthermore, land sales incurred considerable costs to the state in the way of surveying and auctioneering. Indeed. if the colonial state was primarily interested in revenue from land sales to planters, it would have imposed a much higher price and/or a land tax, which it never did.

Looked at from a different perspective, it can be argued that the revenue derived from crown land sales was a forced contribution exacted from the natives, largely the peasantry. The value of the crown lands sold, especially the forest and swidden lands, represents a form of capital accumulation by the state.

Export Duty on Coffee

We have noted that Governor Barnes exempted all cash crops from export duties in 1829. Once the coffee industry got well under way, an export duty was applied to coffee exports (both plantation and peasant) in the late 1830s. This duty was never very large being 1 sh. per cwt. throughout most of the nineteenth century. In 1848, when the coffee industry was faced with a severe depression, Governor Torrington quickly abolished the export duty on coffee and introduced a series of new taxes to make up for the loss incurred by the

---

147. *BPP 1850*, Vol. 12, p. 274.

Plantations and the Colonial State

abolition of the coffee duty.[148] When coffee recovered, the coffee duty was reintroduced in 1857 and again lifted in 1870 when another depression set in.

Unlike the paddy tax which fell on both cultivated and uncultivated land without regard to the cultivators' ability to pay, the export duty on coffee was collected only on the amount exported and was not levied at all when the industry was hard hit. Not only was the state considerate of the interests of the coffee planters, but it also made up the loss it incurred from abolishing the coffee duty by imposing a new set of taxes on the peasantry (discussed later).

Import Duty on Rice

As discussed in Chapter VI, a large percentage of the rice imported from India was purchased by the planters for feeding their laborers. The import duty on rice therefore fell largely on the planter class. In fact, one of the arguments made against the introduction of a land tax to the plantation properties was that the import duty on rice borne by the planters was sufficient means of taxing them. In opposing a general land tax, the Grain Tax Commissioners pointed out in 1878 that while the return from the home grown rice (paddy tax) had increased only threefold between 1823 and 1876, the annual return from the customs duty on imported rice had increased fifteenfold during the same period (see Table 7:5).[149] The point made was that as the import duty on rice was borne predominantly by the planters, the introduction of a tax on plantation lands would be unjust.

Table 7:5

Government Revenues from Grain Taxes

	1823	1876
Customs duty from imported rice/paddy	£12,927	£183,853
Tax on home grown paddy	£36,716	£106,325

Source: Ceylon Government, Sessional Paper No. 29 of 1878, "Papers Relating to Grain," p. 13.

148. *BPP 1850*, Vol. 12, p. 38.
149. *SP 1878*, No. 29, p. 13.

However, it is important to understand that given the stagnation of local paddy agriculture, growth of population, especially the urban population, people outside the plantation sector too came to depend on imported rice. Thus, not all of the imported rice was purchased by the planters, nor the entirety of the import duty on rice borne by them. In 1878,

> ... out of the £177,000 which the rice tax brings in, the planters pay about £65,000, making the number at 260,000 of coolies employed in connection with coffee cultivation. The rest is paid by the floating population, cheifly of Indians who are attracted by the high wages given in Ceylon, who own no land and who contribute scarcely anything in return for the protection they receive.[150]

Thus, the state found in the import duties a convenient means of raising revenue from all classes — not simply the planters, but also those who possessed no land at all such as the Indian laborers who arrived as 'free' laborers to work on government construction projects, the Colombo harbor, or in the urban areas.[151] As mentioned in Chapter VI, the native paddy cultivators themselves came to depend increasingly on imported rice.

To the planters, this import duty, like the export duty on coffee, held many advantages. Not only was the import duty on rice very small, but it also remained more or less stationary (13 cents per bushel of unhusked rice or paddy and 29 cents per bushel of rice) throughout the nineteenth century. The tax on home grown paddy, on the other hand, was increased at each new commutation settlement. The import duty on rice had to be paid only when rice was imported. Similarly, the duty on coffee had to be paid only when coffee was exported. In contrast, the tax on local paddy had to be paid whether the land was cultivated or not, and whether it yielded a harvest or not (except where crop commutation was introduced). Revenues from customs duty on imported rice increased largely due to the rise in the *volume* of imports; but revenues from the tithe on local rice increased largely due to the rise in the *rates of taxation*. The differential treatment of the two sectors of production — export and domestic agriculture — is obvious.

Arrack and Opium Monopolies of the State

Other important sources of colonial state revenue were its arrack and opium monopolies. The state derived revenue by renting the right to sell arrack (distilled coconut alcohol) to the highest bidders at auctions. The renters in turn subcontracted this right to other distributors. The British

---

150. Ibid., p. 9.
151. Ibid., p. 9.

Plantations and the Colonial State 265

inherited this mercantilist practice of renting the arrack monopoly from their Dutch predecessors in the coastal lowlands and later extended it to other regions as well. Like the paddy tax renters discussed in Chapter V, the arrack renters were mostly enterprising Sinhalese from the low country artisan castes. Arrack renting was an important avenue for the accumulation of wealth and the emergence of a local bourgeoisie, particularly among the *karava*.[152]

It was the colonial state that derived the greatest income from these liquor sales. State revenues from arrack renting were quite substantial, ranging approximately from £50,000 to £60,000 a year by the middle of the century.[153] The British were not unaware of the social problems engendered by the widespread sale of arrack. In a speech before the Legislative Council in 1872, Governor Gregory admitted that British rule was responsible for the spread of drunkenness among the Kandyans.[154] This indeed was quite a change from precolonial times, when the Kandyans were known for their traditional abhorrence of liquor.[155] Some aristocratic families were also extinguished by the effects of intemperance, the new evil introduced into Kandyan society. Drunkenness was also common among the Indian estate laborers in the Highlands. It was the colonial state in collusion with the local mercantile classes that were largely responsible for this situation.

Recognizing the seriousness of the problem, the colonial state characteristically attempted to resolve it through the introduction of new legislation. Although the state justified the Excise Reforms of 1912 on moral grounds, some of the more vocal westernized elites were quick to point out that fiscal considerations were still the guiding motive behind the government's initiatives. The agitation against the proposed legislation which evolved into a Temperance Movement in turn became an important element in the emergence of a constitutional reform movement and Sinhalese nationalism during the twentieth century.[156]

Opium, like arrack, was sold by renters who bought the monopoly rights to sell it from the state. Grossholtz notes that opium use was introduced to

---

152. Roberts, *Facets of Modern Ceylon History*, pp. 8, 43.
153. Grossholtz, "Forging Capitalist Patriarchy," pp. 184–85. See also Pieris, "Society and Ideology in Ceylon," p. 96.
154. Pieris, "Society and Ideology in Ceylon," p. 96; Grossholtz, "Forging Capitalist Patriarchy," p. 186.
155. Knox, *An Historical Relation*, p. 159.
156. See Tissa Fernando, "Arrack, Toddy and Ceylonese Nationalism: Some Observations on the Temperance Movement, 1912–1921," *Ceylon Studies Seminar*, 1969/70 Series, No. 9, and P. T. M. Fernando, "The Development of a New Elite in Ceylon with Special Reference to Educational and Occupational Background, 1910–1931," unpublished Ph.D. dissertation, Oxford University, 1968, esp. Ch. 4.

Ceylon (as to China) by the British when the first shop was opened in 1850. By 1905, the number of shops selling opium had increased to 65 and the volume of opium imports by the state had risen from 850 lbs. in 1850 to 20,000 lbs. in 1905.[157]

Colonial State Policy and the Subsistence of the Peasantry

In the early years of British colonial rule, the revenue derived from taxing the peasantry constituted a larger proportion of total state revenues than it did in the later years. This is to be expected given the total dependence of the colonial state on pre-existing sources of revenue at the start. It is impossible to give exact estimates of the revenue borne by the peasantry. Wesumperuma says that the paddy tax alone accounted for approximately one-fifth of the revenue of the colonial government, but he does not say for which years this figure applies.[158] The fact that a part of the tax burden of the peasantry was paid as labor services to feudal overlords further confounds attempts at estimation. In addition, we have seen that the peasants also contributed to state revenues derived from crown land sales and export and import duties.

Perhaps what is more important than the relative contribution of the peasantry and the planters to the state coffers is the proportion of the income of each social class that was appropriated by the state for maintaining itself and the plantation economy. The available evidence demonstrates very succinctly that while the state appropriated a minuscule proportion of the surplus of the higher income groups such as the planters, it took away from the poorer classes the very means of subsistence. The estimates of George Wall (Table 7:6), a prominent critic of the colonial state and of the paddy tax in particular, moved the newly elected Governor Havelock to abolish the tax on paddy cultivation in 1892. To avoid misrepresentation, Table 7:6 is presented without alterations as given by George Wall.

The table shows that the high income classes were exempt from two of the heaviest taxes borne by the paddy cultivators (*goiyas*) — the village labor dues and the paddy tithe. The paddy tax which amounted to approximately fifteen days labor was levied exclusively from the peasant proprietors of paddy fields.[159] Several of the taxes which were uniformly applied such as the road tax and the salt tax, however, added unequal burdens on the different income groups. Whereas the salt tax represented only 0.05 day's imcome for those

---

157. Grossholtz, "Forging Capitalist Patriarchy," pp. 194–95.
158. Wesumperuma, "The Evictions," p. 131.
159. For further calculations on the extent of taxation of peasant cultivators by the colonial state, see Speculum, *Ceylon*, pp. 99–101.

Table 7:6

Incidence of Taxation of a Day's Income on Heads of Families

Classes of People	Goiyas* Paid in Kind	Goiyas* Earning Wages	Person Earning Rs. 500 per Year	Person Earning Rs. 1,000 per year	Person Earning Rs. 5,000 per year	Person Earning Rs. 10,000 per year
One day's income	10 cents	35 cents	Rs. 1.40	Rs. 2.80	Rs. 14.00	Rs. 28.00
Road Tax (Rs.1.50)	6 days of work**	4.3 days work	1.07 days work	0.53 days work	0.10 days work	0.05 days work
Salt Tax (Rs.1.58)	15 days of work	4.5 days work	1.13 days work	0.57 days work	0.11 days work	0.05 days work
Village Labour Dues	12 days of work	12 days of work	—	—	—	—
Paddy Tythe (Rs. 1.50 per acre)	15 days of work (on 8 bushels)	—	—	—	—	—
Customs Duties (on rice, salt fish and bare necessities)	2 days of work (on curry stuff only)	24.5 days work (on 24 bushels of rice)	7.4 days work	3.7 days work	0.74 days work	0.37 days work
Customs Duties on Clothing	2.5 days of work	1.3 days work	1.4 days work	1.1 days work	2.41 days work	1.64 days work
Sum Expended on Clothing per year	Rs. 5.00	Rs. 10.00	Rs. 40.00	Rs. 60.00	Rs. 500.00	Rs. 700.00
Total # of Days per Year of Work Spent Towards Tax Payment	52.5	46.6	11.0	5.90	3.36	2.11
Percentage of 365 days	14.4%	13.0%	3.0%	1.6%	1.0%	0.58%

*'Goiyas' means paddy cultivators in Sinhala.
**The conversion rate set by the Road Ordinance.
Source: Sessional Paper No. 3 of 1892, Enclosure No. 4 – From George Wall to Governor Havelock.

earning Rs. 10,000 and over such as the planters, it represented the value of approximately fifteen days of labor for the paddy cultivating peasantry.

Wall has made an important distinction between the self-employed cultivators ('goiyas paid in kind') and those earning wages ('goiyas earning wages'). In his statistical evidence, and accompanying Despatch to Governor Havelock, he concludes that the wage earning paddy cultivators were financially better off than the owner-cultivators.[160] However, Wall is not explicit as to whether this wage earning class engaged only in supplementary forms of wage labor such as estate work or if they cultivated the paddy fields of others for wages as well. It is likely that peasant commodity producers who received cash incomes, but did not necessarily work for wages, have been included in the category of 'goiyas earning wages.' If they were only supplementary wage earners who possessed paddy fields, they would have been liable to pay the paddy tithe to the state. This seems not to have been the case according to Wall's statistics. However, other evidence suggests that although various forms of tenancy such as sharecropping were widespread in paddy agriculture by the last quarter of the nineteenth century, there was not yet a significant class of paddy cultivators solely dependent on wage labor for their livelihood.

All in all, George Wall's estimates demonstrate very strikingly the class biases of colonial taxation. While a peasant cultivator labored approximately fifty-two days on behalf of the state, a planter was able to pay off his entire tax burden to the state by approximately two days' worth of income.

The relief given to the higher income class necessarily meant an added burden on the poorer classes. This is quite apparent in the manner the state shifted its revenue burden to the peasantry during economic crises. We have already observed that in the late 1870s and 1880s, when the collapse of coffee created a severe economic depression, the colonial state sought to augment its revenue by a policy of exact and systematic collection of the paddy and road taxes. Earlier, when a severe economic depression affected Ceylon's economy in the mid-1840s, Governor Torrington came quickly to the rescue of the planters by abolishing the export duty on coffee. He either abolished or reduced a number of other levies which fell most heavily on the plantation sector such as port duties at the same time. The total loss of income from these reductions amounted to £40,000.[161] The export and import duties thus repealed or modified in order to prop up the plantation sector are indicated in Table 7:7.

In order to meet the deficit that stemmed from these reductions, Torrington imposed a series of new taxes (Table 7:8) which fell most heavily on the

160. *SP 1892*, No. 3, p. 97.
161. K. M. de Silva (ed.), *Letters on Ceylon*, Introduction, p. 7.

peasantry.[162] These included an increase in stamp duties, as well as new levies such as license fees on dogs, guns, carts, shops, and the infamous road tax. It must be remembered that these were introduced on top of the paddy, salt, and other taxes already in operation.

Table 7:7

A STATEMENT of the several Old Taxes Repealed in whole or in part after the Arrival of Lord Torrington, and the expected Loss of Revenue by such Repeal of Modification – 1847 and 1848.

	Old Taxes Repealed or Modified	Estimated Loss of Revenue
Ordinance 9 of 1847	Export duty on cinnamon, reduced from 1s. to 4d. per lb.	£15,000
	Export duties on all other articles (including coffee), abolished	Miscellaneous £3,000
	Import duties modified or reduced	No estimate
Ordinance 4 of 1848	Port dues modified	No estimate

Source: British Parliamentary Papers, vol. 12, 1850, p. 428.

In justifying these new taxes, the Secretary of State for the Colonies, Earl Grey, candidly remarked,

> Nor is to be lost sight of that while direct taxation is, in such circumstances, calculated to promote the progress of society, indirect taxation has the very opposite effect. To create a taste for the habits of civilised life in a rude population, it is requisite that they should have before them the example of civilised men and the gratification of the wants of civilised life should be rendered as easy to them as possible, but with this view imported articles should be rendered cheap, and those branches of trade and industry which require the direction of civilised and educated men, such as the production of sugar and coffee should be encouraged. Hence, the peculiar importance of avoiding the imposition of any taxes which can interfere, with trade and the expediency of adopting the very opposite policy that would be proper in Europe, by endeavouring *in the imposition of taxes, to make them press so far as prudence will admit, rather upon those who are content with a mere subsistence than upon the possessor of property, and the purchasers of luxuries.* [emphasis aded][163]

162. Ibid., p. 7.
163. Ibid., pp. 9–10. Compare policies and justifications of capitalist states elsewhere, e:g: 'Reagonomics' in the U. S. today.

Earl Grey claimed that colonial taxation would encourage the peasantry to follow the example of the civilized and enterprising Europeans. But he did not say how in fact the peasantry were to find the necessary capital when their subsistence itself was so heavily taxed. What Grey had in mind for the peasants was perhaps not entrepreneurship as much as wage labor in European plantations. Moreover, these so-called direct taxes were fixed charges that had no relation to the peasants' ability to pay or their subsistence needs.[164] The new taxes imposed by Torrington during the crisis of 1848 took away the protection from external market forces that the peasantry would have otherwise had as subsistence producers.

In introducing these taxes, the colonial state characteristically did not take peasant reaction into account. Soon it was faced with a widespread rebellion. As Scott has observed in relation to colonial southeast Asia,

> Nothing about the colonial order seemed to infuriate the peasantry more than its taxes. One would be hard pressed to find many demonstrations, petitions, or rebellions involving the peasantry in which the burdens of taxations were not a prominent grievance. Large-scale tax and corvée protests convulsed parts of Indochina in 1848, following floods and crop failures in the Red River Delta, and again in 1908, following a world credit crisis.[165]

One of the leaders in the opposition to the new taxes in Ceylon in 1848 was Dr. Christopher Elliot, the editor of *The Colombo Observer* at the time. Elliot was an Irishman known for his sympathy for the native peasantry. He sought to stamp the ideas of the European Revolution of 1848 in his campaign against the taxes in Ceylon. In a letter published under the pseudonym 'Englishman' in his newspaper, he pointed out the injustice of the taxes.[166] Elliot argued that while most Ceylonese did not receive 10sh. a year, the new taxes alone required them to pay 7sh. or 8sh. a year to the government. Furthermore, he pointed out that 7sh. or 8sh. were sufficient to maintain one person for two whole months. He went on to say that if the Europeans were required to pay the same proportion of their income towards state taxes as the peasants, a European would have to pay £50 out of an annual income of £300.[167]

Torrington later claimed that the Sinhalese translation of Elliot's letter circulated among the peasantry was a major factor in inciting the Sinhalese into rebellion. But historians have found it difficult to calculate the extent of

---

164. Compare, Scott, *The Moral Economy*, p. 93.
165. Ibid., p. 91.
166. Letter by "An Englishman," in *The Colombo Observer*, reprinted in *BPP 1849*, Vol. 36, p. 153.
167. Ibid., p. 153.

Table 7:8

A List of the several New Taxes imposed since the Arrival of Lord Torrington, stating the Date on which each Tax was Passed, and Estimate of the Amount of Revenue expected from the same; stating also the Dates of subsequent Repeal or Modification of any of these New Taxes

(1) New Taxes Imposed	(2) Date of Enactment	(3) Date of Modification or Repeal	(4) Estimate of Amount of Revenue Expected Previous to Modification or Repeal
1) Licence to Possess Fire Arms, Ordinance 13 of 1847	14 Dec. 1847	Modified 23 December 1848, Ordinance 22 of 1848	10,712 10 s.
2) Revision and Augmention of Stamp Duties, Ordinance 2 of 1848	31 Jan. 1848	–	Estimate for 1849 – 36,000 Stamp Revenue 25,152 in 1847 (Blue Book 1847) Increase of Stamps' – Revenue expected 10,848
3) Licensing of Carriages and Boats Used for Hire, Ordinance 3 of 1848	31 Jan. 1848	Modified 23 December 1848, Ordinance 23 of 1848	2,260
4) Licensing of Palanquin and other Carriages used for Hire, Ordinance 7 of 1848	10 April 1848	–	98
5) Registration and Licensing of Retail Traders, Ordinance 5 of 1848	10 April 1848	Repealed 18 December 1848, Ordinance 20 of 1848	3,060
6) Levy of Contributions in Labour or Money for Roads, Ordinance 8 of 1848	13 April 1848	Modified 13 November 1848, Ordinance 14 of 1848	No Return
7) Licences to keep Dogs, Ordinance 9 of 1848	13 April 1848	Repealed 18 December 1848, Ordinance 21 of 1848	2,635

Source: British Parliamentary Papers, Vol. 12, 1850, p. 429.

its circulation or its influence on the 'disturbances' that followed.[168] However, as the various colonial officials and planters who testified before the British Parliamentary Committee on the 1848 rebellion acknowledged, the taxes imposed by Torrington were the immediate cause of that rebellion. A discussion of this rebellion follows in Chapter VIII.

The Colonial State and the Stagnation of Paddy Agticulture

As discussed earlier, the colonial state's policies provided incentives for cash crop production, particularly plantation agriculture, and disincentives for domestic food production — both paddy and chena. Ludovici pointed out that the colonial tax structure mitigated against the native paddy producer from competing with foreign producers in the local rice market.

> The duty on imported paddy is calculated at the same rate as the tax on the home produced grain that is, the import duty of 3d. on the bushel at 2s. 6d. per bushel is exactly equivalent to the one tenth tax on the home producer; but in proportion as the market price of paddy rises so will the rate of duty fall while under the same circumstances the tax rises relatively. The rise of price virtually lowers the duty on the imported grain but the cultivator is not similarly benefited as regards the one-tenth tax. When paddy sells at 2s. 6d. the bushel the native cultivator and the importer are on equal terms; but should paddy rise to 5s. the bushel, the duty falls to one-twentieth while the value of one-tenth rises to one-twentieth.[169]

Furthermore, the colonial state's policies towards irrigation for wet-rice agriculture were haphazard and unsystematic. We have noted earlier in this chapter that some government officials themselves admitted that this was a direct cause of the retrogression of paddy agriculture.

Many critics of the colonial government noted the extremely low yields in local rice agriculture. According to C. S. Salmon, while the average yields in contemporary Burma were between fifty and sixtyfold, and roughly thirtyfold in India, the average yield in Ceylon was only fourfold.[170] Salmon, among others also pointed out that although the acreage under cash crops in Ceylon was steadily increasing, the acreage under paddy was decreasing.[171] The agricultural statistics in Table 7:9 show a generally smaller increase in paddy acreage as compared with the substantial increase in acreage under cash crops. These figures also reveal the increasing disparity between the structures of production and consumption in Ceylon, a characteristic feature of externally oriented colonial economies.

168. K. M. de Silva (ed.), *Letters on Ceylon*, p. 12.
169. Ludovici, *Rice Cultivation*, p. 126.
170. C. S. Salmon, "The Ceylon Starvation Question," p. 12; see also *SP 1867*, No. 4, p. 21.
171. Ibid., p. 7.

Plantations and the Colonial State

In addition to state neglect and excessive taxation, the new property relations and social classes that emerged in the village economy also operated as barriers against the improvement in technology and productivity in paddy agriculture. But as we have argued in Chapter V, these new social relations of production in paddy agriculture were themselves the products of colonial legislation (paddy tax, service tenure reforms, etc.) and new market forces operating in the society.

Table 7:9

Areas Cultivated by Estates and Peasants, Census Years, 1871–1891 (Thousand Acres)

	1871	1881	1891
Estate Land:			
Coffee	214	228	45
Tea	–	12	235
Rubber	–	–	–
Coconuts	200	210	304
Total	413	450	584
Export Smallholdings:			
Coffee	53	57	11
Tea	–	1	26
Rubber	–	–	–
Coconuts	300	315	456
Total	353	373	493
Non-Export Crops:			
Paddy	544	549	563
Others	58	169	186
Total	601	718	750
Total Peasant Area	954	1,092	1,243
Total Cultivated Area	1,367	1,542	1,826
Annual Rate of Increase	–	1.2%	1.7%

Source: Donald R. Snodgrass, *Ceylon: An Export Economy in Transition* (Homewood, Ill.: Richard D. Irwin, Inc., 1966), p. 49.

We have observed differences of opinion within the European community in nineteenth-century Ceylon with regard to the effects of plantation development on the native society – particularly paddy agriculture and peasant subsistence. The sharpest critics of the colonial state were not government officials (although some provincial officials like Le Mesurier were quite vocal) but 'unofficial' members of the European community, like Christopher Elliot and George Wall. But even these critics of the colonial administration agreed that the plantation enterprise was the life blood of the colonial economy and it needed the support and encouragement of the state.[172] These critics differed with their official colleagues only in their idealism that the interests of plantation development, on the one hand, and that of local food production and the peasantry, on the other, were mutually compatible.

Summary

Laissez-faire ideology aside, the colonial state was not a neutral observer of plantation development in Ceylon. It was the officials of the colonial administration that created the plantation economy of Ceylon. But even after a separation was made between planters and officials, the colonial state continued to serve the interests of the plantation economy by providing the necessary legislation, infrastructure, tax policy, and police protection.

In its involvement with facilitating plantation development, the colonial state was compelled to take certain actions that were clearly inimical to local food production and the welfare of the peasantry. There emerged an inverse relationship between the expansion of plantations and the stagntion of paddy agriculture. This relationship was mediated by the colonial state. The dominance of the new plantation agriculture over the pre-existing paddy and chena agriculture was not achieved simply through the operation of free market forces. The intervention of the colonial state through discriminatory legislation and extra-economic coercion played a decisive role in the final outcome.

---

172. Speculum, *Ceylon, passim.*

Part 3: Conclusions, and Theoretical Implications

On the basis of the historical-descriptive material presented in Parts 1 and 2, we will synthesize the different aspects of the colonial transformation and interpret the general dynamic and direction of socioeconomic change which took place in the Kandyan Highlands. The findings of our case study will then be discussed in relation to the theoretical debate in the sociology of development and underdevelopment. Finally, we shall present some formulations towards a more comprehensive theory of colonialism and Third World social formations.

VIII. The Colonial Transformation of the Kandyan Highlands: Socio-Economic Differentiation and Stratification

The 'colonial revolution' of the nineteenth century opened up the previously undeveloped and largely self-contained Kandyan society to outside social and economic forces. Colonial economic development introduced new sources of labor. The population increase that took place during the nineteenth century has not been discussed in this book. However, the population increase in Ceylon from approximately one million in 1800, to three million in 1891, was in many respects a result of changes that came with colonialism.[1] Colonial economic development helped release — at least partially — the entrepreneurial talents of certain groups (especially some of the 'low' castes) which could not be realized within the precolonial caste society. The colonial presence brought a rapid and overall increase in production (through export agriculture) and related service activities (banking, transport, etc.). It achieved a high level of infrastructural development, notably in roads and railways. The British also gave the country a unified administrative and political structure. Although the British continued and adapted some of the worst features of the precolonial society to suit their own needs, they also legislated against some of its most repressive customs such as female infanticide and torturous methods of punishment. Although the new law was administered in favor of the British themselves, it provided the basis for a more rational legal system.

As we have argued, these developments were achieved at the expense of the Sinhalese peasantry and the Indian estate laborers — and not without physical coercion. In the long-run, colonial developments exacerbated the inequities between native social classes and introduced elements of ethnic conflict into the previously homogenous Kandyan society. By concentrating all energies on the supply of a single cash crop to the world market, it made the entire economy and society vulnerable to the vicissitudes of the market. By

---

1. Clarence Maloney, *Peoples of South Asia* (New York: Holt, Rinehart and Winston, 1974), p. 541. See also S. A. Meegama, "The Decline of Mortality in Ceylon Since the End of the Nineteenth Century with Particular Reference to Economic and Social Development" (Ph.D. dissertation, University of London, 1968), *passim*.

neglecting domestic food production, it placed the subsistence of the natives — especially the peasantry — in constant peril.

In the light of these contradictory effects of colonialism, we cannot accept the imperialist or the nationalist perspectives which focus entirely on either the beneficial or the detrimental aspects of the colonial transformation. The interaction between the superimposed politico-economic system, namely the colonial state and the plantation economy, and the pre-existing modes of production and social classes was an inherently conflictive and contradictory process. The foreign sector did not simply destroy the entire native society. Instead it subordinated the native sector to suit its own economic and political needs. But precolonial modes of production and the social classes that represented them were not simply passive victims of external social forces. In resisting and adapting to the external impact (within the available limits) they in turn exercised conditioning effects on the superimposed structures. This complex articulation, fundamentally transformed preexisting economic and social arrangements.

This transformation, however, cannot be adequately understood without a comprehensive examination of the differential effects of the colonial impact on the diverse modes of production, political structures, social classes, ethnic, and caste groups in Kandyan society. Such an examination needs to be informed by the specific manner in which the Kandyan Highlands were incorporated into the world capitalist economy and the Ceylonese economy (itself a creation of colonial politico-economic forces). We will proceed with this analysis on the basis of the historical-descriptive materials presented in Parts 1 and 2 of this book, Additional information on issues which have not been fully discussed in earlier chapters will also be introduced where relevant.

The Incorporation of the Highlands into the World Capitalist Economy

During the nineteenth century, the Kandyan Highlands which had hitherto been isolated and relatively self-sufficient were incorporated into the expanding capitalist world economy as an exporter of a single crop — coffee — and a net importer of food. The nature of this incorporation was determined not simply by social forces internal to the Highlands or the island, but largely by the needs of industrializing Britain. Metropolitan capital in the colonies was invested almost exclusively in the production of raw materials for industries, or, as in the case of the Kandyan Highlands, in the supply of consumption items, such as coffee, for the growing urban populations in the imperial nations. The concentration on a single crop made the colonial economy of Ceylon highly susceptible to the vagaries of the world economy. Depressions in the world market, particularly in Britain, had reverberating effects on the local plantation economy and the lives of the Sinhalese peasantry.

Both plantation and village agriculture as well as the European and native social classes involved in these sectors were hierarchically integrated into the world economy. Within Ceylon, plantation development clearly took precedence over village agriculture, whereas in the context of the capitalist world economy, metropolitan industries took priority over plantation agriculture in the colonies.

The hierarchical structure of the world capitalist economy is best exemplified by the nature of its capital accumulation and reinvestment. As noted elsewhere, very little capital was brought into Ceylon for plantation development; much of it was derived locally. Moreover, the profits from colonial agricultural ventures such as plantations were not reinvested in the colonies but siphoned off to the metropolitan countries for reinvestment and industrial expansion there. Herein lies a fundamental difference between capitalist development in the metropoles and the colonies. In the former, profits from advanced sectors, notably manufacturing, were reinvested in domestic agriculture. Whereas in nineteenth-century Ceylon, as a contemporary British journalist noted critically, this was certainly not the case.

> It follows from the peculiar circumstances herein described that enterprise in Ceylon has to pay a high interest for its capital; that the interest so paid and a great proportion of the profits earned are *exported*, and do not, as in other countries, create a fund of new capital seeking investment, and so nourishing trade and commerce, ...; and that, in short, Ceylon does not derive her proper advantage from the produce of her soil, the fruits of her commerce or even the toil of her labourers. [emphasis in original][2]

A further issue that has an important bearing on this study, but has not been explored in detail, is the relationship that evolved during the nineteenth century between the Ceylonese plantation economy and those regions in South India which exported labor, entrepreneurial groups, and some food supplies to Ceylon. As one writer has noted, during the plantation era, Ceylon was taken as it were into the Tamil heartland.[3] In some ways, specifically with regard to the supply of routine labor, the European plantations had more contact with South Indian districts such as Madura and Ramnad than the neighboring Kandyan villages.

There is little doubt that the plantations in the Kandyan Highlands were a safety valve for relieving the stress of some of the impoverished agricultural labor castes in Southern India. Even after labor migration from India was

---

2. Speculum, *Ceylon*, p. 9. See also ch. 4, p. 80 in this book.
3. Sovani, *Economic Relations of India*, p. 139. See also ch. 6, pp. 195–201 in this work.

The Colonial Transformation of the Kandyan Highlands

stopped in the 1930s, some South Indians continued to come to Ceylon — often illegally — in search of work. As we have noted in passing elsewhere, the tradition of migration from South India to Ceylon goes way back to precolonial times. However, was there during the nineteenth century a deliberate effort on the part of the imperial administration, namely the Colonial Office in London, to coordinate the division of labor and economic development of these two neighboring regions? For example, did the administrators in London plan to 'specialize' Ceylon in plantation agriculture and South India in labor and rice exports? These questions, however, cannot be answered without a detailed study of the articulation between these two regions in the context of the British imperial economy and administration.

The central focus here, however, is not the relationship between the Ceylon plantation economy and the emerging world capitalist economy, but the local manifestation of that relationship, namely the articulation between the plantation and village economies in the Kandyan Highlands. But before we go on to examine this articulation, a few words need to be said about the creation of a national economy in Ceylon and the relationship between the Kandyan Highlands and the southwestern coastal lowlands within the newly evolved Ceylonese economy. In so doing, we will also look at indigenous capitalist development in the southwest coastal regions during the nineteenth century.

Indigenous Capital and Regional Differentiation

The British made the port city of Colombo in the southwest the commercial and administrative capital of the island as the Portuguese and the Dutch did before them. But due to the suitability of its climate and the sparseness of its population, the Central Highlands in the former Kandyan kingdom were chosen for the development of coffee plantations.

The impact of the plantations was most direct and dramatic on the Kandyan Highlands where they were physically located. However, other geographical regions of the island did not remain detached from the plantation enterprise or the socioeconomic forces that accompanied plantation development. The various regions of the island, like the numerous ethnic and caste groups were differentially incorporated into the newly emergent Ceylonese economy. The plantation enterprise and related developments helped create a national economy which did not previously exist. Similarly, colonial policies, especially the reforms of the Colebrooke Commission in 1833, gave the island a unified administrative and political structure and the basis for eventual statehood. It is the political unification given by the British which is now being challenged by the Tamil separatist movement in the northern region of the country. Our concern in the following discussion will be restricted largely to the relationship which emerged between the Kandyan Highlands and the southwestern lowlands in the process of plantation development (see Map, p. p XIV).

The opening up of plantations in the Highlands was accompanied by a massive immigration of laborers from South India. Indian merchant groups such as Chettiyars also came to participate in the rice trade, moneylending, smallholder cashcropping, and other profitable activities. In addition, a significant number of Muslim traders as well as low country Sinhalese belonging largely to the *karawa, durava* and *salagama* service castes also migrated to the Highlands seeking new economic opportunities. As discussed in earlier chapters, these low-country artisan castes provided the specialized labor services needed in the European coffee estates; transported the coffee and estate supplies to and from the sea ports of the southwestern coast; engaged in arrack renting (also the renting of the paddy tax) and other types of trading activities; cultivated coffee smallholdings; bought and sold paddy and high lands in the Kandyan hill country.

In other words, besides the British, a significant non-European population consisting of Indians, Muslims, low-country Sinhalese and some Burghers also came into the Kandyan Highlands with the opening up of plantations. These migrations broke down the relative isolation and ethnic homogeneity which characterized precolonial Kandy.

But like the British who were drawn into the Kandyan hill country in search of profits, these lesser Indian and indigenous capitalists rarely became a settler population. Only a few intermarried with Kandyans and put down roots in the area. The roads, and later the railways, opened by the British allowed these migrant groups to move easily between their native regions and the Highlands.

Except for a handful of Kandyan aristocrats, mostly headmen, the majority of the 'indigenous' capitalist class that emerged during the nineteenth century were non-Kandyans being low-country Sinhalese, Muslims, and Indians. Just as the dominant European capitalist class exported the profits made from coffee plantations in the Highlands out of that region and out of the island, these non-Kandyan native capitalists too exported and reinvested their profits in their home regions and especially in Colombo. Many of the Indian enterpreneurs and merchants repatriated their profits to India.

One major reason for the outflow of profits of the native capitalists from the Highlands was the effective monopoly of coffee plantations by European capital. This is borne out by comparative figures on the extent of land and

The Colonial Transformation of the Kandyan Highlands 281

size of plots bought by Europeans and non-Europeans in the primary plantation region, the Central Province (see Tables 5:1 and 5:2). The subordinate local capitalists were not able to compete successfully with the Europeans for high lands in the plantation regions, credit from British banks or other resources from the colonial state. As the Report by a Commission on Banking noted, as late as 1934, native capitalists were still experiencing great difficulties in obtaining credit from British banks and other European credit agencies in the colony.[4] The benefits that accrued to local capital from the European plantation enterprise were essentially residual.

What resulted in the long-run was the movement of local capitalists (who had accumulated wealth largely from service activities in the plantation economy), into entrepreneurial and mercantile ventures left open by the British. These were generally activities which demanded less capital investment than coffee plantations. A great deal of the newly acquired wealth of native capitalists was also spent on such nonproductive activities as land speculation and conspicuous consumption.

'Crown land' purchases by native entrepreneurs were made predominantly outside the coffee planting regions. This was because of the inability of native capitalists to compete with British planters for crown lands and the general lack of resources and support to undertake large-scale plantation agriculture. It is interesting to note here Patrick Peebles' observations on the ethnic patterns in crown land purchasing during the nineteenth century. Peebles writes,

> Europeans of course bought virtually all of the coffee land. Sinhalese investors preferred coconut land. Dry zone land, much of it in the rapidly developing east coast near Batticaloa was purchased by Muslims and Tamils.[5]

Some of the mercantile activities of the local capitalist class have already been mentioned. In addition, native capitalists achieved a dominance in coconut cultivation. As discussed in Chapter III, acreage under coconut expanded from 200,000 acres in 1860 to 600,000 in 1900, thereby making coconut exports a quarter of total exports and the second largest export commodity from the island.[6] The coconut planting activities of the local capitalists (and peasant smallholders) helped incorporate many of the southwestern lowlands along the coast and the foothills in the Kurunegala district within the expanding world market economy. Coconut cultivation provided the local capitalists a realm of relative freedom from European competition. But it must be noted that coconut cultivation was not strictly a plantation enterprise. The units of

---

4. *SP 1934*, No. 22, "Report of the Ceylon Banking Commission," p. 30.
5. Peebles, "Land Use," p. 75.
6. Rajaratnam, "The Growth of Plantation Agriculture," p. 9.

cultivation were much smaller than coffee plantations; workers were not a large residential or immigrant labor force but rather, Sinhalese villagers who worked on the coconut estates in a shifting capacity. However, the role of coconut cultivation should not be overlooked in the emergence and consolidation of the native capitalist class. Furthermore, as Michael Roberts notes,

> The regional distribution of coconut contributed to some degree towards the manner in which the *Low Country Sinhala and the Ceylon Tamils outpaced the Kandyan Sinhala in the drive for elite status.* [emphasis added][7]

Table 8:1

Waste Land* Use and Ethnic Group, 1860–1889

Land Use	Prominent Sinhalese	Other Sinhalese	Other Ceylonese	Europeans	Total
Colombo town[a]	13	4	4	7	28
Coconut land[b]	366	194	126	43	729
Coffee estates[c]	77	30	21	745	873
Graphite mining[d]	37	35	5	1	78
Dry zone[e]	2	7	212	27	248
Unclassified wet zone[f]	45	99	71	261	476
Totals	540	369	439	1084	2432

Includes all deeds of land sold for Rs 500 or more, 1860–1889.

[a] Includes only those lots within the municipality sold as waste land. Most urban property was sold separately as 'building lots.'
[b] Land in districts in which the cultivation of coconuts increased greatly in the period.
[c] Lots over 50 acres sold for more than Rs 15 per acre in coffee planting districts.
[d] Small lots sold for over Rs 100 per acre in certain localities.
[e] Districts with less than 75" annual rainfall, excluding coconut and coffee land.
[f] A residual category.
*Refers to high lands claimed by the Crown.

Source: Patrick Peebles, "Land Use and Population Growth in Colonial Ceylon," in *Contributions to Asian Studies*, vol. 9, ed. by James Brow (Leiden: E. J. Brill, 1976), p. 75.

In addition to coconut cultivation, native capital also created and dominated the small graphite (plumbago) mining industry. Between 1861 and 1900, "3,347,084 cwts. of graphite were exported for a return of Rs. 23,819,998 (at a rough average of 2,500 tons fetching Rs. 600,000 per

---

7. Roberts, "Export Agriculture," p. 104.

The Colonial Transformation of the Kandyan Highlands   283

year)."[8] The graphite mines, like the coconut estates, were located not in the Kandyan regions, but in the southwestern lowlands. Native capitalists also gained a significant stake in rubber plantation agriculture which opened up in the southwestern Kalutara and Ratnapura districts during the twentieth century.

The various entrepreneurial activities of the native capitalists, and the import and export trade related to the European plantation economy were concentrated in the southwestern coastal lowlands. In addition, the administrative headquarters of the colonial state were located in Colombo. These factors contributed to a rapid urbanization, westernization and population expansion in that region. Uneven regional developments were further accentuated during the twentieth century, so much so that by midtwentieth century over two-thirds of the population in the island were living in the southwestern region.[9] In contrast, despite the plantation presence the processes of urbanization, westernization, and demographic expansion were much slower in the Kandyan hill country. There was a greater cultural resistance on the part of Kandyans, particularly the peasantry and some of the highest noble families to western ideological influences.

The native capitalist class and the emergent petit-bourgeois class (constituting small businessmen, clerical workers, school teachers, etc.) which was to play a highly influential role in the political life of the country during the twentieth century were also located largely in the southwestern coastal lowlands. The secondary schools providing an English education and run mostly by Christian missionaries were also concentrated in the urban centers of the southwestern coast (and the Northern Province). The education received at these schools enabled the sons of the low country capitalists to enter the emerging westernized elite stratum in the colony.[10] It was largely this elite drawn from the low country capitalist class that led the Ceylonese constitutional reform movement in the early twentieth century and finally effected the island's political independence from the British in 1948. The Buddhist revitalization movement beginning in midnineteenth century and the Left movement which started in the 1930s, too, had their origins in the southwestern lowlands.

Thus, in spite of being the heartland of the plantation enterprise, the Kandyan Highlands lagged behind the more dynamic southwestern lowlands in terms of local enterpreneurial activity and during the twentieth century in

8. Roberts, "Aspects of Ceylon's Agrarian Economy," p. 163.
9. Nyrop, et al., *Area Handbook for Ceylon*, p. 4.
10. Tambiah, "Ceylon," p. 56. Wealthy Tamils from the Northern Province also invested in business and real estate in the Colombo metropolitan region.

organized social and political movements. Little of the benefits of the plantation enterprise and related activities accrued to the Kandyans themselves, especially the peasantry. Those who bear the costs of change do not necessarily reap the benefits!

What is clear is that in addition to the British, a significant group of non-Europeans, largely non-Kandyans, derived considerable advantages from the activities of the colonial political economy. It is interesting to note that many of these groups like the *karavas* were considered low in the traditional caste hierarchy, or, like the Chettiyars and Muslims were outside the Sinhalese caste hierarchy. As noted elsewhere, as outsiders without ethnic and kinship ties to the Kandyan peasants, these groups were able to exploit them ruthlessly in their roles as traders, moneylenders, and landlords. The result, then, was not simply uneven economic and social development of the different regions of the island, but also the emergence of an ethnically based 'internal colonialism' within the native population, that is, the exploitation of Kandyans by non-European 'middlemen minorities'.[11]

This, however, should not obliterate the hierarchy of exploitation and the fact that the primary contradiction in the Highlands was between the interests of British capital and the Kandyan peasantry and that the British derived the greatest advantage from the whole colonial enterprise. Lacking competition from the subordinate native capitalists or other European capitalists (since Ceylon was the exclusive domain of the British), the British reigned supreme. It is later in the neocolonial period when British capitalists lost the protections they had under 'classical colonialism' and had therefore to face competition from American and other capital that they began to lose their supremacy in many of their former colonies.

Indigneous capitalist development in Ceylon during the nineteenth century was obviously a significant phenomenon. It was concentrated largely in the cultivation of 'plantation' crops for export. As Edwin Craig notes, the spillover of the European plantation experience to native capitalists (and owner-

---

11. For different uses of the concept of internal colonialism and its application to the U. S. and Britain, see, Robert Blauner, *Racial Oppression in America* (New York: Harper and Row, 1972) and Michael Hechter, *Internal Colonialism: The Celtic Fringe in British National Development, 1536–1966* (Berkeley: University of California Press, 1975) respectively. Some of the characteristics that distinguish 'middlemen minorities' include: ethnicity; merchant (and rentier) capitalism; identification with land of origin (rather than 'host' nation). For some interesting theoretical insights also applicable to 'middlemen' in Kandy, see, Edna Bonacich, "A Theory of Middleman Minorities," in *Majority and Minority: The Dynamics of Race and Ethnicity in American Life*, ed. by Norman R. Yetman with C. Hoy Steele (Boston: Allyn and Bacon, 1982). With reference to the situation in the Kandyan Highlands, see also Samaraweera, "Land, Labor and Capital," p. 140.
12. Edwin Craig, Jr., "Ceylon," p. 222.

The Colonial Transformation of the Kandyan Highlands

producers) in Ceylon seems to have gone much farther than in the Philippines, Java, or elsewhere in the Far East.[12]

Indeed, local capitalist development was not autonomous, but largely defined by and subordinated to European capitalist development in the island. The local capitalist class was a 'comprador' class. As noted earlier, this class either moved into mercantile spheres, such as trade and transport, that British capital did not particularly want to be involved with or production activities, such as smallholder coffee and coconut, where they did not have to compete with the British. In other words, the native capitalist class did not move out of the externally oriented export-import economy which the Europeans developed.

The lack of political power and support from the colonial state reinforced the subordinate status of the indigenous capitalists. Their dependent position is borne out by their inability to develop local food production. Any attempt to compete with rice imports would have been a formidable undertaking in the face of European planter resistance and the colonial administration's partiality towards the European plantation sector. The colonial state's vacillation towards improvements in irrigation for paddy agriculture also prevented paddy from becoming a profitable capitalist investment.

As Tambiah has noted with reference to the midtwentieth century, although a small segment of native capitalists "made the leap from petty commerce to plantation enterprise; . . . the further leap from there to industrial investment has been scarcely made."[13] Hardly any industrial ventures were undertaken by either native or foreign capitalists during the nineteenth century. On the contrary, what little craft industries existed in precolonial times were gradually extinguished by cheap imports. The differences between capitalist development in the metropoles and the colonies are again obvious. Although exhibiting a great deal of ingenuity, the local capitalist class was nevertheless confined to the interstices of the European dominated plantation economy and was in no way able to move in the direction of an autonomous capitalist development.

Unlike in some other colonial situations (twentieth-century India, for example), there emerged no significant tensions or conflicts between the dominant British capital and subordinate local capital in Ceylon. A mutually comfortable relationship was worked out between the two. Local capital performed essential functions for the stabilization of the colonial political economy. These included renting the paddy tax; renting the arrack and opium monopolies; transporting supplies between plantations and ports, etc. For a number of complex reasons such as the colonizers' attempts to cultivate

---

13. Tambiah, "Ceylon," p. 57.

a sense of moral superiority and maintain a social distance from the natives, British capital did not desire to undertake such loathsome tasks. As noted earler, British capital also allowed local capital relative freedom in the spheres of coconut cultivation and plumbago mining. All in all, the activities of the local capitalist class had a stabilizing rather than a disruptive effect on the colonial political economy and European dominance within it. In 1908 some native capitalists declared rather obseqiously,

> Most of us are planters. Our interests are in many respects identical with those of the [European] planters. It is true that many of them have shown us the way, and they deserve the credit for having brought capital into the country and shown us the path along which we may all win prosperity. We have followed in their footsteps and our interests are now the same.[14]

An extremely important ingredient in the creation of a supportive local bourgeoisie was the implantation of western values and lifestyles. As early as the 1840s, a strong western consumer orientation had developed among the privileged natives. This was good for British business and for creating the values and legitimacy for colonialism to be accepted as a civilizing force. An English writer, J. W. Bennet noted in 1843,

> The Sinhalese are partial to Manchester, Leeds, Sheffield and Birmingham manufactures. . . . The higher ranks indulge in the best wines, particularly Madeira and Champagne, which are liberally dispensed at their parties to European guests; and no people in the world set a higher value upon British medicines, stationery and perfumery; or relish with keener zest English hams, cheese, butter, porter, pale ale, cider, sherry, herrings, salmon, anchovies, pickles and confectionery, all of which they prefer to similar imports from France and America except in regard to price.[15]

Socio-Economic Differentiation in the Kandyan Highlands

Having examined the incorporation of the Kandyan Highlands into the world capitalist economy and the national economy of Ceylon and the nature of local capitalist development, we will now turn our attention to the internal developments in the Highlands during the period from 1833 to 1886. Our focus here will be on the differential effects of the colonial impact on the diverse modes of production, political structures, social classes as well as caste, and ethnic groups in Kandyan society.

---

14. *Ceylon National Review.* No. 5, February 1908, p. 169, quoted in Ponnambalam, *Dependent Capitalism in Crisis*, p. 16.
15. Quoted in ibid., p. 8. See also Wickremeratre, "Education and Social Change".

The Articulation of Modes of Production

During the fifty or so years under examination in this study there evolved a complex articulation between several modes of agricultural production in the Kandyan Highlands.[16] Without a doubt, the dominant mode was the superimposed European plantation sector. The relationship of this mode to the several modes of production within the village economy were mediated by the colonial state through the new politico-juridical framework and the coercive powers at its disposal. The modes of production in the village consisted of the pre-existing 'feudalistic' paddy sector, the 'communalistic' chena sector as well as the newly evolved petty commodity (smallholder cashcropping) sector. It is in the context of the dominance of plantations and the colonial state that the ensuing interaction among these modes of production, their internal changes, and resultant class conflicts and alliances need to be understood.

Of all the modes of production in Kandy, the plantation sector was clearly the most capitalist. But the social relations of production here were not entirely capitalist. Extra-economic forces such as debt bondage and the kangani method of labor recruitment and control were essential to the viability of the plantations during the nineteenth century.[17] It is inconceivable that without the middlemen labor headmen or the kanganis, the European planters would have been able to recruit, retain, and discipline the immigrant laborers. It is incorrect, however, to think of debt-bondage and the kangani system as precapitalist or even precolonial phenomena. They were peculiarly colonial adaptations made of certain pre-existing institutions to suit the needs of expanding British capital.

In the long run, that is, during the subsequent tea period of Ceylon's plantation history, as the estate labor force became residential and the kangani system was gradually done away with, social relations of production on the plantations took on a decisively capitalist character. This happened when the estate labor force lost their ties to land in South India and became a 'true' proletariat. Of course plantations in the colonies did not become capitalist in the western sense in that they were forms of 'dependent' capitalist expansion. In other words, plantation profits were exported abroad for reinvestment in the metropolitan nations rather than reinvested in the colonies for expanded reproduction of colonial economies.

16. Please refer to the definition of a mode of production given in Ch. II of this work. Further discussion follows in Ch. IX.
17. For a critique of the characterization of plantations as capitalist modes of production, see Ernesto Laclau, "Feudalism and Capitalism in Latin America," *New Left Review*, vol. 67 (May-June 1971), pp. 26–27. See also Rodolfo Stavenhagen, *Social Classes in Agrarian Societies* (New York: Anchor Press, 1975), p. 221.

It should also be noted that as demonstrated in our discussion of the kangani system, rice imports, etc., the plantation in Ceylon, as in many other colonies, was developed as a 'total institution' having a social and political structure all its own. Here, the European planters reigned supreme with little or no inteference from the colonial state.[18]

Turning our attention now to the precolonial Kandyan village economy, let us bring to mind that it was comprised of two symbiotically related modes of production – the feudalistic wet-rice (paddy) and communalistic swidden (chena) agriculture (see Figure 8:1).

Paddy agriculture was the pivot around which the economic and social organization of the society revolved. As market relations were relatively undeveloped, paddy agriculture remained basically subsistence oriented. However, a substantial surplus was expropriated from the paddy cultivating peasantry by their respective overlords – the king, the nobility, and the clergy.

In the context of the control exercised by overlords over the surplus and the uncertainty of paddy harvests (due to weather conditions, for example), shifting or chena agriculture (as well as garden cultivation) came to provide a supplementary but necessary means of subsistence and a realm of relative political autonomy for the cultivator class in precolonial times. Chena helped mediate the class conflict between overlords and serfs over the surplus and labor retention on the paddy fields.

The traditional integration between the primary (paddy) and the secondary (chena) modes of agricultural production was both complementary and antagonistic. Complementary, in that it provided a supplementary but essential source of subsistence for the cultivators; antagonistic, in that it was an expression of peasant resistance to feudal authority. This traditional articulation between paddy and chena agriculture and corresponding class relations were disrupted and transformed by the intrusion of market forces, plantations, and the colonial state.

The most severe conflict among modes of production in colonial Kandy was that which took place between the two extremes of market and subsistence production, namely plantation and chena agriculture (Figure 8:1). While plantations produced exclusively for the market, chena plots were cultivated to meet the consumption needs of the peasant producers. Plantation agriculture was characterized by private property rights and contractual capital-wage labor relations (with certain qualifications noted earlier). On the

---

18. The term 'total institution' was first used by Irving Goffman to describe self-contained organizational entities, For discussion, see, George L. Beckford, *Persistent Poverty: Underdevelopment in the Third World* (New York: Oxford University Press, 1971), p. 9. See also Section IV on "European Colonialism: Plantation Agriculture," in *Dialectics of Third World Development*, ed. by Vogeler and de Souza.

The Colonial Transformation of the Kandyan Highlands

Figure 8:1

The Articulation of Modes of Production in Colonial Kandy

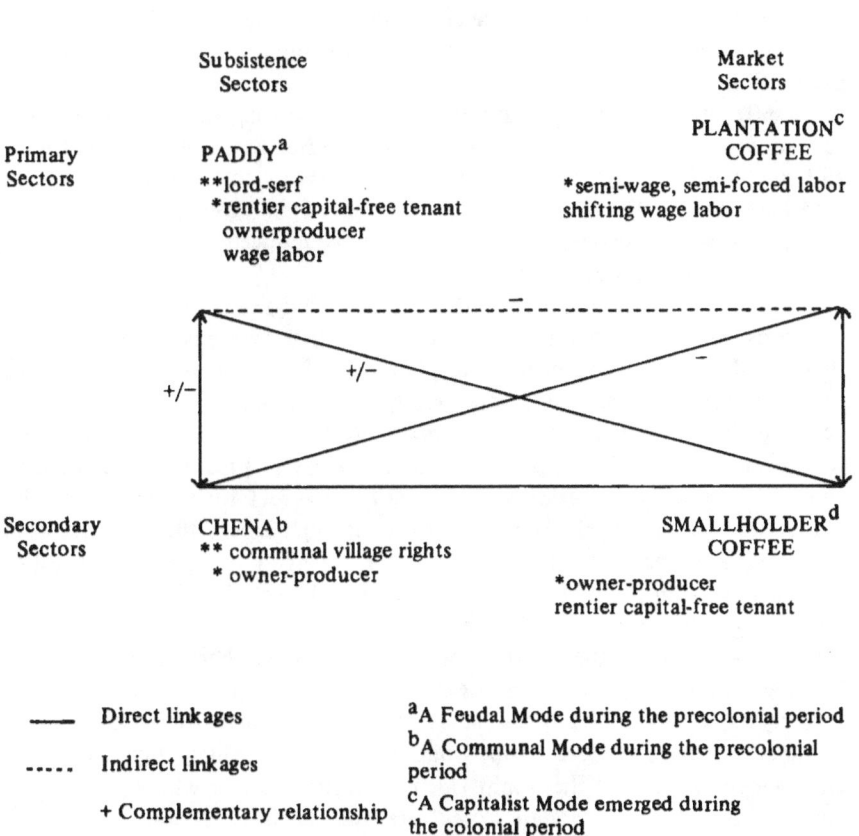

	Subsistence Sectors	Market Sectors
Primary Sectors	PADDY[a] **lord-serf *rentier capital-free tenant ownerproducer wage labor	PLANTATION[c] COFFEE *semi-wage, semi-forced labor shifting wage labor
Secondary Sectors	CHENA[b] ** communal village rights * owner-producer	SMALLHOLDER[d] COFFEE *owner-producer rentier capital-free tenant

——— Direct linkages

- - - - Indirect linkages

+ Complementary relationship

− Competitive relationship

**Dominant social relations during precolonial period

*Dominant social relations during colonial period

[a] A Feudal Mode during the precolonial period

[b] A Communal Mode during the precolonial period

[c] A Capitalist Mode emerged during the colonial period

[d] A Petty Commodity mode emerged during the colonial period

other hand, during the precolonial era, swidden agriculture was characterized by communal property rights and nonhierarchical social relations of production. The most intense form of class conflict in colonial Kandy was that which took place between the European planters and the Kandyan peasantry. This class conflict must be understood in relation to the polarization and conflict between the capitalist plantation and communalistic chena modes of production.

In spite of continuous peasant resistance, in the long run, plantation agriculture emerged victorious over chena agriculture. Expropriation of forest and swidden lands by the colonial state for disposal to the planters, sale of high lands by the feudal lords and the peasants themselves, coupled with the colonial state's campaign against chena greatly reduced the extent and importance of slash-and-burn agriculture.

As the colonial state applied private property rights to high lands, feudal overlords developed an interest in exercising their own customary rights to these lands in order to sell them to planters and speculators, or, as in some cases, to convert them to cashcropping. Thus, in addition to the conflict between European planters, the colonial state and the peasantry, a new conflict over village high lands which did not exist in precolonial times now emerged between the overlords and peasant cultivators. Furthermore, as colonial state policies curtailed peasant access to high lands, the peasants were increasingly restricted to the paddy fields and hence to the greater control of the surplus appropriating class in paddy which included feudal overlords, rentier capitalists, the colonial state, etc.

By the end of the century, the communalistic chena agriculture had become a mode of production in extinction. The extension of private property rights to chena and forest lands and the expansion of the cash nexus and market forces gradually wiped out the communal village rights to forest and swidden lands and the nonhierarchical social relations which prevailed in earlier times. Where swidden agriculture still persisted, it was increasingly subject to new property relations, largely of the smallholder-private property type.

One of the new and important developments in nineteenth-century Ceylon was smallholder cashcropping (Figure 8:1). Although peasant coffee contributed less than one fourth of total coffee exports from Ceylon during mid- to late-nineteenth century, it was the chief monetizer of the Kandyan village economy. Some of the high lands formerly used for swidden cultivation now came to be cultivated with coffee and other cash crops. To a certain extent, then, peasant cash crop cultivation also hastened the demise of chena and became a partial substitute for it.

The Colonial Transformation of the Kandyan Highlands 291

The petty commodity mode of production represented by peasant coffee must be seen as a peasant response to the cash demands placed on them by the colonial state and the new monetized market economy. Rather than becoming wage laborers on European plantations, the Kandyan peasantry adapted themselves to the new colonial political economy by taking up smallholder cash crop production. This enabled them to maintain a certain distance and independence from the surplus appropriators present in other modes of production — feudal lords, rentier capitalists, and planters.

Unlike peasants in many other colonies, the Kandyans had a choice of alternatives not only because they had access to land to cultivate cash crops, but also because the colonizers did not exercise the full extent of their powers to coerce peasants to work on the estates. In settler colonies like Kenya, peasant cashcropping was not allowed and much greater coercion was used to create a labor force for European agriculture.[19] Ceylon, like most of the other Asian colonies of Europe, was not 'settled' by the whites for a number of different reasons. The Kandyan Highlands at the time the British arrived, though isolated and autarkic, was neither a frontier region nor a land inhabited by nomadic people. It had a settled population and a highly evolved feudal social structure and culture. These were factors that inhibited European settlement and attempts to extinguish the native population as white colonizers did in many parts of Africa, the Americas and the Caribbean.

It must be emphasized that the independence the Kandyan peasants derived from cashcropping was, however, a tenuous one. For these same coffee cultivating peasants also cultivated paddy either as owner-producers (paying paddy taxes to the state) or as the tenants of feudal lords or rentier capitalists. In addition, some of them also cultivated chenas and/or worked as casual wage labor on European estates. During the extremely fluid period of rapid and dramatic social change that we have studied, the Kandyan peasants were participating simultaneously in several modes of production.

Owner-production was the dominant relation of production in the sphere of native coffee. However, a substantial amount of lands under smallholder or native coffee was in fact owned by native capitalists, Chettiyars and kanganis. These rentier capitalists had tenant laborers cultivate their lands for them.[20]

---

19. See, for example, Van Zwanenberg, *Colonial Capitalism*, Ch. 4 and 5.
20. For discussion of social relations of production in village cash crop agriculture today, see K. Tudor Silva, "Welivita: The Demise of Kandyan Feudalism" in *The Disintegrating Village*, ed. by Barrie M. Morrison et al., pp. 57–59. For a theoretical discussion of the petty commodity mode and its articulation with other modes of production, see Norman Long and Paul Richardson, "Informal Sectors, Petty Commodity Production and the Social Relations of Small Scale Enterprise," in

As a response to the cash demands made on them by the colonial state and the expanding market economy, the Kandyan peasantry evolved a new form of integration between paddy agriculture and smallholder cashcropping (Figure 8:1). Cash incomes obtained from selling peasant coffee became the chief means of paying the commuted paddy and other cash taxes and of buying imported consumer goods including increasing amounts of food. Peasant coffee then came to subsidize peasant subsistence (as chena had earlier) and the reproduction of paddy agriculture menaced by harsh taxation, cheap rice imports, and neglect of irrigation.

As noted earlier, this particular relationship between paddy and peasant coffee turned out to be highly precarious. When peasant coffee failed as it did in the 1880s, the cultivators were forced to default on their paddy tax payments to the state and loans to creditors. This in turn led to their eviction and the expropriation of their paddy lands by the state or the creditors. The ultimate result of these changes was the substitution of rentier-tenant relations in place of the smallholder private-property relations which had been introduced into the former royal (*gabada*) villages in 1818.[21] These changing social relations of production were detrimental both to peasant security and welfare as well as to the development of paddy agriculture. The elements of both complementarity and antagonism in the relationship between paddy and peasant coffee, then, must be understood in relation to the mediation of these two sectors by outside forces such as the colonial state and the market economy.

The growth of peasant cashcropping demonstrates that the Kandyan peasantry was quick to respond to market stimuli. Their reluctance to become permanent wage labor on the coffee estates does not imply indolence or disinterest in profit maximization as colonial officials, planters, and some theorists have us believe. In fact, the peasantry's decision not to become routine wage labor was quite rational, given the availability of land at the time and the relative economic and political autonomy associated with smallholder cashcropping. It is also important to bear in mind that had the Sinhalese peasantry made a large-scale conversion as plantation labor, it would not have improved their standard of living. The miserable living standards of the Tamil estate laborers were a constant reminder of that fact. It is conveivable that the rates of return from peasant cashcropping were much higher than returns from wage labor on the estates, although middlemen traders probably did not pay a fair price to the peasants for their cash crops.

The New Economic Anthropology, ed. by John Clammer (New York: St. Martin's Press, 1978), pp. 185–86.
21. It must be remembered that colonial state taxes were not collected on paddy fields belonging to the feudal villages of the nobility and the clergy.

The articulation between plantation and smallholder cashcropping was a conflictive one, particularly in the context that both sectors produced the same crop — coffee (Figure 8:1). The competition for land between the two sectors was the most striking feature of this conflict. Native owner-producers and petty capitalists were not able to secure the best land for cashcropping against the European planters who had both money and political force at their disposal. Legislation introduced by the colonial state such as the Coffee Stealing Bill of 1878. protected the interests of plantation agriculture at the expense of smallholder coffee. Furthermore, the taxes that peasants paid to the colonial state from their cash crop earnings, the state in turn passed on towards the creation and reproduction of the plantation sector in the form of infrastructural projects, police protection, etc.

It can be argued that had the peasantry received the institutional support of the state and credit agencies, peasant cashcropping would have become a far more important and dynamic sector than it did during the nineteenth century. In colonies such as the Gold Coast (Ghana), where the plantation was not the dominant agricultural strategy, smallholder cocoa production developed much more extensively than did peasant cash cropping in colonial Ceylon. Nevertheless, some of the residual effects of plantation coffee production did benefit smallholder coffee. For example, the roads, railways, and port facilities, built to further plantation expansion helped smallholders bring down their costs of production as well.

In pointing to the impact that subordinate modes of production have had on the dominant plantation mode, it must be noted that it was peasant coffee which was largely responsible for Kandyan peasants not having to hire themselves out regularly as wage labor on the plantations. In an indirect manner, then, smallholder cashcropping forced the dominant plantation sector to depend on an immigrant labor force, a situation which exercised a determining effect on the organization of plantation production and the reproduction of its labor force. The foreign extraction of the estate labor force continues to be a highly controversial political issue in the contemporary period.

The linkages between the commercial plantation and largely subsistence oriented paddy agriculture are less obvious than the linkages between plantations and the other sectors of the Kandyan village economy, namely chena and smallholder cashcropping (Figure 8:1). The plantations did not compete for the irrigated lands on which paddy was cultivated. Neither were they able to obtain to any worthwhile extent their labor needs or food supplies for the estates from the paddy cultivating Sinhalese peasants. Nevertheless, the expansionary tendency of capitalist plantation agriculture, the activities of the colonial state and market relations in general linked these two sectors, albeit antagonistically.

Part 3: Conclusions and Theoretical Implications

At least a portion of the surplus expropriated from the paddy cultivators in the form of the paddy tax, road tax, and similar taxes was used towards the maintenance of the plantation sector, especially its infrastructure, and the colonial administration. The dualistic policy of the state towards the paddy and plantation sectors (among other factors) contributed to the extension of plantation agriculture at the expense of subsistence paddy agriculture. The refusal of the colonial state to extend the land tax to cashcropping lands and its infrastructural policy favoring roads and railways over irrigation are examples of this dualistic policy.

Almost all observers of social change in Kandyan Ceylon agree that the technology of production in paddy agriculture remained backward during the nineteenth century. In some cases, the technology of paddy agriculture actually retrogressed due to the neglect of irrigation and the decline in the use of animal power. The relationship between plantation development and the decline of buffaloes needed for paddy agriculture due to the expropriation of pasture land by plantations, however, has not been firmly established.[22]

What is quite clear, however, is that the backwardness of technology in paddy agriculture was not due simply to 'traditional' values as dual economy theorists, such as Böeke, have argued.[23] As Arthur Lewis, who popularized a more structuralist variant of dual economy theory, himself has pointed out in relation to Africa, European planters had a direct interest in holding down the productivity in the subsistence sectors.

> Thus, the owners of plantations have no interest in seeing knowledge of new techniques or new seeds conveyed to the peasants, and if they are influential in the government, they will not be found using their influence to expand the facilities for agricultural extension. They will not support proposals for land settlement, and are often instead to be found engaged in turning the peasants off their land.
>
> ... In actual fact the record of every imperial power in Africa in modern times is one of impoverishing the subsistence economy. Compared with what they have spent on providing facilities for European agriculture or mining, their expenditure on the improvement of African agriculture has been negligible. The failure of imperialism to raise living standards is not wholly attributed to self interest, but there are many places where it can be traced directly to the effects of having imperial capital invested in agriculture or in mining.[24]

In addition to the plantation intrusion, the backwardness of agricultural technology and labor productivity were closely linked to the changing social

---

22. For a challenge to this hypothesis, see Michael Roberts, "The Impact of Waste Lands Legislation," pp. 191–97.
23. Böeke, *Economics and Economic Policy*, pp. 37–38. A discussion of dual economy theory follows in Ch. IX of this book.
24. Lewis, "Economic Development with Unlimited Supplies of Labour," pp. 149–50.

The Colonial Transformation of the Kandyan Highlands 295

relations of production within the village economy itself. These new social relations of production in paddy agriculture cannot be understood apart from the overall changes in the society. In other words, the evolution of the village (consisting of several modes of production in a state of flux) and the plantation was inextricably linked.

Social Relations of Production in Paddy Agriculture

Our analysis has shown that although chena agriculture was practically wiped out, the new economic and political forces operating in the society did not destroy paddy agriculture. The vast majority of the peasantry continued to be engaged primarily in paddy cultivation. However, paddy agriculture was reconstituted on a new basis. In the subsequent pages we will summarize the changing social relations of production in the paddy sector (see also Figure 8:2). The picture that emerges is a highly complex one pointing to variations in pace and degree in the dissolution of precolonial social relations in different categories of paddy lands.

In our earlier discussions we noted two categories of villages in precolonial Kandy — royal villages (*gabādagam*) and feudal villages (*nindagam, vihāragam* and *dēvalagam*). The dissolution of precolonial social relations of production started earlier and proceeded much more rapidly in the former royal villages than in the feudal villages held by aristocrats and temples (see Figure 8:2). This was because the colonial state abolished forced labor services in the royal villages as early as 1818 (and again in 1833) and established the tenant cultivators as a class of owner-cultivators paying rent (in kind or cash) to the colonial state. But as described in detail in the text, over the years due to the operation of the commuted paddy tax, many of these owner-producers began to lose their paddy fields to rentier capitalists.

As paddy fields in the crown villages passed into the hands of rentier landlords the precolonial extraeconomic rights of the Crown over these lands began gradually to disappear. Instead, private property norms, contractual economic rights and the concept of land as commodity came to be established over paddy fields in the former royal villages. Nevertheless, as we discussed earlier, some of the native rentier capitalists who bought peasant land grafted some precolonial extraeconomic rights (the exaction of personal labor services for instance) on to the essentially contractual economic relationship with their sharecropping tenants. Some of the reasons for the persistence of such 'feudal' features have been discussed in earlier chapters.

The process of dissolution of feudal social relations was much slower in the villages of the nobility and the clergy. Even today some of the extraeconomic caste services associated with feudal surplus appropriation persist in the monastic or temple villages of the Kandyan Highlands.[25]

However, changes were made in the lord-serf relationship within the feudal villages through the expansion of market forces and the intrusion of the colonial state, especially with the introduction of voluntary commutation of labor and produce rents in 1870. While commutation was widely accepted by the cultivators in the former royal villages, due to a number of reasons discussed earlier, its acceptance in the feudal villages was only partial. Yet, the Service Tenures Ordinance gave the overlord the right to dispossess the tenant of his means of production for default on labor service or rent payments. The extra-economic basis of the feudal relationship was thus undermined providing overlords the institutional framework for reconstituting themselves on a contractual economic basis as rentier capitalists or even capitalist entrepreneurs employing wage labor.[26] The latter option was rarely made use of.

Although the essential nature of the feudal relationship was undermined by external forces, not all feudal lords or even serfs moved with equal speed to break the feudal nexus. The lord's interest in maintaining the right to control people was one reason. Even some of the rentier capitalists who bought paddy fields in the feudal villages attempted to establish extraeconomic rights over the cultivators. The serfs in turn wanted to maintain the security associated with the feudal patron-client relationship. Although the 'feudal' relationship was incorporated within the market economy, the cash nexus and private property norms, feudal forms of surplus appropriation such as caste-defined labor services still persisted. Their dissolution was slow and gradual.

We must reiterate, however, that even where surplus exaction proceeded along extraeconomic lines, the basis for its transformation into a contractual economic relationship was firmly established. This was because the new politico-juridical framework allowed the dispossession of the cultivator from his means of production. The dissolution of feudalism as a mode of production was thus set in motion.[27]

It needs also to be pointed out that whereas the paddy cultivating peasantry had been a relatively homogeneous class (apart from caste differences) in precolonial times, they came to be differentiated into hierarchical economic groups during the nineteenth century. This differentiation proceeded in relationship to the means of production — land. Some continued to labor as serfs of feudal overlords although their hereditary rights to the land were now threatened within the new politico-juridical framework. Many became owner-

25. Gunasinghe, "Production Relations," pp. 130, 132.
26. Compare Hamza Alavi, "India and the Colonial Mode of Production," p. 182.
27. See ch. 5, pp. 154–171 in this work.

producers cultivating small plots. They too faced the ever present threat of expropriation for default on taxes and loans. Still others who were sharecropping tenants of rentier capitalists were dispossessed of hereditary rights to land. Very few were rural wage laborers. Rural wage labor was not very visible during the nineteenth century although it rapidly increased during the twentieth century with population increase, dwindling land supplies and further monetization and commercialization of the village economy. During the nineteenth century (and even today, to some extent) many of the cultivators belonged to several of these cultivator categories. In other words, a strict separation did not exist between owner-producers, and, say, sharecroppers. The increasing insecurity of peasant existence during the colonial era necessitated that cultivators constantly move between different sets of social relations of production. What is clear, however, is that the general direction of change was towards the dispossession of the cultivator and the consolidation of contractual economic rights of the surplus appropriating class.[28]

Much of the debate among neo-Marxist theoreticians on colonial social formations is focused precisely on the issue of social relations of production in the rural agricultural sector. Are these social relations to be characterized as persisting 'feudal' relations? Are they any longer feudal; if not, are they 'capitalist'; or should they be called 'colonial'? Does the persistence of surplus exaction in kind and labor imply that feudalism as a mode of production has survived or has it been transformed into something entirely different? We shall return to these questions in our concluding theoretical discussion in Chapter IX.

Backwardness in Paddy Agriculture

Thus, with the gradual dispossession of the cultivators and the exaction of surplus on the basis of contractual economic rights of the owners, social relations of production in paddy agriculture began to change in a capitalist direction. But this change was inherently slow and uneven. Furthermore, the reinvestment of profits and improvements in technique and labor productivity which are central to the expanded reproduction of capitalist agriculture were absent in the Kandyan Highlands. As writers such as Jairus Banaji have

28. For discussions of the twentieth-century evolution of these social relations of production see Gunasinghe, "Production Relations," and "Agrarian Relations;" Tambiah and Sarker, *Disintegrating Village;* Morrison et al. (eds.), *The Disintegrating Village* (esp. the Introduction and Part III on "The Kandyan Heartland").

pointed out, this contradiction, that is, changes in the social relations of production without changes in the technology of production is a characteristic feature of agricultural underdevelopment in the colonies.[29] What Banaji calles the 'retrograde logic'[30] of capitalist expansion in the colonies lies in such reasons as: the transfer of surplus to metropolitan countries by European capital; the transfer of profits to mercantile activities and export production by local capital; and persistence of archaic social relations within rentier capitalism in rural agriculture.

As discussed earlier in the text, paddy agriculture came to be considered the least profitable form of investment in colonial Ceylon. Often Chettiyar money lenders and Muslim traders became paddy landowners by default — because peasants unable to pay off their loans had nothing else but their small paddy fields to sell. Nonproductive forms of investment such as moneylending and trade in fact, promised higher rates of return than investment in paddy agriculture. Both the feudal lords turned rentier capitalists and the new merchant capitalist classes were therefore more interested in the rent to be collected from the cultivators than in developing paddy production. As elsewhere in the colonial world, the dominance of merchant capital (and particularly 'middlemen' groups) in rural agriculture became a disincentive to agricultural development.[31] As Mamdani has observed in relation to colonial India, "a dynamic economy was not possible without a dynamic dominant class."[32]

The poverty of the cultivators and the tenancy arrangements which allocated a proportion rather than a fixed amount of the yield to the land owner also prevented the peasants from taking an active interest in improving agricultural technique and labor productivity. A British official's observation with respect to Punjabi peasants in colonial India is equally applicable to Kandyan peasants,

> ... there was always before them the knowledge that they might have to pay a higher rent if they sank a well or otherwise increased the productivity of the land, and this knowledge essentially had the effect of permanently checking any disposition on their part to lay out money in improvement.[33]

29. Jairus Banaji, "For a Theory" p. 2501.
30. Ibid., p. 2500.
31. Ibid., p. 2451. See also Charles Bettleheim's observations quoted by Kathleen Gough in "Class and Agrarian Change: Some Comments on Peasant Resistance and Revolution in India — A Rejoinder," *Pacific Affairs*, vol. XIII, no. 3 (Fall 1969), p. 367.
32. Mahmood Mamdani, *The Myth of Population Control: Family, Caste and Class in an Indian Village* (New York: Monthly Review Press, 1972), p. 58.
33. Admission of Colonel W. G. Davies before the Indian Famine Commission of 1878–1879, quoted by Mamdani, ibid., p. 58.

If paddy cultivating peasants were in fact disinterested in profit maximizing behavior, we need to understand that as a reflection of the institutional arrangements of colonial society, including the social relations of paddy agriculture and the impediments placed by the plantation sector and the colonial state.

In the development of capitalism in England, the dispossession of the peasantry was accompanied by improvements in the technology of agricultural production and rural-urban migration causing a large-scale removal of the peasantry from the land into the cities. But in Ceylon — as in many other colonies — the social relations of production changed without improvements in the technology of production or labor productivity. Thus a potentially 'surplus' population (particularly as the rural population increased) was able to remain on the land by intensifying or 'involuting' the age-old methods of production, albeit at the expense of their standards of living.[34]

In addition to the resiliency of intensive irrigated agriculture (in this case — paddy) to absorb increasing population at lower levels of productivity, yet another reason for the absence of a large-scale emigration out of the village was the lack of a significant manufacturing or industrial sector that could employ the surplus rural population. For reasons we have discussed earlier, the Kandyan peasantry refused to become a permanent labor force on the coffee plantations which offered the only major occupational alternative to paddy cultivation. Estate labor did not promise higher incomes or improved standards of living. Even when paddy cultivators began to lose their hereditary rights to paddy fields, they did not necessarily leave their lands. Instead they continued to cultivate their lands in the traditional manner under new and more unfavorable tenancy arrangements. Only a small group became a casual shifting labor force in the coffee estates. The size of this semiproletariat, however, increased during the later tea period. As discussed earlier, in the context of the backwardness of paddy agriculture and the absence of other viable alternatives, smallholder cashcropping became a subsidiary, but extremely important, strategy of peasant adaptation and survival during the nineteenth century.

---

34. S. B. D. de Silva, "Investment and Economic Growth," *passim;* see also Geertz, *Agricultural Involution.*

Figure 8:2

The Transition from Feudal[a] to Colonial Economy (1820s–1880s)

Feudal[b] (Paddy) Economy[a] (circa 1815)	Colonial Economy (circa 1886)		
	Plantation Sector	Village Sector	
		Former Royal Villages (*gabadāgam*)	'Feudal' Villages (*nindagam, vihāragam, dēvalagam*)
1) Unfree labor	1) Semi-wage, semi-bonded labor	1) Small peasant proprietorship in paddy increasingly giving way to rentier capitalism; owner production of cash crops (coffee)	1) Unfree labor persists although basis for its release set in place
2) Surplus exaction on the basis of extraeconomic rights	2) Surplus exaction largely economic but also through extra-economic means (debt bondage and *kanganis*)	2) Surplus exaction by rentier capital on contractual economic basis and by colonial state on extra-economic basis	2) Surplus exaction in labor, produce and money rents on the basis of both extraeconomic and economic rights of appropriators.
3) Fusion of economic and political power at point of production	3) Fusion of economic and political power in the planter-official class until 1845; formal separation later	3) Some extra-economic rights grafted onto the contractual rentier-tenant relationships. Where colonial state taxed paddy, a fusion of economic & political power	3) Extraeconomic rights persist and also grafted on to contractual rentier-tenant relations.

4) Relatively self-sufficient village economy[c]	4) Exclusive production for international market	4) Paddy agriculture largely subsistence oriented; petty commodity production in cash crops (coffee) expansion of market and cash relations	4) Paddy agriculture largely subsistence oriented; some cashcropping; expansion of market and cash relations
5) Simple reproduction	5) Expanded reproduction in the metropolitan nation through exports of profits	5) Simple reproduction of paddy although surplus exacted by state and rentier capital used for expanded reproduction of plantation economy & indigenous capital in other spheres & regions	5) Simple reproduction of paddy although surplus exacted by overlords and rentier capital for expanded reproduction in other spheres and regions

[a] The Feudal Mode was the dominant one in the precolonial village economy. There was also a subordinate communal (chena) mode.
[b] Features of Feudal Mode taken from Hamza Alavi's "India: Transition from Feudalism to Colonial Capitalism," *The Journal of Contemporary Asia*, vol. 10, no. 4 (1980). pp. 363–64.
[c] Some feudal economies, however, had developed market relations.

The Colonial State and the Subordination of Traditional Political Authority

The transition from a predominantly feudal to a colonial economy in the Kadyan Highlands cannot be understood at the level of economic structures alone. As we have noted in several places in this study, the subordination of the precolonial society was not achieved through a simple process of market expansion and the superimposition of the plantation mode of production. The transition that occurred in Kandy did not originate internally; its impetus came from the outside. The power of the colonial state and colonialist ideology were fundamental to the subordination of the indigenous socioeconomic structures. The role of the colonial state in the subordination and transformation of Kandyan society has already been discussed. In this section we shall briefly examine the articulation between precolonial and superimposed political ideologies and authority structures and the conditioning effects of the old and the new upon one another.

The ideology of the colonial state during the nineteenth century was an amalgam of elements drawn from Sinhalese feudalism and contemporary capitalist thinking in the West. This ideology, if indeed it can be called such, was never a well-defined system of thought but an inherently contradictory set of notions that kept changing with the various exigencies facing the colonial state at different periods. The shift from mercantilist to laissez-faire and liberal political views that occurred with the introduction of the Colebrooke-Cameron Reforms in 1833 have been documented in Chapter III.

The self-proclaimed justification for colonial rule was the extension of leadership and democracy to colonized people. But at the same time, the colonial state had to rest itself on the infliction of arbitrary and coercive power upon native people. We have noted in earlier chapters that the justification given by the British for the usurpation of the Kandyan kingdom and the consolidation of British political authority there, was the liberation of the Kandyan people from their tyrannical king. The colonial state avowed to safeguard the ancient customs and institutions of Kandyan society. But as discussed previously in the text, the colonial state adapted feudal theories such as the monarch's right to all the land and precolonial practices such as the exaction of corvée labor and the paddy tax for the wholly new purposes of plantation expansion and the consolidation of colonial political authority.

But once colonial political authority was consolidated and plantation development was underway, colonial ideology shifted from its earlier stress on the conservation of the precolonial order to an emphasis on changing and civilizing the natives. This shift in colonialist ideology must be seen in relation to the shift from the earlier mercantilist phase to the period of plantation development in the island. During the earlier period, radical transformations of the native social structures were not required since mercantile profits were based on extracting local produce under the pre-existing social relations of production. However, when installing the colonial mode of production in the form of plantations, a radical transformation in property relations and labor mobilization came to be required. In keeping with these new needs, a new colonial ideology was also fashioned.

At that time, the disparagement of the Sinhalese as an uncivilized, indolent childlike and inferior race became common place. As illustrated in earlier chapters, the planters, who were exasperated by the Kandyan peasantry's refusal to hire themselves out as estate labor, were not the only ones propagating the myth of the lazy native. Most colonial officials also subscribed to these racist and paternalistic views. The myth of racial superiority of the British became a necessary justification for colonial exploitation. That some provincial officials and governors however held sympathetic views towards the peasantry has been pointed out earlier.

Planters and colonial officials claimed to help the natives through material development and the extension of a civilized way of life. Christian missionary activity and western education which were important components of colonial ideology and practice, have not been discussed in this book.[35] One of the major planks of the new ideology was that the interests of the colonial power and the native society were mutually compatible. Not all planters or colonial officials (for example, Emerson Tennent) believed in this compatibility. But in the absence of other forms of justification for colonial rule, the idea of mutual benefit continued to be put forward for purposes of colonial self-legitimation.

In practice, however, it was precisely the contradictions that occurred between colonial and native (largely peasant) interests that the colonial state was there to mediate. Neither the development of productive forces in the colony (except European plantations), nor the introduction of a western type bureaucratic administration were great concerns of the British during the nineteenth century. The overriding interests were, rather, the security and stability of the colonial state and freedom for the expansion of British capital.

---

35. See, for example, K. M. de Silva, *Social Policy*. See also articles on colonial educational development by L. A. Wickremeratne and Swarna Jayaweera in *History of Ceylon*, ed. by K. M. de Silva, Vol. 3.

The Subordination of Native Chiefs

The early theorist of the colonial state, J. S. Furnivall, made a distinction between two forms of colonial political administration: indirect and direct rule. Indirect rule involved the governance of the colonies through the native chiefs and direct rule involved control primarily through a superimposed European administrative class.[36] In practice, however, there was not muct difference between the two as colonial powers used varying forms of both indirect and direct rule. Furnivall pointed out that in Burma, where direct rule was supposed to prevail, the European officials were nevertheless heavily dependent on the native 'circle headmen' for conducting the affairs of the colonial administration.[37]

Furnivall also argued that the adoption of either indirect or direct rule needs to be understood in relation to the specific strategies of colonial economic development and stages of imperialist expansion. He pointed out that during the earlier period of European merchant capitalism, indirect rule through local chieftains was the cheapest and easiest way of gaining economic control. On the other hand, when western economic enterprises such as plantations were installed in the colonies during a later phase, "large scale transactions ... regulated on western lines" came to be required. At that time. Furnivall argues, there tended to "develop a dual system of administration, half western half tropical...."[38]

Indeed, during the mercantilist phase of British colonial rule in Ceylon, that is. the period preceding 1833, colonial rule took largely an indirect form in that local headmen were used both for the exaction of local produce and political control of the population. But with the Colebrooke Reforms of 1833 a more direct form of European authority was superimposed when the provincial administration was reorganized. The result was a hierarchically organized dual administration. This shift in the form of political and administrative control coincided with the transition from the earlier phase of merchant capital to production capital and the installation of a capitalist plantation mode of production.

However, our Ceylonese case study has shown that direct and indirect rule were not clear-cut alternatives and that the colonial state was composed of both native and European sectors of authority. The two were separate, but inextricably linked. The European officials could not govern without the native headmen and the native headmen had no independent authority but

---

36. Furnivall, *Colonial Policy and Practice*, p. 537.
37. Ibid., p. 42. Gail Omvedt, "Towards a Theory of Colonialism," *Insurgent Sociologist*, vol. 3, no. 3 (Spring 1973), p. 3.
38. Furnivall, quoted by Omvedt, "Towards a Theory," p. 3.

The Colonial Transformation of the Kandyan Highlands 305

that which was conferred upon them by the more powerful European administrators. Like the relationship between the two economic sectors — village and plantation — the relationship of the two political sectors was also hierarchical. Just as the plantation economy was superimposed upon the village economy, European political authority was installed upon the native chiefs. Just as the plantation economy defined the limits and the direction of the evolution of the village economy, European authority defined the limits and the direction of evolution of native political authority. As colonial economic evolution did not necessarily repeat the patterns in the metropoles, the political evolution in the colonies did not result in western bureaucratic type political structures either. E. A. Brett's observations with regard to colonial East Africa have applicability to colonial Ceylon as well.

> These pre-colonial formations were not entirely incorporated by the new colonial system — they were required to change in favor of new demands only up to the point required for the purposes of the colonial political economy but not further than that.... But the continued survival of these dependent structures should not be taken as proof of the continued existence of some earlier "traditional" society. The changes imposed by colonialism were fundamental — they undermined the old structures at their most vulnerable points. The chief might still command his people, but he now deferred to the District Commissioner. When faced with a threat to his authority his ultimate recourse lay with the colonial state, not the pre-colonial social and political sanctions.[39]

Similar to the articulation of modes of economic production, the articulation between the two sectors of political authority was not easy or static but contradictory and changing. The native aristocratic–administrative class did not collaborate with the Europeans in all occassions. During the course of the nineteenth century, the relationship between the native headmen and the European administration shifted from one of collaboration in the deposal of the Kandyan king in 1815 to one of intense rivalry which culminated in the 1818 rebellion. While the aristocracy remained neutral by and large during the 1848 peasant rebellion, a new form of class collaboration was worked out between the headmen and the colonial state following that rebellion.

What is also necessary to understand is that the colonial state was hardly the ideal bureaucratic type of authority described by Max Weber. We have seen that the very legitimacy and basis for operation of the 'modern' colonial bureaucracy was derived from its role as the successor to the precolonial feudal king. Furthermore, the colonial state imposed itself upon Kandyan society promising to uphold the traditional institutions and practices that the deposed Kandyan king himself had violated. As noted earlier, the European

---

39. E. A. Brett, *Colonialism and Underdevelopment in East Africa: The Politics of Economic Change* (New York: NOK Publishers, 1973), pp. 19–20.

sector of the colonial state, like the native sector, was largely an administration of notables and was characterized by patronage rather than impersonal bureaucratic norms.

In the process of contact with the European administration, only selected aspects of the traditional authority structures were changed. The guiding principle in this selective adaptation was the economic and political needs of the Europeans. For example. forced labor was abolished in the crown villages — but maintained in the feudal villages. Just as the European planters were dependent on the Indian labor headmen or kanganis to control their labor force, the colonial officials were dependent on the village headmen to control the native peasantry. Given this state of affairs — that is, the extreme dependence on the native headmen — the colonial state did not make greater efforts than it did to change social relations in the feudal villages. Sudden and dramatic changes in feudal relations would have undermined the authority of the chiefs and their support for the colonial state. The persistence of certain 'feudal' relations of production, then, needs to be understood not simply at the level of economic structures, but also at the level of political and ideological structures and class alliances between the old and the new ruling classes.

Having understood the changing articulations among the diverse economic and political structures in the Kandyan Highlands, we now turn to the changing class, caste, and ethnic configurations there.

Class, Caste and Ethnic Configurations in Colonial Kandy

We have noted earlier that despite the harsh exploitation of the immigrant labor force on the coffee estates, no intense class conflict occurred between planters and their laborers. What little resistance offered by the laborers took the form of refusal to turn up for work, escape to other plantations, and coffee thefts. The relative docility of the plantation labor force during the nineteenth century, we noted, is largely explainable by their foreign character and the patriarchal control exercised by the middlemen — the kanganis. Jeffrey Paige's observations regarding the reformist character of labor agitation in plantation modes of production would be applicable only to the twentieth-century tea plantations of Ceylon.[40] The kangani system and other forms of

40. Jeffrey M. Paige, *Agrarian Revolution: Social Movements and Export Agriculture in the Underdeveloped World* (New York: The Free Press, 1975); see also Arthur L. Stinchcombe, "Agricultural Enterprise and Rural Class Relations," *American Journal of Sociology*, vol. 67 (1961–1962), pp. 165–76.

The Colonial Transformation of the Kandyan Highlands 307

'forced' labor exaction gave way to permanent attachment of labor on the tea estates and their organization along trade union lines by the middle of the twentieth century.

Turning now to the village economy, let us bring to mind our earlier observation that the intrusion of market forces and colonial legislation tended to exacerbate the conflicts between the overlords and the tenants over rent (Figure 8:3). In the early years of colonial rule, tenants had already been avoiding the performance of feudal labor services. But when the colonial state provided a new legitimacy to the overlords through the activities of the Temple Lands Commission, the Service Tenures Ordinance and the commutation option, the overlords began to demand the rent (due in labor, kind, or money) with renewed vigor. The resulting conflicts between lords and serfs did not always take on a precolonial or feudal character because within the new framework of private property rights, absolute ownership and the commercialization of land, the feudal lords could now dispossess the defaulting cultivators of their hereditary lands. The extent of conflicts over land and litigation between the producer and surplus appropriating classes, as well as among the peasants themselves (for example, over the subdivision of family property) greatly increased during the colonial period. These conflicts during the colonial period began slowly to undermine both the patriarchal bond between the lord and the serf as well as the kinship ties among the peasantry, thus leading to a level of peasant insecurity over land, never known in precolonial times.

We have also noted that much of the paddy and some high lands in the former crown villages and some lands in the feudal villages passed into the hands of non-Kandyan rentier capitalists — low country Sinhalese, and Muslim traders, during the period under investigation. The emergence of a class of non-Kandyan absentee landlords introduced new elements of conflict into the lord-tenant relationship. Oftentimes, these conflicts took on caste and ethnic coloration.

It is likely that the reactivation of forced labor services by the colonial state, discussed in Chapter V, was harsher in its impact on the so-called low or artisan castes who performed menial services for the overlords than on the *govi* or cultivator caste. Furthermore, as we have seen earlier, when land passed into the hands of non-Kandyans, the cultivators, who were accustomed to performing personal services only to their caste superiors, often refused to serve outsiders. Thus, pre-existing caste and ethnic cleavages at times facilitated the expression of underlying class hostilities. However, conflicts which took on such expression were sporadic and ultimately restorative in that they looked to the expulsion of the non-Kandyans and the reassertion

Figure 8:3

Economic Sectors, Social Classes,* Ethnic Groups and Castes**
in the Kandyan Highlands — circa 1848

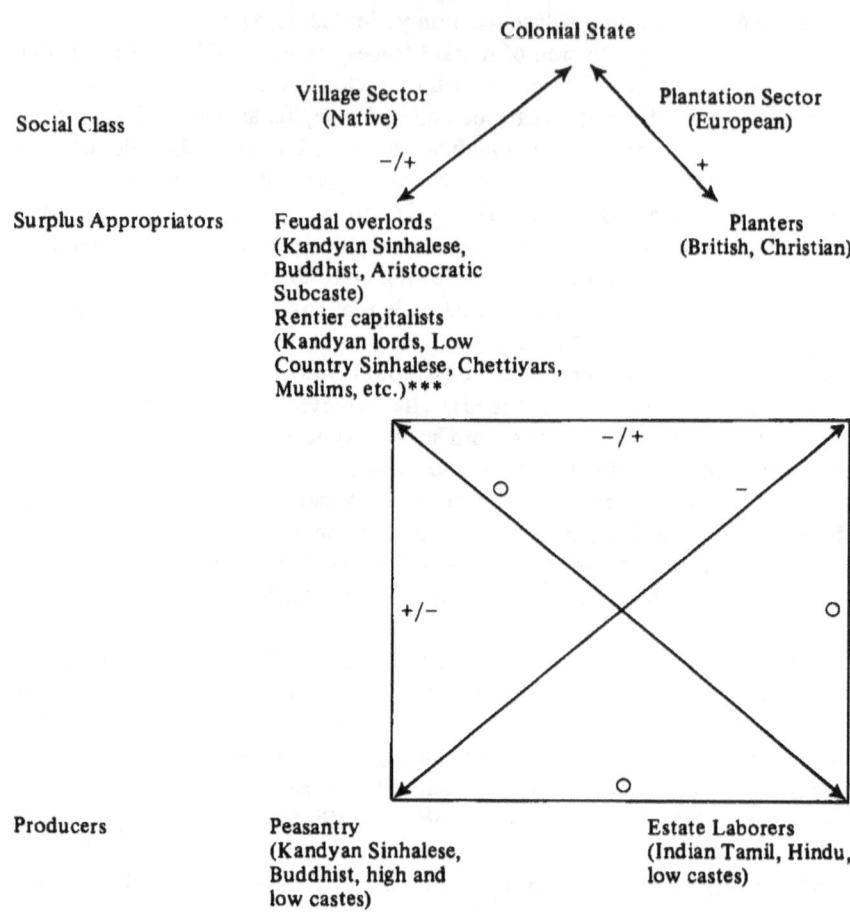

*This is a simplified picture of the class structure. It does not show the
internal differentiation of the producer classes, for example, different types of peasant
cultivators.
**Only high and low caste status indicated.
***The colonial State was also a surplus appropriator.
Primary Relationships Identified: + cooperative − antagonistic,
−/+, +/− changing; 0 neutral.

of the ascriptive caste hierarchy and ethnic homogeneity of precolonial Kandyan society.

Prior to the arrival of the British, Kandyan society was an ethnically homogeneous entity of Sinhalese Buddhists. Sinhalese groups who fled the European-ruled coastal lowlands were gradually absorbed into the Kandyan caste structure, while the Muslims engaged in local trade remained an itinerant group. This relative ethnic homogeneity was the basis of national solidarity between the feudal overlords and the peasantry against successive European invaders from the coastal lowlands.

It must be noted, however, that precolonial Sinhalese societies, especially in the coastal lowlands, received waves of immigrants from India. But there is a fundamental difference in the absorption of immigrants into Sinhalese society during precolonial and colonial times. During the twenty or more centuries of precolonial history in the island, successive immigrant groups were assimilated into the Sinhalese caste structure. Both the *karawa* and *salagama* castes were such recently incorporated Indian immigrant groups in the coastal lowlands.[41] In contrast, during the nineteenth century, the immigrant Tamil estate laborers in the hill country were kept apart as a separate foreign community by the European planters.

Yet, the precolonial situation was different in the case of the northern region of the island where separate indigenous Tamil communities evolved from about the thirteenth century. The Tamil populations there resisted assimilation into Sinhalese communities in the rest of the island. The historical origin of this cultural antagonism between the Sinhalese and the indigenous Tamils (as opposed to the Tamil estate labor force in the hill country) is an issue that is well beyond the scope of the present study.

Upon the cession of the Kandyan kingdom, the Highlands, however, became ethnically heterogeneous (see Figure 8:3) As E. T. Thompson and other writers have pointed out, the plantation is a racially (or ethnically) structured institution.[42] In Ceylon, too, plantation development brought in diverse ethnic groups to the Highlands to play specific roles within the new colonial political economy, such as: the Europeans as planters and administrators; the South Indians as estate laborers; the Chettiyars as moneylenders; the Muslims as traders and the low-country Sinhalese service castes as carpenters, masons, and carters.

---

41. Ralph Pieris, "Caste, Ethos and Social Equilibrium," *Social Forces*, vol. 30, no. 4 (May 1952), p. 413.
42. E. T. Thompson's work as discussed by Beckford in *Persistent Poverty*, pp. 67–73.

The positions these various groups had occupied within their respective precolonial social formations shaped and defined the roles they were to play within the new division of labor in the British plantation economy. The relative landlessness and poverty of the agricultural labor castes in South India compelled them to emigrate to Ceylon in search of plantation work. The Chettiyars, who had historically been a moneylending community were able to continue their usurious and trading activities within the new plantation economy without much difficulty. The low country Sinhalese service castes such as the *karawas* and the *salagama* who were relatively later additions to the Sinhalese caste system did not have the same ties to paddy cultivation as the Kandyan peasantry. They were therefore more willing and able to adapt to the new plantation economy than the Kandyan peasantry rooted in their hereditary paddy fields.

What resulted during the nineteenth century was not assimilation but what Furnivall has called a 'plural society' wherein each ethnic group came to perform a specific function within the hierarchically structured colonial economy.[43] Furnivall, and later theorists working within the 'plural society' framework have argued that due to the ethnically based division of labor and absence of assimilation in plural societies, the different ethnic groups interact with each other only in their occupational roles within the market or economic sphere. In other words, ethnicity takes on caste-like characteristics, i.e., an ascriptive, occupational hierarchy and corresponding social status. Plural society theorists argue that such ethnically heterogeneous societies lack a 'common will' and they must be artificially integrated (though the integration is tenuous) by the external force of the colonial state. The implication is that when this external force is removed, ethnic conflict becomes most severe.[44] Plural society theory has made an important contribution in pointing out that ethnic groups are not inherently antagonistic towards one another merely by reason of the differentiation arising from their cultural patterns. Conflict grows out of the structural positions in which each group is placed within the colonial political economy.[45]

Oftentimes, the class conflicts rooted in the opposing structural positions occupied by these different ethnic groups tend to be expressed simply in ethnic terms. But these apparently 'ethnic' conflicts need to be understood in relation to the economic hierarchy that emerged during the colonial period wherein non-Kandyan groups ranging from the European planters to Muslim

---

43. Furnivall, *Colonial Policy and Practice*, pp. 276–312.
44. Ibid., pp. 276–312. See also M. G. Smith, *The Plural Society in the British West Indies* (Berkeley: University of California Press, 1965).
45. Furnivall, *Colonial Policy and Practice*, pp. 276–312.

traders and low country Sinhalese entrepreneurs were placed in exploitative class relationships vis-à-vis the Kandyan peasantry.

But before we go on to point out specific instances from our case study of class and ethnic conflicts, it is important to bear in mind that ethnic conflict is not a phenomenon restricted to colonial social formations. Nor is it something that can be explained entirely by reference to social class cleavages, as some Marxists attempt to do. Ethnic stratification, like caste, often tends to develop its own system of ranking and associated social consciousness.[46]

The clearest and most intense form of class conflict in the Kandyan Highlands during the nineteenth century took place not between the feudal overlords (and rentier capitalists) and the peasantry or between planters and their laborers, but between planters and peasants. In other words, this conflict took place across economic sectors and not within the productive enterprise (see Figure 8:3) The nature of this class struggle, as we pointed out earlier, must be understood in the context of the contradictions between opposing modes of production; class alliances between the Europeans and the native aristocracy; and Kandyan nationalism.

In spite of the amount of power at its disposal, the colonial state did not win the struggle against the Kandyan peasantry easily. Peasant 'encroachments' on 'crown' and plantation lands and other forms of conflict over high lands (e.g., cattle trespass) continued throughout the nineteenth and well into the twentieth century. The peasantry's resistance against both wage labor on the European estates and forced labor for road construction (particularly after the introduction of the Road Ordinance in 1848) were yet other manifestations of the underlying planter-peasant conflict.

The role of the native overlords, particularly the headmen, was crucial in the mediation of this struggle between the peasantry and colonial economic and political authorities (the planters and the colonial state). In some instances, especially during the early years of British rule, many of the native aristocracy and especially the Buddhist clergy, sided with the peasants in their nationalist attempts to drive out the British. But during the course of the nineteenth century, as the likelihood of ousting the British became remote, the native aristocracy became amenable to a new alliance with the British and to being incorporated within the colonial administration. While the feudal families who entered into partnership with the British thrived under colonial rule, those families who did not do so gradually lost their aristocratic status and privileges. With the incorporation of many of the aristocrats into the

---

46. Gordon's 'ethclass' concept is useful for understanding this; Milton Gordon, *Assimilation in American Life: The Role of Race, Religion and National Origin* (New York: Oxford University Press, 1978).

colonial administration, the potential 'vertical solidarity' between the overlords and the peasants against the British was considerably weakened.

The class conflict between the peasantry and the planters when collectively expressed took on ethnic and nationalist meaning, as we shall see in relation to the 1848 rebellion. The object of peasant resistance in these instances was not so much the plantations themselves as the colonial state. Kitsiri Malalgoda has noted that some of the peasant rebellions in colonial Kandy took the characteristics of Buddhist millennial movements.[47] Peasant rebellions during the colonial period (in Ceylon and elsewhere) were expressed primarily as nationalist revolts rather than class struggles.[48] In many of these rebellions in the Highlands, the Buddhist monks, usually from the lower echelons of the clerical hierarchy, played important roles. Even today the Buddhist clergy is a pillar of Sinhalese nationalism.

In 1883, the Government Agent of the Kegalle District, R. W. Ievers, wrote of "a revival partly religious, partly seditious" which arose in the Seven Korales and gradually spread to other areas.[49] As the historical information pertaining to this movement is scanty, it is not possible to say if it was in any way related to the collapse of peasant coffee and the more rigorous exaction of colonial taxes at the time. But what is known is that a palm-leaf manuscript giving voice to millenial expectations of the arrival of a Buddhist 'Prince of Righteousness' was circulated in that region.[50] The authorship of the manuscript has been attributed to a Kandyan Buddhist monk. Hugh Neville, an Englishman who later obtained this manuscript, wrote,

> This is a modern writing which ... throws light on the native mind. It is written to induce the people to believe that the English rule would not continue, and is a pretended prophecy. It brings an allusion to Saka 1788 or, A.D. 1866, when a king should arrive and therefore restore the good old times.[51]

It must be pointed out that when class conflicts are interpreted simply as ethnic or cultural conflicts — rather than as outcomes of unequal economic and political structures, ethnicity (and caste, where applicable) tends to inhibit the development of class consciousness and the struggles to eliminate the underlying politico-economic hierarchies. This point can be further illustrated by pointing out that because the exploitation of Kandyan peasants by the

---

47. Kitsiri Malalgoda, "Millennialism."
48. Such movements were common occurrences in the colonies, See, for example, Scott's references to the Saya San Rebellion in colonial Burma, *Moral Economy*, pp. 149–50.
49. Quoted by Malalgoda, "Millennialism," p. 437.
50. Ibid., p. 437.
51. Ibid., p. 437.

newly arrived non-Kandyan groups such as Muslim traders, Chettiyar moneylenders and low-country Sinhalese businessmen was more conspicuous, it helped abate the potential conflict between peasants and their native overlords. In this regard, the rioting which broke out between Buddhists and Muslims in 1915 around Kandy (and spread to other areas) is instructive. The common interpretation and the one advanced by the colonial state was that the riots were purely an expression of religious antagonism between the two religio-ethnic groups. But as Kumari Jayawardena has explained, the nature of political and economic development in the preceding years were at the root of the hostilities between the Buddhist majority and the Muslim minority. She notes, "With the aggravated economic hardships the poor had to face after the outbreak of the First World War, there was fierce resentment against profiteering directed mainly against Moor traders."[52]

As noted earlier, the alliance between the British and the aristocracy weakened Kandyan nationalism which had bound the Kandyan overlords and the peasants against the British. Nevertheless, this vertical solidarity was kept alive during the nineteenth century by the cultivation of a new collective Kandyan resentment against low-country Sinhalese, Muslims, and other non-European alien groups exploiting the peasantry. The presence of these non-Kandyan middlemen minorities no doubt helped mitigate peasant antagonism towards the Kandyan overlords, on the one hand, and collective resistance against the British, on the other hand. The ethnically based hierarchy within the colonial economy created disunity among various ethnic groups thereby making it difficult for them to collectively resist the political and economic hegemony of the British. The colonizer in turn encouraged such ethnic disunity, as they did during the 1915 riots noted earlier. Many of the intermediary mercantile groups in fact identified their self interests within the colonial political economy and saw no reason to resist it.

In spite of the increasing social disintegration and pauperization of the peasantry during the course of the nineteenth century, there was a relative absence of peasant revolts since the rebellion of 1848 in the Kandyan Highlands (or elsewhere in the colony). Newton Gunasinghe has attributed the absence of peasant revolts to the emergence of a 'multiclass agrarian bloc' in Kandyan society.

> The aftermath of this revolt [1848 rebellion] witnessed the reactivation of aristocratic authority with the active intervention of the colonial state. This reactivation was accompanied by the formation of a multi-class bloc that bound the landlords and

---

52. Kumari Jayawardena, "Economic and Political Factors in the 1915 Riots," Paper No. 2 in "A Symposium on the 1915 Communal Riots," *Ceylon Studies Seminar*, 1969/70 Series (June 1970), p. 7. Compare role of Indian business groups in East Africa. Mandani, *Politics and Class Formation*, ch. 5.

peasants together; the key link in this bloc was the Buddhist monks, primarily those of the Siamese sect, who by their ideological practice, preserved its integrity. The slogan of the specificity of the Kandyan region was its major ideological plank and the imaginary opposition to the coastal areas provided the bloc with its orientation. The singular absence of peasant revolts — despite peasant pauperization — against colonial-aristocratic authority after the mid-nineteenth century, demonstrates the effectivity of the bloc in overcoming agrarian unrest.[53]

It should be noted that the opposition to the coastal areas was not entirely 'imaginary' as suggested by Gunasinghe. The 'internal colonial' situation we referred to earlier was the basis for this opposition. There is little doubt, however, that the Kandyan aristocrats as well as the British used this opposition to deflect attention away from their own exploitation of the peasants.

A few words about the relations, if any, between the Kandyan peasantry and the Indian estate labor force are necessary before we can conclude this discussion on class and ethnic configurations in the nineteenth-century Kandyan Highlands. As noted in earlier chapters, during the nineteenth century, the Kandyan peasantry had little contact with the immigrant estate labor force. The Sinhalese peasantry generally looked down upon these laborers who were tied to the estates to do the menial work for the Europeans that they themselves refused to perform. But as noted in earlier discussions, some Sinhalese who worked as fieldhands on the estates spoke Tamil and adopted some of the behavioral patterns commonly identified as Tamil. Similarly, the few Indian laborers who had links to the Sinhalese villages spoke Sinhalese and adopted some Sinhalese characteristics. But as noted earlier, such interactions were quite exceptional given the isolation of the estate laborers on the plantations.

The point which needs to be stressed, however, is that during the nineteenth century there were no visible signs of conflict between the two groups. It was only during the twentieth century as Sinhalese villagers began to seek plantation work in increasing numbers (due to population increase and landlessness) that they found themselves in competition with the Indian laborers. It was only at this juncture, in the context of electoral politics and growing Sinhalese nationalism that signs of resentment and conflict became visible between the two ethnic groups. It was also at this time that the citizenship of the Indian estate labor force became a controversial political issue.

We shall now go on to illustrate briefly the changing economic, social class, and ethnic configurations outlined above with three specific instances drawn from nineteenth century Kandyan history: the 1818 rebellion; the 1848 rebellion; and the collapse of coffee from about 1883 to 1886.

53. Gunasinghe, "Agrarian Relations," p. 22. See pp. 275–282 in this chapter.

The Rebellion of 1818

At the time of the Great Rebellion which took place three years after the imposition of British rule in Kandy, in 1818, the precolonial social structures were still intact. The British had imposed themselves upon the mass of cultivators and the feudal overlords. But the relationship between these two native social classes remained unchanged; the market economy had not yet intruded; and the Kandyan Highlands continued to be isolated from the rest of the island and the rest of the world.

The British had been invited into the Kandyan kingdom by a faction of the native aristocracy to depose their king. But upon removing the king, the British usurped the throne for themselves, an outcome unanticipated by the aristocracy. From the beginning of British rule then, the British and the aristocracy were envious and suspicious of each other's powers and privileges. In spite of the agreement made by the British in the Proclamation of 1815 to govern according to the customs and conventions of Kandyan society, the British began to violate some of the Kandyan norms and practices. Very soon dissatisfaction spread throughout the Kandyan society. The loss of political independence was a great blow to the esteem of the Kandyans who had been traditionally proud of their independence. For centuries, when the coastal lowlands were under European domination, the Kandyans had fought to maintain their freedom claiming that they were the legitimate heirs to the glory of the ancient Sinhalese Buddhist civilization of the dry zone.

The Kandyan chiefs were particularly indignant at the racist attitudes and conduct of the British. Even a common British soldier was placed above the highest of the Kandyan nobles. The loss of pride and status on the part of the nobility contributed to their desire to drive out the British and restore the Sinhalese monarchy. There is consensus among analysts that the ensuing rebellion was a post-pacification revolt.

> Indeed taken as a whole the ideology and goals of the Kandyan rebels were not innovative but restorative. They looked back to the *status quo ante*. The rebellion was an attempt on the part of traditional leadership groups to preserve the customary order of things. It was a traditionalist reaction.[54]

The 1818 rebellion was also a nationalist revolt. The leaders of the revolt were some notable Kandyan chiefs and prominent Buddhist monks. The nationalist sentiments shared by the feudal overlord class and the peasantry based on their common Sinhalese Buddhist ethnic identity came to the fore in their attempt to drive out the European Christian intruder. However, as

---

54. Roberts, "Variations on the Theme of Resistance Movements," p. 21; Malalgoda, "Millennialism."

Kitsiri Malalgoda has argued, the series of movements against the British in the early years of their rule in the Kandyan Provinces had their origin in the masses rather than the nobility or the clergy.

> Yet though there is no doubt that some chiefs and some monks gave their support to some of these movements, the origins of these movements were at the wider levels of Kandyan society — among the masses who for centuries had been used to the monarchial form of government, who yearned to return to it, and who resisted all the changes that were being introduced under British rule.[55]

Malalgoda points out that after a pretender to the Kandyan throne named Vilbave was "coronated" in 1817–1818, the rebellion gained greater legitimacy and spread rapidly "from the remote areas to the more central provinces and from the lower to the higher strata of society."[56] At this point the British intervened ruthlessly and put down the rebellion with great difficulty and at much expense. This rebellion, which came so early during their rule over the Kandyan Provinces, was a traumatic experience for the British. From that time on, they were highly suspicious of the Kandyans and acted quickly and harshly at the slightest indication of a 'disturbance' in the area.[57]

Since putting down the rebellion, the colonial state attempted to break down the solidarity between the Kandyan lords and their serfs, which they perceived to be the foremost threat to British political authority in the island. As noted in earlier chapters, they attempted to create countervailing social forces within the native society that could weaken the authority of the chiefs over the masses. The attempt to create a free peasant proprietor class following the 1818 rebellion was one such move. But this did not prove to be successful. The very policies of the colonial state such as the paddy tax and the new market forces worked against the emergence of a strong and independent peasantry loyal to the British. As mentioned before, the peasantry in fact became the strongest opponents of the British.

The Rebellion of 1848

Thirty years later, when the next major upheaval took place in the Kandyan Highlands (and Colombo), radical transformations were well underway in Kandyan society. A network of roads connecting the Highlands to the coast had broken down the isolation of Kandy. The coffee plantations and smallholdings had integrated the region into the global economy. Cash and com-

---

55. Ibid., p. 434.
56. Ibid., p. 436.
57. Ibid., p. 436.

merce, planters, traders, and estate laborers were among the new forces and actors in the region. In fact, the 1848 rebellion was largely a reaction against these dramatic changes that had been taking place during the short time span since the introduction of plantations in the 1830s. We have noted in our earlier discussions that land alienation for plantations and exaction of the forced labor of the peasants for road construction in particular created much peasant antipathy towards the colonial state. As we have discussed elsewhere in this book, the colonial impact was differentially felt by the two broad social classes of Kandyan society — the overlords and the cultivators. The effects being most harsh on the cultivators, the reaction against the colonial state and the plantation economy came from them. As pointed out in several places in this study, many British planters and officials acknowledged in retrospect that plantation development was the underlying cause of the 1848 rebellion.

The immediate cause that sparked off the rebellion was the imposition of new taxes by Governor Torrington which fell most heavily on the peasantry. In the mid-1840s, the Ceylon coffee enterprise suffered a major setback due to the economic depression in England and the decline of coffee prices. The introduction of the new taxes was aimed specifically at shifting the burden of the economic depression from the plantation sector and the colonial state to the peasantry.

In Colombo, the opposition to the taxes was led by Dr. Christopher Elliot, the Irish editor of *The Colombo Observer,* and some Burgher lawyers. As historian K. M. de Silva has noted, for Elliot and the Burgher lawyers, the agitation against the taxes provided an opportunity to introduce some of the ideas of the revolution taking place in Europe at the time. Taking advantage of the 'free press' Elliot published a letter in his newspaper, calling upon the natives to refuse paying the taxes and to agitate for greater democratization of the colonial administration. This was the first occasion when ideas of European radicalism were voiced in the island.[58] It is interesting to note that support for Elliot came in this instance from the most westernized and privileged segment of the local population — the Burghers — an Eurasian population of mixed descent. They, more than any other native group, were in a position to point to the contradictions of colonial rule, particularly the disparities between the democratic ideals upheld by the administration and the suppression of native political rights.

In addition to the protests in Colombo, there was widespread opposition to the taxes in the Kandyan areas. A Sinhalese translation of Elliot's letter

---

58. K. M. de Silva, *Social Policy,* pp. 11, 12. The information on the 1848 rebellion is derived largely from the account given by de Silva. See also K. M. de Silva, "The 'Rebellion' of 1848 in Ceylon," *CJHSS,* Vol. 7, No. 2 (July-December 1964).

(which appeared in *The Observer*) was circulated in the Kandyan area although the extent of its circulation could not have been great given that most peasants were illiterate.[59]

However, the news about the taxes and rumors of still more taxes to come spread quickly through the Kandyan region. On July 6, 1848, a mass protest against the taxes took place in the city of Kandy. On July 8, the colonial administration called a meeting of the Kandyan chiefs to explain the need for the new taxes. But between July 8 and July 29, a mass movement against the taxes had already developed. There were several outbreaks of violence, the most severe of which took place in the Matale and Kurunegala districts between July 29 and July 31, 1848 (see Map p. XIV).[60]

What distinguished the uprising against the taxes in the Kandyan districts from the agitation in Colombo was that a small group of men "sought to channel this discontent in an attempt to drive the British out of Kandy."[61] In this respect, the 1848 rebellion was similar to the Great Rebellion of 1818 although the British did not allow the 1848 revolt to last as long or spread as widely as did the earlier rebellion.

Although the rebellion in the Kandyan districts was essentially a peasant revolt, its most well known leader, Puran Appu, was an adventurer from the coastal lowlands. This rebellion, like the earlier one, was given a nationalist stamp by the crowning of a pretender to the Kandyan throne. The rebels received the support of some segments of the Buddhist clergy in their efforts to restore the Sinhalese monarchy.

While the new taxes sparked off the rebellion, its underlying cause was the contradiction between plantation development and peasant subsistence.[62] Rebel attacks were concentrated on the installations of the colonial state such as jails. *kachcheris* (court houses), and houses of government officials. Few plantations were damaged.[63] Peasant hostility then was directed against the colonial state which was correctly perceived to be the immediate oppressor. But as discussed earlier, most of the state officials at the time were also planters. The 1848 rebellion then was a nationalist revolt against both the colonial state and the plantation economy.

As the situation in the Kandyan region began to get out of hand, the colonial state imposed martial law and ruthlessly suppressed the rebellion.

---

59. Ibid., p. 13.
60. Ibid., pp. 16-17.
61. Ibid., p. 16.
62. A number of the planters who gave evidence before the British Parliamentary hearings on the 1848 rebellion have confirmed this. See, for example, the evidence of H. L. Layard quoted earlier in Ch. 5, p. 104.
63. K. M. de Silva, *Social Policy*, p. 17.

The British had only one soldier wounded, whereas at least two hundred Kandyans lost their lives. One of the reasons for the unduly harsh suppression of the rebellion was the memory of 1818 when the revolt had spread widely because of the failure of the colonial administration to intervene quickly. But another important factor for the ruthless suppression in 1848 was the fear among planter-officials that if the rebellion were allowed to spread, it would cause greater damage to their plantations and the coffee crop. As K. M. de Silva explains,

> The policy of ruthless repression may be attributed to [Governor] Torrington's lack of administrative experience. It is also significant that he and his closest advisors were moved to take these harsh steps for fear that the coffee crop of 1848 would be completely lost. The man on whose advice martial law was imposed was Colonel "Tiger" Fraser who had earned his sobriquet for his ferocity during the rebellion of 1817–18. He was a coffee planter with an estate thirty miles from Matale, the scene of the disturbances. The Government's closest adviser at Kandy was Lieut. General Herbert Maddock, a retired East India Company official who was a coffee planter at Matale. His coffee store in Matale bazaar had been burnt down by the rebels. It was on Maddock that both [Colonial Secretary] Tennent and Torrington relied for advice during the disturbances and he was the evil genius behind the whole policy of repression. During the disturbances Maddock persuaded Tennent to attempt the establishment of colonies of Indians – to work on coffee plantations – on the lands confiscated from the "rebels". Tennent later admitted that the plan was not implemented only because the confiscations had fallen far short of espectations.[64]

Although the British managed to quell the rebellion, it convulsed the British political hegemony and the plantation economy to such an extent that The British Parliament subsequently appointed a high ranking Inquiry Committee (which included Sir Robert Peel, Disraeli, Gladstone, et al.) to investigate the causes for this rebellion. Upon putting down the rebellion, the British insisted that it was engineered and led by the Kandyan aristocracy and the Buddhist monks, and that the pretender to the Kandyan throne and the other leaders of the rebellion were mere puppets of the aristocracy. But as K. M. de Silva has pointed out, the Kandyan chiefs stood aloof from this peasant revolt and at no stage were the British able to provide any evidence in support of their contention. As de Silva argues, if the aristocracy and the clergy had supported the rebels to the extent that the British claimed they did, the rebellion would have become much more formidable and would have taxed British resources much more severely.[65]

---

64. Ibid., p. 19.
65. K. M. de Silva (ed.), *Letters on Ceylon, 1846–1850*, pp. 25–26. There were some parallels between this rebellion in Ceylon and the 1857 Sepoy Mutiny in India, particularly in the resultant changes in colonial administrative policies.

Whether the British actually believed that the aristocracy was behind the rebellion or not, it taught them an important political lesson: that it was impossible to control the masses without the support of the chiefs or headmen. This resulted in a shift of government policy. The rivalry of the British and the chiefs which had climaxed in the 1818 rebellion was quietly forgotten and steps were taken to incorporate the native headmen more closely into the regional administration of the country. Furthermore, since 1848 the colonial state began to take a more cautious approach towards the 'rebellious' Kandyan peasantry. The interest in conserving the peasantry and in restoring ancient irrigational works on the part of some officials such as Governor Ward during the second half of the nineteenth century is partly attributable to the 1848 rebellion.

The Collapse of Coffee: circa 1883—1886

The Great Depression in Britain between 1879 and 1884 and the collapse of Ceylon coffee (due to the leaf disease) brought plantation and peasant interests into direct conflict again in the 1880s. Once more, the colonial state sought to relieve the planters and to pass the fiscal burden on to the peasantry. Having learned its lesson from the rebellion of 1848, this time the colonial state did not introduce any new taxes; instead, it began to collect the already existing taxes, especially the paddy and road taxes, with greater rigor. As we discussed in Chapter V, the peasantry who had lost their cash income due to the collapse of their coffee gardens, were unable to pay the taxes demanded by the state. The result was eviction from their lands for default on tax payments. In this instance, the peasantry who were poverty-stricken and leaderless were in no position to revolt against the colonial state now supported by the native headmen as well. In fact, the 1848 rebellion was the last major upheaval against the British anywhere in Ceylon during the nineteenth century. Minor disturbances such as the religious revival invoking millennial expectations which took place in the Seven Korales around 1883, did not threaten British hegemony as did the rebellions of 1818 and 1848.

By the 1880s, the native headmen class had acquiesced in the colonial administration to such an extent that they sought to take advantage of the peasantry's plight rather than join forces with them as they did in 1818, or play a neutral role as they did in 1848. For example, we have observed that many headmen hastened the eviction of peasants from their lands only to buy up those lands at very low prices from the colonial state. The British then were highly successful in their policy of divide and rule. By incorporating the native chiefs into the colonial political economy as junior partners, they

The colonial Transformation of the Kandyan Highlands 321

ensured that the chiefs did not join the peasantry in their nationalist struggles. At the same time, the Kandyan alliance built around the opposition to the coastal lowlands and Muslim and other alien mercantile groups in the Highlands, helped bind the aristocracy and the peasantry together. These complex alliances of the aristocracy, with the British, on the one hand, and the peasantry, on the other, helped prevent any major revolts during the second half of the nineteenth century.

IX. Theoretical Conclusions: The Characterization of the Colonial Political Economy

Having synthesized the concrete historical materials on the interaction between indigenous and superimposed politico-economic structures in the nineteenth century Kandyan Highlands, it now remains to evaluate our findings in relation to the competing theoretical perspectives in the sociology of development and underdevelopment.

What happens to pre-existing socioeconomic structures in the process of colonial economic and political expansion? What is the nature of the interaction between the indigenous and the superimposed foreign sectors and the general dynamic of change set in motion in the colonized societies? There are a wide variety of competing theories which seek to address this controversial issue. It is impossible to discuss each of these theories in great detail here. Accordingly, only those theoretical positions most relevant for our Ceylonese case study will be outlined. A critique of these various theoretical formulations and their relative merits and de-merits will be presented as they relate to the Kandyan case materials. Attempts will also be made to refine some of the existing theories on the basis of our specific findings and to make a contribution towards a theory of colonialism and Third World transformations.

Development Perspectives

The Modernization School

The dominant social science perspective on the nonwestern world, alternatively referred to as the modernization or development school sees the western impact essentially as a beneficial one. It assumes that underdevelopment — poverty, economic backwardness, etc. — was the characteristic condition of these nonwestern societies at the point of contact with the West. It argues that the western nations laid the framework for the development of these societies by providing the necessary capital, technology, organizational forms, and values. This perspective posits the 'traditional' social structures and value systems of the nonwestern societies as the primary barriers to the successful diffusion of modernity or development from the West. A unili-

Theoretical Conclusions

near evolutionary model wherein all societies would traverse the same path of development as the western capitalist societies is a further assumption of this dominant perspective.[1]

Certainly, from a purely economic growth point of view, the achievements of colonialism were highly impressive. The elaborate communications networks, school systems, and administrative structures developed in colonies like Ceylon have no counterparts in countries like Afghanistan or Ethiopia which did not experience colonial rule. It is on the basis of such aggregate indices as the Gross National Product and massive infrastructural projects that modernization theorists have declared that colonialism, and plantations in particular, were agents of development for the Third World.[2]

But, if in addition to aggregate economic growth, we also apply the criteria of national self-determination, social equity (across regions, social classes, ethnic groups, sexes, etc.) and empowerment of natives, we find that the colonial record was quite deplorable. We have seen, for example, that as Ceylon was incorporated into the world economy as an exporter of coffee and a net importer of food, she lost her national self-determination and became ever-susceptible to the vagaries of the international market. It is by taking into account the effects of colonial expansion and specifically European plantations on the majority of people in the colonies, that writers such as George Beckford have pointed out that plantations were not agents of development as claimed by the modernization theorists, but rather "tributaries of imperialist expansion."[3]

In an attempt to explain some of these obvious contradictions of western capital expansion, specifically the persistence of poverty and backwardness in the colonies in spite of the 'modernizing' presence of the Europeans, a variant of development thinking, popularly known as dual economy/dual society theory came to be fashioned within the modernization school. The earliest

---

1. See Manning Nash's "Introduction: Approaches to the Study of Economic Growth," *Journal of Social Issues* 19 (1963), pp. 1–5, for internal debates within the modernization school.
   For persuasive and powerful critiques of the Modernization perspective from the underdevelopment point of view, see André Gunder Frank, "Sociology of Development and Underdevelopment in Sociology," in *Dependence and Underdevelopment: Latin America's Political Economy*, ed. by James D. Cockcroft, et al. (New York: Doubleday, 1972); Susanne J. Bodenheimer, "The Ideology of Developmentalism: American Political Science's Paradigm-Surrogate for Latin American Studies," *Berkeley Journal of Sociology*, Vol. XV, 1970; and John G. Taylor, *From Modernization to Modes of Production: A Critique of the Sociologies of Development and Underdevelopment* (London: Macmillan, 1979), Part 1.
2. W. O. Jones, "Plantations," in *International Encyclopaedia of the Social Sciences*, 1968 ed., s. v., pp. 154–59; P. P. Courtenay, *Plantation Agriculture*, pp. 3–4.
3. Beckford, *Persistent Poverty, passim*.

324   *Part 3 : Conclusions and Theoretical Implications*

version of this theory — social dualism — was expounded by J. H. Böeke, a Dutch economist, in relation to colonial Indonesia.[4]

According to Böeke, colonial societies are characterized by two fundamentally separate and antithetical sectors — the capitalist or western sector introduced by the colonial powers and the indigenous precapitalist or eastern (read nonwestern in the case of Africa and Latin America) sector. The dynamic western sector is unable to transform the stagnant eastern sector because of the tenacious precapitalist values in the latter. Böeke then argues that "capitalism can only be realized by capitalist minded individuals," and as their traditional prestige and status aspirations thwart interest in profit maximization, the eastern peasantry continues to remain poor and backward.[5]

Dual economy theory asserts the absence of linkages between the native and foreign sectors (for example between subsistence and export agriculture) without seeking to examine the linkages and cleavages that develop between them in the process of colonial political, economic, and cultural expansion. Thus the poverty and backwardness of the indigenous sectors is attributed solely to their supposedly original state of underdevelopment. In the words of dual economy theorist P. T. Ellsworth,

> ... The existence or non-existence of an export industry in itself had little to do with growth or absence of growth in the domestic sector. The failure of that sector to expand and develop must be attributed to its own characteristics ... where, as in most export economies ..., the domestic economy was characterized by an indigenous population addicted to traditional ways, hostile to commercial pursuits, and engaged primarily in subsistence agriculture, the domestic market remained small and the response even to a vigorous export sector slight.... In sum, we are forced to resort to a sociological explanation of dualism. The primitive and stagnant character of underdeveloped economies, burdened with political, social and economic obstacles to development, explains their failure to develop, whether an export industry was present or not.[6]

---

4. J. H. Böeke, *Economics and Economic Policy of Dual Societies* (New York: Institute of Pacific Relations, 1953).
5. Ibid., pp. 37–38. For a critique of Böeke's theory, see Benjamin Higgins, "The Dualistic Theory of Underdeveloped Areas," *Economic Development and Cultural Change* 4 (January 1956). For an elaboration of this essentially psychological approach to development, see David C. McClelland, *The Achieving Society* (Princeton, N. J.: Van Nostrand, 1961).
6. P. T. Ellsworth, "The Dual Economy: A New Approach," *Economic Development and Culture Change* 10 (July 1962): 437. In the dual economy version put forth by Jonathan Levin, the stagnation of the domestic sector is attributed largely to the fact that earnings from the export sector were not diffused into the domestic sector, but were sent abroad. See Jonathan V. Levin, *The Export Economies*, p. 7.

Theoretical Conclusions

The dualistic assumption which has dominated social science thinking on Ceylon (and other nonwestern societies) that the plantation and the village constitute two entirely separate sectors has been completely disproved by our findings. The plantation and village may on the surface appear to be separate. But as this study has demonstrated, a multitude of linkages bound the two sectors together in a relationship of dominance and subordination.

The village was not the static and undifferentiated peasant community, as depicted by theorists such as Snodgrass and Jogaratnam, who have applied the dual economy model to Ceylon.[7] The complex articulation of old and new modes of production within the village with each other and with the dominant plantation mode resulted in new social class, caste, and ethnic relations inside the village. Dual economy theory has ignored a host of socioeconomic forces such as peasant coffee production, indigenous capitalist development, colonial political and ideological structures, as well as a number of other factors which fundamentally transformed the Kandyan village during the nineteenth century. It has also ignored the fact that many native merchant groups and some peasants straddled both plantation and village sectors and engaged in economic activities in several sectors of the village economy (paddy, and smallholder coffee, for example). Dual Economy theorists have merely looked at the backward techniques of production and stagnation in labor productivity in village agriculture. They have completely ignored the changing social relations of production and their relationship to the technology of production and labor productivity for example.

The further assumption of dual economy theory that the village sector remained poor and backward due to its traditional values is indeed too facile. The Kandyan peasantry was quick to respond to market stimuli, a fact borne out by the level of peasant coffee production during the nineteenth century. Many of the barriers to peasant entrepreneurship came from the supposedly 'modernizing presence' of the plantations and the colonial state. This study has demonstrated that the plantation sector was developed at the expense of village agriculture and peasant subsistence.

It is true, however, that precolonial norms such as the tradition of 'land to rule', inhibited capitalist agricultural development in the sphere of paddy agriculture. Barriers to peasant entrepreneurship existed in the precolonial caste structure and religious orientation as well. But these precolonial values and institutions must not be approached in a static manner as dual economy and development theorists often tend to do. Rather, they have to be understood in the broader context of colonial policies favoring European

---

7. Snodgrass, *Ceylon;* Jogaratnam, "The Role of Agriculture."

plantations and the constraints placed on the native comprador capitalist class in developing local food production, and other activities.

The dual economy perspective is both narrow and ahistorical in its conceptualization. It ultimately resorts to psychological explanations of underdevelopment. Dual economy theory which has exercised a tremendous influence on social science thinking has in fact been a barrier to our understanding of the complexity and conflictive nature of social change in the colonies. It is time that we set it aside, at least with respect to Ceylon, if not other Third World societies.

The Classical Marxist School

Like the modernization perspective discussed above, the earlier tradition of Marxist thought has also looked upon the inevitable expansion of Western capital into the colonies as largely a positive force. Marx hailed the new dynamic of growth and capitalist development that it would set in motion in the colonies. This is clearly expressed in the *Communist Manifesto* of 1848.

> The bourgeoisie . . . draws all, even the most barbarian, nations into civilisation. . . . It compels all nations, on pain of extinction, to adopt the bourgeois mode of production; it compels them to introduce what it calls civilisation into their midst, i. e., to become bourgeois themselves. In one word, it creates a world after its own image.[8]

It is sufficient to note, for the moment, that in spite of Marx's references to the precapitalist social structures in the colonies as possible barriers to capitalist development, in his earlier writings, Marx was optimistic about the generalization of the capitalist mode of production throughout the world. Moreover, in anticipating the contradictions of colonialism, he predicted that western capitalist expansion would lay the material basis for future socialist societies in the colonies which had hitherto remained stagnant and backward.

Like the modernization theorists discussed earlier, Marx saw the social structures and values of the colonial societies as the barriers to the expansion of western capital in the colonies. Marx's views on this matter are evident in his conceptualization of the supposedly static and backward 'Asiatic mode of

---

8. *The Communist Manifesto*, quoted by Harold Wolpe in his "Introduction" to Harold Wolpe (ed.), *The Articulation of Modes of Production* (London: Routledge and Kegan Paul, 1980), p. 4. Marx expressed his optimism regarding capitalist development in colonial India in his letters to the *New York Tribune*. See, for example, "The Future Results of British Rule in India," in *On Colonialism: Articles from the New York Tribune and Other Writings*, Karl Marx and Frederick Engels (New York: International Publishers, 1972), p. 82.

Theoretical Conclusions

production' in places like India and China.[9] Although Marx and the followers of his early position on colonialism were ethically opposed to colonialism, they nevertheless envisioned western capitalist expansion as a necessary but transitional phase in the movement towards socialism.

Following upon this early Marxist line of analysis, a few contemporary theorists such as Bill Warren have argued that western capitalist expansion or imperialism has laid the foundation for a vibrant, indigenously rooted capitalism in the colonies.[10] Similarly, in disagreeing with the currently popular neo-Marxist view (coming up) that imperialism has caused the 'underdevelopment' of the colonies, Sanjaya Lall has argued that dependency and uneven/unequal development being equated with underdevelopment are not characteristics peculiar to colonial or postcolonial societies. Rather, he claims that these features – dependency, unevenness inequality – are fundamental to the very logic of capitalist development, whether in the advanced capitalist countries or the colonies. In other words, capitalist development is an inherently contradictory process. A stage theory of capitalist growth and the assumption that nonwestern societies would traverse the same path of evolution as the western capitalist nations are implicit in the writings of both Warren and Lall. In directing his attacks against the neo-Marxist underdevelopment theorists, Lall says,

> ... we are forced to argue that these features of *capitalist* growth in general – in certain stages and in certain circumstances – are not confined to the present condition of the less developed countries.....
>
> ... The desire to promote attacks on the capitalist mode of production causes some dependence and neo-Marxist analysts to concentrate on the appealing but mistaken argument that it can never lead to a repetition of the experience of the developed capitalist countries, when in fact they should be drawing attention to the intrinsic costs of the capitalist system as such, and to its continuously evolving dynamics. [emphasis in original][11]

The conclusion that follows from these polemics is that a separate analysis of capitalist development in the colonies is not necessary and that social change there should be studied as a simple extension or generalization of capitalism on a world scale. But in order to make their arguments persuasive,

---

9. For discussion of the Asiatic Mode of Production, see, for example, Marx's writings in Marx and Engels, *On Colonialism;* Barry Hindess and Paul Q. Hirst, *Pre-Capitalist Modes of Production* (London: Routledge and Kegan Paul, 1975); Karl Marx, *Pre-Capitalist Economic Formations,* ed. by E. J. Hobsbawm (New York: International Publishers, 1964).
10. Bill Warren, *Imperialism: The Pioneer of Capitalism* (London: New Left Books, 1980), *passim.*
11. Sanjaya Lall, "Is 'Dependence' a Useful Concept?" pp. 808–09.

these writers need to distinguish those special situations in the Third World where the capitalist model appears to be working. This necessitates taking into account the changing international political situation, including the super-power struggle, military alliances, etc. Moreover, it is necessary to clarify whether dependency, unevenness, inequality, are simply characteristics peculiar to the capitalist mode of production or whether they are also present (albeit in different forms) in precapitalist and even socialist societies.

The classical Marxist position which envisions the destruction of precapitalist modes of production in the process of western capitalist expansion and its replacement by the capitalist mode of production throughout the colonial world has been qualified by the findings of our Ceylonese case study. The destruction of precapitalist structures in the Kandyan Highlands was a slow and gradual process characterized by continuous conflicts and contradictions between the precolonial and the superimposed colonial politico-economic structures. The social structures and forces that emerged from this interaction differed fundamentally from the outcome of the transformation from feudalism to capitalism in England. As discussed earlier, social relations of production in the Highlands began to change in a capitalist direction. However, the continuous expanded reproduction of the economy, through improvements in techniques and their application to production which characterized capitalist development in the metropole did not necessarily take place in the Kandyan Highlands. Here lies a fundamental difference between developmental and underdevelopmental forms of capitalism.[12] Furthermore, a complete proletarianization of the peasantry, industrialization and other such transformations which occurred in the imperial country were not repeated in the Kandyan Highlands or elsewhere in the colony.

Likewise, the diffusion of capital and technology from the modern/capitalist sectors to the traditional/precapitalist sectors envisioned by both the modernization and Marxist development theorists did not take place in Kandy during the nineteenth century. That the plantation sector deliberately thwarted technological improvements in paddy agriculture has been illustrated in our discussion of colonial policies towards irrigational technology needed for paddy. Furthermore, we have demonstrated that what little surplus was generated in the village sectors was transferred via colonial taxes, market forces, and other factors into the plantation sector and Britain. Native capitalists, too, transferred profits from local agriculture to export agriculture thereby contributing to the continued stagnation of local food production. This has also been discussed in this study.

12. See also Theodore P. Lianos, "Modern Greece: Development or Underdevelopment – Another View," *Monthly Review*, vol. 6, no. 33 (November 1981), p. 62.

Theoretical Conclusions

While it is true that at the point of contact with the West in the early nineteenth century, the Kandyan Highlands was a relatively poor, backward, self-sufficient and subsistence economy, a dynamic of dependent and extraverted development was not there in Kandy when it came into contact with the West. The process of 'dependent capitalism' which emerged during the nineteenth century was the historical product of colonialism. For an understanding of this phenomenon, we need to move beyond both the dominant development perspective and the Marxist capitalist development perspective to the contemporary neo-Marxist underdevelopment perspectives.

Underdevelopment Perspectives

A closer examination of Marx's writings on the contact between capitalist and precapitalist modes of production in the colonies reveals that Marx's position on this subject was neither systematic nor consistent. In his later writings on the colonies, Marx pointed to the resistance of precapitalist modes of production to western capital as well as to the conditioning effects the former exercise on the latter.[13] Moreover, in their writings on Ireland, which they referred to as 'the first English colony', Marx and Engels expressed a great deal of pessimism regarding the benefits of English capital for Ireland.

> The English bourgeoisie ... has in the first place a common interest with the English aristocracy in turning Ireland to a mere pasture land which provides the English market with meat and wool at the cheapest possible prices. It is equally interested in reducing ... the English population to such a small number that *English capital* (capital invested in land leased for farming) can function there "with security". It has the same interest in *clearing the estate of Ireland* as it had in the clearing of the agricultural districts of England and Scotland.... [emphasis in original][14]

The significant differences between Ireland and white settler colonies such as Australia and the nonwestern colonies such as Ceylon, need to be taken into account in generalizing about the relationship between colonialism and underdevelopment. Nevertheless, the observations on Ireland which are rather align inconsistent with Marx's earlier views regarding the British colonial impact on India and other colonies, anticipate to some extent, contemporary Marxist underdevelopment thinking.

---

13. See Wolpe's discussion of Marx's views, "Introduction," in *The Articulation*, pp. 3–4.
14. Marx to S. Meyer and A. Vogt, 9 April 1870 – Marx-Engels, *Selected Correspondence* (Moscow, 1953), pp. 285–86, quoted in Colin Leys, *Underdevelopment in Kenya: The Political Economy of Neo-Colonialism*. See also Marx's discussion of "The Modern Theory of Colonisation" in *Capital*, vol. 1, Ch. 33.

The underdevelopment perspective, first sketched out by Paul Baran, was later elaborated by André Gundar Frank and a number of Latin American theorists.[15] Since then, it has been extended to Africa and less extensively to Asia by numerous scholars.[16] This perspective which emerged as a reaction against the dominant development perspective has inverted some of its basic presuppositions. The following discussion of the underdevelopment perspective will be focused on the formulations of André Gunder Frank, popularly referred to as 'dependency theory'.[17]

Frank argues that underdevelopment is not the original state of the non-western colonized societies, but the product of western capitalism. He points out that western capital subjugated, extraverted, and distorted colonial economies to suit the needs of capitalist development in the imperial or 'metropolitan' countries.[18] Capitalist development of the metropoles was achieved at the expense of the colonial or 'satellite' nations. For Frank then, underdevelopment is synonymous with 'dependency' on the West and the world capitalist economy. The development of the metropole causes the underdevelopment of the periphery; the two are inextricably linked.[19]

Frank also argues that in the process of western capitalist expansion a hierarchical chain of metropolitan-satellite relations are reproduced within the peripheral nations themselves. As examples, he points to the dependent

---

15. Paul Baran, *The Political Economy of Growth* (New York: Monthly Review Press, 1957); André Gunder Frank, *Capitalism and Underdevelopment in Latin America;* Fernando Henrique Cardoso and Enzo Faletto, *Dependency and Development in Latin America* (Berkeley: University of California Press, 1979); see also articles in James D. Cockcroft et al. (eds.), *Dependence and Underdevelopment: Latin America's Political Economy* (New York: Doubleday, 1972). Although Clifford Geertz is not identified as an underdevelopment theorist as such and his work lacks a class analysis, his classic *Agricultural Involution* made many of the same conclusions about the colonial impact (on Java) as the 'underdevelopment' theories.
16. See for example, Colin Leys, *Underdevelopment in Kenya;* E. A. Brett, *Colonialism and Underdevelopment in East Africa;* Van Zwanenberg, *Colonial Capitalism;* Kathleen Gough, "Class and Agrarian Change ... A Rejoinder," and various articles on underdevelopment in Asia in *The Journal of Contemporary Asia.*
17. A wide array of discussions and critiques of the underdevelopment perspective are now available. Noteworthy among these are John G. Taylor, *From Modernization to Modes of Production;* Ian Roxborough, *Theories of Underdevelopment;* Harold Brookfield, *Interdependent Development* (Pittsburgh: University of Pittsburgh Press, 1975); Ivar Oxaal, Tony Barnett and David Booth (eds.), *Beyond the Sociology of Development: Economy and Society in Latin America and Africa* (London: Routledge and Kegan Paul, 1975); Henry Bernstein (ed.), *Underdevelopment and Development: The Third World Today* (Middlesex: Penguin Books, 1978); special issue on Development and Underdevelopment in *The Journal of Contemporary Asia*, vol. 7, no. 1, 1977.
18. This is basically Samir Amin's position as well. See Samir Amin, *Unequal Development, passim.*
19. Frank, *Capitalism and Underdevelopment, passim.*

Theoretical Conclusions

relations between foreign and native agriculture, city and countryside, rich and poor social classes, etc.[20] Turning to the relationship between large-scale foreign agriculture and small-scale native agriculture, Frank argues that the underdevelopment of the latter is caused by the development of the former. He totally disagrees with the dual economy position that backwardness of native agriculture results from traditional values, social structures, or the absence of linkages to modern large-scale agricultural sectors.[21]

The basic assumption of the underdevelopment school, that western capitalist expansion into the colonies subjugated, extraverted, and distorted the colonial economies has been demonstrated by our Ceylonese case study. That the incorporation of Ceylon as a primary exporter and a net importer of food made the nation dependent on the vagaries of the international market and western industrial economies (especially Britain) was pointed out earlier. That plantation growth, and the accompanying expansion of the Gross National Product and infrastructure (roads, railways, etc.) served the interests of British capital and the native comprador bourgeoisie has also been documented. We also showed that these achievements were made at the expense of the native peasantry and local agriculture. To this extent we can agree with Gunder Frank that the process of change set in motion by western capital in the Kandyan Highlands was one of underdevelopment rather than autonomous capitalist development as anticipated by either the modernization or Marxist development theorists.

Frank's argument that the basic relationship of subordination and exploitation between the metropolitan and satellite nations is reproduced within the colonies has also been demonstrated in the Kandyan case materials. This was evident in the hierarchical relationship that emerged between the plantation sector and the village agricultural sectors such as chena, paddy and smallholder coffee. In other words, as Frank would argue, these village agricultural sectors became 'residual' to dominant plantation agriculture.[22]

The spatial or regional dimension of the internal hierarchy that Frank has talked about also finds evidence in our case study. We saw this, for instance, in the evolving relationship between the urban and westernized southwestern coastal region, the home of many native capitalists, and the more rural and tradition-bound Kandyan areas. In other words, as Frank argues, the various economic sectors, regions, and social classes in colonial Ceylon were hierarchically incorporated within the world capitalist economy.

20. Ibid., pp. 37–51.
21. Ibid., 219–29.
22. Ibid., p. 258.

But what was the precise nature of the resultant rural social structures and their specific relationship to the dominant sectors within the colonies (for example, the export enclaves) and the capitalist world economy? It is at this juncture that the various strands within the neo-Marxist underdevelopment perspective and their underlying ideological assumptions begin to confront each other in bitter conflict and competition. Marxist sectarianism is certainly not a phenomenon peculiar to the study of the Third World. Let us take some of the more prominent positions within this neo-Marxist debate on the characterization of Third World social formations and discuss them in relation to the findings of our Ceylonese case study.

Characterization of Colonial Social Formations: The Neo-Marxist Debate

According to André Gunder Frank, as western capital moves to the colonies, each of the economic sectors, regions, and social classes in those peripheral nations is incorporated within the world capitalist economy. Hence they too become capitalist, albeit in a subordinate or dependent position vis-à-vis the metropolitan nations. What has emerged since the fifteenth century, according to Frank, is a single world capitalist system within which different nations, regions, sectors, and social classes are hierarchically positioned.[23] It is important to stress that Frank claims the generalization of capitalism on the basis of the extension of exchange or market relations rather than the installation of capitalist production relations within the colonies.

Frank also argues that in the process of this incorporation into the world capitalist economy, the pre-existing native sectors of production lose their precapitalist basis. He points out that as these sectors become subordinated to large-scale commercial agriculture, they too become commercially determined, hence capitalist. This leads Frank to argue vehemently against what he calls the "myth of feudalism in [Brazilian] agriculture" today.[24]

In many important ways, Immanuel Wallerstein's analysis of the emeregence and evolution of the 'modern world system' is similar to Frank's position on the expansion of the capitalist world economy. Wallerstein, too, bases his concept of the capitalist world system on the generalization of market or

---

23. Ibid., p. 3. See also ch. 3, pp 56–57 in this study.
24. Ibid., pp. 221–77.

Theoretical Conclusions

exchange relations. He insists that although a combination of coercive forms of labor control is characteristic of peripheral nations, they are nevertheless capitalist, having been incorporated into the world capitalist economy through surplus exaction and market forces.[25]

> The point is that the "relations of production" that define a system are the relations of production of the whole system, and the system at this point in time [the sixteenth century] is the European world economy. Free labor is indeed a defining feature of capitalism, but not free labor throughout the productive enterprise. Free labor is the form of labor control used for skilled work in core countries whereas coerced labor is used for less skilled work in peripheral areas. The combination thereof is the essence of capitalism.[26]

Both Frank and Wallerstein then claim that underdeveloped economies of the peripheral nations are capitalist because they have been incorporated into the world capitalist economy through market relations. In other words, their definition of capitalism is based on the criterion of generalized commodity production. Although Frank paints a picture of a hierarchy of metropolitan-satellite relations between and within nations, he provides no *analysis* of the differential incorporation of the various sectors of the colonial economies into the capitalist world economy or the complex interaction of these internal sectors with each other. Frank does not pay much attention to the timing and speed of the processes of incorporation, for example, in relation to different types of metropolitan capital, different forms of precolonial structures, changes in the political and ideological structures of colonialism, or the dialectics of resistance to western expansion. The precise manner in which class formations in the peripheries help create and maintain underdevelopment has not been adequately dealt with either. Although Frank has meant to complement the colonial analysis (i. e., the metropolis-satellite relationship) with a class analysis, what has resulted, as David Booth has noted, is a "conflation of spatial entities and social classes."[27] As Roxborough argues,

---

25. Immanuel Wallerstein, *The Modern World System: Capitalist Agriculture and the Origins of the European World Economy in the Sixteenth Century* (New York: Academic Press, 1974), p. 350.
26. Quoted by Sidney Mintz in "The So-Called World System: Local Initiative and Local Response," *Dialectical Anthropology*, vol. 2, no. 4 (1977), p. 253. For an incisive critique of the Frank-Wallerstein position on the definition of capitalism, see Robert Brenner, "The Origins of Capitalist Development: A Critique of Neo-Smithian Marxism," *New Left Review*, no. 104 (July-August 1977).
27. David Booth, "André Gunder Frank: An Introduction and Appreciation," in *Beyond the Sociology of Development*, ed. by Oxaal et al., p. 78; and Roxborough, *Theories of Underdevelopment*, p. 45.

> ... so that the relationship between landowner and peasant is also characterized as a form of metropolis-satellite tie *exactly comparable* to the links between spatial regions.
> It is this conflation, and the use of the concept of surplus, to replace the Marxist concept of surplus-value, which enables Frank to encompass two apparently disparate phenomena (relations of exploitation among social classes and relations of transfer of value between economic regions) with the simple metaphor of a series of metropolis-satellite links stretching from the Bolivian peasant in an unbroken chain to the rich New York capitalist.[28]

Frank's theory of dependency and underdevelopment has been invaluable in combatting many of the myths perpetuated by the earlier development perspectives. But while his formulations have broad applicability to most colonial situations, they are clearly overgeneralized. We cannot look to Frank or Wallerstein for theoretical direction for understanding the installation of the capitalist mode of production within the colonies or the ensuing contradictions between indigenous and capitalist modes of production and social classes. The neo-Marxist approach, known as 'articulation of modes of production' is more helpful in this respect.

Articulation of Modes of Production

We noted earlier that in his later writings Marx was pessimistic about the transformative effects of British capital on colonial societies. Although Marx retained the assumption that capital accumulation would ultimately transform precapitalist modes of production, he noted that the process of this transformation would be subjected to variation and beset with conflicts and contradictions. He noted also that at times even where the capitalist mode of production is dominant it continues to depend on precapitalist modes for the conditions of its reproduction.[29] With regard to the process of capitalist development in the colonies, Marx noted that

> The obstacles presented by the internal solidarity and organisation of the pre-capitalist national modes of production to the corrosive influence of commerce are strikingly illustrated by the intercourse of the English with India and China.... English commerce exerted a revolutionary influence on these communities and tore them apart only insofar as the low prices of its goods served to destroy the spinning and weaving industries, which were an ancient integrating element of this unity of industrial and

---

28. Ibid., p. 45. For a rejoinder by Frank, see André Gunder Frank, *Lumpen-Bourgeoisie and Lumpen-Development: Dependency, Class and Politics in Latin America* (New York: Monthly Review Press, 1972), pp. 1–4.
29. Wolpe, "Introduction," in *The Articulation*, ed. by Wolpe, p. 4.

Theoretical Conclusions

agricultural production. And even so this work of dissolution proceeds very gradually. And still more slowly in China, where it is not reinforced by direct political force.[30]

The currently popular 'articulation of modes of production' approach seeks to elaborate Marx's rather casual observations on the coexistence of precapitalist and capitalist modes of production, specifically in relation to Third World social formations. While the 'articulation model' has been advanced largely by French Marxist anthropologists, the earlier writings of Ernesto Laclau, a Latin American theorist, can also be included within this general framework.[31]

Ernesto Laclau agrees with André Gunder Frank that the expansion of western capital into the colonies has resulted in a process of underdevelopment in the colonies and that dominance-subordination also characterizes the relationship between sectors of production within the colonies.[32] However, he disagrees with Frank that the subordinated economic sectors are capitalist. He argues that some precapitalist sectors continue to remain precapitalist or feudal in spite of their subordination to the dominant capitalist sectors and their incorporation within the capitalist market economy.

Laclau says that the persistence of precapitalist social structures is not the result of the apathy or the traditional values of the natives as dual economy theorists have argued. Rather, they persist because of the deliberate efforts made by the dominant capitalist sectors to adapt precapitalist structures to suit their own expansionary needs. What results from this adaptation, according to Laclau, is not the generalization of capitalism as Frank has argued,

---

30. Marx, quoted in ibid., p. 4.
31. Ernesto Laclau, "Feudalism and Capitalism." See also Aiden Foster-Carter, "Can We Articulate 'Articulation'?" in *The New Economic Anthropology*, ed. by John Clammer (New York: St. Martin's Press, 1978), p. 212. See also Samir Amin's definition of a social formation as a combination of several modes of production, *Unequal Development*, Ch. 1.
    See the work of Maurice Godelier, Catherine Coquery-Vidrovitch, et al., on Asiatic and African Modes of Production in *Relations of Production: Marxist Approaches to Economic Anthropology*, ed. by David Seddon (London: Frank Cass, 1978). See also Emmanuel Terray, *Marxism and "Primitive" Societies* (New York: Monthly Review Press, 1972).
    For non-Marxist attempts to grapple with the heterogeneous and multistructured forms of production and exchange in the Third World, see the theories on the informal sector and brokerage, as discussed by Norman Long and Paul Richardson, "Informal Sector, Petty Commodity Production and the Social Relations of Small Scale Enterprise," in *The New Economic Anthropology*, ed. by Clammer; and Norman Long, "Structural Dependency, Modes of Production and Economic Brokerage in Rural Peru," in *Beyond the Sociology of Development*, ed. by Oxaal et al.
32. Laclau, "Feudalism and Capitalism," pp. 23–24.

but the coexistence of precapitalist and capitalist sectors within the same economy. The precapitalist sectors, however, are utilized to prop up and expand the capitalist sectors at great expense to the peasantry.[33] Laclau goes on to argue that certain precapitalist social relations of production were in fact accentuated and consolidated by the intrusion of capitalist market forces rather than annihilated by them.

> Now this precapitalist character of the dominant relations of production in Latin America was not only *not* incompatible with production for the world market, but was actually intensified by the expansion of the latter. The feudal regime of the haciendas tended to increase in servile exactions on the peasantry as the growing demands of the world market stimulated maximization of their surplus. Thus, far from the expansion of the external market acting as a disintegrating force on feudalism, its effect was rather to accentuate it and consolidate it. [emphasis in original][34]

There is a fundamental difference between the Marxist version of 'dualism' advanced by Laclau and the dual economy theories of Böeke and others noted earlier. In separating himself from the 'bourgeois' dual economy school, Laclau elaborates on the hierarchy and contradiction that characterize the relationship between the dominant and subordinate sectors within colonial economies.

> ... Dualism implies that no connections exist between the "modern" or "progressive" sector and the "closed" or "traditional" sector. Yet we have argued that, on the contrary, servile exploitation was accentuated and consolidated by the very tendency of entrepreneurs – presumably "modern" in type – to maximize profits; the apparent lack of communication between the two sectors herewith disappears. In such cases we can affirm that the modernity of one sector is a function of the backwardness of the other. ... It is ... correct to confront the system as a whole and to show the indissoluble unity that exists between the maintenance of feudal backwardness at one extreme and the apparent progress of a bourgeois dynamism at the other.[35]

The Frank-Laclau debate as well as the less well-known debates between Kathleen Gough and A. M. Shah in the *Pacific Affairs* and among some Indian Marxists in *The Economic and Political Weekly* on the characterization of colonial (and postcolonial) social formations is largely attributable to the lack of consensus among Marxists on the definition of such central Marxian concepts as mode of production, and the capitalist mode of production in particular.[36] However, this debate is quite helpful in thinking about the rela-

---

33. Ibid., p. 30.
34. Ibid., p. 30.
35. Ibid., p. 31.
36. A. M. Shah, "Class and Agrarian Change;" Kathleen Gough, "Class and Agrarian change ... A Rejoinder." For a discussion of the debate on the mode of production in India, and bibliographic references to it, see Hamza Alavi, "India and the Colonial Modes," and Doug McEachern, "The Mode of Production in India," *Journal of Contemporary Asia* 6 (1976).

Theoretical Conclusions

tive weight to be given to western capitalist expansion and precolonial/precapitalist social structures in the underdevelopment of Third World economies. It is therefore useful for identifying strategies necessary to overcome the conditions of underdevelopment in specific Third World situations as well.

Laclau argues that 'feudalism' persists in the colonies on the basis of continuing coercive social relations of production within the productive enterprise. In contrast, as we noted earlier, Frank argues that enterprises characterized by lord-serf relations are nevertheless capitalist because they are incorporated into the world capitalist economy through market relations.

Laclau argues that a definition of a mode of production must give priority to the social relations of production. A given economic system may consist of several types of social relations of production — lord-serf, capital-wage labor, for example. For Laclau, serfdom is the defining criterion of the feudal mode of production and wage labor, the defining characteristic of the capitalist mode.[37] Accordingly, two or more modes of production can and do exist within the world capitalist economy although combined in a complex hierarchical fashion.

The coexistence and articulation of modes of production have been studied by several other Marxist writers. Claude Meillassoux and Harold Wolpe have approached this issue in terms of the reproduction of the labor force needed by the dominant capitalist sectors (such as mines and plantations) in the colonies.[38] They have shown that in many instances, the dominant capitalist sectors sought to preserve the village economies rather than completely eradicate them. This was because the preservation of the pre-existing village economies allowed the capitalist sectors to shift the costs of reproducing their labor force onto the villages and therefore lower their own costs of production in the capitalist sectors.

In our discussions of the Ceylonese case materials we showed that certain precapitalist institutions such as corvée labor were deliberately preserved by the colonial state. We also showed that the operation of the Temple Lands Commission in the 1860s and the introduction of the Service Tenures Ordinance in 1876 tended to reactivate some of the feudal labor services that had been in decay for many years. We also noted that neither the planters nor the colonial state sought to destroy the village economy or the peasantry entirely but attempted to turn the peasantry into a reliable semiproletariat for the

---

37. Compare also the Frank-Laclau debate with the Sweezy-Dobb debate on the transition from feudalism to capitalism in Western Europe. Rodney Hilton (ed.), *The Transition from Feudalism to Capitalism* (London: New Left Books, 1976); see also David Brenner, "A Critique."
38. Claude Meillassoux, "From Reproduction;" Harold Wolpe, "Capitalism and Cheap Labour-Power;" see also Gail Omvedt, "Migration."

estates. We also explained that the preservation of certain precolonial institutions in the feudal villages was motivated by the necessity to maintain a class alliance with the native aristocracy.

To this extent, we can agree with Laclau that certain precapitalist social relations of production were deliberately preserved and disagree with Frank that 'capitalism' was generalized through and through into the subordinated village sectors in the Kandyan Highlands. However, it is necessary to stress that Laclau's model of the coexistence of the precapitalist and capitalist modes in the underdeveloped economies is a static one. The inherent conflicts and contradictions between these modes, the processes of internal transformation of precapitalist modes and the conditioning effect of these modes upon each other are not captured in Laclau's static picture of coexisting modes of production.

In our case study of the Kandyan Highlands we described in detail the processes of transformation of precolonial social relations of production when several modes of production were articulating with each other. For example, we noted that the colonial state managed to divorce precolonial corvée duty (*rajakāriya*) from landholding and to turn it into a general capitation or head tax. Although the form of its exaction — forced labor — continued, this tax lost its precolonial feudal basis. Furthermore, even the form of its collection began to change with the introduction of a commutation option after 1848. Likewise, labor exaction on the basis of extraeconomic rights persisted, although the introduction of private property rights and the commercialisation of land undermined the feudal basis of coercive social relations of production.

We also noted that in the Kandyan Highlands the speed and degree of change in the various precolonial sectors of production varied a great deal. For example. serfdom was much slower to change in the feudal villages than in the former royal villages. The eradication of communal rights to village high lands was much more rapid than the gradual dispossession of the peasantry from their paddy lands. What all this suggests is that British capital, the colonial state, market forces, and the cash nexus did not wipe out precolonial social relations in one big sweep. The transformation was indeed gradual. But it is not correct to call the resultant social relations feudal or precolonial as Laclau has done in relation to Latin America. The resultant social relations were not feudal, but colonial adaptations of preexisting institutions.[39]

39. One of the strengths of the articulation approach is its ability to take into account not simply the coexistence of two modes (feudal and capitalism for example), but several modes in a given economy. Long and Richardson demonstrate that the articulation approach allows one to recognize the importance of the petty commodity mode. They suggest that while the petty commodity mode was a transitional

Theoretical Conclusions

Several other writers working within the articulation framework have sought to capture the *transitory* nature of the interaction between precapitalist and capitalist modes of production. While Laclau emphasized the deliberate preservation of precapitalist social relations, Charles Bettelheim has pointed out that the process of articulation between opposing modes is a contradictory one of "conservation-dissolution".[40] Meillassoux also points to the contradictions inherent in this articulation between opposing modes as he attacks the conventional dual economy approach.

> The "dual" theory is intended to conceal the exploitation of the rural community, integrated, as we saw above, as an organic component of capitalist production to feed the temporarily unproductive workers of the capitalist sector and supply them with the resources necessary to their survival. Because of this process of absorption within the capitalist economy, the agricultural communities, maintained as reserves of cheap labour, are being both undermined and perpetuated at the same time, undergoing a prolongated crisis and not a smooth transition to capitalism.[41]

Neither Bettelheim nor Meillassoux, however, have analyzed the direction and dynamic of this transition. Meillassoux seems to suggest that eventually the precapitalist mode will be entirely subjugated by the capitalist mode. A similar line of thinking is evident in the work of Pierre-Phillipe Rey (and Dupré) who has provided the most explicit application up to now of the articulation model to a concrete historical case.[42]

Basing his theoretical formulations on a study of 'lineage mode of production' in the Congo, Rey has identified three stages in the articulation of precapitalist and capitalist modes of production. He argues that during the first phase, the initial link between the two modes is made at the level of exchange or trade. At this stage precapitalist features of the lineage mode are reinforced and the lineage mode remains dominant. During the second stage of articulation, capital begins to subordinate the precapitalist mode though still making use of many of its features for capital's own expansionary needs. The role of violence becomes crucial in this transitional phase as the now dominant capitalist mode articulates with the precapitalist mode. According to Rey, violence characterizes the articulation between the capitalist and all

---

form in the development of capitalism in Europe, "recent analysts stress the continued proliferation of small-scale independent activity in less-developed societies," Long and Richardson, "Informal Sector," p. 185.

40. Bettelheim, "Theoretical Comments," pp. 297–98; see also Foster-Carter, "Can We Articulate," p. 213.
41. Meillassoux, "From Reproduction," pp. 198–99.
42. Georges Dupré and Pierre-Phillippe Rey, "Reflections on the Pertinence of the History of Exchange," in *The Articulation*, ed. by Wolpe, pp. 128–60; Barbara Bradby, "The Destruction of Natural Economy," in *The Articulation*, ed. by Wolpe, pp. 93–127; Foster-Carter, "Can We Articulate," pp. 210–49.

precapitalist modes of production except feudalism. The distinction made here is probably based on the unique historical experience of the West, particularly England, where capitalism emerged internally within the feudal mode.[43]

According to Rey, most Third World societies are still experiencing the second, or transitional stage of articulation. Rey claims that during the third or final phase, the precapitalist mode is completely wiped out as capitalist social relations are generalized throughout.[44]

A particularly important feature of Rey's formulation is that he conceives articulation not simply at the level of modes of production, but also at the level of conflicts and alliances between social classes that represent these modes of production. As Rey puts it,

> ... The articulation of two modes of production, one of which establishes its domination over the other ... not as a static given, but as a *process*, that is to say a combat between the two modes of production, with the confrontations and alliances which such a combat implies: confrontations and alliances essentially between the *classes* which these modes of production define. [emphasis in original][45]

The process of articulation that Rey has identified has broad applicability to the Ceylonese case examined in this book. We noted that in the period before the installation of the capitalist mode of production, the mercantilist policies and practices of the colonizing powers did not lead to a dissolution of precolonial social structures, but rather to their intensification. In the subsequent stage of western capitalist expansion, the capitalist mode of production was installed in the form of a plantation economy. At that point the precolonial feudalistic paddy and communalistic chena agriculture began to be undermined. We have examined in great detail the processes of this subordination in relation to the land, labor, infrastructure, and other requirements of the plantations.

The central role played by the colonial state in the process of this subordination has also been discussed in this study. Although the colonial state legitimated its actions through the enactment of a series of new laws and an ideology of welfarism, violence — as in the case of the African lineage societies examined by Rey — played a crucial role in the subordination of Kandyan society. The forcible expropriation of land, exaction of corvée labor, and the ruthless suppression of peasant revolts are some examples of violence perpetrated by the colonial state. Rey's claims to the contrary, the articulation between the capitalist and feudal mode was characterized by a certain degree of violence, at least in the case of Kandyan Ceylon.

43. Ibid., p. 223.
44. Dupré and Rey, "Reflections," pp. 153–62.
45. Rey quoted by Foster-Carter, "Can We articulate," p. 219.

One of the central arguments of this book is that the contradictions of colonial capitalist expansion cannot be understood simply at the abstract level of articulation of modes of production. It is people who act as groups representing different interests. Any attempt to understand the interactions among opposing modes of production has to be approached at the level of social classes as well as ethnic, caste, and other interest groups which constitute the relevant actors within given modes of production. That articulation of modes of production needs to be understood in the context of class relations, the point also argued by Rey, has been elaborated in our study. This was done with reference to the relationship between the dominant capitalist mode and the subordinate 'feudal', 'communal', and petty commodity modes, and the accompanying class, ethnic, and other relations between planters and peasants, peasants and overlords, and so forth.

Does the articulation framework, then, help resolve all the theoretical issues in the delineation of colonial socioeconomic structures? Not quite. As critics of Rey's work have pointed out, he has not distinguished the differences in the processes of articulation between feudalism and capitalism in Western Europe from the processes of articulation between precapitalist and *externally imposed* capitalist structures in the colonies.[46] In attempting to develop a general theory of articulation between precapitalist and capitalist modes, Rey has not made the specificity of imperialism and the external imposition of the capitalist mode central to his analysis of the colonial transformation. Furthermore, Rey and some of the other writers working with the articulation model have not adequately dealt with the issue of underdevelopment that Gunder Frank raised so forcefully.

A particular variant of neo-Marxist thinking which focuses precisely on those issues that the articulation theorists have neglected — the external imposition and the retrograde nature of capitalism in the colonies — is the school which talks about colonial capitalist development as a phenomenon distinct from though interlinked with metropolitan capitalism. We shall briefly turn our attention to this framework now.

Colonial Capitalist Development

Hamza Alavi, Jairus Banaji, and others have argued that neither the model of coexistence of feudalism and capitalism as postulated by Laclau and some Indian Marxists, nor the idea of a single world capitalist economy upheld by

---

46. Ibid., p. 223. See also Roxborough, *Theories of Underdevelopment*, pp. 67–68.

Frank and Wallerstein, accurately describe the nature of Third World social formations structured by colonialism.[47] Alavi and Banaji have outlined a theory of colonial capitalism in different ways. Although there are some significant theoretical differences in their analyses (some of which will be noted shortly) we shall be concerned here with the basic agreements between them on the specificity of colonial capitalist development.

Both Alavi and Banaji argue that as metropolitan capital expands into the colonies, precapitalist modes no longer remain precapitalist or feudal. Although they may appear to retain their precapitalist social relations of production, they are no longer precapitalist but are reconstituted on a new colonial basis. Alavi makes this point very forcefully when he says

> The excessive and misleading emphasis on the *form* of the relationship between the producer and his master has bedevilled discussion of the mode of production; in particular, that has obscured fundamental transformations that were wrought in the nature and the significance of such relationships by virtue of the colonial impact. Although the *form* of such a relationship often remains unchanged, its essential nature and significance undergoes a revolutionary transformation. That is why it is wrong to describe colonial economies to be those in which precapitalist relationships "coexist" with "capitalist" relations. Such relationships, transformed by the colonial impact are no longer "precapitalist". In India "sharecropping" on land has thus been equated with "feudal", just as in Latin America the apparently servile relationships of the hacienda have been defined also as "feudal". But in neither case do they retain, apart from the superficial form, the essential nature of the "feudal" relationships. That is one of the central problems that must be clarified (and the corresponding problem of the so-called "co-existence" of the feudal and capitalist modes of production in a colonial structure). [emphasis in original][48]

Having rejected the characterization of colonial social relations of production as feudal, both Alavi and Banaji go on to reject also the characterization of colonial economies as capitalist. They agree with Laclau (against Frank) that colonial economies cannot be labelled capitalist simply because they are incorporated into the world capitalist economy through market or exchange relations.[49]

Alavi and Banaji distinguish the original transformation of feudalism into capitalism in Western Europe from the capitalist transformation taking place in the colonies. While they point out that imperialist penetration has changed social relations of production in a capitalist direction, they argue that forces

---

47. Banaji, "For a Theory" and "Backward Capitalism, Primitive Accumulation and Modes of Production," *Journal of Contemporary* Asia, vol. 3, no. 4 (1973); Alavi, "India and the Colonial Mode" and "India: Transition from Feudalism;" see also McEachern, "The Mode of Production."
48. Alavi, "India and the Colonial Mode," p. 182. See also Banaji, "For a Theory," p. 2499.
49. Banaji, "For a Theory," pp. 2498–99.

Theoretical Conclusions

of production have not moved in a similar direction. As Alavi points out, the generalization of commodity production and the changes in feudal social relations have not been accompanied by an expanded reproduction of colonial economies through improvements in techniques, labor productivity, and the like.[50] Banaji attributes this retrograde logic of colonial capitalism to the export of colonial profits for reinvestment in the metropoles.

> The colonial modes of production were precisely the circuits through which capital was drained out of the colonies in the form of bullion, consumption goods, raw materials and so on. The financing of primary accumulation outside the colonial world was their chief historical function and it was this fact which determined their peculiarly retrograde logic. We can describe this in the following terms: the colonial modes of production transmitted to the colonies the pressures of the accumulation process in the metropolis without unleashing any corresponding expansion in the forces of production.[51]

Alavi and Banaji argue that to call colonial economies simply capitalist is to overlook the fundamental differences between the processes of capitalist development in the metropoles and the colonies. Thus, in rejecting both the feudal and capitalist characterizations of colonial economies and in specifying the peculiarities of capitalist development in the colonies, these writers prefer to talk of a distinct colonial form of capitalism in Third World social formations.

Our Ceylonese case study too has demonstrated that the Kandyan Highlands lost their precapitalist feudal basis during colonial economic and political expansion. A slow and gradual process of the dispossession of the cultivators from the land was set in motion. Market relations began to replace precolonial extraeconomic relations. However, as Banaji and Alavi have argued, the forces of production remained backward. We have demonstrated that techniques of production and labor productivity remained stagnant in paddy agriculture. In other words, development of productive forces through technological advances and improved labor productivity which characterized capitalist agricultural development in the metropoles, was not repeated in the colonies. To this extent we can agree with Alavi and Banaji that the capitalist development which took place in the Kandyan Highlands during the nineteenth century was a retrograde or peripheral form of capitalism peculiar to colonial societies.[52]

---

50. Alavi, "India: Transition from Feudalism," pp. 391–97.
51. Banaji, "For a Theory," p. 2500.
52. For a discussion of the structural properties of peripheral capitalism as identified by Amin, see *Unequal Development*, Ch. 4 and 5. See also Gunasinghe, "Agrarian Relations," p. 21.

Debate on the Mode of Production

While there seems to be increasing agreement among neo-Marxist underdevelopment theorists that colonial societies are characterized by a form of dependent or peripheral capitalism, there is certainly no consensus among them as to whether colonial capitalism constitutes a single mode of production or the articulation among several modes.

Before we proceed to examine the various positions in this debate, a brief definition of the concept, mode of production, is in order. Although Marx himself did not provide a concise definition of a mode of production, there is broad agreement among Marxist writers that a mode of production is a complex unity consisting of specific forces of production and social relations of production.

The production process involves the transformation of the object of labor (for example, land) into a social product through the combination of labor power and instruments of production. The forces of production which pertain to the various elements in the production process include the combination of labor power, labor organization, and technology of production. Social relations of production, on the other hand, pertain to the relationship between various groups of people brought together by the production process. These social relations are determined principally in relation to the ownership and control of the means of production and the social product. In other words, the social relations of production refer to property relations and the appropriation of the social product.[53]

While most Marxist writers seem to agree on this broad definition of a mode of production at an abstract theoretical level, a number of extremely difficult issues emerge in any attempt to apply this definition to concrete historical situations. In fact, many Marxists concur that a mode of production is a theoretical concept (akin to Max Weber's ideal typical constructs) and that no concrete historical society completely fits one mode of production or the other.[54] Two of the most pressing issues involved in delineating modes of production pertain to the appropriate unit of analysis of a mode of production and the determining criterion of a mode.

---

53. For some attempts at definition, see Hindess and Hirst, *Pre-Capitalist Modes;* Banaji, "Modes of Production;" Alavi, "India: Transition from Feudalism;" Norman Long, "Structural Dependency," in *Beyond the Sociology of Development,* ed. by Oxaal et al., p. 267.
54. Hindness and Hirst, *Pre-Capitalist Economic Formations, passim;* see also Beverly Grier, "Cocoa Marketing in Colonial Ghana: Capitalist Enterprise and the Emergence of a Rural African Bourgeoisie," *UFAHAMU,* Journal of the African Activist Associations, vol. X, nos. 1 and 2 (Fall and Winter, 1980–81), p. 91.

Theoretical Conclusions

As we discussed earlier, writers such as Gunder Frank and Immanuel Wallerstein have defined capitalism at the level of the world economy and on the basis of generalized commodity production. In focusing on these global units of analysis, they have left unanalyzed the constituent elements of these larger world units such as modes of production, and political and ideological structures.[55] As noted earlier, while the macrosociological concepts provided by Frank and Wallerstein provide the essential context for understanding Third World social change, they are not sufficient for the analysis of specific historical situations in the colonies.

Turning now to the other extreme, we find theorists who define a mode of production more narrowly by reference to specific sets of social relations of production. We found, for example, that theorists who work within the articulation framework equate the feudal mode with serfdom and the capitalist mode with wage labor. Taking social relations as the determinant feature of a mode of production, anthropologist Norman Long has identified four main noncapitalist modes of production in rural Peru: the traditional hacienda; the smallholder private property type; the sharecropping type; and, the indigenous peasant community type.[56]

Certainly, this breakdown into several types of social relations of production yields an infinitely richer and more complex picture of the social structure and the dynamics of Third World social formations than is possible with the macroperspectives advanced by Frank and Wallerstein. But the depiction of a multiplicity of modes of production and processes of their articulation, make it difficult to subsume them within a few larger categories such as feudalism and capitalism and to generalize about social change processes across time and space.[57] In order to avoid the pitfalls of narrow empiricism, the articulation process has to be placed firmly within the wider context of the world capitalist economy and the imperialist relationship. We shall develop this argument further in the concluding section of this chapter.

In between the macro- and microlevel definitions of a mode of production lies the concept of the colonial mode of production identified by Hamza Alavi and Jairus Banaji. In criticizing the articulation model, Alavi says that a mode of production cannot be defined simply by the social relations of production. Rather, a mode of production is a complex unity with hierarchically structured relationships. A mode of production then should be defined holistically at several different levels.

55. Foster-Carter, "Can We Articulate," p. 240.
56. Long, "Structural Dependency." Note that Long's discussion is based on the anthropological field work of Rodrigo Montoya.
57. Foster-Carter, "Can We Articulate," p. 240.

> A mode of production is a complex unity. There has been all too often a tendency to reduce that complex dialectical unity to a narrow definition of "relations of production" that focuses on *forms* of relationships between the direct producer, the worker (whether industrial or agricultural) and the class that exploits his labor power. "Relations of production" cannot be understood simplistically in terms of dyadic relationships, i. e., apparently one to one relationships between the worker and his master, for such relationships exist and can only exist by virtue of the totality of the structure- superstructure formation of a society that constitutes a dialectical unity.[58]

Arguing that theorists such as Laclau have defined social relations of production too narrowly, Alavi rejects the notion of articulation between two or more modes of production which is supposedly based on narrow definitions of social relations of production. Instead, Alavi argues that Third World social formations, specifically India, are characterized by a single colonial mode of production. Alavi has identified several defining features of this colonial mode: (1) free labor; (2) surplus exaction on the basis of economic rights; (3) separation of economic and political power; (4) generalized commodity production; and, (5) simple reproduction of the economy.[59] According to Alavi's definition, the social relations of production in the colonies resemble those of metropolitan capitalist societies in many respects. But what distinguishes colonial capitalism from metropolitan capitalism is the fact that reproduction of colonial capital is subordinated to the interests of metropolitan capitalism. It is for these reasons that Alavi chooses to talk of capitalism in the colonies as representing a distinct colonial capitalist mode of production.[60]

Jairus Banaji has also rejected the definition of a mode of production utilized by articulation theorists such as Laclau. He argues that these theorists have mistaken what he calls 'social relations of exploitation' for social relations of production. Banaji claims that relations of exploitation refer simply to the forms of surplus appropriation, for example, serfdom and wage labor. Social relations of production, on the other hand, encompass property relations and the level of development of productive forces in a given society.

> We may define relations of exploitation as the particular form in which surplus is appropriated from the direct producers, not the specific form, e. g., labour rent, rent in kind, but the general form, e. g., serfdom.... Relations of production, on the other hand, are the specific historically determined form which particular relations of exploitation assume due to a certain level of development of the productive forces, to the predominance of particular forms (feudal landed property, etc.) and so on. Thus,

---

58. Alavi, "India and the Colonial Mode," p. 181.
59. Compare Alavi's definitions of the feudal and capitalist modes with his discussion of the colonial mode. Alavi, "India: Transition from Feudalism," pp. 363–64, 391–98.
60. Ibid., p. 362. In his more recent paper on "India: Transition from Feudalism," Alavi talks about colonial capitalism, but does not refer to it as a specific mode of production.

Theoretical Conclusions

in a strict, i. e., scientific or Marxist sense, "feudalism" is not the "same as" serfdom, though the latter constitutes the dominant relation of exploitation in the feudal mode of production not the only one, for slavery survived well into the feudal epoch.[61]

In other words, Banaji argues that although several forms of labor exploitation — serfdom, sharecropping, wage labor, etc. — coexist in colonial economies, they do so within a single colonial mode of production rather than several modes of production as argued by the articulation theorists. But as Foster-Carter points out, Banaji needs to spell out "how a single mode of production can combine so large a number of variant 'forms' [i. e., forms of exploitation] if the term is not to be merely residual."[62]

The concept of the colonial mode of production helps emphasize the differences between colonial structures and precolonial social structures, on the one hand, and between colonial capitalism and metropolitan capitalism, on the other. It also helps identify the broad similarities between different colonial social formations in Asia, Africa, and Latin America. However, this concept runs into severe difficulties when attempts are made to apply it to concrete historical situations.

If the colonial mode of production is a separate entity, with its own laws of motion, what is its precise relationship to the capitalist world economy and metropolitan capitalism in particular?[63] Indeed, both Alavi and Banaji are quite explicit about the exploitative relationship between colonial and metropolitan capitalism. But when the colonial mode is distinguished as a separate entity, there is an implicit suggestion that it 'articulates' with the dominant metropolitan capitalist mode within the world capitalist economy. However, this implication does not accord with the strong positions that both Alavi and Banaji have taken against the articulation approach.

It is important to point out, however, that Alavi does recognize that class struggle in the colonies needs to be understood in relation to the articulation between ascendant and disintegrating modes of production.

> That is the problem of the necessary contradiction between modes of production in historical development; a new emergent mode of production stands in contradiction to the old disintegrating mode of production. If that basic Marxist postulate is accepted, there is a necessity, at each stage of historical development to identify which mode is dominant and therefore represents the principal contradictions in the class struggle. This basic Marxist postulate has been elaborated and explained by Mao Tse Tung in his essay, *On Contradiction*. The issue is not simply whether capitalist relations of production *exist*, nor indeed whether they have completely done away with all feudal survivals, but precisely of the relative weight of each, the alignment of

---

61. Banaji, "For a Theory," p. 2498.
62. Foster-Carter, "Can We Articulate," p. 241.
63. Ibid., p. 236.

classes that represent each mode of production vis-a-vis each other and therefore the thrust of political conflict and the nature of the class struggle.[64]

While the above passage suggests quite clearly the usefulness of the articulation approach for understanding the contradictions between opposing modes of production and resulting class contradictions, the colonial mode as conceptualized by Alavi or Banaji, on its own, does not adequately capture those processes of change and contradictions intrinsic to colonial capitalist development.

Turning to the question of the origin and evolution of the colonial mode of production now, it should be noted, that neither Alavi nor Banaji have indicated at what point a precolonial mode becomes a colonial mode. The impact of metropolitan capital varied across diverse precolonial modes (feudal, communal, lineage, etc.); historical periods of capitalist expansion (merchant capital, financial capital); forms of colonial political control (direct and indirect rule); and colonial economic structures (plantation, smallholder production, etc.). These differences cannot be taken into account in depicting a single colonial mode that supposedly came into being with the earliest movement of metropolitan capital into the colonies.

The inherently uneven and contradictory nature in the transformation of precolonial societies is not captured by reference to a single colonial 'mode'. Rather these contradictory processes need to be described in relation to concrete historical cases before the applicability of the concept of the colonial mode can be determined. In other words, many of the problems of overgeneralization present in the formulations of Frank and Wallerstein are evident in the work of Alavi and Banaji, although at a lower level of abstraction.

Our Ceylonese case study was focused on the period of initial contact between the precolonial social structures of the Kandyan Highlands and the superimposed plantation economy and the colonial state during the fifty or so years between 1833 and 1886. We have explored the fundamental transformations that took place in the Highlands in relation to the articulation of precolonial and superimposed modes of production and political structures and resultant class and ethnic conflicts. We pointed out that plantation dominance led to a virtual annihilation of the communal chena agriculture and a fundamental transformation of feudalistic paddy agriculture. It also resulted in the emergence of petty commodity production in the form of peasant coffee.

---

64. Alavi, "India and the Colonial Mode," p. 171.

Theoretical Conclusions

We noted that everywhere the processes of transformation were uneven and contradictory. The great complexity and differentiation in the colonial transformation cannot be understood by referring simply to a colonial mode of production, a capitalist world economy, or a modern world system. We need to move beyond abstract theoretical formulations in order to understand the specific economic sectors, social groups, and human beings involved in the processes of social change. Abstract theoretical exercises such as the identification of a single or several modes of production in a given social formation are not wholly devoid of practical meaning. They are, for example, crucial in making choices among various social change strategies for particular regions of the world. Nevertheless, we need more concrete historical analyses of specific cases before grand theories and appropriate social change strategies can be more fruitfully discussed.

The Specificity of the Colonial State

One of the obvious shortcomings of almost all the theories in the sociology of development and underdevelopment we have discussed thus far is that they have sought to examine the relationship between colonialism and underdevelopment merely at the level of economic structures. Indeed, the economic motive was the dominant one in western expansion into the colonies. However, even the economic structures the colonizers created cannot be adequately understood without also looking at the political and ideological structures of colonialism. Very little analytical work has been done on these dimensions of colonialism. Studies on the cultural and psychological manifestations of colonialism are especially needed.[65] In the following pages we shall briefly consider two contending views on the political structure of colonial societies and their general applicability or inapplicability to our Ceylonese case study.

The dominant perspective on political change in the colonies is one which is based on the Weberian ideal types of 'traditional' and bureaucratic/modern authority. It must be noted that Max Weber, who identified the traditional and modern *ideal* types, did not project an inevitable evolution of the former

---

65. The writings of Frantz Fanon and Albert Memmi are useful in this respect. See, for example, Frantz Fanon, *Black Skin, White Masks*, trans. Charles Lam Markmann (New York: Grove Press, 1967) and Albert Memmi, *The Colonizer and the Colonized* (Boston: Beacon Press, 1967).

into the latter.⁶⁶ The more recent and popular versions of political dualism, for example, the theories of Parsons and Eisenstadt, claim that the colonial presence which represents modern bureaucratic authority will help generalize 'modernity' into the preexisting traditional authority structures.⁶⁷ These theories of political dualism and modernization obviously complement their economic counterpart, the dual economy theory, which we discussed earlier. Modernization theorists argue that, just as the colonial economic presence would lead to western-style economic development, the colonial state presence would help generalize 'complex' western-style political structures throughout the colonial world.

In our earlier discussions of the colonial state in Ceylon, we noted that it was essentially a dual administration consisting of a subordinate native sector and a dominant European sector. In agreeing with Furnivall, the early theorist of the colonial state, we also noted that the structure and function of the colonial state tended to vary in relation to the changes in the colonial economic strategies.⁶⁸ We also argued that, contrary to the views of the modernization theorists, the colonial presence did not necessarily result in the generalization of 'rational bureaucratic' authority. Instead, it resulted in the amalgamation of precolonial authority structures and the European civil service to meet the varying exigencies of the colonial political economy.

Very little work has been done from a Marxist underdevelopment perspective on the colonial state. The orthodox Marxist position which claims that the economic infrastructure determines the political and ideological superstructures is simply inadequate for understanding the specificity of colonial social formations. Capitalism was introduced externally into the colonies. It was not an endogenous development as in England. It is in the context of this fundamental difference between capitalist development in the colonies and the metropoles, that the peculiarities of the colonial state need to be understood.

We have described in earlier chapters of this book that the colonial state represented by the 'planter-official' class created and developed the plantation economy in Ceylon. It played a direct role in primitive accumulation or the exaction of a surplus from the village economy for purposes of European plantation expansion. It mediated the contradictions between the plantation

---

66. Gerth and Mills, *From Max Weber*, pp. 296–97, 106. We shall not be concerned with Weber's other ideal type, charismatic authority, here.
67. Talcott Parsons, *The System of Modern Societies* (Englewood Cliffs, N. J.: Prentice-Hall, 1966), p. 137; S. Eisenstadt, *Modernisation, Protest and Change* (Englewood Cliffs, N. J.: Prentice-Hall, 1966), p. 1.
68. Furnivall, quoted by Omvedt, "Towards a Theory," p. 3. See ch. 8, pp. 293–301 in this work.

Theoretical Conclusions 351

and the changing modes of production in the village economy to the benefit of the white planter class. The colonial state, then, stood above the contending social classes and modes of production in the Kandyan social formation (see Figure 8:3). As Bipan Chandra notes, the dominance of the political sphere is a characteristic which distinguishes colonial capitalism from metropolitan capitalism.

> The colonial state plays a much greater role quantitatively as well as qualitatively in the colonial system than perhaps in any other social formation. First of all, colonialism is structured by the colonial state. Unlike in the capitalist system, where the state's chief role is to provide the legal and institutional infrastructure for capitalist relations and where the state often does not intrude into the production process till the twentieth century and the system is maintained by the production process itself, the colonial state is not a super-structure erected on the base of colonial economy; it is an integral and intrusive element in the structuring and functioning of the colonial economy. While the "ruling class" of capitalist society is that which owns, and controls the means of production and which is able, by virtue of the economic power thus conferred upon it to use the state as its instrument for the domination of society, under colonialism, the reverse is the case. It is because of its control over the colonial state that the metropolitan capitalism is able to control, subordinate and exploit the colonial society. This is true even of the laissez-faire period.[69]

The primacy of the political sphere is also vital for an understanding of the dialectics of resistance against colonialism. As Bipan Chandra notes, while the metropolitan capitalist state is "the instrument for the suppression of the working class, the colonial state, is the instrument for suppressing entire societies."[70] In suppressing entire societies, the colonial state took on a distinctively racist character. Furthermore, as we discussed in earlier chapters, the colonial state relied much more on its coercive apparatus and racial ideology than on "'leadership' or direction based on consent."[71] While the colonial state was ideologically weak during the early years, it became culturally hegemonic as privileged native classes became assimilated into western cultural patterns. But later on this assimilation engendered its own contradictions as these westernized elites began to question the disparities between the western ideals of democracy and the political realities in the colonies.

As we have discussed earlier, many of the rebellions which took place in the Kandyan Highlands during the nineteenth century, such as the events of

---

69. Bipan Chandra, "Colonialism, Stages of Colonialism and the Colonial State," *Journal of Contemporary Asia*, vol. 10, no. 3 (1980), pp. 280–81. See also, Hamza Alavi, "The State in Post-Colonial Societies: Pakistan and Bangladesh," in *Imperialism and Revolution in South Asia*, ed. by Kathleen Gough and Hari P. Sharma (New York: Monthly Review Press, 1973), pp. 145–73; special issue on "State and Social Formation in the Capitalist Periphery," *The Insurgent Sociologist*, vol. 9, no. 4 (Spring 1980).
70. Chandra, "Colonialism," p. 280.
71. Ibid., p. 283.

1818 and 1848, almost invariably expressed themselves as nationalist revolts rather than class struggles. Furthermore, it was the colonial state, rather than the white planter class that was made the focus of nationalist opposition. The particular forms that these colonial protests took are to a large extent attributable to the dominance of the political sphere in the colonies and the identification of the colonial state as their direct and immediate oppressor by the colonized people.

In its attempts to prevent the various ethnic groups in the native society from coalescing against it, the colonial state was obliged to create ethnic disunity among the various segments of the native population. Even when some conflicts were clearly attributable to the colonial class structure and the vagaries of the world market, such as the 1915 riots between the Sinhalese and the Muslims, the colonial state chose to interpret them as purely ethnic conflicts thereby exacerbating divisions within the local population thus preventing attacks on the colonial politico-economic structures themselves. In fact, the dynamics of the ethnic conflict between the Sinhalese and the Tamils in contemporary Sri Lanka need to be sought in the differential incorporation of these two groups into the colonial political economy, and the specific relationships of the emerging Sinhalese and Tamil bourgeoisie to the colonial state during the twentieth century. This of course is a subject which needs a separate in-depth study.

Towards a Theoretical Synthesis

In this final chapter we have outlined some of the major theoretical positions on colonialism and underdevelopment and considered their relative strengths and weaknesses in the light of concrete historical evidence drawn from the nineteenth-century Kandyan Highlands. What are some of the general emphases and analytical insights that can be derived from these various theories and how can they be combined towards the construction of a more synthetic and holistic theory of colonial capitalist development? We shall consider some of these issues briefly in our concluding remarks.[72] But before we do so, it is important to stress that our focus throughout this book has been on the period of classical colonialism when metropolitan nations exercised direct political control over the colonies. Our remarks here do not

---

72. As the bibliographic references relevant to these concluding remarks have been presented in the earlier sections of this chapter, they will not be repeated here.

Theoretical Conclusions 353

pertain to contemporary neocolonialism and such developments as the emergence of industrialized 'semiperipheral' nations or the oil rich countries of the Third World.[73]

We noted that both the dominant modernization and Marxist versions of the development perspective look upon the western impact on the colonies as inherently developmental. The Marxists have emphasized the inevitable contradictions and inequalities that company capitalist development. Nevertheless the 'classical' Marxist development perspectives and the modernization school have speculated that western capital expansion into the colonies will lead to a repetition of the western model of development in those societies.

On the basis of the historical evidence derived from the Kandyan Highlands, it is fair to conclude that many of the assumptions derived from the West, specifically England, are inapplicable to the Ceylonese case. Moreover, the western experience has not been and is not likely to be repeated in the colonies. Yet, the arguments made by development theorists regarding values and social structures in the colonies as barriers to economic growth should not be completely cast aside as many underdevelopment theorists such as Gunder Frank, often tend to do. However, it is necessary, as demonstrated in this book, to understand that those values and social structures inhibiting progress are not necessarily 'traditional' or precolonial, but the outcome of long years of interaction between precolonial values and social structures and those superimposed upon them during the colonial period.

We found that the neo-Marxist underdevelopment perspective which claims that the western impact has set in motion a dynamic of underdevelopment, generally applicable to the situation of the Kandyan Highlands. Within the broad underdevelopment paradigm, we identified three distinctive strands of thinking each having a specific emphasis. These are the dependency, colonial mode, and the articulation modes of production perspectives. We have shown that each of these schools of thought has much to contribute to our understanding of colonialism and capitalist development in the colonies. But we have also pointed out that each of these positions on its own is inadequate for comprehending the multistructured and highly differentiated nature of Third World social formations and their relationship to the world political economy. We need, then, to synthesize the analytical strengths derived from each of these perspectives in order to arrive at a more comprehensive theory of colonialism and underdevelopment.

---

73. For a discussion of Brazil as an example of semiperipheral development, see Evans, *Dependent Development*.

From the work of André Gunder Frank and other dependency theorists we derive the centrality of the metropolitan-satellite relationship and the incorporation of the colonies into the world capitalist economy. Any attempt to understand social change in the colonies should be made within this wider context. Although Immanuel Wallerstein is not generally regarded as a dependency theorist, his concept of the 'modern world system' provides a similar global context within which Third World social processes have to be understood. We can no longer continue to look at villages, regions, and nation states, as isolated and disparate units but must see them as entities interrelated in hierarchical and complex ways within a single global political economy.

Theorists such as Hamza Alavi and Jairus Banaji have helped us specify two variant but interrelated forms of capitalism within the broader global capitalist economy outlined by Frank and Wallerstein. Alavi and Banaji have made important contributions in helping distinguish colonial capitalism from metropolitan capitalism. Samir Amin's work has also contributed greatly towards a structural specification of peripheral capitalism and the understanding of unequal capitalist development between the central and peripheral capitalist formations.

While dependency, world system, colonial mode, and peripheral capitalism models have each provided the macrosociological concepts and the comparative frameworks within which to understand colonialism and underdevelopment, they have not been very helpful in explaining internal social formations. It is here that the articulation of modes of production approach advanced by Marxist anthropologists becomes quite useful. The articulation model provides a broad framework within which to specify the socioeconomic structures of precolonial societies; their interaction with economic, political, and ideological structures imposed by colonial powers; and the resultant socioeconomic configurations including class and ethnic alliances and conflicts. Although advanced by anthropologists, the articulation approach has not been utilized for understanding the cultural interaction between the colonizers and the colonized or the psychological consequences of cultural imperialism. Much work could be done in this respect by integrating politico-economic analyses with cultural analyses of colonialism and underdevelopment.

What is being suggested here is that the dependency, the colonial mode, articulation model, etc. should not be seen as competing or alternative theoretical frameworks as sectarian Marxists have a tendency to do. Each of these models share the basic presuppositions of the neo-Marxist underdevelopment paradigm formulated in common opposition to the dominant modernization framework. What needs to be recognized is that each of them has been fashion-

Theoretical Conclusions

ed to answer particular sets of questions posed at different levels of abstraction and different units of analysis. While the dependency and the colonial mode constitute general theoretical perspectives, the articulation model is not so much a theoretical perspective *per se* as a broad methodological approach to the study of processes of social change. It is an approach which needs to be utilized and placed within the wider context of imperialism. Dependency, colonial mode, articulation, etc. are not necessarily competing but complementary modes of analysis. They each capture a specific aspect of Third World social reality. But in order to see the reality in its entirety, we need to synthesize these different theoretical models. It is only then that we can evolve a more comprehensive theory of colonialism that can answer a broader range of questions. The test of such a theory ultimately lies in its applicability to alternative empirical case studies.

We have attempted to take up that challenge in this book by applying a variety of theoretical concepts derived from several schools of underdevelopment theory. The dependency and colonial mode perspectives have provided the wider context for our case study of the Kandyan Highlands, while the articulation model has given us the methodological approach for looking at the interaction between the various sectors of the Kandyan village and the plantation economy.

In attempting to develop a comprehensive theory of colonialism and underdevelopment, we need to add several more theoretical foci and emphases which have not been adequately covered by the available underdevelopment theories. Some of these issues and emphases are derived from the findings of our Ceylonese case study.

One such issue that needs emphasis is the complexity and differentiation of precolonial social structures. We need to move beyond the ahistorical and simplistic depictions of precolonial societies as advanced by both the structural-functionalist traditional society ideal type and the Marxist Asiatic-mode concept.[74] As we pointed out in our discussion of precolonial Kandyan society, there was a complex articulation of modes of production and an evolving social class configuration even within a relatively small geographical region of the Kandyan Highlands. A dialectical historical analysis of precolonial socioeconomic structures is a prerequisite if we are to understand the

---

74. For a structural-functionalist depiction of traditional and modern ideal types, see for example, Emile Durkheim, *The Division of Labor in Society* (New York: Free Press, 1964). For bibliographic references to the Marxist concept of the Asiatic mode of production, see note 7, Ch. IX, of this book. The work of Samir Amin is useful for understanding the heterogeneity of precapitalist modes and their differential articulation with the capitalist mode. See Samir Amin, *Unequal Development*, especially Ch. 1.

subsequent direction of these societies as they articulated with superimposed colonial structures.

A further issue that needs to be incorporated within a general theory of colonialism is the heterogeneity of the colonial impact itself. The differentiation of the colonial impact across time and space can be approached by looking at the changing nature of western capital expansion into the colonies, for example, from merchant capital in the earlier period to production and finance capital in later periods. The multiple forms of the colonial impact can also be grasped by focusing on the different economic strategies used by colonizing powers at different times and places, such as mercantile plunder, plantations and mines, smallholder cashcropping, etc. The various methods of political and ideological control that accompanied these shifts in the movement of capital and changes in economic strategies need also to be incorporated within a comprehensive theory of colonialism.

Much of the existing neo-Marxist literature has focused on the destructive effects of western capital and political rule on the precolonial socioeconomic structures of Third World societies. Some of these studies, particularly those written from the dependency perspective, have failed to present the indigenous social groups and individuals as anything but passive victims of the colonial onslaught. The failure to present a dynamic analysis of the strategies of survival and protests of indigenous people is partly attributable to the macrolevel analyses of the dependency and similar perspectives. In any case, as we have attempted to document in our Ceylonese case study, colonialism did not completely annihilate the precolonial social order. The precolonial structures, in turn, exercised conditioning effects on the superimposed economic and political structures. A comprehensive theory of colonialism and underdevelopment should be able to identify and explain native adaptations, protests and influences on the structure and functioning of colonialism. As we discussed earlier, the articulation approach provides a general framework for looking at these issues of interaction between precolonial and superimposed socioeconomic structures.

In pointing out the inadequacies of existing theories and directions for future studies, it should be noted that in spite of the lip service paid to dialectical analysis and class struggle, only a few neo-Marxist theoreticians have given sufficient attention to the specific social conflicts such as class struggles and nationalist movements that emerged in reaction to colonialism. Underdevelopment theories have not adequately explained anticolonial movements in an analytically rigorous fashion. To understand them, we have to move beyond orthodox static analyses. For instance, we pointed out earlier that in order to grasp the nature of class struggle in colonial societies, we need to look beyond the conflicts taking place between the direct producer and

Theoretical Conclusions

the owner within the productive enterprise to conflicts taking place between opposing modes of production, nationalist and millennial movements directed against the colonial state, etc. This also requires that we examine ethnic, caste, and other nonclass forms of social stratification and how they intersect with class stratification rather than simply attributing ethnic or caste conflicts to 'false consciousness'.

Furthermore, as we noted in our earlier discussions, a comprehensive theory of underdevelopment must necessarily come to grips with the political, ideological and psychological dimensions of colonial domination. While some analytical work has been done on the colonial state, a great deal of work needs to be done on the cultural and psychological aspects of colonialism which help to perpetuate the conditions of underdevelopment.

A further shortcoming of the neo-Marxist underdevelopment theory has been its failure to incorporate changes in international politics (e. g., rise of Third World ideology, super-power struggle, militarism) into its analysis. Much work needs to be done in this area in order to go beyond the depiction of underdevelopment as a static phenomenon identical everywhere in the Third World.

The societies of Asia, Africa, and Latin America underwent fundamental socioeconomic transformations during the period of classical colonialism. The processes of change set in motion during that period are continuing apace into the twenty-first century. But in spite of its broad similarities across the Third World, colonialism has historically been a highly differentiated and variable process. In this book we have argued for the need for more studies of alternative particular cases of the colonial experience upon which a more comprehensive theory of colonialism and underdevelopment can be built. These should help us further our understanding of the dynamic of colonialism and the social contradictions and inequities that it has engendered.

The ultimate goal of such research and theory building should be to help resolve those contradictions and inequities. The resolution of the problems created by colonialism and underdevelopment, and now sustained by neocolonialism, however, are far more difficult than their enumeration or analysis. They call not simply for technical but also political solutions. This study has examined only the origins and the consolidation of the colonial political economy of Ceylon in relation to the Kandyan Highlands. Specific strategies with respect to the transformation of the inherited colonial politico-economic structures must depend upon a closer examination of the dynamics of its twentieth-century evolution.

X. Neocolonialism in Sri Lanka, 2020

Sri Lanka's historical narrative has been defined by geopolitical rivalry, external aggression and internal resistance to that aggression. The early historical era experienced successive waves of invasion from South Indian kingdoms. These were followed by European conquest and consecutive rule of the coastal lowlands by the Portuguese (1505–1666), the Dutch (1666–1796) and the British (1796–1815). In 1815, with the British capture of the Kandyan Kingdom in the Central Highlands, the entire island became a British colony. With deception and manipulation, the British conquered the land and built a class of native collaborators; native lords, commoners and Buddhist monks who rebelled were found guilty of treason and banished, imprisoned or killed.

Colonialism in Sri Lanka[1], first published in 1983, provides an extensively documented, in-depth exploration of the political, economic and social transformation of the Kandyan Highlands between 1833 and 1886. The book documents the development of a unified political and administrative structure, new infrastructure, the plantation economy, local and South Indian entrepreneurship as well as the fundamental social changes that came with British colonial authority and associated capitalist development.

It also describes the differential effects of these changes on the island's various sectors of economic production, social classes and ethnic, religious and caste groups. The book discusses the authoritarian and coercive policies used to maintain law and order, land expropriation for plantations, harsh taxation on the local population and the import of indentured labor from South India. The book considers the detrimental effects of these policies on subsistence agriculture, the Kandyan peasantry's land rights and livelihood and the long-term implications for the island's demographic distribution and ecological balance.

Although Sri Lanka's period of 'classical colonialism' with direct political control by Britain ended with its independence in 1948, the socioeconomic and cultural forces set in place during colonialism have continued to dominate the island's development, particularly in terms of economic growth and social class and ethno-religious politics. Neocolonialism – a term introduced

---

1. Asoka Bandarage, *Colonialism in Sri Lanka: The Political Economy of the Kandyan Highlands, 1833–1886*, Berlin: Mouton Publishers, 1983.

by Kwame Nkrumah, the first president of independent Ghana, in the early 1960s – describes a post-colonial state that is 'in theory, independent and has all the outward trappings of international sovereignty,' but 'in reality, its economic system and thus its political policy is directed from outside.'[2] The concepts of neocolonialism and non-alignment in foreign policy that Nkrumah and other leaders of ex-colonial states championed in the 1950s and 1960s still have great relevance for Sri Lanka today.[3]

Sri Lanka is at a decisive historical juncture facing new forms of geopolitical rivalry and external military, political, economic as well as cultural intervention, primarily involving overt and covert expansionist efforts of the U.S., China and India. The beleaguered, small country is struggling to safeguard her sovereignty, territorial integrity and her very ecological survival. Politics is about propaganda, control of narratives and exploiting ignorance and fear. There is therefore a practical need for an in-depth understanding of the colonial experience that goes beyond academic interest. *Colonialism in Sri Lanka*, which has been out of print for many years, is being republished to help meet that need.

Post-Colonial Developments

Since independence, Sri Lanka's political, economic and cultural evolution has centered on a high level of tension between external intervention and local resistance.

In the post-World War II transfer of power from the deflating British empire, the U.S. began its Sri Lankan influence with partisan election interference and political "advisors," as it did in many ex-colonial countries in Africa, South America and Asia. Interference began prior to the pivotal 1956 election, when Secretary of State John Foster Dulles and U.S. ambassador Philip K. Crowe met with Prime Minister John Kotelawala and Governor General Oliver Goonetilleke on March 11. They discussed strategy and a $5 million aid package via the International Cooperation Administration (ICA; a precursor to U.S. Agency for International Development), for "non-agricultural" development and technical assistance

---

2. Kwame Nkrumah, *Neo-Colonialism, The Last Stage of Imperialism*, London: Thomas Nelson & Sons, Ltd., 1965 https://politicalanthro.files.wordpress.com/2010/08/nkrumah.pdf.
3. Ministry of External Affairs, Government of India, *History and Evolution of Non-Aligned Movement*, August 22, 2012 https://www.mea.gov.in/in-focus-article.htm?20349/History+and+Evolution+of+NonAligned+Movement

that had been confirmed in February.[4] The U.S. aid was unofficially announced in the press on February 12, 1956 – with clear description that it was conditional to curbing trade with China and the USSR – in good time to stick in the public's mind for the upcoming election. Strategic pre-election announcements of aid were a common strategy of U.S. electoral interference during the cold war.

Covert electoral interventions then followed in 1960 (twice) and 1965, again in support of the right-leaning and U.S.-friendly United National Party, which finally won in 1965. The full extent of U.S. foreign policy options considered vis-a-vis Sri Lanka remains unknown. As the preface to the Department of State's "Foreign Relations of the United States" compendium of memos, cables and telegrams of U.S. diplomacy of this period states:

> In the Ceylon compilation, withheld material contained speculation about developments in Ceylonese politics and references to intelligence sources and methods. While the overall objectives of U.S. policy in Ceylon are clearly delineated in the compilation, the editors do not believe it reflects the full range of policy options considered by U.S. officials.[5]

One of the "intelligence sources" redacted from these cables and memos is Donald N. Wilber, the propaganda chief for the CIA operation that overthrew Mohammed Mosaddeq in Iran in 1953. The operation in Iran included bribery, disseminating propaganda, and hiring locals to agitate and commit sabotage, including the bombing of religious leader's houses.[6] It is interesting to note that Wilber was stationed in Colombo in 1960, as he described in a 1986 autobiography.[7]

U.S. corporate interest has also continually been advanced in Sri Lanka, and across the developing world, by the IMF and World Bank since 1950, with a strategy of debt-dependency and infrastructure and economic development focused on export (i.e. plantation) economy and, ultimately, foreign

---

4. Dov. H. Levin, 'When the Great Power Gets a Vote: The Effects of Great Power Electoral Interventions on Election Results,' *International Studies Quarterly* (2016), 60, pp.189-201. Appendix 2, pp.2-3; Office of the Historian. Foreign Relations of the United States, 1955–1957, South Asia Vol. VIII - Document 137 "Memorandum of a Conversation, Colombo, March 11, 1956." https://history.state.gov/historicaldocuments/frus1955-57v08/d137.
5. Office of the Historian, *Foreign Relations of the United States, 1958–1960, South and Southeast Asia*. Vol. XV. U.S. Department of State. https://history.state.gov/historicaldocuments/frus1958-60v15.
6. Stephen Kinzer, *Overthrow: America's Century of Regime Change from Hawaii to Iraq*. 1st ed. New York: Times Books/Henry Holt, 2006. p. 123.
7. Donald Newton Wilber, *Adventures in the Middle East: Excursions and Incursions*. Princeton, N.J.: Darwin, 1986.

corporate interest.[8] From the 1980s onwards, U.S. interventions have included military aid and training – which still occurs – labor union imperialism – for example, via the Asian-American Free Labor Institute (AAFLI)[9] – and the soft power tactics of the National Endowment for Democracy (NED), a granting agency and stalwart of U.S. soft power. With the calls for "democracy and freedom" and a budget, in 2018, of $168 million per year, 1600 NED-funded agencies still spread U.S. corporate influence across 90 countries worldwide.[10] As Allen Weinstein of the NED's Center for Democracy said in 1991, "A lot of what we do today was done covertly 25 years ago by the CIA."[11]

These constant and powerful external pressures have reinforced and, in some cases, advanced the old colonial structures and power dynamics. As James Stuart, Master Attendant of the British Colonial State in Sri Lanka (1825-1855) so candidly said, the priority of colonial rule is to "make the culture of the soil profitable to European adventurers" (see page 64). In the modern case, it is to make the environment and the people exploitable and profitable to the investor-adventurer, U.S. descendants of Europeans, as well as the more recent encroachment of Chinese and Indian power. Both historically and in the present, this is achieved by a system that prioritizes land and resource ownership and use by wealthy foreign companies and their local allies, which continually undermines the evolution of a democratic and independent Sri Lanka. The modern form of client-state colonialism operates via the (often covert) power of money "aid" and investment and political and economic "advisors," backed by military, trade and financial threats, under the pretense of Sri Lanka being a self-ruling state.

In the early years, Sri Lankan governments, like those of many ex-colonial states, introduced policies to nationalize foreign-owned plantations and other private enterprises, to foster local industries and develop local culture and identities. The Constitution of 1972 replaced the island's colonial name *Ceylon* with *Sri Lanka*, declaring the country to be a 'free, sovereign, independent and democratic socialist republic.' These designations remain on paper, but many of the nationalist policies backfired, giving rise to massive

---

8. Michael Hudson, *Super Imperialism; the Economic Strategy of American Empire.* New York: Holt, Rinehart and Winston, 1972., p. 8.
9. Tim Shorrock and Kathy Selvaggio, "Which Side Are You On, AAFLI?" *The Nation;* New York: Nation Company L.P., February 15, 1986.
10. Swiss Policy Research. "Organizations Funded by the NED," December 2, 2019. https://swprs.org/organizations-funded-by-the-ned/
11. David Ignatius, "INNOCENCE ABROAD: THE NEW WORLD OF SPYLESS COUPS." *Washington Post,* September 22, 1991.

youth unemployment and violent social class and communal conflicts, specifically the 1971 *Jathika Vimukthi Peramuna* (JVP) Sinhala youth insurrection and Tamil militancy.[12]

In 1977, urged on by the World Bank and the IMF, a newly elected Sri Lankan government introduced an 'Open Economy,' reversing autarkic economic policies, giving free rein to foreign investment and imports and privatizing hitherto state-owned sectors such as transport and telecommunications. This economic 'liberalization' and associated dismantling of the welfare state, as well as the constitution adopted a year later, made 1977 a turning point in the modern economic and political history of the island. Still, it was not a radical departure, but rather an acceleration, of the capitalist development that had begun with the colonial plantation economy in the 1830s.[13]

Sri Lanka's external economic dependence was subsequently deepened by policies and projects including the controversial Mahaweli river development program, labor export to the Middle East and 'export processing zones' offering incentives for foreign investment in export-oriented production. In the post-1977 period, Sri Lanka experienced widening economic inequality, a proliferation of foreign NGOs and an influx of fundamentalist religions, notably evangelical Christianity from the United States and Wahabi Islam from Saudi Arabia.[14]

Despite the authoritarianism of the 1978 Constitution, popular resistance to external economic control persisted and sometimes even prevailed; for example, the legal victory against the U.S. multinational Freeport McMoran's controversial plans for phosphate mining at Eppawala. However, the central concern of this period was the armed struggle of the Liberation Tigers of Tamil Eelam (LTTE), which the United States' Federal Bureau of Investigation (FBI) called 'one of the most dangerous and deadly extremist outfits in the world.'[15] This struggle extended over thirty years, and is covered in the author's book, *The Separatist Conflict in Sri Lanka: Terrorism, Ethnicity, Political Economy* (2009).[16]

---

12. Asoka Bandarage, *The Separatist Conflict in Sri Lanka: Terrorism, Ethnicity, Political Economy* (London: Routledge, 2009), Chaps. 2–3.
13. Asoka Bandarage, 'Women and Capitalist Development in Sri Lanka, 1977–1987', *The Bulletin of Concerned Asian Scholars*, Vol. 20, no. 2, 1988, pp. 57–81.
14. Sasanka Perera, *New Evangelical Movements and Conflict in South Asia: Sri Lanka and Nepal in Perspective*, Colombo: Regional Centre for Strategic Studies, 1998; *EyeSriLanka*, 'Wahhabism on the rise in Sri Lanka?', March 18, 2018 http://www.eyesrilanka.com/2018/03/18/wahhabism-on-the-rise-in-sri-lanka/
15. 'Liberation Tigers of Tamil Eelam (LTTE)', *South Asia Terrorism Portal* https://www.satp.org/satporgtp/countries/srilanka/terroristoutfits/ltte.htm
16. Bandarage, *The Separatist Conflict in Sri Lanka*, op. cit.

In May 2009, Sri Lanka defeated the LTTE in what is considered 'one of the few instances in modern history in which a terrorist group had been defeated militarily.'[17] The decisive military victory did not, however, stop the international Tamil separatist movement. Since the end of the armed conflict, both the political and ideological struggle demanding Tamil regional autonomy, as well as geopolitical intervention by external powers in Sri Lanka, have intensified.[18] The convergence of these forces pose serious threats to the island's peace, security and survival as a united and independent country.

While *Colonialism in Sri Lanka* provides conclusive interpretations of Sri Lanka's political and economic transformation in the nineteenth century, this chapter cannot make such conclusions on rapidly evolving events in the current period. Current important and contentious political, economic and military agreements already signed or under consideration by the Sri Lankan government are discussed below: the lease on the Hambantota port to the Chinese, the 2015 United Nations Human Rights Council (UNHRC) Resolution and the Acquisition and Cross Services Agreement (ACSO) and Status of Forces Agreement (SOFA) and the Millennium Challenge Corporation (MCC) Compact. Any of these may well be changed or discarded before this book is published. It is assumed that future generations of scholars and activists will continue the research and the dialogue.

Despite the uncertainties, the historical narratives and patterns elaborated in *Colonialism in Sri Lanka* are instructive for understanding the complex political economy of contemporary Sri Lanka. Colonialism involves control of a less powerful country by a powerful country, to exploit resources and increase its power and wealth. Essentially, neocolonialism involves the same factors as classical colonialism: militarism, external expropriation of natural resources, deception and manipulation, collusion with local elites, incitement of ethnic and religious differences and local resistance to external aggression. Colonized people must recognize the history and methodology of exploitation and power in order to prevent continued manipulation, deception and domination and to protect the sovereignty and resources of their countries.

---

17. Committee on Foreign Relations, United States Senate, 'Sri Lanka: Recharting U.S. Strategy After the War', Dec. 7, 2009, p.1.
18. Asoka Bandarage, 'The Enduring Impact of Tamil Separatism', *Georgetown Journal of Asian Affairs*, Vol. 3. No. 2, Spring 2017 https://issuu.com/georgetownsfs/docs/gjaa_vol.3_no.2_online; Asoka Bandarage, 'Towards Peace and Justice in Sri Lanka: An Alternative Perspective', *India Quarterly*, Vol. 68, Issue 2, 2012, pp. 103–118.

Neocolonialism and Geopolitical Rivalry

In the era of classical colonialism, a single external power, Britain, controlled Sri Lanka. Today, several powerful foreign countries, with China on the one side and the U.S., India, Japan, Saudi Arabia, et.al. on the other side, are competing for control over the island, which is strategically located in the heart of the Indian Ocean in the ancient East-West maritime trade route. Sea lanes of the Indian Ocean are considered to be the busiest in the world today, with more than 80% of global seaborne oil trade estimated to be passing through choke points of the Indian Ocean.[19]

Chinese Expansion

During the final stages of the separatist war, in March 2009, 'China blocked Western-led efforts to impose a truce through the United Nations Security Council and continued supplying arms to the Sri Lankan Government,'[20] helping to defeat the LTTE. While the United States and its allies pursued a human rights agenda with regard to Sri Lanka, China expanded its economic interests by providing loans 'without any political strings.'[21] China's soft power diplomacy and economic expansion are transforming the political and economic dynamics of Sri Lanka and the entire Indian Ocean strategic environment.[22]

China has invested in infrastructure projects in Sri Lanka since 2005, when Sri Lanka became a participant in China's Belt and Road Initiative (BRI), formerly known as the One Belt One Road Initiative. BRI incorporates 155 countries and organizations across Asia, Africa, the Middle East, Europe as well as Latin America.[23] The $4 trillion BRI planned network of roads, railways, ports and maritime facilities is considered the 'most ambitious infrastructural investment effort in history.'[24] In January 2017, the Sri

---

19. Asoka Bandarage, 'The Transformation of Sri Lanka and the Indian Ocean', *Huffington Post*, Sep. 27, 2016 https://www.huffpost.com/entry/the-transformation-of-sri-lanka-and-the-indian-ocean_b_57ea9c0ce4b095bd8969ffdf.
20. 'Sri Lanka: Recharting U.S. Strategy After the War', *op. cit.*, p. 13.
21. *Ibid.*, p.13.
22. Sergei DeSilva-Ranasinghe, 'Why the Indian Ocean Matters', *The Diplomat*, March 2, 2011 https://thediplomat.com/2011/03/why-the-indian-ocean-matters/
23. HKTDC, 'The Belt and Road Initiative: Country Profiles', https://beltandroad.hktdc.com/en/country-profiles
24. Xu Qinhua, 'Opinion: The BRI is the most ambitious infrastructure project ever', *CGTN*, Jan 23 2013 https://news.cgtn.com/news/3d3d514e77496a-4d32457a6333566d54/index.html; Belt Road, 'The Belt and Road Initiative - A

Lankan government granted China a 99-year lease of Hambantota Port in the island's southwest, near the East-West sea lanes, in exchange for $1.1 billion in debt relief from China.[25]

Given cordial historical relations with China, Sri Lankans tend to see Chinese involvement in their country as essentially benign. However, the debt-for-equity swap over Hambantota port has raised concerns over the loss of a strategic state asset and the island's economic sovereignty. Rural farming families are resisting offers to sell their ancestral land to expand a Chinese industrial zone around the Hambantota port. Clashes between protesters and Sri Lankan government supporters of the Project have turned violent.[26]

Both India and the U.S. are greatly concerned over China's increasing assertiveness in the Indian Ocean. For example, the recent strengthening of the Chinese Navy with aircraft carriers and nuclear submarines.[27] In August 2018, U.S. Vice President Mike Pence warned that the Hambantota port could become a military base for the Chinese Navy.[28]

Among other Chinese BRI initiatives in Sri Lanka is the massive Colombo International Financial City (known as Port City until August 2016); Sri Lanka's 'new Dubai' in Colombo. Construction began in 2014, with the initial phase reclaiming 269 hectares of land from the Indian Ocean. It is the largest single direct foreign investment in Sri Lankan history. This $1.4 billion project is developed by the state-owned Chinese engineering firm, China Communications Construction Company (CCCC), alleged to be 'one of the most corrupt' companies in China.[29] The Port City is reported

---

Road Map to THE FUTURE' https://beltandroad.hktdc.com/en/belt-and-road-basics

25. Asoka Bandarage, 'Demise of Sri Lanka's Independence', *Critical Asian Studies*, Feb. 10, 2019 https://criticalasianstudies.org/commentary/2019/2/10/the-demise-of-sri-lankas-independence; Janaka Wijyasiri, Nuwanthi Senaratna, 'China's Belt and Road Initiative (BRI) and Sri Lanka', https://archivos.juridicas.unam.mx/www/bjv/libros/12/5550/19.pdf

26. Lauren Frayer, 'In Sri Lanka, China's Building Spree Is Raising Questions About Sovereignty', *National Public Radio (U.S.)*, December 13, 2019 https://www.npr.org/2019/12/13/784084567/in-sri-lanka-chinas-building-spree-is-raising-questions-about-sovereignty; Al Jazeera, ' Protest over Hambantota port deal turns violent' 7 January 2017 https://www.aljazeera.com/news/2017/01/protest-hambantota-port-deal-turns-violent-170107080155843.html

27. Daya Gamage, 'US-India tie strongest military knot on Indo-Pacific: Small nations tagged in', *Asian Tribune*, Dec. 25, 2019 http://asiantribune.com/node/93295

28. 'US Vice President warns Sri Lanka on China funded port', *Colombo Gazette*, October 6, 2018 https://colombogazette.com/2018/10/06/us-vice-president-warns-sri-lanka-on-china-funded-port/

29. Hafsa Sabry, 'Environment Issues Of Port City Not Resolved', *Sunday Leader*, Jan. 7, 2020 http://www.thesundayleader.lk/2016/09/11/environment-issues-

to have 'its own business-friendly tax regime and regulations – and possibly a different legal system to the rest of Sri Lanka.'[30]

Sri Lankan activists are concerned about the power a majority-state-owned Chinese corporation would wield as landlord of Port City. There is apprehension that only a certain class of wealthy people, mostly foreigners, would live in the expensive Financial City while services would be provided by Sri Lankans receiving little economic benefit.[31] There is fear that this represents a new form of neocolonialism that could once again make Sri Lankans second class citizens in their own country.

Additionally, environmental activists have raised alarm that coastal sand excavation for Port City and the dumping of chemicals and other waste will cause significant ecological damage and disrupt the livelihood of those in the fishing and related industries. Environmentalists, religious leaders from different communities, fishermen and others have demanded that the project be halted. [32] Additionally, the Human Rights Commission of Sri Lanka, in considering a petition submitted in 2015 by the Center for Environment and Nature Studies, confirmed Port City to be illegal. However, the new set of environmental regulations the Sri Lankan government is said to have negotiated with the CCCC have not yet been made public.[33]

While Sri Lankan activists are protesting against the environmental and social impact of expanding Chinese projects, the US-India-Japan alliance is seeking to involve Sri Lanka in its challenge against Chinese expansion across Asia. As a result, the island is emerging as a battleground of geopolitical rivalry over the Indian Ocean.

Indian Expansion

Following the end of the separatist war with the LTTE, India has tried to consolidate its economic and strategic position in Sri Lanka. Like China, India is seeking to incorporate other smaller neighbors like the Maldives, Myanmar, Nepal and Bhutan within its sphere of influence. Sri Lanka has

---

of-port-city-not-resolved/
30. Michael Safi, 'Sri Lanka's 'new Dubai': will Chinese-built city suck the life out of Colombo?', *The Guardian*, Aug 2, 2018 https://www.theguardian.com/cities/2018/aug/02/sri-lanka-new-dubai-chinese-city-colombo
31. Bandarage, 'Demise of Sri Lanka's Independence', *op. cit.*
32. *Ibid.*
33. Sabry, 'Environmental Issues of Port City', *op. cit.*; 'Writ petition against Port City fixed for Judgement', *Daily News*, Saturday, December 21, 2019 http://www.dailynews.lk/2019/12/21/law-order/206315/writ-petition-against-port-city-fixed-judgement

old and intimate ties with India, its closest neighbor and the ancestral origin of most Sri Lankans. However, India's controversial political and military involvement during the separatist war, especially its impositions of the 13th Amendment on the Sri Lankan Constitution and the Indian Peace Keeping Force (IPKF) deployment on Sri Lankan soil, have left fear and antipathy towards India.[34]

Concerned that the Hambantota port could become a Chinese military base, India is pursuing control over Sri Lanka's other strategic seaports. In an agreement signed between India and Sri Lanka in April 2017, India sought to develop the British colonial era Oil Tank Farm in the eastern seaport town of Trincomalee through a subsidiary of the Indian Oil Corporation, India's largest commercial enterprise. Petroleum trade unions in Sri Lanka immediately went on strike after the signing of the agreement, charging that Sri Lanka was 'handing over [a] national asset' to India and jeopardizing the country's security and independence. The protest was called off when senior Sri Lankan government officials assured the media that they had not agreed to a legally binding agreement.[35]

There have been numerous historic sea battles among rival powers to control Trincomalee, the second deepest natural harbor in the world. Of great strategic military value, it has been controlled in turn by the Portuguese, Dutch, French, and the English. Its capture by the British in 1782 paved the way for Britain's colonization of the entire island (see page 46). In 1942, while Sri Lanka was still a British colony, Japan attacked Trincomalee harbor, sinking three British warships, one of which was raised in 2018. In addition to its strategic value, Sri Lankan researchers believe the area contains large deposits of thorium and titanium, likely further reason for the current interest of external powers in Trincomalee.[36]

To neutralize growing Chinese influence over Sri Lanka, India and Japan are attempting to construct a container terminal at the port in Colombo, next to a Chinese terminal built as part of China's Belt and Road Initiative. Japan is keen for access to Sri Lankan ports given that it is almost completely dependent on energy supplies transported across the Indian Ocean. The Colombo port is 'one of the busiest ports in South Asia and an important

---

34. Bandarage, *The Separatist Conflict in Sri Lanka, op. cit.*, Chap.6.
35. Meera Srinivasan, 'India, Sri Lanka sign energy pact', *The Hindu*, April 28, 2017 https://www.thehindu.com/news/national/india-sri-lanka-sign-energy-pact/article18261624.ece
36. James Rogers, 'Raised from the Deep', *The Sun*, April 3, 2018 https://www.thesun.co.uk/news/5960646/british-warship-world-war-2-ss-sagaing-sri-lanka-harbour/

trans-shipment hub in the region.'³⁷ A previous plan for a terminal between the state-run Sri Lanka Ports Authority and a consortium of firms from Japan and India broke down after backlash from trade unions protesting against the privatization of Sri Lanka's state assets including those being developed by Chinese firms.³⁸

Indeed, control of the ports was the key issue in the disagreement between President Maithripala Sirisena and Prime Minister Ranil Wickremesinghe that led to Sirisena dismissing Wickremesinghe as PM in November 2018, though he was reinstated on Dec. 16, 2018. Wickremesinghe wanted development of the East Container Terminal of the Colombo Port on the basis of an Indian investment while Sirisena argued that it was vital to keep the seaport 'within the ambit of the Sri Lankan government.'³⁹

Another highly controversial agreement between India and Sri Lanka is the proposed Economic and Technology Cooperation Agreement (ETCA) covering trade in services, especially information technology, shipbuilding and engineering. Although the proposal is yet to be made public, given the asymmetry in size and power of the two countries, it has generated tremendous opposition from professional bodies in Sri Lanka who fear that the inundation of doctors and other professionals from India would displace Sri Lankans in their own country.⁴⁰ It brings to mind the massive import of South Indian Tamil labor for the plantations during British colonial rule, which drastically changed the political economy and ethnic dynamics in Sri Lanka (see Chapter VI).

Further recent Indian encroachment in Sri Lanka includes India's proposal to build a sea bridge and tunnel across the Palk Strait, connecting Dhanushkodi in the Tamil Nadu state of India to Talaimannar in northern Sri Lanka, at a cost of more than $5 billion from the Asian Development Bank.⁴¹ Sri Lanka's territorial integrity, sovereignty and unique Buddhist cultural heritage have been maintained historically through its physical separation from its large and powerful neighbor. There is also concern that a bridge would provide the basis for the long-held Tamil separatist dream of Greater Eelam combining Tamil Nadu and northern Sri Lanka. As with

37. Bandarage, 'Demise of Sri Lanka's Independence', *op. cit.*
38. Dipanjan Roy Chaudhury, 'India still to play role in Lanka Port', *The Times of India,* March 19, 2018 https://economictimes.indiatimes.com/news/international/world-news/india-still-to-play-role-in-lanka-port/articleshow/63359686.cms; *World Socialist Website*, 'Sri Lankan riot police attack Colombo port workers', February 7, 2017 https://www8.wsws.org/en/articles/2017/02/07/port-f07.html
39. Bandarage, 'Demise of Sri Lanka's Independence', *op. cit.*
40. *Ibid.*
41. *Ibid.*

Port City, environmentalists also have strong reservations about such a massive infrastructure project threatening the sensitive marine ecosystem in the Palk Strait. Due to popular resistance in Sri Lanka, the proposal was rejected by the Sri Lankan government in December 2015. However, given India's strategic interest in increasing connectivity in the region and Indian Prime Minister Narendra Modi's 'neighborhood first' policy,[42] the Indo-Lanka bridge could be revived in the future.

U.S. Expansion

As the U.S. and its allies became increasingly critical of Sri Lanka's handling of the separatist war and human rights, Sri Lanka aligned itself with China and other non-Western countries like Myanmar, Iran and Libya. Recognizing the new political realities, and claiming that the United States 'cannot afford to "lose" strategically located Sri Lanka,' the U.S. formulated a new policy.[43] The Committee on Foreign Relations of the United States Senate issued a Report in December 2009 entitled 'Sri Lanka: Recharting U.S. Strategy after the war.' It called for

> ... a new approach that increases U.S. leverage vis-à-vis Sri Lanka by expanding the number of tools at our disposal. A more multifaceted U.S. strategy would capitalize on the economic, trade, and security aspects of the relationship. This approach in turn could catalyze much needed political reforms that will ultimately help secure longer-term U.S. strategic interests in the Indian Ocean ...[44]

U. S. political, economic and military agendas towards Sri Lanka are represented respectively by the 2015 UNHRC Resolution, the MCC Compact and the ACSA and SOFA Agreements.

UNHRC Resolution

In January 2015, a U.S.-backed Sri Lankan government led by President Maithripala Sirisena and Prime Minister Ranil Wickramasinghe replaced

---

42. DW Made for Minds, 'Modi woos Sri Lanka, Maldives as India fends off Chinese influence' *Deutsche Welle*, Sep 6, 2019 https://www.dw.com/en/modi-woos-sri-lanka-maldives-as-india-fends-off-chinese-influence/a-49117835
43. 'Sri Lanka: Recharting U.S. Strategy After the War', *op. cit.*, p. 3.
44. *Ibid.*, p. 3.

the Mahinda Rajapaksa government, which had defeated the LTTE. On Oct. 1, 2015, the United States and the new Sri Lankan government co-sponsored a UNHRC resolution in Geneva,[45] with support from the international Tamil separatist lobby. In effect, the resolution has echoes of the Proclamation of March 2, 1815 – the Kandyan Convention – signed by the British and a faction of the Kandyan aristocracy, that turned Sri Lanka into a British colony (see pages 49-50). Two hundred years later, the UNHRC resolution represents a similar strategy to turn Sri Lanka into a client state where the U.S. and the 'international community' can dictate terms for political reform and internal governance.

The controversial resolution must be understood in the broader context of neocolonialism and external political and economic hegemony. Human rights agendas such as a 'responsibility to protect' can be a basis for U.S. and Western intervention, especially in countries like Sri Lanka where ethno-religious conflicts were deliberately promoted under colonialism.[46] Based on highly contested information[47] the UNHRC Resolution calls for accountability and an international investigation of human rights violations in the final stage of the Sri Lankan armed conflict and international monitoring of transitional justice and reconciliation.[48] The aims of investigating and holding to account the international state and non-state actors who supported LTTE human rights violations throughout the war are conspicuously absent from the U.N. resolution.[49]

Clause 16 of the resolution calls on the Sri Lankan government to devolve power on the basis of the controversial 13th Amendment to the Sri Lankan Constitution. The intention is to facilitate the transition of the country's governance structure from a unitary to a federal state. The clause states that the resolution

> *Welcomes* the commitment of the Government of Sri Lanka to a political settlement by

45. United Nations Human Rights Council, 'Resolution adopted by the Human rights Council on 1 October 2015', Oct. 14, 2015 https://sangam.org/wp-content/uploads/2015/12/UNHRC-Resolution-30.1-October-1-2015.pdf
46. Bandarage, '*The Separatist Conflict in Sri Lanka*', *op. cit.*, Chap. 9.
47. G.H. Pieris, 'Encountering 'Death Counts' in the Final Phase of the Eelam War A review article', *Colombo Telegraph*, Feb.9, 204 https://www.colombotelegraph.com/wp-content/uploads/2014/02/here1.pdf
48. Asoka Bandarage, 'Human Rights, Constitutional Reform and Devolution in Sri Lanka', *Huffington Post*, Nov. 20, 2016 https://www.huffpost.com/entry/human-rights-constitutional-reform-and-devolution_b_58325482e4b08c963e3441a7
49. Shenali Waduge, 'Twenty Questions for UNSG and UN Human Rights Council regarding Sri Lanka', March 17, 2019 https://www.spur.asn.au/2019/03/17/30-questions-for-unsg-un-human-rights-council-regarding-sri-lanka/

taking the necessary constitutional measures, encourages the Government's efforts to fulfil its commitments on the devolution of political authority, which is integral to reconciliation and the full enjoyment of human rights by all members of its population; and also encourages the Government to ensure that all Provincial Councils are able to operate effectively in accordance with the Thirteenth Amendment to the Constitution of Sri Lanka.[50]

If accepted and implemented, constitutional reforms that were proposed under the Sirisena- Wickramasinghe government in response to the UNHRC resolution would allow each province in Sri Lanka to become constitutionally independent with the freedom to secede from a federal union.[51] Although only Tamil politicians claiming to represent the Northern Province have, so far, been clamoring for separation, the proposed federal structure is likely to encourage other politicians to take up secession as well. The political fragmentation and destabilization engendered could result in several warring mini-states, greater foreign political and military intervention and increased external economic control over Sri Lanka's strategic assets and natural resources.

The requirements in the U.S.-sponsored U.N. resolution pressure the Sri Lankan government to set up war crimes courts with foreign judges and an office of missing persons comprised of activist-administrators funded by Western NGOs. This has paved the way for the UNHRC and Western governments and NGOs to interfere in Sri Lanka's judicial and security sectors, moving Sri Lanka in the direction of another failed neocolonial state.[52] For example, a Counter Terrorism Act was proposed in 2019 to replace the existing Prevention of Terrorism Act (1979). While the proposed act is designed to protect ex-LTTE elements living abroad, critics have argued that it could be used to 'suppress student unions, trade unions, media freedoms and the Opposition.'[53]

In the name of political settlement, reconciliation and human rights, the

---

50. UNHRC Resolution, Oct. 1, 2015, *op. cit.*
51. Asoka Bandarage, 'Sovereignty, Territorial Integrity and Constitutional Reform in Sri Lanka', *Huffington Post*, Sep. 27, 2017 https://www.huffpost.com/entry/sovereignty-territorial-integrity-and-constitutional_b_59cbcb67e4b028e6bb0a6746.
52. Asoka Bandarage, 'The Easter Attacks and Geopolitical Conflict in Sri Lanka', *Critical Asian Studies*, May 16, 2019 https://criticalasianstudies.org/commentary/2019/5/16/201912-asoka-bandarage-the-easter-attacks-and-geopolitical-conflict-in-sri-lanka; Bandarage, *The Separatist Conflict in Sri Lanka*, *op. cit.*, Chap. 9.
53. Lasanda Kurukulasuriya, 'IS terror in Sri Lanka: Govt dissimulates, as West consolidates', *The Island*, May 6, 2019 http://www.island.lk/index.php?page_cat=article-details&page=article-details&code_title=203773.

UNHRC resolution has been used to pressure the Sri Lankan government to dismiss or imprison intelligence officers and army personnel. Forty intelligence officers who were involved in the anti-LTTE military effort were put in prison apparently 'without sound evidence against them.'[54] These measures weakened Sri Lankan intelligence and security and have increased the country's dependence on India and the 'international community' to maintain peace and stability.

Political Destabilization

The weakened domestic intelligence and security apparatus helped create the circumstances for the coordinated bomb attacks against Christian Churches and five-star hotels – including the Shangri La Hotel in the Chinese Port City, on Easter Sunday in April 2019. The attacks killed 259 people, convulsing the entire island, and were carried out by local extremist Islamist group *National Towheed Jamaath*, and claimed by Islamic State of Iraq and Syria (ISIS).[55]

Despite warnings by Buddhist monks and moderate Muslim leaders prior to the attacks, action was not taken against the spread of extremist Wahabi ideology or *National Towheed Jamaath*. Conflicts were allowed to develop within the Muslim community, and between the Muslim, Buddhist, Christian and other communities. Major factors contributing to the government's failure to curb the spread of radical Islam include its reliance on Muslim politicians and their loyal voters, and the economic and political power wielded by Saudi Arabia and other external forces.[56]

Immediately following the Easter attacks, the Sri Lankan Prime Minister and the President called for foreign intelligence and cooperation to fight the global Islamic threat. Accordingly, the U.S. sent in teams from both the FBI and the U.S. Navy's Indo-Pacific Command. Developments surrounding

---

54. Kalinga Seneviratne, 'Sri Lanka Easter Sunday Attacks Possibly More Than a Religious Conflict', *In Depth News*, April 25, 2019 https://indepthnews.net/index.php/the-world/asia-pacific/2645-sri-lanka-easter-sunday-attacks-possibly-more-than-a-religious-conflict.
55. Bandarage, 'The Easter Attacks and Geopolitical Conflict in Sri Lanka', *op. cit.*
56. Asoka Bandarage, 'Avoiding 'Religious Violence in Sri Lanka', *Asia Times*, March 29, 2018 https://www.asiatimes.com/2018/03/opinion/avoiding-religious-violence-sri-lanka/; Asoka Bandarage, 'Roots of Sri Lanka Attacks and a Way Forward', Other News, April 24, 2019 https://www.other-news.info/2019/04/roots-of-sri-lanka-attacks-and-a-way-forward/; see also Asoka Bandarage, 'Ethnic and Religious Tension in the World: A Political-Economic Perspective', in *Global Political Economy and the Wealth of Nations*, edited by Philip Anthony O'Hara, London: Routledge, 2004.

the Easter attacks in Sri Lanka raise complex and challenging questions: is political destabilization a justification for U.S. intervention and establishment of military bases in strategic locations like Sri Lanka? Is extremist Wahabi ideology exported by Saudi Arabia, and the creation of Islamic terrorism in Sri Lanka and other countries, such as the Philippines and possibly Thailand, a political tool aiding the geopolitical ambitions of the U.S. and its allies in Asia?[57]

The use of terrorism and destabilization – including the intentional and unintentional creation or inflation of "enemies" – is a well-established feature of imperialism. Although it is difficult to distinguish strategic intent from the uncontrollable and complex forces of global and regional power struggles, their place in the arsenal of imperialism is undeniable. For the powerful, chaos, conflict and war make money, propagate individual and national power, make client states weak and dependent and disable potential challengers to their power.[58]

The Millennium Challenge Corporation Compact

The MCC is a United States government corporation established by the U.S. Congress in November 2002 (then known as the Millennium Challenge Account). It is a component of the George W. Bush administration's U.S. National Security Strategy introduced after the terrorist attacks of Sep. 11, 2001, linking economic development with defense and diplomacy. The MCC states its mission as 'reducing poverty through growth,' and chooses countries to receive funding based on MCC criteria on economic freedom, good governance and social investment. Eligible countries must apply to the MCC with specific proposals showing 'ownership' of the compacts they propose.[59]

Critical researchers, however, claim that there is little deviation of

---

57. *Ibid.*; Tony Cartalucci, 'Sri Lanka: How Saudi-Backed Terror Targeted China's Allies', *Mint Press News*, May 3, 2019 https://www.mintpressnews.com/sri-lanka-how-saudi-backed-terror-isis-targeted-chinas-allies/258170/; Peter Koenig, 'Sri Lanka, Candidate for a New NATO Base?' *CounterCurrents*, May 1, 2019 https://countercurrents.org/2019/05/sri-lanka-candidate-for-a-new-nato-base-peter-koenig
58. Naomi Klein, *The Shock Doctrine: The Rise of Disaster Capitalism*, New York, Picador, 2007.
59. Millennium Challenge Corporation https://www.mcc.gov/; Compact Development Guidance https://www.mcc.gov/resources/story/story-cdg-chapter-8-guidelines-for-developing-project-proposals

country proposals from the MCC 'blueprint': '*every single country* independently identified agribusiness, rural entrepreneurial development, and transport infrastructure as their key priorities.' They argue that the MCC's primary commitment is not to poverty reduction but to 'reshape the legal, institutional, infrastructural and financial contexts of poorer countries to better suit U.S. economic interests.' Thus, the MCC is seen as an instrument of the 'new imperialism' pursuing 'economic hegemony through the extension and ever-deepening penetration of neoliberal capitalism.'[60]

The Sri Lankan MCC Compact

Sri Lanka was selected to develop a MCC Compact in December 2016 and the MCC Board approved a five year compact for Sri Lanka on April 25, 2019.[61] A November 2017 'Constraints Analysis' completed by the Center for International Development at Harvard University for the compact identified policy uncertainty; poor transportation and inadequate access to land, especially 'the difficulty of the private sector in accessing state owned land for commercial purposes' as the major constraints to 'private investment and entrepreneurship' in Sri Lanka. According to the Harvard 'Constraints Analysis,'

> Access to land is a binding constraint to growth and economic transformation as well. The state reportedly owns approximately 80 percent of the land in the country and it is held by multiple ministries. Government coordination is poor and the process of acquiring rights to develop land is slow and unclear, resulting in an inability of the government to meet the demand for land needed for new private sector investment, including for export-oriented FDI [Foreign Direct Investment] …, problems with land use and titling are prevalent throughout the country and affect manufacturing, agriculture, construction, residential and commercial development, and tourism. Restrictions on land parcel size, the absence of land titles, and longstanding laws affecting rural land use all reduce agricultural productivity and rural well-being.[62]

60. Emma Mawdsley, 'The millennium challenge account: Neo-liberalism, poverty and security', *Review of International Political Economy*, Vol. 14, Issue 3, 2007. https://www.tandfonline.com/doi/abs/10.1080/09692290701395742; Susanne Soederberg,'American empire and 'excluded states': the millennium challenge account and the shift to pre-emptive development', *Third World Quarterly*, Vol. 25, Issue 2, 2004.
61. Millennium Challenge Corporation, Congressional Notification, April 25, 2019 https://assets.mcc.gov/content/uploads/cn-042519-sri-lanka-intent-to-sign.pdf
62. Millennium Challenge Corporation, Sri Lanka Constraints Analysis, 2017 https://assets.mcc.gov/content/uploads/constraints-analysis-sri-lanka.pdf

The MCC Compact would offer $480 million to Sri Lanka to undertake transportation and land management.⁶³ Article 1 of the draft agreement of the compact states that the objective of the Transport Project is to 'facilitate the flow of passengers and goods between the central region of the country and ports and markets' and the objective of The Land Project is to 'increase the availability of information on private land and under-utilized State Lands in order to increase land market activity.'⁶⁴

MCC funding is to be used to change Sri Lanka's land policy through the creation of a state land inventory based on a 'Parcel Fabric Map,' the conversion of paper deeds into electronic titles and a 'computerized mass appraisal system' for land valuation. MCC Funding would support 'the creation of a digital folio for each land parcel that includes the legal records on land transactions and a linkage to spatial data that identifies the location of each land parcel where possible.'⁶⁵ The goal is to speed up land privatization and commoditization by providing investors, including foreign corporations, easy digital access.

According to the Draft Agreement between the MCC and Sri Lanka's Ministry of Finance, MCC Funding would be used to provide titles to state owned land held by individuals, mostly smallholder farmers, thereby facilitating the sale of their lands to any buyer.

> ... [C]onversion of State Lands to the private domain, creating a marketable and bankable title to this land in the name of the land holder. The Government shall register the absolute land grants in the title registration system, allowing the use of land as collateral for loans and the free transfer of this land without excessive government restrictions. The Land Special Provisions Act (LSPA) is expected to define the process the Government shall use for this conversion of land rights. The availability of MCC Funding for this Activity is dependent on the enactment of the LSPA...⁶⁶

Colonial Land Expropriation

The MCC Compact brings to mind the early stage of capitalist

---

63. Millennium Challenge Cooperation' Highlights of MCC Compact', July 20 2019 https://lk.usembassy.gov/highlights-of-mcc-compact/
64. Millennium Challenge Compact, 'Draft Agreement Between the United States of America and the Democratic Socialist Republic of Sri Lanka', Nov. 5, 2019 http://treasury.gov.lk/documents/10181/519892/MCC+Rescan1.pdf/a5d28fac-22cc-4139-a88e-a37311bafb6b; MCC Sri Lanka Compact, https://www.mcc.gov/where-we-work/program/sri-lanka-compact
65. Millennium Challenge Compact, 'Draft Agreement, *op. cit.*, Annex 1, p. 29.
66. *Ibid.*, p. 30.

development in Sri Lanka, when the British colonial state introduced legislation, infrastructure and other measures to establish the plantation economy (see pages 236-254).[67] Those measures opened up the previously isolated Kandyan Highlands, heralding a fundamental social and economic transformation that benefitted the colonizers and a small stratum of local entrepreneurs and administrators.[68] The infamous 'Ordinance No. 12 of 1840: to prevent Encroachments upon Crown Lands' (see Appendix 4) was introduced to provide the juridical and administrative framework to expropriate land from local people who had customary rights but could not prove 'ownership' and titles to their land as required by the British. The Ordinance stated:

> Whereas divers persons, without any probable claim or pretence of title, have taken possession of lands in this Colony belonging to Her Majesty, and it is necessary that provision be made for the prevention of such encroachments.[69]

Another controversial ordinance, No. 1 of 1897, the so-called 'Waste Lands Ordinance,' overlooked the traditional sustainable cultivation practice of letting land in fallow to maintain the natural productivity. Seeking expropriation and profits and calling uncultivated lands 'waste land', the ordinance introduced a land-grab policy decreeing that '... any land or lands... in respect of which no claim is made... be deemed the property of the Crown and may be dealt with on account of the Crown.'[70]

British colonial policymakers and their latter-day apologists have argued that colonial policies helped advance peasant proprietorship by giving land titles to peasants that previously lacked them. However, as demonstrated in *Colonialism in Sri Lanka*, the long-term results were, in fact, great confusion and conflict over land rights, large scale dispossession from ancestral land and impoverishment of the Kandyan peasantry. Subsistence agriculture and local self-sufficiency were undermined, and the natural environment was disrupted.

Presently, U.S. and Sri Lankan proponents of the MCC Agreement are claiming that the distribution of one million deeds granting outright ownership to individuals holding state land under the compact is a poverty alleviation measure. The draft agreement also states that its Land Project 'is

---

67. Bandarage, *Colonialism in Sri Lanka, op.cit.*, pp.236–254.
68. 'The Establishment and Consolidation of the Plantation Economy of Sri Lanka', *Bulletin of Concerned Asian Scholars*, Vol. 14, no. 3, 1982, pp. 2–22.
69. Bandarage, *Colonialism in Sri Lanka*, op. cit., Appendix 4.
70. Ordinance No. 1 of 1897, 'An Ordinance Relating to Claims to Forest, Chena, Waste, and Unoccupied Lands', *The Legislative Enactments of Ceylon, Vol. II, A.D. 1889–1909*, Colombo: Government Printer, 1923, pp. 384–394.

Neocolonialism in Sri Lanka, 2020   377

unlikely to have adverse environmental and social impacts.'[71] However, the Movement for Land and Agricultural Reform (MONLAR), the National Joint Committee and many other Sri Lankan and diaspora organizations recognize a neocolonial agenda for a massive modern-day land grab, displacement and peasant pauperization:

> ... [L]arge multinational companies have made small time farmers bankrupt and are buying off their agricultural land ... By giving desperate people, an asset that they can sell, the government has ensured that these lands will be sold off.[72]

The MCC Compact includes plans to draw land survey maps and create a digital database of 3.6 million parcels of state-owned land, a task that it proposes to contract for 15 years to Trimble Inc., a U.S.-based geological information and mapping firm. Survey Department trade unions have gone on strike opposing this move, which they see as a threat to both their employment and national security, as well as a wasteful expenditure.[73] Again, these plans mirror the early stage of colonial plantation development, when a single British 'planter-official class' determined rules on land ownership, surveyed and accessed land from the colonial state, employed cheap labor and developed highly profitable plantation companies producing exports for the global market.

The Sri Lanka Physical Plan (2018–2050) and a projected Physical Spatial Structure Map for 2050, upon which the Compact is based, have also raised alarm.[74] There is concern that the proposed 'economic corridor' and

71. 'One Million Land Deeds to be Distributed to the People in Future', *Sunday Times (Sri Lanka)*, 19 March 2019. http://www.sundaytimes.lk/article/1077974/10000-land-deeds-to-be-distributed-to-the-people-in-future-min-karunathilaka; Millennium Challenge Compact, 'Draft Agreement, op. cit., Annex 1, p. 32.
72. Rathindra Kuruwita, 'MONLAR: Land given to the poor will end up with Multinationals', *The Island*, July 8, 2019, http://www.island.lk/index.php?page_cat=article-details&page=article-details&code_title=207148; 'Expats in Los Angeles campaigning against controversial U.S. contracts', *Daily FT*, 1 Aug. 2019. http://www.ft.lk/business/Expats-in-Los-Angeles-campaigning-against-controversial-US-contracts/34-683112; 'The land belongs to the people and all living beings; thou art only the guardian of it ...', *Sunday Times (Sri Lanka)*, June 2, 2019 www.sundaytimes.lk/190602/sunday-times-2/the-land-belongs-to-the-people-and-all-living-beings-thou-art-only-the-guardian-of-it-351773.html
73. 'State surveyors strike to oppose plans to hand over contract to U.S. firm', *Sunday Times (Sri Lanka)*, Dec. 17, 2017 http://www.sundaytimes.lk/171217/news/state-surveyors-strike-to-oppose-plans-to-hand-over-contract-to-us-firm-273640.html
74. Sri Lanka National Physical Planning Department, National Physical Planning Policy and the Plan, 2017–2050. https://drive.google.com/file/d/1TBgPtGflXOJm

highway from Trincomalee to Colombo, reported to cover 1.2 million acres, could 'splinter' Sri Lanka into two separate entities. Given the relationship of the MCC to U.S. National Security Strategy there is fear that the Compact could facilitate greater U.S. control undermining Sri Lanka's sovereignty unity and territorial integrity.[75]

The MCC-Sri Lanka Draft Agreement

In response to persistent public demands for transparency, a draft MCC Agreement was at last published on the Sri Lankan Ministry of Finance website on Nov. 5, 2019, just 11 days before presidential elections. It reveals a range of highly questionable clauses subordinating Sri Lanka to U.S. authority that impinge on the rights of Sri Lankan people and the independence of the country.[76] Only a few of the clauses can be mentioned here.

According to **Annex 1**, a new company called MCA-Sri Lanka is to be established under the Sri Lanka Companies Act of 2007 after the compact is signed. This would be the Sri Lankan government's 'primary agent responsible for exercising the Government's right and obligations to oversee, manage, and implement the Program and Projects.'[77] In other words, the democratically elected Sri Lankan government is asked to voluntarily abdicate its powers and responsibilities to a yet-to-be created private company, thereby contravening its constitutional mandate to protect the country's sovereignty, territory, security and the well-being of its people.

- Article 2.7 (b) states that 'the [Sri Lankan] Government shall ensure that MCC funding is not used for any purpose that would violate United States law or policy, as specified in this Compact or as further notified to the Government in writing including but not limited to . . . any activity that is likely to cause a substantial loss of United States jobs or a substantial displacement of United States

Tn_vVkAmGtJU9AiMckp0/view
75. Neville Ladduwahetty, 'The Millennium Challenge Corporation Compact with Sri Lanka', *The Island*, June 2, 2019 http://www.island.lk/index.php?page_cat=article-details&page=article-details&code_title=205231; See also, 'Rise Up Sri Lanka, Rise Up', *Lankaweb*, Feb 26, 2019. http://www.lankaweb.com/news/items/2019/02/26/rise-up-sri-lanka-rise-up-destroy-the-enemy-as-it-pivots-to-lanka-to-build-an-electrified-eelam-border-wall-and-make-the-island-its-military-hub-in-the-indo-pacific-part-1/
76. Shenali Waduge, 'MCC Agreement & Clauses – how detrimental are they to Sri Lanka?', *Lankaweb*, January 11, 2020 http://www.lankaweb.com/news/items/2020/01/11/mcc-agreement-clauses-how-detrimental-are-they-to-sri-lanka/comment-page-1/
77. Millennium Challenge Compact, 'Draft Agreement, *op. cit.*, Annex 1, p. 34.

production.'⁷⁸ Does this really mean that Sri Lanka is bound to adhere to any future demands made by the MCC including paying for loss of U.S. jobs and U.S. production?
- Article 3.9 states that 'The [Sri Lankan] Government grants to MCC a perpetual, irrevocable, royalty-free, worldwide, fully-paid, assignable right and license to practice or have practiced on its behalf... any portion or portions of Intellectual Property as MCC sees fit in any medium, now known or hereafter developed, for any purpose whatsoever.'⁷⁹ Does this mean that the MCC can claim intellectual property rights over any information or intellectual goods that Sri Lankans create in any area where the MCC Compact operates?
- Article 5.1 states that either party may terminate the compact without cause by giving 30 days' notice, but it specifies that only the MCC can terminate the compact and withdraw funding in whole, or in part, when it wants.⁸⁰
- Article 5.4 states that 'If the Government fails to pay any amount under this Compact or the Program Implementation Agreement when due... the Government shall pay interest on such past due amount.'⁸¹ This contradicts the statement made by the U.S. ambassador to Sri Lanka in June 2019 that the $480 million is a 'gift, not a loan, a gift from the people of the United States.'⁸²
- Article 6.4 states that the compact will be governed by international law and Section 6.8 states that the 'MCC and the United States Government or any current or former officer or employee of MCC or the United States Government shall be immune from the jurisdiction of all courts and tribunals of Sri Lanka for any claim or loss arising out of activities or omissions under this Compact.'⁸³ This affirms that the compact and all its activities will be above Sri Lankan law and Sri Lankan citizens would not be able to seek legal assistance from their country's judicial system. Moreover, Sri Lanka could be taken to international court if it backs out of the compact or contra-

78. *Ibid.*, p. 7.
79. *Ibid.*, p. 12.
80. *Ibid.*, pp. 13–14.
81. *Ibid.*, p. 15.
82. U.S. Embassy in Sri Lanka, 'Remarks of Ambassador Alaina B. Teplitz at 3rd AGM of the Ceylon Chamber of Commerce Sri Lanka-USA Business Council', June 30, 2019. https://lk.usembassy.gov/remarks-of-ambassador-alaina-b-teplitz-at-3rd-agm-of-the-ceylon-chamber-of-commerce-sri-lanka-usa-business-council/
83. *Ibid.*, p. 16.

venes any of its clauses.
- Article 7.1 requires the Compact 'to be submitted to and enacted by the Parliament of Sri Lanka,'[84] which would mean that once it becomes law, it would be exceedingly difficult to make changes to land and other polices that it introduces.

Popular Resistance to the MCC Compact

There is a parallel between the MCC Compact and the UNHRC Resolution in that they both manipulate the Sri Lankan government to turn against itself, giving up its power and responsibilities over the most vital sectors of the state, the resources of the country and the rights of its people. The struggle over the MCC Compact brings to mind the long history of popular resistance against colonial land policies in Sri Lanka. The rebellion of 1848 (see pages 316-320), for example, was a nationalist revolt against imperialist policies such as the Ordinance of 1840, which helped expropriate peasant lands to develop the plantation economy. Today, Sri Lankan activist groups including the National Joint Committee and Sri Lanka Diaspora are demanding that the Sri Lankan government withdraw from the MCC Compact. They are encouraged by the decision of the Sri Lanka Supreme Court on the State Land Special Provisions Act (LSPA) in July 2019, referring the Act to the Provincial Councils, as it would impact passage of land provisions envisaged in the MCC Compact.[85] As shown earlier, the LSPA is vital for the MCC Compact for conversion of land rights, i.e. land privatization and commoditization in Sri Lanka.[86]

Anticipating the electoral defeat of the U.S.-backed Sri Lankan government and in a hurry to seal the MCC Compact, the U.S. Embassy in Sri Lanka issued a statement on Nov. 6, 2019 stating that 'the United States anticipates working toward grant signing and parliamentary approval with the Government of Sri Lanka after Nov. 16, 2019.'[87] On Nov. 6, 2019, the

---

84. Millennium Challenge Compact, 'Draft Agreement', *op. cit.*, Annex 1, p.17.
85. 'Expats in Los Angeles campaigning against controversial U.S. contracts', *op. cit.*; 'State Land s Special Provisions Bill to Acquire 1.2 million acres of land for economic corridor?', *News First*, July 31, 2019. https://www.newsfirst.lk/2019/07/31/state-lands-special-provisions-bill-to-acquire-1-2-mn-acres-of-land-for-economic-corridor/
86. Millennium Challenge Compact, 'Draft Agreement', *op. cit.*, p. 30.
87. U.S. Embassy Sri Lanka, 'Statement on Next Steps for the Millennium Challenge Cooperation Development Assistance Grant', Nov. 6, 2019. https://lk.usembassy.gov/u-s-embassy-statement-on-next-steps-for-the-millennium-challenge-corporation-development-assistance-grant/; See also, Malinda

Government Medical Officers Association also filed a Fundamental Rights Petition seeking to stay all approvals and decisions in respect of the compact as well as the military pacts (ACSA and SOFA, discussed below) with the United States. The petitioners state that if signed or executed, the compact would violate the fundamental tenet of sovereignty of the country, which the constitution expressly upholds to be 'Free, Sovereign and Independent.'[88]

As in the era of classical colonialism, Buddhist monks have also been at the forefront of nationalist resistance against external powers attempting to subordinate the country. A Buddhist monk, the Venerable Ududumbara Kashyapa, for example, began a fast-unto-death on Nov. 5, 2019 against the MCC Compact, and only abandoned it once the government decided not to sign it before the November 2019 presidential election.[89]

Presidential candidate Gotabaya Rajapaksa promised to discard the MCC Compact during his 2019 election campaign. Once in office, his government appointed a cabinet subcommittee to study the compact and has informed the Supreme Court that the compact would 'be revisited and reviewed.'[90] However, the charges that the compact is a tool of new imperialism and neoliberal capitalism, and the demand to discard it, are escalating.

U.S. Military Expansion

U.S. geostrategic interest in Sri Lanka must be seen in relation to broader U.S. initiatives challenging China's military efforts in the Asian region. Among these initiatives is the 2013 'Pivot to Asia' introduced by the Obama administration, aiming to strategically rebalance U.S. interests from Europe and the Middle East toward Asia.[91] Another is the Asia Reassurance

Seneviratne, 'A Political Reading of the U.S. Ambassador's Angst', *Daily Mirror*, 1 Aug. 2019. http://www.dailymirror.lk/opinion/A-POLITICAL-READING-OF-THE-US--AMBASSADOR'S-ANGST/172-172114
88. Lakmal Sooriyagoda, 'GMOA files FR against MCC, ACSA, SOFA', *Daily News*, Nov 6, 2019. http://www.dailynews.lk/2019/11/06/law-order/202146/gmoa-files-fr-against-mcc-acsa-sofa
89. Rohana R. Wasala, 'MCC: Empowerment or Entrapment?', *The Island*, Nov. 10, 2019. http://www.island.lk/index.php?page_cat=article-details&page=article-details&code_title=213581
90. 'Govt. adopting double standards on MCC: JVP', *Daily Mirror*, 16 Dec. 2019. http://www.dailymirror.lk/breaking_news/Govt-adopting-double-standards-on-MCC-JVP/108-179692
91. Matt Shiavenza,'What Exactly Does It Mean That the U.S. Is Pivoting to Asia?', *The Atlantic*, April 15, 2013. https://www.theatlantic.com/china/archive/2013/04/what-exactly-does-it-mean-that-the-us-is-pivoting-to-asia/274936

Initiative Act (ARIA), signed into law by President Donald Trump on Dec. 31, 2018 to increase engagement of the U.S. in the 'Indo-Pacific', which the U.S. defines as the vast strategic region ranging from the western coast of India to the west coast of the United States. The ARIA seeks to strengthen support, including arms sales, for U.S. allies in the Indo-Pacific.[92] The Report on the 2019 U.S. Indo-Pacific Strategy makes it clear that the U.S. will rely specifically on five partners – India, Sri Lanka, the Maldives, Bangladesh, and Nepal – to address shared challenges in the Indian Ocean region.[93]

The United States and India (currently the largest importer of weapons in the world) have agreed to draw the smaller regional states – Sri Lanka, the Maldives, Nepal, Afghanistan and Pakistan – into their alliance. Defense analysts point out that following strengthened military and defense ties and understanding between the United States and India in December 2019, smaller states like Sri Lanka that have already gone into military pacts – such as ACSA and SOFA – may be unable to move away from them.[94]

Military engagement with the strategically located Sri Lanka is considered vital to achieving U.S. objectives in the Indo-Pacific region. In August 2016 the first joint operation between the U.S. and the Sri Lankan military took place in Jaffna with participation of Tamil National Alliance (TNA) politicians at the launching.[95] Since 2016, U.S. military ships have visited Colombo and the U.S. Seventh Fleet vessels and the aircraft carrier USS John C. Stennis have visited the port of Trincomalee. In December 2018, the U.S. Navy announced the setting up of a 'logistic hub' in Sri Lanka to secure support, supplies and services at sea.[96] This announcement came amidst the political chaos in the country resulting from the president's dismissal of the prime minister. Between Jan. 24 and 29, 2019, the Bandaranaike International Airport in Sri Lanka was reportedly 'used for U.S. military planes to bring in supplies, and for aircraft aboard John C.

92. John Xenakis, 'World View: Trump Signs Asia Reassurance Initiative Act (ARIA) Focusing U.S. Military on China', Breitbart.com, Jan.10, 2019. https://www.breitbart.com/national-security/2019/01/10/world-view-trump-signs-asia-reassurance-initiative-act-aria-focusing-u-s-military-on-china/
93. Ankit Panda, 'The 2019 U.S. Indo-Pacific Strategy Report: Who's It For?', June 11, 2019 https://thediplomat.com/2019/06/the-2019-us-indo-pacific-strategy-report-whos-it-for/
94. Gamage, 'US-India tie strongest military knot', *op. cit.*
95. K. Nesan, Tamil Nationalists hail U.S. 'Operation Pacific Angel' in Sri Lanka,' *World Socialist WebSite*, Sept 1 2016. https://www.wsws.org/en/articles/2016/09/01/tami-s01.html
96. Shamindra Ferdinando, 'US sets up logistic hub in Sri Lanka amidst political chaos,' *The Island*, December 18, 2018. http://www.island.lk/index.php?page_cat=article-details&page=article-details&code_title=196293

Stennis to fly in, load, and ferry them back,' in possible violation of Sri Lanka's sovereignty.[97]

Military engagement with Sri Lanka has become even more urgent for the United States since the International Court of Justice ruled in February 2019 that U.S. occupation of the Indian Ocean Chagos Islands, the site of the Diego Garcia military base, is illegal, and that the islands be handed back to Mauritius within six months. The base was established after Britain, the 'illegal colonial owner' of Chagos, forcibly removed its inhabitants between 1968 and 1973. Diego Garcia is one of the United States' most important and secretive military bases[98] and has been central in launching invasions in Iraq and Afghanistan and flying missions across Asia, including over the South China Sea. If the islands go back to Mauritius and the Chagossians are allowed to return, the U.S. will require an alternative base, which could be Sri Lanka.[99] Two US–Sri Lanka bilateral agreements, the Acquisition and Cross Services Agreement and the Status of Forces Agreement, appear headed in this direction.

Acquisition and Cross Services Agreement (ACSA)

Expanding on an earlier 2007 ACSA, the U.S. Defense Department and the Sri Lankan Ministry of Defense entered into a new ACSA on Aug. 4, 2017. This 83-page military pact is considered a 'part of the grand strategy of a united military front between the U.S. and India in the Indo-Pacific.[100] It does not have a specified expiry date and provides open-ended access for U.S. military vessels to use Sri Lanka's airports and seaports. It is designed to facilitate reciprocal logistic support between the U.S. and Sri Lanka for use 'during combined exercises ... or for unforeseen circumstances or exigencies in which one of the parties may have a need for Logistic Support,

---

97. Lasanda Kurukulasuriya, 'Duplicity and Doublespeak About The U.S. Military Logistics Hub in Sri Lanka', Feb 4, 2019. http://dbsjeyaraj.com/dbsj/archives/62829
98. David Vine, 'The Truth About the U.S. Military Base at Diego Garcia' *TruthDig*, Jun 15, 2015 https://www.truthdig.com/articles/the-truth-about-the-u-s-military-base-at-diego-garcia/
99. Asoka Bandarage, 'US Military Presence and Popular Resistance in Sri Lanka' *Covert Action Magazine*, Aug 12, 2019 https://covertactionmagazine.com/index.php/2019/08/12/u-s-military-presence-and-popular-resistance-in-sri-lanka/; see also, Kamalika Pieris, 'Yahapalana and the United States of America (Part 7)', *LankaWeb*, July 30, 2019. http://www.lankaweb.com/news/items/2019/07/30/yahapalana-and-the-united-states-of-america-part-7/
100. Gamage, 'US-India tie strongest military knot', *op. cit.*

Supplies and Services.'[101] Reportedly, it allows, 'every single security or military apparatus in the United States access to Sri Lanka,' making Sri Lanka the 'main supply hub for U.S. armed forces in the Indo-Pacific region.'[102] Analysts argue that if fully implemented, 'it will effectively undermine the Chinese share of geopolitical control in Sri Lanka, by way of military presence in the country.'[103]

Sri Lanka's Cabinet approved ACSA 2017 hastily, under pressure from the U.S. and without careful examination or discussion. It was approved without thorough study by Sri Lankan armed forces commanders and officials, who have expressed serious reservations over some of its provisions. Similarly, ACSA was not presented to the Sri Lankan Parliament[104] and the renewed ACSA has still not been made public despite requests for transparency by opposition political parties, the President of the Bar Association of Sri Lanka (BASL), among others. The then Joint Opposition in Parliament, the JVP and *Yuthukama* civil society organization 'strongly protested against the signing of . . . the ACSA.'[105]

Status of Forces Agreement (SOFA)

The United States has requested that the Sri Lankan Government accept a new SOFA, expanding on the original signed in 1995. On June 30, 2019, The Sunday Times published the new draft SOFA governing U.S. military personnel in Sri Lanka,[106] revealing that it would provide full diplomatic immunity, not only to any member of U.S. armed forces, but also to its contractors and employees, operating in Sri Lanka. SOFA, as drafted, would allow U.S. army personnel the right to:

- Be in any part of Sri Lanka, without restriction;

---

101. 'Embattled President fighting on all fronts', *Sunday Times*, May 5, 2019. http://www.sundaytimes.lk/190505/columns/embattled-president-fighting-on-all-fronts-348051.html
102. *Ibid.*
103. K. M. Wasantha Bandara, 'Indo-American aggression for Geopolitical Control in Sri Lanka', *The Island*, June 12, 2019 http://www.island.lk/index.php?page_cat=article-details&page=article-details&code_title=205742
104. 'Inside story of how Sri Lanka fell into the ACSA-SOFA trap', *Sunday Times*, June 7, 2019 http://www.sundaytimes.lk/190707/columns/inside-story-of-how-sri-lanka-fell-into-the-acsa-sofa-trap-357287.html
105. Shamindra Ferdinando, 'ACSA, SOFA and 2019 prez poll', *The Island*, June 4, 2019 http://island.lk/index.php?page_cat=article-details&page=article-details&code_title=205331
106. 'Sri Lanka's sovereignty and the US', June 30, 2019 http://www.sundaytimes.lk/190630/columns/sri-lankas-sovereignty-and-the-us-355926.html

- Carry arms in uniform;
- Only need U.S. identification to enter and leave Sri Lanka; i.e. would not need passports nor visas;
- Exemption from Sri Lankan law, and not liable for criminal offenses in the country;
- Exemption from all Sri Lankan taxes; and
- Exemption from customs checking at ports of entry and exit to the island.

The U.S. Department of Defense would also be allowed to operate its own telecommunication systems in Sri Lanka without cost to the U.S. Government.[107] With ACSA already signed and SOFA pending, U.S. security companies, notably Sallyport Global, have been running ads to recruit U.S. citizens with 'active TOP secret clearance' to work for U.S. defense operations in Sri Lanka.[108]

There is increasing outrage over, and opposition to, the blatant violation of Sri Lanka's independence and sovereignty that SOFA, ACSA and the MCC Compact represent. It comes from all strata and sectors of Sri Lankan society; for example, the Chief of Defense Staff, the Chamber of Commerce, and the President of the BASL, have all warned of the dangers SOFA poses to national interests. The Sri Lanka Podujana Peramuna political party and the newly formed STOP USA Campaign are organizing media briefings and mass rallies calling for transparency and accountability in making international agreements.

In response to widespread opposition, the U.S. has 'rebranded' SOFA as a Visiting Forces Agreement (VFA). Engaged in a social media campaign to protect the agreements, the U.S. Ambassador Alaina Teplitz stated that the U.S. has 'no intention to build a military base or establish a permanent military presence in Sri Lanka.'[109] However, as Sri Lankan President's Counsel (and former Ambassador to Iran) M.M. Zuhair warns,

> With SOFA in hand, the Americans do not require a military 'base' in Sri Lanka ..., because the whole island will be a U.S. controlled super State operating above the Sri

---

107. *Ibid.*; see also, Lasanda Kurukulasuriya, SOFA with U.S. threatens Lanka's sovereignty', *The Island*, May 26, 2019 http://island.lk/index.php?page_cat=article-details&page=article-details&code_title=204868
108. 'US security firms seek Cleared American Guards for Lanka', *Sunday Times*, July 7, 2019 http://www.sundaytimes.lk/190707/columns/us-security-firms-seek-cleared-american-guards-for-lanka-357298.html
109. 'No intention to build a military base in SL: US', *Daily Mirror*, July 18 2019 http://www.dailymirror.lk/breaking_news/No-intention-to-build-a-military-base-in-SL:-US/108-171333

Lankan laws and State...[110]

At the time of writing (Jan. 10, 2020), there is great concern in Sri Lanka that the country could get unnecessarily pulled into the conflict now brewing between the U.S. and Iran to the detriment of Sri Lanka.[111] While there is antipathy towards Chinese and Indian intervention to grab local resources and control of ports and infrastructure, given the U.S. military record, there is a much greater fear of U.S. military intervention and interference in local governance.

The Way Forward

Gotabaya Rajapaksa, Sri Lanka's former Defense Secretary who led the armed victory over the LTTE in 2009, was elected as the President of Sri Lanka on Nov. 16, 2019. His massive victory was a response to growing concern over national security and widespread opposition to external interventions including the 99-year lease of the Hambantota port to China, ACSA, SOFA, the MCC Compact, the UNHRC Resolution, and other measures undertaken by the former U.S.-backed Sri Lankan government. In the eyes of most Sri Lankans, the defeat of that government, and the departure of the U.S. from the UNHRC on June 19, 2018 have invalidated the U.S.-sponsored 2015 Resolution against Sri Lanka.[112]

The newly elected president and his administration are under pressure from both Sri Lanka's nationalist forces that brought him into office and external powers, especially India and the United States, who want to continue pursuing their own geostrategic and economic interests in Sri Lanka[113]. Local activists are continuing their demands to discard the compact, military agreements and UNCR Resolution, and also renegotiate

---

110. 'Ex-top AG's Dept officer warns of U.S. Trojan Horse', *Ceylon-Ananda.com*, July 28, 2019. https://ceylon-ananda.com/ex-top-ags-dept-officer-warns-of-us-trojan-horse/
111. Shenali D Waduge, 'IRAN-US conflict: Is Sri Lanka unnecessarily caught in the middle?', *Lankaweb*, Jan 8, 2020. http://www.lankaweb.com/news/items/2020/01/08/iran-us-conflict-is-sri-lanka-unnecessarily-caught-in-the-middle/
112. Imogen Foulkes, 'Why did the US leave the UN Human Rights Council?', *BBC News*, June 20, 2018 https://www.bbc.com/news/world-us-canada-44552304.
113. K. Ratnayake, 'US official delivers Trump's threatening message to Sri Lankan president', *World Socialist Website*, 20 Jan. 2020, https://www.wsws.org/en/articles/2020/01/20/slusj20.html?fbclid=IwAR21F297H6V5roICwJZ6HpTYubWeW1j8JG Fkgz8yetes4nDqM8mCydR1VtI

better terms for Sri Lanka on the lease of the Hambantota port and environmental regulation of the Chinese Port City. The demands against Indian projects, the Oil Tank Farm in Trincomalee, ECTA and the Indo-Lanka bridge also persist. Sri Lankan people recognize that these interventions together would thoroughly subordinate their country and turn the government into a mere shell of a state, leaving the island wide open for economic and military exploitation.

It is not easy for a small country like Sri Lanka to forge a foreign policy which uses its geostrategic position to its own advantage. While maintaining cordial relationships with the external powers, the principles of sovereignty, democracy and environmental sustainability must continue to be upheld. In light of the dangers posed by the recent bilateral agreements and the UNHRC Resolution, Sri Lanka has to join with other small countries in Asia and Africa to renew the policy of non-alignment that it championed valiantly during the Cold War.[114] It is also necessary to call on India to do the same. India, herself the victim of two centuries of British colonialism[115], needs to take on an enlightened leadership role in the region, independent of the China-U.S. geopolitical rivalry. In fact, the term 'non-alignment' was coined by Indian Prime Minister Nehru during a speech he made in 1954 in Colombo.[116]

Sri Lanka's National Joint Committee expresses the urgent call for the island's non-alignment in a June 2019 letter written to the then Sri Lankan Prime Minister regarding the MCC Agreement:

> [We are] committed to protect and preserve the unity and territorial integrity of our nation. We believe that Sri Lanka should follow a foreign policy of nonalignment. Due to the fact that Sri Lanka is strategically located in the Indian Ocean the country needs to remain nonaligned and refrain from getting involved in the geopolitical confrontation that is developing between America and China, through agreements that would enable these countries to gain a foothold in Sri Lanka.[117]

---

114. 'Sri Lanka – Non-Alignment Movement Summit, 1976, 6 Part video footage', http://lankapura.com/2008/08/sri-lanka-non-alignment-movement-summit-1976/
115. Dipanjan Roy Chaudhury, 'British Looted $45 trillion from India in today's value: Jaishankar', *The Economic Times*, Oct. 3, 2019 https://economictimes.indiatimes.com/news/politics-and-nation/british-looted-45-trillion-from-india-in-todays-value jaishankar/articleshow/71426353.cms
116. Government of India, *History and Evolution of Non-Aligned Movement, op. cit.*
117. 'The land belongs to the people and all living beings; thou art only the guardian of it ...', *Sunday Times*, June 2, 2019 http://www.sundaytimes.lk/190602/sunday-times-2/the-land-belongs-to-the-people-and-all-living-beings-thou-art-only-the-guardian-of-it-351773.html

Indeed, it is urgent for all countries to uphold the principles of non-alignment and resist the polarization and militarization tearing the world apart. These principles – sovereignty and territorial integrity of states; independence from great power block influences and rivalries; the struggles against imperialism, colonialism and neocolonialism, foreign occupation and domination; disarmament; non-interference into the internal affairs of states; rejection of the use or threat of use of force in international relations; the restructuring of the international economic system; international cooperation on an equal footing – are more urgently needed than ever.[118]

The historical trajectory elaborated in *Colonialism in Sri Lanka* – geopolitical rivalry, external aggression and internal resistance to that aggression – continues with great vigor in this current complex period. The tremendous suffering and destruction caused by this narrative calls for a shift in human relations from domination to partnership, from the exploitative and violent path of colonialism and neocolonialism to one of peace, justice and ecology.[119] This is the transformational challenge facing both Sri Lanka and the world at this decisive time.

---

118. Government of India, *History and Evolution of Non-Aligned Movement*, op. cit.
119. Asoka Bandarage, *Women, Population and Global Crisis: A Political-Economic Analysis*, London: Zed Books, 1997; Asoka Bandarage, *Sustainability and Wellbeing: The Middle Path to Environment, Society and the Economy*, London: Palgrave Macmillan, 2013.

Appendices

APPENDIX I

SOURCES

Given the multiplicity of primary and secondary sources used in this study and the obvious biases of some of these, a note of explanation about the sources is in order.

Primary Sources

The primary sources used are British documents – official and nonofficial. In using these sources, the underlying racial and class biases of the writers have to be constantly confronted. Many of the British who compiled data on Kandyan society were colonial officials who were also directly or indirectly identified with the interests of colonial policy and British capital.

Furthermore, they depended almost exclusively on the native aristocracy and the Buddhist clergy for information on indigenous social institutions. For example, Simon Sawers, who held the position of Revenue and Judicial Commissioner in Kandy between 1815 and 1827 and who authored *The Digest of Kandyan Law* (1826), derived his information from a committee of Kandyan chiefs specifically assembled for that purpose. Their evidence was then systematically arranged by a Buddhist monk of the powerful Malwatte monastery.[1] The evidence of the aristocracy and the clergy by and large favored their own feudal class interests over that of the peasantry who had no voice in the governance of the country in precolonial or colonial times.

However, more objective sources, and sources which are openly critical of the official and planter points of view are not totally absent. *An Historical Relation of Ceylon* (1681), the first book written on Ceylon in English while Ceylon was not yet a British colony, is relatively free of such partisan political and economic interests.[2] Its author, Robert Knox, lived in various parts of the Kandyan kingdom for nearly twenty years between 1660 and 1680. His superb firsthand account of the organization and functioning of the precolonial Kandyan society remains our best source to date.

1. As noted in Hayley, *A Treatise*, p. 16.
2. Robert Knox, *An Historical Relation of Ceylon*.

Appendix 1

As for the British colonial period, the various tracts and pamphlets of the members of the liberal Cobden Club of England, and of local European critics of the colonial government, provide a perspective which is different from the dominant official and planter points of view. The opinions of individuals expressing specific group interests were quoted frequently in this book so as to let the actors speak for themselves and to allow the reader to arrive at his/her own conclusions. However, where necessary, judgment has been made on those quoted passages.

Classification of Sources Used: Official and Nonofficial

The demarcation between the official and the nonofficial sources is quite hazy. A number of private sources such as the *Ceylon Directory* of A. M. and J. Ferguson and newspapers such as *The Colombo Observer* were considered semiofficial sources by the colonial state and widely used for administrative purposes.[3] There was, in fact, little separation between political and economic and official and nonofficial spheres of activity, particularly in the early years of European rule.

Official Sources

The bulk of the sources on nineteenth-century Ceylon consisted of official documents emanating from the colonial bureaucracy. Historian Michael Roberts has related the different official documents to the various levels of the operation of the colonial state.[4]

At the top is the 'macro' or *London-Colombo* level which constituted the area of policy discussion and policy formulation between the Colonial Office in London and the local headquarters in Colombo, notably the colonial governor's office. Among the official sources pertaining to this level and widely used in this study are the *Despatches* exchanged between the Secretary of State for the Colonies in London and the successive British governors of Ceylon. These are filed in the Colonial Office CO 54 series and are invaluable for understanding the policy discussions that preceded policy formulation and assessments that followed their implementation. These Despatches con-

---

3. *The Ceylon Directory* was published annually by A. M. and J. Ferguson in Colombo.
4. Michael Roberts, "A Classification for the Sources on the History of British Ceylon as a Basis for Discussion on their Merits and Demerits," *Ceylon Studies Seminar*, No. 3, 1968/69 Series, p. 1.

tain confidential correspondences between the local governors and the Secretaries of State for the Colonies in London, as well as letters from individuals, officials, and organizations appended to the Despatches sent to London by the governors.

The British Parliamentary Papers, pertaining to colonial Ceylon, specifically the volumes containing the evidence given before the British Parliamentary Committee of Inquiry into the 1848 rebellion, contain a wealth of information on the early British period. In these reports the opinions of the planters and the officials are candidly expressed.

Collections of official correspondence, some of them in print such as "The Private Correspondence of the Third Earl Grey [Secretary of State for the Colonies, 1846–1852] and Viscount Torrington [Governor of Ceylon, 1847–1850]," edited by historian K. M. de Silva, also fall into the same genre as the official Despatches.[5]

The second level of the colonial state operation identified by Michael Roberts is the *Colombo-Provincial* level.[6] The correspondence between the colonial governors based in the capital – Colombo – and Government Agents and Assistant Government Agents in the provinces pertain to this level. The various *Legislative Enactments* promulgated by the colonial state to be implemented by the provincial administrators can be included here. A large number of the letters and minutes from the provincial officials to the governor or colonial secretary in Colombo were appended to the Despatches sent by the governor to London (referred to above), and are to be found in the CO 54 series as well.

Sessional Papers of the Ceylon Legislative Council are in print and available from the early 1860s on. They contain lengthy discussions on a number of important issues such as dry grain cultivation, grain taxes, etc. They also contain conflicting views on these issues presented by members of the various legislative committees.

The Administration Reports of Government Agents and Assistant Government Agents in the plantation districts have been extremely useful for our study. There are annual reports describing the various aspects of the colonial administration and the conditions of the people in specific administrative districts. Provincial officials were keen on impressing their superiors and were not always accurate in their reports of the actual conditions in the provinces. They also depended on the hierarchy of native headmen for much of their information on grassroots level activities. This added further bias into the administrative reports of the provincial officials. Not infrequently, the personalities of the provincial officials and their personal political views

5. K. M. de Silva (ed.), *Letters on Ceylon 1846–1850*.
6. Roberts, "A Classification," p. 1.

Appendix 1

greatly shaped the thrust of their reporting. For example, the Government Agent of Kandy, J. F. Dickson, went to great lengths to point out the efficiency and rigor with which taxes were being collected under his administration, while C. J. R. Le Mesurier, the Assistant Government Agent in Nuwara Eliya, on the other hand, took pain to describe the plight that harsh taxation imposed on the Kandyan peasantry.[7]

The next category of official sources pertain to a still lower level of the administrative network, i.e., what Roberts has identified as the *Provincial (Kachcheri)-Village* level.[8] Manuals and gazetteers of provincial officials such as those by Le Mesurier and A. C. Lawrie, which give detailed information on individual villages in the Central Highlands, are relevant here.[9] The Volumes of material assembled by the Colebrooke-Cameron Commission of Inquiry contain a formidable mass of information on the social and economic life of the early decades of British rule. These manuscripts are filed in the Colonial Office CO 416 Series.

Statistics

Statistical information on land sales, tax revenue, imports and exports, etc., are scattered throughout the official sources, particularly in the various Sessional Papers and Administration Reports.[10] However, as many colonial officials and critics of the government have pointed out, official statistics, especially those pertaining to village agriculture, were notoriously unreliable.[11] The *Blue Books*, which contain official statistics compiled by the colonial state on various topics, as colonial officials themselves often admitted, contained many gross errors. The agricultural statistics for 1877 were found to be "so defective and failed to convey any correct impression of the state of agricultural process and were therefore omitted" from the *Blue Book*.[12] In 1890, the Government Agent for the Sabaragamuwa District wrote that the returns sent in annually to the *Blue Book* were inaccurate and misleading

---

7. *AR 1883*, "Report of the Central Province," by John F. Dickson, Part 1, p. 6A; *AR 1886*, "Report on the Nuwara Eliya District," by C. J. R. Le Mesurier, p. 37A.
8. Roberts, "A Classification," p. 1.
9. C. J. R. Le Mesurier, *Manual of the Nuwara Eliya District of the Central Province Ceylon* (Colombo: 1893); A. C. Lawrie, *A Gazetteer of the Central Province of Ceylon*.
10. Roberts, "A Classification," p. 5.
11. Speculum, pseud. [G. Wall], *Ceylon*, pp. 82–83.
12. Ceylon Government, *Ceylon Blue Book 1877*, p. 6.

and that the government needed to give more attention to the collection and the preparation of agricultural statistics.[13] The statistics on plantation agriculture are generally more reliable and systematic than the data on village agriculture due to the personal interest taken by planters in maintaining reliable information, and the partiality of the colonial state towards the concerns of plantation agriculture.

Censuses of Ceylon published from 1871 on, give fairly reliable demographic estimates. *The Ceylon Directory* compiled by A. M. Ferguson and successors, although a semiofficial publication, was widely used by the colonial administration itself as it contained good information, particularly on the plantation sector.

Nonofficial Sources

Newspapers such as *The Colombo Observer, The Ceylon Examiner* and journals such as *The Tropical Agriculturist* and the *Journal of the Royal Asiatic Society* (Ceylon Branch), contain valuable information. However, they generally express the 'planter-official' view.

In the category of nonofficial sources can also be included the biographies, autobiographies, and travelogues of the British and influential natives.[14] Among these, the works of Knox (noted above), D'Oyly's *A Sketch of the Constitution of the Kandyan Kingdom* (1835), Davy's *An Account of the Interior of Ceylon* (1821), and P. D. Millie's *Thirty Years Ago* (1878) are among the most outstanding and the most valuable.[15]

Tracts and pamphlets pertaining to controversial issues in nineteenth-century Ceylon such as those written by Ludovici, George Wall, and Salmon on the effects of the paddy tax on peasant subsistence have also been extremely useful as alternative sources of nonofficial information.[16]

---

13. *AR 1890*, "Report for Sabaragamuwa," p. J2.
14. For the correspondences of a leading native capitalist, Jeronis Pieris, see Roberts, *Facets of Modern Ceylon History*.
15. John D'Oyly, *A Sketch of the Constitution of the Kandyan Kingdom*, ed. by L. J. B. Turner (Dehiwala: Tissara Prakasakayo, 1975); John Davy, *An Account of the Interior of Ceylon and of its Inhabitants* (London: Longman, Hurst, Rees, Orme and Brown, 1821); P. D. Millie, *Thirty Years Ago*.
16. Ludovici, *Rice Cultivation;* Speculum, *Ceylon;* Salmon, *The Grain Tax in Ceylon.*

APPENDIX 2
KANDYAN CASTE HIERARCHY:
TABLES OF CASTE RANKING GIVEN BY SEVERAL EUROPEANS

TABLE 1: Robert Knox (1681)

>Handuru, noblemen (of two grades, unspecified).
>Smiths (goldsmiths, blacksmiths, carpenters, painters).
>Kuruvē-ättö, elephant-men (reckond equal with smiths).
>Barbers.
>Potters.
>Radava, washers.
>Hangarammu, jaggery-makers (i.e., hakuru, vahumpura).
>Paduvō.
>Weavers, (also astrologers, drummers, dancers).
>Kidiyō, basketmakers.
>Kinnaru, Makers of fine mats.
>Rodi.

TABLE 2: John Davy (1821)

1. Vaisaya-vamsa.

    (1) Goyivamse, cultivators (includes vaddas).
    (2) Nilamakkara (Patti), shepherds.

2. Sudra-vamsa.

    (1) Karāvē, fishermen.
    (2) Chandos (i.e., durave), toddy-drawers.
    (3) Acāri, smiths, etc.
    (4) Hannali, tailors.
    (5) Badahala-baddā, potters.
    (6) Ambättavō, barbers.
    (7) Radā-baddā, washermen.
    (8) Hāli, Chalias, (i.e., halagama).
    (9) Hakuru, jaggery-makers.
    (10) Hunubadda, Chunam or lime burners.
    (11) Pannayō, grass cutters.
    (12) Villi-durayi (Nuvarakalaviya District).
    (13) Dodda Vaddās.
    (14) Padu (Padu, iron-smelters, executioners).
    (15) Berava-baddā or Mahabadda, tom-tom beaters.

(16) Handi (furnished royal stores with baskets and winnows).
(17) Pallaru.
(18) Oli.
(19) Radayō.
(20) Pali (washermen of inferior castes below Potters).
(21) Kinnarabadda.

3. Outcasts

(1) Gattaru.
(2) Rodi.

TABLE 3: John Armour (1842)

(Service castes only, i.e., cultivator caste excluded).

1. Navandanna (artificers).
   Badal (goldsmiths).
   Vadu (carpenters).
   Galvadu (stonemasons).
   Sittara (painters).
   Ācari (blacksmiths).
   Lōkuru (brassfounders).
2. Karāva (fishermen).
   Goda Karāva (hunters).
   Goda Karayo (bullock-carters).
   Karava (fishermen).
3. Durāva (toddy tappers).
4. Radā (washermen).
5. Hannāli (tailors).
6. Badahäla (potters).
7. Ämbätta (barbers).
8. Viyanno (weavers).
9. Hakuru (jaggory [crude sugar] makers).
10. Hanu (lime burners).
11. Panna (grass cutters).
12. Beravā (drummers).
13. Padu (beggars).
14. Gahala (scavengers, executioners).
15. Oli (dancers).
16. Paliyo (inferior washermen).

Sources: Tables 1 and 2 from Ralph Pieris, *Sinhalese Social Organization: The Kandyan Period.* Colombo: Ceylon University Press Board, 1956, p. 191.

Table 3 from H. L. Seneviratne, *Rituals of the Kandyan State.* Cambridge: Cambridge University Press, 1978, pp. 10–11.

APPENDIX 3
Proclamation of 2nd March, 1815.

At a Convention held on the Second day of March, in the year of Christ 1815, and the Cingalese year 1736, at the Palace in the city of Kandy, between His Excellency Lieut.-General Robert Brownrigg, Governor and Commander-in-Chief in and over the British settlements and territories in the Island of Ceylon, acting in the name and on behalf of His Majesty George the Third King, and His Royal Highness George, Prince of Wales, Regent, of the United Kingdom of Great Britain and Ireland, on the one part, and the Adigars, Dessaves, and other principal chiefs of the Kandyan provinces on behalf of the inhabitants, and in presence of the Mohottales, Coraals, Vidaans, and other subordinate headmen from the several provinces, and of the people then and there assembled on the other part, it is agreed and established as follows:

1 That the cruelties and oppressions of the Malabar ruler, in the arbitrary and unjust infliction of bodily tortures and the pains of death without trial, and sometimes without an accusation or the possibility of a crime, and in the general contempt and contravention of all civil rights, have become flagrant, enormous, and intolerable, the acts and maxims of his government being equally and entirely devoid of that justice which should secure the safety of his subjects, and of that good faith which might obtain a beneficial intercourse with the neighbouring settlements.

2 That the Rajah Sri Wikreme Rajah Sinha, by the habitual violation of the chief and most sacred duties of a Sovereign, has forfeited all claims to that title or the powers annexed to the same, and is declared fallen and deposed from the office of king; his family and relatives, whether in the ascending, descending, or collateral line, and whether by affinity or blood, are also for ever excluded from the throne, and all claim and title of the Malabar race to the dominion of the Kandyan provinces is abolished and extinguished.

3 That all male persons being or pretending to be relations of the late Rajah Sri Wikreme Rajah Sinha, either by affinity or blood, and whether in the ascending, descending, or collateral line, are hereby declared enemies to the government of the Kandyan provinces, and excluded and prohibited from

entering those provinces on any pretence whatever, without a written permission for that purpose by the authority of the British Government, under the pains and penalties of martial law, which is hereby declared to be in force for that purpose; and all male persons of the Malabar caste now expelled from the said provinces are, under the same penalties, prohibited from returning, except with the permission before mentioned.

4 The dominion of the Kandyan provinces is vested in the Sovereign of the British Empire, and to be exercised through the Governors or Lieutenant-Governors of Ceylon for the time being, and their accredited Agents, saving to the Adigars, Dessaves, Mohottales, Coraals, Vidaans, and all other chief and subordinate native headmen, lawfully appointed by authority of the British Government, the rights, privileges, and powers of their respective offices, and to all classes of the people the safety of their persons and property, with their civil rights and immunities, according to the laws, institutions, and customs established and in force amongst them.

5 The religion of Boodho, professed by the chiefs and inhabitants of these provinces, is declared inviolable, and its rites, ministers, and places of worship are to be maintained and protected.

6 Every species of bodily torture, and all mutilation of limb, member, or organ, are prohibited and abolished.

10 Provided always that the operation of the several preceding clauses shall not be contravened by the provisions of any temporary or partial proclamation published during the advance of the army; which provisions, in so far as incompatible with the said preceding articles, are hereby repealed.

11 The royal dues and revenues of the Kandyan provinces are to be managed and collected for His Majesty's use and the support of the provincial establishment, according to lawful custom, and under the direction and superintendence of the accredited Agent or Agents of the British Government.

12 His Excellency the Governor will adopt provisionally, and recommend to the confirmation of His Royal Highness the Prince Regent, in the name and on behalf of His Majesty, such dispositions in favour of the trade of these provinces as may facilitate the export of their products, and improve the returns, whether in money or in salt, cloths, or other commodities useful and desirable to the inhabitants of the Kandyan country.

Source: *A Revised Edition of the Legislative Enactments of Ceylon*, 2 Volumes (Colombo: Government Printer, 1923), vol. 1, pp. 59–60.

APPENDIX 4

No. 12 of 1840.

To prevent Encroachments upon Crown Lands.

Whereas divers persons, without any probable claim or pretence of title, have taken possession of lands in this Colony belonging to Her Majesty, and it is necessary that provision be made for the prevention of such encroachments:

1 It shall and may be lawful for the District Court, upon information supported by affidavit charging any person or persons with having, without probable claim or pretence of title, entered upon or taken possession of any land which belongs to Her Majesty, Her heirs, or successors, to issue its summons for the appearance before it of the party or parties alleged to have so illegally entered upon or taken possession of such land, and of any other person or persons whom it may be necessary or proper to examine as a witness or witnesses on the hearing of any such information; and the said District Court shall proceed in a summary way in the presence of the parties, or in case of wilful absence of any person against whom any such information shall have been laid, then in his absence to hear and determine such information ; and in case on the hearing thereof it shall be made to appear by the examination of the said party or parties, or other sufficient evidence to the satisfaction of such District Court, that the said party or parties against whom such information shall have been laid hath or have entered upon or taken possession of the land mentioned or referred to in such information without any probable claim or pretence of title, and that such party or parties hath or have not cultivated, planted, or otherwise improved and held uninterrupted possession of such land for the period of *five* years or upwards, then and not otherwise, such District Court is hereby authorized and required to make an order directing such party or parties to deliver up to Her Majesty, Her heirs, or successors, peaceable possession of such land, together with all crops growing thereon, and all buildings and other immovable property upon and affixed to the said land, and to pay the costs of such information; and in case the party or parties against whom any such order shall have been made shall not, within fourteen days after service thereof, deliver up possession of the said land and premises, pursuant to the said order, or shall afterwards make or cause to be made any further encroachments upon the said land or premises, contrary to such order or in evasion thereof, then and in such case it shall be lawful for such District Court to adjudge such party or parties to pay a fine not exceeding five pounds, or to be imprisoned, with or without

hard labour, for any time not exceeding fourteen days, and to make a further order for the immediate delivery over of the possession of such land and premises to Her Majesty, Her heirs, or successors; and the District Court shall thereupon cause possession thereof to be delivered to Her Majesty, Her heirs, or successors, accordingly.

2 Any person against whom any such order as aforesaid may have been made may, notwithstanding such order, proceed by the ordinary course of law to recover possession of such lands, in case he shall be able to establish a title thereto; and may also in such case recover a reasonable compensation for the damage he may have sustained by reason of his having been compelled to deliver up possession of the said premises, and in like manner, in case of the dismissal of any such information, the part having preferred the same may proceed according to the ordinary course of law, as if no such information had been preferred.

3 Provided always that in case any such information shall be dismissed, it shall be lawful for the said District Court, if it shall think fit, to order payment by Government to the party or parties against whom the same may have been preferred of such sum as the said court may consider to be the amount of costs fairly incurred by such party or parties by reason of such information so dismissed.

4 The forms of the proceedings to be observed on lodging complaints, in issuing summonses, in the examination of the party or parties, in the citation of witnesses, in the making orders, and generally for the complete carrying into execution the powers hereby vested in the said District Court, shall be according to such general rules of practice as the Judges of the Supreme Court may now or hereafter frame thereon.

5 All cinnamon lands which shall have been uninterruptedly possessed by Government for a period of thirty years and upwards, by peeling the cinnamon growing thereon shall be held and deemed to be the property of the Crown.

6 All forest, waste, unoccupied, or uncultivated lands shall be presumed to be the property of the Crown until the contrary thereof be proved, and all chenas and other lands which can be only cultivated after intervals of several years shall, if the same be situate within the districts formerly comprised in the Kandyan provinces (wherein no thombo registers have been heretofore established), be deemed to belong to the Crown and not to be the property of any private person claiming the same against the Crown, except upon proof only by such person of a sannas or grant for the same, together with satisfactory evidence as to the limits and boundaries thereof, or of such customary taxes, dues, or services having been rendered within twenty years for the same as have been rendered within such period for similar lands being

Appendix 4 401

the property of private proprietors in the same districts; and in all other districts in this Colony such chena and other lands which can only be cultivated after intervals of several years shall be deemed to be forest or waste lands within the meaning of this clause.

7 It shall be lawful for any person in the possession of land to make application in writing to the Government Agent of the Province in which such land is situate for a certificate of the Crown having no claim to such land, which application shall contain a full description of the property, together with a survey thereof made by or under the authority of the Surveyor-General, and shall contain a declaration by the applicant, stating the nature of his right, or the manner in which he acquired possession; and if the Government Agent shall, upon investigation, be satisfied that the Crown has no claim to such land, he shall, with the consent of the Governor, grant a certificate to that effect to such applicant, and a copy of such certificate shall be previously entered in a book to be kept in the office of the Government Agent for that purpose, and such certificate, or any copy from such entry thereof, attested by the Government Agent, shall be received by any court as a good and valid title to such land against any right, title, or claim of the Crown thereto existing at the date of such certificate.

8 Whenever any person shall have, without any grant or title from Government, taken possession of and cultivated, planted, or otherwise improved any land belonging to Government, and shall have held uninterrupted possession thereof for not less than ten nor more than thirty years, such person shall be entitled to a grant from Government of such land, on payment by him or her of half the improved value of the said land, unless Government shall require the same for public purposes, or for the use of Her Majesty, Her hiers, and successors, when such person shall be liable only to be ejected from such land on being paid by Government the half of the improved value thereof, and the full value of any buildings that may have been erected thereon.

9 (Repealed by No. 9 of 1841.)

10 All and every encroachment on any public road, street, or highway, by building or other erection, or by enclosure, planting, or otherwise, shall, on information thereof, be immediately abated and removed by judgment, order, or decree of the District Court thereon, and the party or parties offending found liable in damages besides the costs of suit.

11 Any principal or other headman who shall wilfully or knowingly refuse or neglect to give every information within his knowledge or power immediately to the Government Agent of his province, or some Assistant

Agent thereof, of any encroachment made by any person or persons upon any land belonging to Her Majesty, Her heirs, or successors, and situated in the district or village of such headman, shall be liable for every such offence to a fine not exceeding ten pounds.

27th October, 1840.

Source: *A Revised Edition of the Legislative Enactments of Ceylon*, 2 volumes (Colombo: Government Printer, 1923), vol. 1, pp. 120–23.

References

This bibliography is classified under the following headings:
(1) Unpublished Official Material, (2) Published Official Material, (3) Books, (4) Articles, (5) Unpublished Theses and Manuscripts, and (6) Newspapers.

1. Unpublished Official Material
Public Record Office, London (PRO).
Commission of Eastern Enquiry in Ceylon, 1829–1831. C. O. 416 Series, vols. 1–32.
Despatches of the Secretaries of State for the Colonies, the Governors of Ceylon, and other official correspondence. C. O. 54 Series, Colonial Office Papers.
2. Published Official Material
Ceylon Government. *Administration Reports*. Colombo, 1867-annual volumes.
───. *Blue Books*. Colombo, 1862-annual volumes.
───. *Census of Ceylon*. Colombo, 1871, 1881, 1891, 1901.
───. *A Revised Edition of the Legislative Enactments of Ceylon (1707–1909)*, 2 vol. Colombo, 1923.
───. *Papers on the Custom of Polyandry as Practiced in Ceylon*. Colombo, 1898.
Ceylon Legislative Council, *Sessional Papers*. Colombo, 1855-annual volumes.
de Silva, K. M., ed. *Letters on Ceylon, 1846–1850: The Administration of Viscount Torrington and the "Rebellion" of 1848: The Private Correspondence of the Third Earl Grey and Viscount Torrington*. Kandy: K. V. G. de Silva and Sons, 1965.
Ferguson, A. M. and John Ferguson. *The Ceylon Directory*. Colombo: 1859-annual volumes.
Great Britain. *Parliamentary Papers*. London.
Lawrie, A. C. *A Gazeteer of the Central Province of Ceylon (excluding Walapane)*. 2 vols. Colombo: Government Printer, 1896, 1898.
Le Mesurier, C. J. R. *Manual of the Nuwara Eliya District of the Central Province of Ceylon*. Colombo: Government Printer, 1893.
Mendis, G. C., ed. *The Colebrooke-Cameron Papers*. 2 vols. Oxford: Oxford University Press, 1956.
Salmon, C. S. *The Grain Tax in Ceylon: Extracts from Government Administration Reports for the Years 1885, 1886, 1887, 1888 and 1889*. London: Cassell, 1890.
3. Books
Abeysinghe, Ariya. *Ancient Land Tenure to Modern Land Reform in Sri Lanka*. 2 vols. Colombo: Centre for Society and Religion, 1978.
Amin, Samir. *Unequal Development: An Essay on the Social Formation of Peripheral Capitalism*. New York: Monthly Review Press, 1976.
Arasaratnam, S. *Ceylon*. Englewood Cliff, N. J.: Prentice-Hall, 1964.
Armour, John. *Grammar of the Kandyan Law*. Colombo, Examiner Press, 1861.
Arrighi, Emmanuel. *Unequal Exchange: A Study of the Imperialism of Trade*. New York: Monthly Review Press, 1972.
Ashby, Eric. *Universities: British, Indian, African: A Study in the Ecology of Higher Education*. Cambridge: Harvard University Press, 1966.
Balasingham, S. V. *The Administration of Sri Henry Ward, Governor of Ceylon, 1855–60*. Dehiwala-Ceylon: Tissara Prakasakayo, 1968.
Baran, Paul A. *The Political Economy of Growth*. New York: Monthly Review Press, 1968.

Barnet, Richard J. and Ronald E. Müller. *Global Reach: The Power of Multinational Corporations.* New York: Simon and Schuster, 1974.
Bastiampillai, B. *The Administration of Sir William Gregory, Governor of Ceylon, 1872-77.* Dehiwala-Ceylon: Tissara Prakasakayo, 1968.
Beckford, George L. *Presistent Poverty: Underdevelopment in Plantation Economies of the Third World.* New York: Oxford University Press, 1972.
Bendix, Reinhard. *Max Weber: An Intellectual Portrait.* New York: Doubleday, 1962.
Bernstein, Henry, ed. *Underdevelopment and Development: The Third World Today.* Harmondsworth: Penguin Books, 1978.
Blauner, Robert, *Racial Oppression in America.* New York: Harper and Row, 1972.
Böeke, J. H. *Economics and Economic Policy of Dual Societies.* New York: Institute of Pacific Relations, 1953.
Boserup, Ester. *Woman's Role in Economic Development.* New York: St. Martin's Press, 1970.
Brett, E. A. *Colonialism and Underdevelopment in East Africa: The Politics of Economic Change.* New York: NOK Publishers, 1973.
Brookfield, Harold. *Interdependent Development.* Pittsburgh: University of Pittsburgh Press, 1975.
Cardoso, Fernando Henrique and Enzo Faletto. *Dependency and Development in Latin America.* Berekeley: University of California Press, 1979.
Clammer, John, ed. *The New Economic Anthropology.* New York: St. Martin's Press, 1978.
Cockcroft, James D., André Gunder Frank and Dale L. Johnson. *Dependence and Underdevelopment: Latin America's Political Economy.* New York: Doubleday, 1972.
Codrington, H. W. *Ancient Land Tenure and Revenue in Ceylon.* Colombo: Ceylon Government Press, 1938.
Corea, Gamani. *The Instability of an Export Economy.* Colombo: Marga Institute, 1975.
Courtenay, P. P. *Plantation Agriculture.* London: G. Bell, 1965.
Davy, John. *An Account of the Interior of Ceylon and Its Inhabitants.* London: Longman, Hurst, Rees, Orme and Brown, 1821.
de Silva, Colvin R. *Ceylon Under the British Occupation.* 2 vols. Colombo: Colombo Apothecaries, 1953.
de Silva, K. M. *Social Policy and Missionary Organizations in Ceylon, 1840-1855.* London: Longmans, 1965.
―――, ed. *History of Ceylon,* vol. 3. Colombo: University of Ceylon Press Board, 1973.
Dobb, Maurice. *Studies in the Development of Capitalism.* New York: International Publishers, 1963.
D'Oyly, John. *A Sketch of the Constitution of the Kandyan Kingdom.* Ed. by L. J. B. Turner. Dehiwala-Ceylon: Tissara Prakasakayo, 1975.
Durkheim, Emile. *The Division of Labor in Society.* New York: Free Press, 1964.
Eisenstadt, S. *Modernisation, Protest and Change.* Englewood Cliffs, N. J.: Prentice-Hall, 1966.
Evans, Peter. *Dependent Development: The Alliance of Multinational, State and Local Capital in Brazil.* Princeton, N. J.: Princeton University Press, 1979.
Fanon, Frantz. *Black Skin, White Masks.* Trans. by Charles Markmann. New York: Grove Press, 1967.
Ferguson, John. *Ceylon in the Jubilee Year.* Colombo, 1887.
Fieldhouse, D. K. *Economics and Empire.* London: Weidenfeld and Nicolson, 1973.
Forrest, D. M. *A Hundred Years of Ceylon Tea.* London: Chatto and Windus, 1967.
Frank, André Gunder. *Lumpen-Bourgeoisie and Lumpen-Development: Dependency and Politics in Latin America.* New York: Monthly Review Press, 1972.
―――. *Capitalism and Underdevelopment in Latin America: Historical Studies of Chile and Brazil.* New York: Monthly Review Press, 1969.

References

Frykenberg, Robert Eric, ed. *Land Control and Social Structure in Indian History.* Madison: University of Wisconsin Press, 1969.
Furnivall, J. S. *Colonial Policy and Practice: A Comparative Study of Burma and Netherlands India.* Cambridge: Cambridge University Press, 1948.
Geertz, Clifford. *Agricultural Involution: The Process of Ecological Change in Indonesia.* Berkeley: University of California Press, 1963.
Gerth, Hans H. and C. Wright Mills, eds. *From Max Weber: Essays in Sociology.* New York: Oxford University Press, 1958.
Goldthorpe. J. E. *The Sociology of the Third World: Disparity and Involvement.* New York: Cambridge University Press, 1975.
Gordon, Milton M. *Assimilation in American Life: The Role of Race, Religion, and National Origin.* New York: Oxford University Press, 1964.
Gough, Kathleen and Hari Sharma, eds. *Imperialism and Revolution in South Asia.* New York: Monthly Review Press, 1973.
Hayley, F. A. *A Treatise on the Laws and Customs of the Sinhalese.* Colombo: H. W. Cave, 1923.
Hechter, Michael. *Internal Colonialism: The Celtic Fringe in British National Development 1536-1966.* Berkeley: University of California Press, 1975.
Hilton, Rodney, ed. *The Transition from Feudalism to Capitalism.* London: New Left Books, 1976.
Hindess, Barry and Paul Q. Hirst. *Pre-Capitalist Modes of Production.* Routledge, Kegan and Paul, 1975.
Hoselitz, Bert F. *Sociological Factors in Economic Development.* Glencoe, Ill.: Free Press, 1960.
Hulugalle, H. A. J. *British Governors of Ceylon.* Colombo: Associated Newspapers of Ceylon, 1963.
Jayawardena, Visakha Kumari. *The Rise of the Labor Movement in Ceylon.* Durham, N. C.: Duke University Press, 1972.
Jus, pseud. [George Wall]. *The Grain Tax or Native Distress in Ceylon: Its Cause and Remedy.* Colombo: Ceylon Independent, 1889.
Kannangara, P. D. *The History of the Ceylon Civil Service, 1802-1833.* Dehiwala-Ceylon: Tissara Publishers, 1966.
Kay, Geoffrey. *Development and Underdevelopment: A Marxist Analysis.* London: Macmillan Press, 1975.
Kloosterboer, W. *Involuntary Labour Since the Abolition of Slavery.* Leiden: E. J. Brill, 1960.
Knox, Robert, *An Historical Relation of Ceylon*, published as *The Ceylon Historical Journal*, vol. 6 (July 1956-April 1957).
Kumar, Dharma. *Land and Caste in South India: Agricultural Labor in the Madras Presidency during the Nineteenth Century.* Cambridge: Cambridge University Press, 1965.
Levin, Jonathan V. *The Export Economies: Their Pattern of Development in Historical Perspective.* Cambridge: Harvard University Press, 1960.
Lewis, W. Arthur. *The Evolution of the International Economic Order.* Princeton, N. J.: Princeton University Press, 1973.
─── , ed. *Tropical Development, 1880-1913.* London: George Allen and Unwin, 1970.
Leys, Colin. *Underdevelopment in Kenya: The Political Economy of Neo-Colonialism.* Berkeley: University of California Press, 1975.
Ludovici, Leopold. *Rice Cultivation: Its Past History and Present Condition.* Colombo, J. Maitland and Co., 1867.
Malalgoda, Kitsiri. *Buddhism in Sinhalese Society 1750-1900: A Study of Religious Revival and Change.* Berkeley: University of California Press, 1976.

Maloney, Clarence. *Peoples of South Asia.* New York: Holt, Rinehart and Winston, 1974.
Mamdani, Mahmoud. *Politics and Class Formation in Uganda.* New York: Monthly Review Press, 1976.
———. *The Myth of Population Control: Family, Caste and Class in an Indian Village.* New York: Monthly Review Press, 1972.
Mandle, Jay R. *The Plantation Economy: Population and Economic Change in Guyana, 1838–1960.* Philadelphia: Temple University Press, 1973.
Marx, Karl. *Capital.* Ed. by Frederick Engels. 3 vols. New York: International Publishers, 1967.
——— and Frederick Engels. *On Colonialism: Articles from the New York Tribune and Other Writings.* New York: International Publishers, 1972.
———. *Pre-Capitalist Economic Formations.* Ed. by E. J. Hobsbawm. New York: International Publishers, 1964.
McClelland, David. *The Achieving Society.* Princeton, N. J.: Van Nostrand, 1961.
Meek, C. K. *Land Policy and Practice in the Colonies.* London: Oxford University Press, 1946.
Memmi, Albert. *The Colonizer and the Colonized.* Boston: Beacon Press, 1967.
Mendis, G. C. *Ceylon Under the British.* Colombo: Colombo Apothecaries, 1944.
Milie, P. D. *Thirty Years Ago.* Colombo, 1878.
Morrison, Barrie M., M. P. Moore and Ishak M. U. Lebbe, eds. *The Disintegrating Village: Social Changes in Rural Sri Lanka.* Colombo: Lake House Investments, 1979.
Nyrop, Richard F., et al. *Area Handbook for Ceylon* (Foreign Area Studies Series). Washington, D. C.: American University, 1971.
Obeysekere, Gananath. *Land Tenure in Village Ceylon: A Sociological and Historical Study.* Cambridge: Cambridge University Press, 1967.
Oxaal, Ivar, Tony Barnett and David Booth, eds. *Beyond the Sociology of Development: Economy and Society in Latin America and Africa.* London: Routledge and Kegan Paul, 1975.
Paige, Jeffrey M. *Agrarian Revolution: Social Movements and Export Agriculture in the Underdeveloped World.* New York: The Free Press, 1975.
Parsons, Talcott. *The Social System.* Glencoe, Ill.: The Free Press, 1951.
———. *The System of Modern Societies.* Englewood Cliffs, N. J.: Prentice-Hall, 1971.
Pieris, Ralph. *Sinhalese Social Organization.* Colombo: Ceylon University Press Board, 1956.
Ponnambalam, Satchi. *Dependent Capitalism in Crisis: The Sri Lankan Economy, 1948–1980.* London: Zed Press, 1980.
Ramachandran, N. *Foreign Plantation Investment in Ceylon, 1889–1958.* Colombo: Central Bank of Ceylon, 1963.
Ray, H. C., ed. *History of Ceylon*, vol. 1. Colombo: Ceylon University Press, 1960.
Roberts, Michael. *Facets of Modern Ceylon History through the Letters of Jeronis Pieris.* Colombo: Hansa Publishers, 1975.
Robinson, Marguerite S. *Political Structure in a Changing Sinhalese Village.* Cambridge: Cambridge University Press, 1975.
Rostow, Walt W. *The Stages of Economic Growth: A Non-Communist Manifesto.* Cambridge: Cambridge University Press, 1962.
Roxborough, Ian. *Theories of Underdevelopment.* Atlantic Highlands: Humanities Press, 1979.
Ryan, Bryce. *Caste in Modern Ceylon: The Sinhalese System in Transition.* New Brunswick, N. J.: Rutgers University Press, 1953.
Salmon, C. S. *The Ceylon Starvation Question: Its Cause and Remedy.* Colombo: Ceylon Independent, 1889.

References

Sarkar, N. K. and S. J. Tambiah. *The Disintegrating Village.* Colombo: Ceylon University Press Board, 1957.
Scott, James C. *The Moral Economy of the Peasant.* New Haven: Yale University Press, 1976.
Seddon, David, ed. *Relations of Production: Marxist Approaches to Economic Anthropology.* London: Frank Cass, 1978.
Seneviratne, H. L. *Rituals of the Kandyan State.* Cambridge: Cambridge University Press, 1978.
Smith, M. G. *The Plural Society in the British West Indies.* Berkeley: University of California Press, 1965.
Snodgrass, Donald R. *Ceylon: An Export Economy in Transition.* Homewood, Ill.: Richard D. Irwin, 1966.
Sovani, N. V. *Economic Relations of India with South-East Asia and the Far East.* Bombay: Oxford University Press, 1949.
Speculum, pseud. [George Wall]. *Ceylon: Her Present Condition: Revenues, Taxes and Expenditure.* Colombo: Colombo Observer Press, 1868.
Stavenhagen, Rodolfo. *Social Classes in Agrarian Societies.* New York: Anchor Press, 1975.
Stokes, Eric. *English Utilitarians and India.* Oxford: Clarendon Press, 1859.
Taylor, John G. *From Modenization to Modes of Production: A Critique of the Sociologies of Development and Underdevelopment.* London: Macmillan, 1979.
Terray, Emmanuel. *Marxism and "Primitive" Societies.* New York: Monthly Review Press, 1972.
Van Zwanenberg, R. M. A. *Colonial Capitalism and Labor in Kenya: 1919–1939.* Nairobi: East African Publications Bureau, 1975.
Vimalananda, Tennakoon. *Buddhism in Ceylon Under the Christian Powers and the Educational and Religious Policy of the British Government in Ceylon, 1797–1832.* Colombo: M. D. Gunasena, 1963.
Vogeler, Ingolf and Anthony R. de Sousa, eds. *Dialectics of Third World Development.* Montclair: Allanheld Osmun, 1980.
Wallerstein, Immanuel. *The Modern World System: Capitalist Agriculture and the Origins of the European World Economy in the Sixteenth Century.* New York: Academic Press, 1974.
Warren, Bill. *Imperialism: The Pioneer of Capitalism.* London: New Left Books, 1980.
Weber, Max. *The Religion of India.* Glencoe, Ill.: Free Press, 1958.
———. *The Theory of Social and Economic Organization.* Ed. by Talcott Parsons. New York: Free Press, 1964.
Wickizer, V. D. *Coffee, Tea and Cocoa.* Stanford, Calif.: Stanford University Press, 1951.
Wolpe, Harold, ed. *The Articulation of Modes of Production.* London: Routledge and Kegan Paul, 1980.
The Tea Trade. London: The World Development Movement, 1980.
Yalman, Nur. *Under the Bo Tree: Studies in Caste, Kinship and Marriage in the Interior of Ceylon.* Berkeley: University of California Press, 1971.

4. Articles

Alavi, Hamza. "India and the Colonial Mode of Production." *The Socialist Register,* 1975.
———. "India: Transition from Feudalism to Colonial Capitalism." *Journal of Contemporary Asia,* vol. 10, no. 4 (1980).
Ameer Ali, A. C. L. "Peasant Coffee in Ceylon During the Nineteenth Century," *Ceylon Journal of Historical and Social Studies,* vol. 2, no. 1 (January-June 1972).
———. "Changing Conditions and Persisting Problems in the Peasant Sector under

British Rule in the Period 1833-1893." *Celyon Studies Seminar*, no. 3a (1970-/72 Series).
———. "Rice and Irrigation in the Nineteenth Century." *The Ceylon Historical Journal*, vol. 25 (October 1978).
Arasaratnam, S. "The Kingdom of Kandy: Aspects of its External Relations and Commerce, 1658-1710." *Ceylon Journal of Historical and Social Studies*, vol. 3, no. 2 (July-December 1960).
Arrighi, G. "Labour Supplies in Historical Perspective: A Study of the Proletarianisation of the African Peasantry in Rhodesia." *The Journal of Development Studies*, vol. 6, no. 3 (1970).
Banaji, Jairus. "For a Theory of Colonial Modes of Production." *Economic and Political Weekly*, vol. 7 (December 23, 1972).
———. "Modes of Production in a Materialist Conception of History." *Capital and Class* vol. 3 (Autumn 1977).
———. "Backward Capitalism, Primitive Accumulation and Modes of Production." *Journal of Contemporary Asia*, vol. 3, no. 4 (1973).
Bandarage, Asoka. Review of *The Disintegrating Village*, ed. by Barrie Morrison, et.al. *Pacific Affairs*, vol. 54, no. 3 (Fall 1981).
Bechert, Heinz. "Theravada Buddhist Sangha: Some General Observations on Historical and Political Factors in its Development." *Journal of Asian Studies*, vol. 29 (1969-1970).
Bodenheimer, Susanne J. "The Ideology of Developmentalism: American Political Science's Paradigm – Surrogate for Latin American Studies." *Berkeley Journal of Sociology*, vol. 15 (1970).
Bonacich, Edna. "A Theory of Middleman Minorities." In *Majority and Minority: The Dynamics of Race and Ethnicity in American Life*. Ed. by Norman R. Yetman with Steele C. Hoy. Boston: Allyn and Bacon, 1982.
Brenner, Robert. "The Origins of Capitalist Development: A Critique of Neo-Smithian Marxism." *New Left Review*, no. 104 (July-August 1977).
———. "Agrarian Class Structure and Economic Development in Pre-Industrial Europe." *Past and Present*, no. 70 (February 1976).
Brow, James. "The Changing Structure of Appropriations in Vedda Agriculture." *American Ethnologist*. vol. 5, no. 3 (1978).
———. "The Impact of Population Growth on the Agricultural Practices and Settlement Patterns of the Anuradhapura Veddahs." In *Contributions to Asian Studies*, ed. by James Brow. vol. 9. Leiden: E. J. Brill, 1976.
Buchanan, Keith. "Delineation of the Third World." In *Dialectics of Third World Development*, ed. by I. Vogeler and A. R. de Sousa. Montclair: Allanheld Osmun, 1980.
Chandra, Bipan. "Colonialism, Stages of Colonialism and the Colonial State." *Journal of Contemporary Asia*, vol. 10, no. 3 (1980).
Clifford, Hugh. "Some Reflections on the Ceylon Land Question." *Tropical Agriculturist*, vol. 68 (1927).
de Silva, C. R. "Some Comments on the Political and Economic Conditions in the Kingdom of Kotte in the Early Sixteenth Century." *Ceylon Studies Seminar*, no. 10 (1969-1970 Series).
de Silva, Douglas. "The Growth of the Coconut Industry." In *Liberation and Coconut*, Part 1, *Logos*. Published by the Centre for Society and Religion, Colombo, vol. 18, no. 1 (March 1979).
de Silva, K. M. "The Third Earl Grey and the Maintenance of an Imperial Policy on the Sale of Crown Lands in Ceylon, c. 1832-1852." *Journal of Asian Studies*, vol. 27, no. 1 (November 1967).
———. "The 'Rebellion' of 1848 in Ceylon." *Ceylon Journal of Historical and Social Studies*, vol. 7, no. 2 (July-December 1964).

———. "Indian Immigration to Ceylon, The First Phase, c. 1840–1855." *Ceylon Journal of Historical Social Studies*, vol. 4, no. 2 (July-December 1961).
———. "Tennent and Indian Immigration to Ceylon, 1846–1847 – A Rejoinder." *Ceylon Journal of Historical and Social Studies*, vol. 9, no. 1 (January-June 1966).
———. "Studies in British Land Policy in Ceylon I: The Evolution of Ordinances 12 of 1840 and 9 of 1841." *Ceylon Journal of Historical and Social Studies*, vol. 7 (1964).
———. "The Coming of the British to Ceylon, 1762–1802," In *History of Ceylon*, vol. 3, ed. by K.M. de Silva. Colombo: University of Ceylon Press Board, 1973.
———. "The Kandyan kingdom and the British – The Last Phase, 1796 to 1818" In *History of Ceylon*, vol. 3, ed. by K. M. dé Silva. Colombo: University of Ceylon Press Board, 1973.
———. "The Development of the Administrative System, 1833 to C. 1910," In *History of Ceylon*, vol. 3, ed. by K. M. de Silva. Colombo: University of Ceylon Press Board, 1973.
Ellsworth, P. T. "The Dual Economy: A New Approach." *Economic Development and Cultural Change*, vol. 10 (July 1962).
Evers, Hans-Dieter. "Buddha and the Seven Gods: The Dual Organization of a Temple in Central Ceylon." *Journal of Asian Studies*, vol. 27, no. 3 (May 1968).
———. "From Subsistence to Generalized Commodity Production: A Study of the South Indian Money Lenders and the Expansion of the Colonial Mode of Production." Unpublished paper read at the seminar on "Underdevelopment and Subsistence Reproduction in Southeast Asia," University of Bielefeld, West Germany, April 21–23, 1978.
———. " 'Monastic Landlordism' in Ceylon: A Traditional System in a Modern Setting." *Journal of Asian Studies*, vol. 28, no. 4 (August 1969).
———. "Temple Lands and Rājakāriya: The Kandyan Lankātilaka Raja Maha Viharaya." *Ceylon Studies Seminar*, no. 6 (1970–1971 Series).
Fernando, Tissa. "Arrack, Toddy and Ceylonese Nationalism: Some Observations on the Temperance Movement, 1912–1921." *Ceylon Studies Seminar* no. 9 (1969–1970 Series).
Foster-Carter, Aiden. "Can We Articulate 'Articulation'?" In *The New Economic Anthropology*, ed. by John Clammer. New York: St. Martin's Press, 1978.
Gordon, Alex. "Stages in the Destruction of Java's Self-Supporting Rural Economic System." Unpublished paper read at the seminar on "Underdevelopment and Subsistence Reproduction in Southeast Asia," University of Bielefeld, West Germany, April 21–23, 1978.
Gordon, Stewart. "Recovery from Adversity in Eighteenth-Century India: Rethinking 'Villages,' 'Peasants' and Politics in Pre-Modern Kingdoms." *Peasant Studies*, vol. 8, no. 4 (Fall 1979).
Gough, Kathleen. "Class and Agrarian Change: Some Comments on Peasant Resistance and Revolution in India – A Rejoinder." *Pacific Affairs*, vol. 13, no. 3 (Fall 1969).
Grier, Beverly. "Cocoa Marketing in Colonial Ghana: Capitalist Enterprise and the Emergence of a Rural Bourgeoisie." *UFAHAMU* (Journal of the African Activist Association), vol. 10, nos. 1 and 2 (Fall and Winter 1980–1981).
Gunasinghe, Newton. "Social Change and the Disintegration of a Traditional System of Exchange Labour in Kandyan Sri Lanka." *Sociological Bulletin*, vol. 25 (September 1976).
———. "Production Relations and Classes in a Kandyan Village." *Modern Ceylon Studies*, vol. 6, no. 2 (July 1975).
———. "Agrarian Relations in the Kandyan Countryside." *Social Science Review*, no. 1 (September 1979).

Hariss, John. "Agriculture in the Economic Development of Sri Lanka." In *Agriculture in the Peasant Sector of Sri Lanka,* Ed. by S. W. R. de A. Samarasinghe. Peradeniya: Ceylon Studies Seminar, 1977.

Higgins, Benjamin. "The Dualistic Theory of Underdeveloped Areas." *Economic Development and Culture Change,* vol. 4 (January 1956).

The Insurgent Sociologist. Special issue on the "State and Social Formation in the Capitalist Periphery." *The Insurgent Sociologist,* vol. 9, no. 4 (Spring 1980).

Ireland, W. Alleyane. "The Labour Problem in the Tropics." New York: D. Appleton & Co., 1899.

Jayawardena, Kumari. "Economic and Political Factors in the 1915 Riots." *Ceylon Studies Seminar,* 1969/70 Series, (June 1970).

Jogaratnam, T. "The Role of Agriculture in the Economic Development of Ceylon." *University of Ceylon Review,* vol. 20 (April 1962).

Jones, W. O. "Plantations." In *International Encyclopaedia of the Social Sciences,* 1968 ed. s.v.

Journal of Contemporary Asia. Special issue on Development and Underdevelopment. *The Journal of Contemporary Asia,* vol. 7, no. 1 (1977).

Kelegama, J. B. "The Economy of Rural Ceylon and the Problem of the Peasantry." *Ceylon Economist* (September 1959).

Kotelawala, D. A. "Agrarian Policies of the Dutch in South-West Ceylon, 1743–1767." *A. A. G. Bijdragen* 14 (1967).

Kuruppu, N. S. G. "A History of the Working Class Movement in Ceylon." *The Ceylon Historical Journal,* vol. 1, no. 2 (October, 1951).

Laclau, Ernesto. "Feudalism and Capitalism in Latin America." *New Left Review,* no. 67 (May-June 1971).

Lall, Sanjaya. "Is 'Dependence' a Useful Concept in Analysing Underdevelopment?" *World Development,* vol. 3, nos. 11 and 12 (1975).

Leach, E. R. "Hydraulic Society in Ceylon." *Past and Present,* no. 15 (1959).

Lewis, W. Arthur. "Economic Development with Unlimited Supplies of Labour." *The Manchester School* (May 1954).

Lianos, Theodore P. "Modern Greece: Development or Underdevelopment – Another View." *Monthly Review,* vol. 6, no. 33 (November 1981).

Magdoff, Harry. "Colonialism (c. 1450-c. 1970)." In *The Encyclopaedia Britannia,* 15th edition, 1975.

Malalgoda, Kitsiri. "Millennialism in Relation to Buddhism." *Comparative Studies in Society and History,* vol. 12, no. 4 (October 1970).

Marasinghe, M. L. "Kandyan Law and British Colonial Law: A Conflict of Tradition and Modernity – An Early State of Colonial Development in Sri Lanka." Unpublished paper presented at "The Fifth Annual Congress of the International Sociological Association," Uppsala, Sweden, 1978.

McEachern, Doug. "The Mode of Production in India." *Journal of Contemporary Asia,* vol. 6 (1976).

Meyer, Eric. "Between Village and Plantation: Sinhalese Estate Labour in British Ceylon", *Colloques Internationaux du Centre National de la Recherche Scientifique,* Paris, no. 582 (1978).

Mintz, Sidney W. "The So-Called World System: Local Initiative and Local Response." *Dialectical Anthropology,* vol. 2, no. 4 (1977).

Morris, Morris D. "Values as an Obstacle to Economic Growth in South Asia: An Historical Survey." *The Journal of Economic History,* vol. 27 (December 1967).

Munasinghe, Indrani. "The Colombo-Kandy Railway." *The Ceylon Historical Journal,* vol. 25, nos. 1–4 (October 1978).

Nash, Manning. "Introduction: Approaches to the Study of Economic Growth." *Journal of Social Issues,* vol. 19 (1963).

References

Omvedt, Gail. "Migration in Colonial India: The Articulation of Feudalism and Capitalism by the Colonial State." *The Journal of Peasant Studies*, vol. 6, no. 2 (1980).
———. "Towards a Theory of Colonialism." *Insurgent Sociologist*, vol. 3, no. 3 (Spring 1973).
Pathmanathan, S. "Feudal Polity in Medieval Ceylon: An Examination of the Chieftancies of the Vanni." *Ceylon Journal of Historical and Social Studies* (July-December 1972).
Peebles, Patrick. "Land Use and Population Growth in Colonial Ceylon." In *Contributions to Asian Studies*, ed. by James Brow. vol. 9. Leiden: E. J. Brill, 1976.
Pieris, Ralph. ,,Society and Ideology in Ceylon during a 'Time of Troubles,' 1796–1850, III." *University of Ceylon Review*, vol. 10 (January 1952).
———. "Caste, Ethos and Social Equilibrium." *Social Forces*, vol. 30, no. 4 (May 1952).
———. "Some Neglected Aspects of the British Colonial Administration in the Early Nineteenth Century." *Ceylon Historical Journal*, vol. 2, nos. 1–2 (July-October 1952).
Perera, A. B. "Plantation Economy and Colonial Policy in Ceylon." *Ceylon Historical Journal*, vol. 1 (July 1951).
Rajaratnam, S. "The Growth of Plantation Agriculture in Ceylon, 1886–1931." *Ceylon Journal of Historical and Social Studies*, vol. 4 (1961).
———. "The Ceylon Tea Industry, 1886–1931." *Ceylon Journal of Historical and Social Studies*, vol. 4 (1961).
Reimers, E. "Feudalism in Ceylon." *Journal of the Royal Asiatic Society* (Ceylon), vol. 31, no. 81 (1928).
Roberts, Michael. "The Impact of the Waste Lands Legislation and the Growth of Plantations on the Techniques of Paddy Cultivation in British Ceylon: A Critique." *Modern Ceylon Studies*, vol. 1 (1970).
———. "A Classification of the Sources on the History of British Ceylon as a Basis for Discussion on their Merits and Demerits." *Ceylon Studies Seminar*, no. 8 (1968–1979 Series).
———. "Variations on the Theme of Resistance Movements: The Kandyan Rebellion and Latter Day Nationalisms in Ceylon." *Ceylon Studies seminar*, no. 9 (1970–1972 Series).
——— and L. A. Wickremaratne, "Export Agriculture in the Nineteenth Century," In *History of Ceylon* vol. 3, ed. by K. M. de Silva. Colombo: University of Ceylon Press Board, 1973.
———. "Land Problems and Policies c. 1832 to c. 1900," In *History of Ceylon*, vol. 3, ed. by K. M. de Silva. Colombo: University of Ceylon Press Board, 1973.
———. "A Selection of the Documentary Evidence as Aids for the Lecture on 'The Administration of the Waste Lands Ordinance No. 12 of 1840' and its Impact in the Coffee Period, 1840–1880's." *The Archives Lecture Series*, Ceylon (June 20, 1969).
———. "Grain Taxes in British Ceylon, 1832–1878: Problems in the Field." *Journal of Asian Studies*, vol. 27 (1968).
———. "Grain Taxes in British Ceylon, 1832–1878: Theories, Prejudices and Controversies." *Modern Ceylon Studies* vol. 1 (1970).
———. "The Master Servant Laws of 1841 and the 1860's and Immigrant Labour in Ceylon." *Ceylon Journal of Historical and Social Studies*, vol. 8 (1953).
———. "Observations on Computations of the Mortality Rate among Immigrant Indian Labourers in Ceylon in the Coffee Period." *Ceylon Journal of Historical and Social Studies*, vol. 9, no. 1 (January-June 1966).
———. "The Rise of the Karavas." *Ceylon Studies Seminar*, no. 5 (1968–1969 Series).
———. "The Paddy Lands Irrigation Ordinances and the Revival of Traditional

Irrigation Customs, 1856–1871." *Ceylon Journal of Historical and Social Studies*, vol. 10 (1967).
———. "Indian Estate Labour in Ceylon during the Coffee Period, 1830–1880." *The Indian Economic and Social History Review*, vol. 3, no. 1 (March 1966).
———. "Irrigation Policy in British Ceylon during the Nineteenth Century." *South Asia*, no. 2 (August 1972).
———. "Some Comments on Ameer Ali's Paper." *Ceylon Studies Seminar*, no. 3b (1970–1972 Series).
Samaraweera, Vijaya. "Land, Labour, Capital and Sectional Interests in National Politics of Sri Lanka." *Modern Asian Studies*, vol. 15, no. 1 (1981).
———. "Aspects of Ceylon's Agrarian Economy in the Nineteenth Century," In *History of Ceylon* vol. 3, ed. by K. M. de Silva. Colombo: University of Ceylon Press Board, 1973.
———. "*Elite* Formation and *Elites*, 1832–1931," In *History of Ceylon*, vol. 3, ed. by K. M. de Silva. Colombo: University of Ceylon Press Board, 1973.
———. "The Development of the Administrative System from 1802 to 1832" In *History of Ceylon*, vol. 3, ed. by K. M. de Silva. Colombo: University of Ceylon Press Board, 1973.
———. "Economic and Social Developments under the British 1796–1832," In *History of Ceylon*, vd. 3, ed. by K. M. de Silva. Colombo: University of Ceylon Press Board, 1973.
———. "The Colebrooke-Cameron Reforms," In *History of Ceylon*, vol. 3, ed. by K. M. de Silva. Colombo: University of Ceylon Press Board, 1973.
Scott, C. D. "Peasants, Proletarianization and the Articulation of Modes of Production: The Case of Sugar Cane Cutters in Northern Peru, 1940–1969." *The Journal of Peasant Studies*, vol. 3, no. 3 (April 1976).
Seneviratne, L. J. de S. "Land Tenure in the Kandyan Provinces." *Ceylon Economic Journal*, vol. 9 (1937).
Shah, A. M. "Class and Agrarian Change: Some Comments on Peasant Resistance and Revolution in India." *Pacific Affairs*, vol. 13, no. 3 (Fall 1969).
Sievers, Angelika. "Geographical Aspects of Peasant Tradition in the Kandyan Hill Country." *Conference on Ceylon*. Philadelphia: University of Pennsylvania, 1967.
Stinchcombe, Arthur. "Agricultural Enterprise and Rural Class Relations." *American Journal of Sociology*, vol. 67 (1961–62).
Tambiah, S. J. "Ceylon." In *The Role of Savings and Wealth in Southern Asia and the West.* Paris: UNESCO, 1963.
Thiagaraja, K. "Indian Coolies in Ceylon Estates." *The Indian Review* (March 1917).
Van Den Driesen, I. H. "Land Sales Policy and Some Aspects of the Problem of Tenure: 1836–1888, Part 2." *University of Ceylon Review*, vol. 14 (January-April 1956).
———. "Coffee Cultivation in Ceylon (1)." *The Ceylon Historical Journal*, vol. 3, no. 1 (July 1953).
———. "Coffee Cultivation in Ceylon (2)." *The Ceylon Historical Journal*, vol. 3, no. 2 (October 1953).
———. "Some Trends in the Economic History of Ceylon in the 'Modern' Period." *Ceylon Journal of Historical and Social Studies*, vol. 3 (1960).
———. "Indian Immigration to Ceylon – The First Phase c. 1840–1855 – A Comment." *Ceylon Journal of Historical and Social Studies*, vol. 7, no. 2 (July-December 1964).
Wesumperuma, D. "The Evictions under the Paddy Tax and Their Impact of the Peasantry of Walapane, 1882–1885." *Ceylon Journal of Historical and Social Studies*, vol. 10 (1970).
Wickremaratne, L. A. "Grain Consumption and Famine Conditions in Late Nineteenth Century Ceylon." *Ceylon Journal of Historical and Social Studies*, vol. 3, no. 2 (July-December 1973).

"Education and Social Change, 1832 to c. 1900," In *History of Ceylon*, vol. 3, ed. by K.M. de Silva. Colombo: University of Ceylon Press Board, 1973.
Worseley, Peter. "One World or Three?: A Critique of the World System of Immanuel Wallerstein." *Socialist Register*, 1981.

5. Unpublished Theses and Manuscripts

de Silva, S. B. D. "Investment and Economic Growth in Ceylon." Ph.D. dissertation, University of London, 1962.
de Sousa Fernandes, Maria Teresa. "Women and the Wage Labor System – A Theoretical Approach to the Sexual Division of Labor." Ph.D. dissertation, Brandeis University, 1981.
Fernando, P. T. M. "The Development of a New Elite in Ceylon with Special Reference to Educational and Occupational Background, 1910–1931." Ph.D. dissertation, Oxford University, 1968.
Grossholtz, Jean. "Forging Capitalist Patriarchy: The Effect of British Colonial Rule on Sri Lanka." Unpublished manuscript.
Gunasekara, U. A. "Land Tenure in the Kandyan Provinces of Ceylon." B. Litt. thesis, Oxford University, 1959.
Herring, Ronald. "Redistributive Agrarian Policy: Land and Credit in South Asia." Ph.D. dissertation, University of Wisconsin, Madison, 1976.
Hewavitharana, Buddhadasa. "Factors in the Planning and Execution of the Economic Development of Ceylon." Ph.D. dissertation, University of London, 1964.
Jayawardena, Lalith. "The Supply of Sinhalese Labour to Ceylon Plantations (1830–1930): A Study of Imperial Policy in a Peasant Society." Ph.D. dissertation, Cambridge University, 1963.
Meegama, S. A. "The Decline in Mortality in Ceylon Since the End of the Nineteenth Century, with Particular Reference to Economic and Social Development." Ph.D. dissertation, University of London, 1968.
Peebles, Patrick. "The Transformation of a Colonial Elite: The Mudaliyars of Nineteenth-Century Ceylon." Ph.D. dissertation, University of Chicago, 1973.
Pieris, G. H. "Economic Geography of Rubber Production in Ceylon." Ph.D. dissertation, Cambridge University, 1965.
Pieris, P. R. "The Sociological Consequences of Imperialism with Special Reference to Ceylon." Ph.D. dissertation, University of London, 1950.
Rajaratnam, S. "History of Plantation Agriculture of Ceylon, 1886–1931, with Special Reference to Tea and Rubber." M.Sc. thesis, London School of Economics, 1961.
Roberts, Michael. "Some Aspects of Economic and Social Policy in Ceylon, 1840–1871." D.Phil. dissertation, Oxford University, 1965.
Samaraweera, V. K. "The Commission of Eastern Enquiry in Ceylon, 1832–1837: A Study of a Royal Commission of Colonial Inquiry." D.Phil. dissertation, Oxford University, 1969.
Wesumperuma, D. "The Migration and Conditions of Immigrant Labour in Ceylon, 1880–1910." Ph.D. dissertation, University of London, 1974.
Wickramasekara, S. B. W. "The Social and Political Organization of the Kandyan Kingdom." M. A. thesis, University of London, 1961.
Van Den Driesen, I. H. "Some Aspects of the History of the Coffee Industry in Ceylon with Special Reference to the Period, 1832–1885." Ph.D. dissertation, University of London, 1954.

6. Newspapers

The Colombo Observer
Commercial Advertiser and Agrarian Record
The Ceylon Examiner

SUBJECT INDEX*

Afghanistan 323
Africa 294, 324, 330, 335n, 340, 347, 357; East 305; *See also* Kenya (etc.); Mines
'Agrarian bloc' 313–314
Agriculture 12, 89, 331; capitalist 105–106, 237; communal 27–31; export 57, 58, 65–86, 123, 151, 276, 279, 284, 298, 324, 328, 330–331; mixed 70–72, 76, 146; one-crop 76, 79, 146; plough-based 20, 31; precapitalist 19–41, 255–256; statistics of 27; subsistence 20, 25, 30, 57, 102, 115, 121, 129, 178, 182, 213, 217, 251, 266–274, 288, 294, 318, 324, 328, 329; tools of 21, 151; *See also* Coffee; Feudalism; Labor; Land; Landlords; Modes of production; Paddy; Plantations; Slash-and-burn agriculture; Swidden (chena) land and agriculture; Taxes; Tea; Technology; Villages
Alcoholic beverages 54, 229; wine 72; *See also* Arrack
Amiens, Peace of 47
Arabs, as traders 53
Arecanut, as export 43
Aristocracy (Sinhalese) 12, 31–37, 47, 51, 54, 93, 95, 100, 117, 119, 120, 122, 280, 311; and colonial state 47–50, 106, 114, 154, 177, 222ff., 319–320, 338; as government officials 117–118, 222–223, 244, 245, 320; 'new' 229; and peasants 223–228, 288, 320–321, 338; *See also* Chiefs;

Headmen; Labor [both entries], forced; Overlords
Arrack 54, 151, 189, 264–265, 280, 285
Articulation'; *See* Modes of production
Artisans 38, 40, 187, 188–189, 192; *See also* Castes, durava, karava, and salagama
Asia 330, 335n, 347, 357
Assam 85–86
Assessment of land, 125–127, 133, 144
Australia 329
Authority, traditional vs. modern, 349–350
Badulla District (in Uva Province) 95, 104, 130, 137, 138, 139, 179
Banishment, from Ceylon 229
Bank of Deposits 63
Banks 79, 214, 276; British 79, 81, 281
Barter 43–44, 71, 184, 211
Batticaloa District (in Eastern Province) 137, 214, 281
Bengalis 196
Bintanna Province (precolonial) 51
Blue Books, Ceylonese 27
Borahs 117
Bourgeoisie; *See* Capitalists
Brazil 332, 353n; coffee from 75, 136
Bridges, tolls on 75
British; East India Company 46–47, 53, 55, 58, 59–60, 71n, 176, 319; empire 217, 222, 233; *See also* Colonial Office
British administration (of Ceylon) 50ff., 95, 96, 102, 103, 108, 110, 117–118, 124ff., 154, 156, 161–162, 178,

* Sinhala terms are usually explained in the text at first entry.

British 74, 156, 226, 230, 254, 285–286, 303, 329, 331, 334, 338; 'diffusion' of 328; equipment 81; European 63, 70, 182, 278, 281, 333, 348; export of 57, 79–80, 251, 278, 280, 287, 298, 324n, 343, 356; finance 61, 65, 73, 93, 104, 115, 117, 126, 156, 164, 229, 231–233, 240, 242, 243, 246, 276; Legislative Council 61, 119, 133, 174, 223, 230, 235, 265; licensing by 106; officials of 50, 55, 63, 69, 80, 81, 103–106, 127–131, 134, 143, 148, 155–160, 178–180, 181, 183, 191, 193, 202, 214–218, 222, 224, 226, 229–232, 245, 251, 259–260, 273–274, 303, 318, 320; official storehouses of 122, 129; Public Works Department 129, 245; rule by 41–42, 46ff., 100, 104, 176, 193–194, 217–218, 222–223, 227, 238, 244, 283, 315; *See also* Census; Ceylon; Civil service; Coffee; Colebrooke-Cameron Commission; Colonial Office; Colonial state; Government Agents; Governors; Grain Tax; Mercantilism; Monopolies; Ordinances; Plantations; Planters; Revenue (state); Taxes; Tea; Temple Lands Commission

Buddhism 18, 41, 47, 52, 283, 309, 313; clergy of 33–36, 48–51, 93, 95, 100, 110, 114, 117, 119, 122, 154–163, 224, 249, 288, 311, 312, 315–316, 318, 319; code of 163; sects of 36, 110, 304; *See also* Overlords; Temples

Buffaloes 163, 294

Bullion 343

Burghers (of Dutch-Sinhalese descent) 280, 317

Burma 201, 214, 217, 220

Capital 322, 326–327; accumulation of 54, 80, 251, 262, 278, 334, 343; 184, 223ff., 279, 304–306, 316, 318; Board of Commissioners 50; Commissions 54, 115, 119, 160–170, 202, 210, 228, 281; Committees 92, 154, 217, 225, 231, 262, 318; Executive Council 61, 230; judiciary of 59, 348, 356; investment in Ceylon 6, 14, 40, 54, 55, 63, 76, 77, 79–80, 81, 151, 175, 210, 217, 221, 278, 280–281, 298; local (native) 57, 63, 280–286, 291; merchant 52, 348, 356; reinvestment in Ceylon 40, 80, 278, 280, 287, 297; reproduction of 334; *See also* Interest, Mercantilism

Capitalism 230, 241; advanced 195, 212; and colonialism 3–5, 62ff., 104–106, 177, 182, 203, 212, 219, 237, 277, 287–288, 297–299, 323, 329–357; transition to, from feudalism 41–42, 52, 91, 297, 302, 328, 337n, 342; indigenous (native) 9, 325, 327; mercantile (merchant) 56–57, 298, 304, 321; and patriarchy 211–212; and religion 41; rentier 151, 153, 298; 'retrograde' 342–343; world 11, 277, 332; *See also* Labor (under capitalism); Land; Market; Mercantilism; Modes of production; Plantations; Private property in land; Smallholdings

Capitalists 93, 103; Ceylonese 66, 79, 82, 83, 97–99, 126, 133, 151–153, 172, 188–189, 214, 241, 247, 265, 280–286, 293, 296–299, 313, 326, 328, 331; European 97–98, 175; rentier 166, 170, 290–292, 295–296, 298, 307, 311; *See also* Peasants, as proprietors; Planters

Capitals, Sinhalese 53

Carpenters 187, 188–189, 192, 309; *See also* Castes, karava

Cash; *See* Crops, Cash; Money

Subject Index   417

Caste 14, 164, 224, 279, 286, 309, 325, 341, 357; and ethnicity 310–312; under feudalism 35–41, 44, 45, 155, 309; and labor 54, 57, 67, 122, 155, 160, 163–164, 174–175, 296; and land transfers 23, 110, 163–164, 307; pollution 38; and social stasis 40; and new sub-castes 39

Castes 116, 117, 363–365; blacksmith 38, 39; cinnamon peeler (chaliya/salagama) 18, 53–54, 67, 188, 198, 280, 309, 310; cultivator (govi) 38, 110, 164, 307; toddy tapper (durava) 188, 280; forced labor by 67; fishermen (karava) 119, 153, 174–175, 188–189, 220, 247, 265, 280, 284, 309, 310; low Ceylonese 153, 174, 188, 276, 307; low Indian 196–197, 278, 309; moneylender (chettiyar) 55, 117, 119, 149, 152, 186, 214–215; radala 117; weaver 184, 198; See also Chettiyars

Cattle 92, 100, 231, 311

Census 19, 138, 187

Central (Kandyan) Highlands 13ff., 279, 327, 329, 338; precolonial 14, 18–49; roads built into 52, 58

Central Province 19, 30, 74, 97, 105, 106, 120, 124, 129, 131, 133, 135, 136–138, 150, 217, 231, 281

'Certificate of Quiet Possession' 96, 106–107, 117

Ceylon 1ff.; British 39, 46ff., 325–326, 329, 340; as British crown colony 47; Dutch period of 42–45; feudal 175; government of 63, 83, 87, 103, 104, 116, 201, 233; Portuguese period of 42; precolonial 5, 12–13, 14, 18–49, 90–91, 114, 116, 122, 137, 149, 151, 157, 174, 198–199, 236–237, 250–251, 276, 288, 290, 296, 309, 325; provinces of 61; southwestern 19, 53, 56, 67, 83, 84, 188, 279, 280, 283, 331; See also British administration; Central Highlands; Coastal lowlands; Colonial state; Kandy (kingdom); Sri Lanka

Ceylon Association (of London) 230

Ceylon Journal 224

'Ceylonisation' of British administration 227

Chamber of Commerce (of Ceylon) 235

Chena land; See Slash-and-burn agriculture; Swidden (chena) land and agriculture

Chettiyars (moneylender caste) 55, 117, 119, 149, 152, 186, 208, 209, 210, 214–215, 280, 291, 298, 309–310

Chicory 76

Chiefs (of villages) 50–52, 89, 110, 119, 133, 134, 156–157, 160, 164, 177, 223, 227, 244, 315–316, 318, 319–320; See also Headmen

Children, as labor 200, 210–211, 219

China 196, 266, 327, 334–335; indentured workers from 196

Christianity 50; See also Missionaries

Cinchona 84

Cinnamon 18, 53, 54, 62, 67–68, 129, 176, 198; -peeler caste 18, 53–54, 67, 198

Citizenship, of migrant workers 197, 314

Civil service (British, in Ceylon) 224, 225, 227, 230–234

Class 331, 338, 348, 354; analysis 14, 333–334, 341; differentiation 35, 108–109, 116, 242, 276–277, 283, 286–287, 296–297, 325, 355; and karma 35; struggle 25, 31, 39, 170, 288, 290, 311–314, 347, 348, 356–357; working 351

Clergy; See Buddhism, clergy of; Mis-

sionaries; Overlords
Cloth 184; as import 43
Clubs, white only 235
'Coast advances' to immigrant labor 195, 208
Coastal lowlands (of Ceylon) 42, 46–47, 55–56, 67, 68, 75, 83, 84, 89, 176, 225, 227, 246, 265, 279, 283, 309, 314, 315, 321; people from, in Central Highlands 103, 127, 149, 152, 157, 164, 187, 189, 191, 220, 280, 307, 309, 311, 318; *See also* Ceylon, southwestern
Cocoa 84, 293
Coconut 54, 55, 79, 82–84, 130, 133, 151, 260, 285–286; oil of 185; plantations of 189, 281; *See also* Arrack
Coffee 55, 58, 62, 65–82, 119–120, 129, 269; Brazilian 75, 78, 136; collapse of Ceylonese 138, 142, 145, 146, 180, 186, 199, 250, 253, 268, 312, 320; consumption level of 72; duties on export of 72, 123, 206, 261–263, 268; exports of 70, 75, 77, 82, 103, 130, 262–263, 323; harvesting of 174, 183 184, 191, 193, 202; Javanese 75; leaf blight 78–79, 135–136, 153, 161, 259, 320; Liberian 78; peasant-grown 70–72, 76–79, 82, 99, 102–103, 107, 109, 124, 130, 135–140, 142, 146, 161, 179, 185–187, 189, 193, 239, 290, 292, 325, 348; price of 71, 73, 75–76, 78, 136, 142, 317; production of 70–82, 87–88, 174, 177, 191; production lead-time of 76; profit from 79–80; shift from, to tea 14, 84–86, 121–122, 153, 184–190, 194, 200, 219, 259–260; stealing of 103, 207, 239–240, 293, 306; West Indian 72; *See also* Land, high; Market; Ordinances; Plantations; Planters; Smallholdings; Trade
Colebrooke-Cameron Commission (of 1829–33) 131, 228; reforms of 14, 58–59, 61–64, 67, 69, 89, 124, 155, 177, 224, 231, 249, 255, 279, 302, 304
Colombo 55, 206, 216, 220, 229, 247, 279, 280, 283, 316–318; harbor 198
Colombo Observer 112, 233, 252n, 316–317
Colonial Office (British) 59, 90, 184, 230, 233, 279
Colonial Secretaries (in Ceylon) 229; *See also the Name Index*
Colonial state (government of Ceylon) 63, 83, 87, 89, 91–93, 96–97, 100–102, 104, 106–107, 120, 123, 184, 265, 287, 292, 302–306, 338, 340, 348–352, 357; and Sinhalese aristocracy 114–115, 119, 160, 170, 229, 236, 244–245, 311, 315–316, 320; and Buddhism 49–50, 163; diagramed 308; ideology of 302–303, 340; and labor 122, 205, 245, 249–253; and peasantry 107, 109, 121–122, 131, 174, 176, 194, 214, 236, 241–260, 266–274, 276, 290–295, 311, 315–316, 325, 327; and planters 69, 120, 122, 132, 133, 222, 235–241, 244, 245, 264, 274, 288, 290–295; *See also* British administration; Ceylon; Dutch; Governors; India; Ordinances; Taxes
Colonialism 12–15, 100, 132, 171, 179, 284; and capitalism 3–5, 62ff., 104–106, 177, 182, 203, 212, 219, 237, 277, 287–288, 297–299, 304–306, 327–357; and Chettiyars 214–215, 284; classical 1, 5, 284, 352; and economic stasis 41–43, 272, 298–299; 'internal' 284n, 314, 331; neo-284, 353, 357; theory of 47–48,

Subject Index 419

236–237, 297, 305–306, 310, 322–357; *See also* British administration; Ceylon; Colonial state; Development; Dutch; Mercantilism; Portuguese
Communality 20, 287, 288, 338, 341, 348; vs. capitalism 290, 340
Communist Manifesto 326
Commutation: *See* Grain tax, commutation to cash from payment in kind; Road tax, commutation of labor service into
Congo, The 339
Conspicuous consumption 40, 57, 176, 251, 281
Construction work 187, 213
Contractual relations 170, 173, 206, 220, 288, 295, 297; *See also* Debt bondage; Labor (under capitalism), indentured *and* supervisors; Private property in land
Convention of 1815; *See* Kandyan Convention
Copper, deeds written on 95
Corn laws (British), repeal of 60
Corporations 81, 203; multinational 6n
Cotton 66, 68, 123, 184; *See also* Textiles
Courts 61, 130, 156, 165, 167–169, 242, 318; *See also* British administration, judiciary of
Craft production 20n, 285
Credit 63, 75, 76, 77, 79, 85, 161, 172, 281, 293; from Chettiyars 214–215; default on 150, 241, 292; to workers 209, 214–215; *See also* Debt bondage
Crops; cash 54, 55, 62, 66, 71–72, 84, 102, 109, 130, 171, 178, 186, 215, 231, 247, 259–260, 272, 276, 290–295; failure of 127, 138, 142, 145–146, 149, 213, 270; seizure of 135; *See also* Cinnamon; Coconut; Coffee; Paddy; Pepper; Rubber; Spices; Swidden (chena) land and agriculture; Tea
Crown Lands Encroachment Ordinance (of 1840) 93–101, 104, 106, 108, 118, 120, 125, 133, 227, 231, 234, 238, 239, 240, 244; text of 367–370
Cultivators; *See* Castes, cultivator; Labor, Peasants
Curry 134, 211
Customary usage (including rights) 94–95, 108, 114, 115, 166, 237, 238, 254, 290, 296; *See also* Feudalism
Customs duties 62, 69, 75, 261; amount of 215, 262, 264; on cinnamon exports 269; exemption from 58, 262; on exports 67, 75, 123, 206, 254, 262–263, 268–269; on rice imports 132, 154, 211, 215–216, 236, 261, 263–264, 272
Debt bondage 176, 197, 200, 203, 207, 208–210, 220, 245–246, 287; and patriarchy 212; in Peru 209n, 212; tundu system of 209; *See also* Labor (under capitalism), supervisors
Deeds; *See* Land, title to
Defense 32, 36, 47
Democracy 317, 351
Dependency (economic) 287, 327–239, 332, 344, 350; theory of 330–334, 353–354, 356
Depression, economic 75–77, 78–80, 135–137, 252, 261–263, 268, 278, 317, 320
Development (capitalist) 2, 80, 195, 353; in Third World 3–5, 285, 298, 304, 322, 327, 353; in Ceylon 58, 59, 64, 79, 106, 176, 177, 237, 285–286; and underdevelopment 1–12, 14–15, 214n–215n, 218–219, 322–332, 335, 349–350, 354–357; uneven /unequal 327, 344; *See also* 'Dual economy' theory

Differentiation 12; class 35, 108–109, 116, 242, 276–277, 283, 286–287, 296–297, 325, 325, 355; economic 39

Disease 205–206; quarantine of 206; *See also* Labor (under capitalism), and illness

Dissāvas; *See* Governors, Sinhalese

Divide and rule 320

Division of labor 39, 40, 174, 192, 193, 200; ethnic 310; international 60, 67, 217, 279; sexual 13, 35, 183, 211, 243; *See also* Modes of production

Divorce 242, 244

Dry zone (of Ceylon) 18, 19, 20, 41, 42, 122, 130, 256, 281–282, 315

'Dual economy' theory 2–3, 7–8, 9, 12–13, 81–82, 174n, 187, 294, 323–326, 331, 335–336, 339, 350

Dualism, political 350

Dutch 67–68, 97, 191, 225, 280; East India Company 44; in Indonesia 71, 197, 237, 324; mercantilism 41–45, 47, 53–54, 58; rule in Ceylon 42, 44, 46, 49, 127, 176, 237, 265, 279

Duties; *See* Customs duties; Taxes

East India Company; *See* British; Dutch

Eastern Province 135, 138, 214, 258

Ecology 103

Education 13, 61–62, 189, 224, 283, 303

Emigration (from Ceylon) 146

'Enclave economy' 7, 82

Enclosure movement, English 8, 109, 153, 194

England 212, 328, 340, 350, 353; *See also* British administration; Colonial state; Enclosure movement; Great Britain

English language, 61, 224, 283

Epidemics 19

Estate economic sector 7, 81–82; *See also* Plantations, as economic sector

Estates; *See* Plantations

Ethnicity 14, 276–277, 279, 284, 286, 307, 310–314, 325, 341, 348, 352, 354, 357; and division of labor 310–311

Ethiopia 323

Europe, Western 341

Evangelism 60

Exploitation, social relations of 346–347; *See also* Production

Export enclaves 332

Exports (from Ceylon) 7, 43, 44, 53, 54, 62, 67, 81, 83–84, 214, 231; of coconut 82, 260, 281; of coffee 70, 75, 77, 80, 82, 103, 277, 290; of graphite 282; *See also* Agriculture, export; Customs duties

Factories 211–212

'False consciousness' 357

Families 200, 203, 206, 218, 235, 241; migration of 199–200, 219; and wage-rate 182–183, 218

Famines 135, 252; in India 205, 256–257

Feminists 211n

Fertilizer 259

Feudalism 236–237, 345–347; continuation under capitalism 250–251, 332, 335–338, 341–342; European 37, 40, 236; Japanese 37, 40; Kandyan 11, 12, 18, 20–42, 45, 64, 87, 95–96, 152–153, 175, 222–223, 287–288, 340; reciprocity in 166–170; 'semi-' 203; transition from, to capitalism 41–42, 91, 128, 156–157, 197, 295–297, 302, 328–329, 337n, 342; tribute under 114, 155–172; *See also* Aristocracy; Customary usage, Kandy (kingdom); King; Labor [both entries]; Land; Modes of production; Serfdom

Fish, dried 43

Floods, in Indochina 270

Subject Index

Food 179, 183; export of 60, 66–67, 278; import of 81, 277, 292, 323, 331; production of 57, 217, 277, 285, 326, 327; *See also* Gardens; Paddy; Rice; Swidden (chena) land and agriculture

Forests 6, 9, 19, 26, 62, 77, 78, 86, 88–91, 100, 111, 116, 118, 121, 171, 175, 262, 290; clearing of 187, 192; depletion of 103, 144, 189; royal (crown) 21, 28, 89, 93, 101, 237, 246; *See also* Land, high

Four Korales 55

'Free enterprise' 57–58, 63, 216, 235; *See also* Laissez-faire

French, in India 46

Galle District (in Southern Province) 138

Gardens 27–28, 55, 70, 83, 87n, 91, 101, 109, 122, 130, 134, 175, 178, 186, 200, 210, 217; *See also* Coffee, peasant-grown; Food

Gems 53, 54

Gold Coast (Ghana) 293

Government Agents (District heads of British administration) 52, 55, 61, 118, 183, 189, 222, 228, 230, 231, 245, 258; Assistant 95, 130, 178, 228, 230; *See also the Name Index*

Governors (in Ceylon); British 43, 54, 58, 64, 69, 89, 165, 180, 181, 222, 223, 227, 229–230, 234, 237, 255, 257, 303; and planters 235; Sinhalese (Dissāvas) 51, 222, 228; *See also the Name Index*

Grain (paddy) tax 25, 29, 52, 54, 96, 101, 110, 114, 122–154, 177, 215, 233, 237–238, 252, 257, 263, 268, 302, 316; abolition of (1892) 154, 266; amount of 123, 125, 128, 130, 143–144, 238, 263, 266–267; arrears on 136–137, 141–142, 145; aumani aystem of 127–128; Commission (Of 1878) 25, 133–135, 148, 238, 263; commissioners 135, 193; commutation to cash, from payment in kind 128–131, 134, 136, 141, 148, 160–173, 179, 215, 225, 227, 242, 264, 292, 295, 296, 307, 338; debate over 141–142; default on 131, 135, 136–142, 148–150, 172, 179, 215, 250, 292; in England 146; establishment of (1818) 52; exemption from 123, 154–155; farmed out to 'renters' 125–130, 134, 150, 215, 265, 280, 285; increase of 144, 146, 215, 264; methods of collecting 124–135, 228; protest against 141–142, 154, 266; redemption scheme of 124–125, 138; *See also* Tithe

Grains 37, 213; dry 9, 20, 26, 102, 123, 148; East European 43; *See also* Paddy; Rice

Graphite 282–283, 286

Great Britain 75, 77, 328, 329, 331; government of 59, 72, 224, 227, 261; *See also* British administration; Colonial Office; Colonial state; England

Gross National Product 323, 331

Guyana, British 182, 217, 218

Hacienda 342, 345

Hambantota District (in Southern Province) 214, 258

Harvest failure; *See* Crops, failure of

Headmen (of villages) 54–55, 56, 61, 64, 69, 89, 95, 96, 100, 117–118, 138, 149, 155, 204, 225; Burmese 304; as capitalists 280; chief 225; and colonial state 222–229, 230, 235, 245, 250, 304–305, 311; duties of 228; labor headmen, see Labor (under capitalism), supervisors; and/as land assessors 125, 126, 148, 228; as landowners 148, 151, 152, 153, 172; currently in office 123; and peasants 160, 194, 213–228, 304, 311; superior 228; and taxes 123, 128, 131, 132, 134, 148, 154, 292; *See also* Aristocracy; Chiefs

Historians 58, 68n, 106; Sri Lankan 6, 9, 12, 48, 66; feminist 211

Homogeneity (ethnic and class) 276, 280, 296, 309

Honey 26

Hospitals, for plantation laborers 246, 253

Humanitarianism 64, 128, 134, 141, 155, 205

'Hydraulic civilization' in dry zone 18, 20, 38n, 41, 122, 213

Ideal types 344, 349, 355

Illiteracy 204, 208

Immigration 304; banned 219; precolonial 198; routes of 206; *See also* Labor (under capitalism), immigrant, migrant *and* South Indian; Tamils

Imperialism 11, 55, 57, 66, 279, 294, 323, 327, 341, 342, 345, 354–355; *See also* British administration; Colonial state; Colonialism

Imports, to Ceylon 43, 44, 53, 81, 178, 184–185, 247, 277, 323, 331; *See also* Customs duties; Rice, imports

India 46, 53, 60–61, 62, 66, 117, 153, 201, 205, 212, 214, 216–217, 236, 256, 263, 280, 285, 298, 309, 326n, 327, 329, 334, 336, 342, 346; government of 219, 245; Mughal 237n; Sepoy Mutiny (1857) 319n; South 83, 174, 188, 196–200, 203, 208, 210, 245, 278–279, 287; *See also* Labor (under capitalism); Madras Presidency; Malabar; Ramnad; Rice, imports; South Indians; Tanjore

Indian Ocean 53

Indigo 68, 123

Indochina 270

Indonesia 191, 237n, 324; *See also* Java

Industrialization 219, 285, 327; British 52, 59–60, 175, 211, 277; European 57, 60, 66–67

Infanticide 243, 276

Infrastructure 246–247, 255, 274, 276, 293, 294, 323, 331, 340, 350, 351; *See also* Irrigation; Railways; Roads

Institution, total 289

Interest, on capital 278

Ireland 329

Irrigation 26, 32, 88, 101, 102, 176, 214, 216, 217, 251–252, 255–261, 272, 285, 292, 294, 299, 327; *See also* 'Hydraulic civilization' in dry zone

Ivory 53

Jaffna Peninsula 83, 225

Jamaica 72–73

Japan, feudalism in 37, 40

Java 71, 194, 237n, 285; coffee from 75

Jobbers (labor headmen) 203, 212; *See also* Labor (under capitalism), recruitment of *and* supervisors

Jubilee year of Queen Victoria (1887) 140

Judges; *See* British administration, judiciary of

Jungle; *See* Forest

Jute 66

Kalutara District (in Western Province) 283

Kandy (city) 69, 176, 171, 216, 225, 247, 313, 318, 319; population of 19

Kandy (kingdom) 18–19, 56, 58, 61, 88, 109, 114–116, 155; cession of 47–49, 57, 122, 176, 222–223, 302, 309, 315, 365–366; and Dutch 44–45, 49; forest belt surrounding 28, 246; founding of 142–143; invasions of 309; la-

Subject Index

bor system of 36–41, 96, 174, 177, 242, 255, 288–289, 295; land system of 19–36, 90–91, 95–96, 137, 196, 242, 252, 288–289, 295; officials of 32n, 37–38, 45, 48, 251; organization of 37; population of 19; repells Portuguese 44, 49; trade and 42–45; *See also* Ceylon, precolonial; Feudalism; King; Labor (before capitalism); Villages
Kandy District (in Central Province) 129, 138
Kandyan Convention (of 1815) 49, 51, 54, 222; text of 365–366
Kandyan Highlands; *See* Central Highlands
Kanganis; *See* Labor (under capitalism), recruitment of *and* supervisors
Karavas; *See* Castes, karava
Karma 35
Kegalle District (of Sabaragamuva Province) 178
Kenya, colonial 178, 182, 184, 191, 291
Kerosene 184–185
King (of Kandy) 37, 39, 40, 42, 44, 246, 288; and aristocrats 32–33, 35, 47–49; and clergy 33–35, 48–49, 50; deposed by British 33, 47–50, 222, 305, 315; and land 21, 22, 23, 35, 32–35, 50; pretenders 316, 318, 319; royal (crown) villages of 31–32; and trade 44; *See also* Kandy (kingdom)
Kings, Sinhalese 53, 122, 123, 176, 198, 236–237
Kinship ties 154, 201, 206; loosening of 150, 219; *See also* Families
Kurakkan; *See* Millet, finger
Kurunegala District (in North West Province) 281, 318
Labor (before capitalism) 94, 96; communal 27; division of 39, 40; exchanges (attam) 20, 242; forced (corvée) 23,
mobility of 40, 63; scarcity of 196; *See also* Kandy (kingdom), labor 24, 32, 37–40, 45, 51, 52, 54, 63, 69, 114, 122, 152–153, 155, 176, 225, 242, 250, 252, 337; immigrant 198; intensity of 20–21, 31, 194; system of; Serfdom
Labor (under capitalism) 10, 62, 65, 71, 80, 81, 82, 83, 86, 88, 170, 236, 282, 340, 344; absenteeism of 207; coerced 62, 199, 212–213, 220; and colonial state 127, 205, 245, 249–252; contractors, *see* supervisors [below]; 'crimping' of 208; desertion by 199, 207; European 63; forced (corvée) 54–55, 57, 63–64, 67, 68, 74, 80–81, 114, 122, 123, 152–153, 155–173, 176–177, 186, 223, 226, 227–228, 233, 249, 255, 257, 266, 270, 295, 302, 307, 333, 337, 338; 'free' 197, 198, 201, 212, 264, 333, 346; and illness 204, 210; immigrant 7, 74, 77, 129, 132, 174, 181, 195–221, 247, 293, 306; indentured 66, 68, 196, 201, 203; intensity of 13, 31, 154, 194; 'involution' of 194, 199· irregularity of 187–193; legal status of 204; living conditions of 204, 213, 217; migratory 182, 195–196, 201, 219; productivity of 154, 194, 297, 299, 325, 343; recruitment of 198–206, 208, 212, 219, 245, 287; 'reproduction' of 182, 214n–215n, 217–219, 221, 293, 337, 339; resident vs. commuting 187–191, 200. 217–220, 249, 287; semi-wage 220; slave 68, 72; South Indian 9, 14, 72, 73, 74, 76, 79, 84, 85, 153, 174, 181, 192, 195–221, 245–246, 250, 278–280, 304; supervisors (kanganis, jobbers, labor headmen) 145, 182, 202,

213, 220, 287, 306; to pay taxes 179, 183-185, 199; wage 64, 66, 67, 76, 109, 153, 155, 175–221, 228, 241, 245, 264, 268, 288, 291–293, 296–297, 314, 317, 337, 345, 346, 347; *See also* Artisans; Castes; Debt bondage; Land; Ordinances; Paddy; Peasants; Road tax; Tamils; Wages

Laissez-faire 235, 245, 274, 302, 351; *See also* 'Free enterprise'

Land 65, 72, 73–74, 86, 183, 236, 340, 344; alienation of 6, 10, 23, 63, 88–92, 102, 105, 110, 112, 117, 131, 135, 148–151, 155, 163, 166, 171–172, 178, 194, 254; auction of 90, 262; buyers of 140–144, 242; claims 92–101, 105, 112–114, 118–120, 197, 240; as a commodity 128, 157, 171, 307; common 29, 92, 95, 101, 109, 115, 171; co-ownership of 149, 163, 165, 194, 241–242, 307; crown (royal) 63, 74, 75, 91–101, 103, 105, 108, 110, 116, 118, 121, 148, 149, 171, 178, 217, 228, 229, 236–237, 261–262, 281, 302, 311; 'encroachment' on 101, 103, 105, 107, 108, 115, 116–117, 119–121, 194, 240–241, 311; eviction from 141–146, 237, 292, 320; freehold 69, 89, 107–109, 124, 171, 194; grants of 32–35, 45, 50, 58, 63, 69, 89, 93, 95, 106, 111, 118, 119, 122; high 7, 62, 78, 79, 87–96, 100, 102–122, 135–136, 148, 163, 171, 178, 181, 194, 228, 238, 253, 280, 281, 290, 307, 311, 338; inheritance of 241–243; landlessness 196, 314; litigation over 103, 149, 242, 307; marginal 6; measurement of 22, 95–96; mortgage of 23, 150, 152, 241; price of 97, 99, 105, 149, 154, 231; registration of 23, 28, 96, 110, 111, 114–116, 130, 150, 154, 160, 165, 239; rent from 24, 25–26, 31, 32, 39, 122, 152, 163, 166, 173, 238, 298, 307, 346; renting (leasing) of 55, 110, 114, 119, 156, 186, 200, 210; and rulership 151–153, 170, 325; sale of 6, 23, 55, 58, 63, 73–74, 75, 77, 79, 88–90, 93, 96–100, 102–103, 104, 105–108, 110, 115, 116–121, 123, 131, 136–142, 148–153, 157, 163–172, 178–180, 194, 200, 215, 231–234, 240, 250, 257, 261–262, 280, 290, 320; scarcity 6, 44, 194, 297; surplus of 25, 196, 242–243; surveying of 89, 90, 96, 99, 100, 110, 111, 118, 132, 240, 259, 262; tenure 12, 20–25, 27–37, 62, 87–173, 177, 259; title to 21, 24, 28, 93–96, 103, 106, 110–112, 120, 238, 240–241; transfer of 23, 24, 56, 164; use rights to 89, 91–97, 106, 108, 109, 115–116, 119, 157, 166, 171, 237, 238; waste lands 7n, 94, 106, 119, 121, 125, 178, 237; *See also* Assessment of land; Crown Lands Encroachment Ordinance; Customary rights; Feudalism; Forest; Landlords; Market; Ordinances; Paddy; Pasture land; Plantations; Private property in land; Property holding; Smallholdings; Speculators; Swidden (chena) land and agriculture; Taxes; Temples; Tenancy; Villages

Landlords 97–99, 114, 124, 129, 207, 284; absentee 10, 157, 166, 307; Ceylonese 89, 95, 117, 132–134, 152–153, 228; clergy as 33–36, 50–51, 109–116; European 117, 134, 157; feudal 21–26, 28, 31–36, 45, 166; Indian 197, 199, 204, 220; obligations to tenants 152, 161, 166–

Subject Index

170; responsibility for taxes 154; *See also* Land, tenure; Overlords; Plantations, ownership of; Planters; Smallholdings
Language 200, 202, 228, 230
Latin America 324, 329, 335, 336, 338, 342, 347, 357
Laws; *See* Crown Lands Encroachment Ordinance; Ordinances
Liberalism, British 57, 60-61, 64, 141, 302
Liberia, coffee from 78
Looms, Ceylonese hand 184
Low country; *See* Coastal lowlands
Madagama (village) 50
Madras Presidency 46, 58, 197-198
Madura (India) 203, 278
Maize 26, 123
Malabar 53, 197-198, 203, 217, 219
Malaria 256
Malaya 196, 197, 201, 204, 214
Manchester 184
Mannar (town) 206
Manure, use on coffee bush 78
Maritime provinces, of Ceylon, 55, 58, 64n, 69, 127, 133, 223, 246
Market 81, 83, 129, 188, 288, 343; for coffee 71, 72, 75-77, 78, 88, 132, 136, 207; colonies as a 60; economy based on 170, 184, 292, 296, 315; forces of the 13, 20, 29, 37, 43, 62, 107, 173, 180, 193, 270, 273, 288, 296, 316, 328, 338; futures 81; for labor 192; for land 73, 97, 104, 130, 148, 163, 166, 238; for rice 272; for tea 85; world 52, 57, 67, 197, 276, 278, 323, 331-333, 336-337, 342
Marriage 235, 242-245, 281; age of 179; registration of 242-245; *See also* Divorce; Polyandry; Polygyny
Martial law 318-319

Marxism 212, 311, 326-328, 331-332, 347, 350, 353-355; anthropological 335n, 354; Neo- 297, 327-329, 332, 334-337, 341, 344, 353, 356-357
Masons 187, 192, 309; *See also* Castes, karava
Matale District (in Central Province) 138, 206, 318
Matara District (in Southern Province) 138
Matches 184-185
Mauritius 196, 197, 218, 245
Meat 329
Medical facilities, for workers 206, 235, 255; *See also* Hospitals
Mercantilism 17, 340, 356, British 42, 47, 52-55, 58-61, 67, 176, 250-251, 302, 304; defined 56-57; Dutch 41-45, 47, 53-54, 58; European 14, 41-46, 56-57, 67, 264; and land policy 63, 340
Mesuriegama (village) 140
Mexican workers in U.S. 195
Middle East 53
Middlemen 71, 72, 125, 207, 284, 292, 313; labor 306
Military forces 53, 229, 257, 261; *See also* Naval power
Millennial movements 357
Millet, finger (kurakkan) 123, 145, 148, 213
Mines 182, 195, 196, 294, 337, 356
Missionaries, Christian 13, 155, 283, 303
Modernization 2, 6, 62, 67, 322-323, 326-327, 331, 350
Modes of production 11, 12, 14, 19-31, 34, 56, 102, 153, 218-219, 277, 279, 286-297, 305, 325-329, 334-349, 352; 'Asiatic' 326, 355; colonial 303, 338, 341-343, 345-349, 353, defined 344; dominant vs. subordinate 293,

311, 335, 340, 341, 347; 'lineage' 339, 340, 348; *See also* Capitalism: Feudalism
Modliars (headmen) 225
Money 43–44, 56, 70, 96, 103, 106, 114, 117, 126, 142, 253; economy based on 71, 102, 123–129, 150, 151, 160, 163, 170, 173, 179, 196, 215, 290–291; under feudalism 21, 24, 32, 37, 45; land rented for 156; peasants' need for 184, 185, 189, 191, 291–292; taxes paid in 128, 142, 146, 178, 199; *See also* Credit; Labor (under capitalism); Revenue [both entries]; Taxes; Wages
Moneylenders 123, 150, 151, 210, 220, 293; Buddhist clergy as 110; Chettiyars as 55, 108, 209, 280, 309; as landlords 197, 298; Muslim 71
Monopolies 58, 59–60, 71, 188, 203; rice 215; state trade 53–54, 57, 62, 67, 264–266, 285; *See also* Mercantilism
Moors; *See* Muslims
Moratuva (town) 188
Mortality rate, of immigrant workers 205
Muslims 51, 118, 284, 313, 352; as capitalists 280, 321; as landowners 104, 140–141, 149, 152–153, 157, 281; as moneylenders 71; as traders 18, 43, 44, 53, 55, 71–72, 153, 184, 280, 304, 310–311
Mysore (India) 203
Nationalism, Sinhalese 5, 8n, 219, 265, 277, 311–313, 315, 318, 321, 352, 357; historiography and 9, 12
Native reserves 108
Naval power 44, 46
Navigation Acts, British 60
Nayakkar dynasty, princes of 18
Newspapers 90; *See also* Ceylon Journal;

Colombo Observer
Nivitigala (village) 158–160
Northern Province 279, 283
Nuwara Eliya District (in Central Province) 138, 140, 142–143
Oil 353
Ola leaves, deeds written on 95
Opium 123, 264–266, 285
Ordinances 12, 204, 227, 230, 238–239, 243; on coffee 103, 239, 293; Indian 202, 245; on irrigation 258; on labor 245–246, 296, 307, 337; on land 6, 12, 87, 90, 104, 106, 110–111, 114, 119–122, 131, 134–137, 178, 241–243; on marriage 242–245; on roads 100, 179, 239, 249–253, 255, 311; on taxes 126, 143–144, 148, 154, 160–163, 249, 257–258; *See also* Crown Lands Encroachment Ordinance
Oriental Bank (in Ceylon), collapse of 78
Overlords 95, 103, 157, 164, 171, 240, 251, 266, 288; and cultivators (peasants) 25, 119, 164–166, 224, 290, 296, 307, 309, 315; of temple lands 111, 114–116, 119, 161–163, 165–166, 224; *See also* Aristocracy, Chiefs; Headmen, Landlords
Paddy 10, 19–26, 28, 29–32, 91, 95, 100, 108, 115, 117, 170–172, 175, 188, 193, 210, 216, 325, 348; acreage in 27; '-centricity' 194n; crop failure of 26, 27, 31, 101, 199; decline of 141, 144–145, 216–217, 221, 255–260, 264, 272, 274; export/import of 43, 264; extension of 21, 24, 258; hill ('dry') 26, 96, 123; and plantations 293–295, 328, 331, 340; for seed 126; and swidden (chena) land 121, 122, 145, 288–289, 293, 338; tax, *see* Grain tax; technology of 9, 21, 327; yield 21; *See also* Grain tax; Irrigation;

Subject Index

Land; Prices; Rice; Villages
Parsis 117
Pasture land 6, 9, 90, 91, 92, 95, 105, 115, 116, 122, 178, 237
Patriarchy 211–213, 219, 226
Patron-client relation 161
Pay; *See* Debt bondage; Wages
Pearl fishing 54
Peasants (Sinhalese) 101, 114, 118–121, 127, 130, 156–157, 184, 191, 225; and British 107, 193, 217–218, 235, 237, 238, 243; and Chettiyars 213–214; and colonial state 107, 109, 121–122, 131, 174, 176, 194, 214, 236, 241–260, 266–274, 276, 290–296, 316, 320, 337; 'conservation' of 181–182; destitution of 145–146, expropriation of 6, 8–9, 100, 104–106, 109, 131, 137, 148, 153, 161, 166, 170–173, 179–180, 186, 194, 214, 237, 250, 292, 294, 296–297, 319, 343; as fieldworkers 200, 299; 'free' 52, 170; and headmen (aristocrats, chiefs, landlords, overlords) 223, 228, 234, 288–290, 296, 309, 315–316, 320–321; homesteads of 19, 55; 'indolence' of 141, 175, 176, 179–180, 183, 193, 292, 303; and planters 239, 268, 274, 290, 299, 303, 311, 320, 337; as proprietors 7, 70–72, 79, 102, 107, 123–124, 161, 171, 179, 223, 268, 281, 296–297, 316, protests by 100, 136, 149, 164, 166–168, 207, 256–257, 270, 318, 355; self-identity of 30, 213; 'semi-' 182–183, 218, 226, sickliness of 145; sympathy for 140, 180–181, 256, 258, 270, 303; and Tamils 192–193, 195, 200–201, 219, 314; *See also* Caste; Castes; Coffee, peasant grown; Labor [both entries]; Paddy; Rebellion; Smallholdings; Swidden (Chena) land and agriculture; Taxes
Pepper 53, 62, 67, 129
Peripheral nations 5; capitalism in 3–4, 11, 330–333, 343, 344, 354; 'semi-' 5, 353
Peru 196n, 209n, 213, 345
Petitions 149
Philippines, The 285
Plantations 6, 12–14, 81–82, 102–105, 117, 128, 131, 170, 171, 210–213, 228, 309, 323, 337, 356; acreage in 85; coffee 72–82, 87–88, 97, 174–175, 210, 217, 220, 229, 246–247, 280–281; cost to establish 74, 77; decline of 76, 78–79, 82, 135, 143, 153; as economic sector 7–9, 18, 52, 56, 62–63, 65–116, 174, 182, 187, 214, 218, 236–237, 279, 287, 305, 308, 317, 325, 328, 330, 347; elevation of 78, 88–89, 135; expansion of 6, 9, 77, 86, 87, 103, 104, 108–112, 144–145, 173, 182, 189, 231, 254, 273, 293, 317, 350; number of 74; ownership of 70, 81, 84, 99, 234, 240; and paddy agriculture 293–295, 327, 331; pay on 75, 179, 182–183; rubber 84, 283; sales of 76; size of 66; state-owned 67, 68; state bias for 69, 132–133, 222, 230–231, 235–239, 245–247, 255, 257–259, 263, 266, 268–269, 272, 274, 285, 293, 325, 350–351; sugar 100; and taxation 132–134, 262–263; tea 81, 84–86, 121, 209, 213, 220, 230, 306 307; *See also* Capital; Coffee; Labor (under capitalism); Land; Planters; Taxes; Tea; Wages
Planters 5, 84, 105–107, 129, 132, 152, 155, 163, 170, 180, 181, 191, 193, 195, 204–205, 281, 317; Ceylonese

133, 286; and Chettiyars 214–215; coconut 133, 189; coffee 76, 79, 80, 85, 87–88, 90–94, 100, 103, 111, 112, 114, 119, 174, 178, 183–184, 201, 235–236; and colonial state 69, 120, 132–133, 222, 235–241, 244, 245–254, 263, 288, 290–294, legal privilege of 204; lobby of 255; as officials 63, 69, 81, 89, 90, 92, 104–105, 230–234, 274, 318–319, 350; paying wages in rice 211–213, 220; and peasants 239, 268, 274, 290, 294, 299, 303, 310–314, 337; 'Planter Raj' 122; tea 85–86; See also Plantations

Planters Association, of Ceylon 235
Plumbago, mining of; See Graphite
'Plural society' 310
Police 81, 157, 228, 230, 254, 274, 293; magistrates 227
Polyandry 19, 242–245
Polygyny (polygamy) 243–244
Population: increase 189, 194–196, 276, 283, 297, 314; 'surplus' 194, 198, 299; See also Census
Ports; See Seaports
Portuguese (in Ceylon) 225; and Kandyan kingdom 44; mercantilism 42, 44, 53–54, 67; rule by 42, 49, 279
Potatoes 101
Precious stones; See Gems
Prescriptive rights; See Customary usage
Prices 197; of coffee 71, 73, 75–76, 78, 136, 142, 317; fall in 75–76; of paddy (rice) 131, 143, 211, 216, 257
Primogeniture 23, 233, 241
Prisons 250, 318
Private property in land 29, 95, 106, 115–116, 119, 146, 149, 156, 163, 166, 171, 173, 194, 240–244, 288, 307; introduction of 9, 24, 58, 61–63, 67, 89–173, 237, 254, 292, 338
Proclamation of 1815; See Kandyan Convention
Proclamation of 1818 52, 122–123, 154, 161, 223, 315
Production; commodity 343, 345, 346, 348; means of 296, 344, 351; social relations of 220, 287, 292, 295–298, 303, 306, 325, 328, 333, 335–338, 340–342, 344, 346–347; See also Modes of production
Profit 67, 211, 213, 235, 278, 280; maximizing of 182–183, 324, 336; See also Capital, export of
Proletariat 187, 213, 219, 287; 'semi-' 183, 189–191, 193, 197, 218, 299, 337
Property holding 19, 21, 31–36, 171–173, 178, 189, 236–237; See also Feudalism; Land, tenure; Private Property in land; Tenancy
Provinces, of British Ceylon 61, 230
Public works 176–177, 198, 225, 226, 229, 250, 259, 260; See also Infrastructure; Irrigation; Roads
Pussellewa 93
Questionnaire 134
Racism 235, 303, 315, 356
Railways 179, 181, 246–249, 253, 257, 261, 276, 280, 293
Rainfall 19–20
Ramnad (India) 197, 203, 219, 278
Ratnapura District (in Sabaragamuwa Province) 138
Raw materials, as exports 60, 66, 277, 343
Rebellion 229, 351–352; aristocratic 47–52; Great (of 1818) 50–52, 59, 69, 89, 119, 122, 156, 177, 181, 217–218, 223, 231, 246, 305, 314–316, 318–320; individual acts of 207, 306;

peasant (including 1848) 26, 48, 50–52, 55–56, 63, 71, 76, 92, 104–105, 115, 136, 149, 160, 225–226, 249, 252, 256, 270–271, 305, 312, 313, 316–321, 340
Reforms 230, 235, 265, 273; Ceylonese movement for 283; *See also* Colebrook-Cameron Commission, reforms of
Religion 41, 52, 156, 176, 200, 303, 325; *See also* Buddhism; Christianity; Millennial movements
Rent; *See* Land, rent from
'Renters'; *See* Grain
'Renters'; *See* Grain tax, farming out to 'renters'
Reproduction, economic 328, 346; *See also* Labor (under capitalism), 'reproduction' of
Revenue (state) 54, 59, 75, 76, 77, 79, 89, 230, 255; expenditure of 176, 235, 250, 256, 258, 260; need for 136, 143, 249; sources of 55, 57, 97, 112, 124–135, 154, 180, 186, 250, 260–278; *See also* Grain tax; Irrigation; Land, sale of; Monopolies; Public works; Road tax; Roads; Taxes
Revenue (temple) 160, 162
Revolution, European, of 1848 317
Rice 30, 101, 191; dry, *see* Paddy, hill; imports 132, 212–217, 220–221, 255, 256–257, 258, 263, 272, 285, 292; price of 257, 272; riots for 256–257; seed/yield ratio 272; varieties of 216; wages paid in 210–213, 219, 220; wet 31, 70, 71, 72, 87, 102, 111, 116, 122, 123, 144, 152, 155, 174, 213; *See also* Customs duties; Grain tax; Paddy; Prices
Riots 257; of 1915 313, 352
Road tax 132, 137, 179, 188, 249–253, 257, 260, 266, 268–269; commutation of labor service into 244, 250, 252–253; default on 250; *See also* Ordinances; Roads
Roads 101, 145, 217, 228, 235, 248–253, 259–260, 276, 280, 293; commutation of labor service on, to road tax 244, 250, 252–253; construction of 52–54, 58, 69, 73, 75, 77, 80, 100, 176–177, 226, 231, 245, 246, 255, 257; labor service on 55, 176–177, 179, 189, 249–253, 311; maintenance of 176, 249; private 253; tolls on 75
Royal Botanical Gardens, near Kandy 259
Rubber 82, 83, 194, 260, 283
Sabaragamuwa District 109, 118
Sabaragamuwa Province 19, 160, 162
Salaries of officials; increase in 234; reduction in 63, 231
Salt 43, 54, 132
'Satellite' nations and regions, capitalism in 3–4, 330, 333, 354
Sath Korale; *See* Seven Korale Province
Scotland 329
Seaports 43, 44, 47, 75, 246, 257, 280, 285, 293
Secretary of State for the Colonies 90, 120, 133, 175, 224–230, 234, 240, 247, 251, 269; *See also* Colonial Office *and the Name Index*
Sectors, economic 335–336; *See also* Plantation, as economic sector; Smallholdings, as economic sector; Traditional economic sector; Villages, as economic sector
Self-determination, national 323
Serfdom 24–25, 36, 57n, 114, 155, 165, 337, 338, 345, 346–347; *See also* Feudalism; Kandy (kingdom)
Service Tenures Ordinance (of 1876); *See* Ordinances, on labor

Seven Korale Province (precolonial) 68, 163, 312, 320
Sharecropping 24, 153, 170, 186, 194, 268, 295, 297, 342, 347
Shifting cultivation; *See* Slash-and-burn agriculture; Swidden (chena) land and agriculture
Shops, retail 160, 163
Siam 36
Siam Samagam/Nikaya, Buddhist sect 110
Silk 122
Slash-and-burn agriculture 6, 12, 19, 20, 26–32, 109, 290; acreage cultivated by 27; communal aspects of 27–31; *See also* Swidden (chena) land and agriculture
Slaves 192; as labor 66, 176, 212; trade in 59–60; West Indian 72, 196, 205
Smallholdings 66, 67, 74, 151, 171, 178, 191, 215, 280, 287, 291, 299, 356; coconut cultivation on 83–84; coffee cultivation on 70–72, 73, 99, 102, 103, 108, 117, 130, 186, 200, 210, 285, 291–293, 325, 331; as economic sector 293, 348; size of 66; *See also* Capitalists, Ceylonese
Social change 56, 326, 349, 354; in Central Highlands 10, 149–150, 164, 170, 273, 275–277, 279, 291, 295, 302, 306, 314; in Third World 4–5, 327
Social formations 297, 310, 332, 335, 342, 343, 347, 349, 351, 353
Socialism 326–327, 328
South Indians 55; as moneylenders 55, 108, 209; poverty of 196–197, 199, 205, 220, 310; as traders 53; *See also* Labor (under capitalism), immigrant, migratory *and* South Indian, Tamils
Southern Province 135, 150, 153, 214
Speculators in land 91, 100, 114, 119, 149, 163, 262, 281
Spices, as exports 43, 66–67
Squatter movement 106
Sri Lanka 1n, 8; postcolonial 5, 255, 352; *See also* Ceylon
Standard of living 194, 292, 299
Starvation 137, 141–142, 145, 146, 180, 237
Stasis, economic 41–43
Structural transformation 39–40, 56, 149–150, 173
Sugar 68, 100, 123, 182, 197, 209n, 269; use with tea 85
Surplus appropriation 12, 21, 24, 25, 29, 31, 36, 54, 55, 56–57, 61, 71, 80–81, 87, 122, 128, 150–151, 173, 262, 266, 307, 333, 345; and export thereof 57, 298, 328, 329, 336; and modes of production 19, 288–291, 293, 296, 334, 344, 346
Swidden (chena) land and agriculture 7n, 19, 26–32, 90, 91, 95, 96, 100, 115, 116, 123, 130, 134, 144–146, 166, 171, 183, 189, 213, 231, 237, 239, 256, 262, 272, 274, 287–289, 331, 340, 348; acquisition for plantations 88–116, 171, 178, 290; decline of 290, 295; and paddy 121, 122, 145, 288–289; and plantations 293; *See also* Slash-and-burn agriculture
Tamils 117, 133, 140, 189, 192–193, 197–201, 213, 225, 278, 281, 292, 352; 'docility' of 195, 207, 306; separatism in Sri Lanka 280, 309; settlement schemes for 217–218; and Sinhalese peasants 192–193, 195, 200–201, 219, 282, 309, 314; *See also* Labor (under capitalism); South Indians
Tanjore (India) 197, 210, 219
Taxes 12, 34, 55, 59, 62, 69, 75, 76, 79,

Subject Index

80–81, 87, 91, 136, 236, 242, 262–263, 266–274, 312, 317, 320, 328; amount of 267, 270; paid in cash 128–131, 134, 135, 155, 179, 184, 185, 215, 254, 257, 292, 338; on coconut trees 55; default on 320; direct vs. indirect 269–270; evasion of 25, 101, 149; excessive 266–268, 273; exemption from 58, 122, 188, 238; 'head' 252, 338; paid in kind 123, 125–131, 155; on land directly (proposed) 132–135; and land claims 94, 96; paid to landlords (fees) 163, 166, 173; for police 254; records of past payment of 94, 96, 238; on salt 132, 154, 266–269; on shifting cultivation 106, 123; in Southeast Asia 146; stamp tax 132, 154, 269; and wage labor 179, 183–184, 250, 268; water rate 257; *See also* Customs duties; Grain tax; Ordinances; Rebellion; Road tax

Tea 65, 213, 287, 299; consumption level of 85; duties on export of 206; peasant-grown 189; production of 189, 219; production lead-time of 85; shift to from coffee 14, 84–86, 97, 120–122, 153, 189–190, 194, 200, 219, 259–260

Technology 170, 297, 299, 322, 327, 328, 343, 344; of coffee production 77; level of 40, 41, 54, 151, 273, 294, 325; of tea production 85

Temperence movement, Ceylonese 265

Temple Lands Commission 109–116, 119, 155, 157, 170, 227, 307, 337

Temples 33–35, 50, 87; Buddhist 33–35, 50, 87; of deities 33–35, 109, 111, 114, 160; heads (lords) of 35, 152, 161–163; lands of 105, 109, 112, 138, 152, 155, 157, 165–166, 171, 259; shops of 160; villages of 32–36, 64, 87, 111, 132–133, 154, 224, 295–297; *See also* Land, grants of; Overlords; Revenue (temple); Temple Lands Commission

Tenancy 32–41, 105; 154–172; hereditary 23–25, 166, 194, 296, 299; temporary 23–15, 166; *See also* Customary usage; Land, tenure

Textiles 212; imported 53, 184–185; Indian 66, 196; Ceylonese 184

Third World 105, 11, 15, 322, 326, 332, 335, 337, 340, 342, 343, 345–346, 353, 355–357

Timber; cutting of 101, 119; sale of 115

'Tin ticket system' of labor transport 246

Tithe (grain tax) 155, 156, 238, 264; paid in kind 112, 122, 128–129, 160, 224; *See also* Grain tax

Tobacco 54

Tolls, on roads and bridges 75, 76, 80

Torture 276

Towns 19, 25, 34, 39, 153, 213

Trade 18, 41–45, 53–60, 67, 71, 129, 188, 213, 217, 285, 334; Arab 53; overland 43; profit from 53; restrictions on 57; by river 43; *See also* Market; Mercantilism; Monopolies; Muslims; Traders

Trade unions 205, 307

Traders 211, 239, 284, 309, 317; Chettiyars as 214–215, 310; as landowners 150, 157, 298; *See also* Muslims; South Indians

Traditional economic sector 226, 294, 328, 332; and modern sector 2–3, 7–8, 10, 81–82, 277; *See also* 'Dual economy' theory; Villages, as economic sector

Transport 79, 82, 129, 186–187, 189,

192, 211, 213, 247, 272, 280, 285; of labor 246; *See also* Trade
Tribal groups 30
Tribute 36, 37, 67, 95, 114, 116, 122, 128, 160, 234, 251; from merchants 53; *See also* Labor (before capitalism); Land, rent from
Trichinopoly 203
Trincomalee (port) 46
Troops, feeding of 129
Tuticorin (India), immigration via 206
Uda Hewaheta division (in Nuwara Eliya District, Central Province) 255
Udakinda division (in Badulla District, Uva Province) 138–140
Udapalata division (in Nuwara Eliya District, Central Province) 142, 149
Uganda 25
Underdevelopment 352; and development 1–12, 14–15, 182–183, 214, 215n, 218–219, 298, 322–332, 335, 349–350, 354–357; *See also* 'Dual economy theory
United States 212, 284
Urbanization 283, 299
Utilitarianism 61
Uva Province 19, 20, 135, 138–140, 149, 150, 189, 256
Value systems 322, 325, 353
Vellassa Province (precolonial) 51
Villages 70, 87–89, 118, 140–141, 178, 194, 226, 295–297, 354; case studies of 9–11, 157–160; commercialization of 10, 41, 146, 149–152, 171, 250, 290; councils of 61, 257, 293; as economic sector 7, 81–82, 174, 177, 187, 194, 200, 214, 218, 236, 279, 287, 295, 305, 308, 325, 328, 331, 337–338, 350–351; 'feudal' 31–36, 87, 91, 155–172, 224, 306; 'free' 36; granted 32; of headmen 64, 154, 292n; Indian 196–197, 203–204, 208, 209, 210, 218, 219, 220; Javanese 194; and plantation economy 182, 254, 296–297; political structure of 10n; royal (crown) 31–32, 52, 87, 91, 114, 122–124, 152, 156, 161, 170, 171, 192, 223, 224, 292, 306, 338; self-sufficiency of 44; of temples 32–36, 64, 87, 111, 132–133, 154, 224, 295–297; tribunals 227; *See also* Chiefs; Headmen; Land; Peasants
Wages 264; advances of 203–204, 207, 208–209; rate of 75, 179, 182–183, 192, 208, 218; paid in rice 210–213, 219, 220; *See also* Labor (under capitalism), wage; Debt bondage
Walapane division (in Nuwara Eliya District, Central Province) 138–146, 148, 176, 256
Warfare 39; guerilla 47, 246
Water; insufficiency of 30, 144, 145; 'rate' (tax) 257; tanks for 20, 256; village management of 257; *See also* Irrigation
Wealth of Nations, The 60
Weaving 184, 196, 334
West Indies 245, 291; coffee from 72; slavery in 72, 196, 205
Western Province 156
Wet zone (of Ceylon) 42, 122, 130, 256
Wine, consumption of 72
Women 218; labor by 200, 210–212, 218, 219; position of 13, 35, 183, 210–213
Wool 324

NAME INDEX

Ackland, George 92, 231–233, 249
Alavi, Hamza 3–4, 11, 36n, 237n, 341–343, 345–348, 354
Alwis, James 133–134
Ameer Ali, A.C.L. 26–27, 70, 129, 161, 182, 216, 258–259
Amin, Samir 3–4, 330n, 335n, 343n, 354, 355n
Angammana (Ratemahatmaya) 118
Appu, Puran 318
Arasaratnam, S. 20n, 42, 44–45
Arrighi, G 182n
Bailey, J. (Asst. Government Agent, Badulla District, Uva Province) 95, 103–104, 255
Banaji, Jairus 3–4, 24, 297–298, 341–343, 348, 354
Baran, Paul 329
Barnes, Sir Edward (governor 1824–31) 58, 69, 89, 123, 199, 231–233, 247, 249, 262
Barnett, J. Richard 6n
Baumgartner (Asst. Government Agent, Nuwara Eliya District, Central Province) 142, 144, 145, 153, 180
Bennet, J.W. 286
Bentham, Jeremy 59, 61
Bettleheim, Charles 171, 298n, 339
Bird, Major George 69, 89, 199, 231–232
Blackall, Major 233
Bodenheimer, Suzanne J. 323n
Böeke, J.H. 294, 324, 336
Booth, David 333
Boserup, Ester 31n
Bradby, Barbara 196n
Braybooke (Government Agent, Central Province) 106
Brenner, Robert 333n
Brett, E.A. 305
Brow, James 30
Buchanan, Keith 1n
Buller, C.R. (Government Agent, Central Province) 101, 231, 232–233
Cameron, Charles 59
Campbell, Sir Colin (governor 1841–47) 68, 234
Chandra, Bipan 351
Clifford, Sir Hugh governor (1925–27) 6, 8, 234
Colebrooke, William 59, 62–64, 68–69, 124, 155, 177, 224–225, 231, 249, 255
Coomaraswamy, Muttu 132–134
Craig, Edwin 80, 284
Davies, Colonel W.G. 298n
de Silva, Colvin R. 18n, 49, 50
de Silva, Douglas 83n
de Silva, K.M. 1n, 48–49, 63, 88, 208, 225, 227, 317, 319
de Silva, S.B.D. 9, 22, 40, 42, 194
de Sousa Fernandes, Maria Teresa 213n
D'A Vincent 88, 97, 101
Dickson, John F. (Government Agent, Central Province) 136–137, 156, 164, 252
Disraeli, Benjamin 319
Dobb, Maurice 42n, 337n
Doloswala (Disawé), 160
Dupré, Georges 339
Durkheim, Emile 355n
Eisenstadt, S. 350
Elliot, Christopher 270, 274, 317–318
Ellsworth, P.T. 324

Engels, Frederick 329
Evans, Peter 5, 353n
Evers, Hans-Dieter 22, 115, 171, 214
Fanon, Franz 349n
Ferguson, A.M. 80, 180
Ferguson, John 180
Fieldhouse, D.K. 47n
Fisher, F.C. (Government Agent, Uva Province) 149
Forbes, Jonathan 193, 252, 262
Foster-Carter, Aiden 347
Frank, Andre Gunder 3, 323n, 329–336, 341, 342, 345, 348, 353–354
Fraser, Colonel ("Tiger") 319
Furnivall, J.S. 47–48, 304, 310, 350
Ganetirala, Boragolle 142
Geertz, Clifford 194, 330
Gladstone, William E. 319
Goffman, Irving 288n
Goldthorpe, J.E. 206–207
Gordon, Alex 237n
Gordon, Sir Arthur, see Lord Stanmore
Gordon, Milton 311n
Gordon, Stewart 25
Gough, Kathleen 336
Gregory, William (governor 1872–77) 92, 181, 238, 260, 265
Grey, 3rd Earl (Secy. of State for the Colonies) 90, 247, 251–252, 269–270
Grossholtz, Jean 210, 234, 265
Gunasekara, U.A. 23
Gunasinghe, Newton 10–11, 20n, 24, 32n, 229, 313-314
Harris, John 29
Havelock, Sir Arthur (governor 1890–95) 133, 153, 266–268
Hayley, F.A. 23
Herring, Ronald 29
Hewawitharana, Buddhadasa 9
Higgins, Benjamin 324n

Horton, Sir Robert Wilmont (governor 1831–37) 58, 157
Hulugalle, H.A.J. 6
Hume 231–233
Iddamalgoda (Nilemé) 165
Ievers, R.W. (Government Agent, Kegalle District, Sabaragamuva Province) 312
Ireland, W. Alleyane 195
Jackson, Sir Edward 219
Jayawardena, Kumari 219n, 313
Jayawardena, Lalith (Lal) 6n, 7, 9, 107–108, 180, 183, 190
Jogaratnam, T. 7, 325
'Jus' (George Wall) 141
Kannangara, P.D. 223
Kapuwatte (family) 164
Kay, Geoffrey 56
Kelegama, J.B. 8n
King, Aelian A. (Asst. Government Agent, Badulla District, Central Province) 179–180
Kloosterboer, W. 176, 191
Knox, Robert 20n, 25, 34, 38, 39, 40–41
Kotelawala, D.A. 27n
Kuruppu, N.S.G. 198–199
Laclau, Ernesto 56n, 287n, 335–339, 341–342, 346
Lall, Sanjaya 3n, 327
Lawrie, A.C. 118, 164
Layard, C.P. (Government Agent, Western Province) 156, 165
Laylard, H.L. 104–105, 232–233, 318n
Leach, E.R. 38
Lebbe, M.U. Ishak 10n
Le Mesurier, C.J.R. (Asst. Government Agent, Nuwara Eliya District, Central Province) 140–147, 180, 273
Levin, Jonathan 79, 324n
Lewis, W. Arthur 60n, 174n, 196, 217, 294
Long, Norman 291n, 335n, 338n, 345

Name Index

Ludovici, Leopold 97, 141, 151, 255, 257, 272
Macaulay, Thomas Babington 62
Mackenzie, J.A. Stewart (governor 1837–41) 231–232
Maddock, Herbert 319
Magdoff, Harry 59–60
Mahawaletenne (family) 119
Malalgoda, Kitsiri 116, 312, 316
Mamdani, Mahmoud 21n, 25, 298
Mandle, Jay R. 182n
Mao Tse Tung 347
Marx, Karl 56, 326–329, 334–335, 344
McClelland, David C. 324n
Meek, C.K. 22, 160
Meillassoux, Claude 182, 337, 339
Memmi, Albert 349n
Mendis, G.C. 6
Meyer, Eric 179n, 187, 189–190, 200–201
Mill, James Stuart 236
Mill, John Stuart 61
Millie, P.D. 100, 118, 205
Mitford (Government Agent, North Western Province) 157, 160
Moir, R.W.D. (Government Agent, Central Province) 142–144
Molligoda (family) 229
Moore, M.P. 10n
Morris, Morris D. 214n
Morrison, Barrie M. 10–11, 194n
Muller, Ronald E. 6n
Myrdal, Gunnar 195
Neale, Walter C. 21n
Neville, Hugh 312
Newcastle, Lord (Secy. of State for the Colonies) 239
North, Frederick (governor 1798–1805) 58, 64n
Obeysekere, Gananath 24, 138, 149, 150, 152, 153

Omvedt, Gail 197, 203, 210, 218–219
Paige, Jeffrey M. 306
Parantala (Ratemahatmaya) 119
Parsons, Talcott 350
Pathmanathan, S. 18n
Peebles, Patrick 6n, 9n, 89, 97, 116–117, 281
Peel, Sir Robert 319
Perera, A.B. 8n
Pieris, Jeronis 189n
Pieris, Ralph 8n, 21–22, 24–25, 28, 38, 224n, 229
Ponnambalam, Satchi 7–8
Rajaratnam, S. 83
Rajasinghe, Sri Vickrama (king) 47–50, 199
Reimers, E. 42n
Rey, Pierre Philip 43n, 339–341
Richardson, Paul 291n, 335n, 338n
Ridgeway, Sir Joseph West (governor 1895–1903) 230, 234
Roberts, Michael 9–10, 43, 51n, 66n, 68n, 89n, 97, 103, 107–108, 118, 187–188, 192, 205, 211, 234, 235, 236, 257, 283n, 315n
Robinson, Hercules (governor 1865–1872) 175, 246–248, 256
Robinson, Marguerite S. 10n
Roxborough, Ian 4n, 333
Salmon, C.S. 141, 272
Samaraweera, Vijaya 54n, 55n, 58n, 61n, 63n, 250–251, 284n
Sarkar, N.K. 9n, 10
Saunders, F.R. 258–259
Scott, James 25, 27, 146, 270, 312n
Seneviratne, L.J. de S. 28–29
Shah, A.M. 336
Sievers, Angelika 9n
Silva, Tudor 10–11, 291n
Skinner, Major Thomas 226, 229, 231–233

Smith, Adam 60
Snodgrass, Donald R. 6n, 7, 68n, 81–83, 190, 325
'Speculum' (George Wall) 141
Stanley, Lord (Secretary of State for the Colonies) 234
Stanmore, Lord (Sir Arthur Gordon) (governor 1883–1890) 91, 121, 178, 180, 184, 227, 254
Stokes, Eric 60–61
Stuart, James 64
Sweezy, Paul 41–42, 337n
Tambiah, S.J. 9n, 10, 150, 152, 285
Taylor, John G. 323n
Templar (family) 233
Tennett, Sir Emerson (Colonial Secretary, Ceylon) 103, 105–106, 110, 126–127, 132, 155–156, 175, 191, 192, 205, 211, 213, 215, 217–218, 224, 225, 233, 251, 303, 319
Thiagaraja, K. 204, 209
Thompson, E.T. 309
Torrington, Viscount (governor 1847–50) 76, 136, 249, 254, 262, 268–272, 317, 319
Turnour, George (Acting Colonial Secretary, Ceylon) 89, 93, 114, 128, 156–157, 178, 213, 228, 231–233, 236

Tytler, R.B. 73
Van Den Driesen, I.H. 8n, 68n, 70, 72–74, 76, 79, 94, 95, 104, 120, 130, 236, 240–241, 261
Van Zwanenberg, R.M.A. 129n, 178, 191
Vilbave 51
Vimalananda, Tennakoon 6n
Wakefield, Edward Gibbon 63, 89–90
Wall, Goerge (alias 'Jus,' 'Speculum') 141, 235, 251, 261, 266–268, 274
Wallerstein, Immanuel 53n, 61n, 332–334, 345, 348, 354
Ward, Sir Henry (governor 1855–60) 93, 120, 181, 185–186, 242, 251–252, 256, 258, 320
Warren, Bill 327
Watson, Colonel 100
Weber, Max 33n, 36n, 41, 233, 305, 344, 349
Wesumperuma, D. 138, 208, 266
Wickramasekara, S.B.W. 19n, 23, 88
Wijesinghe, Don Domingo 164
Wodehouse, P.E. (Asst. Colonial Secretary, Ceylon) 92, 191, 232–233
Wolpe, Harold 337
Worsley, Peter 1n
Yalman, Nur 10n

www.ingramcontent.com/pod-product-compliance
Lightning Source LLC
Chambersburg PA
CBHW020632230426
43665CB00008B/140